The World Today Series®

Stryker-Post Publications, Harpers Ferry, WV

Latin America 2002

Robert T. Buckman

36th Edition

Next Edition, August 2003

Robert T. Buckman . . .

A journalism professor at the University of Louisiana at Lafayette, he graduated from Texas Christian University where he earned his bachelor's and master's degrees in journalism and political science. He holds a doctorate in journalism from the University of Texas. His writings on Latin America have been widely published in books, newspapers, magazines, and scholarly journals. He has lived and worked in Chile, Panama, and Paraguay. A former lieutenant colonel in the U.S. Army Reserve, he was reserve military attaché to Colombia until his retirement in 1998.

Photographs used to illustrate *The World Today Series* come from many sources, a great number from friends who travel worldwide. If you have taken any which you believe would enhance the visual impact and attractiveness of our books, do let us hear from you.

Adapted, rewritten and revised annually from a book entitled *Latin America 1967*, published in 1967 and succeeding years by

Stryker-Post Publications
P.O. Drawer 1200
Harpers Ferry, WV 25425
Telephones: 1–800–995–1400 (U.S.A. and Canada)
    Other: 1–304–535–2593
    Fax: 1–304–535–6513
    www.Strykerpost.com
    VISA–MASTERCARD

International Standard Book Number: 1–887985–47–5

International Standard Serial Number: 0092–4148

Library of Congress Catalog Number 73–647061

Cover design by MidAtlantic Books & Journals

Chief Bibliographer: Edward Jones

Cartographer: William L. Nelson

Typography by Clarinda

Printed in the United States of America by United Book Press, Inc.
Baltimore, MD 21207

CONTENTS

Stone piece, Tiahuanaco culture, Bolivia

The UN has received into its ranks many small countries, such as those of the Caribbean region. The purpose of this series is to reflect *modern world dynamics.* Thus, we mention only briefly the beautiful nations of the Lesser Antilles and concentrate our attention on the growth of the larger, developing countries.

São Paulo, Brazil, in 1930 . . .

. . . and today

Latin America Today

Latin America, always a land of color and conflict, is undergoing the most dramatic changes of its post–colonial history. These changes—political, economic, technological and cultural—are accelerating as the 21st century begins. It is not an exaggeration to say that Latin America at the dawn of the 21st century bears little resemblance to the Latin America of 1900. Despite some notable exceptions, Latin America gave rise to a stereotype that persists to this day of tropical republics mired in squalor, ruled by self–serving autocrats and lagging decades if not centuries behind the economically advanced societies of Europe and North America.

Such a view ignores the fact that Argentina at the turn of the 20th century was an industrialized and agriculturally rich society boasting a higher standard of living than that of France. Sadly, however, as is true of many stereotypes, there was enough element of truth throughout the rest of the region to reinforce the perception of dictators, destitution and depression. Since World War II, this picture has been slowly, painfully, and sometimes violently evolving into a collection of societies entering the modern world. Some have evolved more than others, but the trend is inexorable. This evolution involves four discrete elements: a democratic revolution; economic diversification and expansion; technological acceleration; and cultural growth and projection.

Democratic Revolution

The sudden collapse of communism and the emergence of democracy in Eastern Europe at the beginning of the 1990s was one of the watershed events of world history. Less dramatic but no less historic was the slow, inexorable shift of Latin America away from its past of *caudillo* strongmen, military juntas and revolving–door regimes and toward constitutionally elected civilian governments. As

recently as the end of 1977, only three of the 20 true "Latin" American republics had genuinely democratic systems with free elections involving two or more political parties and peaceful transfers of power from one to another: Colombia, Costa Rica and Venezuela.

Two other nations had what could be charitably described as imperfect civilian democracies. Mexico had enjoyed civilian rule since the promulgation of its 1917 constitution and peacefully transferred power from one president to another like clockwork every six years, with

re–election strictly forbidden. But until 2000, all those presidents were of one party, the *Partido Revolucionario Institucional (PRI)*, which held government at all levels in a vise–grip and was not above rigging elections to quash the aspirations of upstart opposition parties. In the Dominican Republic, President Joaquín Balaguer was elected in 1966, 1970 and 1974 and showed every indication of hanging onto power indefinitely through extra–"constitutional means if necessary.

Fourteen other republics were governed by military juntas; even the once–envied democracies of Chile and Uruguay had opted for order over chaos in 1973. Finally, Cuba was distinguished by the peculiar totalitarian experiment of Fidel Castro, a model that was still viewed then as a beacon by guerrilla movements and left–wing political parties throughout the region.

Democracy in Latin America, it seemed, was a concept that was unfeasible at best and unwanted at worst. But in 1978, the tide slowly began to turn, until by the late 1980s it had become a tidal wave in favor of duly elected civilian government. In the Dominican elections that year, Balaguer ordered troops to halt the vote–counting when it became apparent the opposition was winning. Under pressure from the administration of U.S. President Jimmy Carter, Balaguer was forced to honor the opposition victory and grudgingly yielded power. After two intervening presidents, Balaguer returned in 1986 for three more terms, retiring as a blind, feeble old man in 1996 and turning over power to a freely elected president of the opposition.

This transition to democracy in all but one of the Latin American Republics is described in detail in the sections on each nation, together with an indication of things to come.

Lest this picture of emerging democracy be misconstrued as overly rosy, it must be noted that two or more consecutive

A beautiful example of Peruvian designed fabric

wielded by divine right by the monarchs of the other colonial powers. When Great Britain granted independence to its colonies, whether voluntarily or involuntarily, it left in place viable political institutions rooted in parliamentary democracy and common law upon which they could build. Washington and Jefferson learned much in the House of Burgesses of colonial Virginia. Spain, Portugal and France, by contrast, bequeathed a legacy of power concentrated in the hands of one man. Or to put it another way, no Spanish king ever signed a Magna Carta.

Thus, although the newly independent Latin America emulated the U.S. Constitution with its three branches of government and checks and balances, in practice the executive enjoyed disproportionate power. Latin America became the living embodiment of the adage that absolute power corrupts absolutely, and such traditions are not easily discarded. In just the past few years, despite the aforementioned advances in Latin American democracy, we have witnessed attempts by several elected presidents to play fast and loose with constitutional rights in the name of

elections, no matter how honest in the eyes of international observers, do not in and of themselves guarantee that the mortar of democratic institutions will set properly. It often takes generations before adherence to liberal principles becomes woven into a nation's social fabric. True democracy flowers best in a climate characterized by such principles as co–equal executive, legislative and judicial branches; tolerance of opposition viewpoints, whether expressed on the floor of a congress, in the mass media or in the streets; unquestioned civilian control over the military; workable constitutions that endure more than a decade or two; eschewal of the temptation to resort to political violence; and public confidence in the integrity of governmental institutions and leaders. Most Latin American countries are still lacking in this regard.

In fairness, however, Latin America should be cut some slack. There is not yet a Utopian society anywhere on Earth. Even in the United States, which has long held a paternal attitude toward its wayward Latin American neighbors, political assassinations and attempted assassinations have occurred with alarming frequency, and local pockets of political corruption, complete with vote fraud, influence peddling and kickbacks, are legendary.

But the United States, Canada and the English–speaking states of the Caribbean enjoyed an advantage over their Latin American neighbors in having had a colonial master that had experienced a Glorious Revolution in 1688. The Enlightenment came late, if at all, to Spain, Portugal and France. The abuses of George III that Jefferson enumerated in the Declaration of Independence seem little more than nit–" picks in contrast to the absolute power

Veracruz, Mexico: The largest of the colossal heads found from the Olmec civilization.

2

expediency. We also have seen the murders of prominent political reformers in Colombia, Mexico and elsewhere.

Another troubling factor is the willingness of democratically elected presidents to employ legal and extralegal measures once employed by their dictatorial predecessors to curtail press freedom, especially critical editorials and investigative reporting. In Peru, for example, Fujimori flouted the constitution in using a bureaucratic technicality to revoke the Peruvian citizenship of an Israeli–born television station owner in 1997 after the station became too aggressive in reporting abuses of human rights by the government. Also in 1997, Panamanian President Ernesto Pérez Balladares, using the labor law as a pretext, attempted to expel a Peruvian citizen who was associate editor of the country's principal daily, which had been ferocious in reporting on the Pérez government's shortcomings. The president backed down only in the face of intense international pressure from press and human rights groups, pressure to which Fujimori proved immune. Colombian President Ernesto Samper's congressional allies enacted a new broadcast law that required all independently produced news programs on the government–owned network to apply for new licenses at the end of 1997, a move aimed at *QAP*, a nettlesome "60 Minutes"–like news show. Presidents Alvaro Arzú of Guatemala and Rafael Caldera of Venezuela were openly hostile to the media, and both applied pressure on businessmen to pull advertising from media that failed to support their governments, pressure that included threats of tax audits. Caldera unsuccessfully attempted at the Ibero-American summit in Venezuela in November 1997 to impose a region–wide regulation that would guarantee "truthful reporting" and impose sanctions on media that violated these government–set standards of "truth." However, his successor, Hugo Chávez, succeeded in having just such a "truth" guarantee inserted into the new Venezuelan constitution approved by voters in December 1999.

Another tactic for dealing with aggressive journalists remains popular in Latin America: murder. According to the Inter American Press Association, 243 journalists were martyred in the Americas from October 1988 to October 2001, including 103 in Colombia, 35 in Mexico, 21 in Guatemala, 19 in Peru, 18 in Brazil and 17 in El Salvador. Eighteen journalists were murdered just between October 2000 and October 2001. Many of the murders can be linked to drug traffickers or guerrillas, but a suspicious number—almost all of them unsolved—were of journalists who were investigating official corruption or who had written critical editorials. Independent journalism in Latin America remains a high–risk occupation, and until it can be practiced without fear, true democracy cannot take root.

The Declaration of Chapultepec, promoted by the IAPA and signed in Mexico City in 1994 by representatives of 22 nations of the hemisphere, acknowledges the importance of freedom of the press and freedom of expression for democratic societies and denounces acts of violence against journalists. Yet, the other 13 countries of the hemisphere have not signed, and abuses continue to occur in the signatory countries. The plight of the media is serious enough that it appeared on the agenda of the second Summit of the Americas in Santiago, Chile, in April 1998. The 34 hemispheric leaders (Castro was not invited) agreed to establish an office within the Inter-American Commission for Human Rights to investigate attacks against journalists.

There have been encouraging signs as well during the past few years that executive branches, and the once-omnipotent military establishments, no longer wield unchecked power. Two presidents, Brazil's Fernando Collor and Venezuela's Carlos Andres Pérez, were impeached and removed from office by their congresses for political corruption. In Paraguay, President Raúl Cubas was impeached by the Chamber of Deputies for abuse of power in 1999 and resigned and went into exile in the face of certain conviction and removal by the Senate. The leaders of the former Argentine junta were prosecuted for human rights abuses committed during the "dirty war" of 1976–1983. Jorge Serrano's attempt to stage a Fujimori–style self–coup in Guatemala in 1993 failed because the army remained loyal to the constitution, and he fled into exile. A coup attempt by a Paraguayan army general, Lino Oviedo, also fizzled out for lack of support in 1996. During the constitutional crisis over the 1998 removal, justifiable or not, of Ecuador's President Abdalá Bucaram, the military remained in its barracks and allowed the civilians to effect a reasonably smooth transition.

Not all signs have been encouraging, however. There was the temporary suspension of constitutional guarantees in 1992 by Peru's Fujimori for reasons of expediency and his shamelessly rigged "reelection" in 2000; the attempted suspension of constitutional rule and imposition of press censorship by Guatemalan President Jorge Serrano in May 1993; the probably unconstitutional removal by Congress of Ecuador's Bucaram in 1998 on the ostensibly justifiable (but unproven) charge of "mental incompetency;" the unquestionably unconstitutional barracks revolt in Ecuador that overthrew President Jamil Mahuad in January 2000 for the unjustifiable reason that his public popularity was too low; the dissolution of Parliament by Haitian President René Préval in 1999; the rigged election in Haiti in December 2000 that brought President Jean-Bertrand Aristide back to power; the spectacle of mob rule in Argentina that led to the resignation of the elected president, Fernando de la Rua, in December 2001 and his eventual replacement with the man who lost the election, Eduardo Duhalde; the almost successful military coup in Venezuela in April 2002 that had President Chávez under house arrest for 24 hours.

A possible indicator of growing self–confidence in the viability of these new democratic institutions is a growing willingness to permit reelection of popular, successful presidents. In a region with its tradition of Stroessners and Balaguers, who remained in control through orchestrated elections, virtually all of these new democracies, and some of the old ones, incorporated a prohibition against reelection, or at least immediate reelection, into their constitutions. Since then, however, the congresses of Peru, Argentina, Brazil and Venezuela amended their constitutions to permit the reelections of

A bus crosses a shallow river in Colombia

3

Presidents Fujimori, Menem, Cardozo and Chávez, respectively. Yet in Panama, when President Ernesto Pérez Balladares called a referendum in August 1998 to seek approval for a second term, a resounding 64% of the voters rejected the idea.

On the down side, it appears some of the old dangers may be resurfacing. After Peru and Argentina opened the door to reelection, Fujimori and Menem began making plans for Rooseveltian third terms. When Peru's electoral court rejected that idea as unconstitutional, Fujimori made an end–run around the judiciary, maintaining that his first election in 1990 was under the pre–1993 constitution and thus did not count. Opinion polls showed overwhelming sentiment against a third term, but when Fujimori's opposition in Congress attempted to call for a referendum to decide the issue as was done in Panama, Fujimori's allies squelched the initiative. Fujimori was "reelected" in May 2000 in an election that was so blatantly fraudulent that the opposition chose to boycott it and international observers withdrew rather than participate in a flawed vote count. Fujimori was inaugurated for his third term in July 2000, but public indignation and mounting evidence of scandal forced him to resign in November, paving the way for a new presidential vote in April and June 2001, which international observers pronounced fair.

In Argentina, Menem declared in February 1998 that he would not seek a third term, then coyly hinted that he would accept a draft, then aggressively began pushing for a constitutional amendment. It was a moot issue, however, because not only did Menem's Justicialist Party lose its majority in Congress in 1997, but polls showed Menem had become so unpopular that he would be badly beaten even if he could run. By the end of 1998, Menem pragmatically had disavowed another run in 1999, but bombastically began vowing a comeback in 2003. With the chaos reigning now in Argentina, he may do it.

Another possibly disturbing trend is the public's fascination in several countries with former military strongmen or charismatic military figures who have entered the political arena. In Bolivia in 1997, former strongman Hugo Banzer was elected to the presidency by the Congress after he won a plurality of the popular vote. In Guatemala, opinion polls continue to show that the most popular political figure in the country remains former military dictator Efraín Ríos Montt, who is barred by the constitution from serving again as head of state. The political movement he heads remains an influential force nonetheless. In 1999, his Guatemalan Republican Front won an absolute majority in the Congress, which then named Ríos Montt president of that body for the second time, and his chosen candidate scored a landslide election as president of the republic.

A similar situation occurred in Paraguay in 1998. Former General Oviedo, who had attempted a coup in 1996 and who was convicted and placed under house arrest, won the Colorado Party nomination for president over the opposition of incumbent civilian President Juan Carlos Wasmosy—himself of the Colorado Party. Polls indicated that Oviedo, who could not even leave his quarters to campaign, would win the May 1998 election hands-down, causing Wasmosy to threaten to postpone the vote. The Supreme Court intervened and declared Oviedo's candidacy illegal, whereupon his running mate, Raúl Cubas, was elected president. Cubas then ordered the release of Oviedo, widely seen as the power behind the throne, a move that sparked a governmental crisis. The public's fascination with Oviedo, however, dimmed after the assassination in March 1999 of Vice President Luis María Argaña, Oviedo's leading opponent within the Colorado Party. The day after President Cubas' subsequent resignation, Oviedo fled to Argentina, then to Brazil, where he was arrested in June 2000. The Supreme Court ordered his release in 2001, and he has vowed to return to Paraguay and run for the presidency.

But the most dramatic case of a would-be *caudillo* continues to unfold in Venezuela. Former Lieutenant Colonel Hugo Chávez, who spent two years in prison for leading a failed attempt to overthrow President Carlos Andres Pérez in 1992, capitalized on public disgust with the corruption of the two traditional parties to run for president as an independent populist. In December 1998, after the two desperate parties agreed on a unity candidate, Chávez won a landslide victory. Upon assuming office in February 1999, he expressed his contempt for the legislative and judicial branches, then called for an election for a constituent assembly to rewrite the 1962 constitution. His adherents won 90% of the seats in that assembly, which then forged a new organic law that would allow Chávez to serve for two consecutive six-year terms, besides granting him broad new powers. Voters overwhelmingly approved the new constitution in December 1999, whereupon Chávez called for a new presidential election for May 2000, postponed at the last minute until July. Chávez won with 59% of the vote, an even greater landslide than in December 1998. An open admirer of Cuba's Fidel Castro, Chávez has openly expressed contempt for freedom of the press and the voices of dissent. He has voiced the familiar siren song of *caudillos* past who assume dictatorial powers: It is the only way to solve the country's problems. Mounting opposition to Chávez's heavy-handed methods erupted into violence in April 2002, which led to an abortive military coup. Within 48 hours, however, additional violence by pro-Chávez mobs effected his return to power. Ironically, Chávez, like Argentina's Juan Perón, is an elected autocrat, a political oxymoron if there ever was one.

There is nothing new about people in struggling societies turning to a strong–willed, charismatic leader who promises to bring order out of chaos, in Latin America or elsewhere. It evokes memories of the infamous explanation by

The Tikal Altar Stone, Guatemala

View of Montevideo, Uruguay

an Italian woman for why Mussolini remained popular for so long: "Because he made the trains run on time." The fact that a former military leader is elected president in a free, honest popular vote does not in and of itself represent a threat to democracy; Brazil's Getulio Vargas and Chile's Carlos Ibáñez both were returned to power in free elections. Indeed, it is the very manifestation of the people's will. It can be argued that the United States has elevated a number of military heroes to the presidency—most recently in 1952 and 1956—without undermining its democracy. But the United States and Latin America have vastly different traditions where military presidents are concerned, and the question that remains unanswered at this juncture is whether military men who win power through the ballot box are committed democrats or Trojan horses who will disregard the democratic process if it becomes inconvenient to them.

Despite these obvious shortcomings, when the Latin America of 2001 is compared with the Latin America of 1977, there can be no disputing the advances that have been made toward meaningful democracy, so in fairness the Latin American glass should be viewed as 4/5 full rather than 1/5 empty.

Economic Diversification and the Trend Toward Free Trade

For more than a hundred years, most of the post–colonial Latin American countries languished in the economic doldrums while North America experienced robust economic growth and prosperity. Only Argentina experienced growth similar to that of the United States and Canada. Several factors condemned Latin America to the poverty from which it is only now beginning to emerge.

To begin with, just as Spain, Portugal and France had failed to bequeath a democratic tradition to their former colonies, neither did they leave behind sound economic infrastructures. Sadly, these colonial powers were more concerned with exploitation than with development. Spain in particular was obsessed with how

much precious metal could be extracted from the ground, not with building roads, schools or financial institutions. Granted, the Jamestown colonists had come in search of gold, but when it became apparent that there was no gold in Virginia, the English recognized that the fecund soil offered other opportunities. The demand created for tobacco generated the wealth that gold did not. Subsequent English immigrants to the New World, whether to escape prison or religious persecution, came prepared to exploit the wealth of the soil or to engage in mercantilism. This fostered an independent, entrepreneurial spirit that was carried over into the post–independence period.

The Industrial Revolution was exported successfully from Britain to America. Industry, agriculture and the advent of public education led in the 19th century to the rise of a literate middle class of independent farmers and merchants with political rights sandwiched between those who amassed great wealth and those left behind in destitution. The unique concept of homesteading, providing free title to land in return for working it, further broadened the base of this independent–minded middle class. The opportunities it offered for self–advancement also sparked a wave of immigration that brought with it new zeal and new ideas.

There was no corresponding industrialization, democratization or mass education in Spain or in most of its erstwhile colonies in the 19th century. The result was a dual class structure in which a tiny, educated, wealthy elite, a disproportionate number of them Caucasian, held absolute economic and political power over a mass of desperately poor, illiterate Indian and *mestizo* peons. This structure was enforced in some countries for decades by a lone dictator, such as Paraguay's Rodrigo Gaspar de Francia or Mexico's Porfirio Díaz. Thus, social inequality enforced at bayonet point became the second major obstacle to Latin American development. Industrial growth requires a literate workforce.

The third major obstacle was monocultural dependency, the reliance of a country's economy on a single resource for export. This handicap persisted throughout the late 19th century and in some cases well into the 20th century. Thus, Brazil and Colombia depended on coffee, Bolivia on tin, Chile on copper, Peru on guano fertilizer, Cuba and the Dominican Republic on sugar, Venezuela on petroleum and Ecuador and the Central American republics on bananas. The derogatory term "banana republic" is another unfortunate Latin American stereotype, but again it had some basis in fact. The products upon which these countries depended for foreign exchange were at the mercy of the world market. To use an old analogy, when the world tin market sneezed, Bolivia caught pneumonia.

Compounding this situation was a fourth obstacle, undercapitalization that could only be overcome by surrendering control of the nation's one valuable resource to those who *did* have capital: foreign investors. Consequently, foreign–owned companies, mostly British and U.S., came to dominate these underdeveloped economies, exercising considerable political influence over their host governments. Probably the most egregious example was that of the United Fruit Company of the United States, which treated the Central American countries as private fiefs.

These deplorable conditions persisted decade after decade, as those with the power and money were able to maintain the status quo through force if necessary. Those lacking power could only submit. In those countries where democracy did manage to gain a temporary foothold in the late 19th and early 20th centuries—Argentina, Brazil, Chile and Uruguay—it is not surprising that socialist, communist and anarchist movements won adherents, much as they did in the United States during the same era. If misery existed under a capitalist system, the logic went, capitalism must be the enemy. Foreign capitalists were especially popular whipping boys. Expropriation of foreign holdings came into vogue, beginning with Mexico's nationalization of the oil industry in 1938. Latin American intellectuals, from the 1960s until the early '90s, almost universally followed like sheep a school of thinking known as "dependency theory," which held that Latin America was economically and culturally "dependent" upon the developed countries, especially the United States. Occasionally even reform–minded military officers would seize power with a

PER CAPITA INCOME 2001 in U.S. dollars	
Argentina	$7,680
Uruguay	$5,900
Mexico	$5,460
Venezuela	$5,283
Chile	$4,873
Costa Rica	$4,450
Panama	$3,663
Brazil	$3,300
Dominican Republic	$2,303 (2000)
El Salvador	$2,100 (2000)
Peru	$2,074
Colombia	$1,927
Guatemala	$1,729
Cuba	$1,700 (1999 est.)
Paraguay	$1,552 (1999)
Ecuador	$1,353
Bolivia	$1,019
Honduras	$720
Haiti	$520
Nicaragua	$470

Source: U.S. Department of State

Balsa boats in Lake Titicaca, Peru

promise to redress social wrongs, such as the military government in Peru from 1968–1980 that sought to impose a socialist system based on the Yugoslav model. Marxism came to power by force of arms in Cuba in 1959 and in Nicaragua in 1979 and through the ballot box in Chile in 1970. Fidel Castro was an enticing role model. Even conservative military regimes created state–owned corporations to run utilities, airlines, railroads, ports, mines and oil refineries. The realization that a cumbersome bureaucracy was a woefully inefficient way to provide reliable telephone or electrical service came slowly.

Other economic experiments were aimed at what were seen as sinister outside forces: high protective tariffs and regional trade blocs. Alas, these also proved a disappointment. Tariffs designed to protect fledgling local industries often created bloated monopolies that produced substandard and overpriced products. And trade blocs such as the Central American Common Market and the Andean Pact proved ineffectual because the member countries were not producing products for export that the other members wanted to import.

The Pinochet government in Chile proved to be the regional trend–setter when it withdrew from the Andean Pact and scuttled its protective tariffs to create a free–market economy. The initial result was a disastrous recession as local businesses proved unable to compete with

better and cheaper foreign imports. But gradually the economy equalized, showing real growth with single–digit inflation, something unattainable under the Marxist government of Salvador Allende. Pinochet also broke Chile's dependency on copper exports, promoting the export of fresh fruits. Chile's free–market strategy proved so successful that Pinochet's civilian successors have left it in place and it has been emulated by its neighbors.

Not long after the creation of Chile's free–market model, the Soviet Bloc collapsed, taking down with it the discredited notion of a state–run economy. Like a chain of dominos, Latin American countries began privatizing decades–old, state–owned corporations: Argentina, Brazil, Mexico, Peru and others. New policies, some of them draconian, also permitted Argentina, Brazil, Mexico and Peru to tame the hyperinflation that had become a seemingly permanent fixture throughout the 1970s and '80s. Two presidents who are the very embodiments of Latin America's conversion from public sector to private sector dominance are Brazil's Fernando Henrique Cardoso (1994–2002), an erstwhile Marxist economist and leading dependency theorist, and Argentina's Carlos Saúl Menem (1989–1999), a Peronist who steered the country on a course 180 degrees from that set by his patron saint, Juan Perón.

By the mid–1990s, Latin America was in the midst of an economic boom that had U.S. and European economists predicting

that the region could repeat the success story of the robust export–oriented economies of Asia. This expectation was heightened by the catastrophic collapse of the Asian stock markets in late 1997. Mexico was welcomed into the North American Free Trade Agreement (NAFTA) in 1993, and four new vibrant and stable economies in the Southern Cone of South America have formed *Mercosur*, a meaningful trade bloc that is showing moderate signs of success.

Following up on the concept of NAFTA and *Mercosur*, U.S. President Bill Clinton invited the Western Hemisphere's heads of state, minus Cuba's Fidel Castro, to Miami in 1993 for the first Summit of the Americas. There, the idea of establishing a hemisphere-wide Free Trade Area of the Americas (FTAA), with membership limited to democratic countries, was first advanced. In late 1997, Clinton suffered a setback when an odd coalition of Republicans and pro-labor Democrats blocked the president's request for so-called "fast-track" authority to negotiate trade pacts.

Nonetheless, at the second Summit of the Americas in Santiago, Chile, in April 1998, the 34 heads of state (once again, Castro was not invited), approved blueprints to establish the FTAA by 2005. Also recognizing that true economic development is dependent upon an educated workforce, the summit's communique called for the expenditure of $6.1 billion over three years to improve education. It also set a goal that 100% of the hemisphere's children would have access to elementary education and 75% would have access to secondary education by 2010. No longer seen as bogeymen, foreign investors are not only welcome but openly courted, and the political stability spreading through the region makes it an attractive target for investment.

The third Summit of the Americas was held in Quebec City, Canada, in April 2001, and once again the FTAA was the top agenda item. Thirty-four heads of state from democracies in the hemisphere attended; again, Cuba was excluded. The new U.S. president, George W. Bush, appeared to be an even more enthusiastic advocate of the FTAA than had Clinton. The heads of state set a target date of December 31, 2005, for establishment of what would become the world's largest free-trade bloc, encompassing 800 million people and accounting for an estimated $15 trillion in trade. The concept was not without its naysayers, however. In the streets of Quebec, protesters representing labor unions, environmental groups and various anti-capitalist organizations engaged in violent clashes with police in an attempt to break up the summit. Inside the summit, Venezuelan President Hugo Chávez charged that the lofty goals of the Miami and Santiago summits of reducing poverty had not been met, while Brazilian

President Cardoso complained about U.S. anti-dumping laws.

By the late 1990s, Latin America was experiencing regional economic growth that averaged a healthy 3% per year. In September 1998, however, uncertainty over the Russian ruble caused a chain–reaction market panic that hit the United States, the major Asian stock markets, and then Brazil, Argentina and Mexico. The crisis worsened in January 1999 when the bottom dropped out of the Brazilian stock market; its government allowed its currency, the *real*, to float, and it lost 46% of its value. The panic spread to neighboring stock markets, and for a time it appeared a massive regional recession was likely. The market crisis coincided with a dramatic drop in the world market price of petroleum which affected the economies of Venezuela, Ecuador and Mexico. The situation has since stabilized.

As with the trend toward democracy, however, the dramatic improvement in the Latin American economy has had its negative aspects, as well as nagging, unremedied problems: the continued gap between the very wealthy and the very poor; environmental pollution; overpopulation; and an underground economy based on the illegal traffic of drugs.

According to a report released in September 1996 by the U.N. Economic Commission for Latin America and the Caribbean, one third of Latin Americans live in poverty and 18 percent of them live in *dire* poverty, earning less than $1 a day. Even in comparatively affluent countries such as Uruguay, the wealthiest 10 percent of the population have access to 15 times the resources of the poorest 10 percent; in Honduras and Peru, the figure is 80 times. In these emerging democracies, however, these squalid masses do have access to something else—the ballot box. Unless such social inequality is addressed, Latin America could see a rebirth of the now-discredited movements of the left, with their siren song of help for the underprivileged. The election of the populist, and eccentric, Abdalá Bucaram as president of Ecuador in 1996, and the constitutional crisis he precipitated, could well prove to be a harbinger, as could the election of Venezuela's Chávez in 1998.

Such newly industrialized countries as Mexico, Argentina, Brazil and Chile are learning quickly what it took the United States and other developed economies more than a century to discover: that industrialization carries an expensive environmental price tag. The air pollution in Mexico City, Santiago and São Paulo is legendary, and a serious health hazard. Rivers and coastlines have become dumping grounds for the toxic waste by-products of heavy industry. Brazil, meanwhile, only began to take action in 1998 to slow the destruction of its rain forests in the name of agriculture, an environmental

rape that had raised international concerns for its exacerbation of global warming. Yet, in most of these still-underprivileged countries, this is a price they have been willing to pay in order to provide jobs for growing urban populations. But unless some solutions are found soon, those who are "lucky" enough to find work in the major cities may find that they have condemned themselves and their children to early graves.

Unchecked population growth has been problematical in countries ranging from industrial giants such as Mexico and Brazil to desperately poor agrarian Haiti. Too often social scientists in developed countries, many of whom apparently never visit Latin America, are too quick to single out the Roman Catholic Church's ban on contraception as the primary culprit. Although this is a factor, one would find that the urban middle classes in Latin America are just as willing to practice birth control in defiance of the pope as Roman Catholics in North America or Europe. Most of the population growth occurs in the lower economic strata, but not because they are more devout Catholics.

There are long–standing cultural factors at play as well. The *macho* ethic holds that the number of children a man sires is an outward manifestation of his virility, his very manhood. Moreover, as is the case in Africa and Asia, poor Latin Americans dependent upon agriculture for their existence see children as future fieldhands, someone to help them carry their burdens as they themselves age. Also, it is believed, a large brood is one way to guarantee security for one's old age. Such traditions cannot be overcome by government decree, but until some way is found to ensure that the number of new job-seekers does not exceed supply, Latin America's newly affluent cities will continue to be ringed by slums populated by those with high expectations, waiting their turn for a better life that may never come.

The drug trade has created in some areas the illusion of prosperity. In reality, it has brought back the monocultural dependence of poor farmers on a single cash crop. In the cities, it has brought fabulous wealth to a tiny cadre of drug lords, wealth which has trickled down in droplets to the veritable army of lab processors, transporters and others who have been enticed away from legitimate pursuits by the promise of quick, if venal, wealth.

It has been estimated that the Rodríguez Orijuela brothers, Gilberto and Miguel, the incarcerated leaders of the Cali Cartel of Colombia, are worth $250 billion. But the wealth drugs generate is illusionary—there is so much of it there is nothing left on which to spend it. Further, the real economies within which the drug trade operates cannot officially incorpo-

rate it. Governments cannot tax billions in revenue which is not legal and not claimed. Moreover, it proves a drain on the economy because governments must spend millions on enforcement that proves futile, and the very governmental institutions that seek vainly to bring this illicit industry to bay are themselves corrupted from the top down by the drug barons.

The futility is exacerbated by the rather naive counter–narcotics policies of the consuming countries of the north. For years the hope has been that somehow impoverished peasants can be made to see that they are endangering lives in Los Angeles or Chicago and that they can be persuaded to substitute cultivating coca with another cash crop—whose yield per hectare may be one tenth as much. Unless the insatiable demand for narcotics can be curbed in the consuming countries, there will be poor Latin Americans willing to run the risks to cultivate, process and transport drugs.

Technological Emergence

Yet another stereotype of Latin America, persistently reinforced by Hollywood, is of a backward region with muddy streets and antiquated technology. In the rural areas, that is still too often the case. But in the major cities, the economic boom has led inevitably to investment in modernizing the technological infrastructures. The impetus is the very essence of free-market capitalism: the necessity to compete. Visitors to even the poorer capital

Panamanian equestrian Fernando Senderos

A trainer with a playful porpoise in Nassau, Bahamas . . .

cities of most Latin American capitals will find computers literally everywhere, in hotels, banks, newspapers, universities and even small businesses. To ignore computerization is to fall behind the competition.

The communications revolution also has pervaded Latin America. For example, the tallest structure on the Santiago, Chile, skyline, just two blocks from the Moneda (presidential) Palace along Avenida Bernardo O'Higgins, is the Entel Tower, bristling with antennas and satellite dishes linking Santiago with the interior and with the rest of the world. Guests at even mid–priced hotels in a country like Guatemala may be surprised to find CNN and HBO on their television sets. Again, competition demands this.

As is the case in developed countries, the technological revolution has been an upward spiral, with innovation breeding innovation. Some of these countries, such as Brazil and Chile, now manufacture their own computer hardware and software. Free–trade agreements facilitate the transfer of technology across international boundaries.

If there is a negative picture at all in the technological emergence of Latin America, it is that there is still a long way to go. If public investment is made in upgrading public transportation, perhaps with modern subway systems such as Santiago's, it could help lessen the air pollution crises in the capital cities; as bad as Santiago's air quality is, it would be worse if the subway had not supplanted hundreds of buses belching oily exhaust from the combustion of cheap fuel. Despite advances in medical technology, more funds need to be invested in that sector to acquire state–of–the–art equipment. If the current economic expansion continues, it is inevitable that technological expansion will continue in its wake.

Cultural Growth and Projection

There is no more a "Latin American culture" than there is a homogenous U.S. or European culture. Which music, for example, is indicative of U.S. culture: jazz, blues, country–western, bluegrass, rock 'n' roll, rap, or grunge rock? The answer, of course, is all of the above. Is there a typically European art, literary style, music, architecture, fashion or cuisine? They vary, of course, from country to country.

Latin American culture—or better described, cultures—also are regionalized. The stereotype of the Latin American as a devout Catholic *mestizo* who speaks Spanish, wears white campesino cotton clothing, listens to mariachi music and eats spicy food is as far from reality as the Latin American stereotype of the "typical" *gringo* as a rich, Anglo–Saxon Protestant who wears Calvin Klein jeans, listens to rock and eats nothing but steak or hamburgers. (All right, maybe there's a kernel of truth to the rock and hamburger part.)

The North American view of Latin America understandably has been geographically influenced by neighboring Mexico. As Don Podesta of the *Washington Post* wrote a few years ago, Mexico is "a prism through which all Latin culture is viewed." But it is a woefully distorted view. In reality, the majority of the South American population are Portuguese–speaking Brazilians. Chile has a Lutheran minority of more than 10% stemming from German immigration in the 19th century, while nearly 40% of Guatemalans are converts to evangelical Protestantism. Mariachi music is no more, nor less, representative of Latin America than are Argentina's tango, Brazil's samba, the salsa of the Caribbean countries, the flute music of the Andean highlands, Chile's *huaso* music or the harp–based folk music of Paraguay. An Argentine accustomed to his bland meat–and–pasta diet would probably gag on the chili–pepper–laced *ceviche*, a concoction of raw fish and lime juice peculiar to the Pacific coast countries.

Ethnically, the Hispanic colonies evolved far differently from their counterparts in North America, or for that matter, in Brazil. The English colonizers pushed the Indian tribes back beyond the ever–expanding frontier, or simply exterminated them, while for manual labor in the fields they imported black slaves from West Africa. The Portuguese followed a roughly similar policy in Brazil. The Spanish, meanwhile, enslaved the Indian populations they found there, pressing them into service in the mines and on the *haciendas*. But while miscegenation was limited between the English on the one hand and the Indians and black slaves on the other, it was widespread in Brazil and the Spanish colonies, producing a mixed race of *mestizos* in the Hispanic realm, and of *mulattos* in Brazil. But this ethnic mosaic

was not woven evenly, however, providing for cultural discreteness today. The Argentines, like their counterparts in the United States, followed a shameless policy of genocide against the indigenous inhabitants, with the result that its culture is preponderantly Caucasian–European. So is that of Costa Rica, but there the white settlers found the land largely uninhabited. In Guatemala, Peru and Bolivia, the undiluted Indian races are in the majority. Perhaps the most diversified cultural tapestry is that of Panama, where apart from whites, *mestizos* and Indians there are the descendants of black laborers brought from the Caribbean early in this century to construct the canal, and Orientals who came later.

Just as the Anglo–Saxon stereotype is fading in the United States, so is the Hispanic stereotype no longer *apropriado* in Latin America, and for the same reason: successive waves of massive immigration beginning in the late 19th century and continuing to the present. Roughly half of all Argentines, for example, are of Italian lineage, descendants of migrant farmworkers who came to harvest grapes because of the reversed seasons and decided to stay. Germans, British and other Europeans also flocked to Argentina, Uruguay and Chile, as did European Jews seeking escape from persecution. Spanish Republicans seeking refuge after their defeat in the 1936–1939 civil war settled throughout the region.

Most Latin American countries also have unassimilated colonies of Arabs, Gypsies, blacks, and Orientals. To underscore just how much of a melting pot Latin America has become, we have only to consider the surnames of some of the recent presidents in one third of the former Spanish colonies: Sanguinetti in Uruguay (Italian), Fujimori in Peru (Japanese), Frei in Chile (Swiss), Wasmosy in Paraguay (Polish), Menem in Argentina and Bucaram and Mahaud in Ecuador (Arab) and Fox in Mexico (English). By contrast, of its 42 presidents, the United States has had but six without Anglo–Saxon surnames: Van Buren and the two Roosevelts (Dutch), Kennedy and Reagan (Irish) and Eisenhower (German).

Language, religion and ethnicity may be the roots of a culture, but its flowers are thoughts, ideas and expressions. In this regard, Latin America represents a veritable cultural nursery, one that finally has begun achieving recognition from the rest of the world. To be sure, U.S. and European cultural influences are much in evidence, ranging from Coca–Cola, McDonald's and Calvin Klein to the *plan europeo* practiced by the hotels and the architecture that makes cities like Buenos Aires, Rio de Janeiro and Santiago appear like New World copies of Madrid, Milan or Lisbon. The dependency theorists who warned that Latin America was economically subjugated by the United States also wrung their hands over perceived U.S. cultural intrusion; for some reason, they never seemed threatened by European influences. However, despite Coca–Cola, McDonald's, Calvin Klein, Rambo, rock music and the ubiquitous "I Love Lucy" reruns, the *dependentistas* wasted a great deal of bile for nothing. The Latin American cultures not only were not supplanted, Latin American art, music, literature, cinema and television have grown into distinctive genres in their own right, and these cultural expressions have been projected to the developed world.

Because Latin American art, music, literature and cinema are so individualistic according to nation, they are described more fully under the "Culture" section of each nation contained in this book.

Latin American televison development lagged well behind that of the United States and Europe, and because of its higher price tag it was usually the governments that led the way. This made television, like radio, an important political tool and a pawn in the quest for power. An exception was in Chile, where the first three stations were licensed to major universities. In recent years, state–owned television stations have yielded increasingly to privatization; in some countries, as in Britain, privately owned stations compete with the government station. In its early days, television programming in Latin America was crude, unreliable and heavily dependent on translated imported programs from the United States, which were cheaper than producing programs locally. This reality lent grist to the argument of the cultural dependency theorists. That has changed dramatically since the 1970s, however, with Mexico, Brazil, Argentina, Venezuela, Colombia and Chile all producing that uniquely Latin American soap opera, the *telenovela*, both for domestic consumption and for export. Variety shows are reminiscent of those of the United States in the 1950s and 1960s. One that reaches a hemispheric audience is *Sábado Gigante*, transmitted every Saturday from Miami but emceed by a Chilean, Mario Krutzberger, better known by the stage name Don Francisco.

Also following the U.S. model are sitcoms and news magazine shows, such as the not-very-original *Sesenta Minutos* in Argentina. U.S. imports are still in evidence, such as *Casado—con hijos* ("Married—with Children"). But the dependency theorists' fears that they would outpace demand for programs produced in the native language have not been realized.

Looking Forward ...

In attempting to digest this description of the political, economic, technological and cultural realities of Latin America today, one must invariably return to the analogous glass that is half full rather than half empty. Much cheer can be taken from the advances that have been made, while the remaining shortcomings must be acknowledged and addressed.

Another indicator of hope is Latin America's seeming abandonment of its policy of paranoia vis–à–vis its neighbor to the north. Granted, the United States did much to warrant paranoia with its policy of gunboat diplomacy and CIA–sponsored intrigue. A sardonic joke underscored the Latin American view of the United States: Why are there no military coups in the United States? Because they don't have an American Embassy! The most recent U.S. intervention in the region, in Haiti in 1994, however well intentioned it may have been, inevitably raised eyebrows anew in Latin American capitals.

Yet, the relationship of old that bordered on praetorianism has yielded to one of equal partnership in terms of trade. Even that most xenophobic of nations, Mexico, accepted President Clinton's offer of a $13.5 billion loan to bail it out of its 1994–1995 recession and entered into NAFTA. Despite dire predictions from members of the U.S. Congress that the loan was throwing good money after bad, Mexico repaid the loan in January 1997, with interest—and three years ahead of schedule, albeit with money borrowed in Europe at lower interest rates.

Other issues must be addressed, however, if Latin America is to continue to develop democratically, socially and economically. Press freedom must be respected as an independent check on would-be autocrats. Environmental pollution, that inevitable by-product of development, threatens the health of the next generation. Most importantly, there is the need to provide that next generation with a better education. Latin America continues to lag behind the developed world and the emerging countries of Asia in educational quality. The next generation must be more than merely literate; it must join the computer age.

The hemisphere's greatest remaining blight, the anachronistic totalitarian system in Cuba, must inevitably acquiesce to the weight of history. A false hope was raised with Pope John Paul II's historic visit to Cuba in January 1998, an event that Castro marked by allowing a revival of religious expression and by releasing some of his political prisoners. Alas, since then, Castro has continued to imprison dissenters—230 at last count—and to resist international calls for reform. In response to the "Varela Project,"a petition signed by 11,000 courageous dissenters in 2002 that called for a referendum on free elections and freedom of expression, Castro responded with a "petition" of his owned, signed by a suspicious 8.2 million people, for a constitutional amendment that would make his dogmatic Marxist system "untouchable." The National Assembly dutifully passed this constitutional amendment-to-outlaw-constitutional amendments, 557-0. The 75-year-old Castro has thus thrown down his gauntlet before the domestic and international chorus for reform, raising the specter of a violent struggle for power when he finally dies.

The overall trend in Latin America toward greater political freedom, economic affluence, technological expansion and cultural individuality is evident. There have inevitably been setbacks. There will be more. But for the moment, Latin America appears to be investing in its future, and its stock is clearly on the rise.

Robert T. Buckman
Lafayette, Louisiana, July 2002.

. . . while silvered dolphins decorate the fountain in a flower–filled patio in mid–town Port–of–Spain, Trinidad

The Early Americans

THE GEOGRAPHICAL FACTOR

The development of few civilizations have been so influenced by geographical factors as those in Latin America. Contrary to long held beliefs, the land of Central and South America is neither young nor generally fertile. Old and trampled by several civilizations, large territories had already been abandoned by the Indians, even before the arrival of the Spaniards. The Mayas probably exhausted their initial homeland, and the Incas called the vast desert regions between Peru and Chile "the land of hunger and death." Furthermore, the continent had few and scattered ports and is internally divided by rugged mountains, jungles, turbulent rivers and arid zones, which constitute formidable obstacles for communication or exploitation of natural resources.

Thus, since pre–Columbian times, human societies developed in sort of isolated clusters having little contact with other communities. The Spanish policy of building cities as centers of political power increased this basic pattern of concentration and regionalism. Consequently, once the unifying authority of the Spanish king collapsed, it was impossible to keep all those remote and distant cities under a common authority. Immediately, almost every important urban center felt capable of demanding and asserting its own independence.

Geography not only contributed to this fragmentation, but also greatly determined the acceleration of two negative social trends which continue to hinder Latin American progress: (1) the abnormal growth of cities, especially capitals, constantly attracting masses of impoverished peasants—Mexico City's population jumped from less than 5 million in 1963 to 16.5 million in 1986 and the estimate for the year 2000 is 30 million!—and (2) the lack of balance in the national population distribution. In almost every Latin country, the population is concentrated in one–third to one–half of its national territory, leaving large zones almost totally uninhabited. Such conditions make the exploitation of the hinterland's resources a difficult and costly enterprise.

Indian Civilizations

When the Spaniards and other Europeans reached the New World, they found the native Americans in various stages of cultural development. Thinly scattered nomadic tribes of hunters and fishermen who also practiced simple farming populated much of the region. In contrast, three groups of natives—the Mayas, the Aztecs and the Incas—developed comparatively sophisticated and complex civilizations. They constructed large cities with imposing architectural styling, organized empires, acquired a knowledge of mathematics and astronomy and worked in precious stones and metals. The majority of these Indian civilizations had a sort of fatalistic concept of life and the universe; their worship halls and temples were full of terrifying gods who incessantly demanded sacrifices, usually human. Their societies were stratified by class division and were based more on communal interest and units than on individual achievements. Furthermore, vast distances and geographical obstacles hindered enlightening inter–cultural relations, while the absence of horses, cows or any pack animals limited their economic expansion or mass mobility. Perhaps because of such limitations, only one of these civilizations, the Mayas, developed some form of primitive writing, while none discovered the practical use of the wheel. In spite of intense research by scientists and archaeologists, we don't have yet a clear picture of the intricate aspects of the social systems and collective beliefs of pre–Columbian Indian society. Many questions remain to be answered.

The Mayas (Guatemala, Mexico, Belize, Honduras, El Salvador)

As the most advanced and sophisticated of the early American civilizations, Mayan culture flourished for more than 1,000 years, reaching the peak of its development in the 7th and 8th centuries A.D. Mayan life was sustained by a single basic crop: corn, which grew in such abundance that it allowed them time to engage in a multitude of activities other than raising food, thus raising their lifestyles above that of the other Indian societies which remained tied to the soil in order simply to exist. Apparently the Mayas lived mostly in independent city states, tied together by an extensive road system and a common culture. A warlike people, the Mayas placed most political power in the hands of an extended royal family and priests. Mayan religion was based on the worship of many gods, but the practice declined with the growing sophistication of the society. Initially, religious ceremonies called for frequent human sacrifices. Art and architecture were not greatly inferior to that of Europe at the time. As pioneers in the use of mathematics and astronomy, the Mayas refined an advanced calendar as early as the 4th century B.C. They also devised the mathematical concept of *zero* and developed a highly complex form of writing based on hieroglyphics (picture writing) which until today remains partially undeciphered.

Among the greatest achievements of the Mayas was art, including sculpture, pottery and textiles. Foremost was architecture. Major reminders of the Mayan civilization survive today in the form of thousands of monumental temples, soaring pyramids and majestic palaces. Many of these impressive structures have been discovered only recently, enveloped in the lush, tropical jungles of Central America and southern Mexico. These vestiges of the past, however, have yet to reveal why the Mayas suddenly abandoned their great cities long before the arrival of the Spaniards. Was it due to massive crop failure? Was it pestilence? Military defeat? Rebellion by slaves? The answer to this question is slowly being revealed—it probably involved the split-up of a large empire because of rivalries, followed by succession of unnumbered small states each with its own fortification and the fascination of the people with constant warfare. The techniques of siege were probably perfected, and they killed each other off to an extent that those remaining simply disappeared into the thick foliage to live as primitives.

Aztec goddess *Coatlicue*

The Aztecs (Mexico)

When Hernán Cortés landed on the Mexican coast in 1519, the Aztec empire was at the very height of its power and development. Assimilating the knowledge and achievements of previous civilizations such as the Olmecs and the Toltecs, the Aztecs developed into a harsh and efficient military society which allowed them to conquer all of central Mexico from the Atlantic to the Pacific. This brutal form of domination provoked constant rebellions among the tribes they subjugated, from whom they extracted slaves and human victims for sacrifice to their gods. In one especially dry season, Montezuma I, claiming that "the gods are thirsty," sacrificed 20,000 human beings on Aztec altars.

The Aztec social system rested on a rigid class structure with most manual work being performed by slaves captured during military campaigns. The economy was based on corn. Aztec architecture was impressive and their capital city of Tenochtitlán, now the site of Mexico City, was described by the conquering Spaniards as being equal to any in Europe. Although not as advanced as the Mayas had been in the use of science, mathematics or writing, the Aztecs did develop a more cohesive empire, even though it was based on force. The widespread resentment among enslaved neighboring groups was shrewdly exploited by Cortés to topple the Aztec empire.

Incas (Peru, Ecuador, Bolivia)

The empire carved out of the rugged Andes by the Incas reached its greatest level of development about a century before the arrival of the Spaniards. Through conquest of weaker Indian tribes in the region, the Incas expanded their realm from Peru through southern Colombia, Ecua-

Mayan ruins at Tikal, Guatemala

Detail of an Inca stone wall in Cuzco, Peru

dor and Bolivia, and northern Chile—a combined area of more than 350,000 square miles. Facilitated by an efficient administrative command, a courier communications network and an impressive road system rivaling that of the Roman Empire, the Incas were able to weave their vast domain into the most highly organized and efficient civilization of all the native Americans. At the head of the entire system was the ruling god–emperor called Inca. Under him was a highly structured noble class and priests, followed by lower level officials. The rigid chain of command permeated every corner of the empire. The Incas integrated newly conquered tribes into the realm by imposing a single language, *Quechua*, religion and social structure. Except for the highly rigid caste system of the ruling elite, the Inca state came close to being a totalitarian socialist state. All property was owned by the state and all work was organized on a communal basis. Through a system called "mita" (which the Spaniards later immediately adopted in the region) all

members of the lower classes were obliged to work free for the empire for a period of four months every year. In return, the empire provided for the needs of its citizens. The result was a rather dull life for the masses—with little incentive, capability or effort to rebel. The heart of the empire was the capital of Cuzco (literally "navel" in Quechua). A magnificent city by almost any standard, Cuzco glistened with enormous palaces and temples (many of which were lavishly gilded with gold) and other imposing dwellings which housed the elite. Even today, some of these structures are still in use, having withstood for centuries the abuses of man and the elements.

Although the Incas were less developed than the Mayas in the skills of writing, mathematics and astronomy, they surpassed the Mayas in architecture, water works, stonework and engineering. Indeed, some lengthy Inca suspension bridges were found when the Europeans reached the area and remained in use until the middle of the 19th century. Inca sys-

tems of irrigation, pottery, textiles, medicines and even surgical techniques were remarkable. The Incas' greatest gift to the world, however, was the potato, which in time would save tens of thousands of Europeans from starvation. Despite its vast power, the Inca empire quickly fell to the *conquistadores*. The reasons for the sudden collapse of America's greatest Indian civilization were numerous: the Spaniards possessed superiority in firearms, employed advanced military tactics, exploited the advantage of horses and were relentlessly driven onward by the lure of gold. In contrast, the Inca empire was mortally weakened by a rigid social system in which the vital administrative structure was paralyzed once the top Inca was captured. In addition, a devastating war of succession between two royal Inca brothers had left the empire exhausted and divided. As a result, the Incas fell easy prey to a band of only 184 con- querors led by a cunning Francisco Pizarro.

Other Indian civilizations that reached a high level of development were the

Major Native Cultures About 1500

Chibchas of northern Colombia and the Pueblo Indians of New Mexico. Indeed, the 16th century Spanish conquerors of Latin America—in contrast to the 17th century English, French and Dutch settlers in North America—encountered civilized natives whose social level was not greatly inferior to their own.

The impact of the conquest destroyed the Indian civilizations and looted their priceless treasures. To this was added the seizure of their valuable lands, forced labor and the spread of diseases unknown to the Indians, which decimated their population. The Spanish intermarried with the women of the former Indian ruling classes and built their empire on the social and economic foundations of the vanquished civilizations. Unsuited to plantation labor, especially in the tropics, the Indians were replaced by slaves imported from Africa and indentured laborers from Asia.

One of the most impressive and lasting achievements of the Spaniards was the conversion of the Indians to Catholicism. Devoted missionaries, still imbued with the religious fervor of the "glorious crusade" which had expelled the Arabs from Spain, risked their lives to preach the new faith among the Indians, learned their languages and defended them from the greed of the *conquistadores* and even the Spanish crown. Thanks to their examples and sacrifices, Catholic religion, or at least some variation of Catholicism, penetrated deeply among the Indian masses, transforming the Church into a powerful and influential institution in Latin America from the colonial period; its influence is waning as Indians migrate to the larger cities.

Scattered remnants of Indian civilization retreated from Spanish influence to the mountains of Guatemala, Ecuador,

Peru and Bolivia, while the majority remained under Spanish rule. Until recent times, many of the Indians have succeeded in preserving their ancient communal life and customs. Today, the Quechua-speaking Indians still number some 6 million in Bolivia and 2 million in Ecuador. Although their living conditions have scarcely improved since Pizarro's time, Andean Indians have remained detached and suspicious of meager government efforts to incorporate these survivors of the Inca Empire into a modern social and economic structure.

Efforts to modernize traditional Indian lifestyles have also been painfully slow in Central America and Mexico. In Guatemala, the descendants of the Mayas have largely continued to cling to their traditional customs despite government programs to encourage change. Even in Mexico, the most *mestizo* (mixed European–Indian ancestry) country in Latin America, many of Aztec and Mayan ancestry, particularly in the southern area, still have only marginal contact with the 20th century—even though modernization of Indian lifestyles has been a

nominal objective of the Mexican government.

The process of social change has accelerated since World War II with the aid of modern communications—particularly the transistor radio—which have helped to penetrate the isolation that has allowed outmoded social, economic and political conditions to persist in the remote hinterlands.

Recently some Latin American governments, particularly those of Mexico and Peru, have begun to show an increasing appreciation of the contributions and heritage of the early American civilizations. This growing interest has not been without cost. The rising appeal for Indian art has led to large-scale looting of ancient monuments and graves. In Central America and in the Andes, art thieves have stolen priceless stonework, jewelry and pottery—irreparably damaging some of it in the process—in an effort to satisfy the modern demand for genuine ancient art. In that sense, today's art thieves are continuing the same traditions of the *conquistadores* who plundered the early American Indian civilizations.

The ruins of Machu Picchu, the remote mountainous retreat of the Inca rulers, so well hidden that it was only discovered in 1911

13

Conquest, Colonization,
and the Challenge of Independence

Cortés and the ambassadors of Moctezuma

Cortés began his conquest of Mexico in 1519; Pizarro invaded Peru in 1531 and Quesada and others began the conquest of Colombia in 1536. The Spaniards' superiority in weaponry and cavalry does not fully explain the victory of so few over so many. The decisive factor was the different character of the contending armies. Based on individual initiative, the Spanish regiments could face and fight formidable odds no matter what the losses. Based on strict authority and command, the Indian armies usually disintegrated when the general or high priest was captured or killed. In the battle of Otumba, Cortés had no gunpowder and only sixteen horsemen, while the Aztecs were 20,000 strong. When a desperate Spanish charge killed the Aztec commander, the Indian army remained paralyzed while Cortés and his small group marched toward the safety of Tlaxcala, the capital of a powerful Indian tribe which had become Cortés' ally.

The conquest and colonization of Brazil followed a different pattern. By the Treaty of Tordesillas of 1494, Spain and Portugal divided South America between them along the 45th Meridian—Spain to the west, Portugal to the east. As early as April 22, 1500, Admiral Pedro Alvares Cabral established Portugal's authority over the region, but as further explorations found no traces of gold and silver, and since Portugal was then fully engaged in its profitable Asian trade, Brazil received scant attention. For many years, colonists occupied only a narrow belt of coastal land. The "*bandeirantes*," rough adventurers and *mestizos* organized in groups called "bandeiras," were the ones who in their search for Indians and wealth slowly opened the interior of Brazil, pushing the nomadic Indian tribes into further remote areas. Portugal's declining Asian trade ultimately stimulated emigration to Brazil. In 1549, after the appointment of the first royal governors, a better system of land distribution was established and the Jesuits opened their first schools.

The strategic position and potential of Brazil attracted foreign attacks. French and Dutch attempts to hold Brazilian territories failed, however, and by 1645 the expanding colony was under Portugal's firm control. Initially sugar production flourished in the north, but the discovery of gold in what is today the state of Minas Gerais made the south the economic and political center of the colony, a position consolidated by subsequent discoveries of diamonds and precious stones. At the beginning of the 19th century, Brazil was a growing but still basically rural colony, with a vast and untouched hinterland.

During the colonial period, Spain created a highly centralized government, with most power concentrated in the monarch, and an internal balance of power which functioned remarkably well for three centuries. The region was divided into four viceroyalties: New Spain (capital, Mexico

14

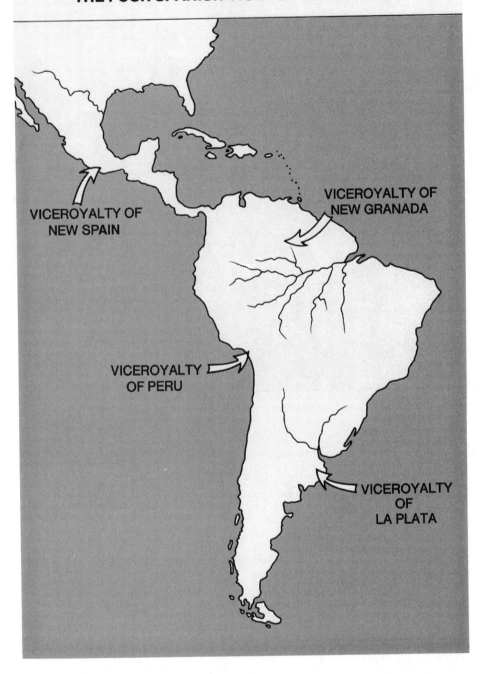

THE FOUR SPANISH VICEROYALTIES: 1790

VICEROYALTY OF
NEW SPAIN

VICEROYALTY OF
NEW GRANADA

VICEROYALTY
OF PERU

VICEROYALTY
OF
LA PLATA

America displayed important cities like Mexico and Lima, impressive cathedrals, a few universities and even famous writers like Sor Juana Inés de la Cruz and Carlos de Siguenza y Gongora.

At the beginning of the 18th century, the ruling elite became increasingly divided between the *criollos,* or creoles (those born in America) and the *peninsulares* (mainly functionaries recently arrived from Spain or Portugal). The creoles generally controlled the land, the *peninsulares* wielded political power. The aspiration of the creoles to be treated as equals and to share political power intensified the friction between the two groups. Aware of Spain's and Portugal's decline as European powers, the creoles turned to France for cultural guidance.

Thus, the French Revolution had more impact in Latin America than did the American one. In Haiti, the division of the French white ruling elite brought about by France's political turmoil, sparked a rebellion of the black slaves under Toussaint L'Overture, which after a bloody and devastating war, ended with the liberation of the island. In the rest of Latin America, though, the creoles were far from being *Jacobins* (revolutionaries). A minority sympathized with the Declaration of Human Rights, but the majority was aware of the dangers which an open rebellion against Spain and Portugal could bring. Fearful of the surrounding masses of Indians and *mestizos,* most of the creoles wanted reforms, not revolution. Only the collapse of the Iberian monarchies could prompt them into action. In 1808 Napoleon gave them the opportunity. Invading the Iberian peninsula, he imprisoned the Spanish king and forced the Braganças, Portugal's royal family, to escape to Rio de Janeiro. Confronted with this political crisis, the creoles were forced to act.

City), New Granada (capital, Bogotá), Peru (capital, Lima), and Rio de la Plata (capital, Buenos Aires). Several captains–general ruled less important territories. All judicial matters were dealt with by the *audiencias,* and the designation of ecclesiastical posts remained in the king's hands. At the end of his term, every viceroy had to submit to a *juicio de residencia,* a sort of trial where everyone could accuse him of improprieties or abuses of power. Although initially some authority had been granted to city councils (*cabildos*), eventually their autonomy was greatly reduced by royal control. Consequently, the colonies gained little experience in self–government or administration of public affairs.

The Church was in charge of education, but private religious orders, especially the Jesuits, made determined efforts to modernize learning. Nevertheless, a humanistic, non–scientific type of education became traditional in Ibero–America. Under the patronage of the Church and the Crown, architecture and schools of painting flourished, and the Baroque style, perfectly suited to dazzle the masses, became dominant in all artistic expression. By the middle of the 18th century, while Brazil, whose development was much slower, had only scattered rural towns, Hispanic

Cathedral of Cuzco, built about 1535

15

General José de San Martín proclaims Peru's independence, July 1821

Independence and Its Aftermath

While the Spanish people rebelled against Napoleonic armies, and the Brazilians proudly received their sovereigns, Hispanoamericans were left in a political vacuum. Their initial reaction was to swear fidelity to Ferdinand, the captured Spanish king. Soon, however, *they* realized their power. Deprived of legitimacy and without hope of receiving reinforcements from Spain, colonial authorities were practically paralyzed. By 1810 the creoles had moved from tentative autonomy to open independence. Significantly, Mexico and Peru, the two viceroyalties where Indian population was in greater proportion, remained under Spanish control. Immediately, regionalism and individualism began to fragment colonial unity. In the principal cities of the continent, hastily formed governments adopted republican constitutions and strove to extend their shaky authority over the surrounding territories.

In 1814, Napoleon's defeat brought absolutist Ferdinand back to the Spanish throne. The prestige of the restored king, and some military reinforcements, gave the colonial authorities the upper hand. By 1816, with the exception of Buenos Aires, including the Viceroyalty of Rio de la Plata, Spanish rule had been reestablished over most of the empire. Abso-

lutism, however, could no longer appeal to the creoles. Furthermore, Spain's political troubles had not ended: in 1820 a poorly equipped army destined to fight in America rebelled against the king, occupied Madrid and imposed a liberal constitution. In the meantime, inspired by the leadership of Simón Bolívar and José de San Martín, the creoles renewed the war. After organizing an army in Argentina, San Martín crossed the Andes and defeated the Spaniards in Chile. Bolívar obtained similar victories in Venezuela and Colombia. After invading Peru and meeting Bolívar, San Martín abandoned the struggle and retired to France, the first in a long list of disillusioned liberators. Bolívar marched into Peru and on December 9, 1824, his best commander, Antonio José de Sucre, defeated the last royalist army in the battle of Ayacucho.

Two years before that decisive battle, with less violence, Mexico and Brazil achieved independence. In Mexico, the successive rebellions of two priests, Father Miguel Hidalgo and Father José María Morelos, backed mostly by Indians and *mestizos*, had been defeated by an alliance of conservative creoles and Spanish forces. In 1820 the proclamation of a liberal constitution in Spain induced those conservative allies to seek independence. Their instrument was a creole army officer, Agustín de Iturbide, whose mission

was to defeat the remnant republican guerrillas and to proclaim a conservative empire. Instead, Iturbide gained popularity by appealing to *all* factions, entered Mexico City in triumph and was proclaimed Emperor Agustín I! In Brazil, Portugal's liberal revolution produced similar consequences. The new government in Lisbon recalled the king, and tried to reduce Brazil back to a colonial status. Before departing Brazil, the king designated his son Pedro as regent and gave him sound advice: if the Brazilians want independence, don't *oppose* them, *lead* them. Shortly after his father's departure Pedro received a peremptory summons from the Lisbon parliament. Encouraged and supported by the Brazilians, he refused to go. When Portugal sent him a rash ultimatum, Pedro answered by proclaiming the independence of Brazil. On December 1, 1822, he was crowned emperor of Brazil. By 1825, Portugal had lost its American colony and only Cuba and Puerto Rico remained under Spanish rule.

The Challenge of Independence

The first 50 years of independence were marked by political turmoil, regional confrontations and economic decline. The only exceptions to this were Chile, where a small territory and a rather homogenous population allowed the creole elite to

ACTA DE INDEPENDENCIA

DEL

IMPERIO MEXICANO,

PRONUNCIADA POR SU JUNTA SOBERANA,

CONGREGADA EN LA CAPITAL DE EL, EN 28 DE SETIEMBRE DE 1821.

La Nacion Mexicana, que por trescientos años, ni ha tenido voluntad propia, ni libre el uso de la voz, sale hoy de la opresion en que ha vivido.

Los heróicos esfuerzos de sus hijos han sido coronados, y está consumada la empresa, eternamente memorable, que un génio, superior a toda admiracion y elogio, amor y gloria de su patria, principió en Iguala, prosiguió y llevó al cabo, arrollando obstáculos casi insuperables.

Restituida, pues, esta parte del Septentrion al ejercicio de cuantos derechos le concedió el Autor de la naturaleza, y reconocen por inenagenables y sagrados las naciones cultas de la tierra, en libertad de constituirse del modo que mas convenga á su felicidad, y con representantes que puedan manifestar su voluntad y sus designios, comienza á hacer uso de tan preciosos dones, y declara solemnemente, por medio de la Junta Suprema del imperio, que es Nacion soberana é independiente de la antigua España, con quien, en lo sucesivo no mantendrá otra union que la de una amistad estrecha, en los términos que prescribieren los tratados: que entablará relaciones amistosas con las demas potencias, ejecutando, respecto de ellas, cuantos actos pueden y están en posesion de ejecutar las otras naciones soberanas: que va a constituirse con arreglo a las bases que en el plan de Iguala y tratado de Córdoba estableció sabiamente el primer gefe del ejército imperial de las tres garantias; y en fin, que sostendrá a todo trance, y con el sacrificio de los haberes y vidas de sus individuos, si fuere necesario, esta solemne declaracion, hecha en la capital del imperio a veintiocho de setiembre del año de mil ochocientos veintiuno, primero de la independencia mexicana.

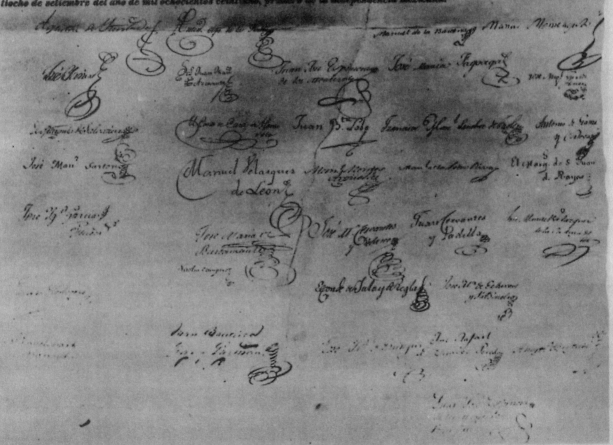

Mexico's Declaration of Independence with Iturbide's signature, top left–hand corner.

develop a strong and stable government, and Brazil, where the monarchy provided a moderate unifying force. In the rest of Latin America, the lack of concensus on who should rule, massive ignorance, racial differences and a tradition of authoritarianism, opened the doors for *caudillos*, strong leaders who temporarily commanded the loyalty of armed groups and imposed their authority over congresses and constitutions. There were *caudillos* of all sorts: enigmatic men like Gaspar Rodríguez de Francia, who closed Paraguay to foreign influences; barbarians like Bolivian Mariano Melgarejo, who "executed" his uniform for hurting his neck; ultra Catholics like Ecuadorian García Moreno and liberals like Venezuelan Gusmán Blanco. But almost all of them, even Argentine Juan Manuel de Rosas, represented more a consequence than a cause. They filled a political vacuum and, to a certain extent, contributed to uniting the nations they ruled.

Around 1870, Latin America entered a period of political stability and economic progress. In Argentina, Buenos Aires' liberal oligarchy finally imposed its authority over the provinces. Brazil became a republic in 1889 and even Mexico, a land plagued by internal dissention and foreign military interventions, attained political stability under the firm control of dictator Porfirio Díaz. Almost simultaneously, expanding European markets, especially England's, which had become the dominant economic power in Latin America, increased the demands for Latin American products, ushering in a period of growth and economic dependence.

During this period, waves of European immigrants poured into Argentina, Brazil, Chile and, in lesser numbers, into other Latin American nations. Political parties appeared, government control over the remote territories expanded thanks to better communication and the creation of professional armies, and large towns like Buenos Aires, Rio de Janeiro and Mexico became burgeoning cities.

In 1898, the United States intervened in the Cuban war of independence, defeated Spain and occupied Cuba and Puerto Rico. Cuba became "independent" in 1902, but about the same time, Panama severed itself from Colombia (an event arranged by the United States) and signed a treaty with Washington authorizing the opening of a canal in an "American" territorial zone which was to extend from the Atlantic to the Pacific, physically dividing Panama. In spite of those ominous notes, which sent a wave of anti–imperialism throughout Latin America, at the beginning of the 20th century a mood of optimism reigned in the hemisphere.

Many of the old problems, though, remained unsolved. Unequal distribution of wealth, economic dependence, landless peasants, regional concentration of power, all hampered genuine development. Very soon, hemispheric and international events demonstrated the fragility of Latin American political stability. In 1910, the Mexican Revolution began; four years later, World War I exposed the vulnerability of the hemispheric economies; after the Russian revolution of 1917, communist parties appeared in almost every Latin American country. Another economic crisis shook the continent in 1919; thus the 1920s were years of political turmoil crowned by the devastating economic crisis of the worldwide depression of 1929–1939. Few Latin American governments survived the impact of the Great

U.S. troops camp in front of the Presidential Palace in Havana, 1898

View of the Zocalo, Mexico City's main square

Depression. Only World War II and the emergence of the United States as a global power temporarily revitalized the economy of the hemisphere. But the period after the war also brought the economic competition of new underdeveloped nations, the decline of Latin exports, and, finally, with Cuba's revolution, the entrance of Latin America into the ideological struggle between the U.S. and the Soviet Union.

In 1961, Castro's Cuba, the first socialist regime in the Western Hemisphere, launched a continental offensive under Marxist banners. The emergence of Castroite guerrillas in almost every corner of the continent disrupted the slow but steady progress toward democracy experienced in the 1950s when military regimes were toppled in Argentina, Venezuela, Colombia, Brazil and Peru. Threatened by this new enemy, Latin American armies, occasionally backed or tacitly supported by equally alarmed civilians, responded with a series of military coups, which reduced the number of democratic governments to only four. Simultaneously, Washington initiated an ambitious "Alliance for Progress" to lessen Latin American economic and so-

cial problems, and increased its military aid to the armies. By 1975, the guerrillas had been defeated, dictatorial regimes dominated most of the continent, and under new economic guidelines, encouraging progress on industrialization and agricultural development had been achieved. In the 1970s Latin America spent more money on education (in relative terms of national budgets) than any other region in the world.

The stormy economic winds of the early 1980s brought a sudden halt to that effort. The oil crisis, accompanied by the subsequent economic recession in the U.S. and Western Europe, hit Latin America hard. With astronomical external public debts, plummeting prices for its products and sources for further loans drying up, Latin America plunged into its worst economic crisis of the last five decades. While austerity measures triggered popular protests in several countries, the emergence of another Marxist–oriented regime in Nicaragua brought forth U.S. intervention and an expansion of the crisis demonstrated by the re–emergence of the guerrilla threat and of communist exploitation of social woes. By mid–1985, in spite of

heartening democratic victories in Argentina, Guatemala, El Salvador, Uruguay and Brazil, a cloud of uncertainty and gloom hovered over the entire continent— a condition which continues.

During the 1960s, many observers felt the major problem facing Latin America was to save it from Castro–inspired revolutionaries. In the 1990s many see the major problem as one of maintaining fledgling democratic regimes. Regardless of the political system now in each Latin American nation, most face similar problems that confront the region (and the world) as a whole: widespread poverty, hunger, illiteracy and disease as well as one–product economies that suffer from fluctuations of prices in world markets and—all too often—underdeveloped social and political systems.

The daring liberators of the 19th century were successful—perhaps too successful—in their zeal to destroy the prevailing political, social and economic order. Today, some four centuries later, Latin America is still trying to construct a workable replacement for these shattered systems. Developing such institutions for the future remains the challenge for the present.

U.S.–Latin American Relations

The history of the relationship between the United States and Latin America can be divided into five relatively distinct periods: **1820–1880,** the era of the Monroe Doctrine and U.S. paternalism; **1880–1934,** the era of open U.S. imperialism, intervention, and the policies of gunboat diplomacy and the "big stick;" **1934–1945,** the "Good Neighbor Policy;" **1945–1990,** the Cold War, the Alliance for Progress, the Cuban and Nicaraguan revolutions and U.S. support for anti–communist dictators; and **1990–present,** the post Cold War era, the emergence of democracy in Latin America and a growing U.S.–Latin American trade partnership.

Even a brief summary of U.S.–Latin American relations usually begins by mentioning how the example of American independence stirred rebellious ideas among the creole elites in colonial Latin America. Actually, geographical, cultural and political barriers greatly reduced the impact of American "revolutionary" wars in the southern hemisphere. Only a tiny minority of cultivated creoles had some notion of what had happened in North America. Beyond the general satisfaction of witnessing the defeat of England and a vague reverence toward the figures of George Washington and Thomas Jefferson, it is difficult to find concrete traces of North American influence in the Latin American elites of the 18th century.

For a long time, the United States, following President Washington's isolationist policy, remained indifferent to the affairs of the southern neighboring nations. While Latin America struggled and achieved independence, the United States concentrated on purchasing Florida from Spain in 1821 and avoided any act or declaration which could endanger those negotiations.

In 1823, President Monroe delivered his famous message to Congress, quickly raised to the rank of a "doctrine," warning European powers that any attempt to extend their system to any portion of this hemisphere would be considered as a threat to the United States. In spite of its significance, the Monroe Doctrine was a U.S. unilateral declaration which did not imply any concern or interest in Latin American problems. When three years later Simón Bolívar, dreaming of unifying the newly born Latin American states, convened the ill–fated first Pan-American Congress, the United States reacted with little enthusiasm. The United States did not invoke the Monroe Doctrine in 1833 when England occupied the Falkland Islands claimed by Argentina nor in 1838–_1840 when France took military actions against Mexico and Buenos Aires. In 1848 a victory in its war with Mexico allowed the United States to acquire vast territories from that country and extend its territory to the Pacific Ocean.

Historical circumstances prevented Latin America from expressing any strong criticism of the United States during Mexico's debacle. Fragmented into several fledgling states, facing almost continuous internal political turmoil and poorly informed of international events, Latin America was not ready for any continental or racial solidarity. Furthermore, during almost the entire 19th century the dominant power in Latin America was Great Britain, not the United States. By 1880 the situation had changed. Political stability and economic progress in Latin America coincided with the emergence of expansionist or imperialist trends in the United States.

In 1889 the United States showed its growing economic interest in the southern regions by holding in Washington the first Pan–American Conference and establishing the basis for an Inter–American regional system under U.S. domination. Shortly after that conference, American expansionism transformed the image of the United States from a "model" to be copied by Latin America into an aggressive "Colossus of the North," bent on dominating the entire continent.

In 1898 the United States intervened in the Cuban rebellion against Spain, defeated Spain and occupied Puerto Rico and the Philippines. Cuba proclaimed its independence in 1902 only after accepting an amendment in its constitution (the Platt

International Conference of American States, Washington, D.C., 1889

Amendment) which gave the United States the right to intervene on the island under certain conditions (determined by the United States). The acquisition of the Panama Canal and the Roosevelt Corollary to the Monroe Doctrine, by which the United States acquired the right to decide when a "flagrant wrongdoing" had occurred in a Latin America state that merited "preventive intervention," defined a new imperialist U.S. policy.

Woodrow Wilson, a self–professed progressive on domestic policy, soon proved that he could be as jingoistic as Theodore Roosevelt in the name of imposing his vision of democratic morality on the nations to the south. After the odious Victoriano Huerta overthrew and murdered the democratic reformer Francisco Madero _in Mexico just days before Wilson's inauguration in March 1913, Wilson soon signaled that it would be U.S. policy to promote democracy in Mexico and elsewhere. When U.S. intelligence determined that a shipment of German arms was bound for Veracruz, Wilson ordered U.S. Marines to seize the Mexican port in 1914 to prevent the guns from reaching Huerta, a move that backfired by causing Mexican public opinion to rally around the dictator. After Huerta was toppled in 1915, Wilson threw his support behind the new president, Venustiano Carranza, who was opposed by such rebel leaders as Emiliano Zapata in the south and Francisco "Pancho" Villa in the north. Wilson could do little in the south, but he allowed Carranza's troops to use U.S. railroads to outflank Villa. Enraged, Villa attacked the town of Columbus, New Mexico, in 1916, killing about 40 Americans and prompting Wilson to dispatch Gen. John J. Pershing on a "punitive expedition" into Mexico to pursue Villa. Once again, the U.S. intervention had the effect only of galvanizing the various Mexican warring factions against the *gringo* invaders. The expedition was a total failure, and even long after the end of the Mexican Revolution, Mexico's distrust of its trigger–happy northern neighbor lingered.

Also during his first term, before he became more preoccupied with the threat from Germany that led to U.S. entry into World War I, Wilson sent the Marines at one time or another to occupy Nicaragua, Honduras, Costa Rica, the Dominican Republic and Haiti. The Marines remained in Nicaragua throughout much of the 1920s, battling a rebel leader who was to become a martyr and would lend his name to a Marxist movement 50 years later: Augusto César Sandino. The occupation of Haiti endured for 19 years, under five presidents of both parties, until 1934.

World War I diminished Great Britain's influence and facilitated U.S. economic expansion in the hemisphere. Between 1913 and 1920 U.S. commerce with Latin

The President of Colombia addresses the OAS conference, Bogotá, March 1948.

America increased by 400%. In 1929, U.S. investment in the region amounted to over $5 billion, exceeding Britain's by almost $1 billion. Latin American bitterness, however, worried Washington. By 1928, the time of the sixth Conference of American States in Havana, Nicaraguan guerrilla leader Sandino, then fighting the Marines in his country, had become a Latin hero and the United States began to reconsider the wisdom of the "big stick" policy. The economic crash of 1929 increased interest in a policy change. In

1933, President Franklin Roosevelt proclaimed the Good Neighbor Policy.

From 1933 until 1945, U.S.–Latin relations experienced a considerable improvement. Economic recovery and better trade agreements, the rise of fascism, adoption by the Communist parties of a conciliatory tactic known as the "popular front" and the spirit of solidarity provoked by World War II contributed to raise the Good Neighbor Policy and Panamericanism to a real level of continental unity.

Roosevelt died in 1945, the war ended, and the United States once more relegated Latin America to a secondary position. From the end of World War II to the Cuban Revolution, U.S.– Latin American relations steadily declined. While Washington concentrated its attention on Europe and on meeting the Soviet global challenge, Latin America confronted old and pressing economic and social problems. Population growth, unstable economies, populist movements and military interventions agitated the continent. The United States seemed exclusively interested in creating a solid anti–communist bloc in the hemisphere.

In 1954, when a "leftist" government in Guatemala posed a threat to the unity of the bloc, the United States used the first conference of the new Organization of American States (OAS), created in Bogotá in 1948, to pressure Latin delegates into an anti–Guatemalan declaration. After a vague anti–communist declaration was issued, the American delegation paid little attention to the rest of the agenda. A few months later, the Arbenz government in Guatemala was toppled by a U.S.–backed invasion from Honduras. Democratic leaders and parties in Latin America expressed their criticism of what they considered U.S. favoritism toward anti–communist dictators. This criticism found a favorable echo when a powerful upsurge of democratic movements seemed to be sweeping the continent. The *MNR (Movimiento Nacionalista Revolucionario)* came to power in Bolivia in 1952; in 1955 Perón fell in Argentina, and in the following years, Generals Odría, Rojas Pinilla and Pérez Jiménez were toppled in Peru, Colombia and Venezuela, respectively. "Democracy is on the march," proclaimed Costa Rican leader José Figueres in 1959. That year General Batista was forced to abandon Cuba as Fidel Castro entered Havana in triumph, hailed as a democratic hero. Contrary to general expectations in and outside the island, the Cuban revolution moved radically to the left, creating an entirely new situation in Latin American history.

Immediately after seizing power, Fidel Castro demonstrated his decision to revolutionize the entire Latin continent by encouraging and aiding guerrilla groups in several countries. This policy, the rapid socialization of the revolutionary regime and increasing anti–American propaganda, strained relations with the United States. In the summer of 1960 President Eisenhower reduced the Cuban sugar quota allowed to enter the United States, the Soviet Union announced its intention to purchase the total amount of the reduction, and arms from the communist bloc began pouring into Cuba. In January 1961, after several conflicts and mutual recriminations, the United States, which was already preparing a military operation

against Castro, broke diplomatic relations with Cuba.

John F. Kennedy was inaugurated just days later and inherited from Eisenhower a CIA plan for an invasion of Cuba by anti–Castro exiles. The force of 1,200 men had been training clandestinely in Guatemala, again governed by a president friendly to the United States. At the last minute, however, Kennedy withdrew crucial air support for the operation, fearing a Soviet response. The Bay of Pigs invasion ended in a disaster, raising Castro to the level of an international hero in the eyes of some, and damaging the United States' reputation as a military power. Emboldened by this American failure, the Soviets began placing missiles in Cuba. A dangerous Soviet–American confrontation followed. In October 1962 the Soviets pulled the missiles out of Cuba, but at the same time, obtained a guarantee from Washington that no further aggressive action would be taken against Castro. The U.S. anti–communist bloc in the Western Hemisphere had been broken.

Protected by the U.S.–Soviet pact, Castro increased his guerrilla campaign in Latin America. The United States, which had managed to isolate Cuba diplomatically in 1961, answered with the Alliance for Progress, to promote economic progress in Latin America and renewed military aid to Latin American armies. The second aspect of the strategy proved more successful than the first. While few economic advantages were accomplished by the Alliance for Progress, Latin American armies defeated the guerrillas everywhere on the continent. Unfortunately, victory was usually preceded or followed by military coups. By the end of the 1960s a few democracies had survived the military onslaught. The trend continued in the 1970s; the Uruguayan army crushed the Tupamaros, a leftist terrorist organization, the Chilean armed forces toppled socialist president Salvador Allende, and military rule was imposed on those two traditionally democratic countries. In both cases, American covert intervention played a significant role.

The guerrillas' defeat, and the continuous deterioration of Cuba's economy, saved and sustained by increasing Soviet aid, forced Castro to abandon his independent guerrilla path and accept Soviet control of Cuba. From 1973 to 1975 U.S-Cuban relations seemed to be improving. Many Latin American nations reestablished relations with Cuba, while several influential voices in the United States asked for an end to the commercial embargo imposed on the island. In 1975 the conciliatory trend was halted when Castro sent troops to Angola to aid a faltering socialist regime, and publicly denounced American "colonialism" in Puerto Rico.

Castro was not the only crisis facing the United States in Latin America during the

1960s. In January 1964, less than two months after Lyndon Johnson succeeded the assassinated Kennedy, riots erupted in Panama when foolhardy American high school students in the U.S.–controlled Canal Zone tore down the Panamanian flag which, under a decree from President Eisenhower, flew beside the U.S. flag in the Zone. U.S. troops opened fire on the rioters as they spilled over into the Zone; a total of 22 Panamanians and six Americans were killed in the bloodshed. Panama still honors its slain citizens on every anniversary of the riots, and Fourth of July Avenue in Panama City was renamed "Avenue of the Martyrs."

The following year, the left–wing Juan Bosch came to power in the Dominican Republic, sparking civil unrest, and an alarmed Johnson feared that the country would become "another Cuba." He dispatched the 82nd Airborne Division to restore order, but not before there was considerable fighting and loss of life. The back–to–back incidents of U.S. military force in Panama and the Dominican Republic reinforced Latin America's distrust of its powerful neighbor, and greatly enhanced the prestige of Fidel Castro among left–leaning, anti–U.S. movements in the region. It may have been apocryphal, but the earthy LBJ was reported to have commented at the height of the Dominican crisis, "Those people down there couldn't pour piss out of a boot if they had instructions written on the heel." True or not, it epitomized what Latin Americans regarded as U.S. arrogance and condescension. In 1967, Johnson enjoyed a modest triumph with a CIA operation to train a Bolivian ranger battalion that ultimately tracked down and killed Ernesto "Che" Guevara.

Republican President Richard Nixon did little to dissipate Latin American distrust in 1970 when the CIA made a clumsy attempt to bribe Chilean congressmen into blocking the election of the Marxist Salvador Allende as president after he had received a narrow plurality, but not a majority, of the vote. As another example of both the prevailing Cold War mentality and traditional U.S. arrogance toward Latin America, National Security Adviser Henry Kissinger reportedly said, "I see no reason to allow a country to go communist because of the irresponsibility of its own people." Allende was elected, and he promptly nationalized most U.S. businesses. Nixon responded with an economic embargo against Chile, which brought Allende sympathy even from non–Marxist Latin Americans. Like Castro, he was viewed as a heroic David standing up to the American Goliath. It wasn't revealed until 1975 that Nixon's CIA also waged a clandestine effort to destabilize the Allende government by instigating public protests and strikes by independent truck drivers. The CIA also was tangentially involved in the military coup that overthrew Allende in 1973. Allende died in the bloody coup, and although it was not clear whether it was by his own hand or at the hands of the military, another anti–U.S. martyr had been created.

Democratic President Jimmy Carter reversed long–standing U.S. policy of supporting military dictatorships in the name of anti–communism and embarked on a moralistic crusade reminiscent of Woodrow Wilson's. He appointed ambassadors who aggressively confronted the generals in Brazil, Chile, Argentina, Uruguay, El Salvador, Nicaragua and Paraguay for alleged human rights violations and curtailed or cut military aid to those countries. He also strained relations with Brazil just weeks into his presidency in 1977 by condemning its nuclear program, which provoked Brazil into canceling its mutual–defense treaty with the United States. At the same time, Carter sought to ameliorate long–standing distrust of the United States by signing the historic Panama Canal treaties—somewhat hypocritically—with a dictator, Omar Torrijos. The signing ceremony at the Organization of American States in 1977 was a major hemispheric event, with all the Latin American heads of state except Castro in attendance.

The *Sandinistas* toppled strongman Anastasio Somoza—a West Point graduate—in Nicaragua on Carter's watch in 1979, but they exhibited little gratitude to the United States for withdrawing its traditional support for Somoza. They vilified the United States, turned to Cuba and the Soviet Union for support and began establishing a Marxist state with little regard for the human rights that Carter seemed to cherish.

Carter faced another Latin American crisis in 1980 with the so–called Mariel boatlift. When Castro declared that anyone who wished to leave Cuba was free to do so, thousands of boats owned by Cuban–American expatriates in Florida sailed to Cuba in a Dunkirk–like evacuation and carried about 125,000 Cubans to the United States. Too late was it discovered that thousands of them were common criminals and lunatics Castro had removed from prisons and asylums and forced onto the boats. Carter's inept handling of the crisis was a major issue in the 1980 election.

In that election, Republican Ronald Reagan defeated Carter in a landslide and immediately ordered a 180–degree course change in Latin American policy. He reversed Carter's human–rights policy and began patching up relations with the military strongmen. He restored military aid and enlarged the training programs for Latin American officers and NCOs at the U.S. Army's School of the Americas (which Carter had relocated from Panama to Georgia) to combat Marxist insurgencies. Despite congressional objections, he lavished military aid on the military regime in El Salvador to combat that insurgency, and he fired the Carter–appointed ambassador there who had the audacity to criticize the regime after four American

nuns were murdered by right–wing death squads.

In October 1983, Reagan ordered U.S. forces into the Caribbean island nation of Grenada after its Marxist president, Maurice Bishop, was overthrown and murdered by a cabal of pro–Cuban, Marxist–Leninist soldiers. The invasion, all too reminiscent of the era of gunboat diplomacy, was denounced throughout Latin America, even by the anti–communist strongmen Reagan had been courting. Moreover, Reagan provided military and financial aid to the Nicaraguan *Contras*, who were battling to topple the *Sandinistas* and whom Reagan praised as "the moral equivalent of our founding fathers." All this was part of Reagan's overall strategy of defeating the Soviet Union and winning the Cold War with a massive military buildup and confronting the Soviets vicariously with surrogate warriors on such far–flung battlefields as Afghanistan, Angola and Central America.

Reagan's support for the *Contras* almost proved the undoing of his presidency, however. When the Democratic-controlled Congress prohibited any further aid to the *Contras,* Reagan's minions made an end–run around Congress by secretly selling arms to Iran, then at war with Iraq, and diverting the profits to the *Contras.* When the deal became public in late 1986, a major scandal erupted that lingered until Reagan left office in 1989. By then, however, Reagan's strategy of spending the Soviet Union into oblivion was well on its way to success.

With the collapse of the Soviet Union, Reagan's successor, Republican George Bush, had the opportunity to usher in a new era of mutual understanding and cooperation between the United States and Latin America without the old issue of communism vs. anticommunism hanging over both parties. During his first few months in office, he attended an anti–drug summit in Cartagena, Colombia, and promised closer ties with Latin America in return for its cooperation on drug control. But Bush's military intervention in Panama in December 1989, no matter how justifiable in light of strongman Manuel Noriega's provocations, was denounced throughout the hemisphere as just another example of the United States' application of naked power to enforce its will in Latin America.

Another obstacle in U.S.–Latin American relations left over from the Reagan era was effectively eliminated when the *Sandinistas* finally were removed from power—by free election—in 1990.

Toward the end of his single term in office, Bush negotiated the North American Free Trade Agreement (NAFTA) with Canada and Mexico, and he openly advocated a hemisphere–wide free trade zone.

By the time Democrat Bill Clinton came to office in 1993, virtually all the dictator-

ships had been replaced by democratically elected civilian governments. He had to contend neither with gross abuses of human rights, as Carter had, nor with the problem of communist insurgencies, as Reagan had. In his first year in office, Clinton invited the heads of state of all the nations of the hemisphere except Cuba to a Summit of the Americas in Miami. There, he resurrected Bush's proposal for a Free Trade Area of the Americas (FTAA), open to any country with a democratic form of government. Toward that end, he made a state visit to Brazil, Uruguay, Argentina and Chile in 1997.

Meanwhile, however, Clinton found himself in the position of resorting to armed intervention just as his two Republican predecessors had. After the military strongmen who had overthrown the democratically elected Haitian President Jean–Bertrand Aristide refused to acquiesce to international pressure to restore Aristide, Clinton ordered in the 82nd Airborne Division in September 1994 to keep order and to effect the transition back to democracy. Although this invasion was a benevolent one and there was minimal loss of life, the televised images of American paratroopers landing in Haiti in full battle dress evoked the old spectre of Theodore Roosevelt's "big stick."

The Americans withdrew in 1995 and were replaced by United Nations peacekeepers, and the memory of this latest U.S. intervention soon began to fade.

Clinton was able to turn his attention again toward the upcoming second Summit of the Americas in Santiago, Chile, but in late 1997 the Congress blocked his request for "fast-track" authority to negotiate trade agreements on his own initiative. Nonetheless, when the 34 hemispheric leaders (once again, Castro had been excluded) met in Santiago from April 17–19, 1998, they issued a communique that called for establishment of the FTAA by 2005. Clinton praised Latin America's advances in democracy, but called for "a second generation of reforms" to consolidate the region's fragile democracies.

Although the Santiago summit was marked by unprecedented good will between the U.S. president and his Latin American counterparts, there were still some nagging complaints about U.S. hegemony. Among these were the continued U.S. embargo against Cuba, with which nearly all the Latin American countries now have diplomatic and trade relations, and the U.S. policy of "certifying" countries as cooperating allies in the war against drugs as a condition for financial aid, which the Latin Americans see as

demeaning. The drug issue as a whole continues to strain North–South relations, with the United States pushing for support at eradicating coca, marijuana and heroin poppy cultivation at their sources and Latin America arguing that there would be no market for illegal drugs if the United States would curb the demand for them at home. Both sides, of course, have a point.

Clinton's successor in January 2001, Republican George W. Bush, has shown a greater interest in, and sensitivity toward, Latin America than most of his predecessors, including his father. A former governor of Texas, he is fluent in Spanish and openly courted Hispanic votes in the 2000 presidential race. Indeed, the Cuban-American vote in Florida provided the narrow victory in that state that gave him an Electoral College victory over the Democratic candidate, Al Gore. Accustomed to dealing with Mexican authorities as governor, Bush made a state visit to Mexico weeks after his inauguration to meet with the newly inaugurated President Vicente Fox; in the past, new U.S. presidents made their first trip abroad to Western Europe. Both conservatives, Bush and Fox got on well. Bush also hosted Chilean President Ricardo Lagos and Brazilian President Fernando Henrique Cardoso at the White

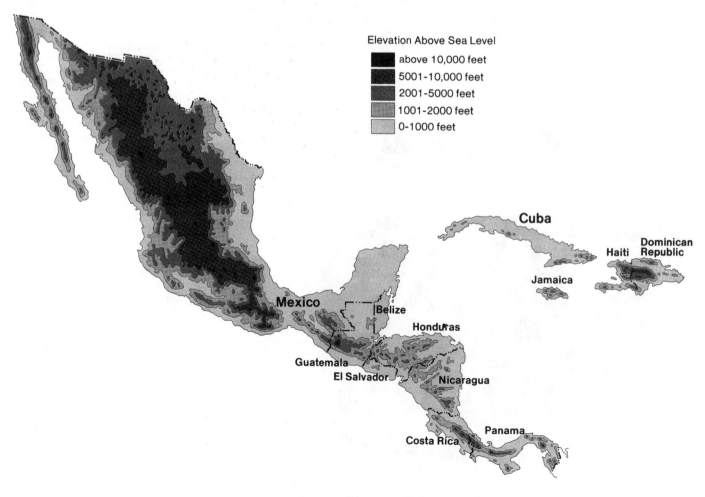

Elevation Above Sea Level

- above 10,000 feet
- 5001–10,000 feet
- 2001–5000 feet
- 1001–2000 feet
- 0–1000 feet

Cuba

Dominican Republic

Haiti

Jamaica

Mexico

Belize

Honduras

Guatemala

El Salvador

Nicaragua

Costa Rica

Panama

House soon after the visit to Mexico. In April, Bush attended the third Summit of the Americas in Quebec, where he conversed in Spanish with his Latin American counterparts and voiced his strong commitment to the FTAA. The leaders agreed to a target date of December 31, 2005, and made adherence to representative democracy a condition for participation.

Much of Bush's hope for expanded free trade in the hemisphere depends on Congress granting him what it had denied Clinton: fast-track trading authority, now called trade promotion authority, or TPA. The Republican-controlled House of Representatives, which had denied that authority to Democrat Clinton, approved it for Republican Bush in late 2001—by one vote. The Senate, in which the Democrats have a one-seat majority, finally approved TPA on August 1, 64–34.

A few months after Quebec, U.S. Secretary of State Colin Powell flew to Lima, Peru, to attend an important summit of OAS foreign ministers, ostensibly to emphasize again the Bush administration's commitment to regional integration and democracy. The date: September 11, 2001. Within hours of his arrival, Powell made a hasty departure for Washington to deal with the crisis of the terrorist attacks on New York and Washington. Although his Latin American colleagues were sympathetic and understanding, there could have been no more symbolic reminder of where U.S. priorities lay in the world.

Perhaps mindful of the need to mend fences in the wake of the shift of global priorities after September 11, Bush made a whirlwind, four-day tour of Mexico, El Salvador and Peru in March 2002. In Mexico, he attended a U.N. summit on poverty in Monterrey, to assure Latin America and other developing regions that the United States was concerned with more than the war on terrorism. In El Salvador, he held a summit with several Central American presidents to assure them of his commitment to a U.S.-Central-American free-trade pact (In June, Costa Rican President Abel Pacheco met with Bush at the White House and announced that negotiations for such a pact would begin later this year). In Lima, Bush told his Andean counterparts that he was trying to get a recalcitrant Democratic-controlled Senate to reinstate preferential tariffs that had expired the month before, and he urged their continued cooperation on combating terrorism and drug trafficking. On all three stops, he reiterated his support for democracy.

But then two events occurred that called into question the depth of the Bush administration's commitment to Latin American democracy.

The first was the abortive military coup in Venezuela in April 2002 that had

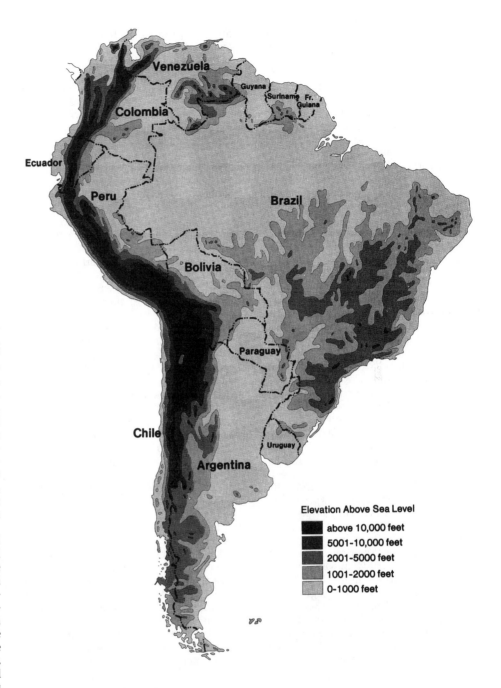

Elevation Above Sea Level

- above 10,000 feet
- 5001-10,000 feet
- 2001-5000 feet
- 1001-2000 feet
- 0-1000 feet

President Hugo Chávez under house arrest for 48 hours. Chávez had long been a thorn in the side of the United States because of his close ties to Cuba, Iraq, Iran and Libya and for his opposition to the FTAA (see Venezuela). The statements emanating from the State Department within hours of the coup clearly conveyed the idea that the Bush administration regarded the overthrow of Chávez, who has twice been elected by overwhelming majorities, as the will of the Venezuelan people and said, essentially, that Chávez had it coming. When Chávez was reinstalled two days later, President Bush's national security adviser, Condoleezza Rice, said in a televised interview that she hoped Chávez had learned something from his experience. The message regarding U.S. policy toward Latin America was unmistakable:

We're all for democracy—as long as you don't elect someone we don't like.

That message was underscored in the second event two months later in Bolivia, just days before the June 30 presidential election. One of the candidates was Evo Morales, leader of the coca farmers, who had pledged to reverse the incumbent administration's coca-eradication policy. U.S. Ambassador Manuel Rocha, in an incredibly stupid breach of diplomatic protocol, declared in a public speech that voting for Morales could jeopardize U.S. aid. Bolivians were justifiably furious over this interference in their internal political affairs. The result: Morales, whom polls had predicted would receive no more than 12% of the vote, finished in second place, with about 21% of the vote (see Bolivia).

In sum, the United States is still sending mixed signals to its Latin American neighbors—just as it has for 200 years.

Latin America and the World

One of the most dramatic changes taking place in Latin America is its progressive integration into the rest of the world. Almost totally isolated during most of the 19th century and until World War II under the tutelage first of Britain and then of the United States, Latin America has since then experienced a progressive "opening to the world."

After 1960, Canada increased its economic and cultural ties with Latin countries, principally Brazil, Cuba and, with NAFTA in 1994, Mexico. The most important nations of Western Europe, especially Germany, Italy and Spain, reinforced their influence in the hemisphere through economic aid, cultural programs and support for political groups or parties attuned to their predominant ideologies.

During the Cold War, the Soviet presence was prodigious. The Cuban socialist regime, which transformed the island into a formidable military base, opened the door for further Soviet influence in Latin America. The Peruvian military regime of 1968-80 enjoyed close ties with the Soviet Union, which re-equipped the Peruvian army with T-62 tanks and its air force with MiGs. The Nicaraguan army under the Sandinistas also became equipped with Soviet weapons, including tanks, helicopter gunships and a host of various types of the latest armaments. Every year, thousands of Latin American students received grants to study in Moscow, and Marxist publications multiplied on the continent. Latin America, a region once relegated by the Kremlin to a secondary position, became one of its top priorities (as foretold by Lenin before his death). But one factor was overlooked by most observers: the Soviet largesse directed at

Latin American was at the expense of the Soviet workers.

Then–General Secretary Gorbachëv planned to visit Mexico, Argentina, Uruguay and possibly Brazil in the summer of 1987. This was canceled because such adventures were inconsistent with his programs of democracy, *perestroika* and *glasnost*. These countries were dependent upon U.S.–dominated sources for continuing loans and financial backing. The Soviets were devoid of spare foreign exchange to offer. (In fact, they applied for membership in the International Monetary Fund to bolster their sagging economy; the request was denied.) His 1989 visit to Cuba indicated substantial differences with Fidel Castro and was otherwise uneventful, except for a strong hint that Cuba should export more to the Soviet Union.

In recent decades, there has been increased Japanese interest in investment in Latin America. With its huge surplus from a favorable balance of foreign trade for years, the supply of money is ample. Needless to say, the Japanese insist on control and security of their investments and, above all, efficiency, productivity and competitiveness. Nothing could be healthier for Latin America; local entrepreneurs may decide to adopt Japanese styles of production, which would greatly assist in long–term solutions to chronic economic ills.

Since 1991, the heads of government and key ministers of Spain, Portugal and the 19 Latin American countries they once colonized have met every November for the Ibero-American Summit. Unlike the OAS and the Summits of the Americas, the United States is not included but Cuba is. The agendas usually include such topics as trade and human rights. Although these summits have accomplished little of substance, such as persuading Cuba to clean up its human rights act, they have provided a forum for a healthful exchange of ideas of mutual importance to the Latin American leaders and their Iberian

counterparts. They also have helped give Latin America a toehold in European trade, as Spain and Portugal are both members of the European Union. At the 2001 summit in Lima, Peru, the agenda was expanded to include the Argentine financial crisis, drug trafficking and terrorism, which was of importance to both Spain, with its Basque terrorist group *ETA*, and Colombia, plagued by both left-wing guerrillas and right-wing paramilitaries. The final resolution condemned the terrorist attacks on the United States as "barbaric acts" and a "threat to democracy." Cuba's Fidel Castro, usually the central attraction at these summits, did not attend because of Hurricane Michelle.

As an outgrowth of the Ibero-American summits, the first summit of leaders of the European Union, Latin America and the Caribbean was held in 1999. Spain hosted another two-day summit in Madrid in May 2002, which was attended by about 50 heads of government and their foreign and economy ministers. Trade and terrorism dominated the agenda. As one of the major accomplishments, the EU and Chile ended their "association" agreement, the first step to beginning a free-trade agreement to be signed in late 2002; Mexico already has such an agreement with the EU. In its final declaration, the EU pledged to initiate separate free-trade talks with the Andean, Caribbean and Central American trade blocs; *Mercosur,* the free-trade bloc consisting of Argentina, Brazil, Uruguay and Paraguay, already has entered into an "association" agreement with the EU like the one Chile had. The EC also acceded to a request from the Colombian president to add the Revolutionary Armed Forces of Colombia *(FARC)* to its list of terrorist organizations. The trade potential of these summits is enormous, but they also represent a lessening of Latin America's traditional dependence on the United States and its increasing involvement in world affairs.

The Argentine Republic

Downtown Buenos Aires

Capital City: Buenos Aires (Pop. 13 million, including suburbs).

Climate: The northern *Chaco* region is wet and hot; the central plains, or *Pampas*, are temperate with moderate rain-fall; southern Patagonia is arid, becoming wet and cold in the southernmost part.

Neighboring Countries: Uruguay and Brazil (East); Paraguay and Bolivia (North); Chile (West).

Official Language: Spanish

Other Principal Tongues: English, German, Italian.

Ethnic Background: European (predominantly Spanish and Italian) 98%; *Mestizo* (mixed Spanish and Indian ancestry) 2%.

Principal Religion: Roman Catholic Christianity.

Chief Commercial Products: Meat, grain, oilseed, hides, wool.

Currency: Peso (replacing the former *Austral*).

Gross Domestic Product: U.S. $289 billion in 2001 ($7,680 per capita).

Former Colonial Status: Spanish Crown Colony (1580–1816).

Independence Date: July 9, 1816.

Chief of State: Eduardo Duhalde (b. October 1941), interim president (since January 2, 2002).

National Flag: Sky blue, white and sky blue equal horizontal stripes with "the sun of May" centered in the white stripe.

Argentina varies widely in terrain and climate. Four main regions are generally recognized. The northern region (*Chaco*) is heavily forested, low, wet and hot; the central plains (*Pampas*) are flat, fertile and temperate, well watered along the coast and increasingly dry to the west; the southern region (*Patagonia*) is an arid, windswept plateau, cut through by grassy valleys; the fourth region (Andes) runs the length of the Argentine–Chilean frontier—the mountains are low and glaciated in the south, high and dry in the central part and gradually widen into the high plateau of Bolivia in the north.

Argentina's most important river is the Paraná, with tributaries that flow into the Rio de la Plata estuary north of Buenos Aires. A 25-mile-long bridge connecting Argentina and Uruguay, reaching a height of 1,200 feet over the shipping lane, is now under construction. Three-quarters of Argentina's land is too dry for cultivation without irrigation. The capital city and adjoining *Pampas* have 98% of the population. Temperatures vary from the hot, humid *Chaco* to the cold and damp Patagonia in the south.

History: The Río de la Plata estuary was first visited in 1516 by Spanish explorers who were driven off by hostile Indians. Magellan visited the region in 1520 and

Area: 1,072,745 sq. mi. = 2,771,300 sq. km. Argentina claims 1,084,120 square miles, including the Falkland Islands, in dispute with Great Britain, and other territories claimed by Chile.

Population: 37.8 million.

Spain made unsuccessful efforts to establish colonies on the Paraná River in 1527 and 1536. The Spanish moved up river to the Paraná's junction with the Paraguay River, where they founded Asunción, the center of Spanish operations in southeastern South America for the succeeding 50 years. In 1573, an expedition from Asunción established a settlement in the vicinity of modern Buenos Aires and subsequently Spain transferred its base of colonial government from Asunción to the new town.

Argentina was settled by two main streams of colonists: one crossed the Andes from Peru and occupied the fertile oases along the areas on the eastern slopes of the Andes, founding Córdoba and Tucumán; the other arrived directly from Europe and settled in and around the port of Buenos Aires. Thus, from the start, two distinct groups of Argentine people developed. The people of the interior, a mixture of Spanish and Indian heritage, were dependent on the grazing of cattle on the plains of the central *Pampas* and upon small home manufactures. Far removed from any aid, these people developed a

rude, self–sufficient civilization fiercely resistant to encroachment and disdainful of the ruling authority established in Buenos Aires by urban intellectuals.

The people of Buenos Aires, a mixture of Europeans (Spanish, French, English, Italian and German) who came to the port for trade, to defend the region or to govern it, had little interest in the Latin Americans and sought to re–create in Buenos Aires the standards of living of the European cities from which they originated. The nobility, which governed the defending military, and the clergy, retained special privileges; they could neither be tried in the local courts nor be held accountable to the people for their actions.

Under the Spanish colonial system, Latin America was held by a few people who administered their grants as feudal holdings. Far removed from the restraints of the Spanish court, the Argentine people

evolved into a somewhat wild and free civilization that allowed the development of community and regional pride. In 1806 and 1807, British expeditions attacked and temporarily occupied Buenos Aires; in both cases, almost without Spanish aid, the creoles rallied and defeated the British. The following year, Napoleon's invasion of Spain turned the British into allies, but the exhilaration of those victories did much to imbue self–confidence among the creoles.

On May 25, 1810, the cabildo of Buenos Aires declared it would govern the viceroyalty of La Plata in the name of the deposed King Fernando VII; rebel envoys and armies were sent to the provinces to

forge national unity, but, as in the rest of Hispanic America, attempts to hold the former viceroyalty's territories under Buenos Aires' control were far from successful. A provincial assembly eventually declared independence on July 9, 1816. Paraguay proclaimed its own independence and Uruguay, under the guidance of its popular hero José Manuel Artígas, insisted on autonomy, ushering in a long period of Brazilian–Argentine conflict over the region, which culminated in a precarious Uruguayan independence in the 1840s. Even in the interior of what is today Argentina, the provinces constantly rebelled against Buenos Aires. The first 50 years of Argentine history is the history of

City Hall in Buenos Aires, 1846

the struggle between Buenos Aires and the provinces, and of political turmoil in the capital, where different types of government were tried in a desperate search for stability.

Patriotically, Argentina's greatest hero, General José de San Martín, refused to be dragged into such internecine disputes and concentrated on organizing an army to invade and liberate Chile. Like Bolívar in the north, San Martín was convinced that independence could not be assured until no Spanish stronghold remained in South America. Subsequently he crossed the Andes with his army, battling the Spanish into submission in Chile. He then turned to Peru, fighting his way to the north of that country where he met the liberator of northern South America, Simón Bolívar. Disappointed by Bolívar's refusal to take command of the two armies, San Martín, feeling that his presence as a military man might adversely affect the Peruvian revolution, retired and left for France, where he remained for the rest of his life.

Argentina started its independent history with great territorial losses and a division between its social groups—those of the port and the interior, the metropolis and the countryside. The elimination of Spanish control created a series of conflicts among the regional contenders for power. There was immediate strife between the ranchers controlling large estates on the coast and the merchants in Buenos Aires, who insisted that all trade pass through the port, with duties and taxes used for the capital city rather than for the country. The interior provinces in turn demanded a federal form of government, with autonomous sovereign states and a national capital outside Buenos Aires.

To foster economic development, the leaders of Buenos Aires wanted to promote agriculture and expand European immigration to farm the land as was being done in the United States. The coastal ranchers, knowing that small farms would destroy their great *estancias*, made common cause with the interior to overthrow the Buenos Aires leaders and installed their own leader in 1835, Juan Manuel de Rosas. In the name of federalism, he brutally imposed "national unity" and stubbornly opposed French and British intervention in Río de la Plata, preserving Argentina for future generations. Unfortunately, his enemies belonged to one of the most brilliant generations of Argentina, producing quantities of great literature, including Domingo Faustino Sarmiento and Bartolomé Mitre, both destined to become Argentine presidents. A combination of Brazilian forces and Argentine *caudillos* finally overthrew Rosas' government in 1852.

A constitution of 1853 provided for a federal system and moved the seat of government to Paraná, 150 miles north of Buenos Aires. The former capital seceded from the union, was defeated, renewed the war and was again defeated by national forces. In 1861 the provinces accepted Buenos Aires' supremacy and the first constitutional president, Bartolomé Mitre, assumed office. During the years of the non–urban leadership, the fertile *Pampas* lands were seized and distributed to large estate holders, a policy which continued for several years; the governments used the army "to open" the interior of Argentina, eliminating Indians and *gauchos* and gaining further territories. For a considerable period after independence, Argentina was simply a cattle–raising country, importing all manufactured goods and even food from Europe.

In the late 19th century, the demand for chilled beef led to changes in the meat industry, requiring better cattle and grains for both cattle–feeding and human consumption. Despite the changes in production, however, Argentine economic and political power remained in the hands of a small group of planters, cattle raisers and the merchants in the port city.

Contemptuous of the cattle–herding *gauchos*, the *porteños*, residents of the port, Buenos Aires, opened the doors of Argentina to European immigrants. From 1852 to 1895, hundreds of thousands of Italians, Spanish, Germans and British poured into the nation. In 1852, of a total population of 1,200,000, non–Argentines were less than 5%, but by 1895 of almost 4 million inhabitants, over 1 million were foreigners. By the beginning of the 20th century, the demands for political equality of this mass of immigrants transformed the political scene. The Radical Party had become the most popular among the immigrants and emerged into the first really populist party of Argentina. Organized by an enigmatic leader, Hipólito Irigoyen, the Radical Party has maintained its influence, in one form or another, up to the present day.

Industrialization came late to Argentina and was largely due to British investment during the last half of the 19th century. Concentrated in Buenos Aires and in the hands of a few large investors, industry centered on the supply of local needs and the transportation and processing of Argentina's export commodities. Although industrialization changed the ratio of national earnings from agriculture and cattle raising to include industrial products, it provided little increase in total earnings.

The formation of labor unions, largely through the efforts of immigrants, posed

General José de San Martín

29

the first threat to the historic domination of the country by landed interests and industrialists, both Argentine and foreign. The unions also included displaced agricultural laborers and were initially disorganized and effectively excluded from participation in political or economic power until the first decades of the 20th century. The ruling elite chose compromise: in 1912 electoral laws were democratically modified, providing for a secret ballot and minority party representation. The first elections held under this system in 1916 resulted in a Radical Party victory under Irigoyen and the defeat of the large landowners' and industrialists' Conservative Party. The populist Radical Party ruled Argentina from 1916 to 1930. Its programs included expansion of the democratic system and social reforms to benefit workers, but these fell short of expectations. Political and social unrest soon appeared—in 1918 there was a rebellion of students at the University of Córdoba and a year later widespread strikes provoked bloody confrontations with the police. Social unrest soon caused the downfall of the Radical Party. A restless army, weary of turmoil and fascinated by Italian dictator Benito Mussolini and his totalitarian efficiency, found its opportunity in 1930 when the international depression gripped the country. An elderly Irigoyen was deposed and the armed forces seized the government "to save the nation from chaos." The "saviors" remained in or behind power for more than *five decades* and remain a force to be reckoned with to this day. The Conservative Party was restored to power. For the next 13 years, a combination of landowners, bankers, merchants and generals controlled the government. But in 1943, a group of pseudo–fascist army officers, who feared the government's progressive inclinations toward the Allied powers, used "official corruption" as a pretext to seize power. Lacking a program, and with limited leadership abilities, the government failed to cope with internal problems and mismanaged foreign relations.

The Perón Eras

From the rubble of political confusion there emerged a new leader, Colonel Juan Domingo Perón, a classic charismatic *caudillo* who, wittingly or unwittingly, united forces which had resisted conservative efforts to reestablish political dominance. He brilliantly saw that no government could exist in Argentina without the support of the middle classes, which had grown substantially, and, more important, the lower laboring class.

Attaining the office of labor minister under the conservative military government, he devoted his efforts toward seizing control of the labor unions from the Radical and Conservative parties. Tre-

General Bartolomé Mitre

mendous assistance came from popular radio announcer Maria Eva Duarte. The military–conservative element sensed too late that he had acquired an immense power base. When an attempt was made to remove Perón in 1945, masses rallied to his support and forced the government to desist. In the elections of 1946, Perón became president with a substantial majority of the vote.

Perón married the glamorous and even more charismatic radio announcer, who became popularly called "Evita," and they used their abilities well, gaining firm control of labor and creating a popular mass organization called the *Descamisados* ("shirtless ones") which some erroneously identified with the Fascist Italian regime. Despite the fact that Perón threatened conservative interests, he was able to gain and hold vital army support through pay raises and military expenditures. He also received support of the clergy through advocacy of programs of religious education and by adopting a moderate position on church–state relations.

While Perón and Evita built their strength through propaganda and blatant patronage, certain of their accomplishments were significant. The working class was brought into the political arena and made aware of its massive power. Evita's charitable social works provided health and welfare benefits to the poor that could not be withdrawn (all, of course, widely publicized). The increased wages paid to labor and the practice of "featherbedding" in the government of Buenos Aires was deceiving, as rising prices canceled the increased earnings of the people. Mass

housing, schools and hospitals and a flood of labor laws favorable to the workers dominated Perón's programs. Costly and often inefficient industries were created to provide jobs for the thousands streaming into the cities. Agriculture, the backbone of the economy, was taxed heavily to pay for disorderly industrialization. The natural result was a drop in farm output which in turn caused a drop in exports and foreign trade. The problem of importing more than is exported is one that persists in Argentina to this day.

Perón's handling of foreign relations was astute and restored Argentina's international prestige; however, his efforts to establish Argentine political leadership in Latin America were resented and resisted by most of the other nations of the continent. The death of Evita in 1952 from cancer marked the beginning of the decline of Perón's power. Within a short time the bankrupt state of the economy became apparent and thereafter the moral bankruptcy was difficult to hide. Resorting to repression to silence opposition to his regime, Perón alienated the Church and coerced opposition businessmen and landowners into burying their complaints against his rule. Popular unrest and increasing economic problems gave the armed forces, which had resisted Perón's attempts to control them, an opportunity to intervene. In September 1955, a military insurrection ended his rule.

The army seized the government and installed a provisional president. Honest, but timid, he was unable to cope with the overwhelming problems inherited from Perón. After serving for two months, he was replaced by another general who was able to restore civil order and hold elections in 1958.

Arturo Frondizi, elected in 1958, was capable, but also was a stern disciplinarian; he sought to repair the damage created by the Perón regime. He lasted until 1962 when he was overthrown and replaced by the military. His replacement, Dr. Arturo Illia, lasted until mid–1966 when *he* was deposed by another military coup.

Lieutenant General Carlos Ongania was installed as the next president; known as "El Caño" (The Pipe), he was said to be straight on the outside but hollow within. His solution for Argentine problems was to ban political parties, dismiss the Congress and neutralize the courts. It was not long before he envisioned a regime modeled after that of Mussolini with himself (of course) as permanent head. By late 1969, however, his dream turned into a nightmare, replete with riots, strikes and general unrest.

Three years of near–anarchy and frequent changes in military government leadership ensued. The generals ordered elections which were set for March 1973 and most political parties were legalized, including Perón's *Justicialista* movement.

President and Mrs. Perón

Long–standing criminal charges against the former leader were dropped to permit his return from Spain where he had been in exile, maintaining control of his movement by balancing one rival faction against another and issuing vague political statements.

When the military refused to permit Perón to run for the presidency, he instructed his party to nominate Héctor J. Cámpora, a colorless party worker. Campaigning on the slogan "Cámpora to the presidency, Perón to power," the *Justicialistas* gained 49.5% of the vote, plus large majorities in congressional and provincial races.

Inaugurated in May 1973, Cámpora pledged to revitalize the economy, increase benefits for labor and seek closer ties with "neutralist" countries. However, Cámpora's efforts to cooperate with the restive leftists within the party quickly alienated its conservative members. Street fighting between rival factions became common; when one bloody shootout left 25 dead and hundreds wounded at an airport reception for Perón, Cámpora and his entire cabinet were forced to resign after only 49 days in power. The son–in–law of Perón's private secretary was named interim president and new elections were set for September. With anti–Perón military leaders having been forced into retirement, Perón was free to run for president.

Ironically, many of those who supported *El Líder* included such former enemies as the military, the large landowners and business leaders—all of whom welcomed his increased conservatism. Perón's main support, however, came from his traditional base of power: organized labor. As his running mate, Perón chose his wife, Isabel, a 42–year–old former cabaret dancer. Certain of victory, he ran a leisurely campaign based on vague promises of national unity. Election results gave him 61.9% of the vote, while the candidate of the opposition Radical Civic Union received 24.3%. A third center–right coalition candidate won less than 15%.

The problems facing Perón were immense. The economy was plagued with low growth and high inflation; leftist terrorism was rampant and his own political movement was badly divided. As President, Perón concocted an unrealistic mixture of a leftist foreign policy and a conservative domestic program. He sought closer economic and political ties with "Marxist" and "Third World" countries and even hoped to make an official visit to Moscow. Huge credits ($1.2 billion) were offered to Cuba; at the same time, greater restrictions were placed on foreign private investments in Argentina.

Perón's domestic policies, however, were staunchly conservative. He openly courted right–wing union and political leaders. At his direction, liberal government and school officials were dismissed and leftist publications closed. He publicly berated leftist *Peronista* youths as "mercenaries at the service of foreign forces." These conservative policies merely widened the rift within his political movement. Having played an important role in bringing Perón back to power through their struggles with the military government, the leftists now refused to be pushed out of the *Peronista* movement. Instead, left–wing guerrillas continued their attacks against conservative union leaders, right–wing government officials and foreign businessmen. Conservatives responded with counter–terror. The basic functions of the government ground to a halt as the rift between the right and the left, as well as between *Peronistas* and anti–*Peronistas*, polarized the nation.

Perón's hapless plight was perhaps best seen in his 1974 May Day speech: while he was calling for "peace and conciliation" among his followers, rival *Peronista* factions broke into bloody street fighting even before his speech was ended. The continued jockeying for position became even more intense as Perón's health began to fail; in hindsight, he was senile when he returned from Spanish exile. Each faction hoped to be able to seize control of the party should *El Líder* die in office.

By 1973, the aging Perón, almost 78 years old, tiring easily, had difficulty concentrating for more than brief periods. In November he suffered a mild heart attack from which he never recovered; death came from heart failure in July 1974.

With the passing of Juan Domingo Perón, most national leaders quickly pledged their *oral* support for constitutional government and the new president, María Estela Martínez de Perón, widely known simply as "Isabel." A crucial difference, however, existed between loyalty of the people toward *El Presidente Perón* and *La Presidente Perón*. His wife lacked the personal magnetism and immense power base formerly held by her late husband and was totally unimaginative. Actually, her husband had selected her as his running mate only to allow him additional time to choose a more likely successor.

Occupying the highest office ever held by a woman in the Western Hemisphere, Isabel held conservative views that were bitterly opposed by leftists, while old–line *Peronistas* resented any replacement of Perón's beloved first wife, Evita. More ominous, the old guard regarded her background as a nightclub dancer with a sixth grade education as woefully inadequate. The upper classes dismissed her as a commoner, as they had Evita. Feeling herself thus isolated from traditional sources of power, Isabel began to rely heavily on the advice and counsel of José López Rega, minister of social welfare, a close confidant of the late president and somewhat mysterious practitioner of the occult. He favored staunch conservative measures which, needless to say, were opposed by moderates and bitterly resisted by leftists.

Frail and reclusive, Isabel delegated broad power to López Rega and other key officials in the hope of pulling the nation out of an economic nosedive caused by (1) runaway inflation (2) growing shortages of industrial and consumer goods, (3) a thriving black market, (4) huge budget and foreign trade deficits, (5) declining domestic and foreign investments and (6) a disastrous drop in farm output. Part of the fiscal plight was caused when Isabel permitted large wage increases in violation of an earlier wage–price freeze. Although the move was popular with the large labor movement, it triggered widespread business losses which in turn led to a fresh round of price increases and a further escalation of inflation, which by 1975 was at an annual rate of 330%.

During the same period, the government policies of overtaxing farmers to subsidize the immense urban population had caused a major decline in farm exports which traditionally furnished the bulk of Argentina's foreign exchange earnings. As a result, the nation faced a trade deficit of $600 million in 1975. Worse, some $2 billion in foreign debts were due the same year; although foreign reserves stood at $1 billion when the *Peronistas* took office in 1973, they plummeted to an all–time low of only $2 million by early 1976. To finance the government, the money supply was expanded by 200%.

In spite of further attempts at austerity (which failed) the economic picture worsened until there was virtual paralysis. Political conditions also declined—violence became the worst in the nation's history.

La Presidente **Isabela Perón**

Assassinations by leftist and right–wing terrorists claimed 1,100 lives during 1975. One leftist group, the *Montanaros*, collected huge fees by kidnapping business leaders. A single kidnapping netted the guerrillas $60 million!

Although the *Peronistas* scored well (46.5%) in regional elections in the normally conservative province of Misiones, the victory did not hide the disintegration of the *Peronista* movement. During the 21 months she was in office, Isabel reorganized the cabinet 10 times. The conservative labor movement—long a pillar of support for Perón—continued to increase the distance between itself and Isabel. The loss of this vital support paved the way for the collapse of the Perón presidency. Increasingly erratic, *La Presidente* took a leave of absence from her job in the latter part of 1975. Compounding the economic and political malaise was a growing public resentment against increasing reports of widespread political corruption. Among those implicated was Isabel, who was accused of transferring half a million dollars from a public charity to her own bank account. A formal congressional probe of the incident was averted, however, only after the *Peronista*–controlled legislature voted along strict party lines to drop the inquiry.

Government corruption, rising terrorism, a reeling economy and disintegrating government control of national affairs prompted a long expected military coup on March 24, 1976—the sixth within the prior 21 years. Army Lieutenant General Jorge Rafael Videla, 50, was named president and head of the three–man *junta*.

The "Dirty War"

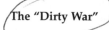

To combat Argentina's mounting problems, the generals vowed to fight for three key goals: an end to political terrorism, a drastic cut in the inflation rate and economic development.

To control inflation, wages were frozen, taxes increased and prices were allowed to rise to their natural levels. Also, the peso was devalued by 70%, government spending was reduced and farm prices raised to stimulate agricultural growth. These measures helped cut inflation from 35% *a month* to about 10% by early 1978. Political corruption was a special target, and the *junta* moved swiftly to prosecute those who profited illegally under the *Peronista* government; Isabel Perón was so charged and placed under house arrest.

Upon seizing power, the military rulers were able to boast of dramatic improvements in the national economy. Foreign reserves jumped from $20 million in 1976 to $10 *billion* by mid–1980. Farm output also grew, paced by a 52% rise in wheat production during the 1978–79 season over the previous harvest. Oil and natural gas exploration was increased as the gov-

Lt. Gen. Jorge Rafael Videla

ernment sought to attain self–sufficiency in energy by 1982.

Such rapid economic expansion carried a high price tag, as the liberalization of monetary policies helped to undermine confidence in the peso. The cost in human lives was even greater. Hoping to improve domestic stability—and thereby stimulate economic investments—the government unleashed a campaign of terror against the leftists. Between 1976 and 1981, some 6,000-15,000 persons simply disappeared after having been arrested by security forces. To protest these human rights abuses, the Carter administration suspended military aid to Argentina.

In doing this, the U.S. administration failed to realize that there are two sides to every conflict. The leftists didn't have the words "human rights" in their vocabulary. Summary executions of military personnel by leftists using clandestine, terrorist and guerrilla tactics were ordinary occurrences in Argentina at the time.

Retaliation by the military was equally grisly. It was revealed in 1995 that a naval school used as a prison was the point of departure for many imprisoned by the military. A prison guard wielding a hypodermic loaded with a hypnotic drug would inject a shackled prisoner. When he became unconscious, he was loaded aboard an airplane which flew over the Atlantic for an appropriate distance. The unconscious (but not dead) prisoner would be unceremoniously dumped overboard. Dissidents thus did indeed disappear, without a trace. The school also served as a torture center.

Economic Woes

The nation's impressive economic boom proved short–lived, and by mid–1981 the country was mired in a recession and disenchanted with military rule. To enhance its public image, the *junta* tried several moves. In July 1981, the government bowed to the demands of the *Peronistas*

32

and freed Isabel; she promptly took up a luxurious and quiet exile in Spain.

Still, the opposition to military rule persisted. In December 1981 the *junta* fired moderate President Roberto Viola, replacing him with hardline Army Commander Leopoldo F. Galtieri. In contrast to Viola, who attempted to deal with the banned political parties, the new president sought to reaffirm the military's control of the government and its commitment to free–market economic policies. Although Galtieri pledged to deal more firmly with the nation's economic problems, the recession intensified, driving the inflation rate to 130% and unemployment to 13–16%. Argentina was in its worst economic crisis of the century. By March 1982, labor unrest was spreading throughout the land and the outlawed political parties were agitating for a return to constitutional government.

The Falkland Islands War

At that point, Galtieri and some top military commanders made a momentous decision. Taking advantage of a dispute between Argentina and Britain over some rather worthless islands, the Falklands (*Malvinas* to the Argentines), the president ordered the armed forces to seize them in April 1982. So, after an absence of 149 years the Argentine flag once again flew over this disputed territory. Overnight, Galtieri and his military conquerors were the heroes of Argentina. For the next 74 days, Argentina was at war.

The dispute over the Falkland Islands started in the 1500s. On the basis of initial occupation, the Argentine historical claim does seem to have somewhat greater validity.

Despite treaties, the British did establish colonies on the islands in the 1770s,

ARGENTINAZO: ¡LAS MALVINAS RECUPERADAS!

ACCION CONJUNTA DE NUESTRAS FUERZAS ARMADAS; MARCHAN AVIONES Y BARCOS EN GRAN OPERATIVO; EL TIEMPO CONSPIRA

¡Las Malvinas están incorporadas, definitivamente, a nuestro territorio! La frase y la fecha, ya históricas, fueron escuchadas esta madrugada en círculos oficiales y políticos, mientras todo el país, sin distinción de banderías, grita, más que nunca ¡Argentina! ¡Argentina!
La esperada resolución de las Fuerzas Armadas Argentinas

del uso de la fuerza" y la "indiferencia" del gobierno del Reino Unido frente a las propuestas argentinas para considerar por vías pacíficas y de negociación el diferendo. En su presentación ante la OEA, la Argentina denunció que los actos del gobierno británico han creado una "situación de grave tensión que podría llegar a poner en peligro el mante-

Buenos Aires' *Cronica* (April 2, 1982) hails Argentina's "recovery" of the Malvinas (Falkland Islands)

but they were soon abandoned. The Spanish claims to the islands were transferred to Argentina when the nation achieved independence from Spain in 1816. Four years later, Argentina reaffirmed its sovereignty over the archipelago as parts of the islands were settled and land grants were awarded. Apparently the Argentines also used the territory as a penal colony.

At the urging of the U.S. consulate in Buenos Aires, the British forcibly occupied the islands in January 1833. At that time, all Argentine residents were deported. For the next 149 years, Argentines were prevented from living on the islands, and

until 1999 Argentine citizens had to buy a round–trip ticket before they are even allowed to *visit* the islands. Since 1851 the islands have been largely controlled by the Falkland Islands Company, a London–"based firm that owns 40% of the main two islands.

Economically, the Falklands have little to offer except offshore oil deposits. Charles Darwin called them "the miserable islands" when he visited them in 1833. Most of the residents today are engaged in sheep ranching and associated production of wool.

The Argentine invasion of 1982 *did* violate two basic principles of internation-

General Leopoldo F. Galtieri

Argentine troops man the Falkland beaches

33

al law: (1) use of force to settle international disputes and (2) the right of self–determination. As a result, the United Nations Security Council voted to demand that they withdraw. There is widespread sentiment in Latin America in favor of returning the islands to Argentina and the United Nations also voted overwhelmingly in the 1960s and 1970s to ask Great Britain to negotiate on the islands' "decolonization."

The British position in 1982 was for 25 more years of control over the islands. Argentina warned that it might seek "other means" to resolve the dispute. It was this frustration with diplomacy that set the stage for the invasion by Argentina. The conflict quickly escalated to include a British nuclear submarine. Ten weeks later, there had been 1,700 Argentine casualties, including 650 dead or missing. The beaten Argentines left enormous amounts of military equipment worth millions of dollars. There were 11,000 war prisoners held by the British. After a lengthy delay they were returned to remote ports in Argentina where they were received amid great security (in part to prevent media coverage) and with little fanfare. The battle cost the British $2 billion—$1 million for each Falklander.

For Argentina, the war was a disaster. The army was humiliated, the military dictatorship was discredited and the economy was pushed toward bankruptcy. In Buenos Aires, angry crowds marched on the Plaza de Mayo demanding to nail "Galtieri to the wall!" The writing was already on the wall for the dictator. In order to prevent elimination of its power, the *junta* promptly fired the president. That was the easy part.

For the next week, the government remained virtually paralyzed while the three armed forces quarreled over a successor. Having just lost on the battlefield, the army—the largest of the three services—had no intention of going down in defeat on the home front as well. Unable to reach an agreement, it finally named one of its own to the presidency: retired Major General Reynaldo Benito Antonio Bignone, age 58. In dismay, the navy and air force said they would not actively participate in the new government.

The United States was put in an awkward position by the conflict. Its endorsement of a 1947 Inter–American Treaty of Mutual Defense (better known as the Rio Treaty) appeared questionable when it refused to side with Argentina. By supporting the British, the significance of the Monroe Doctrine came into question in the minds of many Latin Americans. When it cut off military aid to Argentina, its reliability as a supplier of weapons became questionable. Argentina's support of U.S. efforts against communists in Nicaragua and El Salvador was terminated.

Democracy

Demoralized by defeat and besieged by monumental social and economic problems, the Argentine military government had no other expedient but to allow the electoral process to run as fast and smooth as possible while attempting a rear guard action to protect the power of the armed forces from future judicial action. Encouraged by political freedom, human rights activists demanded more information about the *desaparecidos* (disappeared ones) during the "Dirty War" and stern punishment for those responsible for the crimes. The military *junta* answered with (1) a declaration that the *desaparecidos* should be considered dead and (2) in September 1983 with a law granting amnesty to military security personnel involved in the anti–terrorist campaign of 1976–1982. An outraged public opinion forced the presidential candidates to announce they would repeal the law as soon as civilian authority was reestablished.

One was sentenced to 10 years imprisonment for "illegal association." Many of those sentenced to prison were quietly released within a few months or years.

On October 30, 1983, general elections were held. The winner, Raúl Alfonsín of the Radical Civic Union (*UCR*), represented a more moderate tendency in the Argentine political spectrum. The *Peronistas*, poorly organized, were waiting for Isabel to return, but she preferred her more peaceful life in Spain.

The new democratic government, which ended an eight–year period of military rule, faced a multiplicity of urgent problems, but three appeared as the *most* pressing: control of the armed forces, labor demands and a depressed economy. The full extent of the military's crackdown became clear in late 1985 when nine military leaders, including Videla, Viola and Galtieri were placed on trial. Furious with an attempt by the military to whitewash the gruesome activities of elite military and paramilitary units, the civilian courts assumed jurisdiction. The trial furnished lively media material describing in detail methods of torture and execution. The defense presented by the generals was predictable: (1) they were fighting a war against a subversive enemy financed from abroad and (2) they did not know the extent of the excesses being perpetrated by those under their control. Further, in typical military fashion, lesser officers and personnel claimed they were simply following military orders.

General Videla and Admiral Emilio Massera (Navy member of the Videla *junta*) were sentenced to life for 62 murders; three others were given nominal sentences. Galtieri and two other principals were acquitted, but Galtieri was sentenced by a court martial to 12 years imprisonment for "negligence" in directing the armed forces

during the Malvinas war. His son, killed in the conflict, was buried on one of the islands. Human rights activists numbering 3,000, led by the Mothers of the Plaza de Mayo, who sought information as to their absent loved ones, paraded to protest the leniency of the sentences. This illustrated a well–known fact about the military in Argentina—the country cannot exist without it and cannot stand living with it. Nevertheless, court action against thousands of former military and police strongmen was commenced in 1986, with orders that they be expedited. This, however, led to extreme unrest and in 1987 a serious threat of revolt by the military. To dispel this, President Alfonsín requested the legislature to grant amnesty to all military personnel below the rank of colonel—an action which the liberals (but not the *Peronistas*) denounced. The president was obviously under heavy pressure from the military when this move was made in May. The net result was that of 7,000 potential defendants who could have been tried for atrocities, perhaps 50 actually were charged; there were few convictions.

The year 1985 also marked action against former *Montanaro* leaders (*Peronista*) who had touched off the "Dirty War" of the 1970s. The defense to charges of murder and kidnapping was also predictable: the organization was only exercising political rights and responsibilities. Labor demands were temporarily appeased by some concessions and appeals to democratic patriotism. But it was on the international economic front where Argentina gained its most impressive, even if quite indecisive, battle. Under the burden of a public debt estimated at about $48 billion, Argentina threatened to ignore a March 31, 1984, deadline for paying $500 million in interest to creditors around the world. After several complicated maneuvers, the alarmed bankers agreed to new terms and better payment conditions. Argentina temporarily gained an essential respite and showed other debtor nations that they were not without bargaining power.

The program of austerity, which was necessary to support economic reorganization on even a modest level, sharply lowered living standards in Argentina. A basic problem involved investment funds. There was and is an annual trade surplus which was eaten up by the need to pay interest. It was necessary to borrow additional funds to pay that interest, pushing the external debt to $64 billion.

Although Alfonsín initially appeared to be an astute politician, his knowledge of economic policy was low and this showed quite visibly. Further, he had no competent advisers. The result was hyperinflation caused by spiraling wages and prices (as much as 400% per month!). A new currency, the *austral*, was introduced, but it was devalued so many times it became meaningless.

Alfonsín tried repeated wage–price

freezes that didn't work. Strikes became commonplace. Although the country could have been self–sufficient in oil production, he demanded 50% of production from potential foreign producers as the price of exploration.

The *Peronista* movement splintered into two factions, but loosely reconsolidated in 1987 and in 1988 it nominated Carlos Saúl Menem, popular governor of the impoverished province of La Rioja in the northwest, for president.

Menem proved to be a most colorful candidate, promising everything to everybody. One of his campaign posters showed him reclining on a couch in a bikini bathing suit. He was known for his love of movie starlets and fast cars. His opponent from Alfonsín's *UCR* received 32.5% of the vote in mid–1989 elections but Menem (of Syrian descent) received 47.4%. Alfonsín had vowed to serve until

Raúl Alfonsín

the end of his term in November, but, beset with riots and a host of unsolvable problems, he stepped down in July; Menem was sworn in. He was faced with a debt of $69 billion.

The Menem Presidency

What those attending the inaugural heard was quite different from that which they heard before the election. "I do not bring easy or immediate promises . . . I can only offer my people work, sacrifice and hope," he said. "We must tell the truth, once and for all: Argentina has broken down." He forthwith announced a number of measures calculated to bring order to the country.

Prices went up, restaurants emptied and pasta became a disliked meat substitute. By the end of 1989 all military were

Carlos Saúl Menem

pardoned, including Galtieri and later, Videla, infuriating many; 1 million signed a resolution of protest. He normalized relations with the British. His popularity plummeted sharply. He took an ominous step in March 1990, signing a decree authorizing the military to act in the event of "social upheaval." Further, it would command all state and local police in such an event. The economy continued its downward spiral and the middle class became poor.

In an ingenious move, he announced the privatization of about 90 state monopolies. Part of the purchase price was the purchase of a portion of Argentina's external debt, worth about 30¢ to the dollar. The first to go was the antiquated telephone system, which fetched more than $1.8 billion in hard currency. In early 1992 he effectively tied the latest Argentine currency, again called the peso, to the U.S. dollar to encourage North American and European investment. These and other dramatic measures have helped to put Argentina together again. The continued parity of the peso with the U.S. dollar as of 1999 is an indication of the stability achieved with far–reaching reforms.

Under the programs of President Menem the economy has turned sharply upward, at least on the surface. The improvement has not involved all sectors, however. In a hurry to placate union workers and the economic elite, the government tended in the 1990s to overlook the small business sector and the white collar workers. Privatization has taken its toll among relatives and party favorites— as economists express it, "redundancies" were sharply pared. In other words, unless a person actually did something productive, he or she was fired. In the past this was unheard of; favoritism was not

limited to the elite owner class, but also heavily involved unions. The result was the same: low productivity.

Investors from abroad were unwilling to provide funds in such a setting, so Menem energetically set about changing age–old employment patterns. The result speaks for itself. Both the gross national product and the annual per capita income more than *doubled* after 1990. The external debt rose by almost $2 billion since 1992 and now is still the $69 billion owed when Menem took office (but it has not grown). Inflation is in single digits.

Not all has been a bed of roses. Scandals and corruptions involving Menem's in–_laws (and therefore attributed to him) tarnished his image (although he never pretended to be an angel). When a dispute arose with his wife in 1990, he simply threw her out of the presidential palace. She provided exciting copy for the media, particularly the tabloids.

Desiring that the positive work he had started continue, Menem began in 1993 to devise a way to circumvent the constitutional limitation which forbade a president more than one consecutive term. His term would end in 1995 under the present document. In order to have it changed, it was necessary to have the cooperation of the *UCR*. This was made possible in part by the election of former President Alfonsín as leader of the party in November 1993. A deal was made (the Olivos Pact) between the Peronist *Justicialista* Party of Menem and the *UCR*, for a constituent assembly, the prime purpose of which was to enable Menem to run for a second term. The two parties had a majority (211 of 305 seats) adequate to adopt a proposed constitutional amendment in August 1993 allowing the president to run for a second term in 1995. The bill also created the office of prime minister and gave the president the power to nominate Supreme Court justices, subject to a two-thirds vote in the Senate.

Having won the right to seek reelection, Menem was blessed with incredibly favorable political and economic timing. He easily won his historic reelection bid in May 1995 with about 50 percent of the vote, thus avoiding a runoff. No sooner did he win his second term, reduced to four years, than the effects of the Mexican peso devaluation struck Argentina, plunging it into recession. Unemployment soared to 18%.

Menem kept his campaign promises to modernize the economy through privatization and other free-market reforms, and he accomplished the unthinkable by reducing inflation to single-digits. Still, the painful remedies cost Menem his popularity. In June 1996, the *Peronistas* were dealt a severe blow when Fernando de la Rua, the *UCR* candidate for mayor of Buenos Aires, won a decisive victory in that *Peronista* stronghold. In 1997, the Radicals en-

Edición
Internacional
Vía Aérea

LA NACION

Una selección
de la semana

Año 120 - Nros. 42.255 al 42.261 - Ed. Int. N° 1502 - Año 28   Buenos Aires, lunes 3 de julio de 1989   Bouchard 557, C. P. 1106, Tel. 313-1003, 1453 y 312-3021/9

Menem dispondría la libertad de militares

Lo reveló implícitamente, al sostener que no puede ver encerrados "ni a los pájaros"; viajará a los EE. UU., en septiembre, por el problema de la deuda externa

Por César Ivancovich

(Enviado especial de LA NACION)

Jueves 29

LA RIOJA.– El presidente electo, Carlos Menem, reiteró que hay que cerrar las heridas entre militares y civiles y reveló implícitamente que todos los hombres de armas condenados por la Justicia recuperarán su libertad, al utilizar la expresión: "Yo no puedo ver encerrados ni a los pájaros".

También anunció que viajará en septiembre próximo a los Estados Unidos, en un intento por revertir la "extrema dureza" advertida en los medios financieros internacionales respecto de la Argentina.

"No hay vuelta que darle, todo pasa por allí", comentó el todavía gobernador riojano al justificar la aceptación del convite formulado por el presidente norteamericano, Georges Bush.

Menem no sólo se refirió a las dificultades que enfrenta la economía en el plano externo –en su reciente viaje a Washington, el canciller designado, Domingo Cavallo, se estrelló contra una dura muralla construida por los centros financieros–, sino también en el ámbito local.

Admitió, por ejemplo, que esos 2500 millones de dólares que según versiones aportarían empresas locales para el arranque de su plan económico son, por ahora, algo así como un espejismo en el medio del desierto. Nadie sabe, empero, si al seguir avanzando la imagen corresponderá efectivamente a un oasis.

Por lo que dicen los allegados de

Lo que sí dijo ayer el presidente electo es que la dureza que implica va a ser mayor después de los cien días que al comienzo de su gestión. Cree que las medidas de shock para aplicarse de entrada serán efectivas para bajar la inflación, pero que las requeridas para mantenerla en ese nivel, después de los tres primeros meses, podrían llegar a ser mucho más duras.

Este enviado le preguntó si creía que los operadores retirarían su capital del circuito financiero para invertirlo en la producción. "Sí. Los especuladores deberán replegarse, pues habrá créditos baratos para la producción. Las mesas de dinero tendrán que adaptarse o desaparecer", sentenció.

Formalizaron sus renuncias Alfonsín y Víctor Martínez

Las presentaron en el Congreso; serán aceptadas el 8, antes de que jure Menem

Sábado 1

El presidente Raúl Alfonsín y el vicepresidente Víctor Martínez presentaron ayer al Parlamento sus renuncias, para que la Asamblea Legislativa del 8 del actual las acepte momentos antes de que preste juramento como nuevo mandatario el doctor Carlos Saúl Menem.

Se formalizaron así las dimisiones anunciadas por Alfonsín en su discurso del 12 de junio, cuando anticipó su decisión de resignar el cargo a partir de ayer.

El sobre lacrado con la renuncia del jefe del Estado llegó al Congreso en manos del secretario general de la Presidencia, Carlos Becerra, quien lo entregó a Víctor Martínez en su carácter de titular del Senado.

Al recibir la renuncia –en una breve ceremonia realizada en su despacho– Martínez sumó la suya, también en sobre cerrado. Ambos fueron entregados al secretario parlamentario de la Cámara alta, Antonio Macris, y sólo serán

a la formalidad o un mensaje extenso con consideraciones o pronunciamientos políticos.

"Misión histórica"

"Presentar la renuncia me apena un poco, pero nos complace saber que esto lo hacemos en beneficio del país", dijo Víctor Martínez a los periodistas tras el acto en su despacho.

Becerra, por su parte, declaró que se sentía "muy honrado por esta misión histórica que me encomendó el Presidente: este acto cierra el capítulo de la consolidación de la democracia".

Agregó que el radicalismo acompañará "con alta responsabilidad" la nueva etapa política que comienza el 8 del actual.

Alfonsín en el Congreso

Martínez confirmó, asimismo, que pasado mañana Alfonsín concurrirá al Congreso, a las 17, para saludar protocolarmente al nuevo titular provisional

La Nación headlines two watershed events on July 3, 1989: President–elect Menem's declaration that he would release jailed military officers as a gesture of reconciliation, and the resignations of President Alfonsín and Vice President Martínez, which allowed Menem to take office five months early.

---

tered into an opposition alliance with *Frepaso*, a Peronist splinter group, to contest the October congressional elections. The Alliance wisely chose not to attack Menem's successful free-market policies, because the economy was still growing at a robust 8%. Instead, the Alliance hit the president where he was most vulnerable: the rampant corruption within his administration, which had grown so bad that Economy Minister Domingo Cavallo, the architect of the new economic miracle, resigned in disgust in 1996. In the elections for 127 of the 257 seats in the lower house, the *Peronistas* suffered another serious setback by losing their absolute majority, dropping from 131 seats to 119; their share of the popular vote plummeted from 43% in 1995 to 36%. The Alliance won 106 seats, while other parties held 32 seats and the balance of power.

There was a hostile relationship between Menem and the press. Unlike years past, the Argentine media now enjoy unprecedented freedom and they dutifully exposed scandal after scandal in the Menem government. In January 1997, José Luis Cabezas, an investigative photographer who was probing alleged police corruption, was found beaten, shot and burned to a cinder in his car. The crime shocked the nation and brought international pressure on Menem to bring the killers to justice. The scandal reached a head in May 1998 when the wife of one of two policemen arrested in connection with Cabezas' murder publicly revealed that they had been hired by Alfredo

Yabrán, a powerful, influential and secretive tycoon who was rumored to have Mafia ties and who for good measure was a close friend of Menem's. Cabezas had surreptitiously taken the first published photographs of the reclusive Yabrán, who, like Menem, was of Arab descent. On May 20, as police closed in on Yabrán's *estancia* to arrest him for Cabezas' murder, the tycoon apparently shot himself to death. There was no autopsy, and he wasn't even buried before rumors circulated that the Mafia had murdered him to silence him. Quipped the U.S. ambassador: "Yabrán committed suicide, but we don't know who did it yet."

Yabrán's mysterious death was not to be the last to rivet the attention of the press and public. In August 1998, former navy Captain Horacio Estrada, who had just been subpoenaed to testify in controversial and illegal arms sales to Ecuador and Croatia, was found dead in his apartment with a gunshot wound to his head. In October 1998, businessman Marcelo Cattaneo, who was expected to appear in court in connection with another high–profile scandal involving alleged bribes by Banco Nación and the U.S. computer firm IBM, was found hanged on a communications tower. Both deaths were ruled suicides, but the press has raised allegations of organized crime connections. A defensive Menem responded, "We can't jump to conclusions."

Ghosts from the Past

The past came back to haunt Argentina in 1998, beginning with controversial statements by two former naval officers that scraped open the still-healing wounds of the Dirty War. One, Adolfo Scilingo, voluntarily traveled to Spain, where he was wanted for human rights violations against Spanish citizens in Argentina, and served three months in jail. Upon his release, he openly expressed remorse in a press interview that he had participated in the so–called "death flights," in which naked prisoners were thrown to their deaths into the ocean from aircraft. He called for war-crimes trials for his fellow officers.

The other officer, Alfredo Astiz, was arrogant and unrepentant. Astiz had been sentenced to life in prison by France in absentia in 1990, and was also wanted by Spain and Italy for Dirty War atrocities against nationals of those countries. He, too, admitted in a magazine interview that he had killed prisoners, but justified the killings as necessary. His remarks sparked a public outcry, and Menem ordered him jailed. He was soon released, still defiant, but Menem stripped him of his former rank. (In December 2001, Astiz was arrested at the request of Sweden, which wanted him extradited to stand trial for the death of a Swedish girl during the Dirty War.)

The Astiz incident prompted *Frepaso* to introduce legislation repealing the amnesty granted to military officers after the return to civilian rule, but this caused a strain between the Alliance coalition partners because the amnesty had been adopted during the administration of the Radicals' Alfonsín. In the end, Congress passed a watered-down version. Almost simultaneously, the public expressed outrage over Menem's plan to raze the Navy Mechanics School, the most notorious of the military's torture centers during the Dirty War, and replace it with a park containing a memorial to the victims. Most Argentines evidently preferred to convert the school into a museum, much like the museums dedicated to Holocaust victims. In March 1998, a judge issued an injunction against plans to demolish the building, not on sentimental grounds but on the pretext that destruction might destroy criminal evidence.

The past again came crashing down on the present on June 10, 1998, when former President Videla was arrested on charges he participated in selling the babies of "disappeared" dissidents to adoptive parents. Videla's 1990 pardon on war crimes charges did not cover these new allegations. The so-called "baby–stealing" probe widened after Videla's arrest. In November, former Admiral Emilio Massera, navy chief during the Dirty War, was arrested after DNA tests showed that two women adopted as babies were children of parents who had disappeared after being arrested; one of them was adopted and raised by an aide of Massera's. In January 1999, former President Reynaldo Bignone was arrested for possible involvement in the baby kidnapping scheme but was not charged with a specific crime. Since then, several more officers have been detained in the baby-stealing investigation, most recently a retired army general, Guillermo Suárez Mason, in December 1999. Suárez Mason, who allegedly was involved with Massera in the operation of the Navy Mechanics School, was among 98 former officers indicted by Spanish Judge Baltasar Garzón for alleged human rights abuses in November 1999.

The investigations have continued. In March 2001, three weeks before the 25th anniversary of the 1976 coup that presaged the "Dirty War," a federal judge ruled in a case brought against army officers in the disappearance of a young couple in 1978 that the amnesty laws absolving the military of wrongdoing in human rights cases are unconstitutional. Six months later, a judge ordered the arrest of 12 former military men and six civilians at the request of Judge Garzón, the same judge who had requested the arrest of former Chilean strongman Augusto Pinochet by the British in 1998.

In July 2002, former President Galtieri and 41 others were detained in connection with the disappearance of 20 *Montanaro* suspects during his presidency.

The Elections of 1999

No sooner had the 1997 congressional elections ended, it seemed, than the jockeying began for the October 24, 1999, presidential election, among both the Justicialists and the Alliance. Eduardo Duhalde, the Peronist governor of Buenos Aires Province, regarded himself as the logical heir apparent to Menem and began running for the nomination. But Menem shocked the country—and infuriated Duhalde—by coyly hinting in early 1998 that he would be amenable to a constitutional amendment permitting him to run for a third term. For most it seemed a moot point because the Peronists had lost their majority in the Chamber of Deputies, but Menem nonetheless began talking more and more like a man running for reelection. Yet, faced with increasing opposition within the party, a chorus of criticism from the press, the near-impossibility of pushing such an amendment through Congress and opinion polls showing him running in the single digits, Menem subsequently declared that he would not run for reelection. But in October 1998 he boasted to a French newspaper that he would return to power in the 2003 election. Meanwhile, he ramrodded through a vote in a party conference that would keep him as leader of the party until 2002, even if another Peronist were to be elected president of the republic. In February 1999, a court invalidated that vote.

By early 1999, Menem was hinting *again* that he would accept a "draft." Tension between Menem and Duhalde mounted, and Duhalde pulled off an astute political maneuver by scheduling a referendum in Buenos Aires Province for March 28, 1999, on whether or not the constitution should be amended to allow Menem to run again. It was a classic poker player's bluff; it could have backfired if the vote were yes, but Duhalde was confident the vote would go against Menem. Menem realized it, too, and folded. He definitively withdrew from the race, Duhalde canceled the referendum, and the party postponed the date of the party primary to select the presidential candidate from April 11 to July 4. Duhalde won easily and selected a former pop music star, Palito Ortega, as his running mate.

The Alliance, meanwhile, had a schism of its own between two sexagenarians, the *UCR*'s Fernando de la Rua, 61, mayor of the city of Buenos Aires, and *Frepaso*'s Senator Graciela Fernández Meijide, 68, mother of one of the "disappeareds" of the Dirty War. Preference polls in 1998 showed Fernández Meijide with a slight lead over either de la Rua or Duhalde, but in the Alliance's primary election on November 30, 1998, de la Rua handily defeated her 63% to 36%. About 2 million people voted. To keep the Alliance intact,

de la Rua chose as his running mate a *Frepaso* strategist, Carlos Alvarez. As a consolation, Fernández Meijide became the Alliance's candidate to succeed Duhalde as governor of Buenos Aires Province. Her opponent was Menem's retiring vice president, Carlos Ruckauf.

The disgruntled Domingo Cavallo, Menem's erstwhile economic adviser, launched an independent candidacy for president.

The ensuing campaign was the most dramatic the country had seen since the restoration of democracy 16 years earlier. The lead see-sawed back and forth between de la Rua and Duhalde in the polls. But 10 years of Peronist rule, coupled with nagging public concerns over official corruption and an alarming 14.5% unemployment rate, proved too much of an encumbrance for Duhalde. In the balloting on October 24, de la Rua scored a decisive first-round victory, receiving 48.5% of the vote to Duhalde's 38% and Cavallo's 10.2%. With characteristic bombast, Menem declared on election night, "I could have won easily," a claim that is highly debatable. Nonetheless, the president graciously telephoned de la Rua to congratulate him. The Alliance's victory carried over into the elections for the Chamber of Deputies. It increased its number of seats from 106 to 123, just six short of a majority, while the Justicialist Party fell from 122 seats to 101, its worst showing since it won 97 seats in the 1985 off-year elections. The Justicialists could console themselves with victories for a number of governorships, among them that of Buenos Aires; Ruckauf defeated Fernández Meijide 48.3% to 41.5%. Moreover, they still controlled the Senate, which will require de la Rua to govern by consensus.

While domestic politics consumed much of the public's attention in 1999, a major foreign policy event took place in July. Foreign Minister Guido di Tella and British Foreign Secretary Robin Cook signed a bilateral agreement that in effect ended the diplomatic hostilities over the Falkland Islands. Argentine nationals were once again permitted to visit the islands.

Even before he took office, de la Rua also found himself involved in foreign affairs. On November 4, Spanish Judge Baltasar Garzón, the same judge who had sought the extradition of former Chilean strongman Augusto Pinochet from Britain, issued indictments against 98 former Argentine officers for alleged human rights abuses committed during the Dirty War. Both President Menem and President-elect de la Rua denounced the indictments as an infringement on Argentine sovereignty and refused to recognize them. (In August, Menem also demonstrated his disagreement with Spain in the Pinochet case by joining Chile in boy-

The *gaucho*—free on the plains . . .

. . . and the socially elite at the glittering Colón Theater in Buenos Aires

cotting the Ibero-American summit in Cuba.)

Faced with a strained relationship with an old European friend, de la Rua made an effort to further improve relations with a long-time European foe. While in Paris in November to represent the Alliance in the Socialist International convention, he held a 20-minute dialogue with British Prime Minister Tony Blair. The two men reportedly discussed mostly economic and trade issues, but they agreed in principle to expand upon the bilateral agreement reached in July on the Falkland Islands. As another indication of the thaw in the relations between the former adversaries, Blair announced that Prince Andrew, a Falklands War veteran, would represent Britain at de la Rua's inauguration.

De la Rua's Aborted Presidency

De la Rua was sworn in on December 10, 1999. The new president soon demonstrated that his administration represented not merely a change in parties and personalities but in style as well. Breaking with Menem's image as a flamboyant spendthrift, de la Rua announced he

would sell Tango 1, the ostentatious presidential jet, a Boeing 757 that cost Argentine taxpayers $66 million and a small fortune to fly and maintain as well. When de la Rua visited Sweden in January 2000, he flew by commercial jet.

To combat the recession and budget deficit bequeathed by the Menem government, de la Rua advocated a stinging $2.5 billion tax increase to reduce the $7.1 billion budget deficit. The IMF expressed its approval over the tax hike by extending a $7.4 billion loan. The tax increase was far less popular with the Argentine public, but they did not seem to be holding it against the new president. Polls taken two months into his term showed that while his government had only a 42% approval rating, the president himself was riding high at 63%. That would soon change.

De la Rua then introduced a far more controversial labor reform bill that would allow more flexibility in labor contracts, a move seen as a gesture to wary foreign investors but also to satisfy IMF expectations. Among its provisions were a reduction in employer contributions to payroll deductions, an increase in the probation period for new employees from 30 to 90

days and decentralization of collective bargaining. It was essentially an Argentine analogy to the Taft-Hartley Act of 1947 in the United States, and it had a similar effect of waving a red flag at the still-powerful trade unions, which took to the streets to protest the new measure after it passed the Chamber of Deputies. In April 2000, union militants, primarily garbage workers and truck drivers, surrounded the Congress and clashed with police, who used truncheons and rubber bullets to disperse them. Thirty people were injured, 43 were arrested, and 12 policemen were suspended for excessive use of force. It was merely a taste of what was to come.

The Peronist majority in the Senate temporarily delayed discussion of the bill, but a week later the upper chamber passed, 57-4, a compromise version that precluded salaries from being reduced in collective bargaining. Organized labor found itself split over the modified plan, reportedly because de la Rua slyly promised entrenched labor bosses that he would not probe their operations if they would support the bill. The measure then returned to the lower house to resolve the disparities in the two versions, as union hardliners continued to protest by calling a one-day general strike on May 5. It disrupted traffic, but not the functioning of the country as organizers had hoped. The Chamber of Deputies passed the bill on May 11 by a vote of 121-84.

At the height of the uproar over the labor bill, and just two days after the one-day strike, de la Rua and the Alliance received an important vote of confidence. The Alliance candidate to succeed de la Rua as mayor of Buenos Aires, Anibal Ibarra of the Radicals' left-of-center *Frepaso* coalition partner, defeated the still-disgruntled Domingo Cavallo, 49.4% to 33.1%. On election night, Cavallo lashed out at the victor, charged that the election was tainted by fraud and boasted that he would overtake Ibarra in the runoff. The following day, however, faced with the brutal reality of mathematics, a contrite Cavallo apologized for his intemperate remarks and withdrew from the race, handing the mayoralty to Ibarra.

Weeks later, however, fissures began to appear in the Radical-*Frepaso* Alliance after de la Rua announced $938 million in budget cuts and reductions of from 12% to 15% in the salaries of civil servants. This time, 14 *Frepaso* members of Congress revolted against the president, as did the *Frepaso's* moral guardian, Graciela Fernández Mejía, the social development minister.

Another one-day work stoppage was called for June 9, which was much more widely observed than the stoppage of May 5 and represented the most serious expression of public disapproval to date of de la Rua's austerity measures, which the public has nicknamed *"el Ajuste,"* or, the Adjustment. Even by the most conser-

Fernando de la Rua

vative estimates from the government, 60% of the labor force took part, closing banks and other offices, blocking highways, paralyzing public transportation, and largely bringing business to a standstill in the capital and elsewhere. There were sporadic acts of nonlethal violence, and at least 50 people were arrested. It was the largest such stoppage in years. The unions estimated the participation at 85%. De la Rua steadfastly maintained that the austerity program, painful as it was, was necessary to balance the budget and would eventually be successful.

Left-wing members of the Alliance also were grumbling over what they regarded as undue influence on de la Rua by his close friend Fernando de Santibañes, a prominent and conservative banker whom de la Rua had named head of the National Intelligence Service (SIDE). Santibañes, critics charge, had been dabbling in economic policy and lobbied openly to push the labor bill through Congress, matters clearly outside the purview of the spy director.

In mid-2000, the executive and legislative branches became embroiled in a scandal; accusations arose that the government had paid $10 million in bribes to 11 senators to secure passage of the labor reform bill. There was no substantive evidence, but the scandal droned on for months before finally dying out. Despite the lack of concrete evidence, a poll indicated that 70% of the corruption-jaded Argentine public believed the charges were true; chief among the critics was none other than the reform-minded Vice President Carlos Alvarez of Frepaso, who presided over the Senate.

Partly in response to the scandal, and partly to deal with public discontent over a nagging recession then in its third year, de la Rua shuffled his cabinet in October.

But when he retained Santibañes and promoted Labor Minister Alberto Flamarique to presidential chief of staff—both men had been implicated in the bribe scandal—Vice President Alvarez called a news conference the following day to announce his irrevocable decision to resign. He delivered a stinging denunciation of corruption in government, but insisted, unconvincingly, that he and the party he helped found would remain loyal to de la Rua. Hours later, Flamarique also resigned, although Fernández Mejide remained as social development minister, preserving for a time the illusion that Frepaso was a partner in the government. Alvarez's resignation proved fateful, and it would confront Argentina with a constitutional crisis 14 months later. Meanwhile, the role of Economy Minister José Luis Machinea was strengthened to deal with the recession.

At year's end, de la Rua publicly admitted that the country's economic performance had been disappointing again in 2000, with GDP down by 5% and unemployment remaining stubbornly around 15%. About the only bright spot was a $40 billion economic rescue package approved by the IMF. Among the terms of the package: Argentina had to reduce its budget deficit from more than $9 billion to $6.5 billion by the end of 2001.

The economy continued to preoccupy the government and the public during the first half of 2001. In March, Machinea, yielding to public pressure, resigned; the Argentine bolsa, or stock market, gleefully responded with a 2% jump same day. De la Rua replaced him with a conservative technocrat, Ricardo López Murphy, more trusted by investors than was Machinea but detested by the Peronists and Frepaso. He would last only two weeks. During his brief tenure, he provoked the last remaining Frepaso cabinet members, including Fernández Mejide, to resign by announcing $4.5 billion in budget cuts. Rumors flew that Argentina would default on its IMF package, even that de la Rua planned to resign; the bolsa plunged, and international banks and investors looked nervously at Argentina. On March 20, a desperate de la Rua stunned the country—but delighted the international financial markets—by resurrecting the irrepressible Domingo Cavallo to replace López.

Cavallo lost little time in proposing extraordinary measures to comply with the IMF bailout terms and to jumpstart the flagging economy. His first round of proposals was a half-percent tax on financial transactions and a crackdown on tax evasion, which he said cost the government $25 billion in revenue—half the total amount. One method: requiring all transactions of more than $1,000 to be by check or credit card. The Chamber of Deputies quickly passed Cavallo's plan; the Peronist-controlled Senate soon followed suit.

His next proposal was even more controversial: Granting emergency powers for one year to the president—in reality, to Cavallo himself—to deal with the economic crisis by decree. Among the principal proposals he advanced were to convert state institutions into state-owned companies; to lower some taxes to stimulate economic growth; to lower tariffs on capital goods needed to stimulate the economy but raising them on some consumer goods; and eliminating some tax exemptions. The lower house passed the so-called "superpowers" on March 26 by a vote of 151-81. Cavallo's small Action for the Republic party, which had 12 seats in the Chamber, helped offset Frepaso defectors. However, the lower house clipped Cavallo's claws somewhat with amendments that prevent him from privatizing state-owned firms, from reducing the pay of civil servants or from tinkering with pension plans or labor laws. In a display of multipartisan cooperation similar to that on the labor reform bill the year before, the Peronist-dominated Senate approved the emergency powers by an even more lopsided 50-4; the IMF expressed its immediate approval.

In April, Cavallo came up with another offbeat idea: Instead of pegging the peso solely to the dollar, the inflation-busting technique he had fathered a decade earlier, he proposed pegging the peso to the average of the dollar and the euro, the European Union's new monetary unit. Although Cavallo argued that it would add stability to the peso, the bolsa and international markets reacted negatively, and the proposal caused consternation in Brazil, Argentina's leading trading partner. Within a week, near-panic ensued after former President Menem suggested Argentines trade in their pesos for dollars before the peso weakened. The bolsa plummeted 6.3% on April 20, even as de la Rua was visiting with President George W. Bush at the White House en route to the Summit of the Americas in Quebec. On April 22, a Sunday, Argentina suspended issuance of $700 million in treasury bills, and its international risk rating jumped more than 10% to 1,049—a rate worse than Russia's. Cavallo went before the television cameras to reassure investors that his recovery plan was "on track."

Cavallo next turned his attention to getting rid of Central Bank head Pedro Pou, who had opposed Cavallo's call to ease up on monetary policy to stimulate the economy. Pou already was under investigation by Congress for his lackluster attitude toward money laundering. After some vacillating, de la Rua sacked Pou and replaced him with Roque Maccarone, a Cavallo bedfellow.

Simultaneous with the currency panic and the Pou controversy, a separate development unfolded that threatened to jeopardize Peronist cooperation with Cavallo's emergency measures. A federal prosecutor accused Menem of being the intellectual author of illegal arms sales in 1991 to Ecuador, then in a virtual state of war with Peru, and to Croatia, then under a United Nations arms embargo. Peronists rallied to the defense of their former chief, who denied the charges. Always flamboyant, the 70-year-old Menem splashed back into the international deadlines on May 26, 2001, by marrying Cecilia Bolocco, a 36-year-old former Miss Universe from Chile. He splashed into the headlines again on June 7 when he was placed under house arrest on the arms sale charges He was formally indicted in July, but in November the Supreme Court threw out the charges.

The last of Cavallo's bold proposals to reduce the budget deficit to levels acceptable to the IMF was a "megaswap" of $25 billion worth of short-term bond indebtedness for longer-term bonds. This would save the country $5 billion in interest payments in 2001. With the bond exchange approved, Cavallo said he would turn his attention to stimulating the economy.

In July, de la Rua announced his seventh painful austerity plan to cut the budget deficit and stave off defaulting on Argentina's foreign debt, which at that point was $128 billion. The plan included a 13% pay cut for civil servants, which sparked labor protests. De la Rua obtained a grudging endorsement within the Alliance, but on July 12 the *bolsa* plummeted 8.16% over uncertainty whether the Peronists would agree; Argentina's country risk indicator jumped to 1,616 points—worse than Ecuador's! However, on July 13, the 13 Peronist governors also rallied around the austerity plan and pledged to balance their provincial budgets as well. The austerity plan was approved by the Chamber of Deputies by 83-64 on July 21 and by the Senate on July 30. The IMF responded with another $8 billion loan.

The austerity plan may have pleased the IMF, but it proved highly unpopular to the Argentines, especially the restriction on savings withdrawals. By October 2001, de la Rua's approval rating was 18% and Cavallo's was 16%.

It was bad timing for the Alliance. In the October 14 elections for the entire Senate and half the Chamber of Deputies, the Peronists strengthened their majority in the upper chamber and increased from 102 to 116 in the lower chamber, replacing the Alliance as the largest bloc. The *UCR* dropped from 84 seats to 71, while *Frepaso* dropped from 23 to 17; Cavallo's party dropped from 12 to nine seats. In the popular vote, the Peronists received 40%, the Alliance only 23%. Duhalde remained politically viable by winning a Senate seat from Buenos Aires. But 30% of Argentines angrily cast blank ballots or nullified them by writing in names like Bart Simpson or Mickey Mouse. The public mood was dangerously ugly.

Less than a week after the election, de la Rua's political woes were compounded when the last *Frepaso* cabinet member, Juan Pablo Cafiero, who has succeeded Fernández Mejide as social development minister, resigned after Cavallo cut his department's budget by 75%.

For the next two months, de la Rua and Cavallo desperately tried to deal with the deepening economic crisis and to avoid default on the national debt, which had increased to $132 billion; if it happened, it would be the largest default in history, one that could generate global shock waves. To do it, de la Rua had to appease the IMF by trying to balance the budget in the face of declining revenues while trying to sell the idea of greater belt-tightening to a Peronist-dominated Congress, powerful Peronist state governors, the trade unions and domestic and foreign investors. In November, he announced a "debt swap," that traded $95 billion worth of existing bonds that paid 11% for longer-term bonds that paid only 7%; for investors, it was a no-brainer. Then the Peronist governors dealt the president a setback by rejecting his proposed reduction in federal remittances to the state governments, something he needed to meet the terms for a $22 billion international rescue plan. Also in November, rumors resurfaced in financial circles that Argentina would replace the peso with the dollar or the euro; de la Rua announced he was sticking to the dollar-parity plan.

Descent into Chaos

By December 2001, fears of an imminent Argentine debt default and economic meltdown had Argentines makings runs on their banks, emptying ATM machines and exchanging pesos for dollars in a near-panic. De la Rua infuriated his countrymen by reducing the monthly limit on savings withdrawals from $1,500 to $1,000. The IMF did not help matters on December 5 by freezing a scheduled $1.3 billion installment on its $22 billion line of credit because of displeasure with the government's lack of progress in meeting demands on deficit reduction and because it felt the peso had become unreasonably overvalued by the dollar peg. Cavallo flew to Washington for emergency talks with the IMF; the World Bank and the Inter-American Development Bank froze another $1.1 billion in loans pending the results of the talks. Argentina, and the world financial markets, held their breaths.

Events then began exploding in chain reaction. On Tuesday, December 11, the government pleaded for consensus with the Peronists to cut the budget from $49.6 billion to $42.5 billion—a whopping 14% decrease—to obtain the desperately needed help from the IMF. The budget deficit

Rounding up sheep for market

was $11 billion, about double what de la Rua had assured the IMF it would be by year's end. The media reported the Peronists were demanding de la Rua's resignation as their price for cooperation. On Thursday, December 13, there was a massive general strike to protest continued high unemployment, then at 18.3%; police had to protect a grocery store in Rosario from being looted. On Friday, December 14, the government announced it had allayed defaulting on the debt by making a loan payment of more than $700 million, but the good news was muted by the sudden resignation of the deputy finance minister, ostensibly for personal reasons but which embarrassed the president. The same day, a new poll showed that a majority of Argentines wanted Cavallo, whose appointment they had cheered nine months earlier, to resign. For the next six days, Argentina was a powder keg. On Wednesday, December 19, it exploded.

The spark was a demonstration by mostly middle-class Argentines, frustrated over the decline in their living standards and weary of their financial insecurity. The demonstrations began peacefully with the traditional banging on pots and pans, but soon there were the inevitable violent clashes with police, who fired rubber bullets and tear gas. Full-scale rioting then erupted in the capital and several cities in the interior. Rioters began looting grocery stores and carting off food—and wine. Five people were killed that first day, and de la Rua declared a 30-day state of siege—the first since the riots of 1989 that shortened the Alfonsín presidency. The riots carried over into Thursday, December 20, as demonstrators tried to storm de la Rua's office. More people were killed, as de la Rua pleaded for calm. With the republic literally falling apart, the entire cabinet, including Cavallo, resigned in a vain attempt to quell the violence. The number of rioters in Buenos Aires alone was estimated at 20,000. Simultaneously, thousands of people rushed to banks to withdraw their monthly limit. The *bolsa* closed indefinitely; the Central Bank declared a partial holiday.

That evening, de la Rua himself resigned, two years and 10 days after he was inaugurated, and at sunset he was ignominiously whisked away from the Casa Rosada by helicopter, a scene eerily like that in 1976 when the military overthrew Isabel Perón. The mobs cheered the news, but it was a hollow celebration at best. By Thursday night, the death toll had climbed to 22, many of them looters shot not by police but by shopkeepers defending their property.

Despite de la Rua's resignation, the rioting continued, as a leaderless government desperately tried to cope with the violence as well as with a constitutional crisis. With the vacancy in the vice presidency caused by Alvarez's resignation 14 months earlier, de la Rua's constitutional successor was the Senate president, Ramón Puerta, a Peronist. But Puerta, feigning ill health, let it be known that he had no stomach for his constitutional mandate, which he said made him president for only 48 hours. It was hard to blame him; that same day, the Economy Ministry delivered still more bad news: The gross domestic product for the third quarter declined by 4.9% compared with the third quarter of 2000.

Thus, Argentina was quite literally on the brink of anarchy by Saturday, December 22, when Congress called new elections for March 3 and the Peronists tapped their governor of San Luis, Adolfo Rodríguez Sáa, 54, as their choice for interim president until then. He was elected on a 169-138 vote in a joint session of Congress and sworn in on Sunday, December 23. Rodríguez Sáa brought cheers—temporarily—by announcing that he was lifting the state of siege, suspending payment on the foreign debt, and channeling the money instead into the creation of 1 million new jobs, the first 24,000 to be public service jobs created within days. The decision did not sit well with the IMF or with U.S. President George W. Bush, who urged Rodríguez Sáa to seek "technical advice" from the United States.

It seemed that the country at least was no longer rudderless, as calm temporarily returned; the final death toll from the riots was 27, with hundreds more injured or taken into custody. Seven deaths alone had taken place in the Plaza de Mayo, in front of the Casa Rosada. Argentines settled down for an uneasy Christmas, bracing themselves for an expected currency devaluation, which could bring back the long-dead bogeyman of hyperinflation. Plans were announced to issue a new currency in January, the *argentino*, to circulate alongside the peso and the dollar. The idea was abandoned within a week because of speculation. On Saturday, December 29, pot-beating protesters took to the streets again to protest Rodríguez Sáa's decision to continue the limit on savings withdrawals. Again, the protests turned violent, although not deadly. Protesters, screaming their rage not just at the banking restrictions but at politicians in general, tried to storm their way into the Casa Rosada and the Congress, but were expelled by riot police. Twelve policemen were injured and 33 protesters were arrested.

If Rodríguez Sáa had had illusions that he would have more success than de la Rua at achieving a consensus, he was soon disappointed. He huddled with the Peronist leaders and desperately called on them to offer solutions that might quell the popular uprising without worsening the economic crisis and reach a consensus on how to select the Peronist candidate for the March 3 election. They could not—or would not.

On Sunday, December 30, after exactly one week in office, Rodríguez Sáa resigned in disgust, bitterly lashing out at the members of his own party for failing to support him on the tough decisions that had to be made. Mob rule, it seemed, was close to prevailing in Argentina.

With Puerta out of the running, the next hapless interim president was Eduardo Carmoña, speaker of the Chamber of Deputies, who like Puerta would keep the presidential chair warm for 48 hours until a joint session of Congress met on New Year's Day 2002 to select the nation's fifth president in 12 days. Meanwhile, on New Year's Eve, Congress canceled the March 3 election and decided to appoint an interim president to fill out de la Rua's term, which would have expired December 10, 2003.

The unfortunate "winner" of the January 1 balloting: The former Vice President, Buenos Aires governor and newly elected senator from Buenos Aires, Eduardo Duhalde, 60, the Peronist presidential candidate who lost to de la Rua in 1999. The vote was 262-21, with 18 abstentions. He was sworn in on Wednesday, January 2. He told the Congress and the nation that he was scrapping the "exhausted model" of free markets and neoliberal economic policies that he blamed for the country's woes (even though they had succeeded in Brazil, Chile and Mexico) and that he would "recreate the conditions" to attract investors. "Argentina is bankrupt," he bluntly told his countrymen, "Argentina is destroyed. This model destroyed everything." He thus was calling for a return to the pre-Menem Peronist ideals of populism and protectionism. In a closing statement reminiscent of Franklin D. Roosevelt's assurance to Depression-weary Americans that "the only thing we have to fear is fear itself," Duhalde urged Argentines "never to doubt even for a minute that Argentina has a future." Also like Roosevelt, he promised to guarantee deposits to prevent further panic—or violence. He also continued the moratorium on foreign debt payments. But he avoided mention of the two most sensitive topics—a possible peso devaluation and whether he would lift the detested restriction on bank withdrawals, which Argentines had nicknamed *"el corralito,"* or little corral.

In his first days in office, Duhalde appointed a bipartisan cabinet but with the key posts going to Peronists. As economy minister, by far the most-watched appointment, he named Jorge Remes Lenicov, an internationally respected economist who had served as economy minister of Buenos Aires province under Governor Duhalde. He shared Duhalde's aversion for Menem's free-market policies, but had been seen as more fiscally responsible than the governor on budget matters. As foreign minister Duhalde appointed the current Buenos Aires governor—and another former vice president—Carlos Ruckauf.

Duhalde and Remes immediately submitted to Congress an emergency economic plan which, among other provisions, granted Duhalde and Remes *carte blanche*, authorized devaluation of the peso and froze job layoffs for six months. Meanwhile, on Thursday, January 3, Argentina missed an interest payment on a $28 billion loan; the country was officially in default. The Chamber of Deputies quickly approved it on Saturday, January 5, and the Senate followed on Sunday. That night, Remes announced that the decade-old peg of the peso to the dollar had ended. He devalued the peso 40%, to an official rate of 1.40 to the dollar for exports and imports, but said it would be allowed to float freely to find its levels on international exchanges. He extended the banking holiday and the moratorium on foreign currency exchanges until Friday, January 11, to minimize the shock. He also said he would begin negotiations in February to restructure the foreign debt, which had grown to a staggering $141 billion.

On Thursday, January 10, the demonstrators were back in the streets banging on pots and pans, demanding access to their savings. On January 16, they began smashing their way into banks and destroying ATM machines. Tens of thousands more engaged in another pot-banging demonstration on January 26.

Besides having to cope with angry protesters, the government also had to deal with an angry IMF board of directors, which sent a letter criticizing Duhalde's economic plan as incoherent. Deputy

Economy Minister Jorge Todesca angrily responded that the letter was "offensive to Argentina." The IMF was not alone in its criticism, however. In a speech to the OAS in Washington on January 17, President Bush warned that Argentina would face a "bleak and stagnant future" if it returned to the old Peronist protectionism and called on Duhalde to come up with a coherent, long-term recovery plan. He said free markets were still the greatest means to ensuring prosperity.

On February 2, the Supreme Court got into the act by declaring the restrictions on savings unconstitutional, presenting Duhalde with yet another complication. Remes responded with another bank holiday on February 5, as depositors began arming themselves with court orders directing the banks to give them their money. Remes also declared that the peso would be allowed to float freely and that bank withdrawals and government transactions would henceforth be in pesos. This announcement led to even more violent demonstrations on February 19.

On February 27, Duhalde succeeded where de la Rua had failed by persuading the powerful Peronist governors to agree to a revenue-sharing plan that the IMF had demanded. Duhalde hammered out a budget plan, and tensions between Argentina and the IMF eased temporarily.

But the economic situation has worsened. The unemployment rate increased to an alarming 23.8% in April—about what it was in the United States during the depths of the Great Depression. On March 26, the peso hit an all-time low of 4.00 to the dollar; when this book went to press in July, it had improved only slightly, to 3.575. The percentage of Argentines living below the $200-a-month poverty line mushroomed to 57%. Then, suddenly, another old enemy had returned: Inflation. One thing that could be said for Menem's dollar-parity plan and de la Rua's austerity plan was that they controlled inflation. In the first three quarters of 2001, in fact, Argentina had experienced *deflation*. In April 2002 alone, prices rose 10%, and for the first five months of 2002, inflation was already 26%. The combination of double-digit unemployment and double-digit inflation defied the laws of economics and have created a climate of desperation.

In April, Remes abruptly resigned after Congress rejected his proposed bank reform plan, adding to the existing turmoil. Later that month, Duhalde won a major victory when Congress passed a law that would prevent depositors who receive court orders allowing them to withdraw their savings from doing so until the banks appealed the orders. Soon thereafter, he appointed Roberto Lavagna, a trade expert and former ambassador to the European Union and the World trade Organization, as economy minister—the country's sixth in 14 months.

President Eduardo Duhalde

In a separate, unrelated development, former Economy Minister Cavallo was arrested on April 3 in connection with the alleged sale of illegal arms to Ecuador and Croatia that had implicated Menem. At the same time, an appeals court ordered the presiding judge in the case to reopen the investigation of Menem and several others.

The government tried to come up with a plan to allow depositors to withdraw savings without bankrupting the banking system. In April, it devised a scheme requiring depositors to accept five- and 10-year bonds in exchange for some accounts. Needless to say, depositors reacted with fury.

On May 21, Duhalde received the best news he had had in his first four months: the managing director of the IMF agreed to give Argentina another year to pay a $136 million loan that was due.

The protests continued throughout May and June, and Duhalde, ironically, was trying to persuade the Congress and the 14 Peronist governors to enable him to take the same difficult austerity measures to guarantee additional IMF support that had brought down de la Rua; he reportedly threatened to resign at one point unless they cooperated. At mid-year, he was still negotiating with the IMF, and the Central Bank director said he anticipated a new deal would be reached in August.

On June 26, one protest turned deadly when riot police opened fire, killing two demonstrators. The deaths of two peaceful protesters sparked further riots the next day. Duhalde denounced the deaths, and two policemen were arrested.

On July 2, a frustrated Duhalde announced that he was advancing the presidential elections by six months, from September to March 2003. He clearly is in a hurry to turn the hopeless, thankless job he had once wanted so badly over to someone else. Congress had already enacted legislation providing for open party primaries to select the candidates (see The Future).

Culture: Unlike most of the South American colonies, Argentina did not develop a *mestizo* race (European-Indian) because the indigenous inhabitants were driven ever westward beyond the expanding frontier or were exterminated outright. This military policy, which bordered on genocide, extended into the late 19th century. Unlike the United States or neighboring Brazil, there was no importation of African slaves. Instead, what was to become the laboring class in Argentina stemmed from a wave of European immigrants, chiefly from Spain and Italy, who were attracted during the 19th century by work on the cattle ranches and in the wheat fields, vineyards and emerging industries.

Consequently, Argentina's ethnic make-up today is almost wholly European, with Italian descendants accounting for nearly half the population. This also has given Argentine Spanish a distinctly Italian inflection, an unmistakable accent that is the butt of jokes in other Latin American countries. Lesser influxes of British and German settlers, many of them well-to-do investors, also have colored Argentina's social fabric, as have Jews, Arabs and Gypsies.

Which is not to say that Argentina lacks a rich cultural heritage of its own. As occurred in the United States, the romanticism associated with the conquest of the frontier and the development of vast stretches of rich farming and grazing lands of the *Pampas* gave rise to a uniquely Argentine folk hero: the *gaucho*, or cowboy. As with the North American cowboy, it is difficult to separate myth from reality, but unquestionably the raw-boned *gauchos* with their baggy cotton pants, sheepskin chaps and *bolas*, (the device used to ensnare the legs of running calves) greatly shaped Argentine culture and folklore. Their drum-based music, *malambo*, is as identifiable with Argentine culture as the tango.

One of the great works of the so-called golden age of Argentine literature of the late 19th and early 20th centuries was the epic poem *El gaucho Martín Fierro*, written by José Hernández in two installments in 1872 and 1879. Martín Fierro occupies much the same place in Argentine folklore as do Paul Bunyan or Pecos Bill in the United States. It is not uncommon to see truckstops in northern Argentina today named for this folk hero. The legacy of the *gauchos* also is exploited today for tourist purposes in such Buenos Aires steakhouses as *La Estancia*, where waiters dress in traditional *gaucho* garb and *malambo* groups provide live music.

The wealth of the *estancias*, or ranches, also shaped Argentines' meat-based diets. The most popular eating places in Argentina, except perhaps for the ubiquitous pasta bars, are *parrilladas*, which specialize in assorted meats grilled over wood embers; often an entire goat is staked out on a metal frame and roasted in front of a *fogón*, or bonfire. The most common social gathering is the *asado*, a barbecue on a massive scale in which sometimes dozens of guests consume a variety of meats and wash them down with copious amounts of domestic wine, which can be excellent.

The relative enlightenment that followed the Rosas dictatorship in the mid–19th century allowed a rich literary tradition to take root. Two of the greatest writers of this period also were leaders in the struggle for democracy. Bartolomé Mitre served as president of the republic during the pivotal period of 1862–68, and two years after leaving the presidency he founded the daily newspaper *La Nación*, still published by his descendants today and regarded as one of the world's great newspapers. Domingo Faustino Sarmiento was forced into exile during the Rosas era and nettled the dictatorship from neighboring Chile, where he edited *El Mercurio*, then based in Valparaiso. Sarmiento's writings proved inspirational not only for Argentines but for other Latin Americans saddled with dictatorship, and he is revered as one of the premier figures of Latin American letters. He succeeded Mitre in the presidency, serving from 1868–74. Another great newspaper of record, *La Prensa*, was established in 1869; it served as a conduit for the poems, stories and essays of the great writers of the golden age. Both it and *La Nación* also developed a reputation for resisting the will of dictators; *La Prensa*, published by several generations of the Gainza and Paz families, was closed by Perón from 1951–55.

This tradition continued into the 20th century, when *La Nación* made space available for the verse of a blind man acknowledged as Argentina's greatest poet: Jorge Luis Borges (1899-1986). His reputation was global, although the Nobel Prize eluded him all his life. Like many of Latin America's great writers, artists and musicians, he spent much of his career in Europe, in part because of Argentina's periodic reversions to dictatorship and the chilling effect that invariably had on the arts. He died in Switzerland in 1986.

Other notable 20th century Argentine writers include Julio Cortázar (1914-1984), a novelist, playwright and poet, perhaps best remembered for the plays *Los reyes* (1949) and *Bestiario* (1951) and the novels *Los premios* (1960), *Rayuela* (1963), *62/Modelo para armar* (1968), and *Libro de Manuel* (1973); and Ernesto Sábato (b. 1911), a renowned essayist and author of three memorable novels: *El túnel* (1948), *Sobre héroes y tumbas* (1961), and *Abbadón el exterminador (1974)*. Both Cortázar and Sábato achieved recognition throughout the Spanish-speaking—and reading—world, and their works have been translated into numerous other languages. Manuel Puig (1932-1990), wrote a tale of two political prisoners sharing a cell that was adapted

to the stage and the screen: *El beso de la mujer araña* ("The Kiss of the Spider Woman.") Another Argentine writer, Adolfo Pérez Esquivel, received the Nobel Peace Prize in 1980 for his courageous opposition to military rule.

In music, Argentina has produced its share of classical composers, the most renowned being Alberto Ginastera (1916-1983). But when one thinks of Argentine music, one thinks of the tango. The dance and music that has become synonymous with Argentina emerged as an erotic art form in the sleazy nightclubs and brothels of La Boca, the port district of Buenos Aires. Its contagious rhythm and sexual innuendo won it ready acceptance in the *avante–garde* circles of Paris during the 1920s, and from the Left Bank its popularity spread throughout the bistros and cabarets of Europe and the Prohibition–era U.S. nightclubs and speakeasies. Ironically, the tango composer and singer who came to be most identified with the genre was an immigrant from France at age 3: Carlos Gardel (1890-1935). Killed in a plane crash in Colombia at age 45, Gardel even today is the center of an Elvis-like cult following. Posters of the forever-young Gardel, his slick black hair parted in the middle, are a ubiquitous symbol of the nation's cultural identity. Eventually, through the talents of the internationally renowned composer Astor Piazzolla (1921-1992), the tango emerged into a classical form acceptable in polite society. One literally cannot escape the sounds of the tango in Argentine restaurants, so ingrained is it in the life of the nation. Two U.S.–made movies, "Scent of a Woman" and "Evita," have revived interest in the tango abroad.

Argentine cinema, established in the 1930s, enjoyed something of a boom during the first Perón era, but lapsed into mediocrity during subsequent military regimes, particularly that of 1976–83, when political repression and artistic censorship forced many leading actors and directors into exile. Since 1983 it has enjoyed a renaissance and has won some international accolades. The film *La historia oficial*, ("The Official Story") an account of a middle–aged housewife who comes to realize that her adopted daughter was taken from two slain dissidents during the "Dirty War," won the Golden Palm at the Cannes Film Festival.

Radio in Argentina enjoyed a golden age in the 1920s and '30s, just as it had in the United States, the exception being that tango enjoyed equal billing with that of the Big Band sounds. Soap operas were popular, and provided the boost to stardom of an ambitious young actress named Eva Duarte—later Eva Perón. Television began as a state venture and wallowed in mediocrity for decades for much the same reason as did the cinema: the flight of talent from the censorship of military re-

gimes. The result was a dependence on dubbed imported programs, mostly from the United States. Today's less–encumbered Argentine television has seen a boom in locally produced programs, many of them the ever–popular *telenovelas*, which often are exported.

Economy: Argentina is well–endowed with some of the richest farmland in the world and as a result, the economy has traditionally been based on agriculture, primarily cattle, wheat and wine. A favorable balance of trade led to industrialization as well, and at the turn of the 20th century, Argentina was one of the four wealthiest nations in the world.

After World War II, the economy was plagued by the fiscal policies of the first Perón administration. When he took office in 1946, reserves stood at a respectable $1.5 billion. By 1955 that surplus had vanished and the nation was deeply in the red. Every government since then has added to the debt. Agriculture was penalized in order to promote industrialization. Food prices were held artificially low and taxes were placed on farm exports in order to finance the construction of factories. The government role in the economy also expanded. The state controlled more than half of all heavy industry—most of which has been inefficient, overstaffed and unprofitable. Because of a lack of capital investment in newer techniques, it became the equivalent of the "rust belt" industry of the northeast United States, which has been undergoing replacement by facilities erected in the southern United States because of onerous taxes, wages and workers' benefits in the North.

Argentina has for the last 50+ years enjoyed the most evenly distributed and largest per capita income in Latin America. Much of this wealth, however, was eroded by runaway inflation, particularly during the 1980s. Perón taught the nation to live beyond its means, printing more and more pesos, establishing a precedent which was repeated over and over.

Once the *Peronistas* returned to power in 1973 the economy was harassed by widespread strikes, a shortage of consumer goods and high job absenteeism. Even more damaging was the disastrous drop in farm exports, which usually had counted for 70% of the nation's foreign earnings. Although poor weather was a contributing factor, most farm problems stemmed from government policies which maintained low food prices for the people of Buenos Aires and the cities, where 80% of the nation lives. Beef exports dropped to their lowest level of the century when the European Common Market reduced imports of Argentine meat. At the same time, beef consumption rose because of lowered prices. By 1975 Argentines consumed 220 pounds of beef per person annually, twice the U.S. figure.

The major customer for Argentine wheat was the former Soviet Union, but this has been questionable since it dissolved. Agreements provided that Argentina had to import substantial amounts of Soviet goods, most of which were of poor quality. The successors of the Soviet Union have no hard currency reserves and are now haunted by galloping inflation. Having no money to pay for Argentine grain, the Russians are getting it from the United States, using credits (loans) that have been generously granted to further U.S. interest in keeping the state afloat in Moscow.

Industrial output fell in Argentina, partially due to a shortage of parts, frequent strikes and low capital reinvestment. The nation's once–mighty auto industry also broke down, with eight foreign–owned assembly plants losing $160 million on their Argentine operations in 1975. During that period, the growth in the nation's gross national product dropped to zero. It went as low as '"9% in the late 1980s.

Controlling of the country from 1976-83, the military rulers sought to return Argentina to a free–market system—a dramatic about face from the state planning which had dominated the economy since Perón first took office. The impact of the changes was limited—partly because 60% of the economy was under government control or ownership.

The worst depression, coupled with hyperinflation, corruption, overspending, a bulging bureaucracy in Buenos Aires and the provinces, and the excessive demands of labor unions, all took the starch out of the economy during the presidency of Raúl Alfonsín, of the Radical Civil Union (1983-89). One observer noted, "In the U.S. and Europe, things are either automatic or predictable. Here, nothing is automatic or predictable." Riots forced Alfonsín to relinquish power to his successor several months early.

Under Peronist President Carlos Menem (1989-99), things at last began changing (although a bitter pill for many). In 1992, he announced he was pegging the peso to the U.S. dollar, one-to-one. The effect was almost immediate. Inflation dropped from 40% per month to less than 10% per year, which enabled Argentina at last to engage in intelligent financial planning. It also attracted foreign investment in substantial quantities that was vitally necessary for continued growth. Menem also abandoned protectionism and embraced free-market economics, which for a Peronist was heretical. But there was no questioning its success.

Capital which used to migrate abroad began staying within Argentina, and funds began returning there from overseas. The return on investment was attractive in the 1990s, and Argentina imposed fewer and fewer restrictions on withdrawal of profits by investors, in stark contrast to much of the rest of Latin America.

The devaluation of the Mexican peso in 1994 presented a major threat to Argentine economic stability since it, just as Mexico, had been presumed to be a place for safe investment. Menem responded energetically to preserve Argentina's reputation, and did so successfully. He almost immediately instituted an austerity program to reduce imports and wages, two unpopular moves which had to be made just before the May 1995 elections. The program enabled Argentina's banking system to defend its currency.

By early 1998, Argentina was experiencing a negative aspect of globalizing its economy. It had successfully overcome the effects of the 1994–95 Mexican peso crisis, only to begin feeling the effects of the crisis in the Asian markets. Growth was still in the neighborhood of 8%, and though unemployment was down it was still an uncomfortable 13%. Inflation for 1998 was a mere 1%. Overall, these were the best aconomic times Argentina had seen in decades. But it was not to last.

Foreseeing a coming slump, the IMF approved a three–year, $2.8 billion loan for Argentina in February 1998. Nonetheless, the country slid into recession in July 1998. Meanwhile, in a surprise move apparently aimed at shoring up his traditional support among the once–powerful labor unions, Menem swung the pendulum back from his policy of appeasing the needs of big business by proposing new labor regulations that essentially left in place the *Peronistas'* liberal severance benefits. It also nullified a 1995 law that allowed companies greater leeway in hiring part-time workers without paying payroll taxes.

Responding to renewed fears of inflation, the head of the central bank announced in January 1999 that he favored a monetary treaty with the United States that would actually make the dollar the official currency of Argentina, as it is in Panama, within three years. Former President Alfonsín scoffed at the suggestion, saying it would make Argentina an economic vassal of the United States, like Puerto Rico.

Year-end figures for 1999 graphically demonstrated the severity of the recession incoming Radical President Fernando de la Rua had inherited from Menem. Real GDP declined by 3.5%, and unemployment was 14.5%. About the only good news was that once-feared inflation *declined* by 2%. De la Rua's painful austerity measures and the labor reform bill were needed to obtain funds from the IMF, but experts warned that it could be some time before the benefits were felt. Those experts proved correct. De la Rua made an ill-advised prediction in mid-2000 that Argentina would end the year with positive growth of 3.5% to 4%, a prediction that returned to haunt him and cost him even more of his credibility and popularity Argentina's economy *shrank* another 0.5% in 2000; the only cheer came from the fact that it was a fraction of the decrease of 1999. Unemployment was still a troubling 14.7%, and it has grown steadily worse since then.

Under de la Rua, there was no further talk of embracing the dollar as Ecuador did in early 2000. Instead, de la Rua publicly called for *Mercosur* to emulate the European Union by adopting a common currency for the trade bloc. He predicted monetary union could be in place within three years, but financial experts said it could take 10. De la Rua also was an advocate of the Free Trade Area of the Americas (FTAA).

In late 2001, the recession deepened as unemployment grew to 18.3% and de la Rua sought desperately to meet the deficit-reduction goals he had set to ensure continued IMF support so Argentina could avoid default on its $132 billion foreign debt. When he imposed strict limits of $1,000 a month on savings withdrawals, angry Argentines took to the streets. The demonstrations erupted in violence that left 27 people dead and forced de la Rua to resign. After three interim presidents proved unwilling or incapable of dealing with the crisis, Congress elected a Peronist, Eduardo Duhalde, on January 2, 2002 as interim president until the next elections (see History).

Within days, the new president pushed an emergency economic reform package through Congress, after which he revoked Menem's 10-year-old dollar-parity plan. In March, the free-floating peso hit an all-time low of 4.00 to the dollar; when this book went to press in July, it had recovered only slightly, to 3.575. Another consequence of devaluation: After ending 2001 with an inflation rate of only 1%, inflation for the first five months of 2002 was 26%; prices of many food staples, such as flour and cooking oil, had increased by more than 130%.

The economic crisis had plunged more and more Argentines into poverty, and bartering was becoming common in the cash-strapped country. In March 2000, a study by the Social Development Ministry had reported that 37% of Argentines liveded below the poverty line of $200 a month. My mid-2002, that figure was a staggering 57%, a damning statistic for what remains, even with the crisis, Latin America's most affluent country.

GDP growth for 2001 was down another 1%, and in July 2002 Argentina entered its fifth year of recession with unemployment still above 20% and no end in sight before the end of the year. The IMF issued dire predictions that GDP in 2002 could decline by 10-15%, which could be cataclysmic. The Economist Intelligence Unit in London was more optimistic, predicting a decline of "only" about 8%, with growth returning in 2003. The head of the central bank said in July that he expected a new deal with the IMF to be reached in August. Unless something happens, the unprecedented combination of spiraling inflation, record unemployment and declining living standards could well lead to far greater violence.

The Future: This is being written, coincidentally and appropriately, on July 9—Argentine Independence Day. Thousands of Argentines "celebrated" with yet another noisy demonstration in front of the Casa Rosada demanding that the politicians be "thrown out." But replaced with whom? It has always baffled this author how such a literate country, with such diversified natural wealth and rich cultural traditions, could perennially make such a mess of itself politically and economically.

Who is going to follow Duhalde next March in the thankless job of Argentine president? Foreign Minister Carlos Ruckauf, a Peronist, is known to covet the job, God knows why. Polls in July showed a left-wing Peronist deputy, Elisa Carrio, the "frontrunner" with 15% and Peronist Governor Carlos Reutemann, who enjoys name recognition as a former race car driver, in second place.

But a more likely possibility is former President Menem—unless he goes to jail first for his alleged involvement in illegal arms sales to Ecuador and Croatia in 1995. When he left office under an ethical cloud in 1999, people laughed when he vowed to make a comeback in 2003. So did this author. No one—including me—is laughing any more. Love him or loathe him, he is the only president since Hipólito Irigoyen in the 1920s who left the country in better shape than he found it. He may very well rise Phoenix-like from his own ashes.

What is truly historic about the social, political and economic meltdown of 2001-02 is what did *not* happen: There was no military coup, as there has been during so many times of crisis. There never apparently was even a suggestion that the generals and admirals might intervene. A cynic might ask, could they do any worse than the five bumbling civilians who have served in the past year?

Based on their last performance from 1976-83, the answer is yes, they could. Perhaps they learned a valuable lesson from their last intervention and realized they were better off staying in the barracks this time. Duhalde is no Irigoyen, but he's no Videla or Galtieri either. At least he has been willing to try to pull Argentina out of the quicksand it is in,

and he has done it without murdering anyone.

Alas, Duhalde's worst enemy, and that of any Argentine president, is not the generals or the political opposition or the IMF. It is the Argentine people themselves, with their weather-vane shifts in public opinion, their lemming-like self-destructiveness and their fondness for resorting to mob rule to bring down their governments without a moment's thought as to what will happen after they do. Granted, much of their rage is justified; the corruption of Argentine politicians is so notorious it makes Louisiana politicians look like naughty schoolchildren by comparison. Even the president of neighboring Uruguay this year undiplomatically called Argentina's rulers "a band of thieves."

Still, the replacement of an elected president with the man he defeated sends an ominous message: If you don't like the guy who won, just stage some riots and the guy who lost will come to power. Democracy Argentine style? It is not a model for others to emulate. Argentines are like a spoiled, irresponsible adolescent from an affluent, privileged family, and it is time for them to grow up, to accept their responsibilities, and to work to realize their potential, which is considerable. If they ever can, Argentina once again could enter a Golden Age.

Belize

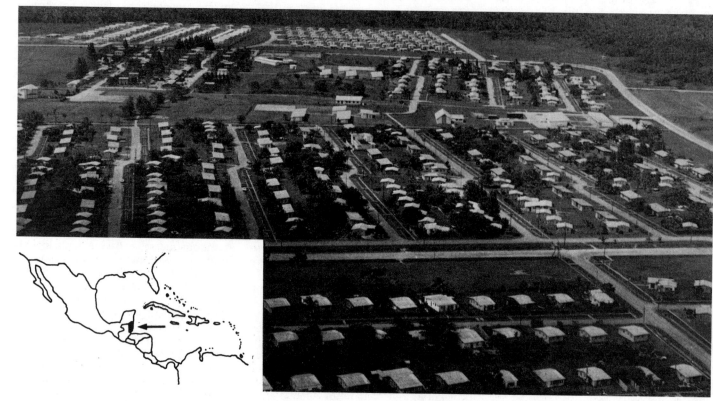

Aerial view of Belmopan

(pronounced Beh–*lees*)

Area: 8,866 sq. mi., somewhat larger than Massachusetts.

Population: 243,000 (estimated in 1999).

Capital City: Belmopan (Pop. 4,000, estimated).

Climate: Hot and humid.

Neighboring Countries: Mexico (North); Guatemala (West); Honduras lies 50 miles to the southeast across the Gulf of Honduras.

Official Language: English.

Other Principal Tongues: Spanish and some Indian dialects.

Ethnic Background: African (65%); Mestizo, Creole and those of Mayan ancestry, European.

Principal Religions: Roman Catholicism, Anglican Protestant Christianity.

Chief Commercial Products: Sugar, citrus fruit, lobster, shrimp, forest products.

Currency: Belize Dollar.

Gross Domestic Product: U.S. $675 million in 1999 ($2,772 per capita).

Former Colonial Status: British Colony (1862–1981).

National Day: September 21 (Independence Day).

Chief of State: Queen Elizabeth II of Great Britain, represented by Colville Young, Governor General.

Head of Government: Said Musa, Prime Minister (since August 1998).

National Flag: A white circle on a blue field, with red horizontal bars at top and bottom. The circle shows two workers and symbols of agriculture, industry and maritime activity.

Wedged between Mexico's Yucatán Peninsula to the north and Guatemala to the west and south, and calmed by placid waters of the Caribbean Sea on its eastern coastline, Belize is a warm to hot and humid country about 174 miles long and 69 miles wide across at its widest point. Flat and swampy on the coast, but mercifully relieved by pleasant sea breezes, its beaches are unspoiled and beautiful. The terrain slowly rises toward the interior to about 3,000 feet above sea level into pine forests and pasturelands. At lower altitudes, tropical growth predominates.

Some 15 miles offshore there is the longest barrier reef in the Western Hemisphere stretching 190 miles, offering a spectacular variety of tropical fish and coral formations, a delight for the experienced snorkel diver. The land is thinly inhabited; its largest town is Belize City with a population of about 50,000—which, however, has an international airport.

History: Originally settled about 1638 by bands of British woodcutters illegally harvesting the timber in Spanish domains,

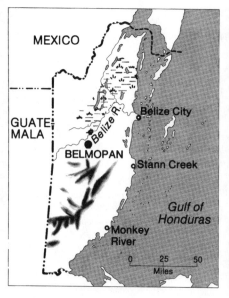

Belize settlers managed their own affairs and government, although the Spanish tried many times to eject them. In 1786 Britain finally appointed a superintendent for the territory; in 1840 it was termed a colony, called British Honduras, although it was not officially a colony until 1862 when it was made subordinate to Jamaica. In 1884 it was made a separate crown colony. Colonial status continued until 1964 when the colony was granted full internal self–government. In June 1973, its

46

name was changed to Belize. Guatemala long had claimed Belize as an integral part of that neighboring country, but despite its loud protests, the colony was given its independence in September 1981. Guatemala refused to acknowledge the country's independence, and Britain maintained a force of some 1,800 troops to maintain its security. Guatemalan President Vinicio Cerezo generally conceded that Belize's independence was negotiable, provided Guatemala obtained access to the Atlantic via one or more of its ports. The dispute was settled in late 1992 when such rights were granted, and Guatemala formally recognized Belize.

Government consists of a 29–member House of Representatives and an eight-member appointed Senate. The People's United Party (PUP) of George Price held power from independence until 1984, when it was defeated by the United Democratic Party (UDP) led by Manuel Esquivel, running on a free-trade platform. But in late 1989, the PUP returned to power by a narrow margin of 15 to 14, later increased to 16–13 when a UDP member deserted his party.

Price made many friends during almost three decades of public service—particularly popular was his "clinic day" on Wednesdays, whereby any Belizean could drop in his office in Belize City and tell him of his concerns. His successors have continued this popular tradition.

In early 1993 the British announced that it would withdraw its force from Belize within 15 months, which created quite a stir. Price, hoping to gain from the recent years of prosperity, mandated elections to be held in June 1993, 15 months before they were due.

But security was the main issue. Guatemala had repudiated the treaty recognizing Belize. The UDP seized the issue, typified by a song: "We don't want no Guatemala!" It won narrowly, 16 to 13 seats, and Esquivel again became prime minister.

The new UDP government charged that Price's party attempted to bribe two members to cross over party lines to aid in a takeover. Governor–General Minita Gordon was accused of being involved, and of interfering in the government and was asked to leave. The treaty with Guatemala was repudiated by Belize. British troops departed on January 1, 1994; security became the responsibility of the Belize Defense Force. There is at present a British team designated a "jungle training" unit.

The UDP government, alleging mismanagement by the PUP, began raising taxes early in its five–year mandate. Most controversial was a 15% value-added tax; the government also raised utility rates. These unpopular measures returned to haunt Esquivel, and in the general election of August 28, 1998, the pendulum swung sharply back to the PUP, which had chosen Said Musa, a former attorney general under Price, as its standard bearer.

In the campaign, Musa denounced Esquivel's "killa taxes" which he said were frightening away foreign investors. He pledged to cut utility rates and to create 15,000 new jobs. The appeal paid off; the PUP won in a landslide, taking 23 of the 29 seats in the Assembly. The PUP carried some districts by 3–1. This time, Esquivel would not be around as leader of the opposition; he was defeated in his own district by the mayor of Belize City, José Coye.

Culture: Belizeans are friendly and arm–hearted people, about 65% of whom are of African origin, about 25% of Mayan and *mestizo* background and there is a small percentage of Europeans. A colony of German-speaking Mennonites produces almost all the country's dairy products. There also are sizeable colonies of Taiwanese and Sri Lankans in this harmonious ethnic gumbo. Belmopan, the capital city, was built in 1971 in the center of the country about 50 miles west of Belize City, its largest urban area with a population of about 50,000+. For the tourist, the city is not safe for a lone pedestrian, especially after dark. This also is true of those traveling alone to remote tourist facilities. Armed robbery and muggings are growing in number in spite of efforts by the government to control crime.

U.S. baseball is immensely popular; both men and women spent hours watching the games. Great disappointment was noted when the 1994 strike canceled the World Series. Excellent fishing, sailing, scuba diving and other sports abound. A Teacher's College provides a two–year intramural program followed by a year of supervised internship in the classroom.

Mayan ruins, numbering 700 and about 1,000 years old, can be seen on guided tours. Unusual wildlife is prolific. Youths and young men in urban areas have an appearance similar to "street children" found everywhere in Latin America, but are more probably teenagers with little or nothing to do. As in the United States, spray-painting seems to fascinate them.

Economy: Until recent times, forestry was the most important activity in Belize, but as the timber supply grew sparse, sugar cane growing took on more importance and now is the leading industry. Although the country has a great deal of land which is well suited for agriculture, only a small portion is farmed, and it is necessary for Belize to import millions of dollars in foodstuffs. Belize's major trading partners are the U.S. and the United Kingdom—about two–thirds of its exports and imports are with these nations, and now that it is a member of the Caribbean Community (CARICOM), it is hoping for a greater market for its potential grain and livestock surpluses.

The lush lower altitudes of Belize, with their tropical climate, are favorable locations for two crops: marijuana and oranges for juice. The first presented a problem both to Belize and the United States in the 1980s. Production rose quickly to more than 1,000 tons annually and Belize became the second–largest supplier to U.S. dealers. After 1984 this was curtailed and virtually eliminated by a spraying program, but not before a high government official was arrested and indicted in Miami (1985) on charges of conspiring to export 30,000 tons annually to the United States. Production is now closely monitored and is less than 100 tons per year.

Cocaine proved to be a far more serious problem. As alternative routes of transportation from Colombia to the United States were restricted, Belize took up the slack. Small airplanes would land on rural roads for refueling. In order to stop this, the government erected poles on the sides of the roads to break the wings of the craft. Local people bent the poles to eliminate their effectiveness.

The Coca–Cola Company was lured to Belize by its potential for citrus crops, primarily oranges, for production of concentrated juice. A relatively enormous tract was purchased for about $172 an acre, but local opposition, coupled with that of Florida citrus growers, made the project impossible. Most of the land was donated to conservationists after opposition groups proclaimed that Coca–Cola sought to destroy 700,000 acres of virgin rain forest to plant orange trees.

Unable to obtain insurance for the project, it was largely discontinued. But the soft drink firm and its two Texas partners in the venture retained about 50,000 acres of the choicest land.

Belize is relatively more prosperous than its Spanish-speaking neighbors, with a per capita GDP of about $2,800 in 1999. Real GDP in 1999 totaled $675 million, marking a healthy increase of 6.2% from 1998; the previous year, growth was only 1.4%. Unemployment remains high however, 12.8% in 1999, down from 14.3% in 1998. was a troublesome 13%. Inflation declined by 0.8% in 1998 and 1.2% in 1999.

The Future: Tourism, and settlement of affluent people in retirement homes (not centers) is being emphasized. This country has all the advantages and disadvantages of a tropical Caribbean nation, but its biggest advantage is few people. For the bold, it offers out–of–the–way retirement possibilities at relatively modest prices (together with exotic insects and other creatures).

The Republic of Bolivia

Nestled in the rugged mountains is a shimmering Andean lake

Area: 424,052 sq. mi.

Population: 8.5 million in 2001.

Capital Cities: La Paz (Pop. 1.25 million, estimated) and Sucre (110,000, estimated).

Climate: The eastern lowlands are hot all year round; they are wet from November through March, dry from May through September. The highland climate varies greatly with the altitude. The high plateau, or *altiplano*, is dry and cold all year round.

Neighboring Countries: Brazil (North and East); Paraguay (Southeast); Argentina (South); Chile (Southwest); Peru (Northwest).

Official Language: Spanish.

Other Principal Tongues: Quechua, Aymara and Guaraní.

Ethnic Background: Indian (70%); *mestizo* (mixed European and Indian (25%); European (5%).

Principal Religion: Roman Catholic Christianity.

Chief Commercial Products: Tin, lead, zinc, silver, tungsten, gold, natural gas, agricultural products. Coca production, used to make cocaine, is a major source of income.

Currency: Bolivian Peso (subject to erratic valuation).

Gross Domestic Product: U.S. $8.66 billion in 2001 (1,019 per capita).

Former Colonial Status: Spanish colony known as Upper Peru (1538–1825).

Independence Date: August 6, 1825.

Chief of State: Gonzalo Sánchez de Lozada (b. 1930), president (since August 6, 2002).

National Flag: Equal red, yellow and green horizontal stripes.

Bolivia, the fifth-largest nation in South America, is landlocked. Stretching 1,000 miles from north to south and 800 miles each to west, it is divided into two highly contrasting regions—the *altiplano* (a high mountain plateau) and the eastern lowlands. The Andean mountain range reaches its greatest width—some 400 miles—in Bolivia. The *Western Cordillera,* which separates Bolivia from Chile and Peru, contains snowy peaks of 19,000 to 21,240 feet, with numerous rough volcanoes along the crest. The narrow passes to the Pacific coast exceed 13,000 feet in altitude. The *altiplano*, lying to the east of the *Western Cordillera*, is an arid, windswept, treeless plateau some 85 miles wide and 520 miles in length and much of it is above 13,000 feet.

Split into basins by spurs from the *Western Cordillera*, the southern portion is parched desert, uninhabited except for mining camps; the northern portion, containing chilly Lake Titicaca (3,400 square miles at 12,500 feet), has many small settlements along the river flowing into the lake, and around the shore there is a large and prosperous Indian farming population. The eastern *cordillera*, separating the *altiplano* from the lowlands, reaches 20,000 feet in the north, but is much lower in the south.

The mountains drop sharply to the northeast and the hot, humid Amazon basin. Further to the south they form a stepped descent to a region called the *Puno* and then into the *Chaco* plains of Paraguay and Argentina. The valleys that cut into the eastern slopes of the mountains are fertile, semi–tropical and densely inhabited. These valleys, called *yungas*, produce a wide variety of cereals and fruits, but the task of transporting them to the cities of the *altiplano* is formidable. The lowland tropical plains of the northeast, once heavily populated, are now largely abandoned because of their inaccessibility.

History: The Aymara Indians living in the Lake Titicaca region had a relatively high level of development between 600 and 900 A.D. This civilization disappeared from some undetermined disaster and the Quechua–speaking Inca invaders found the surviving Aymaras living among monuments and ruins which they could not explain. Bolivia was still in Inca hands when the Spaniards arrived from Peru in 1538.

The Spanish development of Bolivia began with the discovery of a silver

mountain at Potosí in 1545, followed by additional discoveries at Oruro. The capital, Sucre, was founded in 1539. La Paz (the actual capital), founded in 1548, was an important terminal for treasure convoys preparing for the difficult passage to Peru. The Inca social and economic organizations were abandoned in a mad effort to extract and process the metallic wealth of the mountains—tin, silver, lead and zinc. Jesuit missionaries penetrated into the tropical lowlands, gathering the Indians into prosperous farming communities which endured into the 18th century. However, they aroused little interest on the part of the Spanish authorities and

had even less influence on the social and political development of the country. The Spaniards intermarried with the Indians and a large group of multi–ancestry *mestizos* was the result, which would affect the course of Bolivian history.

Revolutionary movements against Spanish rule began early in Bolivia—revolts by *mestizos* broke out in La Paz in 1661 and at Cochabamba in 1730. Indian revolts occurred in Sucre, Cochabamba, Oruro and La Paz from 1776 to 1780. The University of San Francisco Xavier in Sucre issued a call in 1809 for the liberation of all colonies from Spain. Although several attempts were made to free Bolivia in the years following, they were unsuccessful until 1825, when Simón Bolívar sent General Antonio José de Sucre to free Upper Peru. Independence was declared on August 6 of that year.

No other South American nation faced greater initial handicaps than Bolivia. There were few competent patriotic leaders among the landed aristocracy and there was no middle class. The apathetic Indians and the *mestizos* were simply pawns in a game they did not under-_stand. The military, which had been trained in the campaigns of San Martín and Bolívar, seized power. The history of independent Bolivia's first fifty years is a dismal recitation of misrule and violence as jealous rivals struggled for power. Following its defeat

Exacting Inca stonework

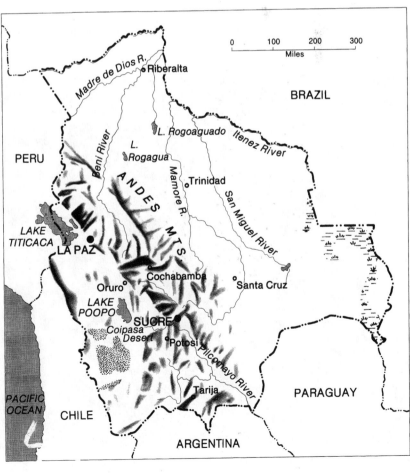

in The War of the Pacific (1879–1883), Bolivia lost its Pacific provinces to Chile and became a landlocked nation.

During the 1880s and 1890s several able men occupied the presidency. Silver mining was revived, a few schools were opened and political parties were developed. Traditional Liberal and Conservative titles were adopted, but their memberships represented little more than opposing factions of the nation's ruling elite. One of the principal Liberal demands was for the transfer of the capital from Sucre to La Paz. After seizing the presidency by revolt, a Liberal regime made La Paz the seat of government.

Under Liberal leadership, Bolivia achieved a degree of stability in the first two decades of the 20th century. Economic reforms were undertaken, disputes with Chile and Brazil were resolved—with losses of territory but with receipt of indemnities—mining was expanded and the building of roads and railroads was pushed. The motive behind this limited "modernization" was the increasing world demand for tin, a mineral that quickly became Bolivia's basic export, transforming the small group who controlled its extraction—the "tin barons"—into powerful international millionaires. In the 1920s a party carrying the label Republican came to power. Foreign capital was sought for mining and petroleum interests, attracting U.S. investors.

By the 1930s, United States interests controlled most of Bolivia's mineral concessions. While some of the investment capital went into roads, railroads and agriculture, much of it was wasted in irresponsible spending. When the world depression of the 1930s hit Bolivia, its economy collapsed, the treasury defaulted on its bonds and the Republican president was ousted.

In 1931 elections, Daniel Salamanca, a competent businessman, became president amid hopes that he could bring order out of chaos. This optimistic mood was shattered the following year with the outbreak of war with Paraguay. Blame for this senseless conflict lies with the miscalculation of the leadership of both countries. Humiliated by a long series of military disasters, both nations overestimated their own capabilities and underestimated those of the other. Though ostensibly more powerful than Paraguay, Bolivia, in a monumental display of military incompetence, suffered a crushing defeat in which 52,000 of its soldiers were killed. Fought to exhaustion on both sides, the war ended with Paraguay in possession of the disputed *Chaco* region in 1935. Soldiers returning home, angered by their shabby treatment during the war, joined with university students and labor agitators in demanding reforms.

In 1936, a group of socially conscious military officers led by Colonel David Toro overthrew the civilian government and proclaimed Bolivia a "socialist republic." This short–lived government established the first labor ministry and expropriated the holdings of Standard Oil. After only a year and a half, Toro was overthrown by an even more radical officer, Colonel Germán Busch, a hero of the Chaco War.

He implemented the first labor code, encouraged organization of the tin miners and imposed governmental control over the tin companies. Busch died suddenly in 1939, and it remains an enduring mystery whether he died by his own hand or those of conservative economic interests alarmed by the pace of his reforms. At any rate, his death temporarily brought social reform to an abrupt halt.

Conservative military elements took control of the ballot boxes in 1940 elections and installed their man as president. For the next three years, the country was ruled by these right–wing elements, but during this period there arose a number of civilian–based political parties and movements, ranging from Trotskyite on the left to the Bolivian Falange, modeled after the movement of Spain's Generalisimo Francisco Franco, on the right. The one that was to have the most profound impact on the country, however, one that endures to this day, was the Revolutionary Nationalist Movement, or *MNR*, led by Víctor Paz Estenssoro, who had been an economic adviser to Busch. When another group of military reformers overthrew the conservatives in 1943 and installed Major Gualberto Villarroel as president, they invited the *MNR* to participate in the new government. Although Villarroel was enlightened in his treatment of the Indian population and was sympathetic to the miners, he proved too conservative for ultra–leftwing elements that overthrew him and publicly hanged him in 1946.

The 1952 Revolution

The following six years were marked by exceptional political turbulence and instability, even for Bolivia. The end of this volatile period, in which Bolivia was ruled by a wearisome series of military *juntas*, was marked by the beginning of what scholars regard as one of Latin America's four genuine social revolutions, along with those of Mexico, Cuba and Nicaragua.

In 1952, the *MNR* led a revolt that left about 3,000 dead and led to the installation of Paz Estenssoro as president. His revolutionary government took three remarkable steps: it temporarily abolished the army and replaced it with armed militias of Indians and tin miners; it extended universal suffrage to the illiterate masses, giving them genuine political power for the first time, and it implemented true land reform, breaking up huge estates and giving Indian peasants title to their own plots. The *MNR* also established itself within the unions and Indian communities, making it then, as now, the country's premier civilian political force.

The revolution was hampered by a lack of trained administrators, inadequate financial resources, opposition from both internal and external elements and, above all, by a steady decline in tin prices that

A Bolivian miner gazes into the icicled entrance of a tin mine near La Paz

50

View of La Paz

put Bolivia in chronic economic crisis. Nonetheless, for its first 12 years the revolution gave power to the powerless and brought an end to revolving–door governments. When Paz Estenssoro's four–year term expired in 1956, he was succeeded by another *MNR* leader, Hernán Siles Suazo. Paz Estenssoro, however, returned to power in the 1960 election, but when he made overtures toward reelection in 1964, the newly organized revolutionary army proved as skillful at staging a *coup d'etat* as had its predecessors. The vice president and former air force commander, General René Barrientos, came to power in November 1964, and Paz Estenssoro was forced into exile. Despite the *MNR's* failure to retain power, its 12 years of revolution proved to be a *fait accompli* from which there was no turning back to the "old order."

The flamboyant and charismatic Barrientos proved a highly popular president, and he was given a resounding mandate in a 1966 election. The following year, a U.S.-trained counterinsurgency battalion captured and executed the legendary Argentine-born revolutionary, Ernesto "Che" Guevara, who had attempted to launch a Cuban-style revolution among Bolivia's rural Indians. Barrientos was fond of making personal visits to the interior by helicopter, and on one such trip, in April 1969, he died when his helicopter crashed. He was succeeded by his vice president who was quickly overthrown by General Alfredo Ovando, a leftist and nationalist who expropriated the holdings of Gulf Oil Co. He was in turn overthrown by the even more left-wing General Juan José Torres in 1970. Torres replaced the Congress with a Soviet-style

"People's Assembly" and forged a coalition of Marxist intellectuals and tin miners. However, he failed to win the support of the peasants, as Barrientos had, or most workers. Even worse, he alienated the U.S. Embassy.

Coup No. 187 (the best estimate) in 145 years of independence ensued in 1971, bringing to power a more conservative military strongman, Colonel Hugo Banzer Suárez. By 1975, Banzer had fended off 13 coup attempts, and by 1978, after seven years, he had held power continuously longer than any Bolivian president of the 20th century. The formula for his longevity was a three–point strategy: elimination of major political opposition, economic improvement and increased emphasis on foreign affairs to divert popular attention from unsolved domestic problems. Perhaps the best example of this last strategy was Bolivia's renewed demand for access to the sea through Chile.

In July 1978 Banzer called for an open presidential election in which he had intended to relinquish power to his hand–picked successor, Colonel Juan Pereda Asbún. But in the balloting, former President Siles Suazo won a plurality, while Pereda ran a poor third. Congress was to decide the outcome, but rather than risk the anti–military Siles Suazo coming to power, Banzer suddenly resigned as Pereda proclaimed himself president. Banzer's departure thus created a power vacuum that was to return Bolivia to political turmoil for two years.

The usurpation of power lasted only four months. General David Padilla, the latest reform–minded military officer, overthrew Pereda in November and pledged to pave the way for yet another

free election in July 1979. In that contest, Siles Suazo again polled a plurality but not a majority, throwing the decision to the Congress. Under the watchful eye of the jittery military, Congress opted for a compromise choice for president: Walter Guevara Arce, a civilian leader of the 1952 revolution who later split from the *MNR* and therefore was acceptable to conservative military elements. This good–faith effort at restoring civilian rule also would last only until November 1979, when an overly ambitious colonel, Alberto Natusch Busch, led a successful coup.

His motive for seizing power apparently was for personal gain rather than any lofty reform goals; he immediately found himself faced with overwhelming domestic and international opposition to his naked power play. After only 19 days in power, he was forced to resign and he fled into exile, taking an undetermined amount of cash from the national treasury with him. Congress then chose Lidia Gueiler as Bolivia's first woman president. She had no sooner taken office, of course, before speculation began as to when she would be overthrown and by which officer. She called still another election in June 1980 to choose a president, and once again the victor was Siles Suazo. Coup No. 191 took place and General Luis García Meza seized control of the government.

Thus, in the 24 months between Banzer's resignation in July 1978 and García Meza's coup in July 1980, Bolivia had had a total of seven presidents.

García Meza's 13 months in power marked the harshest crackdown on personal freedom in Bolivia's modern history. Hundreds were arrested, some labor leaders were murdered and strict

General García Meza

censorship was imposed on the press. The new military regime seemed determined to muzzle—and if possible to exterminate—the opposition in the labor movement. Reports held that 500 to 2,000 political prisoners were jailed. The Carter Administration suspended all aid to the country and Bolivia had to turn to neighboring military governments for assistance.

Seeking to consolidate his control over the government, García Meza jailed his opponents and allegedly bribed key members of the armed forces with payoff money from drug traffickers.

Such heavy–handed tactics combined with depressed economic conditions fomented widespread opposition to the military. In August 1981, reformist military officers forced García Meza to resign. The coup was rather gentlemanly by Bolivian standards; as a consolation prize, the discredited strongman was allowed to live in the Presidential Palace for a month following his ouster. An attempt to bring García Meza and his collaborators to trial before the Bolivian Supreme Court in 1986 had to be aborted within two days—two justices died, the prosecutor claimed five others were closely associated with the defendants and the defense attorney claimed that other justices were communists.

Named as the new head of the three–"man military *junta* was General Celso Torrelio Villa. Political conditions remained unstable as the nation chafed under harsh military rule. In November, tin workers mounted widespread strikes to demand a return of their union and political rights which the *junta* suspended in 1980. Hoping to ease criticism of the regime, Torrelio promised to (1) reduce human rights violations, (2) slow the rampant flow of illegal cocaine out of the country and (3) to reduce the state's role in the economy while expanding the opportunities for private enterprise.

Although such policies pleased the United States, which resumed full diplomatic ties after a 16–month delay, the promises prompted skepticism at home. Efforts to impose austerity measures touched off widespread strikes in early

1982. When the peso was allowed to float, it promptly fell 76% to a new rate of 44 to the U.S. dollar. This was only a precursor of that which was to come.

Return to Democracy

To reduce growing criticism, the *junta* promised to lift its ban on political activity and to hold elections for a constituent assembly early in 1983, but as the national economic crisis worsened and popular agitation spread, the government was forced to lift the ban on the activities of political parties and labor unions. The president resigned in mid–1982 and the remainder of the *junta* decided to shorten the political process by recalling the democratically elected Congress of 1980, which confirmed the results of those elections which had been won by Hernán Siles Suazo; in late 1982 he and Jaime Paz Zamora, a Socialist, were officially proclaimed as president and vice president of Bolivia.

The situation inherited by the civilian government bordered on total chaos. The public debt amounted to about $3 billion, inflation was utterly out of control, unemployment was rampant and the corruptive influence of the drug traffic had reached alarming proportions. During the first months of 1983, the government made brave, but disorganized, attempts to impose a program of economic austerity and public honesty. Its partial success immediately provoked opposition and social unrest.

By the middle of 1984, battered by worker strikes and interminable rumors of impending military coups, the civilian government had managed to survive against formidable odds. Exemplifying the extent of the regime's troubles, in mid–1984 President Siles Suazo encouraged private sectors to invest in the country, rejected a demand for a 500% rise in worker' wages, proclaimed a new war against drug dealers, promised to reduce inflation to 45%, reaffirmed his confidence in the loyalty of the armed forces and appealed to international institutions to lend more money to Bolivia to save the nation from a "desperate economic situation."

The president was abducted one month later and held for some hours before being released in what appeared to be a clumsy attempt to stage a military coup.

Social unrest, several more labor strikes and inflation, which at the beginning of 1985 was running at an astronomical annual rate of 24,000%, led Siles Suazo to advance presidential elections to 1985. It appeared that General Hugo Banzer would win, and he actually received more votes than the runner–up in an election riddled with corruption, particularly in the La Paz area. Although former President Paz Estenssoro, age 77, received 26.4% of the vote, about 2% less than Banzer, he was elected president by the new Congress, in

which Paz Estenssoro's party received more seats than that of Banzer.

Paz Estenssoro successfully undertook renegotiation of Bolivia's foreign debt when he took office in August 1985 (it had reached $4.9 billion); he reduced the value of the peso by 1 million to one. (It had been traded on the black market at 1.4 million per $1 U.S.) He promised decentralization of the economy, particularly the state mining and petroleum monopolies. As might have been expected, these moves and others increased food prices tenfold and provoked strikes and violence which led to the declaration of a state of siege. About 1,500 hunger–striking trade unionists were arrested and sent into internal exile. Surprisingly, Banzer and his supporters joined in the efforts of Paz Estenssoro for economic reform. As a result of dramatic change, the International Monetary Fund, the World Bank, the United States, Japan, China and European countries were willing to resume loans to Bolivia.

The years 1985–1988 were not kind to Bolivia. Part of this was because of internal human factors, but most were natural or external in nature. The bottom dropped out of world tin prices in 1985. The basic causes were a vast stock oversupply (one year) and, more ominously, increased substitution of aluminum. Further complicating Bolivia's problems was the discovery of Brazilian deposits which can be mined with much greater ease. Bolivia wound up in the position of marketing tin for less than one third the price of production. By 1989, a single province of western Brazil was producing more tin than all of Bolivia, using modern technology in contrast to Bolivia's antiquated methods.

The government had no choice but to close the most inefficient mines, causing unemployment to rise to 32%. Huge numbers of workers marched in opposition ("March for Life").

Heavy flood damage in early 1986 occurred because of heavy rains and rising waters of Lake Titicaca, leaving 150,000 Aymara Indians destitute.

Finally, the United States decided to tackle its growing cocaine problem by destroying (hopefully) the sources. Coca production, from which cocaine is derived, produces more revenue for Bolivia than any other source. At first, a mild approach was attempted: an offer of $350 for every hectare of coca leaf taken out of production was made. Since up to $10,000 _per hectare can be made by cultivating the narcotic leaf, the plan was not only poorly received, it was actively resisted by farmers who threatened violence. Then, in "Operation Blast Furnace," the United States persuaded the Bolivian government to cooperate in destroying the facilities used to process the coca into cocaine with the assistance of American helicopters and armaments.

The operation was approved, but was carried out in an incredibly clumsy way. Clusters of U.S. helicopters and military appeared at major Bolivian airports and sat idle for four days while "planning" went on. Needless to say, no one was home when they ultimately reached their target. The result: crowds demonstrated in front of the U.S. Embassy shouting *"Viva coca!"*

U.S. efforts against coca from 1986 to 1997 were hampered for several reasons. First, there was a demand for cocaine. If Bolivian coca production went down, it rose in neighboring nations. Second, coca production was an informal government industry. It successfully functioned because of an elaborate, ever-changing system of bribery which had even invaded the Supreme Court. Third, paid informants were useless because drug figureheads had counter-informants up to the highest level of the military and police.

Coca production underwent two important changes. First, it was no longer a "cottage" industry—plantations were used for production, which hired help at low wages for the menial work (they would otherwise be unemployed). The growers could raise large crowds for anti-government demonstrations quite easily. Second, instead of producing coca "paste" using kerosene and shipping it to Colombian cartels, Bolivia had a tremendous number of "factories" producing the treasured final product—white powder. This latter transformation reflected a local desire for immense profits formerly reaped by Colombian cartels, not because those elusive organizations have been seriously damaged by U.S. efforts to control cocaine production.

May 1989 presidential elections produced two top candidates out of nine—Gonzalo Sánchez de Lozada, 58, candidate of the *MNR*, received 23% of the vote and Banzer received 22%. Jaime Paz Zamora, nephew of Paz Estenssoro, but a leftist, received 19.5%. Three months of meetings in smoke–filled rooms ensued. Finally, in August the doors opened and number three was declared the new president. How? Number two, Banzer, who while in power had jailed and exiled Paz Zamora in the 1970s, threw his support behind his former arch foe in exchange for 10 out of 17 cabinet posts and virtually assured his control of the government.

Paz Zamora pledged to continue the style of government of his uncle and did so. Unrest did not cease; his term was typified by a nationwide teacher's strike and a murky plot to assassinate him, the chief drug enforcement officer and the U.S. ambassador in late 1990. Drug raids with U.S. assistance were only moderately successful and highly resented by Bolivians.

The next elections were held in mid-1993. Cabinet ministers resigned from government to support Banzer. In spite of this, Sánchez de Lozada won a plurality of 36%; Banzer then threw his support to his rival, making a runoff election unnecessary. The Congress decreed Sánchez de Lozada president in August 1993.

Like many other Latin American presidents of the 1990s, Sánchez de Lozada undertook a pragmatic program of privatizing cumbersome state-owned enterprises, including the national airline, the oil company and the telecommunications infrastructure. He also sought to decentralize power, placing unprecedented control in the hands of the departments. He also began welcoming foreign investors to Bolivia with red-carpet incentives.

Faced with strikes and protests by the majority Indian community for this seeming betrayal of the 1952 revolution, Sánchez reached a new land-reform agreement with Indian leaders in October 1996, the most significant such law since the transcendental land-reform law of 1952. Unlike the earlier law, the new statute not only gave peasants title to their land but also permitted them to sell it. Previously, they could only bequeath it to their children, with the result that individual plots became too small to be economically viable.

Banzer Returns to Power

The reforms proved to be the leading issue of the June 1, 1997 presidential elections, which drew 10 candidates and were marked by the stunning political comeback of the former strongman Banzer, now 71. All the major candidates embraced Sánchez's reforms, but Banzer capitalized on the discontent among the poor by running on a foggy populist platform which included his promise to "humanize" the reforms, whatever that meant. Nevertheless, the ploy worked, and Banzer, now a zealous democrat who pledged to respect human rights, emerged as the front runner with 22% of the vote. The *MNR* candidate was second with 18% and former president Paz Zamora was third with 17%. There was a 70% turnout of 3.2 million voters.

Because no one received a majority, Congress again was required to select the president, but this time Banzer's Nationalist Democratic Alliance (*ADN*) forged an unusual alliance with populist and left-wing parties to assure him of victory. In the balloting on August 5, Banzer received the necessary majority of 79 of the 157 deputies after only two thirds of them had voted. The new vice president was Jorge Quiroga, 37, a previous finance minister under Paz Zamora, a former IBM executive and an engineering graduate of Texas A&M who was married to a Texan. They were sworn in the next day, Independence Day, for a term that had been constitutionally extended from four to five years.

Though not specified in his inaugural address, Banzer soon issued a controversial pledge to eradicate Bolivia's coca production before the end of his term in 2002. Though the news gladdened the Clinton administration, the Republican-controlled U.S. Congress nonetheless began making noises that it would increase drug–control aid to Colombia while reducing Bolivia's aid from $34 million to $12 million. This prompted a visit to Washington in March 1998 by English–speaking Vice President Quiroga. He met with Clinton's drug policy adviser Barry McCaffrey, who assured him the Clinton administration wanted to increase the aid to $45 million.

Back at home, the powerful Confederation of Bolivian Workers (*COB*) soon began engaging in the country's second most popular pastime after soccer: general strikes. The *COB* was demanding an increase in the monthly minimum wage from the admittedly paltry $45 to an unreasonable and inflationary $667. The government made an offer of $54, which the *COB* predictably rejected. It called three 48–hour general strikes between August 1997 and March 1998, which were observed mostly by teachers, cleaning workers and some miners. When the government still refused to budge, an open–ended strike began in early April. Coupled with this, coca–growing peasants in the Chapare region, furious over the government's decision to eliminate their livelihood, joined the strike by setting up roadblocks on the Santa Cruz–"Cochabamba highway. Hundreds of troops and police were dispatched to disperse them, and violence erupted.

Meanwhile, the negotiations between the government and the *COB* broke down when the government refused to accept the participation of Evo Morales, the leader of the coca growers, who had been elected to Congress in 1997. Morales made the seemingly reasonable argument that the government should offer incentives for the peasants to switch to alternative

Former President Hugo Banzer Suárez

crops, which, in fact, already has been done, and non–traditional crops in Chapare now outnumber coca acreage three–to–one. The government also has paid farmers up to $2,500 per hectare—almost all of it provided by the United States, of course—to uproot coca plants, but the incentive program was not to be extended beyond 1998. Cooperate now and get paid, or be an outlaw, was the strategy. Miffed, Morales accused Banzer of having had ties to drug traffickers, which the president vehemently denied. The strike turned violent, and before it died out, 18 people were killed. But in the test of wills between the strong–willed Banzer and the strong–willed Morales, the president prevailed. He reported to Congress that of the estimated 40,000 hectares of coca cultivation, 7,000 were eradicated in 1997 and 11,620 in 1998. Critics maintained that new cultivation reduced the net eradication in those years to 2,000 and 8,000, respectively. Moreover, Morales and younger, less moderate spokesmen for the growers complain that the ostensible markets for the alternative crops do not exist.

Banzer faced another challenge in late 1998 when former President Sánchez de Lozada called for an investigation into Banzer's role in the human rights abuses committed during his military regime, when an estimated 200 people were killed. The call no doubt was inspired by the arrest in London days earlier of former Chilean strongman Augusto Pinochet and by the ongoing investigation of Argentine military men for atrocities committed during the "Dirty War." Banzer justifiably accused the *MNR* of hypocrisy and called on the opposition party to examine its own complicity with military regimes. Bolivian public opinion seemed to concur with Banzer that this was little more than political sour grapes on Sánchez's part.

In September 1999, the government announced even more impressive figures in the coca-eradication program than it had the year before. According to the information minister, the army and police had removed 11,670 hectares from cultivation, slightly more than the entire number of hectares for 1998, and predicted that another 14,000 hectares would be removed by the end of the year, which would leave only 16,000 hectares under cultivation.

General strikes continued to plague the country. In September 1999, both La Paz and Sucre were shut down for a day by a peaceful strike protesting increases in bread, fuel and transportation prices. But in April 2000, a seemingly routine local protest in Cochabamba against an increase in water prices turned violent and presented Banzer with his gravest domestic crisis to date. Before the unrest subsided nine days later, the protests had spread to five of the nine departments, five people were killed and 40 injured,

dozens were arrested, and the president issued a 90-day state of siege, the seventh since the restoration of democracy.

The unrest was sparked by a $70 million contract to a London-based engineering firm to build a tunnel that would bring water across the Andes to Cochabamba, which would have required an increase of from 20% to 80% in water rates. In February, the New Republican Force *(NFR)*, one of the members of Banzer's congressional coalition, had opposed the price increases, prompting the president to expel the group from the coalition. Public discontent in Cochabamba over the price increase soon escalated into violence fueled by general frustration over the depressed economy in the wake of coca eradication. Clashes erupted between soldiers and protesters in several locations, none more violent than in the town of Achacachi on April 10, where two soldiers and three protesters were killed. One of the soldiers, a captain, was dragged by a mob from a hospital room and killed in the town square. The protesters also looted government offices.

The unrest quickly spread, as angry farmers erected roadblocks in five departments. In one town, even policemen, angered by their low pay, seized their station; in La Paz, other policemen fired on soldiers. After Banzer declared the state of siege, which suspended basic civil liberties, the COB sought to mount a nationwide general strike. However, Banzer's pragmatic decision to cancel the water project contract, coupled with negotiations between the government and the protesters mediated by the Catholic Church, largely defused the crisis, and by April 13 the protests had lost their steam.

New, more broadly based protests flared up again in September 2000, principally by coca farmers protesting Banzer's eradication programs, but they were joined by other peasant farmers, teachers and transport workers. Banzer's response to the protests, which consisted mainly of blockading main roads, was relatively measured, leaving "only" about 10 people dead. The protests forced him to cancel a state visit to Japan. By April 2001, it was street vendors in La Paz who began demonstrating to protest new regulations on them. Those protests, while noisy, were nonviolent.

Shortly before Christmas 2000, in an elaborate ceremony at a military base in Chapare, Banzer officially declared the successful culmination of the coca eradication program, claiming 40,000 hectares had been removed from cultivation. Under the government's program, only 12,000 hectares in Yungas are allowed to be cultivated for "traditional" purposes, a concession to the sentiments of local Indians. Still, there is intense resentment against the crop-substitution plan, as the peasants complain that other crops, such

as coffee, earn them only a fraction of what they made from coca.

As an offshoot of the mounting discontent with the Banzer government, what could be an important new variable was added into the Bolivian political equation. On November 14, 2000, a new Indian-based political party, *Movimiento Indígeno Pachacuti* (the Aymara word for "revival"), was established on the site of the execution by the Spanish in 1783 of Tupac Katari, the leader of an Indian revolt. Its leader is Felipe Quispe, the head of a peasant labor confederation, also known by the sobriquet Mallku, which means condor.

Perhaps in response to this new movement, as well as to the frequent protests, Banzer pushed through Congress in February 2001 an ambitious, 50-point constitutional reform that in principle would broaden Bolivian democracy. The reforms take aim at election fraud by removing local elections from the control of local kingpins, providing for referenda, and empowering the Supreme Court rather than Congress with the decision to revoke congressional immunity in corruption investigations. The opposition *MNR* grudgingly supported the plan, but accused Banzer of having political motives.

A political era came to an end in Bolivia on June 7, 2001, when four-time former President Paz Estenssoro, the intellectual author of the 1952 revolution, died at the age of 93. He died on the 59th anniversary of the founding of the *MNR*. His funeral in Tarija attracted thousands of peasants, who mingled with the elite of various parties who came to pay tribute to the man and his legacy.

The incumbent president would soon follow him. On July 1, 2001, Banzer, a heavy smoker, was admitted to Walter Reed Hospital in Washington; six days later he was diagnosed with lung and liver cancer and his condition was reported as "grave." He remained for 30 days for chemotherapy. Banzer resigned effective August 6, Independence Day and the fourth anniversary of his inauguration, and Vice President Quiroga was sworn in the following day for the remaining year of his term. Banzer, 75, succumbed in Santa Cruz on May 5, 2002. Thousands filled the streets to pay homage to this dictator-turned-democrat as his funeral cortege passed.

A lame duck from the start, Quiroga, known to Bolivians by the nickname "Tuto," nonetheless seemed determined to make a mark during his brief occupancy of the presidential palace. He pledged to continue Banzer's coca eradication policy, and he pushed several reform measures through Congress, including a civil service, non-partisan electoral courts, expanded powers for the comptroller-general and financial accountability for public officials. In October 2001, a member of

Former President Jorge Quiroga

Congress was stripped of his legislative immunity from prosecution for allegedly mishandling $60 million in public funds. Armed with his new power, the comptroller-general has been investigating other congressmen and other public officials without regard to party. One problem that still has gone unaddressed, however, is the rampant corruption in the national police.

In November, when Quiroga issued a decree that prohibited the drying, shipping or sale of coca leaves in open markets, something that heretofore had been legal, Morales and his minions protested that the decree was unconstitutional. When police attempted to close such a market near Cochabamba in January 2002, the protests flared into three days of violence that left seven people, including four of the policemen, dead. A congressional panel then sought to strip Morales of his seat for allegedly inciting the violence. That sparked still more violence, in which two more people died. In the end, Quiroga and Morales reached a compromise on the decree.

Quiroga boycotted a summit meeting on terrorism and drugs in Peru with the presidents of the United States, Peru, Ecuador and Colombia in March 2002 in a fit of pique over a U.S. State Department report that Bolivia had not been doing enough to crack down on coca cultivation in Chapare Department. Quiroga fired back a letter that claimed that 8,000 hectares of coca had been taken out of cultivation in the seven months since he assumed office.

The Election of 2002

The presidential race of 2002 was the usual free-for-all. Two former presidents, Gonzalo Sánchez de Lozada of the *MNR* and Jaime Paz Zamora of the Movement of the Revolutionary Left *(MIR)* entered the race. As Quiroga was barred from running, the *ADN* nominated Ronald MacLean. Evo Morales, the leader of the coca farmers, entered the race as the candidate of the Movement to Socialism *(MAS)*, while Felipe Quispe, as expected, ran as the candidate of the Pachacuti Indigenous Movement *(MIP)*. Rounding out the cluttered field of major contenders was the long-time mayor of Cochabamba and a former army captain, Manfred Villa Reyes, the standard-bearer of populist-oriented New Republican Force *(NFR)*.

Early polls showed Sánchez and Paz the two frontrunners, but then Reyes surged ahead of Paz into a statistical tie with Sánchez, with Morales a distant fourth. Sánchez, 72, pledged to continue the free-market reforms and to make Bolivia more attractive to investors, initiates he had taken as president. Paz and Morales both denounced free-market capitalism. Paz said he would return some of the country's vast natural gas wealth to state control, while Morales, 42, who chewed coca leaves at his rallies as a political statement, vowed to discontinue the coca erad-

ication program and bombastically declared he would expel the *"yanquis."* Reyes, 46, offered only vague generalities, other than to say he would double the size of the armed forces—although what or whom they would be fighting against was unclear.

Then, just five days before the June 30 election, U.S. Ambassador Manuel Rocha, in a stunning breach of diplomatic protocol, warned during a ceremony he attended with President Quiroga that voting for Morales could jeopardize continued U.S. aid. The reaction was immediate and ferocious, as Bolivians of all political stripes denounced this U.S. intrusion into domestic politics. (Many Bolivians already were sensitive to U.S. intrusion, as their first lady, Virginia Gillum de Quiroga, still held U.S. citizenship.) Rocha's importune remark was to boomerang in a way he neither wanted nor expected.

The vote tabulation was electoral drama at its highest, as the count proved agonizingly slow and tantalizingly close. Sánchez de Lozada, as expected, forged into an early lead that was slim but unchanging, with Reyes Villa close behind. But to everyone's surprise—and to the consternation of the loose-mouthed Ambassador Rocha and the Bush administration—Morales surged into a convincing third place, several points ahead of Paz Zamora. Over the course of the next week, as votes trickled in from the remote altiplano—coca-growing country—Morales edged closer and closer to Reyes. On July 8, with 99.2% of the vote counted, Reyes' lead had dwindled to fewer than 1,000 votes. And on July 9, the Bolivian press reported what was once unthinkable: With the count 99.78% complete, Morales had a 706-vote lead over Reyes, with only 475 votes left to count in the country! The final margin was 721 votes. The effect was as stunning as that of ultra-rightist Jean-Marie LePen's unexpected placing in the French presidential runoff the month before.

A total of 2,993,708 Bolivians had voted, a respectable turnout of 72.04%. The complete official count gave Sánchez 624,126 votes, or 22.46%; Morales, 581,884 votes, or 20.94%; Reyes, 581,163, or 20.91%; Paz, 453,375, or 16.31%; Quispe, 169,737, or 6.09%; Johnny Fernández of the Civic Solidarity Union *(UCS)*, 153,175, or 5.51%; MacLean of the *ADN* had a pitiful 94,333, or 3.4%. Sánchez and Morales each carried four of the nine departments; Paz carried one, Reyes Villa none.

Pending a recount, Congress thus would be choosing between Sánchez and Morales before August 6, after this book's deadline, and the jockeying for alliances in the new Congress was underway. On July 10, the Bolivian press was reporting that Reyes Villa's *NFR* had decided to remain in the opposition in the new Congress, although that did not mean it

55

would not in the end throw its support behind the election of Sánchez. The press also was reporting that the *MNR* was negotiating a coalition with Paz's *MIR*, the *UCS* and the *ADN*, which still would not constitute an outright majority. In such a case, the *NFR* would prove the balance of power between a minority Sánchez government on the one hand and the *MAS* and the *MIP* on the other. The press was also reporting that Ambassador Rocha was again thrusting himself into domestic politics by actively participating in an inter-party meeting and that he was applying "pressure" on behalf of Sánchez and against Morales.

For his part, once his second-place finish was established, Morales suddenly began sounding more conciliatory. Interviewed by the Spanish-language edition of CNN, he insisted that there was a difference between coca cultivation and narcotrafficking, which he said he has always opposed, but he blamed the problem on the demand for cocaine in the developed countries. He also pragmatically made conciliatory remarks about the World Bank and the IMF, as radicals who suddenly find themselves on the brink of power often do.

On August 4, Congress elected Sánchez de Lozada, known to Bolivians as "Goni," over Morales, 84-43. He was inaugurated on August 6.

Culture: The Spanish conquerors and settlers of Bolivia built new cities and tended to concentrate there, leaving the interior to the indigenous Aymara Indians.

Today, the majority of Bolivians still speak Aymara as their first language, learning Spanish as a necessity to conduct official business. A substantial minority of the population also speaks Quéchua, the ancient tongue of the Incas. The populations of the cities of La Paz and Potosí are about 70 percent indigenous Indian, 25% *mestizo* and only 5% European.

Bolivian culture, consequently, remains essentially Indian with only a thin veneer of European Christianity superimposed upon it. Bolivia has produced few cultural figures of international note, although the flute–based folk music of the *altiplano* has become internationally popular. It is not unusual to see *altiplano* flute bands in colorful Indian dress playing on street corners from New Orleans to New York to Paris to Venice. Bolivians insist that the Brazilians "stole" the music for the mega–hit dance *Lambada* from Bolivia.

Because of the abysmally low literacy rate, Bolivia never developed a strong literary tradition. There were two newspapers of note, however, both published in La Paz: *El Diario*, founded in 1904, and *Presencia*, established by the Catholic Church during the revolutionary year 1952. *Presencia* ceased publication in 2001. Other current dailies now include *Los Tiempos, El Deber, La Prensa* and *La Razón*.

Economy: Bolivia's economy has been based on the extraction of its mineral wealth for more than 400 years. The vast sums produced have been exported, with little or no benefit accruing to the Bolivian people. Mismanagement and the decline

of world demands for its minerals have resulted in the *de facto* bankruptcy of the Bolivian government. While the 1952 revolution largely ended serfdom, a lack of technical and financial resources limits a more even distribution of wealth and income. The nation's major source of income, the tin mines, are a thing of the past and has been replaced at least in part by exports of petroleum and natural gas.

The other mainstay of the Bolivian economy is an underground one: coca leaf. President Banzer's program to eradicate coca cultivation was largely successful, but it created social unrest among the impoverished peasants who depend on it for their livelihood. The government's proposal to replace coca with alternative crops has a hollow ring, as any crop suitable for the humid Bolivian plains, such as soybeans or peanuts, will bring only a fraction of the price of illegal coca.

Bolivia remains one of the hemisphere's poorest nations, and its agricultural- and mineral-based economy has shown but modest growth in recent years. Growth has fallen from 4.2% in 1997 and 4.7% in 1998 to 2.0% in 1999, 2.5% in 2000 and 1.5% in 2001. Even the reduced growth of 1999 could have been worse, considering its three much more prosperous neighbors—Brazil, Argentina and Chile—slid into severe recessions. GDP stood at $8.66 billion in 2001. Per capita income surpassed the $1,000 mark for the first time in 1999. Unemployment officially was 8.0% in 1999 and 7.6% in 2000, but as with many Latin American countries, the

President Gonzalo Sánchez de Lozada

"employed" include the underemployed with menial, part-time jobs who can barely feed their families. Inflation was 4.0% in 2001.

The Future: Bolivia is the classic case of viewing the glass as half full rather than half empty. The country remains beset by serious political, economic and social problems, among the worst in the hemisphere. The influence of the drug trade in national life remains powerful. Yet, when viewed in the historical context of Bolivia's turbulent past, there is reason for cautious optimism. Although the military remains an undeniable sword of Damocles, since 1982 there has been a steady succession of civilian presidents who have served out their terms. The election of a former military dictator through the democratic process in 1997 is not unprecedented in Latin America—Brazil's Getulio Vargas and Chile's Carlos Ibáñez come to mind. But it was the first such case since the democratization process began in Latin America, and Bolivia was still a democracy, albeit a troubled and imperfect one, when the dying Banzer resigned in 2001. Banzer's legacy may be to show that perhaps old dictators can change their spots.

For his second term, Sánchez de Lozada is going to face a badly fragmented Congress, which is nothing new; Banzer and his predecessors governed reasonably successfully after receiving small pluralities of the popular vote. What *is* new is the strength of the indigenous movements of Morales and Quispe, both Aymaras. Between them, the *MAS* and the *MIP* should have about a fourth of the seats in Congress, large enough to become power brokers with the older, established parties. What is not known is whether these two political newcomers, who showed that they could mobilize mass protests that often turned violent, will have the wisdom not to abuse power now that they have a share of it. An alliance between them, however, is not a foregone conclusion, as there is no love lost between them; they bitterly attacked one another during the campaign, apparently an intra-Aymara turf battle.

Another question that this author would like to have answered is whether U.S. Ambassador Manuel Rocha was acting under State Department orders when he foolishly interjected himself into the campaign by threatening Bolivian voters if they voted for Morales, thus catapulting Morales into second place. If so, it could seriously jeopardize the good will that the Bush administration has carefully tried to nurture with Latin America (see U.S.-Latin American Relations). If he was acting on his own, he should be fired for stupidity.

The Federative Republic of Brazil

Seen from the Brazilian border, encircled by dense jungle, Iguassu Falls—about three miles wide—plummets its violent waters for a drop of 284 feet

Courtesy: Mr. and Mrs. Schuyler Lowe

Area: 3,286,500 square miles

Population: 169 million (2000 census).

Capital City: Brasilia (Pop. 2.3 million, estimated).

Climate: The northern lowlands are hot, with heavy rainfall; the central plateau and northeastern regions are subtropical and dry; the southern regions are temperate with moderate rainfall.

Neighboring Countries: French Guiana, Suriname, Guyana, Venezuela, Colombia (North); Peru, Bolivia (West); Paraguay, Argentina, Uruguay (Southwest).

Official Language: Portuguese.

Other Principal Tongues: English, French, German and other European languages.

Ethnic Background: Black African/Mulatto (48%), European White (48%); Other (3%); Native Indian (1%).

Principal Religion: Christianity (Roman Catholic 75%, Protestant Evangelical 20%).

Chief Commercial Products: Coffee, refined metal ores, chemicals, cacao, soy-beans, sugar, cotton, wood, automobiles and parts, shoes.

Currency: Real (established July 1, 1994).

Gross Domestic Product: U.S. $570 billion in first quarter of 2002 ($3,300 per capita).

Former Colonial Status: Colony of Portugal (1500–1815); Kingdom of the Portuguese Empire (1815–1822).

Independence Date: September 7, 1822.

Chief of State: Fernando Henrique Cardoso, President (Since Jan. 1, 1995, b. 1931).

National Flag: Green, with a yellow lozenge enclosing a blue sphere with 21 stars, five of which form the Southern Cross, and the motto *Ordem e Progresso* (Order and Progress).

Brazil occupies almost half of the South American continent and is almost as large as the continental United States. It stretches some 2,700 miles from the Guiana highlands in the North to the plains of Uruguay in the South and an equal distance from the "hump" on the Atlantic Coast to the jungles of Bolivia and Peru in the West. Almost half of this area is the hot, humid basin of the mighty Amazon River and its thousands of winding tributaries.

The northeast Bahia region, the interior of the "hump," is a semi–arid region; to the south and inland is a plateau drained to the northeast by the São Francisco River. This is a region of forests and plains which attracts migrants from other parts of Brazil and from abroad. The plains of the extreme south drain into the Paraná River valley. The southern states from Minas Gerais to Rio Grande do Sul comprise the effective Brazil, where approximately 90% of the population lives on less than 30% of the land. In an effort to draw settlers into other areas of the interior, the capital was moved in 1960 from pleasant and coastal Rio de Janeiro to inland and not so pleasant Brasilia. A modern city as planned, the capital is now surrounded by outlying shantytowns with almost one million people within 12 miles of the central area.

History: Pedro Alvares Cabral first raised the Portuguese flag in Brazil on April 22, 1500 after having been blown off course while enroute (he thought) from Portugal to India. The Portuguese government, preoccupied with its India trade, took little interest in the American claim until 1530 when it established a colony at Rio de Janeiro and in 1532 founded São Vincente. The land was quickly divided into vast estates with a frontage on the Atlantic Ocean and ran west to the line of demarcation between Spanish and Portuguese areas for discovery and colonization—approximately the 45th meridian west, set by the Treaty of Tordesillas in 1494. These estates, called *capitanias,* were granted as feudal holdings to the nobles who were to build towns and forts, explore, settle colonists and (most importantly) enrich the mother country. Thirteen of these estates were laid out, but the poor quality of the colonists sent out and the oppressive climate gave them a poor start.

In spite of this, several towns were founded—Olinda in 1535, Santo Amaro, Itamarca and Pernambuco in 1536, Bahia in 1549—and from these towns expeditions explored the interior.

From 1580 to 1640, Brazil was under Spanish control—Philip II of Spain had inherited the Portuguese throne. During this period, explorations were pushed beyond the demarcation line, but few towns were established in the dense interior. From 1630 to 1654, the Dutch briefly held the northeast coast from Pernambuco to Parnaiba. During most of its colonial period, Brazil was in reality a coastal colony with an immense, unexplored interior. That the colonies prospered and remained under Portuguese control was largely due to the politics of Europe and to the efforts of two capable leaders—General Tomé de Souza and General Mem de Sá—and to the efforts of a few Jesuit missionaries.

For almost one and a half centuries following Spanish rule, Brazil was neglected by the Portuguese government. It did, however, benefit from the liberal policies of the Marquis of Pombal, the Portuguese prime minister under Joseph I (1749–1777), who did much to improve the public services. In general, Brazil's communities were ruled by the municipal councils with little interference from the Portuguese monarchs. By the end of the colonial period, cities had developed power and prestige reminiscent of the feudal ones of Europe. The smaller municipalities were at the mercy of the militia commanders, and the great estates were under the absolute rule of their owners.

Probably the most cohesive force in the Brazilian colonies was the Catholic Church, and the most influential of the churchmen were the Jesuits. The Portuguese church had been influenced by modifying cultures at home, both Moslem and Oriental, and was subject to still more change in Brazil because of the primitive Indian and African Negro cultures. The Jesuits took as their first responsibility the protection of the Indians. Despite the opposition of the planters, who needed labor, the fathers gathered their charges into fortified villages, taught them useful arts and crafts, and improved methods of agriculture simultaneously with the fundamentals of Christianity.

The ouster of the Jesuits in 1759 was simply political reaction to the fact that they were so successful in their work of protecting the native Indians that they were bad for the colony's businessmen.

The settling of Brazil's interior was the work of a few pioneers, the celebrated *bandeirantes,* the boldest of whom were the missionaries and the slave raiders of São Paulo. The latter were foremost in establishing Portuguese rule in the interior; their raids forced the remaining Indians to withdraw deeper inland and served as a counter-force against Spanish penetrations. In their wake came planters and, later, gold prospectors. As African Negro slaves were introduced, the slave raiders turned to commerce and industry, making São Paulo the most prosperous of the Brazilian states. The colonial economy was based on sugar and forest products until the end of the 17th century, when the lure of gold depopulated the plantations as owners with their slaves migrated to Minas Gerais. Gold was also found in Mato Grosso and Goiás; about the same time it was learned that the bright stones found in Minas Gerais were diamonds. This wealth brought an influx of immigrants and pushed the frontier further inland. In 1763 the capital of Brazil was transferred from the north to Rio de Janeiro.

The cities furnished only the middlemen, the brokers and the hucksters, in the development of colonial Brazil. Its theoretically rigid class society was in fact for many decades a bizarre mixture of aristocracy, democracy and anarchy. At the top

Rio de Janeiro about 1825

was the ruling class from Portugal; next came those of Portuguese origin born in Brazil—which included a majority of the estate owners; then followed in descending order mixed bloods, slaves and native Indians.

Actually, the system was elastic. The *mulatto* children born of the owner and his slaves might be reared equally with his legitimate children, and the Negro with the capacity to win wealth or influence took precedence with the elite. By the end of the colonial period, the whites had declined in number and influence, while those of mixed ancestry showed strength and a high degree of adaptation to the Brazilian environment. Brazil's society was tolerant, and the freedom from interference from Portugal allowed it to develop a one–class people—Brazilians.

Brazil's history as an independent state may be divided into two periods: Empire and Republic, and these in turn have their subdivisions. Certainly, loyalty to the crown kept the regional factions from creating small states, as happened in the Spanish states of *Gran Colombia* and Central America.

Empire and Republic

In 1822, Pedro I, Crown Prince of Portugal and titular Prince of Brazil, refused an order to return to Portugal and on _September 7 declared Brazil independent. Surviving republican and separatist movements, he was able to create a constitutional monarchy. With his father's death in 1826, he inherited the throne of Portugal, which he renounced in favor of his five–year–old daughter to appease those Brazilians who feared a reunion with Portugal. However, through mismanagement and corruption, Pedro alienated the Brazilians, who in 1831 forced his abdication in favor of his five–year–old son, Pedro II. Fortunate in his tutors and regents, Pedro II proved to be a capable leader who retained the affection of the Brazilian people for a period of 49 years.

Although the abdication of Pedro I left Brazil on the verge of anarchy, the regents who governed during the minority of Pedro II were able to suppress rebellions. They made many liberal changes in the constitution, and Brazil avoided the series of tyrannical dictatorships experienced by many of the former Spanish colonies.

From his coronation in 1841 until 1850, Pedro II was occupied with establishing his authority to rule. The Brazil of this era consisted of population centers at Rio de Janeiro, Minas Gerais, São Paulo and Pernambuco. The population numbered some 7 million—between 1 and 2 million whites, 3 to 4 million Negro slaves, a million free Negroes and people of mixed blood and a half million Indians. The immense Amazon River basin was largely unexplored and while the cattle–raising south and the states of São Paulo and Minas Gerais were showing progress, the remainder of Brazil was still little more than a fringe of Atlantic coast settlements.

Although Pedro II's government was patterned after that of Great Britain, it lacked the popular base of the British government; the illiterate mass of Brazilians had no vote, and effective control fell to landowners, merchants and the learned men of the cities. Pedro's government was conducted by his ministers, while he exercised the role of arbitrator. The period of the 1840s was devoted to the suppression of separatist movements and consolidation of the nation; the 1850s and 1860s were spent in resolving Brazil's foreign disputes and in enlarging the national territory. The 1870s and 1880s were marked by much liberal legislation, the growth of republican ideas, the abolition of slavery and the end of the Empire.

From the 1850s to the 1870s, Brazil's economy expanded in a manner similar to that of the United States. Railroads, industry, agriculture and land speculation attracted large amounts of capital and a stream of immigrants who brought technical skills missing from Brazil's own population. By the mid 1870s, Brazil was earning a net profit of some $20 million from its foreign trade. During this period, Pedro

Dom Pedro II, Emperor of Brazil

II fostered education and Brazilian cultural expression developed. Through the 1860s his popularity and support were such that he could have governed under any title—king, emperor or president.

Liberal in his religious views, he respected freedom of worship; when in 1865 the pope published a ban against Freemasonry, Pedro refused to permit its adoption in Brazil. Despite his stand, the conflict between church and Masonry grew to the point that he personally became involved, losing support from the church and the clergy without satisfying the Masons. Following the Paraguayan War (1865–70) the Emperor became involved in a dispute between the army and the Liberal Party; while keeping the army under civilian control, he insisted upon supporting its legitimate needs for maintaining professional competence. These measures satisfied neither group and cost him the support of the elements whose interests he was defending.

The support of landowners was lost when slavery was abolished in 1871; the law also safeguarded the owners' economic interests and provided for the training of the emancipated slaves. Again, neither side was satisfied with Pedro's moderation and he was forced to abdicate in 1889 in the face of an impending military coup.

General Deodoro da Fonseca announced by decree the creation of the Federative Republic of Brazil, composed of 20 states. Pledged to recognize and respect the obligations created under the empire, the new government won popular acclaim. A constitution based on that of the United States was imposed on the country by decree in 1891. Although theoretically founded under democratic principles, the constitution gave less voice to the populace than it had under Pedro II. Fonseca later proved to be an inept leader and was replaced in 1893 by Marshal Floriano Peixoto, an even more capricious figure who provoked the navy into a rebellion which was followed by a short–lived civil war.

A reign of terror followed the rebellion—previously unknown in Brazil; in 1894 Peixoto peacefully turned the government over to a more moderate Civilain president, Prudente de Morais Barros, the first of three consecutive presidents from São Paulo.

The government was badly demoralized, and had an empty treasury, and people were widely split in a military–civilian standoff. Further complicating the scene were the *conselheiros*, a group of fanatics in the northeast who held out against the army until the last man was killed. The president was able to spend his last year in office in peace.

The years to 1910 saw the republic develop under a series of three capable presidents. Two decades of turmoil ensued, which tested the strength of the federal republic. Problems centered around political meddling by the military, anarchic regionalism and an ailing economy, all of which were complicated by World War I. The military–civilian division worsened and continued for some 20 years; in the states, state loyalty was greater than national loyalty and was compounded by various militia loyal to local political leaders.

The Vargas Era

Asian rubber production, the decline of coffee prices and the loss of foreign markets, rubbed salt in already sore wounds. Foreign debts and unwise fiscal policies in Brazil brought it to the verge of bankruptcy. The world–wide depression of the 1930s and political blunders of the gov-

Getulio Vargas, 1934

ernment brought on military intervention and the installation of Getulio Vargas, who ruled as dictator for 15 years. He combined a shrewd sense of politics with managerial ability and personal honesty. Sometimes compared with the Jesuits who defended the Indians against the landlords, Vargas posed as a defender of Brazil against the military and the powerful state governors, while trying to unify the laboring classes and grant the right to vote to the entire population.

Vargas rehabilitated the economy and forced state cooperation with the new national government. A new pseudo–fascist constitution in 1934 enfranchised women and provided social legislation to protect workers. Peace endured for a year, but was followed by communist and fascist attempts to seize power. Profiting from the scare, Vargas suspended the constitution, extended his term and ruled by decree. An amiable but forceful dictator, he selected capable men to administer gov-

ernment services and accomplished much to improve the living standards of the poor. His management of the national economy was sound and Brazil made notable progress in industrialization and in production. He also brought Brazil into the war on the side of the Allies and sent troops to fight in Italy. Despite the generally popular nature of his rule, by the end of World War II, opposition had developed to the point that Vargas could only retain his position by the use of force. On October 29, 1945, a committee of military officers persuaded Vargas to resign. Vargas already had ordered free elections for December, in which General Eurico Gaspar Dutra won the presidency by a decisive margin. Colorless and inept, he was unable to control the economy. Overspending and corruption and inflation spelled the end of his career.

In the elections of 1950, Vargas entered the competition as a candidate of the Labor Party and announced himself to be the champion of democratic government. The National Democratic Union was unable to stop his demagogic appeal. But his new term in office was not impressive; his appointees were largely incompetent and many were corrupt.

By 1954, general discontent was highly apparent; both the military and civilian elements were in a mood to unseat Vargas— events were triggered by an attack on the editor of a leading Rio newspaper. Faced with the evidence that his own bodyguard was implicated, and under military pressure for his resignation, Vargas instead committed suicide.

His successor proved to be no solution; by the time Juscelino Kubitschek finished his term, there was a flurry of strikes and refusals of the International Monetary Fund and Washington to advance further sums to an extravagant Brazil. Campaigning on a platform of austerity and competent government, Jãnio Quadros won the 1960 elections by the largest plurality of any president in Brazilian history. However, he was embarrassed by a last-minute round of wage increases granted by his predecessor and the election of a controversial leftist, João Goulart, as vice president. Quadros faced staggering problems, including large foreign debts, mounting inflation, widespread opposition to his plan for trade with the communist bloc and moderation toward Cuba. This led to feelings of frustration and his sudden resignation in August 1961.

Goulart was permitted to take office the following month only after agreeing to demands by conservative military officials to a drastic limitation of presidential powers. Brazil thus became a rudderless ship, headed by a president with no authority and a congress bitterly divided among 12 political parties. Faced with a stagnant economy, growing inflation which had reached an annual rate of 100% by 1964

Brasilia's Alvorada Palace, the presidential residence

and deepening social division, the president fought for and obtained greater power through a plebiscite in 1963. Relying increasingly on leftist support, he sought to divide the military and use mass demonstrations to intimidate his opposition.

Military–*ARENA* Rule, 1964–1985

Fearing the nation might be plunged into chaos, the armed forces ousted him on April 1, 1964, and replaced him with General Humberto Castelo Branco. This began a series of military governments that altered the political and economic face of Brazil.

Regarding themselves as authentic "revolutionaries," the military imposed a presidential government controlled by the high command of about 12 top officers better known as the *Estado Maior* or general staff. Their basic goal was not a social revolution, but an industrial revolution to enable Brazil to become a major world power. Relying heavily on technicians, the military government was relatively honest and nonpolitical. Indeed, the traditional politicians were suspect, "social" programs had low priority and human rights were respected only when they did not interfere with the "revolution."

The military quickly imposed austere economic measures to control inflation. In addition, all political parties were disbanded and replaced by two new ones: the Alliance for National Renovation

(ARENA), and the Brazilian Democratic Movement *(MDB)*.

In theory, *ARENA* was to be the dominant, government party, while the *MDB* was to furnish token opposition. In reality, both parties were powerless to challenge the military. After assuming dictatorial powers, ruling by decree, the military saw to it that *ARENA* won a large majority in carefully supervised 1966 elections. Following instructions, legislators then chose as the next president Marshal Arthur da Costa e Silva in 1967. In late 1968 he dissolved Congress, instituted press censorship and jailed prominent political opponents, including Kubitschek. In addition he suspended judicial "interference" with prosecution for "crimes against the state."

When Costa e Silva suffered a paralyzing stroke in mid–1969, General Emilio Garrastazu Médici was named president. Prosperity and repression were the two prominent traits of his regime, which believed that the first is possible only because of the latter. Under his tutelage, Brazil developed a prosperous economy, forcing even critics to admit that the "Brazilian miracle" economically compared with the post-war boom in Germany and Japan, albeit at tremendous loss of liberty.

The expanding economy helped finance ambitious government projects in education, health and public works. The mammoth Trans–Amazonian highway linked

Brazil's Atlantic coast with the Peruvian border, hacked 3,250 miles through vast empty stretches of the national heartland. (A continuing battle with the encroaching jungle has been waged since that time.) The cost of economic boom was high; industrial growth was financed largely through exploitation of workers. During the first 10 years of military rule, the economy grew by 56% while real wages dropped by 55%. The result was a severe decrease in purchasing power for the lower classes. In the same period, government expenditures for education were reduced by half and investments in health and social services also declined in real terms. While the upper 5% of the population saw its share of the national wealth jump by 9% to a total of 36%, the lower half's share dropped by 4% to a total of 14%. Although Brazilian business executives were among the world's best paid, the bottom 40% of the people were underfed. Government officials said this squeeze on the masses was necessary to raise exports. Foreign investments were attracted by the fixed low wage scale of less than 50 cents an hour.

The political situation was even more rigidly controlled—the 1967 constitution, imposed by the military, provided for a strong executive and a powerless congress. Through the Institutional Acts Nos. 5, 13 and 14, the regime systematically silenced its critics. Torture of political opponents was condemned by the Human

Rights Commission of the Organization of American States. Despite ironclad censorship of the arts and media, some criticism of the regime was evident. Most outspoken was the Catholic Church. The regime in turn charged that church work with the poor was communist–oriented. Paramilitary government secret police frequently raided church offices, seizing property and harassing leaders. The regime conducted a major crackdown in 1973 on church activities that offended it.

Unknown to many Brazilians, presidential elections were held in early 1974. The official government candidate—selected by the military high command—was retired Army General Ernesto Geisel, a portly 68–year–old former head of the Brazilian oil monopoly, *Petrobras*. The only opposition candidate was denied meaningful access to the press and television during the campaign; he could not speak out against the regime, but he called the election a "farce." There was no direct vote for president in Brazil; the "electoral college" formalized the selection of the new president by a vote of 400 to 76.

Although he promised a degree of moderation, at the same time he cautioned that social reform must wait until the nation's economic problems were solved. Nevertheless, press censorship was greatly reduced, although not eliminated, and police repression was also less evident. Efforts were made to improve strained relations with the Catholic Church and organized labor; small steps were taken to increase wages for the workers.

After allowing politicians a greater voice in national affairs, despite objections from hardliners within the ruling military councils, Geisel went ahead with plans to hold elections in late 1974. The results proved to be a disaster for the regime and its *ARENA* organization. The opposition *MDB* received twice the vote of the military–backed slate. As a result, the *MDB* picked up 16 of 22 Senate seats and a third of the Chamber of Deputies. The military favored a return to the "good old days" while the civilian population appeared more restless after a decade of military rule. Geisel tried to walk a tightrope between the two sides—he decided not to overturn the election results, but at the same time he appeared to have placated the conservative military by permitting a rise in right–wing "vigilante" acts against suspected leftists and petty criminals. Reports of torture of political opponents continued to circulate; most of this activity was conducted by the government's Intelligence Operations Detachment (*DOI*).

STATES AND TERRITORIES

The president also appeared to have turned on his critics—in 1976 he revoked the political rights of three opposition legislators who charged that Brazil was being run by "an aristocracy wearing uniforms." The regime also brought charges against 21 critical journalists.

Economic decline had a dramatic impact on Brazil's foreign policy—in mid-1975 it became the first nation in Latin America (aside from Cuba) to recognize the Soviet- and Cuban-backed revolutionaries in the Angolan civil war.

This surprising move by the staunchly anti-communist regime was largely due to economics, as Brazil hoped to buy Angolan oil and wanted to include that country in an international coffee cartel to raise the price of that commodity. It also viewed this Portuguese-speaking African nation as a potential customer for Brazilian products.

Although Brazil always had maintained cordial relations with the United States, there was a strain in 1975—in addition to recognizing Angola, Brazil voted in the UN to equate Zionism with racism. (Brazil currently imports much of its oil from Arab states).

Further questions centered around development of atomic power based on West German technology. Although Brazil said it would not build *the bomb*, the United States and other countries feared Brazil's entry into the nuclear field would accelerate the race for nuclear weapons then shaping up in the "Third World." The final upsetting factor was Brazil's growing alignment with Third World economic aims. This centered on a belief that the price of raw materials from developing nations had not kept pace with the price of machines from industrialized states.

Brazil's trade deficit with the United States steadily mounted to _crisis proportions.

When the Carter administration reduced military aid until Brazil showed greater respect for human rights and called on Brazil to terminate its nuclear program, the response was cancellation of the entire 25-year-old military pact with the United States. Geisel faced serious conflict with the business community, which openly complained that it was being elbowed aside by huge, state-run industries and fast-growing multi-national corporations. Small farmers (as in the United States) were forced off their land by huge farm combines and other modern agricultural techniques. Political tensions mounted. After the Congress abruptly dismissed Geisel's proposal for judicial changes in 1977, the president dismissed the legislature for two weeks. By decree, he ordered changes that made Brazil a one-party state. Under the plan, the president, all state governors and a third of the Senate would be elected indirectly, and in a manner so as to force them to remain under permanent control of *ARENA* and the military. The measure further gave the president another year in office.

President Geisel chose his successor, announcing in early 1978 that General João Baptista de Oliveira Figueiredo, head of the national intelligence agency, would become the next chief executive. There followed an almost meaningless presidential campaign. Virtually unknown to the public at the time of his nomination, the new president sought to project the image of a Harry Truman style "man in the street"—a campaign model which sharply contrasted with Brazil's normally stern and colorless military leadership. The obedi-

ent electoral college, with the military looking over its shoulder, officially named Figueiredo to a six-year term. In contrast, unusually free congressional elections were held throughout the nation in late 1978. To the chagrin of the military, the opposition *MDB* won a majority of the 45 million popular votes, largely because of big margins in urban areas. Nevertheless, since Brazilian law prohibited any opposition party from winning control of Congress, *ARENA* wound up with 231 of the 420 seats in the lower house and 42 _of the 67 Senate seats. All 21 state governors and most city mayors were appointed directly by the military.

Installed in March 1979, the new president pledged to "open this country up to democracy"—a promise which dismayed some army officers who distrust civilian government. This was not empty political talk. Under a new plan, free, direct elections were to be held for every office except the president. Brazil suddenly came alive with political activity. For the first time, government opponents were allowed access to the news media and the last political prisoner was released. At least *six* parties fielded candidates, compared to only one official and one opposition party permitted to exist under the old order. The plan put all Chamber of Deputies seats and one-third of the Senate seats up for grabs.

Maintaining the government-proclaimed policy of gradually returning the country to democratic rule, on November 15, 1982, peaceful elections were held for 479 seats in the Chamber of Deputies, one third of the seats in the Senate, the state governorships and assemblies, and the municipalities. Five parties participated—one pro-government, the *Partido Democratico Social (PDS)*, and four opposition groups, the most important of which is the *Partido Movimento Democratico Brasileiro (PMDB)*. The *PDS* gained an overall victory in the elections, retaining vital control of Congress, but the opposition, mainly the *PMDB* and the *Partido Trabalhista Brasileiro (PTB)*—Brazilian Labor Party—managed to win the state governorships of the three most important states: São Paulo, Rio de Janeiro and Minas Gerais.

However, expressed in intense (but sporadic) demonstrations of dissatisfaction and unrest in the principal cities, public attention was focused on the presidential elections. The majority of the opposition leaders expressed the will of the people shown in the rallies: direct presiden-_tial elections. The military-backed *PDS* convention in Brasilia nominated Paulo Salim Maluf, a wealthy businessman of Lebanese heritage. At the same time, a coalition of the *PMDB* and dissident *PDS* delegates calling itself the Democratic Alliance met and selected a widely known and revered public figure, Dr. Tancredo Neves. This elderly gentleman had the

Cattle-drawn cart

unique ability to attract the support of not only military elements, but communists and leftists. José Sarney, who had recently resigned as head of the *PDS*, was selected as vice presidential candidate of the alliance. The government opposed direct elections, arguing that they would break constitutional provisions. Instead, President Figueiredo proposed an amendment to the constitution which, while holding to indirect elections in 1985, would allow direct popular elections for the presidential period 1988–92. As the electoral college meeting drew close, political allegiances hardened. Charges (probably true) were made that Maluf had bribed and bought the nomination of the *PDS*. Popular support for Dr. Neves grew by leaps and bounds—the public sensed correctly that he was a person of great dedication and integrity. President Figueiredo, beset with illness and the military, correctly foreseeing a victory of Neves, made peace with him in an unwritten agreement. Sensing the tide running against him, Maluf attempted to make party allegiance binding on all delegates of the electoral college. The effort failed.

Return to Democracy

In early January 1985, indirect presidential elections were held, and an electoral college formed by 686 members representing most political parties elected Neves by a majority of 480 to 180 for Maluf; the majority included the dissatisfied members of the *PDS*.

Neves would have been sworn into office on March 15, officially ending a period of military rule of 21 years. Popular celebrations were cut short by the sudden illness of the president–elect, who was rushed to the hospital the day before his inauguration; after multiple operations he died on April 21, 1985, plunging the country into mourning.

Vice President Sarney, who had been acting president during Neves' illness, assumed the presidency and proclaimed that he would follow "the ideas and plans of Tancredo Neves." He inherited a coalition of Neves' center–left *PMDB* and a numerically smaller rightist Liberal Front Party *(PFL)* formed by a faction of the *PDS* of which party Sarney had been president before his resignation prior to the elections. Bickering between the two factions erupted almost immediately. Sarney initially ruled somewhat timidly and it appeared that he lacked the leadership necessary to move Brazil forward.

Labor unrest was rampant—a strike by a half million truckers, who in early 1986 blocked highways, threatened the food supply of the cities. This was topped by 1985 strikes by 2 million other workers.

Sarney did nothing to lessen governmental corruption which existed for a

Former President and Mrs. Figueiredo

century and grew worse under the military. He spent the nation into virtual bankruptcy but did nothing for the immense number of poor.

Nature was not kind to Brazil in the last quarter–century. A killing frost in the 1970s destroyed millions of coffee trees; as soon as the industry had recovered, a murderous drought killed or stunted the plants, reducing production by 50%. Floods in the northeast and southeast in the 1980s followed by a five–year drought in the northeast left more than a million homeless. In late 1994, killing frosts again hit the coffee trees, resulting in a 100% rise in the price of Brazil's favored *Arabica* coffee. These natural disasters increased migration of unskilled, penniless people to the cities.

Economic Reforms and External Debt

Sarney's only attempt to rid the country of its economic unevenness and chronic programs was "The *Cruzado* Program." Prices were frozen, and wage increases of 20% in many sectors were decreed. Violators of the price freeze not only had to face the law, but vigilante committees. The *cruzeiro* was abolished and the *cruzado* took its place, worth 1,000 units of the former currency. A freeze on government hiring was commenced (in name only) at both the federal and state level. The staggering foreign debt (the largest in the world at $108 billion) was hesitantly rescheduled by the "Paris Club," a group of creditor nations representing commercial and national banks which had loaned money to Brazil. Sarney announced that Brazil would not "pay its foreign debt with recession, nor with unemployment, nor with hunger," but that is precisely

what happened. The IMF, accustomed to inspections of and "recommendations" to debtor nations, was told it had to keep these activities at a minimum in Brazil.

A four–year moratorium was announced on income tax refunds. An ambitious land reform plan, however, had to be watered down to include only a distribution of government–owned acreage. Although the plan had originally included the purchase of sub–marginal producing land, the landowners hired gunmen _in many areas to drive out the peasants who had resettled. "Liberation theology" priests and bishops of the Roman Catholic Church who supported the poor were infuriated and fomented unrest. Pope John Paul II had to remind the National Conference of Brazilian Bishops that the clergy had to stay out of politics, although he, too, supported land reform in Brazil.

Former President José Sarney

Glamorous Rio de Janeiro from the ocean . . .

should have been nationalized. Brazil should have gone even further: allow foreign enterprise to come into the country according to capitalist principles—i.e. the investor keeps the profits, not Brazil.

Fernando Collor de Mello

After five years of economic chaos under Sarney, capped by an inflation rate of 1,700% in 1989, it was inevitable that the 1989 elections would center around the economy. Although 30 candidates entered the fray, three emerged as the frontrunners. Because candidates of the left–wing *PTB* had been so successful in municipal elections during 1988, its leader, Luis Inacio "Lula" da Silva, was initially the front–runnner. Leonel Brizola of the also leftist Democratic Worker's Party was second. Both were quickly outpaced by Fernando Collor de Mello, of the hastily organized, right–of–center National Reconstruction Party *(PRN)*.

This wealthy, handsome, 6'1" governor of poverty–stricken Alagoas State on the central Atlantic Coast, trained as an economist, began his career as a reporter and went on to own a number of media organizations. He contrasted sharply with da Silva, a lathe operator with a sixth-grade education and a bad case of fractured grammar. While governor, Collor had undertaken an energetic program to fire almost half of the bureaucracy, particularly the *maharajas*, in order to bring solvency to the state. His action was reversed by the state Supreme Court. He quickly was able to gain the confidence of the owner of the largest private television network and the battle began. He made a bold promise: economic measures would ensure a 7% annual growth in the economy. If there was anything left over, it would be used to retire foreign debt.

High interest rates were established to discourage the flight of capital from Brazil. Taxes were raised on just about everything, including the purchase of U.S. dollars (25%). Additional taxes were imposed on the purchase of cars, and compulsory "loans" to the government were part of the purchase arrangement. Although there were loud murmurs of discontent from both the wealthy sector and from the labor movement, these sweeping reforms were generally greeted with initial acceptance by a country which had been sapped economically for too many years. But the *maharajas*—persons with low or nonexistent work at government "jobs"—continued in a leech–like fashion to suck the economic blood out of the country.

The *PMDB* and *PFL* increased their majority in the Chamber of Deputies in late 1986 elections to a combined total of 374 out of 487 seats; the largest losses were incurred by the labor-supported *PTB*.

Due to inflation and currency instability, a vigorous black market in just about everything developed in which most consumer goods were bought and sold. Currency reform in 1988 was useless—it was followed by numerous devaluations. A price freeze was tried, and lifted after it failed. Brazil sank into actual bankruptcy; Sarney made it official in early 1987: Brazil would suspend payment of principal and interest on its foreign debt *indefinitely*.

Of course, all international credit instantly ended. The moratorium lasted a year and cost far more than had been gained. Further, the moratorium worsened economic chaos within Brazil to the extent that there was a genuine threat of resumed military control. Western banks responded by extending repayment of existing debt over 20 years and lowered interest rates.

Although heavily indebted, nevertheless Brazil became number 10 of the industrial nations of the world. It developed a lively business in aircraft and armaments worldwide, selling products of good quality and easily repairable. It surpassed Bolivia's tin production and experimented in enriched nuclear fuels, while avowing not to develop weapons. Nevertheless, it insisted on classifying itself as an underdeveloped nation of the "Third World." One observer likened it economically to a "hulking teenager." To this might be added "with a huge allowance, 24-hour use of the family car and little ambition."

Brazil's only hope was to get rid of at least half of the top–heavy government bureaucracy, at least half of the armed forces, punish government and union corruption with heavy penalties and make its currency non–exchangeable with any other currency except through a single, honestly managed central bank. Private banks

66

The campaign was dirty and spirited. Personal attacks were the rule of the day. When the dust settled, Collor had 28.5% of the vote and da Silva 16%. About 17% cast blank ballots (voting is compulsory over the age of 18 in Brazil). After an equally heated runoff, Collor won 43% to da Silva's 38%. He took office on March 15, 1990.

He inherited a Brazil in which *sleaze* had become so much a part of the very culture of the country. The work ethic of government employees (arrive late, if at all, take a long break for lunch and leave early, keeping any activity resembling work at a minimum) had been about as bad as can be imagined. Many jobs were "make work" situations distributed as patronage among relatives.

If the people thought Collor's campaign promises were stiff medicine, they gasped when decrees started to issue from the presidential palace. All banks were closed for three days and all savings accounts were limited to withdrawals of the equivalent of $1,200. Industries were allowed to withdraw only enough to pay *current* salaries; this resulted in wholesale layoffs. Although this initially landed about $88 billion, it quickly dwindled to about $16 billion through corruption. The *cruzeiro* was reconstituted the national currency at a vastly increased value (they could not be printed in advance, lest the consequences of Collor's plans be revealed). Much of Brazil reverted to a barter economy because of currency shortages. But, oddly, 80% of the people stood solidly behind Collor although undergoing personal sacrifices.

The president had vowed to get rid of 360,000 unneeded government workers. He reached the figure of 260,000, but stumbled badly when the Supreme Court overturned him. Civil "servants" had tenure under the constitution and could not be fired. Collor oversaw the sale of 4,675 government limousines, formerly seen idling daily in the cafe district of Brasilia with waiting chauffeurs.

Things began to fall apart in 1992, however. As it later became apparent, Collor was caught up in a four–part storm which had no precedent and hopefully will have no repetition.

First, the unprecedented righteousness he displayed in his election campaign inflamed the passions of his supporters to a degree he never anticipated. Second, his loose-cannon younger brother decided to play to the tabloid media in a series of exposés starting in the spring of 1992 which were sensationalized and reprinted tirelessly by supposedly responsible media sources. They had no concern for truth or honest judgment, but only wished to sell as many newspapers as possible and command as wide an audience as they could on Brazil's TV networks.

Even more shabby, a series romanticizing anti–government teenage fighters replete with oriental karate skills appeared for late spring–early summer fare, inflaming Brazil's youth to an incredible degree. Third, Collor had virtually no support in either house of the legislature, and his cabinet turned out to have the loyalty of hyenas. Finally, he had used about $2.5

. . . seen from Corcovado crowned by Christ the Redeemer, and then to . . .

... the city's dark side where poverty and desperation live side by side in the favelas

month, devaluing the currency to the point that it was virtually worthless. About half the people lived outside the wage economy. The authority of the state disappeared. Murder, which had been frequent, became ordinary. Few people bothered to hire a lawyer and sue—they just hired a hit man. This is done through an elaborate method that usually involves intermediaries and advance scandalous publicity about the soon–to–be victim so that no one will get excited when the plan is carried out. The price: $700 to about $7,000 depending on the station in life of the person killed. As in inner U.S. cities, only a very small number of homicides are "solved" and there are almost no convictions.

The killing of homeless "street children" in Rio and other large cities reached dreadful levels. They are almost all black and have been kicked out of their homes as early as age 6 because there is not enough to feed them. Prostitution at age 8 is common. Shanty towns around the cities (*favelas*) were controlled largely by drug gangs.

An effort was made in November 1994 to assert control by sending the military with armored vehicles into areas close to Rio de Janeiro, which has the third largest slums in Latin America. This was done when it became apparent that innocent people were being frequently killed during police forays in pursuit of drug criminals. The operation lasted a day and a half and when it ended, drug gangs set off firecrackers to announce they were back in business.

The Congress wallowed eyeball deep in its own scandals; with Collor disposed of, the media turned on it, reporting generally at the level of U.S. tabloids. Indifferent to all criticism, it sat only on Wednesdays, if at all. The judiciary and police were openly corrupt.

After wearing out four finance ministers, Franco appointed Fernando Henrique Cardoso in 1994. It was an unlikely choice; Cardoso was a longtime Marxist economist and one of the loudest of the *dependentisas*, who viewed foreign investments as a threat to national identity. His book, *Dependency and Underdevelopment in Latin America*, was the Koran of dependency theorists. When it was published, Cardoso was exiled by the military government. Once in office as finance minister, however, and equipped with power rather than theories, Cardoso underwent a conversion as dramatic as that of St. Paul on the road to Damascus. He pragmatically replaced the inflation–riddled and devaluation–prone *cruzeiro* with a new currency, the *real*, which like Argentina's new currency was pegged to the U.S. dollar. Cardoso also began welcoming foreign investors and dismantling inefficient and costly state–owned utilities and other enterprises. Under Cardoso's guidance,

million in campaign contributions for personal purposes, including the luxurious remodeling of his mansion's back yard in Brasilia. The stage was set for the disgracing of a popular public figure (except in the eyes of political traditionalists).

The attacks by non–Collor–owned media were so vicious that Collor literally did not know what had hit him. The alleged offenses he was charged with were commonplace and overlooked in Brazil for more than a century. But incited particularly by a TV national network, popular demonstrations against Collor became commonplace.

Collor was removed by Congress in 1992, which some felt was like the pot convicting the kettle. He resigned rather than face a televised, months-long trial, but was convicted of "lack of decorum" (whatever that is). Criminal charges were dismissed by the Supreme Court because

of "insufficient evidence," the legal language for a "fix." He benefited from the unwritten Brazilian law that no former political leader is convicted—of anything.

Itamar Franco

Collor's successor, Itamar Franco, was an unintelligent, colorless, temperamental hack who had bubbled to the top of the Brazilian political cauldron. His career was noted for utter silence on anything important and nit–picking on everything of little or no consequence. He showed poor judgment in personal matters while in office, permitting himself to be shown on TV holding hands with and kissing a young pornography actress during the 1994 *Carnaval* celebration.

During most of the 27 months of Franco's tenure, Brazil went from disorganized to chaotic. Inflation neared 40% per inflation plummeted from 2,500% annually to double–digit levels. He became a national hero, an economic David who had slain the Goliath of hyperinflation. In October 1994, Cardoso was the presidential candidate of a coalition of his own Social Democratic Party and Franco's larger *PMDB*. He handily defeated da Silva, the perennial candidate of the left.

In his final months in office, Franco also attempted to deal with Brazil's endemic political corruption, which was yet another impediment to the recovering economy. He created an audit bureau that almost immediately began reducing waste and fraud in the government, saving tens of millions of dollars in questionable expenditures.

The Cardoso Era

Cardoso was inaugurated before an enthusiastic crowd in January 1995, and he has arguably been the most effective democratic president of this century. His economic measures stabilized the *real* and provided real GDP growth that was a steady 3–4% throughout his first term. He also followed through with his privatization program, as billions in foreign investment flowed into the country. At the end of 1997, unemployment was a mere 4.84%.

On the negative side, corruption remained ingrained, resisting attempts to combat it from the top. The problem was spotlighted further in late 1995 when Pelé, the former soccer star who had become a sports minister, declared that politicians were corrupt, that the Congress was full of thieves and that Brazil is a "decadent country."

Pelé also implied that he would like to become Brazil's first black president. About 64 million Brazilians have at least some African blood, but although U.S.-style racial conflict has not been a problem in Brazil, the fact is that most blacks live in poverty, are excluded from the political elite and suffer from low self-esteem. An important political development in 1996 was the election of Celso Pitta as the first black mayor of São Paulo, although his administration, too, would be marred by corruption.

Riding a crest of popularity, Cardoso persuaded Congress in 1997 to amend the constitution to allow him to seek a second term, arguing that no president could successfully deal with the country's prodigious problems in one four–year term. His popularity was only marginally affected by the impact of the Asian market crisis that October that caused him to impose a tough, painful austerity plan to shore up the *real*. Even so, unemployment shot up sharply in January1998.

Former President Franco sought the nomination of the *PMDB* for president in the October 4, 1998 elections. But in March, Franco's party opted to nominate

Former President Itamar Franco

Cardoso; Franco charged later that Cardoso had "bought" the nomination with promises of pork–barrel projects. That left da Silva, again, as his only major opponent.

Cardoso also came under fire in 1998 for alleged inaction in dealing with the fires in Roraima state (see Economy) and insensitivity to the victims of the *El Niño*–related drought in the northeast. The campaign between Cardoso and da Silva took a nasty turn in June when da Silva accused Cardoso of offering to sell off the state–owned communications firm, Telebras, below market value: Cardoso responded by filing a defamation suit against his opponent.

The presidential contest of 1998 was largely a rematch of 1994, with da Silva making his perennial, quixotic run for the post. Early in the year, polls showed Cardoso comfortably ahead, possibly enough to receive the 40% plurality needed to win without a runoff. But by June, da Silva had almost closed the gap, raising the possibility that minor candidates could throw the outcome into a Cardoso–da Silva runoff.

Then, in early September, the world financial jitters, stemming from the previous year's Asian market crisis and uncertainty over the Russian ruble and debt payments, suddenly came crashing down on Brazil. Rumors spread that Brazil would devalue the *real*, which caused a market panic in São Paulo. On one day, the market dropped 13%, and the panic quickly spread to the markets in Argentina, Mexico, Venezuela and Colombia; shock waves also were felt in New York, Europe and Asia. To defend the *real*, the government began selling off its reserves of dollars; in September alone, dollar reserves dropped by $30 billion. Interest rates were drastically raised, from 29.75% to 49.75%. On September 25, Cardoso

boldly reacted to the crisis by pledging an austerity program to reduce the huge budget deficit, a move sure to reassure the IMF and nervous foreign investors, but highly risky for a politician just nine days away from an election.

Yet, on October 4, voters gave their president a resounding mandate to continue for another four years. Cardoso crushed da Silva 53% to 32%. He reiterated his determination to impose an austerity program, but put off the details until the crucial governor's races on October 25. The outcome of those races tempered Cardoso's elation over his presidential landslide. A friend and ally, Mario Covas, was reelected in São Paulo, but two leftists were elected in Rio de Janeiro and Rio Grande do Sul. More ominous for Cardoso, former President Franco, Cardoso's erstwhile boss and now a bitter enemy, was elected governor of Minas Gerais.

Days later, Cardoso announced a $23.5 billion austerity plan of tax increases and spending cuts. On December 23, nine days before his inauguration, Cardoso announced his selection of a cabinet, which was little changed from the existing one except for the creation of a new development ministry, which was given an annual budget of $20 billion.

The 1999 Economic Crisis

Cardoso was inaugurated for his second term on January 1, 1999; the same day, Franco was inaugurated as governor of Minas Gerais. Cardoso's austerity plan seemed to have quieted the fears of foreign investors and lending institutions.

President Fernando Henrique Cardoso

The slide of the *real* had stopped, and it was still pegged to the dollar; sanity had returned to the stock market, and inflation had remained under control. Suddenly, the willful Franco, known to be consumed with jealousy against Cardoso because his former minion had received all the credit for rescuing Brazil from economic chaos, decided to toss a boulder into this tranquil pond and precipitated a financial crisis with global repercussions. On January 6, Franco announced a 90–day moratorium on the payment of his state's $13.5 billion debt, triggering another market panic that far surpassed the one in September. Wall Street responded negatively to the crisis, as did other markets around the world. International condemnation was heaped upon Franco, who seemed to relish the attention. It was to backfire on him, however; the World Bank froze $209 million in development loans for Minas Gerais.

This time, the central government could not keep propping up the *real* by selling dollars. On January 15, the government was forced to abandon the five–year–old *Real* Plan—which Franco and Cardoso had introduced together—and announced that the *real* would be allowed to float against foreign currencies. The reaction was immediate; at one point, the *real* plummeted 46% in value, before beginning a slow climb. The devaluation raised the specter of renewed inflation. On the other hand, it pleased manufacturers by making Brazilian exports more attractive.

The crisis continued for two months, as Brazil slid into a recession. By March, however, international fears that the Brazilian economy, burdened by the huge budget deficit, would collapse proved unfounded. Cardoso's painful austerity measures dragged down his approval rating in the polls, especially as unemployment remained stubbornly high.

When Cardoso presented his budget in August 1999, he predicted that the economy would show a 1% decline for 1999 but would record a 4% growth rate in 2000, with 8.5 million new jobs. The old economic wizard proved close to the mark: the economy shrank by .4% in 1999, not as bad as he had predicted, and grew by 2.6% in 2000. In April 2000, Brazil paid off the last of the $41.5 billion of the international loan package the IMF and other institutions had advanced during the January 1999 market panic. Clearly, the economy was back on track.

There was a significant governmental restructuring in 1999 that had historic overtones. Cardoso created a new defense ministry, consolidating the three armed services and placing them under a civilian minister for the first time. The three chiefs of the uniformed services simultaneously were removed from the cabinet. Cardoso reportedly intended for the change to show how far the country had emerged from the 1964–85 dictatorship.

Dancing in the streets . . . then after Carnaval

But a scandal erupted when Cardoso was forced to fire the new defense minister, Elcio Alvares, for demurring over firing his chief of staff and longtime friend, who had been linked to drug trafficking. Cardoso then named Attorney General Geraldo Magela Quintao to replace Alvares.

On April 22, 2000, Brazil observed the 500th anniversary of the landing of Portuguese sailor Pedro Alvares Cabral in Brazil in 1500. But what Cardoso had intented as a major celebration of Brazilian national identity and unity turned into an ugly spectacle when nearly 200 Indian tribes protested the event as an insult to their own cultural identity. They had a point; there were 5 million indigenous inhabitants when Cabral landed, but there are only 330,000 today. One of their banners asked a logical question: "Who says Brazil was discovered?" The Indians were soon joined by some African Brazilians, who said that to celebrate the Portuguese arrival was to celebrate the legacy of slavery. About 3,000 Indians descended on the town of Porto Seguro, near Cabral's landfall, to stage a "countercomemoration." Five thousand policemen were called out to discourage disruption of the planned celebration. Cardoso patiently acknowledged the Indians' right to protest, but warned against violence. Still, the police

and the Indians inevitably clashed. The police used clubs and tear gas to break up the demonstration, and 140 Indians were arrested. Cardoso cut short his appearance in Porto Seguro, his carefully planned party in ruins.

On the heels of the protests against the 500th anniversary celebrations came an even more violent confrontation in early May between authorities and landless peasants who squatted on unused lands and even forcibly occupied government buildings in Brasilia. About 30,000 peasants of the Landless Rural Workers Movement, or *MST*, took part in the protests, which left one peasant dead and 47 injured in clashes with security forces. Cardoso organized a special police force to deal with illegal squatters, but at the same time he acceded to some of the their demands, agreeing to parcel out 5 million more acres of land to the peasants in addition to the 40 million acres that already had been distributed during his administration.

Brazilian voters went to the polls on October 1 and 29, 2000, to elect mayors and councilmen in more than 5,500 municipalities, a closely watched quadrennial bellwether of the public mood midway between presidential elections. For the first time, reelection was permitted. If there was a clear victor, it was da Silva's

Workers Party *(PT)*, which increased its share of the popular vote from 10.6% in 1996 to 14.1% and the number of mayors from 112 to 174. In the 31 cities holding runoffs on October 29, the *PT* won 13 of the 16 that it contested. None created more excitement than the landslide victory in São Paulo of Marta Suplicy, 55, a former television sex psychologist in the 1980s who later served in Congress. Her husband, Eduardo, a member of the city's elite, is currently a federal senator, also from the *PT*. She is popular with housewives because of her frank talk about sex and abortion and with homosexuals because of her advocacy of gay rights. She received nearly 59% of the vote against veteran former mayor and governor Paulo Maluf of the conservative Brazilian Progressive Party. She was aided greatly by the rampant corruption that had occurred during the administration of the incumbent, Celso Pitta, who was so tarnished that he chose not to stand for reelection. The *PT* also retained the mayoralty of Porto Alegre and won control of Goiania and Recife. In Rio de Janeiro, Cesar Maia of the Brazilian Labor Party scored an upset victory over incumbent Luis Paulo Conde of the conservative Liberal Front Party *(PFL)* with 51%. Overall, however, the *PFL*, one of the four parties in Cardoso's governing coalition, strengthened its holdings of mayors from 962 to 1,027. Another coalition party, the *PMDB*, dropped from 1,323 to 1,253. Despite the impressive showing of the left-wing opposition, coalition parties still control a preponderance of local governments.

During the first half of 2001, Cardoso's political troubles came not from the opposition but from what can only be called a congressional foodfight within his coalition that left stains on the coalition's reputation.

What eventually resulted in an ungluing of the coalition began in February with the elections of the presiding officers of the Senate and the Chamber of Deputies. The powerful and influential Senate president, Antonio Carlos Magalhaes of the *PFL*, desperately sought to block the election of his arch-rival, Jader Barbalho of the *PMDB*, as his successor. Each accused the other of various corrupt acts, even publishing books that specified the wrongdoing. Barbalho won, and Magalhaes' chosen candidate for speaker of the Chamber of Deputies lost to Aecio Neves of Cardoso's own *PSDB*. Apparently miffed that Cardoso had done nothing to block Barbalho's election, Magalhaes publicly alleged high-level corruption in the executive branch. Days later, Cardoso sacked two *PFL* ministers for alleged disloyalty. This further infuriated Magalhaes, who then accused Cardoso of harboring corrupt officials in the executive branch. The exchange of accusations within the governing coalition delighted the opposi-

tion *PT*, which called for a full congressional investigation.

For two months, Cardoso urged Congress against embroiling itself in an investigation that would delay his own economic reform measures. He sought to allay congressional and public demands by firing more officials and appointing a federal inspector general. Just as it seemed Cardoso would prevail, two separate scandals unfolded in April that ultimately would bring down both Magalhaes and Barbalho. First, a news magazine reported leaked tapes that supported Magalhaes' allegation that Barbalho had enriched himself with funds earmarked for *SUDAM*, an Amazon development agency, while he had served as governor of Para state. A newly appointed *SUDAM* director fueled the scandal with the revelation that $820 million was unaccounted for. Barbalho found himself testifying before the Senate ethics committee to explain how he managed to enjoy his affluent lifestyle on a public official's salary. In May, Cardoso abolished the agency.

But Magalhaes could not savor his triumph over his hated rival for long. In April 2001, a Senate report alleged that he and floor leader Jose Roberto Arruda had accessed a list showing how senators had voted on the expulsion of Senator Luiz Estevão in June 2000 for misconduct. Senate votes are secret, and rules violations are grounds for expulsion. Both Magalhaes and Arruda vehemently denied the report,

but irrefutable evidence surfaced against them. On April 19, Arruda resigned as floor leader, and four days later made a tearful public confession that he had accessed the list. In May, both Magalhaes and Arruda resigned their Senate seats. The executive branch, meanwhile, was engaged in an aggressive in-house investigation in order to mollify the Congress. During this tawdry affair, Cardoso's approval rating in the polls dipped to 26% in March at the height of scandal, but at mid-year an improving economy had raised it back to the mid-30s—still well below the 50% following his reelection. His political position was bolstered in September when one of his allies within the *PMDB*, Michael Temer, won the party's presidency

Recent Developments

In June 2001, new charges surfaced in the press against Barbalho, who allegedly was involved in the sale of $4 million in government notes in 1988 while he was agrarian reform minister. In September, he resigned as Senate president, and in October, he resigned from the body altogether. Cardoso's minister of national integration, Ramez Tebet, was elected to succeed Barbalho as Senate president. In February 2002, Barbalho was formally arrested and jailed, precipitating the breakup of the governing coalition and derailing the candidacy of a promising presidential candidate. What happened?

The Cathedral, Brasilia

Fishing in the waters of the mighty Amazon River near Manaus

By the end of 2001, da Silva had declared his fourth candidacy for the presidency, and this time the polls consistently showed him in the lead against a field of lesser known candidates with about a third of the votes. Among those candidates were Health Minister Jose Serra, 60, of the *PSDB* and Cardoso's acknowledged choice as his successor; Rio de Janeiro State Governor Anthony Garotinho of the Brazilian Socialist Party, 41, a mellowed Marxist and a former agnostic who became an evangelical Presbyterian after surviving an automobile accident; Ciro Gomes, of the moderate-left Popular Socialist Party; former President Itamar Franco of the *PMDB*, now governor of Minas Gerais but still a pariah; and Maranhão State Governor Roseana Sarney, 46, daughter of former President Jose Sarney of the *PFL*, then still part of the governing coalition. At year's end, Sarney's candidacy was clearly on the ascendancy, edging into second place for the runoff spot; by January 2002 polls showed her with 25%, just two points behind da Silva. But then, as often happens in Brazilian politics, everything suddenly came unraveled.

Two weeks after Barbalho's arrest in February 2002, as part of the on-going investigation into the *SUDAM* scandal, police raided the office of a company owned by Sarney's husband, Jorge Murad, who also served as her state planning minister, and discovered 1.34 million *reais* ($570,000) in cash. Murad made several feeble and contradictory attempts to explain the source of the money, finally confessing that it was money he had raised illegally for his wife's presidential

campaign; under the law, candidates cannot start raising money until the June before the election. Sarney's standing in the polls began dropping like mercury after a cold front, and in March she withdrew from the race. Bitterly, she accused Cardoso of staging the raid to damage her candidacy and to aid Serra's. Her brother, Jose Jr., resigned as Cardoso's environment minister, and two other *PFL* cabinet ministers also resigned in protest; the four-year-old coalition officially was no more. Cardoso denied complicity in the raid, noting that it had been carried out by state police, but there is no question that Serra was the chief beneficiary of Sarney's withdrawal.

Serra moved for a time into the undisputed second-place spot for the October 6 election, and he received a boost on June 15 when the *PMDB* endorsed him. At that point, da Silva still had a daunting lead of 40% to 23%. Garotinho was third and Gomes was fourth, both scoring in the teens. But two polls published in July as this book was going to press showed Serra was in trouble. A Vox Populi poll gave da Silva 39% while a Datafolha poll gave him 40%. The Vox Populi poll showed Serra had slipped since its last survey from 21% to 17%, while Datafolha showed him falling from 21% to 20%. But the most stunning finding was that Vox Populi showed Gomes eclipsing Serra, moving up from 16% to 18%. Datafolha also showed Gomes with 18%, a gain of seven points. With the two polls' margins of error, Serra and Gomes were in a statistical dead heat to make the runoff, although Gomes seems to be the one with the momentum. Garotinho increased from 11% to 12% in the Vox Populi poll but dropped from 16% to 13% in the Datafolha poll.

Prospects of a da Silva victory have sent a chill through international financial markets, prompting the candidate and his party to engage in some frantic public relations maneuvering. The *PT* pointed to the sound fiscal records of the states and municipalities under its control, and da Silva pledged to continue Cardoso's rational policies and to continue servicing the $274 billion debt; he even began wearing suits and ties at his campaign appearances! Moreover, in a bold shift toward the political center, the *PT* entered into an alliance with the center-right Liberal Party on June 19, and da Silva named Jose Alencar, a Liberal senator, as his running mate. It was a masterful, if unlikely, political stroke; the *PT* already has close ties with the progressive wing of the Catholic Church, while the Liberal Party draws support from the Universal Church of the Kingdom of God, a large evangelical congregation that controls a television network and claims an estimated 4 million followers. Nonetheless, two days later market jitters caused the *real* to drop to its second-worst showing ever of 2.84 against

the dollar, leading da Silva to state that he may appoint people from outside the party as finance minister and central bank president.

The Congress was occupied with other matters besides the Magalhaes-Barbalho affair in 2001 and 2002. In August 2001, Congress approved a long-debated revision to the country's archaic 1916 civil code. The revised code legitimizes the civil status of people born out of wedlock, lowers the age of majority for marrying or signing contracts from 21 to 18, and eliminates the preferential legal status of men over women. Previously, for example, a man could annul his marriage if he discovered his bride was not a virgin. Under the new code, neither spouse can go into debt without the consent of the other, and divorced fathers have equal custody rights with mothers. In May 2002, Cardoso endorsed a bill before Congress that would legalize homosexual unions, a move that probably was politically motivated to steal some thunder from da Silva's *PT*, which has long advocated gay rights.

Brazil's alarming crime problem, and the methods being used to deal with it, have remained in the international spotlight. Reports of extrajudicial executions of criminal suspects, especially youths in the country's squalid *favelas*, are commonplace. In October, the London-based human rights group Amnesty International issued a report alleging that torture was still a widespread practice by Brazilian security forces nearly two decades after the end of military rule. Yet, so desperate are Brazilians for a solution to a crime problem that has them living in abject fear for their persons and properties, that they tend to turn a blind eye to such abuses. They were reminded again of the evil nature of the problem in early June 2002 when Tim Lopes, an award-winning investigative reporter for the Globo network, was murdered while conducting an undercover investigation into sex abuse and drug use in a Rio de Janeiro *favela*. His burned and desecrated corpse was found in a cave. The killing outraged the country. Four people were arrested, and a drug lord believed responsible for Lopes' death was in hiding.

Culture: Brazil is culturally unique among the Latin American republics, with its mix of Portuguese and African accents in religion, music, architecture and food. There was little interplay between the invading Portuguese colonizers and the indigenous Indians, and what scattered tribes remain are isolated and unassimilated in the vast interior Amazon rain forest. It was the influx of African slaves that shaped modern Brazil's ethnic and cultural composition.

It can be argued that Brazilian culture today is tripartite. In the far southern temperate zone, characterized by wheat farming, cattle ranching and coffee production, the population is predominantly Caucasian, a cross–current of European immigration. As in Argentina, the cattle culture produced a distinct sub–culture with a meat–based diet. The Brazilian equivalent of the Argentine *asado* is the *churrasco*, a variety of grilled meats and sausages. This region is the home of Brazil's national dish, *feijoada*, a culinary orgy traditionally served on Wednesdays and Saturdays and consisting of various meats and sausages, black beans *(feijão)*, rice, greens and orange slices.

In the northeast, on the "hump" of Brazil, the population is predominantly black and the culture has its roots in Africa, a mere 1,000 miles across the Atlantic. Despite the ostensible dominance of the Roman Catholic Church in Brazil, blacks still practice *macumba*, a voodoo–like tribal religion based on black magic. In this equatorial climate, there is little cattle ranching, and the diet is based more on seafood and the universal Brazilian staples, black beans and rice. The Bahian style of cooking is characterized by stewing fish, shellfish or chicken in dende oil, derived from a palm nut, and coconut milk. Perhaps the region's greatest contribution to Brazilian culture, however, is its music. Here is where the samba was born, and like Argentina's tango it began in the slums and won mainstream acceptance and an international following.

The third element of Brazilian culture is in the cosmopolitan and industrial urban centers, chiefly Rio de Janeiro and São Paulo, where the other two cultures converge. Here, Catholicism and *macumba* have intertwined to give the world one of its most distinctive cultural offerings: *Carnaval*, the Brazilian version of *Mardi Gras*, the great explosion of revelry and hedonism before the onset of the somber season of Lent.

One of Brazil's great anomalies, however, is that although racial tolerance has been practiced for generations and intermarriage between whites and blacks is relatively commonplace, the country's social elite and its political power structure remain virtually entirely Caucasian, while blacks still occupy a disproportionate share of the bottommost rung of Brazil's social and economic ladder.

While the Portuguese influence is most keenly felt in Brazil's architecture and literature, the African contribution has been greatest to Brazilian folklore, art and music. Moreover, there was considerable French influence during the immediate post–independence period. During the reign of Emperor Dom Pedro I (1825–31), the French–founded Royal School of Science, Arts and Crafts was incorporated into the Academy of Fine Arts. French influence on Brazilian art was especially strong.

Nineteenth century Brazilian literature also was influenced by French naturalism. The two leading Brazilian representatives of this style were Aluísio de Azevedo, author of the novels *Ó mulato* and *O Cortico (The Slum);* and the mulatto novelist, poet, playwright and story writer Joaquim Maria Machado de Assis. In the early 20th century were published two novels that remain classics of Brazilian—and Latin American—literature: *Os sertões*, by Euclides da Cunha, and *Canaã*, by Jose Pereira de Graça Aranha, for whom one of Brazil's modern literature prizes is named.

Arguably the country's most internationally renowned writer of the 20th century was Jorge Amado, born in 1912, whose novels *Terra do sem fin, Dona Flor e seus dois maridos* and *Gabriela, cravo e canela,* have been translated and marketed worldwide. His death on August 6, 2001, four days before his 89th birthday, was a cause for national mourning, and his passing was noted around the world. Other noteworthy contemporary writers include the poet and essayist Carlos Drummond de Andrade and playwright Nelson Rodrigues.

In music, the samba and other styles of African origin bridge the gap between folk and popular. Brazilian composers whose works incorporated Brazilian folk styles include Claudio Santoro and Heitor Villa–Lobos. Brazilian popular music, or *MPB* as it is called in the press, is a major domestic industry. Perhaps the best known abroad were Sergio Mendes, whose group Brasil 66 was especially popular in the United States in the 1960s, and Antonio Carlos Jobim, who wrote "The Girl from Ipanema" and "The One–Note Samba." Brazilian pop singers whose popularity spread throughout Latin America included Roberto Carlos and the late Elis Regina.

Internationally known Brazilian artists included Waldemar Cordeiro, sculptor Mario Carvo Jr., and the naturalist painter Candido Portinari. In the field of architecture Brazil boasts the internationally famous Oscar Niemeyer, whose most enduring creation is Brazil's futuristic capital city, Brasilia, constructed in the 1950s during the presidency of Juscelino Kubitschek.

The Brazilian film industry, one of the region's oldest, received an impetus in the 1960s and 1970s through the creative genius of director Glauber Rocha and his *Cinema Novo* movement. Brazilian films, long exported to other Latin American countries and to Portugal, have won increasing critical acclaim elsewhere. Two outstanding examples are the comedy *Dona Flor e seus dois maridos*, adapted from the Jorge Amado novel, and *Peixote*, a dark film about the lives of Brazil's street children, which won actress Marilia Pera the New York Film Critics' Award for best actress in 1982.

After that, Brazilian cinematic creativity went into a slump that lasted nearly a decade. After the state-owned firm *Embrafilme* was abolished in 1990, ending government subsidies, only a handful of films was produced each year in the 1990s and only 1% of the films shown in Brazil were domestically produced, compared with 40% during the era of *Cinema Novo*. But in the late 1990s, a new law allowed film companies a tax write-off if they invested up to 3% in new films. The incentive helped spark a revival. Thirty films were produced in 2000, and Brazil has seen a new generation of directors achieve international acclaim. For example, *O Quatrilho*, a story about Italian immigrants to Brazil directed by Fabio Barreto, and *O Que E Isso Companeiro*, whose English title is *Four Days in September,* the true story of the kidnapping of a U.S. ambassador directed by Barreto's brother, Bruno, were nominated for Oscars in 1996 and 1998. In 1999, *Central do Brasil (Central Station)*, a story of an elderly woman who befriends an orphan boy directed by Walter Salles, was nominated for Best Foreign Film and its star, Fernanda Montenegro, was nominated for Best Actress. *Eu, Tu, Eles* (Me, You, Them), a true story of polygamy in the Brazilian outback directed by Andrucha Waddington, received widespread acclaim at the 2001 Cannes Film Festival and won prizes at festivals in Cuba and the Czech Republic.

Brazilian radio and television developed along U.S. lines, though in its early days Brazilian television depended heavily on U.S. imports. That has changed, and Brazil now exports its translated *telenovelas* throughout Latin America. The mammoth Globo Network, with 75 million viewers, claims the largest audience of any network in the world.

Educational reform was late in coming to Brazil, and it lags behind some of its neighbors in literacy and newspaper readership per 1,000 people. For decades Brazil's most respected daily has been *O Estado de São Paulo*, owned by the Mesquita family, which resisted the press controls imposed by both Getulio Vargas and the military regimes of 1964–85. Rio's two elite newspapers are *Jornal do Brasil,* founded in 1891, and the circulation leader, *O Globo,* which also owns the like–named television network. Numerous tabloid newspapers boast large circulations throughout the country. There are several high–quality magazines, including *Manchete, Veja* and *Isto É.*

Economy: Occupying half the continent, Brazil has immense natural wealth, including a diverse agricultural sector in which tropical and subtropical products flourish. A significant cattle industry in the south provides meat for domestic consumption and leather for export. With the exception of petroleum, the country also has been blessed with mineral wealth, including gold, iron, manganese, chromium and tin. Brazil also is the world's third–leading producer of bauxite, the raw material from which aluminum is refined. Manufacturing began early in the 20th century, but domestic industry, protected from imports by high tariffs, failed to match that of neighboring Argentina. Like many Latin American countries, Brazil adopted a quasi–socialist mixed economic system characterized by public sector control of utilities and transportation. Brazil's economic growth has long been hamstrung by one of the world's highest birthrates, which largely accounts for the high percentage of people living below the poverty line.

The military governments that ruled the country from 1964–1985 reversed policy in the late 1960s by inviting foreign investors into Brazil, offering attractive tax incentives. The resulting capitalization led to a boom that international economists referred to as the "Brazilian economic miracle." Foreign automobile manufacturers put Brazil on wheels, and Volkswagen remains the country's largest manufacturer today. An aggressive effort was made to increase nontraditional exports, including automobiles, tractors, military vehicles, weapons, aircraft and shoes. In 1967 the government declared the port of Manaus near the mouth of the Amazon a free–trade zone, which still produces about $10 billion worth of goods, mostly consumer items for export.

The miracle abruptly halted in 1974–75 because of a dual blow. The first was OPEC's quadrupling of petroleum prices, which sparked a worldwide recession that was felt especially keenly in Brazil, which imported 90% of its oil. The second blow was a devastating frost in the south that virtually destroyed Brazil's coffee crop, still the leading export item. The military

rulers sought a two–fold solution. Because coffee trees require seven years to produce marketable beans, farmers were encouraged to replant much of the destroyed coffee acreage with soybeans, an annual crop that provided immediate export earnings. The second was to begin manufacturing automobiles designed to burn pure alcohol, distilled from domestically grown sugar cane. Exploitation of newly discovered offshore oil deposits also helped ease Brazil's dependence on foreign oil, and with the drop in petroleum prices in the mid–1980s, alcohol became more expensive than gasoline.

As in neighboring Argentina, efforts by the military to deal with the recession sparked hyperinflation, which continued into the post–military period. Inflation peaked in 1994, when then–Finance Minister Cardoso implemented the "Real Plan," named for the new currency unit. Inflation dropped to double–digit, then single–digit levels by 1997, when the Asian economic crisis forced President Cardoso to adopt a drastic austerity plan that included a 40% increase in interest rates and $18 billion worth of public savings, paid for through a combination of spending cuts and tax increases. Still, unemployment in January 1998 jumped to 7.25%, the highest in 13 years. In order to further shore up the *real* and prevent a flight of foreign capital, Cardoso urged congress to streamline the civil service and make social security cuts, which sparked violent protests in the capital.

Despite the economic advances of recent years, however, Brazil's economy remains perhaps the least equitable of any industrialized country. According to a U.S. State Department report issued in January 1998, the top 10% of Brazil's 163 million people account for 48% of the income, while the bottom 10% make only 1%. An estimated 17% of the work force

earns less than the minimum wage of $105 a month. This situation is not likely to improve markedly until some effort is made to keep Brazil's burgeoning birthrate lower than the ability of the economy to absorb new workers, but producing babies is an inherent part of the male–oriented culture.

On a positive note, Brazil's Congress seemed willing to take action to deal with a problem that had brought Brazil international condemnation for more than a decade: the destruction of the Amazon rain forest. In its zeal to foster growth, a succession of Brazilian presidents, both military and civilian, had given agricultural development of the vast, virgin Amazon Basin a high priority. Developers were given *carte blanche* to use slash–and–burn methods to cut away trees to make room for cultivation, despite protests by national and international ecologists that the destruction of the rain forest could have a global impact. The clearing of vast areas of oxygen–producing trees, they argued, would further contribute to the worldwide buildup of greenhouse gases and contribute to global warming. One Brazilian environmental activist was murdered in the 1980s for his high–profile efforts to save the forest, while president after president ignored the issue in the name of economic development. But in an encouraging about face, the Cardoso government acknowledged in January 1998 that deforestation had reached a peak in 1995 of 11,621 square miles, double the 5,958 square miles cleared in 1994. The rate in 1996 was down to 7,200 square miles, and an estimated 5,200 in 1997. Since 1978, the report said, 200,000 square miles, or one eighth of the forest, had been lost. Days later, Congress approved legislation giving the federal environmental agency legal power to enforce environmental protection laws and providing criminal penalties for violators. Ironically, the law was no sooner on the books when a devastating fire in Roraima state, exacerbated by an *El Niño*–related drought, burned out of control for weeks, destroying the forest at a pace even more rapid than man had.

The Brazilian market collapse of September 1998 is reflected in the figures for real GDP growth: 2.8% in 1996, 3.2% in 1997, only .7% in 1998—and that was before the market meltdown of January 1999. Unemployment has risen steadily over the same period: 5.4% in 1996, 6.0% in 1997 and 8.0% at the end of 1998. The economic malaise has at least had one positive effect: inflation was only 2.0% in 1998, down from 4.3% in 1997 and 9.1% in 1996.

By mid-2000, there were clear signs that Brazil had weathered the crisis. It finished 1999 with a slight GDP growth of about 1%, which was far better than the predictions of deep recession. The growth rate

A rural church in Curitiba

WORLD BANK Photo

for 2000 was an encouraging 4.5%, but in 2001 in dropped back to 3%, barely enough to keep up with the growth in the workforce. In the first quarter of 2002, it was back up to 4%.

The *real* also appears to have stabilized, though it experienced dramatic fluctuations in the first half of 2001. Its fall against the dollar in March 2001—the lowest since the 1999 market crisis—nonetheless proved a boon for Brazilian exporters. As another positive indicator, the Central Bank announced in April 2000 that it was repaying $10.5 billion of the $41.5 billion emergency loan package the IMF had extended in 1999 to rescue the economy, bringing to $18.2 billion the amount that had been repaid.

Unemployment has remained stubbornly high at 8% in 1999, 7.9% in 2000 and 8% in 2001 and the first quarter of 2002, although urban unemployment still was only half that of neighboring Argentina. Inflation, meanwhile, has moderated from 5.9% in 2000 to 4% in 2001.

President Cardoso hosted the *Mercosur* summit in Rio de Janeiro in May 2000 and created a stir by suggesting the trade bloc could adopt a common currency, as the European Union had done, possibly within five years. But just two days later Cardoso's own finance minister threw cold water on the idea, saying it would take much longer.

Cardoso met with new U.S. President George W. Bush at the White House in late March 2001. Both men are enthusiastic free-trade advocates, and Bush proposed a U.S.-Brazilian free-trade pact, but a skeptical Cardoso questioned Bush's sincerity by pointing out protectionist U.S. anti-dumping measures aimed at Brazilian steel and produce. Cardoso repeated his criticism at the Summit of the Americas in Quebec in April. The steel dispute worsened in March 2002 when Bush, yielding to demands from domestic steelmakers, imposed a 30% tariff on most steel imports. In June, Brazil protested the U.S. tariff before the World Trade Organization.

Periodic drought in 2000 and 2001 led to an acute power shortage as the nation's hydroelectric dams became unable to meet national demand. The energy crisis, very similar to that then facing the state of California, led President Cardoso to impose power rationing that included mandatory blackouts of up to four hours per day beginning June 1, 2001. The goal was to cut electricity usage by 20% the first month. The rationing was lifted in September 2001, after rains began refilling the lakes, although some states were still plagued by power shortages. To cope with the crisis, the Cardoso government announced a short-term plan to build 55 new thermoelectric plants by 2003 to provide 21,000 megawatts and a long-term plan for eight new hydroelectric plants over seven years. The crisis was becoming a political issue as the 2002 presidential election campaign got underway. The energy crunch probably was a factor that slowed economic growth in 2001.

Brazil's unusually high population growth of 1.3% annually, coupled with the economic slowdown of 1999-2001, led to a dramatic drop in per capita GDP, from $3,600 in 2000 to $3,100 in 2001. In the first half of 2002 it had regained some of the ground it lost, but was still only $3,300.

By June 2002, polls showing former the socialist union leader Luiz Inacio Lula da Silva with a strong lead for the October 6 presidential election led to concerns among international lenders and investors that as president da Silva could default on payments of Brazil's huge $274 billion debt. Despite assurances by the candidate that he had abandoned his erstwhile Marxist thinking (as had Cardoso before him), the jitters continued, affecting Brazil's bond rating. In response, the Cardoso government announced it would draw down $10 billion from an IMF loan to stabilize the markets and reassure foreign investors. On June 20, U.S. Treasury Secretary Paul O'Neill made an injudicious comment, saying Brazil's problems were more political than economic and questioning the wisdom of U.S. aid to stabilize the economy. The next day, the

real to dropped to 2.84 against the dollar, its second-worst showing on record; O'Neill hastily retracted his comment the following day and insisted he believed the Cardoso government was "implementing the right economic policies."

The Future: President Cardoso is approaching the end of his two four-year terms, and there seems to be a dearth of candidates of his stature to replace him. As this book was going to press, it appeared a foregone conclusion that the perennial candidate of the now-center-left Workers Party *(PT)*, Luiz Inacio Lula da Silva, would finish first in the October 6 presidential election. But who will be his runoff opponent, and which of them will win? For months it appeared that runoff opponent would be Cardoso's handpicked favorite, his former health minister, Jose Serra. But polls in July show Celso Gomes of the Popular Socialist Party forging into a strong second-place showing and that Gomes would be much more difficult for da Silva to defeat than Serra would be. In fact, da Silva and Gomes were in a statistical tie.

The unknown variable may well be the center-right Liberal Front Party *(PFL)* of Maranhão Governor Roseana Sarney, who was forced from the presidential race in March 2002 by a campaign finance scandal; the *PFL* withdrew from Cardoso's four-party governing coalition as a result (see History). What will the 25% of the voters who once indicated they would vote for her do on October 6? With the vicissitudes of Brazilian politics being what they are, it is anybody's guess.

In short, anything could happen by October 6. After the topsy-turvy course the presidential campaign has taken in the past year, this author is not about to make any predictions, and certainly no bets.

But a much larger question than who will win on October 6 is, will whoever win prove as able a president as Cardoso? Brazil is famed as a shoe-manufacturing country, but Cardoso's shoes are going to prove extremely difficult to fill.

The Republic of Chile

La Moneda, Santiago

Area: 286,322 square miles.

Population: 13.6 million (estimated).

Capital City: Santiago (Pop. 5.1 million, estimated).

Climate: Northern coastal lowlands are very hot and dry; the central valley is warm and dry from October through April and mild and damp through September; the southern regions are wet and cold.

Neighboring Countries: Peru (Northwest); Bolivia (Northeast); Argentina (East);

Official Language: Spanish

Other Principal Tongues: German, Quechua and Araucanian.

Ethnic Background: The majority are *mestizo* (mixed European and Indian).

Principal Religion: Roman Catholic Christianity.

Chief Commercial Products: Copper, nitrates, iron, steel, foodstuffs, processed fish, agricultural products.

Currency: Peso.

Gross Domestic Product: U.S. $74.123 billion in 2001 ($4,873 per capita).

Former Colonial Status: Spanish Crown Colony (1541–1818).

Independence Day: September 18, 1810.

Chief of State: Ricardo Lagos, President (since March 11, 2000).

National Flag: White, blue and red, with a white star in the blue stripe.

Chile, which has a name derived from an old Indian word meaning "land's end," sixth in size among the South American countries, is a strip of land 2,600 miles long and averaging 110 miles wide, lying between the Andes and the Pacific Ocean. Nearly one–half of this territory is occupied by the Andes Mountains and a coastal range of peaks. Because of its north–south length, Chile has a wide range of soils and climates; the country's frontier with Peru runs from Arica on the Pacific coast east to the crest of the Andes. The frontier with Bolivia and Argentina follows the crest of the Andes—18,000 feet high in the north, rising to 23,000 feet in the center and dropping to 13,000 feet in the south. The coastal range runs from the north to deep south, dropping abruptly into the sea with few ports. The heartland of Chile is the central valley between the two ranges.

Chile is divided into five natural regions. The northern, extending 600 miles south from the Peruvian border to Copiapo, is one of the driest regions of the world. Here are found rich nitrate deposits and major copper mines for which Chile has been famous. From Copiapo 400 miles south to Illapel, there is a semi–arid region; however, there is sufficient rainfall to permit the raising of crops in the val-

leys. Chile's iron ore is found in this region. From Illapel 500 miles south to Concepción is the fertile area of the lush, green central valley. With adequate rainfall in the winter (May to August) the valley is intensively cultivated. Here also are the three principal cities and the major portion of the population. From Concepción to Puerto Montt there is a forest region, with large, sparkling lakes and rivers where rainfall is oppressively heavy during the fall and winter. The fifth and last zone stretches south 1,000 miles from Puerto Montt. This is an almost uninhabited wild region of cold mountains, glaciers and small islands. Rainfall is torrential and the climate stormy, wet and chilling.

History: Prior to the arrival of the Spaniards, Chile was the home from time immemorial of the Araucanian Indians, a loosely grouped civilization of primitive people who were completely isolated from the rest of mankind.

In the early 15th century, the Incas pushed across the desert and conquered the northern half of the fertile valley where present–day Santiago is located; however, they were unable to penetrate south of the river Maule. The Spaniards later occupied the area held by the Indians and founded Santiago in 1541, but their efforts to extend their holdings further south were fiercely and successfully resisted by the Araucanians. About a century later, the Indians entered into a treaty with the Spanish to retain the land south of Concepción. Despite the treaty, war continued between the Araucanians and their would–be conquerors until late in the 19th century.

During the conquest, the land was divided into great estates among the army officers; soldiers and settlers married Araucanian women captives, producing a *mestizo* population with qualities of both conquerors and the conquered. The colonial period was one of savage warfare and internal dissension. Particularly sharp were clashes between landowners and the clergy over the practice of holding Indians in slavery. During the 17th century, slavery was replaced by a system of sharecropping which only recently has abated.

To the wars and dissensions which marked Chile's history must be added a long list of natural disasters. Earthquakes and tidal waves have repeatedly destroyed its cities. An additional difficulty was presented by the fact that from the end of the 16th century until independence in 1817, Chile's coasts were infested with British and French pirates.

For the entire Spanish period, Chile was part of the Viceroyalty of Peru, governed from Lima; trade with areas other than the colony was forbidden, which led to wholesale smuggling. Reports of the early 18th century indicated some 40 French ships engaged in illegal trade with Chile. Not until 1778 was trade permitted between Chile and Spain. Neglected by both Spain and Lima, the landowning aristocracy felt little loyalty to their own overlords and developed their estates as semi–independent fiefs.

General Bernardo O'Higgins

Chile declared its independence from Spain on September 18, 1810, which was followed by seven years of bitter war between the Chileans and Spanish forces. Finally, victory was achieved in 1817

Punta Arenas, the only city on the Strait of Magellan

Courtesy: Mr. & Mrs. Schuyler Lowe

when General José de San Martín led an army from Argentina across the Andes to help the Chileans. The Chilean revolutionary hero, General Bernardo O'Higgins, became the first president of the republic—under his leadership the first constitution was drafted. Almost revolutionary in its liberal democratic ideas, it served as a model for the famous constitution later adopted in 1833.

Opposition of the landowners to O'Higgins' efforts concerning the distribution of land to small farmers, the separation of church and state and the encouragement of free education, resulted in his ouster in 1823. For nearly 100 years, the country was ruled by a small oligarchy of landowners, or *latifundistas* who still own the major share of valuable land. Conservatives, advocating a strong central government, dominated the political scene until 1861. Their autocratic rule enlarged the economy and united the country; however, the repression of the Liberal Party laid the basis for years of bitter conflict.

Liberals came to power in 1861 and were successful in modifying some of the more restrictive measures of the conservative regime. However, they made little progress against the landowners or the church. Liberals ruled until 1891, during which time longstanding disputes with Peru and Bolivia led to the War of the Pacific (1879–1883). Although unprepared for war, Chile quickly defeated Bolivia, overran the disputed nitrate fields and occupied Lima from 1881 to 1884.

Dictating the victor's terms, Chile took possession of both Bolivian and Peruvian provinces and the ports Arica and Antofagasta. Liberal José Balmaceda, elected to the presidency in 1886, decided the time was ripe for major reforms to improve the lot of the poor and curb the power of the landlords and the church. By 1890, he had created a crisis in urging these programs and in 1891 the Congress voted to depose him and installed a naval officer to head a provisional government. With the support of the army, Balmaceda resisted the action; the result was a civil war resulting in the deaths of some 10,000, with widespread damage. Balmaceda was ultimately forced to seek asylum in the Argentine Embassy, where he committed suicide.

Balmaceda's death also marked the death of the Liberal era and ushered in the phenomenon of congressional rule that predominated over the executive—definitely an anomaly for Latin America. The conservative oligarchy wielded virtually unchecked control for the next three decades through a political machine known as *La Fronda*. This same period, however, witnessed a proliferation of political parties that supplanted the traditional Liberals and Conservatives: Radical, National, Democratic, Socialist and Communist, among others. Moreover, there was an industrial revolution that led to greater agi-tation for reform by organized labor movements. World War I saw a boom in the demand for Chilean nitrates, although the wealth that flowed into the country, as usual, failed to trickle down to the lower economic strata. At the end of the war, the same social ferment that led to the Bolshevik Revolution in Russia erupted in Chile in the form of strikes. Revolution seemed imminent.

Alessandri and Ibáñez

In 1920, a so-called Liberal Alliance of Radicals, Democrats, some Liberals and other factions, coalesced behind the nomination of Arturo Alessandri Palma for president. Like Franklin D. Roosevelt and John F. Kennedy, Alessandri was a handsome, wealthy patrician with a charismatic personality who convinced the working classes that he had their interests at heart. His message paralleled that of President Hipólito Irigoyen in neighboring Argentina, whose social reforms had defused a revolution there and caught the fancy of Chileans. Alessandri advocated separation of church and state, women's suffrage and increased taxes on the wealthy, including an income tax, to fund social welfare programs. Alessandri's popular appeal was such that he eked out a narrow plurality despite the *latifundistas'* control of the rural vote. Faced with the prospect of a genuine revolution, such as the one that had just unfolded in Mexico, the oligarchy's representatives in Congress pragmatically realized that Alessandri represented the lesser of two evils and voted to ratify his victory.

It was a largely hollow victory, however, because although the Liberal Alliance controlled the Chamber of Deputies, the right still controlled the Senate and frustrated virtually all of Alessandri's reform measures save the income tax; it was a situation uncannily similar to the gridlock in Chile's Congress today. Congress' obstinance, however, was to prove its undoing, because one of the measures that was tied up was the army's appropriation, always a mistake in Latin America. In September 1924, a band of officers invaded Congress and not so subtly demanded that it approve Alessandri's reform package (as well as their back pay). The officers then demanded that the president sign the measures. He complied, but to protest this undemocratic intervention, he resigned and left for self-imposed exile, first to Argentina, then to his parents' native Italy.

A power vacuum resulted, into which stepped in January 1925 a young colonel who would have a direct or indirect influence on Chilean government for more than 30 years: Carlos Ibáñez del Campo. Ironically, it was this military man who would implement much of the remainder of the reforms Alessandri had called for in 1920, and he somehow did so without alarming the oligarchy. Moreover, he promulgated the 1925 constitution, largely inspired by Alessandri, that returned power to the executive and served as the cornerstone for a reborn but shaky democracy that would last until 1973. Hardly a democrat himself, however, Ibáñez ruled from behind the throne for two years until he was "elected" in a highly suspect election in 1927. Although he enjoyed widespread public approval for a time, not even this military strongman could control events in New York. With the Stock Market Crash of 1929, the world price of copper plummeted, dragging Chile into the Great Depression. Ibáñez was overthrown in 1931, and there was a bewildering succession of revolving–door governments, including a socialist one, for the next 15 months. During this period of chaos, Alessandri returned from Italy and his leadership–starved countrymen returned him to the presidency for a six-year term in October 1932.

The Alessandri of the 1930s, however, was a changed man from the fiery reformer of the 1920s. His exile in Benito Mussolini's Italy had taught him the value of order and stability. Nonetheless, women's suffrage became a reality in 1935. He skillfully placated the discrete elements of the power structure—the military, the church, the wealthy landowners and industrialists, the middle class—when necessary; he resorted to a heavy hand to keep the social ferment from exploding. He once dissolved Congress, and he threw strike leaders in jail, causing the Socialists and Communists to break away and form a European–style Popular Front then in vogue.

The Popular Front's presidential candidate in 1938, Pedro Aguirre Cerda, an intellectual, won by a narrow plurality. His government was responsible for the creation of Latin America's most comprehensive social welfare program, made possible largely by the jump in copper and nitrate prices caused by the outbreak of World War II, and it became something of a model for the left–wing reformers in Latin America and Europe. It also proved a training ground for a generation of left–wing politicians at home; Aguirre Cerda's minister of health, for example, was a young physician named Salvador Allende. The war also caused a breakup of the Popular Front because of the nonaggression pact between Hitler and Stalin.

President Aguirre died in 1941 and a Radical, Juan Antonio Ríos, defeated Ibáñez, the candidate of the right, in the ensuing election. Ríos, who was considerably to the right of his predecessor, oversaw a booming wartime economy and, largely because of German influence, maintained a neutral course until just before the end of the war, when Chile declared war on the all–but–defeated Axis.

Ríos, too, died in office, and in the election to choose a successor in 1946 the vote was fragmented among several candidates. Congress then selected another Radical, Gabriel González Videla, who unwisely formed a coalition government that included Socialists and Communists. Not only did the United States exert pressure on González Videla because of the Communist influence, but the Communists began engaging in intrigues aimed at seizing absolute power. In 1948 González Videla purged the Communists not only from his cabinet but from Congress, including the world–renowned poet and future Nobel Laureate, Pablo Neruda.

Chile swung even farther to the right in the election of 1952 when Ibáñez, then 75, finally succeeded in finishing in first place in another fragmented election. Labeling himself above politics, this quasi–fascist managed to draw votes from poor laborers and farm workers. Congress, following its tradition to ratify the top vote–getter, returned him to power. Despite fears that he would seek to become another Juan Perón, whom he admired, Ibáñez presided over a largely do–nothing government for six years. When he failed to take strong action to deal with spiraling inflation, the populace became bitterly disillusioned with this once–dynamic leader.

In 1958, the Socialists and Communists, in their most determined effort, united behind the candidacy of Salvador Allende, a committed Marxist. The Liberals and Conservatives rallied behind a moderate, Jorge Alessandri, son of Arturo, while a new force, the Christian Democrats, nominated Eduardo Frei Montalva. Alessandri finished just 1% ahead of Allende, giving the establishment a scare. Alessandri proved quite conservative, and although he helped stabilize the economy, he failed to address the perennial social ills that were providing grist for the far left.

By 1964, it seemed the impatience of the lower classes for some remedies to their plight could well give Allende a plurality of the popular vote and, if Congress followed tradition, the presidency. Fearing that eventuality, the rightists gradually abandoned their own candidate and rallied behind the Christian Democrats' Frei, who represented a middle course of reform without revolution. Frei easily defeated Allende with 55% of the vote, the first time in decades that a candidate had won with an absolute majority. Frei made good on many of his promises, initiating land reform and making the first steps toward nationalization of the foreign-owned copper mines. But he found himself in a damned–if–you–do–damned–if–you–don't dilemma. The right vilified him for going too far, the left for not going far enough.

Allende and Pinochet

In 1970, Allende was again a candidate, this time of a Socialist–Communist–Radical coalition called Popular Unity. But this time the right split with the Christian Democrats and nominated former President Alessandri, by then quite elderly, while the Christian Democrats nominated a left–of–center candidate, Rodomiro Tomic, who tried unsuccessfully to steal Allende's thunder. Polls showed the race a tossup between Allende and Alessandri, and the world watched with expectation to see if Allende would usher in the world's first democratically elected Marxist government. Ironically, only 29% of the electorate turned out for what would become the most fateful election in Chile's history. Allende won by an eyelash, 36.4% to Alessandri's 35.2%. Under the 1925 constitution, the choice fell again to Congress. Despite a clumsy attempt by the CIA to bribe Christian Democratic congressmen to vote for Alessandri, Congress confirmed Allende, and Frei placed the presidential sash over the shoulders of his Marxist successor on November 3, 1970.

The victory of Popular Unity seemed to have caught even Allende and his dogmatic supporters by surprise. Despite their shaky mandate, they set off to turn Chile into a Marxist state, gradually alienating the centrist Christian Democrats who initially provided them with the congressional votes they needed to pass legislation. The government implemented a hastily devised economic program that nationalized the U.S.–owned copper mines and telephone system, which resulted in economic sanctions by the Nixon Administration. The Soviet Union and China, for a time, willingly came to Chile's economic rescue. In other action, the government increased wages and froze prices, which temporarily created the illusion of prosperity; Chileans went on a spending spree, and in 1971 municipal elections voters expressed their gratitude by giving Popular Unity 49% of the vote.

Old Marxists were suspicious in spite of the apparent economic success; some foresaw the disaster that lay ahead. The Soviet Union started to worry about being burdened with the support of an expensive second Latin American nation. Fidel Castro warned Allende in 1973 during a state visit that Chile's economic plans were the opposite of Marxism, in which consumption is held to a minimum. Allende replied that he was working in a system where he had to win reelection until a "dictatorship of the proletariat" could be established, and rejected Castro's advice.

View of downtown Santiago

Salvador Allende

Although general disintegration of the economy was well underway by the time of 1973 congressional elections, thirst for continued consumerism resulted in an increased share of the vote for Allende's coalition to 44%. Voter enthusiasm could not save the economy, which was experiencing a "domino" style collapse in which one sector would bring down others. First to fall were the retail stores. With prices fixed and wages raised, stores could not afford to restock sold items; when everything on the shelves was gone, the stores closed, idling thousands.

The result in agriculture was the same. Instead of orderly land redistribution, Allende simply broke up plantations of wealthy persons regardless of productivity. Owners refused to plant crops which would be harvested by others. Political cronies were appointed to administer the nationalized farms; as production dropped by 20% it became necessary for Chile to increase food imports.

The government seized the copper mines owned by large U.S. companies to end what Allende termed foreign exploitation. Virtually no compensation was offered. Spurred on by widespread public support for his expropriation of the mines, Allende then ordered the nationalization of other key industries—including those owned by Chileans. Taking their cues from the government, workers (and outside agitators) began seizing farms and factories throughout the country. To the great dismay of Allende's economic planners, workers did not hesitate to strike against newly expropriated state industries. These work stoppages—combined with inept management of nationalized firms, led to a catastrophic decline in economic output.

Allende isolated Chile in foreign affairs and trade. The availability of loans from non-communist nations and institutions

predictably disappeared. The Soviets and Chinese heaped praise on Chile, but offered precious little monetary support. The United States even declined Chilean offers to buy food for cash.

The people found themselves wasting hour upon hour in lines to buy what few consumer goods were left. As the government continued to "finance" itself by printing more money, inflation ran absolutely wild. Food was scarce, spare parts for machinery were nonexistent; only the black market flourished. Strikes and street fights between rival political factions became common. Political bickering in the Congress froze all constructive activity.

As things crumbled, the opposition became more unified. The right–wing National Party and the fascist Fatherland and Freedom Party began to sabotage operations of the government. The culmination of resistance came when a two–month strike by the nation's truck owners opposing nationalization—a strike a U.S. congressional inquiry later determined to have been partly financed by the CIA—virtually cleared the roads at the same time protesting housewives were filling the streets. With civil war imminent, the military staged its long–expected coup on September 11, 1973. Quickly seizing control, they announced that Allende had allegedly killed himself with a machine gun given to him as a gift by Fidel Castro.

During his brief but stormy term as president, Allende left a lasting mark on the nation. He sought to increase the living standards of the poor, to distribute farms to those who worked the land and to provide a full spectrum of social and economic benefits. He might possibly have succeeded if a unified, workable plan had first been developed and if at the same time he had been given enough time and had control of his followers.

Although Allende was unable to control his supporters, civil liberties were largely respected. A small number of political opponents was sent into exile, but none was harmed. The vigorous opposition press (two–thirds of the total) remained free. Opposition parties thrived while critics of the government spoke out without fear of reprisal. Congress and the courts continued to function normally. Yet his administration was a disaster. When the Congress and courts opposed his policies, Allende felt free to ignore them.

Allende never received a majority of votes in any election, thus he lacked the necessary public support for changes that were so radical. He came to power because of a divided opposition rather than because of his own popularity.

Once it decided to move against the Allende government, the *junta* left no holds barred. Leftists and suspected opponents of the *junta* were promptly exterminated

General Augusto Pinochet Ugarte

or rounded up in huge detention centers. Catholic Church officials in Chile estimated that one out of every 100 Chileans was arrested at least once during the $16^1/_2$ years the military held power. Many, according to the government, were "shot while trying to escape." Others simply disappeared while under detention. Other opponents of the regime were expelled from the country. By 1980, though, the government allowed many to return safely.

A major victim of military repression was Chile's long–standing tradition as a pioneering Latin American democracy. Upon seizing power the *junta* immediately closed Congress and pointedly used its chambers to store records of political prisoners. The constitution was suspended and the courts neutralized. Freedom of the press disappeared and suspected books and publications were destroyed. Schools, factories and the nation itself, were placed under rigid control to discourage dissent and—most importantly—to "root out Marxism."

Political parties (except selected right–wing groups) were placed "in suspension." The large Christian Democratic Party newspaper was closed and its leader, former President Frei, was forced to muzzle his biting criticism. Not surprisingly, Marxists suffered most. Socialist and communist leaders were arrested, killed, exiled or forced into hiding.

The only group which continually dared to speak out against the generals was the Catholic clergy. The *junta* responded by banning some religious festivals and arresting priests and nuns suspected of leftist sympathies. At one point, the church's prisoner relief agency was ordered to discontinue its attempts to locate persons who disappeared following their arrest by security agents. The church disregarded the directive and reported 750 such disappearances in 1975.

When the Catholic Church published a book by former President Frei in 1976 calling for a return to democracy, the government quickly outlawed public discussion of it. In his sermons, Raúl Cardinal Silva Henríquez boldly criticized the regime's rigid austerity program, which he said was pushing the nation's impoverished masses to the edge of starvation.

A major goal of the military rulers had been to pull Chile out of an economic tailspin caused by the Allende administration. Skilled managers were sent to farms and factories while property seized by the previous government was returned. Taxes and interest rates were increased and the amount of currency in circulation was reduced by cuts in government spending of 15% to 20%. Strikes were strongly "discouraged," while the nation's high unemployment rate in the months following the coup forced wage levels downward.

To increase farm output and industrial production, prices of consumer goods—including food—were allowed to rise to their natural levels. Soaring food costs, however, threatened fully a third of the nation with hunger in the months following the coup. To prevent starvation, the government provided the most destitute with limited food handouts and low-paying public works jobs.

Although the *junta* consisted of four military men, real power was in the hands of General Augusto Pinochet Ugarte. Pinochet initially said that democracy could not be restored during his lifetime or the lifetime of his successor. Military rule, he had insisted, could not be lifted until "the ills of democracy" had been erased. On freedom of expression, Pinochet was once quoted as saying, "We're not against ideas; we're just against people spreading them." In terms of human rights, the cure appeared to be worse than the disease. But economically, it was a tremendous success. Pinochet surrounded himself with a clique of civilian economic technocrats, many of whom had studied under free–market guru Milton Friedman at the University of Chicago, and who quickly won the monicker, "los Chicago Boys" (see Economy).

Chileans surged to the polls in January 1978 to give a simple "sí" or "no" vote in a plebiscite testing support for the military rulers. The *junta* received a lopsided 75% approval. Elated at the "solid support," President Pinochet declared that no further elections needed to be held for 10 years.

Even as Pinochet savored his electoral triumph, however, he was confronted with a serious threat from abroad. Neighboring Argentina suddenly revived an old territorial claim over three rocky, uninhabited islands at the mouth of the Beagle Channel in faraway Tierra del Fuego. At Argentina's suggestion, the two countries submitted their competing claims to the islands—Lennox, Picton and Nueva—to the British Crown for arbitration. The British ruled that Chile had legitimate sovereignty over all three islands, whereupon the Argentine military government of General Jorge Rafael Videla renounced the decision it itself had sought and threatened to seize the islands by force. By December 1978, both countries were on a war footing, and hostilities appeared imminent. Literally at the 11th hour, the two military strongmen, who after all were bound philosophically by their hatred of communism and democratic institutions, agreed to a second arbitration, this time by the Vatican. The Italian cardinal assigned to review the matter also concluded that Chile had the stronger claim. Despite occasional saber–rattling, Argentina eventually dropped the matter. But Pinochet had the last laugh. When Argentina foolishly invaded the Falkland Islands in 1982, precipitating war with Britain, Pinochet secretly allowed the Royal Navy to use Chilean territorial waters and islands, even as Chile was echoing the denunciation of other Latin American countries of the perceived British aggression against their sister republic.

Despite widespread national and international criticism of its harsh political and rigid economic policies, the *junta* could point to some dramatic successes: the inflation rate dropped from 600% per year in 1973 to just under 10% in 1981—one of the lowest in Latin America. In addition, foreign investment rose rapidly.

Repression had also been reduced. The regime became increasingly tolerant of public criticism, and arrests of political opponents declined. At the same time, a limited number of Chileans sent into exile following the coup were allowed to return home.

Another "sí" or "no" plebiscite was put before the voters in September 1980. By a two-to-one margin, they approved President Pinochet's desire to remain in power for another eight years. Some observers charged that the balloting was rigged. His term was technically scheduled to end in 1990 after an election to choose his successor. But the strongman still enjoyed an added insurance policy: the *junta* had the power to reappoint him for *another* eight years—which in theory could stretch his term until 1997, the year that constitutional safeguards were slated to become effective. His intentions were made known in July 1986 when he scheduled another "yes" or "no" plebiscite to be held in October 1988. A yes vote would have returned him to power for another eight years.

Human rights violations by Chile's military rulers touched off widespread international protest and complicated relations with the United States. After Chilean secret police were linked with the 1976 assassination of Allende supporter Orlando Letelier in Washington, the Carter administration cut off most military aid to the Pinochet regime in 1979. When a member of the military involved in the murder identified the masterminds of the plot in 1986 the subject came up again as demand for their extradition to the U.S. was made; it was ignored by Pinochet.

But the Reagan administration, favorably impressed with the *junta's* anti–communist leanings, sought to improve ties between the two countries. Thus, in 1981, some trade barriers were removed and the United States invited Chile to participate in joint naval exercises. The U.S. Senate voted in 1981 to resume military aid to Chile—on the condition that Santiago complies with "internationally recognized standards of human rights."

The economy, though, continued to deteriorate. Chile suffered the worst slump in all of Latin America in the recession of 1981–82, resulting in a reduction of about 13% in the gross domestic product and forcing the government to intervene in private enterprise to prevent an increasing number of bankruptcies. By May 1983, it was estimated that 21% of the urban force was unemployed. The following month a strike of truck drivers and copper miners—the first important labor challenge to the military government since 1973—appeared to be the beginning of a deep social crisis. The government's swift reaction, combining repression with conciliation, defused the danger.

When the *Alianza Democrática* (Demo-

Entrance of La Moneda, the presidential palace

cratic Alliance), a group of five opposition parties formed in 1983, tried in late 1984 to expand tenuous dialogue with the government and to pressure Pinochet for more political concessions, the government answered by declaring a stage of siege (the first in its 11 years in power), imposing a curfew and tightening its control over the media. By June 1985, however, it appeared as if the regime had softened its stand and was willing to listen to the group's more moderate members. Another attempt at reconciliation was attempted, this time spearheaded by "liberation theology" Catholic priests and bishops, a movement which ripened into the National Assembly of Civil Society, a gathering of professional associations, academics, students, teachers, bus drivers, shopkeepers and two large union groups.

In order to reinforce its demands for a return to democracy, the organization called for a general strike on July 2–3, 1986. Although the leader of the organization called the strike a "gigantic success," (which it was) it proved to be a mistake—the equivalent of tweaking the tiger's tail. The strike resulted in several deaths, many wounded and more than 1,000 arrests.

The regime's forces claimed to have discovered over 70 tons of munitions in August 1986, allegedly from the Vietnam war period, including Soviet–bloc manufactured items and U.S. M–16 rifles. The caches of arms had been unloaded from Cuban trawlers for use by insurgents and guerrillas trained in insurrection in Cuba and Nicaragua, according to Chilean intelligence sources. For several months after this, conditions were extremely unsettled, with leftist groups resorting to widespread terrorism and the Chilean regime responding in kind. As one astute Chilean politician stated (rough translation): "it is open season on everyone." Right–wing terrorists felt quite justified in shooting and bombing leftist radicals and vice versa.

In September 1986, Pinochet narrowly escaped death in an ambush by left–wing terrorists on his motorcade that left five of his bodyguards dead. The radical Manuel Rodríguez Patriotic Front (*FPMR*) claimed credit for the deed; predictably, Pinochet responded with a new 90–day state of siege and announced he would "expel or lock up all those people talking about human rights and all those things."

In keeping with his intention to schedule a 1988 plebiscite to install himself in office for another eight years, in an effort to bolster sagging relations with the United States and to placate moderate politicians at home, Pinochet announced the legalization of political parties in March 1987 (except Marxists). But there was a catch in the measure: no party could be affiliated with one which had existed before. During a visit by Pope John Paul II in

1987, there was widespread violence, with clashes between dissidents and forces of the regime virtually every day; this indicated that there was still deeply seated resentment of many with the Pinochet regime.

Return to Democracy

As the time for the October 7, 1988 plebiscite drew near, Pinochet underwent a marked change. Instead of his former elitist, aloof style, he tried, with some success, to promote the image of a kindly old father–figure. He counted on the division of the opposition (17 parties) and actually believed he would win. In August, after changes were made in the *junta,* it voted him in for another eight–year term as provided for in the questionable 1980 constitution. This met with widespread disfavor. The numerous political parties were highly united into The Command for No by a single ambition: to oust Pinochet.

The voting was relatively close because of a single reason: economic prosperity. By 1988 inflation had descended to 8% and Chile enjoyed a trade surplus of more than $1.5 billion. The outcome was 54% to 43% against Pinochet. The country held its breath, wondering what the elderly leader would do. Somewhat hesitatingly, he announced that as provided for by law, elections would be held in December 1989.

Patricio Aylwin, a centrist Christian Democrat who had been a senator when the 1973 coup occurred, was the presidential candidate of a coalition of 17 center–left parties called the *Concertación.* The Communists were not part of the coalition but

Angelmo Market

gave tacit support to Aylwin. In a three–way contest, Aylwin received 55% against Hernán Büchi, a former civilian finance minister during the military regime and Pinochet's hand–picked candidate, who received only 29%, and Francisco Javier Errázuriz, an enigmatic, Ross Perot–style tycoon who polled 15% as an independent. Election night saw an outpouring of jubilation as *Concertación* supporters filled the streets to celebrate the end of 17 years of authoritarian rule. On March 11, 1990, Pinochet placed the presidential sash on the shoulders of his civilian successor, marking a major milestone in the life of the country.

Not surprisingly, however, friction soon developed between the two over the issue of civilian control. Aylwin asked Pinochet to resign as army commander, but the general steadfastly refused, saying his presence provided stability for the transition to democracy. There was little Aylwin could do, as the 1980 constitution permitted Pinochet to remain in command until the end of 1997, and the *Concertación* lacked the votes in congress to amend the constitution. In fact, the constitution also allowed Pinochet to name nine permanent "institutional" senators to the 47–member upper house of Congress when he left office, which has given the conservative opposition a narrow majority and consequent veto power over legislation passed by the *Concertación*–controlled Chamber of Deputies. (One of those senators has since died). The opposition also enjoys a disproportionate number of elected seats in both houses because of the peculiar double–member districts, in which the top two vote–getters are both elected. It is classic gridlock. Among other things, the opposition–controlled Senate repeatedly blocked executive branch efforts to abolish the national holiday for September 11, the anniversary of the coup. The holiday was finally abolished in 1999.

Aylwin was heavily pressured to try all major military figures responsible for disappearances for so many years. A valid question was posed to him without being stated: if the military was to be tried, why also should not the left–wing, anti–military subversives also be tried? Lacking an answer, in the style of a skilled politician, he appointed a commission to investigate and study the matter.

The commission found that 3,197 people had been killed outright or disappeared at the hands of the military following the coup, but in the midst of prosperity, most Chileans seem to prefer to let the past rest in peace and not fan the flames of renewed conflict.

The Supreme Court, in an unusual and imaginative decision, heard a case involving the validity of the amnesty laws which protected the military against charges of alleged crimes. It was argued that because Chile was in fact at war, criminal charges

**Former President
Eduardo Frei Ruiz–Tagle**

could not be sustained. The court agreed about the state of war, but held that even so, the terms of the Geneva Convention forbidding the murder of prisoners was applicable.

The continuing dispute vividly illustrates an ongoing problem of today's world: how can law and justice during times of unlawfulness and injustice be applied retroactively? The question first arose at the Nuremburg trials following World War II. Pinochet summed up the dilemma very tersely, saying, "During wars, crimes are always committed."

Chile prospered under Aylwin, and for a time saw its economy expand at a rate approaching an average of 10% per year. It still has a thorny problem with the perpetually poor, but the government has shown a willingness to tackle this problem, too. Prosperity and growth has been the product of free trade (few, if any tariffs) and foreign investment, the latter flowing in at a rate of more than U.S. $1 billion a year.

In December 1993, voters affirmed their satisfaction with the status quo by electing Eduardo Frei Ruiz–Tagle, son of the president who preceded Allende, to the presidency by a resounding 59 percent of the vote against five opponents. Almost simultaneously, Congress extended the presidential term from four to six years, as it was before the military coup. Like Aylwin, Frei is a Christian Democrat who was the candidate of a coalition of centrist and left–wing parties, less the Communists. The two conservative opposition parties, National Renewal (RN) and the ultra–rightist Independent Democratic Union (UDI), bickered until just two months before the election before agreeing on a single candidate, Arturo Alessandri, grandson and namesake of the presi-

dent of the 1920s and 1930s and nephew of the late President Jorge Alessandri, predecessor of Frei's father. Conservative unity came too late, however, as Alessandri polled only 29 percent, only slightly more than Pinochet's hand–picked candidate in 1989.

One of the most historic aspects of this election, however, was that the once-mighty Communist Party received only about 3 percent. Frei's coalition retained its majority in the lower house, but the eight remaining "institutional senators" named by Pinochet allowed the conservative opposition to keep control of the upper chamber and thus serve as a brake on the majority.

Frei, an engineer by training rather than a politician, was elected to the Senate in 1989 and as president of the Christian Democratic Party two years later. Following the counsel of a group of influential advisers, Frei wisely kept the successful economic policies in effect, and Chile's economic growth continued to be the envy of Latin America. The combination of stable civilian government and free–market economics made Chile a favorite target of foreign investors, who have increasingly sought new opportunities in the region as they once did in the Pacific Rim countries of Asia. Frei also emerged as a leader of regional importance, hosting a Latin American summit in Santiago in 1996 and visiting with President Clinton at the White House in 1997 for trade talks. Clinton included Chile in his four–nation tour of South America in October 1997.

Like Aylwin before him, Frei experienced friction with Pinochet, who successfully resisted efforts to curtail the extraordinary authority granted to him in his personalized 1980 constitution. The general further annoyed the president, and generated great public controversy, by postponing his promised retirement from the announced date of January 26, 1998. Pinochet finally retired as army commander, at age 82, on March 10 in a fanfare-filled ceremony in which he tearfully bade farewell to the troops he had commanded for nearly 25 years and to the institution to which he had belonged for more than 60. He was succeeded by Major General Ricardo Izurieta, 53, a cavalry officer and former chairman of the National Defense Council.

But Pinochet's long–awaited retirement did not mean he was withdrawing from public life—or from the controversy that continues to follow him. The day after his retirement ceremony, and still adhering to a right given to him in the constitution as a former head of state, the former strongman put on a civilian business suit and assumed a lifetime seat in the Senate, joining the other non–elected "institutional senators" who give the conservative opposition a majority. Pinochet's transfer to

the Senate angered left–wing lawmakers, and there were public demonstrations to protest such an antidemocratic measure. Efforts to block Pinochet by judicial means failed, as did an impeachment motion in the Chamber of Deputies, which was rejected in an unusual secret ballot 62-52. Once again the aging general demonstrated he was still a force to contend with, whether his detractors liked it or not.

Congressional elections in December 1997 failed to alter the balance of power, but voters sent some confusing signals. The lineup in the Chamber of Deputies remains 70–50 in favor of the Concertación, although its popular vote dropped to 50.5%. It also lost one Senate seat, giving it 20 of the elected seats to 18 for the conservatives. With the "institutional" senators, including Pinochet, the opposition holds a commanding seven–seat majority. The Christian Democrats remain the largest party in Congress, but their popular vote fell from 27% to 23%. The Christian Democrats' main coalition partner, the center–left Party for Democracy (PPD), broke even. There were two major surprises: the ultra–rightwing UDI became the second ranking party in the Senate, moving ahead of its opposition partner, the RN. And on the left, the Communists showed their first modest gains since they abandoned their adherence to Marxism-Leninism. Perhaps most troubling for Chile's reborn democracy was that one sixth of eligible voters registered to vote and only 83% of registered voters turned out, even though voting is mandatory.

The Pinochet Arrest

Chilean government and society were suddenly thrust into turmoil in October 1998. Pinochet flew to London, where he underwent back surgery. On October 16, as he was recuperating in a clinic, the British government formally placed him under arrest, acting on an extradition request from Spain. A Spanish judge, Baltasar Garzón, acting largely on his own initiative, requested Pinochet's extradition ostensibly to account for Spanish citizens tortured and killed during the military regime. But the warrant eventually was broadened to take advantage of the 1988 International Convention Against Torture, promulgated by the United Nations, by which a country can seek the arrest in a second country of someone accused of torture committed in a third country. Twelve days after his arrest, judges in Switzerland and France submitted similar extradition requests for the aging general, while Chilean exiles–by–choice in France, Denmark, Italy and Belgium also filed petitions accusing Pinochet of human rights abuses.

The news of Pinochet's arrest made headlines around the world, particularly in Chile, where the news was greeted with glee by Pinochet's detractors and with outrage by his supporters. But the Spanish warrant and the British arrest also struck at the core of Chilean nationalism, and moderate Chileans, even some Pinochet–haters, denounced the action as a violation of Chilean sovereignty. There were anonymous threats made against the British and Spanish embassies in Santiago and against resident nationals from those countries—even against some Chileans of British and Spanish descent!

The Chilean government, meanwhile, found itself on the horns of a diplomatic dilemma. President Frei, despite his own personal animosity to the general, dutifully added his voice to those urging Pinochet's release on the grounds that as a member of the Chilean Senate he enjoyed diplomatic immunity from arrest. Rumors circulated that the military might take action if the government did not, a reminder of the Sword of Damocles that continues to hang above Chile's civilian rulers. In a case of delicious irony, Foreign Minister José Miguel Insulza, who himself had been arrested after the coup and spent years in exile, was dispatched to London to plead Pinochet's cause.

The Pinochet case then began a torturous (no pun intended) 16-month journey through the British court system. After his release from the clinic, Pinochet was placed under house arrest in a rented mansion on the outskirts of London. There his visitors included his old philosophical ally, Lady Margaret Thatcher, who strongly advocated his release. Pinochet won the first legal skirmish on October 28, 1998, when the London High Court ruled that as head of state when the crimes were committed, Pinochet was immune to arrest in Britain, but declined to

release him pending an appeal. On November 3, the case was heard before a panel of five Law Lords, jurists who are members of the House of Lords, Britain's court of last resort. While this hearing was underway, the Spanish cabinet called for Pinochet's extradition, prompting Frei to recall Chile's ambassador from Madrid for consultation. On November 25—Pinochet's 83rd birthday—the Law Lords voted 3–2 that Pinochet's arrest was legal. The decision then fell upon Home Secretary Jack Straw whether to grant Spain's extradition request. About this time, the pro–Pinochet press in Chile reported that as a student visiting Chile in the 1960s, Straw had visited with then–Senator Salvador Allende.

Pinochet's lawyers raised a stronger case of bias when, in December, they asked for a new hearing because one of the five Law Lords and his wife were active in the human rights group Amnesty International. The following day, the proud general was required to undergo the ignominy of appearing in court for a bail hearing. He huffily declared in Spanish that he did not recognize the jurisdiction of a non–Chilean court, and the judge remanded him on bail. On December 17, Pinochet's prospects appeared brighter once again when the House of Lords agreed that he was entitled to a new hearing, this time before a seven–judge panel. The new, 12–day hearing opened on January 18, 1999.

On March 24, the Law Lords handed down a decision that left both Pinochet supporters and opponents perplexed, not knowing whether to celebrate or not. The judges ruled 6–1 that Pinochet's arrest was legal and that the extradition request could proceed, but they agreed with Pinochet's lawyers that the general could not be held accountable for any crime al-

legedly committed before September 29, 1988—the date that Britain incorporated the international torture convention into its criminal laws. This effectively dismissed 29 of the 32 charges in the Spanish warrant. However, the general remained under arrest on the other three counts. Judge Garzón angrily denounced the decision as "inhumane" and busily began raising new allegations of cases committed after 1988.

The decision of whether to proceed with the extradition once again fell upon Straw, who on April 15, 1999, decided that it could. Pinochet's lawyers were given more time to appeal, while a judge scheduled the extradition hearing for September 27.

As the hearing approached, Chile requested that Spain agree to an international arbitration panel to decide Pinochet's fate. Spain refused, and President Frei angrily withdrew Chile's ambassador to Madrid temporarily. Chile also boycotted the Ibero-American summit in Havana in August to protest Spain's extradition request, and Argentina followed suit to express support for Chile. Meanwhile, Pinochet's health deteriorated in September as he suffered two minor strokes. Nonetheless, the hearing was held as scheduled, with Pinochet's lawyers arguing that Spain lacked jurisdiction to try the general for alleged crimes that occurred in Chile and also that he was too ill to stand trial. Eleven days later, and eight days short of the first anniversary of Pinochet's arrest, the magistrate rejected Pinochet's arguments and declared that he could be extradited. Once again, Pinochet haters cheered; once again, Pinochet's lawyers vowed to appeal; and once again, the decision fell upon Home Secretary Straw, who found himself in the unenviable position of choosing between releasing what the international community regarded as a war criminal or sending a feeble old man to Spain, where in all likelihood he would die in captivity.

Straw vascilated for another three months, finally ordering that Pinochet undergo a series of medical examinations to determine whether he were too ill to be extradited. The general, who turned 84 on November 25, 1999, underwent the exams in mid-January, 2000, and the Santiago daily *El Mercurio* carried a large front-page picture of Pinochet seated in the back seat of his limousine, obviously exhausted after the seven-hour ordeal. The picture did little to ameliorate Chilean public opinion toward the British or Spanish. On January 13, Straw decided that Pinochet was indeed too ill to be extradited, setting off a torrent of outrage by human rights groups. He further angered the governments seeking Pinochet's extradition by refusing to make the medical report public.

Torres del Paine

The Chilean public's divided view on Pinochet as shown in leaflets showered on the crowds awaiting his arrival in Santiago . . .

Inevitably, there were more appeals, but in late February Straw at last made the fateful decision that Pinochet would be freed and returned to Chile. A Chilean air force plane was dispatched to Britain, and on March 3, 2000, after 16 months under house arrest, the once-proud Pinochet was returned to his native soil—in a wheelchair. However, his travails were far from over. Charges at home brought by survivors of those killed following the coup, and on May 29 the Santiago Court of Appeals voted 13-9 to strip him of his legislative immunity as senator-for-life to allow him to stand trial. Pinochet's lawyers immediately appealed to the Supreme Court, arguing once again that he was too frail and ill to face a trial. Moreover, the U.S. government announced in March it planned to investigate whether Pinochet were the intellectual author of the 1976 car bomb assassination of Orlando Letelier, a former Allende cabinet minister; Letelier's secretary, a U.S. national, also died in the blast.

On August 8, 2000, the Supreme Court voted 14-6 to uphold the lower court's decision to strip Pinochet of his legislative immunity. Judge Juan Guzmán, who had been appointed to handle the domestic complaints against Pinochet, found a loophole around the amnesty law that protected members of the military from being tried for atrocities committed following the coup. There are a total of 189 complaints filed against Pinochet, but the focus of the charges against Pinochet was his alleged complicity in the infamous "Caravan of Death," a helicopter-borne squad of soldiers that scoured the country after the coup and carried dissidents away to their deaths. More than 70 dissidents were believed slain during the Caravan of Death, although 18 were never accounted for. Guzmán opted to treat these as kidnappings rather than murders—which are not covered by the amnesty law.

Guzmán generated headlines around the world on December 1 by announcing that Pinochet would stand trial and ordering him placed under house arrest. An appeals court quickly overturned his order, on the grounds that Guzmán never interrogated Pinochet before arresting him. Pinochet's lawyers, meanwhile, continued to argue that their client was too frail to

stand trial, whereupon Guzmán ordered Pinochet to undergo more medical testing. At first, the proud Pinochet huffily refused, but on January 10, 2001, he yielded to his lawyers' advice and subjected himself to the exams. Later, Pinochet again ignored his lawyers and agreed to be interrogated in his seaside home by Guzmán. As a result, the judge declared Pinochet mentally competent to stand trial. On January 29, Guzmán again issued an arrest warrant, which was served on the defendant at his home. On July 9, an appeals court ruled that Pinochet was mentally incompetent to stand trial. But in August, the Supreme Court voted to overturn that decision, keeping alive the hopes of Pinochet's opponents that the general may still be brought to trial.

For 11 more months the lawyers wrangled, until the Supreme Court ruled 4-1 on July 2, 2002, that Pinochet was mentally incompetent to stand trial. Three days later, Pinochet resigned his lifetime Senate seat. His 29-year political career, and an era in Chilean history, were over.

The armed forces were caught in a dilemma with their former commander's arrest. Although the military had protested vigorously to President Lagos, it seemed to realize that it is a new day in Chile, and that it would be bad public relations to undermine a duly elected government. Moreover, the military has felt compelled to own up to the whereabouts of the bodies of many of the "disappeared." Once a death is confirmed, it is covered by the amnesty law and can no longer be treated as a kidnapping. Alas, the military has acknowledged that many victims were dumped at sea.

The Elections of 1999-2000

As the Pinochet drama unfolded during 1999, Chileans prepared to elect their third president since the restoration of democracy. At first it seemed the *Concertación* might break apart if the Christian Democrats and the *PPD*, the *PDC*'s main coalition partner, could not agree on a candidate. In a coalition primary election, the *PPD*'s Ricardo Lagos, 61, a neo-socialist economist, handily defeated Andrés Zaldivar, a moderate Christian Democrat, with 70% of the vote. The *PDC* leadership duly rallied around Lagos, who had served as education minister under Aylwin and public works minister under Frei and who had spent most of the Pinochet regime in self-imposed exile on a faculty in North Carolina. *Concertación* unity was preserved—or so it seemed. Meanwhile, the two right-wing opposition parties, *RN* and the *UDI*, also held a joint primary, and the overwhelming winner was the *UDI*'s Joaquín Lavín, 46, also an economist and a former mayor of the affluent Santiago suburb of Los Condes. During the Pinochet regime, Lavín had been one

Precio: $ 250
Regiones I-II: $ 330; XI y XII: $ 400

TIEMPO EN LA CAPITAL
Mín. **11** Máx. **29**

UNIDAD DE FOMENTO
$ 15.087,36

la TERCERA

Lunes 17 de enero de 2000, Año 50, Número 18.112

Conéctese hoy a
www.tercera.cl

ELECCIONES: Descargue el
resultado electoral ▸

ENCUESTA: ¿Volverá
Pinochet esta semana? ▸

MOUSE: Guía de libros de
computación ▸

Todo sobre la victoria de Lagos

PRESIDENTE2000

The front page of the Santiago daily *La Tercera* the morning after the january 16, 2000, presidential runoff shows the victorious Ricardo Lagos, right, with his defeated opponent, Joaquín Lavín, in a display of gracious goodwill.

of the "Chicago Boys," the University of Chicago-educated economists who engineered Chile's free-market economic miracle. The Communist Party leader Gladys Marín mounted a separate candidacy, while three lesser candidates completed the field.

At mid-year, all the polls agreed that Lagos' election was inevitable and that he would win, like Aylwin and Frei before him, without the need for a *segunda vuelta*, or runoff. But by late 1999, Chile found itself in its first recession in 15 years, and as unemployment increased, Lagos' stand-

ing in the polls decreased in inverse correlation. Moreover, like Aesop's tortoise, the dogged Lavín campaigned energetically and soon began making inroads among conservative and moderate Christian Democrats who had voted for Aylwin and Frei but who were leery of both La-

President Ricardo Lagos
Photo by the author

gos' socialist past and his avowed agnosticism. Lavín, by stark contrast, not only is a devout Roman Catholic but is a member of the conservative Catholic organization Opus Dei. Lavín had another powerful asset: Lagos himself, who proved cold and stuffy as a candidate. Lavín campaigned U.S.-style, often without a coat or tie and with rolled-up sleeves, which Lagos dismissed condescendingly as "unpresidential." As the election approached, however, polls predicted correctly that a runoff would be necessary for the first time. The results of the first round on December 12 were breathtakingly close: 3,359,679, or 47.96 percent, for Lagos, to 3,328,652, or 47.52 percent, for Lavín; the tortoise almost pulled it off. Marín received only 223,000 votes, or 3.2 percent, but those votes would prove crucial in the January 16, 2000 runoff.

This author spent two weeks in Chile observing the runoff campaign as a freelance journalist and had the opportunity to speak briefly with both candidates. By then, Lagos had heeded the advice of his advisers and was beginning to campaign in a more laid-back style, much to the derision of Lavín supporters. Lagos was addressing crowds without a coat, although he couldn't quite bring himself to remove his tie. Both candidates tried to outdo each other with lavish, U.S.-style campaign promises that left analysts wondering how they expected to pay for them. For example, Lagos promised southern milk producers he would guarantee a price of US$1.73 per liter, up from the current unprotected price of 77 cents. Promising protective tariffs on imported milk represented a dramatic shift from Chile's free-market policy. Lagos also promised to spend $14.2 billion on the public works infrastructure and to add 5,200 Caribineros, or national policemen, to the force to com-

bat crime, one of Chile's push-button issues. Lavín countered with a promise to spend US$17.5 billion on social spending, including health, education, housing, old-age pensions and police protection. He also pledged to spend US$40 million for 80,000 college loans and to increase aid to poor schools outside the capital by 40 percent. Of Lagos' promises, Lavín sneered, "What they haven't done in 10 years they aren't going to do now."

An amusing spectacle of the campaign was the devoutly Catholic Lavín and the agnostic Lagos pleading for votes from evangelicals, who now comprise 7 percent of the population.

Buttonholed after the campaign speech to milk producers and asked why he had done so much worse than expected in the first round, Lagos told me, "It just means we're going to have a second round of voting, nothing more. The results were the result of a difficult economic situation. Any coalition government that faces 12 percent unemployment is going to have difficulties." Asked pointblank if he wanted to see General Pinochet prosecuted if he were allowed to return to Chile, Lagos replied carefully, "I think it's a judicial issue. The Chilean courts have jurisdiction. We have to create the necessary conditions for anyone to be judged," an apparent reference to Pinochet's legislative immunity as a senator-for-life.

The Pinochet case was a political minefield for both candidates. The left-wing militants backing Lagos wanted their pound of flesh from Pinochet. But front-page pictures of the exhaused 84-year-old former strongman after undergoing seven hours of medical exams in London offended average Chileans, most of whom had, at least tacitly, supported the 1973 coup. For his part, Lavín already was sensitive to criticism that he had served as an adviser to the dictator and eventually declared that he would respect whatever the Chilean courts decided to do with his former boss. As an indication of his sensitivity on this subject, I tried to ask Lavín about Pinochet after a campaign stop in Puerto Montt and he snapped, "Oh, why don't you ask something else?" and stalked off.

Fortunately for Lagos, by election day the unemployment rate had ameliorated to 10.5%, hinting that a recovery was beginning. Still, polls showed the race a statistical tie, and the outcome was almost as dramatic as the first round had been: 3,677,968 or 51.31% for Lagos, to 3,490,561, or 48.69% for Lavín. The loser stunned the winner by coming personally to his hotel to congratulate him, then the two of them went to the balcony together where, to the delight of the cheering Lagos supporters, Lavín magnanimously pledged his support to the president-elect. It was a refreshing conclusion to what had at times been a bruising battle.

Lagos was inaugurated on March 11.

Recent Developments

The first major litmus test of the Lagos government's popularity came in the mu-

Supporters of rival presidential candidates Ricardo Lagos and Joaquín Lavín compete for space on the same street corner in downtown Puerto Montt in January 2000.
Photo by the author

nicipal elections of October 29, 2000, in which 341 local governments were up for grabs. The results were less than a ringing endorsement for the *Concertación* which, despite renewed economic growth projected at 5.5% for the year, was still battling a stubborn 10% unemployment rate. Although it wanly claimed victory because it polled 52% of the popular vote nationwide, that was down from 56% in the 1996 municipal elections. Moreover, it lost about 40 cities and towns to the conservative opposition. Nowhere was the rebuke to the ruling coalition more stinging than in the Santiago mayor's race. Joaquín Lavín, who had narrowly lost the presidency just nine months earlier, handily defeated Marta Larraechea, wife of former President Frei, 62% to 28%. The *Concertación* also lost control of Concepción and Viña del Mar.

The next major showdown came in the congressional elections of December 16, 2001. The popular vote seemed to reflect a mandate for the *Concertación*, which received 51.4% of the 1.7 million votes cast, compared with 44% for the conservative coalition Alliance for Chile and 2.6% for the Communists. But in the tabulation of seats, the *Concertación* lost ground. Even with former President Frei assuming a lifetime Senate seat, and the continued absence of Pinochet, the election resulted in a tie in the upper chamber. In the Chamber of Deputies, the *Concertación* barely held its majority, dropping from 70 to 63 deputies. The major losers were the Christian Democrats, which fell from 16 to 14 Senate seats and from 38 to 24 deputies. The major winners were Lagos' *PPD*, which increased its number of senators from three to four and its number of deputies from 16 to 21; and the right-wing *UDI*, which increased its showing from 10 to 11 senators and from 24 to 35 deputies.

Culture: One of Spain's least–developed colonies, since independence Chile has made cultural contributions far out of proportion to its size, particularly in literature. During the 19th century, Chile's intellectual climate produced not only outstanding writers but attracted others seeking greater freedom of expression. Two outstanding examples are Venezuela's Andrés Bello, whose statue stands in front of the University of Chile, which he founded, and Argentina's Domingo Faustino Sarmiento, who spent several years in exile as editor of *El Mercurio* during the dictatorship of Juan Manuel de Rosas in his native land. During this era Chile produced a number of its own realist prose writers, the best known of whom was probably the novelist Alberto Blest Gana, author of such enduring classics as *El niño que enloqueció de amor.* The late 19th century also produced a golden age in art, though it was heavily influenced by contemporary French impressionism.

In the 20th century, Chile enjoys the distinction of being the only Latin American country to have produced two Nobel Prize–winning poets, Lucía Godoy Alcayaga (1886–1957) and Naftalí Reyes (1904–1973). But the world does not remember them by the names with which they were born; it remembers them as Gabriela Mistral and Pablo Neruda. Both achieved international acclaim, and both represented Chile abroad for a time as diplomats. Mistral taught for several years in the United States. Two of Chile's best–known writers today are the novelist Isabel Allende, a distant cousin of the Marxist president, who now lives in California, and Ariel Dorfman. Two of Allende's novels, *La casa de los espiritus,* and *De amor y sombras,* were adapted for the English–language films *The House of the Spirits* and *Of Love and Shadows.* Dorfman's play, *La muerte y la doncella,* was adapted for the U.S. movie *Death and the Maiden.*

Chile's folklore is grounded in the tradition of the *huaso,* a trans–Andean version of Argentina's gaucho. Its guitar–based music is similar to Mexican *ranchero.* Distinctly Chilean, however, is the national folk dance, the *cueca,* which traditionally is performed in conjunction with Chilean independence day on September 18 but is performed in touristy cafes year–round. Perhaps Chile's best– known folk singer was Violeta Parra, best remembered for her song *Gracias a la vida,* known throughout Latin America. She committed suicide because of a love affair gone bad in 1967, but her likeness is seen on copper wall plaques sold in tourist shops.

Chile's reputation as a haven for political and artistic expression disappeared during the 1973–90 military regime. Many of its own artistic, literary and musical figures were either killed or exiled. One of Chile's best–known popular singers, Victor Jara, was killed in the Santiago stadium after the 1973 coup. Film director Miguel Littín fled to Cuba. After 1990 many such artists returned, but a new generation emerged, less tied to the Marxist traditions of its predecessors. A promising young film director is Ricardo Larraín, whose 1991 movie, *La frontera,* won international acclaim.

Television came to Chile in 1960, but rather than the first stations being private or government–owned as in other Latin American countries, the first three stations were put on the air by the University of Chile, Catholic University of Santiago and Catholic University of Valparaíso; these universities still operate the stations today. The government launched *TV Nacional* in 1967. It wasn't until the early 1990s that the first two private franchises were awarded. Chilean television has become increasingly less dependent on foreign programming and has produced a number of creditable programs of its own,

some of which are exported to other Latin American countries.

Chile was the birthplace of the Latin American press. The region's first regularly published newspaper, *La Aurora de Chile,* appeared in 1810 and lasted nearly a decade. The press used to print it is on display in the National Library. Chile also is the home of the oldest continually published newspaper in Latin America, *El Mercurio,* which began as a weekly in Valparaiso in 1837, became a daily a few years later, and began publishing in Santiago in 1900. Today six dailies are published in the capital, and the provincial press also flourishes.

Economy: Few countries in the world have been whipsawed as violently from one political or economic extreme to another as has Chile. The country was long dependent on copper for foreign exchange, which as late as the 1970s still accounted for 60 percent of exports. As with Bolivia's dependence on tin, fluctuations in the world copper market often led to recessions in Chile. Moreover, the copper mines, as well as many of the country's utilities, were owned by foreign corporations, a fact that provided the Communist and Socialist parties with election–year ammunition. The elder Eduardo Frei tried to steer Chile on a middle course between Marxism and capitalism in the 1960s, an effort rewarded by President Lyndon Johnson, who lent Chile substantial foreign aid. Frei's halfway economic and social reforms proved of limited success, however, and in the end were criticized by the right as too radical and by the left as inadequate.

The result was the narrow minority victory of Salvador Allende's Popular Unity coalition in 1970, which jerked the country abruptly to the left. Allende quickly nationalized the copper mines and utilities, moves that were applauded even by Allende's conservative opponents at first because of nationalist pride. But signing a decree nationalizing an industry is one thing; running it efficiently and profitably proved to be quite another. The result was one of the many economic disasters of the Allende regime. Another was land reform, through the breaking up of the huge *latifundias* of wealthy and often absentee owners. On the surface, such reform seemed a long-overdue application of social justice. In reality, it destroyed agricultural operations that often were operating well, replacing them with small communal plots which were not commercially useful and run by peasants with little or no knowledge of efficient agricultural techniques. Marxist distribution policies also resulted in severe, Cuban–style shortages, which eroded what little confidence the regime still enjoyed. To compound its woes, the regime was beset by hyperinflation of 1,000 percent annually. It was with the country on the verge of social and economic chaos that the military intervened on September 11, 1973.

The military government of General Pinochet moved quickly to restore order, and it reversed virtually every policy of the Marxist experiment. Land holdings were restored to their original owners, although a new homesteading law was implemented to provide land to small farmers who were able to demonstrate they planned to make it produce something beyond the basic needs of their families. For a time, nationalized industries were run by the state, but by the 1980s they were privatized.

The Pinochet government made it clear it intended a dramatic break with the past, that it would not merely restore the *status quo ante* Allende. With the government's encouragement, Chilean entrepreneurs began to exploit the wealth that had lured the first permanent Spanish settlers to the out–of–the–way colony: the extraordinarily rich, nitrate–laden soil. Because of the reversal of seasons in the Southern Hemisphere, Chile began exporting enormous quantities of produce to the United States, Europe and Japan during the Northern Hemisphere winter. By the time Pinochet relinquished power in 1990, agricultural exports exceeded those of copper, thus breaking the traditional dependence on that mineral. Yet, even copper began contributing to the Chilean economy as never before in the 1990s as exports from other copper–mining countries, such as Zaïre and Zambia, declined because of inefficiency and instability.

The most dramatic economic transition of the Pinochet regime, however, was the move to almost pure free–market economics. Pinochet surrounded himself with a "kitchen cabinet" of civilian economic technocrats, many of whom had been schooled under Milton Friedman at the University of Chicago. Thus, the press quickly dubbed this team of economists "los Chicago Boys." Chile withdrew from the Andean Pact in the late 1970s and slashed its high protective tariffs, which led to a flood of cheap imported goods. At the same time, government subsidies that had kept inefficient domestic industries afloat were eliminated, forcing them to sink or swim; more than a few sank. After a brief period of seeming prosperity, the new policies plunged Chile into a severe recession in 1981. Large and small industries, unable to compete with foreign imports, foundered. So did many banks. The economic crisis lasted more than three years before the new economic realities took hold.

New Chilean industries proved capable of holding their own in the international marketplace. One such example was Chile's new arms industries, born out of necessity from the cutoff of U.S. military aid because of Pinochet's human rights vi-

olations. Chilean wineries are another international marketing success story, and there even are beginning computer hardware and software industries.

By 1990, when Pinochet turned over power to Patricio Aylwin, Chile was in the midst of an economic boom. Ironically, while the new civilian government publicly reviled Pinochet for his human rights abuses, it grudgingly acknowledged the success of his free–market policies by retaining them. It was an especially bitter pill for the Socialists who were part of the governing coalition. The result, however, was an economy that for several years was the envy of Latin America—and the world. Real GDP growth between 1990 and 1997 has averaged a dazzling 8% annually, exceeding 12% in 1992 and 10% in 1995. Contributing to Chile's success, and to its attractiveness to foreign investors, are wage costs lower than Mexico's or South Asia's and an educated workforce; the literacy rate is 96%, compared with Brazil's 83%. In addition to robust growth, inflation was trimmed to 6% and unemployment to 4%. Chile also is widely admired for its private pension system, implemented during the Pinochet era and continued since, which has provided retirees far greater returns than the government's social security system. Even U.S. congressmen have been eyeing Chile's retirement system as a possible model.

Chile is an associate member of the four–nation *Mercosur* free–trade pact (Argentina, Brazil, Uruguay and Paraguay), but because its tariff policies differ so sharply from the other four, it has opted against full membership for the moment. Chile was expected to become the fourth member of NAFTA. President Eduardo Frei discussed the issue with President Clinton during a state visit to Washington in February 1997, but his pitch to the U.S. Congress was to a mostly empty chamber. The two presidents discussed the issue again during Clinton's visit to Santiago the following October. But in late 1997 the Republican–controlled U.S. Congress denied Clinton's request for "fast–track" trade authority, which effectively scuttled Chile's membership. Still, Chile already has free–trade agreements with the other two NAFTA members, Canada and Mexico, and the three countries have greatly expanded their trade. Canadian Prime Minister Jean Chretien and a delegation of 400 businessmen visited Santiago for talks in January 1998.

In 1997, the economy became a victim of its own success. Frei was twice forced to raise interest rates to prevent the economy from overheating and to keep inflation under control. Two unforeseen external factors soon helped cool down the economy: a drop in the price of copper, which despite diversification still accounts for 42% of export earnings, from $1.19 to 75 cents a pound, and the Octo-

ber market panic in Asia, which buys about a third of Chile's exports.

The fallout of the Asian market crisis was still being felt in 1998. In September, Frei addressed the nation and announced that the 1999 budget would increase only 1.5% in real terms and called on the private sector to restrict pending. Frei predicted a 5% rise in GDP for 1998 and only 3.8% for 1999, but that was before the Brazilian market meltdowns of September 1998 and January 1999. Chile weathered that crisis better than Argentina, Venezuela or Mexico, but Frei's prediction for 1998 still fell short; the growth rate turned out to be only 3.3%, compared with the steamroller of 7.1% in 1997 and 7.2% in 1996. Worse still, the economy shrank 2.8% in the last quarter of 1998 and 2.3% in the first quarter of 1999 compared with the same quarters the previous years, meaning Chile officially was in recession for the first time in 15 years.

Year-end figures for 1999 hit just as Chileans were voting in the two rounds of the presidential election, and the recession almost proved the undoing of the ruling *Concertación*. Real GDP declined by 2.7% compared with 1998, when it had grown by 3.3%, while unemployment leaped from 6% to 11% and per capita income fell slightly from $5,100 to $5,000. Reflecting the recession, inflation was only 2.4%, compared with 4.7% the year before.

President Lagos had reason to celebrate his first year in office: real GDP growth snapped back from the negative column to a healthy 4.3% for 2000, later revised to 5.4%; it was up 4.0% in 2001. Unemployment dropped slightly from 9.7% to 8.0%. Preliminary estimates for 2001 put it back up at 9.0%. Inflation declined slightly, from 4.5% in 2000 to 3.5% in 2001.

Like Brazil's Fernando Henrique Cardoso, the one-time socialist appears to have undergone a dramatic conversion to free-market principles and has followed an economic course that has been so conservative that the opposition has had little to quibble with. He traveled to Quebec in April 2001 for the third Summit of the Americas and embraced the concept of a Free Trade Area of the Americas. While the U.S. Congress hesitated at approving a free-trade agreement with Chile, Lagos concluded a $7.6 billion free-trade accord with the European Union in May 2002.

Chile can boast one major success story, in recent years: wine, long recognized for its quality. Since 1985, wine exports have skyrocketed 5,000%, from $10.9 million to $526 million in 1999, accounting for 5.4% of total exports. The trend, though plateauing, continues upward, as large new tracts in the central region are planted with grapes.

The Future: The arrest of General Pinochet had the unfortunate side–effect of scraping the scab off Chile's slowly healing body politic. This writer covered the 1989, 1993 and 1999–2000 presidential elections as a free–lance journalist and spent a semester in Chile as a Fulbright Scholar in 1991. In 1989, I had been struck by the lingering hatred between right and left, even by Chileans who had been born after the Allende period. I interviewed then–Senator Frei in 1991, who told me that the most common words uttered by politicians were *"transición,"* meaning from military to civilian rule, and *"reconciliación."* "We seem to have accomplished the first," he said, "but we still have a way to go with the second."

Very true. The bitterness I heard in conversations with scores of Chileans from all classes and political persuasions reminded me of the century–long resentment of Southerners after the U.S. Civil War, which I experienced as a boy in Texas. Yet, in 1993–94, I was astonished at how much the bitterness had subsided. Chileans were enjoying unprecedented prosperity and had adopted a don't–rock–the–boat mentality. It seemed that, at last, they were prepared to put the tragedies of the Allende and Pinochet eras behind them and look to the future. The Pinochet case has resurrected all these old ghosts. One wonders whether they can be put to rest again even with Pinochet's eventual death, or whether they will linger as long as there is anyone alive who remembers that traumatic episode in Chilean history.

Hopefully, they will not be passed down from generation to generation, as happened in the U.S. South.

Nonetheless, democracy appears to have become rerooted in Chile, although there are some decidedly undemocratic features in the current 1980 constitution, such as the non–elected "institutional senators" and the peculiar double–member district system of electing members of Congress, which allows the opposition virtual parity. There is also the nagging question of the lingering influence of the military over the civilian government. The Lagos government has pledged to address these and other issues, but it now lacks the necessary votes in Congress to implement meaningful changes.

Chilean newspaper

The Republic of Colombia

Area: 439,405 square miles. **Population:** 40 million.

Capital City: Bogotá (Pop. 7 million, estimated).

Climate: The lowlands are generally hot, with heavy rainfall except for the Guajira Peninsula, which is arid. Highland climate varies with altitude, becoming quite temperate and pleasant in the higher elevations.

Neighboring Countries: Venezuela (East and Northeast); Brazil (Southeast); Peru and Ecuador (South); Panama (Northwest).

Official Language: Spanish.

Other Principal Tongues: Isolated Indian dialects.

Ethnic Background: *Mestizo* (mixed European and Indian, 58%), European (20%) Mulatto (mixed Black and White, 14%), Negro (4%), Mixed Negro–Indian and Indian (4%).

Principal Religion: Roman Catholic Christianity.

Chief Commercial Products: Refined cocaine, a technically illegal export worth over $10 billion U.S., coffee, petroleum, cotton, tobacco, sugar, textiles, bananas, fresh–cut flowers.

Currency: Peso.

Gross Domestic Product: U.S. $83.057 billion in 2001($1,927 per capita). This does not include money from drug trafficking, which, if included, would increase this figure by an estimated 25%.

Former Colonial Status: Spanish Crown Colony (1525–1819).

Independence Date: July 20, 1810.

Chief of State: Alvaro Uribe Vélez, (b. July 4, 1952), president (since August 7, 2002).

National Flag: Yellow, blue and red horizontal stripes.

Colombia is the fourth largest state in South America and the only one with both Atlantic and Pacific coasts. The high Andes mountains divide the country into four ranges from the *Pasto Knot* just north of the border with Ecuador and occupy about two fifths of the land. To the east of the mountains are the great, seemingly endless plains (*llanos*) and the western tip of the Guiana Highland. The majority of Colombia's population is concentrated in the green valleys and mountain basins that lie between the ranges of the Andes.

Eleven of Colombia's 14 urban centers are in the mountain valleys; the remainder are on the Caribbean coast. The vast plains along the base of the eastern range contain cattle ranches, but the extensions of the plains into the jungle–filled Amazon Basin are almost unpopulated. The northern ends of the mountain valleys, which fan out to the Caribbean coast, are wet, hot and almost uninhabited.

Because travel between the populated areas is difficult, Colombia's people live in quite distinctive communities that vary from white, Indian and black populations to combinations of mixed ancestry. The rivers of Colombia have been its most important means of communication—the Magdalena is navigable for nearly 1,000 miles and still is the principal means of transporting cargo to and from the vicinity of Bogotá. The second great river is the Cauca, not important for transportation but for furnishing water for irrigation and power for industry in the Cauca Valley.

In recent years a major construction program, similar to that of the Tennessee Valley project, has been undertaken to further develop the Cauca Valley's resources. As in all countries near the Equator, altitude is the principal factor, modifying an otherwise oppressive climate. Throughout the country rainfall is ample—there are no seasons applicable to the whole country. Summer is generally considered the dry season and the rainy season is winter; however, in some regions along the Pacific, rains, either violent thunderstorms or warm, steady showers, fall every day in the year. From sea level to 3,000 feet the climate is tropical; from 3,000 to 6,500 feet it is temperate; above 6,500 feet it is chilly. Crops are grown at elevations up to 10,000 feet, but above this level trees thin out and tall peaks are covered by snow year around.

History: The Spaniards first discovered the coast of Colombia about 1500, but the Indians proved so hostile that the explorers quickly withdrew. The first settlement was later established at Santa Marta in 1525, and Cartagena was subsequently founded in 1533. The interior was not penetrated until 1536 when Gonzalo Jiménez de Quesada explored the Magdalena River seeking its source. Climbing the eastern range, he found the Chibcha Indians in several of the mountain valleys, conquered them and founded Bogotá, the present capital. The Chibchas were sedentary, agricultural people who had developed a fairly high level of civilization.

More or less simultaneously, an expedition from Ecuador under Sebastián de

Bolívar crossing the Andes

Belalcazar discovered the Cauca Valley and founded Pasto, Popayán and Cali in 1536. Nicolaus de Federmann led an expedition toward the site of Bogotá from Venezuela. Belalcazar reached Bogotá in 1538 and came into contact with Federmann in 1539. Similar to other conquests, the period of settlement was marked by conflict among the various groups of conquerors. Sugarcane, wheat, cattle, sheep and horses were introduced by the Spaniards and a royal government was established at Bogotá in 1550 for the administration of most of the land in modern Colombia.

Gold was discovered in Antioquía about 1550, rapidly reducing further interest in the agricultural regions around Bogotá and Cali. Almost simultaneously with the start of gold shipments to Spain, English and Dutch pirates started their attacks on Spanish shipping and the Caribbean ports. However, the interior of the country was at peace and, unmolested, gradually developed. Descendants of the conquerors amassed large estates, worked by Indian or black slaves and established a semi–feudal system of agriculture that still persists in the remote parts of Colombia.

During the colonial period, what is modern-day Colombia was part of the viceroyalty of New Granada. The movement for independence from Spain started in the 1790s following publication of the French Revolution's Declaration of the Rights of Man. This was not a popular movement, but rather one of young intellectuals from the aristocratic families of Bogotá. Revolts erupted in Venezuela in 1796 and 1806, followed by an abortive

attempt to set up an independent government at Bogotá. However, the provinces were divided and the Spanish reestablished control. When news reached New Granada in 1810 that Spain's King Fernando VII had been deposed by Napoleon, the restive creoles revolted again. This time they seized Cartagena, then town after town in the Cauca and Magdalena valleys. On July 20, 1810, today observed as independence day, the *cabildo* in Bogotá arrested the viceroy and assumed control. Independence came after eight years of see–saw warfare in which Simón Bolívar and his generals, José Antonio Páez, Francisco de Paula Santander and Antonio José de Sucre victoriously marched and countermarched across Colombia, Venezuela and Ecuador. Following the defeat of the Spanish forces at the Battle of Boyacá, the Republic of Gran Colombia was proclaimed December 17, 1819, incorporating Venezuela, Colombia and Ecuador in a political union.

The allies in the war for independence divided over the form of government that should be established for the new state; Bolívar wanted a strong central government while Páez and Santander pressed for a federation of sovereign states. Later, this discord would be expressed by two political parties which developed and which still control the country today: the Conservatives, in favor of central government and close relations with the Catholic Church, opposed by the Liberals, favoring a federation of states and separation of church and state. The Republic of Gran Colombia lasted only 10 years. Venezuela separated from the union in 1829 and Ecuador declared its independence a year

later; the remaining provinces took the name of New Granada. The name Colombia was restored in 1861 as the United States of Colombia and became the Republic of Colombia in 1886.

From its inception, the new republic was torn with dissent. Bolívar sought to create a "Great Colombia;" Santander believed there was little hope for uniting diverse people with few common interests into an effective union. Dissent grew during the period of the wars of liberation of Peru and Bolivia (1822–1824). In 1826, Bolívar assumed dictatorial power. By 1830, opposition to him led to revolt; the republic was broken up and the *el Libertador* died on his way into exile.

Santander became the actual founder of Colombia. Recalled from exile in 1832, he brought a degree of order from the chaos of war. Despite his own championing of democratic ideas, he imposed a strict discipline on the country, organized its finances and set up central government services with an iron hand. He and his successor pursued moderate policies concerning the church and the differences between the Conservatives and Liberals on the form of government. However, the radicals of both sides, as well as regional interests, sought their goals by force of arms; from 1839 to 1842 civil war was waged intermittently by constantly changing forces. By 1840 the gap between the Conservative and Liberal views had widened; the Liberals were characterized as blasphemous and disorderly while the Conservatives gained power as defenders of order, godliness and good government. The Conservatives (as usual during this period) represented an alliance of the landowners, the church and the army. From 1840 to 1880, the two parties alternated in power, each using its position to persecute the other and generally provoking recurrent strife bordering on civil war. In spite of this turmoil, by 1880 the economy had broadened, the population had doubled since independence, communication and trade were improved and Colombia had few international problems.

The election of Rafael Núñez in 1880 marked a major change in Colombia's history. A long–time Liberal, he united the moderates of his party with the more moderate Conservatives and formed the National Party. Surviving another Conservative–Liberal civil war in 1884–85, Núñez secured adoption of Colombia's 10th constitution and brought order to the country. The Liberal regime became progressively conservative and subsequently dictatorial—the privileges of the church were restored, peace was maintained and political dissent was suppressed. His death in 1899 left the government in the hands of conservatives without a leader capable of avoiding the consequences of 20 years of repression. Civil war raged for three years as Liberals sought to oust

Conservatives. The so–called Thousand Day War left more than 100,000 dead, widespread destruction, a ruined economy and a demoralized people. These losses were soon followed by the revolt of the province of Panama in 1903 (arranged by the United States; see Panama).

The Colombians demanded a leader capable of reuniting the country and rebuilding the economy. A Conservative seemed to fit the bill; a proud and energetic man, Rafael Reyes assumed dictatorial powers. His five–year term was stormy—despite an empty treasury and a bitter people, he was able to reorganize the national finances, restore Colombia's credit, initiate the construction of roads and railroads and encourage the development of the coffee industry. Opposition forced his resignation in 1909.

Five Conservative presidents followed him (1909–1930). This era was marked by advances in political realism and cooperation. Elections became more honest, a semblance of a two–party government was developed and censorship of the press was reduced. During the same period, the economy improved, production rose, petroleum was discovered and business grew with the boom years of the 1920s. The ready money brought on an expansion of industry: railroads and power plants were built and coffee production expanded. The affluence also corrupted public officials and led to overexpansion and inflation.

The break in world prices in 1929 associated with the rampant depression produced a financial disaster which discredited the Conservatives, and in 1930 a Liberal government came to power.

The peaceful transfer of power in 1930 was in marked contrast to the violence found in other parts of Latin America and to Colombia's past. So, too, the Liberals of 1930 were quite distinct from their predecessors. Most of the issues which had produced the civil wars of the previous century were dead or no longer important. The Liberal Party of 1930 was interested in economic and social reforms to protect the interests of labor and of the growing middle class.

The first of three elected Liberal presidents who would govern for the next 16 years, Enrique Olaya Herrera (1930–34), satisfied reform–minded Liberals while his moderation reassured Conservatives. The second, Alfonso López (1934–38), a wealthy publisher and intellectual, was far more outspoken and dynamic. To secure needed social reforms, he implemented radical changes in the constitution that frightened Conservatives. However, he tempered their fears with more moderate legislation. His successor, Eduardo Santos (1938–42), publisher of the influential Liberal daily *El Tiempo*, moved the country sharply back to the right, bringing denunciation from López and creating the first signs of the growing schism between the left and right wings of the party.

López returned to power in the 1942 election and brought the country into World War II on the side of the Allies, much to the displeasure of pro–Axis Conservatives and neutralists within his own party. Compounding López's problems, a corruption scandal erupted during his second administration that embroiled members of his own family. Increasingly, moderate Liberals joined with Conservatives in Congress to block his proposals. There were numerous plots against him, and he faced discontent from underpaid government employees. Under mounting pressure, he resigned in 1945 and was replaced by an interim president until the 1946 election.

La Violencia

The Liberal split led to the election of a Conservative, Mariano Ospina Pérez, in 1946 with a plurality of 42% of the vote. A timid man in the wrong job at the wrong time, he was incapable of controlling either the growing militancy of the Liberal left or the fanaticism of the crypto–fascists in his own party. Bloodshed erupted between elements of these two political extremes, and there were revolts in several departments.

The murder in April 1948 of Jorge Eliécer Gaitán, a popular leader of the Liberal left, touched off a riot in the capital of such violence that the term *Bogotazo* was coined to describe a situation in which a whole people rioted. Some 2,000 deaths resulted as mobs roamed the streets, burning, looting and shooting. The conflict spread to the country as Liberals and Conservatives fought for control of villages and rural communities. The president declared martial law and gradually restored an appearance of order. It was in this atmosphere that the elections of 1950 were held. The Liberal Party, badly split, expected trouble at the polls and stayed away; the Conservatives elected their candidate, Laureano Gómez.

President Gómez was an admirer of Franco and Hitler, and installed an ultra-rightist regime. Ruling as a dictator, he used the army and police to hunt down and exterminate the Liberals. From his regime there developed an undeclared civil war that caused an estimated 200,000 deaths and a way of life known as *La Violencia* (The Violence). In 1953, he was ousted by a military coup, and General Gustavo Rojas Pinilla was installed as president. The change, accompanied by an amnesty, brought a lull in the fighting. However, his administration proved cruel and incompetent. The sole redeeming feature of his rule was that he did not discriminate between Liberals and Conservatives, forcing these enemies to arrange a truce in order to oust him in 1957.

Democracy Takes Root

There followed a Liberal–Conservative coalition that agreed to alternate Liberal and Conservative presidents for 16 years. A Liberal, Alberto Lleras Camargo, took office on August 7, 1958. Having to cope not only with the conflict between the parties but with the equally bitter internal party strife, Lleras Camargo nonetheless succeeded in separating the political antagonists from rural bandits who were capitalizing on a continuing reign of terror. He pursued moderate policies in social and economic matters while attempt-

Coffee plantation

ing the political union of Colombia. His moderation restored a degree of stability to Colombia, but the political party in Congress and government imposed by the coalition soon showed its basic weakness. The government, lacking a majority, was unable to enact any of the needed reform measures; the people, unable to influence their destiny by political effort, lost interest in the democratic process.

His Conservative successor in 1962, Guillermo León Valencia, unable to obtain legislative cooperation for even the routine functions of government, was forced to rule by decree.

The Liberal regime that followed from 1966 to 1970 was forced to use the same system. Under President Carlos Lleras Restrepo, Colombia enjoyed a comfortable rate of economic growth and continued decline in traditional rural banditry and violence that had racked the nation for nearly three decades. The Liberal–Conservative truce, known as the National Unity Agreement, served to postpone renewed competition between the political factions. Misael Pastrana Borrero, a Conservative, was elected by a slim 1.5% majority over former dictator Rojas Pinilla in the 1970 elections. A politically unknown Conservative economist, Pastrana sought to diversify the nation's farm–based economy. Although exports soared and certain sectors of the economy improved, runaway inflation and increasing unemployment became major issues in the 1974 election campaign.

With the National Unity Agreement expiring at the presidential level in 1974, Colombians voted in the nation's first open election in more than 20 years. Alfonso López Michelsen, a Liberal, was elected with 52% of the vote. In second place was the Conservative candidate, while Rojas Pinilla's daughter ran a strong third as an independent. Although the Liberals also had won large majorities in both houses of Congress, the Constitution required that all appointive offices be divided equally between the Liberals and Conservatives until 1978; this requirement was extended informally through 1986.

To carry out his program, the president declared a "national economic emergency" just five weeks after taking office in mid–1974. Permitted under a 1968 law, the action allowed López to bypass the slow–moving Congress and institute by decree certain economic reforms. Highlights of the plan included raising the daily wage by 40% to $1.50 a day, imposing a hefty tax increase on the wealthy and on luxury imports and instituting a special tax on idle farmland to encourage greater agricultural output. In addition, various steps were taken to cut the inflation rate from 30% in 1974 to an estimated 20% in 1976.

These bold economic measures met stiff opposition. Conservatives charged that the new business and personal taxes were causing a recession and discouraged new investments. On the other extreme, leftists demanded even more radical change, particularly in the rural sector. The top 4% of the population owned 68% of the farmland while the bottom 73% of the people held just 7%, consisting of small plots that provide a living only for a small family. Largely as a result of such a wide difference in living conditions, fully two thirds of the nation's youth suffered from malnutrition.

During his final year in office, President López Michelsen maintained a firm grip on the presidency—even though his administration was troubled by labor unrest, corruption charges, cabinet shuffles, guerrilla terrorism, high unemployment and inflation.

The Liberal Party candidate, Julio César Turbay Ayala, defeated his Conservative opponent in 1978 by a mere 140,000 votes. He immediately implemented his law-and-order promises by ordering an all–out military campaign against political violence, drug smuggling and general lawlessness.

Harsher tactics against guerrillas led to worldwide charges of violation of human rights. Yet the M–19 guerrilla front continued its sensational terrorism throughout 1980: seizure of 15 diplomats, murder of an American missionary and a 300-man attack on two provincial towns punctuated violence. In a murderous shootout with government troops in March 1981 in which much of the M–19 high command died, more than 400 people were killed.

Although the Liberal Party captured a majority of seats in the Congress and provincial assemblies in 1982, party dissent ultimately resulted in a Conservative victory in the 1982 presidential election. The new president, Belisario Betancur, quickly adopted an internal populist policy to help the lower classes, and a foreign policy more independent of the United States. The government was able to persuade some guerrillas to become part of the lawful political process.

Return to *La Violencia*

The next several administrations found themselves trying to deal with escalating violence from guerrillas, drug traffickers and right-wing paramilitary elements that was to make Colombia one of the most dangerous countries on Earth. President Betancur ordered a crackdown on rampant drug trafficking in 1984. The powerful Colombian drug barons retaliated against the judiciary, contributing heavily to the various guerrilla movements active in the country. When the president in turn authorized the extradition of the drug lords to the United States for trial, the cocaine producers hired guerrillas to wipe out the judges involved in such proceedings.

During the 1980s, about 100 revolutionary groups and/or coalitions were active, all dedicated to terrorism. The terrorist threat was amply illustrated in 1985 when the *M–19* stormed the Palace of Justice using mortar fire and grenades. Betancur ordered the army to storm the building, resulting in the deaths of 11 Supreme Court justices together with a large group working on extradition cases. After the event, one Colombian judge said, "You either have the choice of accepting a $500,000 bribe from these people or be killed." In all, 350 judges and prosecutors were killed during the 1980s. Frozen with fear, the Colombian Supreme Court ruled the extradition treaty unconstitutional.

The next president, Virgilio Barco, a Liberal (1986-90), also declared war on the drug barons. Fearful of being extradited, the drug cartels paralyzed efforts to control leftist guerrillas. They bribed or killed uncounted local police and eluded the national police and army. Crusading journalists also were assassinated. When a leading candidate for president was gunned down, Barco responded by reinstating the extradition laws. The terrified justice minister resigned, going into hiding in the United States with her son, fearful for their lives.

However, the lives of *Los Extraditables* also was hell on Earth. They knew that the army was *always* in pursuit of them and they stood little chance of escaping death on the spot if caught. Anyone who saw them was capable of informing the authorities (for a suitable price). There was no point in having hundreds of millions of dollars if one cannot have the pleasure of spending them. They increasingly became interested in a trial in Colombia and the possibility that bribes and favors would produce a lenient sentence in a country-club prison. In the interim, their drug business could be operated by their lieutenants.

Disillusioned by events in the former Soviet Union and Eastern Europe, *M–19* guerrillas began laying down their arms in 1989. Presidential elections were held in May 1990, and the notoriously bloodthirsty Medellín Cartel of Pablo Escobar disposed of another candidate. Yet another candidate, Carlos Pizarro, a former guerrilla commander, was assassinated by right-wing elements. Although traditional spirited rallies in the principal cities and towns were the custom, this campaign was conducted on television—it was too dangerous to venture out. Running on a promise to continue the war on drug leaders, César Gaviria of the Liberal Party won with less than a majority.

The war on the cartels was costly—there were 40 or more murders a day in Colombia. The cost of having a policeman killed was $4,000 and a judge was $20,000—pocket change for the wealthy drug barons. All officials traveled in armored vehicles in motorcades. The drug cartels proclaimed a unilateral truce in mid–1990 and the level of violence abated sharply. Gaviria did not wait for a scheduled 1991 constitutional convention: he decreed that any drug baron who surrendered and confessed would (1) not be extradited to the United States and (2) would have his Colombian jail sentence cut in half. These promises would prove to be costly.

In early 1991 several of the drug kingpins (Escobar and the Ochoa brothers) surrendered. Escobar was allowed to build his own luxurious "jail" close to Medellín, his home town. It was virtually an open house. Rated as one of the wealthiest men in the world, he enjoyed the company of 11 of his associates, claiming that the walls of the "jail" were in place to keep his enemies out. A deal obviously had been struck.

But even these pleasant conditions bored Escobar. He started running his cocaine business from the "jail," and used it as a site for the execution of real and imagined rivals. This was too much for the government and, exasperated, it sent a government force to seize the "jail" and its prime occupant. But Escobar was forewarned by one of his agents in the police and departed in July 1992 before the force arrived. He was "at large" but in misery until December 1993, pursued not only by federal forces, but by an impromptu group of former henchmen turned into reward-seekers (the United States and Colombia had posted $8.7 million for his capture). Loosely organized, they were known as *"Pepes"* (People Persecuted by Pablo Escobar). Weary, he offered to surrender in the spring of 1993, but the terms were impossible. He hid for several weeks in Medellín in late 1993, but was located by means of a traced telephone call. He and his bodyguard "offered resistance" and were shot dead on December 2 trying to elude pursuers on the rooftop of the building in which he had hidden. His funeral was sheer pandemonium as thousands sought to pay him tribute; he had "given generously" to many people and causes during his lifetime who wished to remember him. The fact is that he had a huge surplus of money that *had* to be given away.

The reward money was divided in unknown quantities between the police and survivors of Escobar's countless victims—he always had ample money for assassinations, crude torture and bombings. He was well–known for recruiting very young boys to carry out death sentences.

After 1990, Cali replaced Medellín as the center of the cocaine with its own cartel of drug overlords, chiefly the Rodríguez Orejuela brothers. It now controls 80% of the world's cocaine production and trade. Its leadership has changed several times in theory. When jailed, the drug kingpins operate from cells and their orders are carried out by an army of lieutenants, the membership of which is constantly changing. An elaborate system of distribution and money laundering is in place and functions smoothly. The profits are enormous, and now no longer being made by distribution using small aircraft. There are ample airports in Mexico where a 747 can land and quickly unload during the wee hours of the night on a remote pad. It leaves quickly, averting interception.

This is known to U.S. authorities who are powerless to do anything to prevent such shipments. An elaborate and sophisticated radar system is now in operation showing such flights. Mexico is now the route of transport of an estimated 70% of the cocaine entering the United States.

A new prosecutor general was appointed, Gustavo de Greiff, under the constitution adopted in 1991, with wide powers and discretion calculated to deal with the drug kingpins. He initially appeared to be a source of hope that basic changes could be made to make the law effective in dealing with the Cali Cartel, but in 1994 this turned sour (or realistic, in the opinion of some). There had been close cooperation between the U.S. authorities and his office until it became obvious that either his office had been penetrated by drug cartel informants or he was becoming too accommodating with regard to drug trafficking. When the names of witnesses were disclosed to his office in early 1994 by the United States, their close relatives were murdered.

De Greiff was no stranger to controversy during his term. He angered both U.S. Attorney General Janet Reno and many Colombian officials by suggesting that the legalization of drugs be given serious

A view of Medellín

95

consideration. He met with three kingpins of the Cali Cartel to discuss a plea bargain whereby none of them would receive more than five years in prison—and a country–club prison at that. U.S. and Colombian officials again were dismayed when the details of the meeting leaked out. De Greiff resigned when he reached the mandatory retirement age in August 1994 and the Supreme Court named as his replacement Alfonso Valdivieso. The new special prosecutor's tenure thus began at precisely the same time as a new president's, one who was shrouded with scandal even before taking office and who never shook it off.

The Samper Presidency

Ernesto Samper, the candidate of the Liberal Party in 1994, bragged in his presidential campaign that he bore 11 bullet wounds from an assassination attempt by drug traffickers. Indeed, he had survived an attempt on his life in 1989 by the Medellín Cartel. He emerged the front–runner in the first round of voting in May 1994, and he was elected president in the June runoff by a razor–thin margin over his Conservative opponent, Andrés Pastrana. Between his election victory and his inauguration in August, however, a series of audio tapes of telephone conversations between Samper or members of his campaign staff and kingpins of the Cali Cartel were leaked to the press, which quickly dubbed them the "narcocassettes." Thus, Samper was sworn into office under a cloud. In his first year in office, his defense minister, who had been his campaign manager, was arrested and admitted that the Samper campaign had accepted about $6 million in assistance from the Cali Cartel. Samper became a pariah to the United States, and in March 1996 the Clinton Administration revoked Colombia's certification as an ally in the war against drugs.

Samper, just midway through his term, also was under pressure at home to resign because of the embarrassing revelations. When he refused, the lower house of Congress brought impeachment charges. But in June 1996, the House of Representatives voted decisively not to remove Samper from office; even the opposition Conservatives voted by a two–vote margin against impeachment. Why? Some observers contended that the House of Representatives was fearful of the political turmoil that would result from removing a president from office. Still others believed that the Congress wanted to send a signal to the United States not to interfere in Colombia's internal affairs.

Whatever the reason, the exoneration of Samper, despite convincing evidence against him, infuriated the United States. U.S. Ambassador Myles Frechette opened an almost daily war of words, not only against the president but the Colombian government as a whole. For example, within days of the congressional vote, he accused the Colombian intelligence agency of tapping his telephone, a charge the intelligence director hotly denied. The United States took an extraordinary step in July when it revoked Samper's visa to visit the United States, a stunning rebuke of a sitting chief of state. In September, Samper was again humiliated when a stash of heroin was discovered on the presidential aircraft just as it was about to take the president to New York to address the United Nations—on the war against drugs! Authorities impounded his plane, and he had to fly to New York on a commercial aircraft. (The following May, three Colombian Air Force soldiers were charged with having smuggled the heroin onto the aircraft.) In 1997, the Clinton Administration again refused to certify Colombia as an ally in the drug war. Still, Samper hung tough, and vowed to serve until the end of his term in 1998.

Meanwhile, Valdivieso began to enjoy some success in his campaign against the Cali Cartel. In early 1996, the Rodríguez Orejuela brothers, Gilberto and Miguel, surrendered separately to authorities and were incarcerated in La Picota, a country–club prison, to await trial. A third Cali Cartel kingpin, José Santacruz Londoño, also surrendered but later opted to escape. He subsequently was gunned down, ostensibly by a rival drug gang. In January 1997, a judge sentenced Gilberto Rodríguez Orejuela to $10^1/_2$ years in prison; Miguel subsequently was sentenced to terms of 9 and 22 years. Both the U.S. and Colombian governments expressed outrage over the lightness of the sentences for men who had smuggled hundreds of tons of cocaine into the United States and other countries. The sentences were another factor in the continued decertification of Colombia as an ally in the drug war.

The government experienced yet another embarrassment in March 1997 when Defense Minister Guillermo Alberto González resigned after acknowledging that a drug kingpin may have contributed to his 1989 Senate campaign. Ambassador Frechette had warned against González's appointment in January, alleging he was tainted by drug ties. The resignation followed the arrest in October 1996 of former Attorney General Orlando Vásquez Velásquez, who was dismissed from his post by the Supreme Court on charges of abuse of power and drug–related corruption.

U.S.–Colombian relations began to improve dramatically in October 1997 with the resignation of Ambassador Frechette. He was replaced in March 1998 by Curtis Warren Kammen, a career diplomat seen as far less combative than Frechette. Foreign Minister María Emma Mejía labeled the change "a breath of fresh air." A month after Frechette's departure, the Colombian Congress extended an overture of its own by acceding to a longstanding U.S. request to repeal the ban on extradition of Colombian nationals. It was only half a loaf for the United States, however, because the law was not made retroactive and thus exempts the Rodríguez Orejuela brothers and another major kingpin, Helmer "Pacho" Herrera, who was sentenced in March 1998 to six years and eight months in prison. Herrera was murdered in his jail cell in November 1998, apparently in a contract killing by a rival drug gang.

Nonetheless, the thaw in bilateral relations accelerated in December 1997 when

Plaza de Bolivar, Bogotá

the Clinton administration lifted its ban on military aid, suspended because of alleged human rights abuses by the army and the paramilitary groups it was accused of supporting. The United States attached some peculiar strings to the $37 million it promised, however; it could be used only for operations against guerrillas suspected of dealing with narcotics traffickers, and those operations were to be confined to a classified area in the south referred to as "the Box." But the most dramatic improvement in strained relations came in February 1998, when for the first time in three years the Clinton administration "certified" Colombia as an ally in the drug war. It was certified again in 1999, 2000 and 2001.

Guerrilla Warfare Stalemates

Coupled with the Colombian government's inability to come to grips with drug trafficking has been its stalemated war against the guerrilla groups, principally the Revolutionary Armed Forces of Colombia (FARC) and the National Liberation Army (ELN). Another once-nettlesome group, M-19, abandoned its armed struggle to participate in the electoral system, with minimal success. The FARC and ELN continue to hold sway over vast areas of the rugged interior of the country, but with a new twist. There is increasing evidence that in the wake of the collapse of the Soviet Union the two groups have become motivated less by ideology and more by greed, and that they have become mercenary forces in the hire of the drug traffickers. As one U.S. Embassy official put it, they have become common outlaws, much as Jesse James and other former Confederate guerrillas did after the U.S. Civil War.

The engagements have become increasingly bloody, grimly reminiscent of the guerrilla warfare in Vietnam, only more protracted. At least 35,000 people, military and civilian, have been killed since the insurgency erupted in the early 1960s. Another Vietnam analogy is that an army of low-paid conscripts is fighting a well-motivated guerrilla force that has considerable support from the rural populace and now controls as much as 50% of Colombia's land area—even more, by some estimates. The rebels have disrupted the country's vital oil pipeline to the Caribbean coast regularly, they continue to assassinate local, state and national officials, and they frequently kidnap domestic and foreign businessmen for astronomical ransoms that help them purchase sophisticated arms on the international black market. Unlike Vietnam, however, the rebels cannot rely on the support of a foreign power any longer and lack the military strength to take Bogotá by storm, although they operate freely in its environs. What is occurring at present, in short, is a classic military stalemate.

The Colombian army suffered a major humiliation in a FARC attack on its base at Las Delicias in Putumayo Province in August 1996, in which 26 soldiers were killed and another 70 taken prisoner. They were held for 10 months before Samper agreed, against the bitter opposition of the army, to the ignominious conditions to demilitarize a large area of Caquetá Department and to exchange the soldiers for FARC prisoners. The victory was a major boost for the FARC's international prestige and credibility. Samper responded to the vocal criticism of his armed forces chief, General Harold Bedoya, by sacking him in July 1997 and replacing him with General Manuel José Bonnett.

More embarrassments were to come. In September, Bonnett ordered a major offensive, called Destructor II, with 3,000 men in the south-central region. The military expended 84,000 rounds of ammunition and more than 300 bombs, but it killed only nine Indian civilians and 40 cows, while taking one suspected guerrilla prisoner. Then, in early October, Bonnett himself narrowly escaped death when guerrillas ambushed his car. The army suffered another setback in December when the FARC killed nine soldiers and took 18 prisoners in an attack on a mountaintop communication outpost at Cerro de Patascoy in Nariño Department.

But the worst was yet in store for the beleaguered army. During the first week of March 1998, the FARC launched a Tet-like offensive designed to disrupt the congressional elections. The rebels inflicted the worst defeat to date on the army in the heaviest fighting in 30 years of warfare. The brunt of the fighting took place along the Caguan River in Caquetá, near the town of El Billar. According to both sides, the combat was at close quarters, sometimes hand-to-hand. At least 83 soldiers were killed and another 61 were captured. Compounding the army's humiliation, _43 of the prisoners were members of an elite counterinsurgency unit. The army claimed it was attacked by 700 rebels and killed 40 of them; the FARC responded that it had committed only 300 men and had lost only six dead. The truth probably was somewhere in between.

Bogotá, Colombia

Former President Andrés Pastrana Arango

The guerrillas and the armed forces are not the only key players in this protracted guerrilla war. Another is the various right–wing paramilitary groups that have committed numerous atrocities against civilians, mostly peasants, who are suspected of rebel sympathies. International human rights groups have alleged that these groups have the tacit support of the army, which the army continues to deny. In April 1997, Carlos Castaño, leader of the most notorious of these groups, brought 5,000 paramilitary fighters together under the umbrella of the so–called United Self–Defense Forces of Colombia (*AUC*). In 1997 and 1998, the *AUC* was believed responsible for several civilian massacres in different departments, many of which brought reprisals from the guerrillas.

Pastrana Seeks Peace

Colombian politics proved as volatile as ever as the country neared the two rounds of the 1998 presidential election on May 31 and June 21. In municipal elections on October 26, 1997, guerrillas murdered dozens of candidates and frightened hundreds of others into withdrawing. Tens of thousands of voters, intimidated by rebel threats of violence, stayed home.

In January 1998, the Liberals formally nominated President Samper's hand-picked candidate, former Interior Minister Horacio Serpa, for president. But Serpa's nomination threatened to split the party as anti–Samper reformers, led by Representative Ingrid Betancourt of the so–called Liberal Oxygen faction, denounced the nomination. The Conservatives, meanwhile, renominated Andrés Pastrana, who narrowly lost to Samper in 1994, while retired General Harold Bedoya, whom Samper had sacked the

previous July, launched an independent candidacy, as did Noemí Sanín, who had served as a cabinet minister under both Betancur and Gaviria.

The congressional elections on March 8 should have been cause for jubilation for the Liberals, who won 53 of the 102 Senate seats to 27 for the Conservatives and about the same proportion of seats in the 161–member House of Representatives. Moreover, turnout was a higher–than–expected 44%, despite the backdrop of a guerrilla offensive and the usual voter apathy. But the party regulars were stunned when the maverick Betancourt won her Senate seat by the largest majority of any candidate.

The presidential race turned into a free–for–all. Pastrana adroitly distanced himself from the banner of a party that had lost the last three elections. He anointed his movement the Grand Alliance for Change and reached out to Liberals disaffected with Samper and Serpa. He named as his running mate Gustavo Bell, a former Liberal governor of Atlántico Department. The Pastrana–Bell ticket won the endorsements of such prominent non-Conservatives as Senator Betancourt, former Special Prosecutor Alfonso Valdivieso and Nobel Laureate Gabriel García Márquez. The polls leading up to the first round on May 31 all showed Pastrana with a strong lead. But on election day, which this author observed first–hand, Serpa defied all the predictions with a razor–thin first–place finish of 34.3% to Pastrana's 34.0%. Only 26,000 votes separated the two men. Sanín drew 26.6%, the largest vote for an independent candidate since Rojas Pinilla in 1970. The guerrillas behaved themselves this time, permitting a record turnout of 10.7 million voters.

In the June 21 runoff, the polls this time showed Serpa with a strong lead, and this time they might have been right but for two dramatic last–minute developments. Four days before the election, the media reported that a Pastrana representative had met with Manuel "Tirofijo" Marulanda of the *FARC*, who declared that Pastrana was the candidate with the greater chance of negotiating peace. This crippled Serpa, whose slogan was "The road to peace." The next day, Sanín, while not endorsing Pastrana and never mentioning Serpa by name, assailed Samper for allegedly using government–owned media for pro–Serpa propaganda and said, "Colombians cannot have another four years of doubt about the legitimacy of their government." Meanwhile, her top campaign advisers and her own husband publicly endorsed Pastrana. In a record turnout of 12 million voters, 59% of those eligible, Pastrana won with 50.4% to Serpa's 46.5%, almost the identical margin by which Pastrana had lost to Samper four years before. The remaining 3.1% cast blank ballots in protest.

President Pastrana, 44, son of former President Misael Pastrana, was schooled as a lawyer but eschewed that profession in favor of broadcast journalism, which he practiced until he was elected to the Bogotá city council in the 1980s. He was elected mayor in 1988 and a senator in 1991. In his victory speech, he graciously praised Serpa, who responded in kind, but in a dig at Samper, Pastrana pledged to restore Colombia's international reputation. Retorted Samper: "I just hope he has more loyal and dignified adversaries than I had." Nonetheless, Samper dutifully placed the presidential sash over the shoulder of his arch-nemesis on August 7, 1998, the 40th anniversary of Colombia's post–Rojas democracy.

Shortly after his inauguration, Pastrana met again with the *FARC*'s Marulanda. Much to the army's displeasure, Pastrana agreed to the demand the *FARC* had made to Samper to demilitarize an area the size of Switzerland in Caquetá Department as a pre–condition to peace talks, which subsequently were scheduled for January 7, 1999. Pastrana fired army commander Mario Hugo Galán because of his opposition to the demilitarization. Pastrana rejected, however, a guerrilla proposal to exchange captured soldiers and policemen for 452 rebel prisoners.

Those who had hoped for a cessation of hostilities in anticipation of the peace talks were cruelly disillusioned on November 1, 1998, when the *FARC* launched its biggest push since the Caguan offensive in March, this time in coca–rich Vaupes Department in the southeast. An estimated 800 rebels overran the departmental capital, Mitu, near the Brazilian border, killing 60 policemen and 10 civilians in a pitched, 12–hour battle; another 40 policemen were taken prisoner. This came even as the army was complying with the ordered demilitarization in Caquetá. The army suffered heavy casualties retaking the now–destroyed town.

Despite the rebel offensive, the army meekly completed the demilitarization in Caquetá. Twelve days later, the *FARC* launched an attack on a local *AUC* headquarters in Urabá Department, in northwestern Colombia, and claimed they killed 32 paramilitary fighters in their sleep; *AUC* commander Carlos Castaño put his losses at 19 and guerrilla deaths at 16. The *FARC* attacked Castaño's own camp at the end of December, just nine days before the peace talks were to begin, and announced they may have killed Castaño himself, a report that proved to be wishful thinking.

In a separate surprising development, the U.S. Congress in December tripled the amount of aid to the Colombian police for its drug–fighting efforts, from $88.6 million in 1998 to $289 million in 1999. In February, the Clinton administration, which had not requested the dramatic increase in counter–drug aid, recertified Colombia as an ally in the drug war.

The peace talks began on schedule on January 7, 1999, but days later the *AUC* went on another of its trademark killing sprees, killing 130 alleged guerrilla sympathizers. A perplexed Pastrana flew to Havana and on January 17 met with Fidel Castro and Venezuelan President–elect Hugo Chavez to solicit their intercession with the guerrillas. Nonetheless, the *FARC* broke off the talks three days later, demanding that Pastrana clamp down on what it called government sanctioning of the paramilitaries; it also gave the government a list of officers suspected of paramilitary links. Meanwhile, Nature intervened to halt the bloodshed temporarily. On January 25, a devastating earthquake struck the city of Armenia, killing about 900 people. In the aftermath, *FARC* and army elements actually cooperated for a time to maintain order and to deter looting in the stricken city. Alas, the killing soon resumed; in the heaviest fighting since the Mitu battle, 12 soldiers and 30 guerrillas died in a clash in Arauca Department on February 18.

Perhaps as part of an effort to placate the *FARC* and jump–start the peace talks, Prosecutor General Alfonso Gómez announced on March 31 the arrest of an army lieutenant colonel in connection with the grisly July 1997 massacre by paramilitary forces of about 30 peasants in the town of Mapiripán, in Meta Department. He was the highest–ranking officer ever arrested for alleged paramilitary ties. (On May 21, the brigadier general who had commanded the army brigade near Mapiripan also was arrested and charged with failure to respond to repeated telephone calls for help as the massacre unfolded.) Pastrana also cashiered two army brigadier generals in April whom the guerrillas and human rights groups had accused of paramilitary links. The government denied that was the reason for their dismissals from active service, though it did not offer another explanation. Another general was arrested in July 2001 and formally charged with organizing paramilitary forces in Antioquía Department, while the navy's second-ranking admiral was being investigated for permitting the massacre of 27 people by paramilitaries in January 2001.

Apparently, some army officers have not taken the firings seriously. In August 1999, paramilitary forces killed another 36 people in two towns in Antioquía Department. Two weeks later, Pastrana again sacked the brigadier general in command of the army brigade in the area, after evidence surfaced that he ignored repeated reports that the paramilitaries would strike there. Also in mid-1999, paramilitaries allegedly assassinated a political satirist and an economist who were high-profile activists in the peace process.

Despite Pastrana's concessions, both the peace talks and the fighting dragged on simultaneously. In November 1999, government and *FARC* representatives met in Sweden, and Pastrana held out an olive branch by suggesting a cease-fire for the holiday season. Within days, the *FARC* responded with one of its largest offensives in months, launching coordinated attacks in six outlying departments that left 10 soldiers or policemen dead. Pastrana angrily denounced the attacks as "demented" and said they amounted to a betrayal. In mid-December, the *FARC* attacked a naval base near the Panamanian border, killing 23 marines. Despite the renewed fighting, government and *FARC* representatives met again at the Vatican in February 2000 with a representative of Pope John Paul II, with inconclusive results. In late March, the *FARC* launched another offensive in Chocó and Antioquía departments, killing 11 policemen and 11 civilians, including two children. By May, a frustrated, angry Pastrana was threatening to break off the talks. The *FARC*'s blasé response: If you want to.

Meanwhile, in April 2000, the *FARC* announced the creation of a new political group, the Bolivarian Movement for a New Colombia, which claims to be reaching out to all disenchanted sectors of society (which would in theory include almost everyone!). It was unclear whether the new group is designed as a political party to compete for power within the system, or whether it is a sign that the *FARC* is attempting to establish a parallel national government within the large area it controls. It may be the latter, as the *FARC* has begun passing "laws" in the area it controls that impose taxes and provide harsh penalties for what it perceives as "corruption."

The talks sputtered off and on for several more months, until in November 2000 the *FARC* suspended them indefinitely, ostensibly to protest the government's failure to curtail army involvement with the right-wing paramilitaries. Pastrana offered to extend the terms of the euphemistically named demilitarized zone—in reality a safe haven for the highly militarized guerrillas—if the *FARC* would return to the bargaining table. The *FARC* let Pastrana dangle until February 2001, when the president met with Marulanda again in the jungle. Among the concessions Pastrana made were an eight-month extension of the safe haven and a purging of the army's ranks of suspected collaborators with the *AUC*. In February 2001, an army tribunal convicted a brigadier general of failing to stop the 1997 Mapiripán massacre. He was sentenced to only 40 months, but the conviction was nonetheless historic. Pastrana also pushed through a law mandating that armed forces personnel accused of human rights violations would henceforth be tried in civilian, not military, courts. That did

not stop the U.S. State department from releasing a new report in late February 2001, just days before Pastrana visited Washington again, assailing the human rights record of the Colombian army.

Nor did the government's concessions do anything to allay the killing. Although the armed forces scored a few impressive tactical victories, they also suffered some humiliating setbacks at the hands of the *FARC*. In October 2000, at a time when the talks were still in progress, the *FARC* attacked the town of Dabeiba, in Urubá state, in force with 800 guerrillas. Five of the much-touted Blackhawk helicopters brought elite troops to the rescue. One was shot down by ground fire, killing all 22 men on board; a second was grounded by mechanical failure; the other three reached their landing zone, but the 60 troops were annihilated after they landed. In March 2001, the *FARC* killed 17 marines in an attack on a vital telecommunications tower in the south. In another incident, the *FARC* "executed" 13 policemen it had taken prisoner after capturing the town of Roncesvalles in July 2000. Apparently, the *FARC* was competing with the *AUC* to seize the moral low ground.

Rumors had circulated for nearly a year of an imminent prisoner exchange, something finally begun on June 6, 2001, when the *FARC* released a badly wounded police colonel and three other officers. In exchange, the government released 73 ill prisoners. On June 28, the *FARC* released 242 more prisoners, leaving only an estimated 42 still in its hands. Some hailed the exchange as the most positive product of the two and a half years of "peace" talks, while some skeptics claimed that the *FARC* was only ridding itself of a logistical burden.

The public had good reason to be skeptical. A report released by the president's human rights office showed that in the first four months of 2001 the number of killings by non-governmental forces had actually *increased* by 75% over the previous year. Of those deaths, 529 were attributed to the *AUC*, 190 to the *FARC* and 50 to the *ELN*.

For its part, the *ELN* began reminding the government that it is still a force to be reckoned with. The *ELN* demanded that the government create a demilitarized zone for it in the north as it had for the *FARC* in the south, although it was more modest in its demand: "only" 2,300 square miles. As a show of force, the *ELN* blocked the highway between Bogotá and Medellín in February. The rebels did little more than create mischief, shooting out tires of cars and holding about 1,000 people hostage until soldiers supported by helicopter gunships drove them off. Amazingly, despite the failure of the concessions to the *FARC* to bring peace, Pastrana announced in April that he was agreeing to demilitarize three municipalities in

Santuario (sanctuary) de las Lajas in Nariño State in southwestern Colombia, partially built into the rock of the mountain.

Courtesy: Embassy of Colombia

Bolívar and Antioquía departments, a total of about 1,800 square miles, as a precursor to peace talks with the *ELN*. Unlike the *FARC*-controlled zone, however, this area is a hotbed of activity by the right-wing *AUC* paramilitary group as well as the left-wing *ELN*, and the "demilitarization" has not led to an end to clashes between the two.

The government and *ELN* representatives met in Geneva in July 2000, but the talks were unproductive. Pastrana at first refused to yield to the demands for a safe haven, but after the *ELN* staged some spectacular kidnappings as a show of force, the jelly-spined Pastrana acquiesced in February 2001, agreeing to a reduced area of about 1,100 square miles, still larger than Rhode Island. Residents in the area, spurred in part by the *AUC*, protested their government's surrendering them and their lands to the *ELN*'s control in exchange for—nothing. The local army commander complained that he was on the verge of capturing the *ELN* headquarters in Bolívar when he was ordered to withdraw. The withdrawal of government forces began on March 29. Interestingly, U.S. Ambassador Anne Patterson endorsed the safe haven as a step toward peace. For one thing, the *ELN*, unlike the *FARC*, agreed to international monitors in

its area. Also, it was believed, the *ELN* was on its last legs, under increasing pressure both from the army and the paramilitaries and was more likely to be willing to talk peace. The *AUC* launched an offensive in April against the *ELN*, which caused the deaths of seven guerrillas and four paramilitaries. The *ELN* suspended the talks on April 19, although it released 34 employees of Occidental Petroleum it had kidnapped.

The other major player in the conflict, the *AUC*, has actually been strengthened, in part perhaps because of the government's willingness to make concessions to the guerrillas that many rank-and-file Colombians regarded as too much in exchange for too little. Its strength was estimated at 8,000 in 2001. It continues to flout the rules of warfare, preferring massacres of civilians to achieve its nebulous goals. One such atrocity was a raid on the town of Naya in Cauca state on April 14, 2001, in which 32 civilians were reported killed; the arms of a 17-year-old girl were severed with a chain saw. That same month, the U.S. government formally declared the *AUC* a terrorist organization, and in September it added it to the list of terror organizations to which Americans may be prosecuted for contributing money. Also in 2001, the Colombian army

launched a crackdown against the paramilitaries called "Operation Dignity," mostly to convince the *FARC* that it was serious. The yield: 10 paramilitaries killed and 61 captured, figures that were unprecedented. Also seized was the chain saw believed to have been used in Naya. A milestone for the *AUC* came with Castaño's resignation in August 2001, ostensibly because he could not control the more bloodthirsty elements. He was succeeded by Salvatore Mancuso, scion of an affluent Italian immigrant family, who is perceived as more of a hardliner than Castaño, even advocating attacks against army troops as well as against guerrillas. Days after he assumed command, the *AUC* massacred 11 people in a town in Tolima Department. A month later, they massacred 24 more in the town of Buga, Valle del Cauca Department, and 12 in Magdalena Department. In an interview with the Associated Press at a mountain hideout in February 2002, Mancuso boasted that the *AUC* now numbers 14,000 effectives and promised even greater bloodshed.

In August 2001, the *FARC* launched offensives in Cordoba, Arauca and Caquetá departments in the northwest, but this time the army proved a match for the guerrillas, killing about 100 of them and

Children swimming in the river near Monteria, Colombia

destroying 16 of their camps while losing 21 dead. Ten days later, the rebels responded with two more bombings of the Caño Linón pipeline in Arauca, belonging to Occidental Petroleum, polluting a river for 50 miles. A week later, the army, supported by the air force, scored another major victory in Meta, Guaviare and Meta departments in the southeast against a *FARC* force of 1,200, killing at least 50. In September, the army killed another 24 *FARC* members in a pitched battle near San José de Guaviare, which the army turned into a media event. The triple defeats were believed the costliest ever for the *FARC* in such a short time period.

The *FARC* found itself with a public relations problem in late September after it had kidnapped Consuelo Araujo, Pastrana's former culture minister, a prominent and highly popular patron of the arts, in a highway abduction. Her body was found a few days later, and the crime outraged the nation. Suddenly, the *FARC* announced on October 5 that it would desist from highway kidnappings and negotiate seriously for a cease-fire. Still grasping for his peace straw, and against the advice of his generals, Pastrana unwisely reciprocated the gesture just when the *FARC* was reeling, extending the safe haven for another three months, until January 2002. The *FARC* then refused to return to the negotiating table until December 15. The same day, the government and the *ELN* reached an agreement in Havana to resume talks in January 2002. Two days later, the *ELN* declared a truce for Christmas and New Year's, which it kept. Not so the *FARC*, which launched attacks on several towns in Cauca at New Year's. But the *FARC* met unexpected resistance from civilians, who staged protests. The *FARC* relented, while the rest of the nation cheered the gutsy townspeople who at last dared to stand up to the bullies. Clearly, the *FARC* was losing the battle for hearts and minds.

On January 10, 2002, Pastrana announced the *FARC* had broken off talks again and gave it 48 hours to abandon the demilitarized zone, and he dispatched troops into the area. The *FARC* responded with a 14-point negotiating plan that appeared to address some of Pastrana's concerns for security along the border of the DMZ. The president briefly acted as though he had developed a backbone and rejected the proposal, but within days he acquiesced to the *FARC* once again. Within hours, the *FARC* responded to the president's show of good faith by setting off bombs in a town 30 miles from Bogotá and by attacking a prison and freeing 39 rebels; four soldiers were killed in the attacks. Despite this perfidy, on January 20 Pastrana, his new backbone gone, caved in again and agreed to resume cease-fire negotiations, to be brokered by the United Nations, setting a deadline of April 7.

The *FARC* showed once again how serious it was about peace by bringing urban terrorism to the capital. On January 25, it set off a car bomb in Bogotá that killed five people; on January 29, it dynamited 50 electrical towers and the dam that provides Bogotá with its water supply. The next day, thousands of residents of the capital poured into the streets for a mass demonstration against the *FARC*, banging on pots and pans, a traditional Latin American form of nonviolent protest.

Events then began to explode in a dramatic and violent chain reaction. On February 20, after the *FARC* hijacked a domestic airliner and forced it to land, kidnapping a prominent senator who was on board, Pastrana finally realized the futility of attempting to negotiate with people of bad faith and broke off the peace talks. He sent the army into the safe haven and ordered the air force to bomb and strafe *FARC* base camps and landing strips in the zone; the military met surprisingly feeble resistance as the zone was "remilitarized." Apparently in retaliation and as a show of defiance, the *FARC* committed still another outrage on February 24 by kidnapping independent presidential candidate Ingrid Betancourt. She remains a hostage. On March 3, the *FARC* assassinated a Liberal senator. In early April, the *FARC* set off a pair of bombs in Villavicencio that killed 12 people and wounded 70. On April 11, it kidnapped 12 members of the Cali departmental legislature. On April 14, it made an unsuccessful attempt to assassinate the front-running presidential candidate Alvaro Uribe, who was calling for a military victory over the *FARC* (see The Elections of 2002). On April 21 it kidnapped the governor of Antioquía. But the worst was yet to come.

On May 2, about 1,000 *FARC* and 600 *AUC* fighters engaged in a bloody battle for the village of Bella Vista, in the district of Bojaya, in Chocó Department near the Panamanian border. The area, strategic as a corridor for imported arms and cocaine exports, vital to both sides, was the scene of the bloody *FARC* attacks in March 2000 that left 11 policemen and 11 civilians dead. More than 500 civilians were huddled in a church for safety during the battle when a *FARC* gas-cylinder mortar shell crashed through the roof and exploded, killing and dismembering 117 people, including 40 children and a woman who was nine months pregnant. The *FARC* admitted it had fired the mortar round but claimed the church had been hit by accident. It cynically blamed the *AUC* for the appalling death toll, saying the civilians should not have been in the town—where they lived. It took the army eight days to reach the area. The atrocity shocked an already numbed Colombia, as well as the international community. The U.N. human rights representative to Colombia initially called it a "war crime." Pastrana

asked a U.N. human rights investigating team to visit the area, but he was not prepared for the scathing report it issued a few weeks later. It concluded the *FARC* was directly responsible for the deaths, but it blamed the *AUC* for putting the civilians in harm's way and it assailed the Pastrana government for ignoring warnings the United Nations had given it on April 23 that paramilitary forces were moving into the area and that a violent confrontation was imminent. It also castigated the army for its tardiness in reaching the town. The U.S. Congress, meanwhile, demanded to know why the army, which was the beneficiary of so much U.S. aid, had responded so slowly. Once again, the *FARC* found itself with a public relations nightmare. In early June, the European Community finally acceded to a request from Pastrana to follow the U.S. lead in declaring the *FARC* a terrorist organization; the Bojaya incident was the catalyst. Yet, the bloodletting continued. On June 3, fighting involving the *FARC*, the *AUC* and the army in Caquetá, near the border of the "RMZ," left another 49 people dead.

If there were any lingering doubts about the *FARC*'s ruthless nature, they were dispelled in June when it declared it would begin killing mayors who do not resign. As this book was going to press, dozens had resigned.

The guerrilla war also has soured Colombia's relations with neighboring Venezuela. In February 2001, the government of President Hugo Chávez, long suspected of being sympathetic to the Colombian guerrillas anyway, admitted it had captured, then released, an *ELN* member suspected in a 1999 airplane hijacking. Pastrana and Chávez met at the remote Venezuelan mining town of Puerto Ordaz on March 24. By then Venezuela had rearrested the hijack suspect, José María Ballestas, and Pastrana was pressing for his extradition. The two presidents announced at the conclusion of the two-day meeting that Venezuela would serve as an active partner in the negotiations between the Colombian government and the guerrillas and that their two armed forces would exchange intelligence information. However, Colombian intelligence is aware that aircraft regularly flew between Venezuela's border region and the *FARC* safe haven.

A potentially important new variable was added to this already complex equation in February 2002 when the Bush administration asked Congress to approve additional military aid for Colombia. In a major policy shift, Secretary of State Colin Powell said the aid should be used against the guerrillas, not just against the drug traffickers. The U.S. government is especially concerned about security for the vital Caño Limón oil pipeline, which the *FARC* and the *ELN* have attacked nearly

,000 times. Moreover, the United States sees the *FARC* as just another international terrorist organization to be included in its war on terrorism in the wake of the September 11, 2001 attacks on the United States by Islamic extremists. The *FARC's* alleged international links had been spotlighted the previous August when three suspected members of the Irish Republican Army were arrested in Colombia, accused of providing the *FARC* with terror training. In fact, the *FARC's* bombings in Bogotá in January had distinct IRA fingerprints. By April, when Pastrana made one of his perennial visits to Washington, the Bush administration was asking for $133 million to protect the pipeline and $439 million in long-term military aid.

"Plan Colombia"

As the peace talks and the fighting both droned on, Pastrana outlined a six-year, $7.5 billion plan to destroy the drug trade. Called *"Plan Colombia,"* it includes expanded enforcement as well as incentives to farmers to plant alternative crops. The Clinton administration asked Congress in January 2000 for $1.6 billion for aid to both the Colombian police and army for their counter-drug operations. Among the hardware included for *Plan Colombia* were 30 sophisticated Blackhawk helicopters. As usual, the administration insisted that the new aid money for the army would be used only against drug traffickers, not against the guerrillas, thus seeking to perpetuate the myth that the two were distinguishable and unrelated.

The House of Representatives approved the measure to which the Colombian aid was attached in March, but it hit a snag in the Senate. In April, Pastrana personally flew to Washington—where he had once worked as a television correspondent—to personally lobby for the aid money. As he had humbled himself before both guerrilla groups, Pastrana now humbled himself before Senator Trent Lott, leader of the Republican majority, to plead for the money. Lott told Pastrana he supported the Colombian aid in principle but that he objected to the "bloated" $13 billion appropriation bill to which it was attached. Lott essentially told Pastrana to be patient, and the president went home empty-handed. Eventually, in June, the Senate approved a drastically reduced $934 million aid package, which also replaced the 30 sophisticated Blackhawks with 60 aging Hueys. In the end, the two houses agreed on a $1.3 billion aid package in August, which Clinton quickly signed into law. Colombia thus became the third-largest recipient of U.S. military aid after Israel and Egypt. Days later, Clinton met with Pastrana in the colonial city of Cartagena.

Since then, U.S. Special Forces, or "Green Berets," have trained a special counter-drug brigade of three battalions, totaling 3,000 men. The brigade received 16 Blackhawks and 25 SuperHueys. The *FARC* denounced *Plan Colombia*, using it as a convenient pretext for scuttling the peace talks, and in February 2002 it demanded that it be ended and foreign military advisers withdrawn. Clearly, they were feeling the pinch.

The new U.S. president, George W. Bush, upped the ante for *Plan Colombia*. In mid- 2001, Congress approved an additional $676 million to battle the Colombian drug trade, a 50% increase. However, with all that money, some of it was bound to go bad. In May 2002, the U.S. Congress partially suspended further aid for the drug war when Colombian media and the U.S. Embassy reported that $2 million in anti-drug money had disappeared. The commander of the national police's anti-drug unit, General Gustavo Socha, fired six officers believed responsible for the pilferage. Days later, Socha was himself demoted and subsequently resigned, being replaced by General Jorge Linares.

A major event in the drug war occurred in September 2001 when Fabio Ochoa, an alleged kingpin of the old Medellín cartel, was extradited to the United States. It was a major departure for Colombia, which had not extradited such a notorious suspect in more than 10 years.

The Elections of 2002

Meanwhile, the hapless president's Conservative Party also proved a spectacular failure in the departmental and municipal elections on October 29, 2000, a bellwether for the presidential contest on May 26, 2002. The Conservatives failed to win a single governorship, while the Liberals and independents each won 15. Independents also won the mayor's races in four of the five largest cities, including Bogotá. There, Antanas Mockus, a flamboyant and somewhat eccentric philosophy professor who served as mayor in 1995-97 and once mooned a heckler, won the post again. The campaigns were marked by the usual violence and intimidation; more than 20 candidates were killed either by left-wing guerrillas or right-wing paramilitaries, others were kidnapped and another 100 withdrew. There was evidence of *FARC* intimidation and even some ballot-stealing in the areas it controls, although an independent defeated a *FARC*-backed candidate in the largest town under its control, San Vicente del Caguan.

The presidential field then began taking shape. The Liberals once again nominated Horacio Serpa, who lost narrowly to Pastrana in 1998, hoping he would make the same sort of comeback Pastrana had after his 1994 defeat. The Conservatives nominated Juan Camilo Restrepo, who had been Pastrana's finance minister and ambassador to France. Once again, there were several independent candidates, seemingly assuring the race would be thrown into a runoff again: Noemí Sanín, who polled over a fourth of the vote as an independent in 1998; Senator Ingrid Betancourt, a prominent Liberal renegade who had supported Pastrana in 1998; and Alvaro Uribe, a former Liberal governor of Antioquía, candidate of a movement called *Primero Colombia*, who pledged to get tough with the guerrillas. Rounding out the field was Luis Eduardo Garzón of the far-left Social and Political Front. It looked like Colombian politics as usual. But the 2002 election would not be usual.

Serpa, who had promised to continue peace talks with the guerrillas, forged to an early lead, but as the peace talks droned on and the *FARC* outrages continued, Uribe suddenly broke from the pack by promising to double the size of the military and seek an all-out victory over the guerrillas. After the peace talks collapsed on February 20 and Betancourt was kidnapped on February 24, he soared to 59% in the polls.

There was another bellwether of the public mood on March 10, when Colombians voted for a new Congress. The turnout was 44%,despite the usual rebel threats. The Liberals retained their majorities in both houses, but at least 27 new senators publicly declared their support for Uribe (the *AUC* claimed that 35% of the new Congress were its sympathizers, a claim that could neither be verified nor discounted). Voters clearly were in a get-tough mood.

On March 12, Restrepo, who had been receiving only1-2% in the polls, dropped out. It left the Conservative Party without a presidential candidate for the first time since it was founded in 1849. He made no endorsement.

Uribe's tough anti-*FARC* rhetoric was not lost on the guerrillas. On April 13, they attempted to assassinate the candidate by setting off a remote-controlled bomb under a bridge on a highway near Barranquilla as his motorcade passed. He escaped unhurt, but three bystanders were killed and 15 injured. Ignoring the danger, he stopped and offered comfort to the injured. For Uribe, the attack was *déjà vu*; in 1983, his father had been killed when he resisted a *FARC* kidnap attempt.

The assassination attempt backfired on the *FARC*; not only did their nemesis survive, but the attempt on his life boosted his standing in the polls. Desperately trying to regain his early momentum, Serpa alleged that Uribe was drawing support from the right-wing paramilitaries, a charge that Uribe denied. Even if it had been true, with the mood the Colombian voters were in, it probably would have helped him further.

The results on May 26 were a veritable landslide, not just a mandate in favor of the hawk, Uribe, over the dove, Serpa, but a repudiation of the guerrillas. A total of 11.2 million Colombians voted, a turnout of 46.3%. Uribe scored a decisive first-round victory with 5.7 million votes, or 52.9%; Serpa received 3.5 million, or 31.7%. Garzón was a distant third, followed closely by Sanín; Betancourt, still in *FARC* captivity, was a poor fifth.

A day after his election, the president-elect sounded far more conciliatory than the truculent candidate had been, saying he still favored a U.N.-brokered peace with the guerrillas. The *FARC*, however, probably will reject his overtures, setting the stage for a bloody, winner-take-all showdown. Uribe also said he was willing to engage in peace talks with the paramilitaries, something his predecessors had eschewed. He further promised to continue the war against drugs , to reduce corruption and increase efficiency in government, and somehow to increase social spending. A Harvard-educated lawyer, who turned 50 on July 4, 2002, Uribe had a positive record as an efficient governor of Antioquía. Three weeks after the election, the president-elect held talks in Washington with President Bush and other senior officials and in New York with U.N. Secretary-General Kofi Annan. Back home, he advocated a constitutional amendment to allow him to declare a state of emergency to deal with the guerrillas, a proposal that gave chills to human rights advocates.

Uribe was inaugurated on August 7. *FARC* launched a mortar attack near the National Palace in an attempt to disrupt the inauguration, killing 19 people.

Culture: The blend of the European and Indian races was more thorough in Colombia than in the nations of the southern areas of Latin America. Moreover, refugee blacks from the Caribbean settled along the northern coast and, as elsewhere, have made their contribution to Colombian music and art. However, the so-called Bolivarian countries of the northwestern tier of South America, those liberated by Simón Bolivar, have not been characterized by the comparative freedom of expression and political stability of the countries of the southern part of the continent.

Colombia's long history of dictatorship, political turmoil and domestic violence conspired to retard its cultural development until the latter half of the 20th century. The overthrow of the Rojas Pinilla dictatorship, and the truce reached between the warring Liberal and Conservative parties in 1958, marked a watershed in Colombian cultural expression. Bogotá's self-proclaimed title of "the Athens of South America" is a bit boastful, but there is no question that the country has made a regional impact.

This is especially true in the plastic arts, as a visit to the top floor of the *Museo* *Nacional* in Bogotá will attest. As in Chile, the influence of France on 19th century Colombian art is unmistakable, but in the late 20th century a number of talented Colombian painters and sculptors have won international reputations. Perhaps the three best known are Edgar Negret, the abstractionist Alejandro Obregón and Fernando Botero.

The premier figure of Colombian literature remains Gabriel García Márquez, who received the Nobel Prize in 1982. His landmark novel was *Cien años de soledad*, but later novels that have won international critical acclaim include *Crónica de una muerte anunciada* and *El Amor en los tiempos de cólera*. García Márquez's leftist policies have brought him controversy. He is a close friend of Fidel Castro's and maintains a residence in Havana as well as in Paris. Despite his international prestige, he was denied a visa to visit the United States during the Reagan Administration.

A newer, if older, star among Colombian writers is Alvaro Mutis, a novelist and poet who has achieved acclaim in the Spanish-speaking world with the fictitious character, Maqroll el Gaviero; such novels as *La última escala del Tramp Steamer* and *Amirbar*; and the book of poetry, *La mansión de Araucaíma*. At the age of 79, he received Spain's coveted Cervantes Prize in April 2002, becoming the first writer from any country to win all three of Spain's most prestigious literary awards.

Bogotá and the major provincial capitals of Medellín, Cartagena, Cali and Barranquilla have active theatrical and musical communities, though much is still borrowed from abroad. Colombian popular music has definite Caribbean influence.

Colombian cinema is still in the developmental stage, compared with the more established industries of Mexico, Brazil and Argentina, but a few feature-length films are produced each year. Colombian television has become largely self-sufficient in programming, and some of its *telenovelas* are exported.

The Colombian press, like so much else in the country, has been shaped by the Liberal-Conservative rivalry and in recent years has been the target of drug-related violence. Involvement of newspaper owners in politics has been commonplace, most notably former Presidents Laureano Gómez, who established the Conservative mouthpiece *El Siglo*, and Eduardo Santos, whose family still publishes the prestigious pro-Liberal daily *El Tiempo*. Ironically, these two rival newspapers both were intimidated by the Rojas Pinilla dictatorship, forcing them to collaborate editorially against the dictator. The dean of the Colombian press and its circulation leader is another pro-Liberal paper, *El Espectador*, which has won international plaudits for its courageous editorial at-

tacks against the drug cartels. Its editor, Guillermo Cano, was murdered by the Medellín Cartel in 1986, just one of scores of Colombian journalists who have given their lives in the line of duty. Several high-quality news magazines are published, the most widely read being *Cromos* and *Semana*.

Economy: The informal economy of Colombia is based on production and smuggled export of refined cocaine and far outweighs the formal economy based on agriculture. The coca leaves are not generally grown in Colombia, but come from Peru, Ecuador and Bolivia, where an acre can yield $10,000 a year. The final stage of processing takes place in Colombia, which traditionally has had but loose control over illicit activities. Small "factories" are easily moved, and with police double-agents abounding, when there is a raid on a facility, no one is home.

Most of the population, however, was employed in agriculture, which is handicapped by inefficient techniques and misuse of resources—produce and labor. Rural violence is common and has stimulated migration to the cities since 1948 where many of the newcomers are unemployable because of lack of education and skills. Now, only 1.7% of the people work the land. An estimated 60% are engaged in the cocaine traffic in one capacity or another. The resources of Colombia are capable of supporting the growing population without the cocaine industry, but numerous problems, principally poor distribution of wealth, must be resolved before there can be major economic gains.

Government programs were undertaken to end the traditional dependence on coffee exports, and by 1973 other goods and products produced more foreign income than coffee. Manufactured goods are slowly gaining a larger share of total exports.

The López administration sought to revitalize the rural sector through agrarian reform and government investment. Tighter controls over foreign-owned firms and banks, together with new taxes on the wealthy increased government revenues 50%. High unemployment (17%) persists and a relatively high population growth rate of 2.3% annually also hampers progress.

Colombia has a thriving coal industry; it is not only self-sufficient in oil, but is a major exporter. Honda makes motorcycles here, with production exceeding 50,000 units per year.

One bright spot for the economy in 1996, albeit a temporary one, was a disastrous frost in Brazil that destroyed much of its coffee harvest. The result has been skyrocketing coffee prices on the world market, much to the benefit of Colombia, whose coffee growers already had embarked on an aggressive marketing campaign with its "Juan Valdez" character in the industrialized countries.

The overall economic picture in Colombia has been bleak for several years. Chronic high unemployment, along with the endemic corruption within the Samper government, was one of the major issues in the 1998 presidential election that saw an end to 12 years of Liberal rule. The jobless rate that year was 16%, second only to Haiti among the 20 Latin republics, while inflation also was among the highest in the region at 18%. Real GDP for 1998 was $96.9 billion, up 3% since 1997. Growth in 1999 was 4.3%, which dropped to 2.8% in 2000; preliminary figures for 2001 put growth at 3%.

The already dismal unemployment picture has gradually worsened: 18.1% in 1999, 19.7% in 2000 and 20.5% in 2001, still the worse in Latin America. Inflation has moderated slightly, from 9.2% in 1999 to 8% in 2001.

The combination of sluggish economic growth, population increases, joblessness and inflation have steadily dragged down Colombians' living standards. Per capita GDP has declined from $2,440 in 1997 to 2,081 in 1999 to $1,927 in 2001.

The Future: President Pastrana's four years in office were a dismal failure. Like Neville Chamberlain, who naively attempted to ensure peace by appeasing Adolph Hitler, Pastrana is a decent man who had noble intentions, but he was no match for his ruthless adversary. His Chamberlain-like approach to appeasing the *FARC*—yielding to all their unreasonable demands in the vague hope that their intentions were good—proved fruitless, not to mention gutless, and his legacy will be that of a pitiful failure. What he never seemed to grasp is that the *FARC,* and to a lesser degree the *ELN,* had no incentive to make peace. The *FARC* enjoyed actual control of an area the size of New Jersey,

which Pastrana handed to them on a silver platter without regard for the people living there, just as Chamberlain sacrificed Czechoslovakia, and tacit control over an area the size of California; the *ELN* had free rein over an area about the size of Delaware. Within these safe havens, the guerrillas operated with impunity—except for the occasional attacks by the outlaw *AUC.* The *FARC* is making an estimated $600 million a year from the drug trade, more than the GDP of most countries. The guerrillas lack the military strength to storm the capital and take complete control of the country, as the Sandinistas did in Nicaragua in 1979, but what matter? They already enjoy power in a state within a state.

Will the $2 billion the United States has allocated for *Plan Colombia* produce results? Only up to a point. For every coca field and clandestine laboratory destroyed by these U.S.-trained battalions, others will crop up to replace them in the vast, incredibly rugged and inaccessible Colombian hinterlands. At best, the U.S. anti-drug effort will run in place, as on a treadmill. Why? Because, as the Latin Americans have complained for years, U.S. and European demand for illegal drugs is insatiable, making the trafficking of them an endeavor too lucrative to abandon and so lucrative to make it worth the risks.

How can demand be reduced? One way could be through more effective public education in the consuming countries, something far more effective than Nancy Reagan's "Just say no"campaign. This author was the Army Reserve attaché to Colombia from 1994-1998, and I learned a great deal about cocaine production. The three principal ingredients needed to refine coca leaves into that coveted, exorbitant powder that addicts need so desperately are gasoline, powdered cement and hydrochloric acid. Public service messages

showing in graphic detail the disgusting process of how cocaine is actually made ought to persuade any reasonable person never to try it—and maybe even to give it up.

Two major events occurred in 2002 that possibly augur a long-overdue breakthrough in a 38-year-old war that to date has claimed 40,000 lives. First, President Bush proposed, and the Congress disposed, to end the ridiculous restriction that U.S. military aid be used only against drug traffickers but not against the guerrillas. The mood in Washington changed decidedly after September 11, 2001, and liberals in the U.S. Congress finally saw the *FARC* for what it is—a terrorist organization, one in league with the narcotraffickers and even the IRA, not a band of social reformers. Second, Colombian voters gave a resounding mandate to Alvaro Uribe to double the size of the military and to crack down on the guerrillas and stop pussy-footing with them as Pastrana had for four years.

But tough rhetoric is one thing and delivering on it is another. One cannot presuppose that the Colombian armed forces, even with the hundreds of millions of extra dollars they will be receiving from Bush and Uribe, will prove up to the task of achieving a battlefield solution. It hasn't in 38 years, in part because the army is made up of conscripted, underpaid cannon fodder. To achieve a military victory will require more sophisticated training, state-of-the-art technology, better pay for troops at all echelons and—something impossible to purchase—more professional leadership.

This probably will require more than one four-year presidential term. But if Uribe can make some strides in that direction, he almost assuredly will enjoy a more positive legacy than Pastrana's. The trick for him, however, will be to stay alive long enough to accomplish something.

The Republic of Costa Rica

Costa Rican cowboys—campesinos

Area: 19,647 square miles.
Population: 4.0 million (estimated).
Capital City: San José (Pop. 800,000, estimated).
Climate: The coastal lowlands are hot and tropical, with heavy rains from April to December. The valley of the central highlands is temperate, with moderate rains during the wet season.
Neighboring Countries: Nicaragua (North); Panama (Southeast).
Official Language: Spanish
Ethnic Background: Overwhelmingly Spanish European descent, blended with some Indian lineage. A few Indians with African heritage are found along the Atlantic coast; some pureblood Indians live in the highlands.
Principal Religion: Roman Catholic Christianity.

Chief Commercial Products: Coffee, bananas, sugar and cacao.
Currency: Colon.
Gross Domestic Product: U.S. $15.85 billion in 2001 ($4,450 per capita).
Former Colonial Status: Spanish Crown Colony (1522–1821).
Independence Date: September 15, 1821.
Chief of State: Abel Pacheco de la Espriella, president (since May 8, 2002).
National Flag: Blue, white and red horizontal stripes.

Costa Rica, literally *Rich Coast*, is next to the smallest of the Central American republics. Lying between Nicaragua and Panama with coasts on both the Atlantic and Pacific oceans, the distance from ocean to ocean varies from 75 to 175 miles.

The country is divided into three distinct regions: the Atlantic coastal plains, the central highlands and the Pacific coast. The central highlands are part of a chain of scenic mountains rising in Nicaragua and running southeast through Costa Rica into Panama. They contain lofty peaks reaching 12,500 feet and several steep–_sided inter–mountain valleys. The green central valley, some 40 miles wide and 50 miles long, lying between 3,000 and 6,000 feet above sea level, is the most densely populated part of Costa Rica.

The two principal cities, San José and Cartago, share the valley with four volcanoes, two of which are still violently active. Mount Irazú, close to the capital, littered the city with ashes and cinders in 1962. Arenal erupted in 1998.

Costa Rica's coffee is grown on the slopes of the hills and volcanoes which rim the valley. The Atlantic coastal plains are moist and low, heavily forested and sparsely settled. Costa Rica's main port in the east is Puerto Limón, the only city of commercial importance in the area.

The Pacific lowlands, drier than the Atlantic plains, are quite narrow except for the Nicoya and Osa peninsulas. Thinly settled, the region produces bananas and fiber on large plantations. The port of Golfito on the Pacific coast handles most of the country's exports. Lying in the tropical rainbelt, Costa Rica has more than abundant rainfall, particularly in the rainy season from April to December of each year. Some parts of the oppressive Atlantic coast region have rain during 300 days of the year.

History: The Spaniards discovered the Nicoya Peninsula in 1522, settling in the Central Valley, where a few sedentary Indian farmers were found. They organized into a *hacienda* system of independent farm communities. The Spaniards intermarried with the Indians, who were assimilated into the Spanish culture. Cartago was founded in 1563, but no expansion of this settlement occurred for 145 years, during which time the Costa Ricans evolved as a community of small farmers. With the assimilated Indians and a few slaves, the Costa Rican worked his own land, developing a system of small, efficient and independent landowners and a tradition of industry not usually found in Hispanic society. Settlers from Cartago founded Heredia in 1717 and San José in 1737; by 1750 the population had reached approximately 2,500, divided into some 400 family groups.

Independence from Spain was achieved on September 15, 1821 as a result of actions in Guatemala, Mexico and other colonies. Costa Rica fell victim to the civil wars which followed the separation of the

Central American Republics from the short–lived Mexican Empire. However, remoteness from the scene of the bitter quarrels between conservatives and liberals in Guatemala and El Salvador minimized the effects of the civil war in Costa Rica. The most significant events of Costa Rica's history as an independent state have been its efforts to develop the economy to provide the revenues required to support the people.

The government encouraged the production of coffee in 1825, offering free land for development. From 1850, the coffee trade attracted new settlers and inspired the development of roads and the settlement of areas outside the central valley. The building of railroads between the 1870s and 1890s introduced banana growing to provide traffic for the new system. At the same time, West Indians were brought in to build the railroads, clear the forests and to work the Atlantic coast plantations.

Subsequently, irrigated banana plantations were developed on the Pacific coast, resulting in the building of ports at Golfito and Puntarenas. On the Nicoya Peninsula and in the northwest, cattle raising became and remains an important industry.

Politically, the Costa Rican experience was tranquil. The first experiments in government were hardly more than gentlemanly agreements among the principal families. The constitution of 1848 abolished the army and replaced it with a civil guard. Costa Rica has had only one _major experience with dictatorial government. Tomás Guardia came to power in 1870 and ruled as an undisguised dictator until 1882. Exiling opposition leaders and spending money with a lavish hand, he broke up the traditional parties, installed his friends in office and undertook to modernize the rural agricultural state. During his term of office, roads, railroads, schools and public buildings were constructed; the production of sugar and coffee was increased and international trade was encouraged.

Costa Rican political freedom was recovered in elections of 1889 which were free and honest. Three subsequent attempts were made to seize the government: in 1917, which lasted two years, an unsuccessful attempt in 1932 and a communist—inspired effort in 1948 was ended by a brief civil war. José Figueres, a hero of the civil war, won election in 1953; a capable farmer and businessman, he did much to renew public works and increase government revenues. An outspoken critic of Caribbean dictatorships, he was denounced as a communist and an invasion force from Nicaragua moved to unseat him.

An appeal to the Organization of American States ended the conflict; Figueres disbanded the force he had raised for defense and pressed for both economic and social development. Subsequent presi-

dents representing conservative and liberal parties have maintained the tradition of responsible, democratic government which was the ideal of Figueres. Like most countries dependent upon agricultural exports for its revenues, Costa Rica has had its economic problems, but also has shown a remarkable ability to handle them peacefully.

Between 1945 and 1974 the presidency alternated between conservatives and liberals while the single–chamber legislature was dominated by the liberal National Liberation Party (PLN). This pattern was reversed with the election of Daniel Oduber Quirós to succeed President Figueres.

With 42% of the vote, Oduber's victory was credited to the superior organization of the PLN and to the divided opposition of seven other candidates. The new president, a former head of the legislature, promised agrarian reform and constitutional changes to increase the power of the executive branch. However, in 1978, voters ousted the ruling PLN, electing Rodrigo Carazo of the Democratic Renovation Party. He won by 50% to 49% over the

PLN candidate, former union organizer Luís Alberto Monge Alvarez.

The right–of–center president soon found his administration beset by scandals and fiscal problems. For years, Costa Ricans imported more than they exported and spent more than they earned. Somehow, it worked until 1980, when the nation's imported oil bills and international interest charges skyrocketed while earnings from exports nosedived.

Rather than impose needed austerity measures (the government subsidizes food, fuel and luxury imports), Carazo sought to stave off disaster by printing more paper money. International lenders responded by cutting off credit.

The crisis exacted another toll: Carazo became the most unpopular president in recent years. In 1982 presidential elections, voters rejected his Unity coalition in favor of Monge 56, who this time took 58% of the vote. During his years in office, his popularity remained high in spite of an unpleasant task: austerity measures to bolster a sagging economy.

By mid–1984, democratic Costa Rica appeared besieged by several problems. The armed conflicts in neighboring Nicaragua and El Salvador threatened to interfere with the national political process at a time when economic conditions in the nation reached a dangerously low level; the national public debt increased to $4.4 billion by 1986, placing the government on the brink of bankruptcy. Significantly, in mid–1984 the government asked the United States for $7.3 million in order to improve its military capability to resist

increasing *Sandinista* pressure on its Nicaraguan border. By the middle of 1985, the first U.S. military advisers were already training the Costa Rican National Guard.

Costa Ricans went to the polls in early 1986 and elected Oscar Arias Sánchez of the *PLN* president by a majority of 52.3%. A highly educated and respected man, he was expected to perform as well as might be possible in the face of adversities which surrounded the country and which it had been experiencing from communist infiltration of the labor movement from within. His performance was mostly steady, but sometimes erratic. During a visit to Washington in mid–1987 he strongly urged President Reagan to discontinue aid to the *contras* of Nicaragua, stating that they were fomenting unrest in Central America. But a few days later, he declared that so long as the *Sandinista* regime of Nicaragua existed, there would be a danger that communism would spread throughout Central America.

President Arias was the architect in late 1987 of a peace plan for Central America, a scheme that was immediately embraced by liberals in the U.S. House of Representatives who had been trying to end aid to the anti–communist *contras*. He received the Nobel Peace Price for this effort, which appeared doomed to failure. But those who had this opinion did not take into account the fact that the Soviet Union was in a state of rapid economic collapse.

The *Sandinistas* found the economic rug being abruptly yanked out from under their regime, and out of sheer desperation, accepted the Arias plan, which included democratization of that country.

Arias was not eligible under law for a second term, and was succeeded by the then 40–year–old Rafael Angelo Calderón, a lawyer from the Social Christian Unity Party (*PUSC*). He significantly cut the number of civil employees and undertook a number of measures to modernize the economy.

In the 1994 election, the *PLN* returned to power with the candidacy of José María Figueres, son of the former president. He narrowly defeated Miguel Angel Rodríguez of the *PUSC*, despite the cloud hanging over Figueres that he may have been involved in a murder when he was a teenager and charges, dismissed because of a statute of limitations, of corruption while he was a government minister. Figueres' campaign also was helped by a Washington–based political consulting firm, which ran U.S.–style television commercials that smeared Rodríguez as a shady businessman who once was forced to file for bankruptcy.

Although the Harvard–educated Figueres was elected on a promise to retain the Uruguayan–style social welfare system his father had engineered, once in office he did what so many other Latin Ameri-

Oscar Arias Sánchez

can presidents have done in recent years. Confronted with economic reality, including a cumbersome public debt of $3.5 billion that represented 40% of GDP, he abandoned his party's idealistic social principles and sought pragmatic solutions to the country's economic woes. His greatest feat was in touting Costa Rica's low labor costs and highly literate work force to persuade transnational high–tech firms to locate assembly plants in Costa Rica. His major prize was Intel Corp., which agreed to build a $300 million assembly plant that will export $3 billion per year in Pentium processors. Among Figueres' other economic successes, he lowered the unemployment rate from 6.2% in 1996 to 5.4% in 1997, cut inflation to 11.2% in 1997, the lowest in four years, and oversaw a robust GDP growth rate of 4% in 1997. Yet, Figueres proved the most unpopular president since Carazo. Despite his economic successes, Costa Ricans still grumbled that their glass was half empty rather than half full. The Figueres administration was plagued by a number of low–level scandals, hardly more than peccadillos by Latin American standards but which undermined public confidence in his government. The public also was concerned over an alarming increase in common crime, including violent crime, once rare. Finally, Figueres was faulted for neglecting the nation's infrastructure, especially the sorry condition of streets and highways.

The time was ripe for the *PUSC*'s Rodríguez to make a Nixon–like comeback in the February 1, 1998 elections. The *PLN* candidate, former soccer star José Miguel Corrales, sought to distance himself from the unpopular Figueres by attempting to seize the moral high ground and purging the party of congressional and municipal candidates with allegedly questionable

backgrounds. This move merely alienated Corrales from the rank and file of his own party. While Corrales made grand promises to pay housewives a minimum wage and to provide more free bonds for private home construction, Rodríguez's campaign strategy might well have been summed up, "It's the potholes, stupid." Indeed, at times he sounded more like a candidate for county commissioner than for president, promising to repave highways, to expand water purification systems, even to remove the hated turnstiles from the front of buses and to allow passengers to exit from the rear. The outcome was closer than the polls had predicted, with Rodríguez winning by a 46–43% margin over Corrales and 11 other candidates. He was inaugurated on May 8, 1998.

In his term, Rodríguez managed to do something unusual for a Latin American president: keep his promises. He expanded the San José airport and embarked on an ambitious road-building program. He also was aggressive in luring more foreign investors, an initiative that appears to be paying off (see Economy). However, Rodríguez was met with vigorous street protests when he attempted to privatize state-owned companies as has been done in virtually every other Latin American country except Cuba and Uruguay. Rice farmers also protested his free-trade initiatives.

The 2002 election reflected Costa Ricans' growing disenchantment with what they regard as a lack of choice between the two major parties. For the first time in Costa Rica's venerable 53-year-old democracy, a third-party candidate emerged who threatened the traditional parties' power monopoly. In 2001, Otton Solís, a 48-year-old economist and *PLN* dissident, formed the Citizen Action Party (*PAC*).

President and Mrs. Abel Pacheco

The *PUSC* nominated a 68-year-old psychiatrist and congressional deputy, Abel Pacheco, while the *PLN* nominated Rolando Araya, 54, a chemical engineer. Both Pacheco and Araya had high name recognition from having been television commentators. Solís attacked what is widely perceived as the two main parties' corruption; Pacheco pledged to crack down on common crime, which has become a major problem and a threat to the all-important tourist industry; Araya placed his emphasis on improving education. Polls showed the three candidates at one point in a statistical three-way tie. In the balloting on February 3, 2002, however, the two major parties won the upper hand, but Solís prevented either of them from receiving the necessary 40% to avoid a second round. Pacheco finished first with 38.5%, Araya was second with 30.9% and Solís was a strong third with 26.3%. Besides throwing the election into a runoff for the first time, Solís' *PAC* also emerged as the kingmaker in the new Congress with 14 seats; the *PUSC* won 19 and the *PLN*, 17. Voter turnout was 69%, as anemic as it had been in 1998.

In Costa Rica's first-ever runoff, Araya attempted to win over Solís' voters by pledging a crackdown on official corruption, but he had little success because of the bitter attacks he had made on Solís in the first round to move up from third place in the polls. Araya also attempted unsuccessfully to portray Pacheco as a neoliberal; in truth, both candidates adhered to the popular sentiment against privatization of government–owned enterprises like telecommunications and insurance. In the April 7 runoff, Pacheco won with a resounding mandate of 58%. It was the first time the *PUSC* had won two successive elections. Pacheco was inaugurated on May 8.

Culture: Costa Ricans are Christian, nominally Roman Catholic. Basically they are of Spanish ancestry; the country has the lowest percentage of Indians and *mestizos* of any Central American country. Early in the colonial era, what few Indians native to the area were assimilated into a uniform, friendly society of middle class merchants and small farmers.

The pure Spanish emerged as a small, rich elite controlling the wealth of Costa Rica. Popular cultural expression is found in music and dance. The most characteristic art expression is the brilliantly decorated ox carts still found in rural Spain and Portugal; they are accepted as a national symbol, although they are rapidly being replaced by trucks and tractors in the national economy. Through energetic promotion of education, Costa Rica has achieved the highest literacy rate in Central America—93%—greater than that of the United States. Fifteen television stations provide a wide variety of entertainment.

This is one of the most pleasant of the Central American countries to visit. The train journey from San José to Limón is scenically spectacular. Of course, the usual precautions against thievery must be taken where there is great disparity in wealth, particularly in the bustling city of Limón.

Economy: Costa Rica's sources of external income are coffee and bananas. Industrial activity once was limited to processing agricultural products for market and the production of import substitutes for domestic consumption. In recent years, foreign firms have established assembly plants, such as Motorola and Intel.

Improved economic conditions have encouraged the elite upper class to retain more capital funds within Costa Rica which formerly would have been invested abroad. There is no immediate threat to the economy, and there is also a growing sense within the elite that the wealth of the nation must be shared more widely. Tourism is growing rapidly, lured by beautiful beaches on both coasts and a number of rain forest reserves. There is room for many more luxury resorts on the west coast and inland areas which would attract North American patronage during the winter months in particular, but also year–around. Bilateral agreements with Canada would be most useful in this respect.

Another area of wealth is starting to open up which offers tremendous opportunities. Costa Rica is an ideal site for a relatively luxurious retirement at a modest cost for U.S. citizens. Stability and lower prices for everything but imported goods is very attractive to persons with reasonable but not unlimited means and annual income. This is now being carefully advertised in U.S. newspapers as an excellent place for individual (not communal) retirement, attracting widespread interest. About 30,000 Americans already have settled here.

Costa Rica has been cursed (or blessed) by a flood of illegal Nicaraguan workers whose labor actually is necessary to prosperity. The problem is crime—major, violent crime—which they are prone to commit.

There was a major disappointment in 1998 when Motorola announced it would begin scaling back the output of its Costa Rican plant, but the impact was more than neutralized by the opening of Intel's Pentium processor plant. The plant's $2 billion in exports in 1999 gave Costa Rica a $93 million trade surplus, compared with a $702 million deficit in 1998, its first surplus in 13 years. It also generated a disproportionate growth in real GDP of 8.2%,

Typical Costa Rican ox cart

the highest in Latin America, but experts warned that it would drop when the Intel plant was fully operational in 2000. It did; growth for 2000 was a meager 1.4% and only .5% in 2001.

These positive factors, plus political stability, an educated labor force and President Rodríguez's eight-year tax exemption for manufacturers of export products, have proven attractive to foreign investors. One target: the cumbersome government-owned electricity and telecommunications company, which Rodríguez attempted unsuccessfully to privatize. Costa Ricans have proven stubbornly reluctant to dismantle the quasi-socialist public sector, apparently out of fear of the unknown and despite the privatization trend that has swept Latin America. Even celular telephone service and insurance are state-owned in Costa Rica. In the next few years, high-tech and ecotourism are expected to transform the Costa Rican economy, replacing the far more market-sensitive coffee and bananas as the mainstays of the economy.

The Future: For the first time, Costa Ricans have elected a *PUSC* president for two consecutive terms, a significant vote of confidence from a people notorious for being spoiled and fickle. For all their complaining, however, Costa Ricans enjoy one of the highest standards of living in Latin America, perhaps one reason they are so fearful of dismantling their cumbersome public sector and replacing it with privately owned enterprises. They will admit that the telecomunications system is not working all that well, but they don't seem to think that it's broke bad enough to fix. Rodríguez made good on his promise to improve the terrible road and highway infrastructure. If Pacheco does as well with his promise to combat the alarming increase in street crime, which is frightening tourists, Costa Rica will be well served.

The Socialist Republic of Cuba

Señores Imperialists: We are not in the least afraid of you!

Photo by Sheila Curtin

Area: 44,217 square miles; with the Isle of Pines, 45,397 square miles.

Population: 11 million .

Capital City: Havana (Pop. 2.4 million, estimated).

Climate: Tropical with little daily or seasonal change. Cuba is buffeted by occasional tropical hurricanes from July to October.

Neighboring Countries: Cuba is an island, the largest and most westerly of the Greater Antilles islands, lying 90 miles south of Florida and separated from Hispaniola by 40 miles.

Official Language: Spanish.

Ethnic Background: Mulatto (mixed black and white, 51%), white (37%) black (11%) Other (1%).

Principal Religion: Roman Catholic Christianity.

Chief Commercial Products: Sugar, minerals and tobacco.

Currency: Peso.

Gross Domestic Product: U.S. $18.6 billion in 1999 ($1,700 per capita). These figures are estimates derived from various factors and may be the result of government distortion or exaggeration. No direct estimate is possible.

Former Colonial Status: Spanish Crown Colony (1492–1898).

Independence Date: May 20, 1902. (Spanish rule ended on December 10, 1898).

Chief of State: Fidel Castro Ruz, President. (Since 1959; b. 1927).

National Flag: Three blue and two white horizontal stripes; a white star in a red triangle at the staff.

Cuba, an island 745 miles long and not over 90 miles wide at any point, lies east and west across the Gulf of Mexico, 90 miles south of Key West, Florida. Cuba is gifted with moderate temperatures, adequate rainfall and excellent soils. While the general impression of Cuba is one of rolling hills, it is in fact quite mountainous in parts. To the west of Havana is the Sierra de los Organos, with elevations of up to 2,500 feet; toward the center of the island are the Trinidad Mountains rising to 3,700 feet; in the east the Sierra Maestra has peaks reaching 6,500 feet. About one sixth of the land is forested. The rough, stony headlands east of Guantanamo Bay are semi–arid and the source of copper, nickel, chrome and iron ores.

History: Cuba was discovered by Columbus in 1492 and conquered by the Spanish in 1511. Indians offered little resistance and, decimated by hard labor and epidemics, disappeared fairly rapidly. By the end of the 16th century only small, dwindling groups survived in the mountainous areas of the island.

The Spanish conquest of the continent relegated Cuba and the other islands in the Caribbean to a secondary position in the rapidly expanding empire. Lured by the news of gold and glory coming from Mexico and Peru, Spanish immigrants abandoned Cuba to join further exploration and conquests. Two factors, though, compelled Spain to pay special attention to Cuba: its strategic geographical location, dominating the entrance to the Gulf of Mexico, and the increasing attacks by pirates which forced Spain to concentrate its naval resources in "convoys," or fleets, for better protection of its rich cargoes. These fleets, one departing from Veracruz, Mexico, and the other from Cartagena, Colombia, joined in Havana and then, under the protection of the Spanish navy, sailed for Europe. Consequently the port of Havana had to be extremely well forti-ied, and the sporadic presence of these fleets allowed for a flourishing degree of commerce.

During the 18th century the development of the island gained some momentum. The decline of gold and silver production on the continent convinced many Spaniards that they should remain on the island. Garrisons were kept to protect several ports besides Havana; smuggling with other islands—principally Jamaica and Haiti, by then British and French possessions—increased trade. The rising demand for the island's first valuable export, tobacco, created favorable conditions for steady economic growth. The strategic importance of Cuba was highlighted in 1762 when Havana was attacked and captured by a large British expeditionary force. The British did not expand their occupation beyond the port, and they stayed less than two years. However, the attack jolted Spain. More fortifications were built along the shores of the island, more capable officials were sent to govern the colony and a program of road construction began into the interior of Cuba. Almost simultaneously, the island's sugar production began to demonstrate its rich potential.

The independence of the United States in 1783 opened a close and expanding market, and the collapse of Haiti's sugar production in 1799–1801 following its devastating war for independence gave Cuba a truly golden opportunity. In the first three decades of the 19th century the island changed rapidly from a slowly developing "factory" into the world's leading sugar producer.

The production of sugar, however, required a growing number of black slaves. Fearing a repetition of Haiti's experience, and enjoying unhindered prosperity—the Napoleonic wars and affairs in South America had kept Spain occupied in other areas—Cubans were not eager to risk all in an attempt to break with the mother country. After 1830, however, this situation began to change. Concentrating her attention on Cuba, Spain increased taxa-

tion, imposed arbitrary rules for its own benefit and completely alienated the creoles (native born Cubans of mixed ancestry), by denying them any voice in the government. Seeking annexation to the United States, a now powerful nation where slavery was accepted, many slave owners promoted armed expeditions from southern American ports, but the North's resistance to the incorporation of *more* slave territories into the Union, and the eventual defeat of the South in the American Civil War, put an end to those efforts. By 1865 the majority of the creoles still held hopes of obtaining reforms from Spain. Only a minority proclaimed the necessity of fighting for independence. An international economic crisis which hit the island in 1866 and Madrid's dismissal in 1867 of a Cuban delegation demanding reforms set the stage for the *independentistas*. In 1868, in the town of Yara, Carlos Manuel de Céspedes raised the banner of independence.

Using guerrilla tactics, and under the guidance of able military leaders, the Cubans fought valiantly against an increasing number of Spanish troops for 10 years. Their failure to invade the rich western provinces (the struggle was limited to the eastern regions), internal dissension, exhaustion of resources and renewed Spanish promises of reforms, brought peace in 1878. But in spite of the Cuban Autonomist Party's efforts, few reforms materialized. By 1890, Cuban discontent was growing and a new, exceptional leader had appeared: José Martí. Poet, essayist and patriot, Martí managed to unite almost all Cuban exiles, organized a conspiracy on the island and prepared to renew the struggle. He dreamed of a short, popular war which would avoid the destruction of wealth, the rise of military *caudillos* and U.S. intervention. In 1895 the

war began and Martí was killed in one of its first skirmishes.

U.S. Domination

From 1895 until 1898 the Cubans fought Spain's military might. This time, able to carry the war throughout the entire island, the rebels burned and destroyed most of Cuba's wealth. Increasingly alarmed, and stimulated by imperialist groups and a "yellow" (sensationalist) press, the United States finally intervened in 1898 when the explosion of the battleship *Maine* in Havana harbor raised to _a peak the clamor for war. The "splendid little war" against an exhausted Spain lasted a few months and ended with the military occupation of Cuba. After reorganizing a country ravaged by war and disease, the U.S. military forces abandoned the island in 1902. That year, the Cuban people proclaimed a constitution which (through the Platt Amendment by the U.S. Congress) gave the United States the right to intervene in case of crisis, and elected its first democratic president, Tomás Estrada Palma.

Estrada Palma's honest administration was marred by political turmoil when the president sought reelection in 1906—reluctantly, the United States was forced to again occupy the island for two years. After building a Cuban army and watching the election of Liberal José Miguel Gómez, the United States once more pulled out its military forces. The next 20 years witnessed rapid expansion of sugar production, increased American investment, persistent political corruption and economic instability of a one–product economy. Nevertheless, the republic progressed in many areas. Education improved, communication was expanded and a new

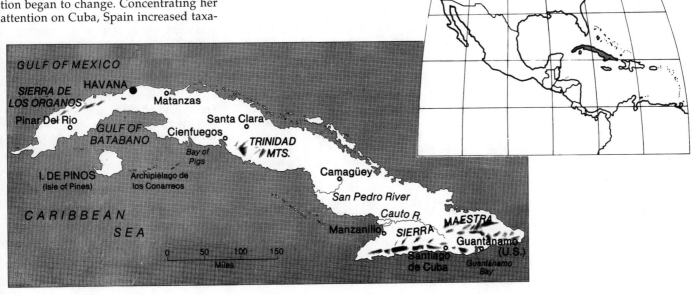

President Batista deposits his ballot

nationalistic awareness matured. An economic crisis of 1919–21 resulted in a rising crescendo of popular demands for the abrogation of the Platt Amendment and strong protests against official corruption.

Liberal Gerardo Machado was elected president in 1925 and initiated a vast program of national regeneration and public construction. His popularity declined in 1928 when he imposed his candidacy for reelection on the Cuban people—it plunged after the economic collapse of 1929–30. Faced with widespread misery and violent opposition spearheaded by university students as well as a secret organization known as A.B.C., Machado responded with brutality. By 1933, in spite of increased terrorism on the part of the government, the struggle had reached a stalemate; the opposition had no realistic hopes of toppling Machado and the government was unable to eliminate its opponents. It was time for Washington again to intervene.

Constrained by his own "Good Neighbor Policy" which precluded the use of military force, the recently elected President Roosevelt sent his trusted aide Sumner Welles to seek a legal solution for Cuba; his mission was to prevent a revolution and avoid American military intervention. Posing as a mediator, Welles pressured Machado into making concessions, encouraged the opposition and eroded the army's loyalty to the president. In 1933 a general strike decided the issue: Machado fled the island. Immediately Welles organized a provisional government with the cooperation of the A.B.C. and the majority of the opposition. But the revolutionary momentum disrupted his plan. There was a purely military insurrection of Army sergeants headed by Fulgencio Batista which was transformed by

university students into a revolutionary movement that toppled the provisional government. For four turbulent months under a temporary president, the students and the sergeants (by then *colonels*) tried to enforce a radical and ambitious program of social reforms. Sternly opposed by Welles, the government collapsed in January 1934 when Batista shifted to the opposition. As soon as a moderate president was installed, Washington abrogated the Platt Amendment. For the following decade, *real power* centered around Batista.

Batista was not a bloody dictator or a counter–revolutionary. A man of humble origins, both shrewd and ambitious, he preferred bribery and corruption over brutality. Well aware of the importance of the nationalistic and social forces unleashed by the revolutionary episode of 1933, he tried to use them for his own benefit. Encouraging the emergence of political parties and the return to the island of political exiles, he quickly restored stability. Labor unions were legally protected, social legislation approved and a modest plan for national recovery announced. After Batista harshly repressed a general strike in 1935, the Cuban political atmosphere became calm. Supported by several parties, including the Communist Party, Batista convened a Constitutional Assembly, and in 1940 one of the most advanced social constitutions in all of Latin America was issued. That same year Batista was elected president.

With the price of sugar climbing, Batista's term of office coincided with a return of economic prosperity. In 1944 Batista crowned his accomplishments by allowing free elections. Ramón Grau San Martín, hero of 1933 and head of the *Autentico* Party, obtained the overwhelming majority of the votes. The *Autenticos* ruled

from 1944 to 1948, with a positive record of benefits for the workers, respect for democratic values, a more equitable distribution of wealth, continuing economic recovery and rising living standards, but was tarnished by public corruption on an unprecedented scale. Grau was succeeded in 1948 by a fellow *Auténtico*, Carlos Prío Socarrás, who proved equally venal. Before the people could repudiate the *Auténticos* in 1952 elections, Batista dis-

The U.S. and Cuba
1902–1959

Despite the unevenness of U.S.–Cuban relations politically, the two nations developed close economic ties during the post–independence period through the 1959 Cuban Revolution. U.S. investment was encouraged and protected, and in fact became a mainstay of the Cuban economy. In spite of domestic Cuban upheavals, there was an unwritten understanding that neither U.S. investments nor Cuban tourist facilities calculated to attract Americans would be disturbed.

Some aspects of this relationship were resented by many Cubans, particularly the common U.S. notion that Cuba was a paradise for those seeking sexual adventures not explicitly described, but well–known. Many "French" postcards (pornography, judged by then–prevailing standards in the United States) had their origin in Cuba. Numerous films "for private exhibition" were produced and made in the island nation. Tourists relished in the decadence offered by the casinos and nightclubs, many controlled by organized crime figures, chief among them Meyer Lansky.

Havana and other coastal resorts and towns were favored ports of call for resort and cruise ships and there was regular steamship service catering to vacationers. A luxurious train regularly departed from New York—"The Havana Special"—which ran down the east coast through Miami and went on to Key West over a rail causeway. From there, the cars were loaded onto seagoing ferries which took them to their ultimate destination, loaded with fun–seeking vacationers. This ended in 1936 when a devastating hurricane wiped out the causeway.

As airline traffic came into its own after World War II, Havana was a favorite destination of tourists and vacationers. This pleasant state of affairs continued right up to 1960, with all political considerations being put aside.

rupted the political process with a military coup.

Trying to keep up appearances, Batista promised elections in 1954. But the illegitimacy of the government prompted political parties and numerous sectors of the population to demand a return to "true democracy." Soon more radical opponents appeared. The students organized violent acts and on July 26, 1953—now a holiday in Cuba—a group of young men under the leadership of Fidel Castro made an unsuccessful attack on the military barracks at Santiago de Cuba. The sheer brutality of its repression mobilized popular support for the rebels. With Castro and his surviving group in prison, Batista renewed his effort to gain legitimacy.

Elections were held in 1954; Batista was elected to the presidency and he allowed *all* political prisoners to go free—including young Fidel Castro. But his opposition increased; while a Student Revolutionary Federation resorted to terrorism to achieve Batista's overthrow, Castro, who had been in self–exile in Mexico, landed an expedition of 80 young men in Oriente Province in December 1956 and took immediate refuge in the Sierra Maestra mountains of eastern Cuba.

Weakened by adverse propaganda and its own corruption, with a demoralized army incapable of mounting any serious operation, the regime consistently lost ground. When in 1958 Washington showed its disapproval by proclaiming an arms embargo, Batista was doomed. In December he fled the island (with millions of dollars stashed safely in Swiss banks), and Fidel Castro entered Havana in triumph on New Year's Day 1959.

The Cuban Revolution

For the vast majority of the Cuban people, Batista's downfall represented the end of an illegitimate and violent episode in their history and a quick return to the democratic process. Fidel Castro, and other leaders of the 26th of July Movement (named after the attack on the Moncada Army Barracks) had repeatedly promised the restoration of the 1940 constitutional freedom of expression, elections within 18 months and an end of political corruption. Thus, the young leader, enhanced by his heroic image, received the almost unanimous applause of the Cuban people. Batista had fallen into such disrepute in the United States that Castro was considered to be a liberating hero of Cuba; there was widespread discussion and speculation about how firm and friendly ties with the new government on the island could be forged, together with enhanced U.S. investment. Castro, however, had other ideas.

The illegitimate son of a wealthy Spanish landowner, Castro had very early shown inclinations toward violence and unlimited ambition: he wanted unrestricted, absolute power. Increasing his power with a series of laws which, at least temporarily, benefited the masses—agrarian reform, increased wages, a reduction of the cost of public services—he simultaneously used his popularity, or his charisma, as a weapon to crush his opponents. The Student Directory was reduced to a secondary role through a pointed television campaign; Dr. Manuel Urrutia, the same man he had appointed president six months before, was forced to resign under a barrage of insults in mid–1959. Soon a new slogan appeared: "Revolution first, elections later!" Special tribunals dealt harshly with *Batistianos* and later with anyone accused of counter–revolution; about 550 were executed by firing squads. In late 1959, one of the heroes of the revolution, Major Huber Matos, resigned to protest an increasing communist influence in the government. He was sentenced to 20 years in prison. By the end of that year, almost all of the media was under government control. Ominously, another slogan proclaimed that "to be anti–communist was to be counter–revolutionary." Quietly, Castro began building a formidable military apparatus, commanded by his brother, Raúl. He also appointed his former revolutionary comrade, the Argentine dentist Ernesto "Che" Guevara, as minister of industry. Guevara embarked on a disastrous plan to communize Cuba's means of production. Tens of millions of dollars worth of U.S. land and business holdings were expropriated, further souring bilateral relations. In 1960, the United States retaliated with an economic embargo of the Castro regime, still in effect four decades later, and in January 1961 the outgoing Eisenhower administration severed diplomatic relations.

Meanwhile, there was widespread disillusionment in Cuba. Thousands left the island (with their descendants, the figure is now more than 2 million); others organized a resistance. Anti–communist guerrillas appeared in the central mountains and acts of sabotage became common.

Encouraged by this show of resistance, the U.S. CIA and Cuban exiles in Florida hatched up a scheme to have Cuban expatriates invade the island. The people, supposedly fed up with Castro, were anticipated to join the invaders in a groundswell movement that would envelop and suffocate the newborn regime. In April 1961, an expedition of about 1,200 Cuban exiles invaded at the *Bahia Cochinos* (Bay of Pigs) on the southern coast of Cuba. Although the size of the force, the anticipated response by Castro's forces and the terrain involved, all mandated the use of air support, no provision in the plans had been made for this. Further, no coordination had been undertaken with internal Cuban resistance forces, which had little, if any, organization. The invasion force was a sitting duck target for Castro's army. The whole plan was, in the words of Sir Winston Churchill, "a wretched half–measure." About 100 of the invaders were killed and the remainder captured.

Castro triumphantly announced that total victory had been won against "American imperialism," and he proceeded to wipe out all remaining internal resistance and to pose as a conquering hero. Defiantly, he proclaimed Cuba a socialist state. Emboldened by what appeared to be an indication of U.S. weakness, the Soviet Union, which until then had refrained from any military commitment, began sending vast amounts of military equipment to Cuba—including intercontinental missiles with nuclear warheads.

In October 1962, President John F. Kennedy, still smarting from the Bay of Pigs fiasco, blockaded the island, placed U.S. military forces on alert and demanded withdrawal of the missiles. For 13 days, the world teetered on the brink of thermonuclear war. Soviet Premier Nikita Khrushchëv, furious, nevertheless complied with the U.S. demands, but only after obtaining a costly oral promise of

Fidel Castro, Ernesto "Che" Guevara, and the USSR's Anastas Mikoyan, 1963

vast significance from Kennedy: the U.S. would never invade Cuba. Kennedy thus verbally abrogated a cornerstone of U.S. Latin American policy—the long-"standing Monroe Doctrine. Protected by that assurance, Castro embarked on a series of continental revolutionary adventures.

Castro's formula for revolutionary success was guerrilla warfare modeled on the Cuban experience. From 1962 to 1968, Havana became a center of support for leftist revolutionaries who spread their activities from Mexico to Argentina. Nevertheless, the formula failed. Opposed by communist parties which rejected *any* revolution they did not control as the "vanguard of the proletariat," and confronted by armies much better trained than Batista's, the guerrillas were defeated everywhere. In 1967, "Che" Guevara was killed in Bolivia, thus becoming an international Marxist icon. A dangerous deterioration of Cuba's economy forced Castro to fold the guerrilla banner and to accept the orthodox communist line demanded by the Soviet Union. Significantly, in 1968 Castro applauded the Soviet invasion of Czechoslovakia and publicly criticized China's Mao Tse–tung.

Communism in Cuba

Nothing resembling the structures of government envisioned in the tortured writings of Karl Marx came about in Cuba, nor did anything similar to the dual party–government structure of the Soviet Union emerge under Castro. Three stated goals of 20th century communism were achieved with remarkable success: the eradication of illiteracy, universal medical care and public housing. The centrally planned economy of the Soviet Union did not appear. Even though he had no skills in economics, Castro nevertheless waded in without hesitation, wrecking the economy with record speed.

Erratic planning, concentration of total power in Castro's hands and burgeoning bureaucracies, capped by the maintenance of a huge military force (once about 450,000) resulted in declining sugar productivity and failure to develop other resources for trade and income. The United States imposed an economic blockade in 1960, effectively isolating the island from the only significant source of foreign income and investment.

Increasing Soviet aid became vital for the survival of the revolution. When in 1968 Moscow was forced to apply a minimum of economic pressure to avoid pouring increasing amounts of economic aid into what seemed to be an endless chasm, Castro had to surrender more of what had become Cuba's limited independence. He made an urgent effort in 1970 to obtain desperately needed hard currency by mobilizing urban people, sending thousands of them into the fields to bring in the sugar cane, hoping for a 10-million-ton crop. The effort failed; the mobilization totally disrupted the economy for months. In the next year, Castro ostensibly began a process of "institutionalization" (creating organizations theoretically capable of sharing his power) while at the same time yielding increasing control over economic planning to Soviet advisers.

The Cuban debt to the Soviet Union, in spite of its annual purchases of the sugar crop at a level above the prevailing world price, increased at a rate of $2 billion annually, a figure which gradually rose to more than $5 billion. In an effort to repay the Soviets, Castro was receptive to a request for the use of his troops for international communist adventures. In 1975, 20,000 soldiers left for Angola to try to prop up its tottering communist regime; by 1989 this force had grown to almost 60,000. Having no stake in the outcome of Angola's ongoing struggle, Cubans turned out to be poor fighters, not caring to expose themselves to the cost of open warfare. They were overwhelmingly black; their return to Cuba, many infected with AIDS, and without a "victory," ended an unfortunate chapter in communist adventurism. Further Cuban involvement in Ethiopia, Yemen, Nicaragua, El Salvador and Guatemala also occurred during the 1970s and 1980s.

Both the United States and Cuba were humiliated in early 1980. Hundreds of Cubans stormed into the compound of the Peruvian Embassy in Havana, begging for political asylum. In a bold and unprecedented move, Castro suddenly announced that any Cuban who wished to leave the country was free to do so. The result was a frantic exodus, as thousands of small privately owned boats crossed the Florida Straits to the port of Mariel to pick up refugees in a Dunkirk-like evacuation. About 125,000 so-called *Marielitos* departed the island. Most were honorable and were assimilated into the Florida Cuban community as well as in other places. But a significant number were lunatics, criminals and/or homosexuals, some forced onto the waiting boats at gunpoint, who wound up in already overcrowded U.S. federal prisons.

It had been a master stroke by Castro, a means of emptying his prisons and asylums as well as getting rid of potentially troublesome dissenters. But even he realized that he had overplayed his hand. After tedious indirect negotiations with the United States, Castro finally agreed to accept the undesirables back. Many of the prisoners rioted, however, preferring life as detainees in the United States to life in Cuba. The so-called "Mariel Boatlift" became a political issue in the 1980 U.S. presidential campaign, a foreign policy disaster of President Jimmy Carter that contributed to the victory of Ronald Reagan.

There followed eight years of increased bilateral hostility and U.S. military opposition to Cuban adventurism in Nicaragua, El Salvador and Grenada, among other places. The U.S. invasion of Grenada in 1983 and the increasing presence of American advisers and troops in Central America made Castro more cautious. As a further demonstration of its submission to the Soviets, Cuba declined to attend the 1984 Summer Olympics in Los Angeles. Relations with the United

Typical apartment housing in Havana

Photo by Sheila Curtin

The forbidding La Cabaña military prison where thousands of Cuban dissidents have spent countless years for their anti–Castro views.   Photo by Sheila Curtin

States appeared to thaw briefly in 1984, but then resumed their frozen state when "Radio Martí" started broadcasting from Miami with U.S. government support. Cuba quickly jammed it.

Changes in the Cuban Politburo since 1966 have occurred twice, and although minorities were included, such as blacks, women and younger people, they were in fact meaningless. Castro's performances at party congresses in 1986 and 1991 were long, boring and virtually identical. First, he heaped praise on the achievements of Cuba under socialism. Then his mood turned to one of rage—he berated the assemblage, delivered a withering attack on the shortcomings of the Cuban people, made a devastating attack on capitalism and then vented his anger on the United States, the trade embargo in particular, Americans in general and then zeroed in on U.S. presidents from Kennedy to Clinton, with particular enmity expressed towards Nixon, Reagan and Bush (not in that particular order). All problems of Cuba were blamed on these sources, but never associated with poor Cuban leadership. Later added to his list pariahs was the former Soviet Union and its ex–president, Mikhail Gorbachëv.

Cuba's foreign interests were identical to those of the Soviet Union when the latter existed. Now they are centered upon Cuban survival and include the cautious wooing of capitalist nations perceived not to be an imminent threat to Castro's continuation in power.

Its foreign ventures, financed by the Soviets, were costly. For reasons difficult to explain, Castro decreed that Cuban troops in Angola would not leave until *apartheid* was ended in South Africa and Namibia was independent. Cuban activities in Central America alienated most of Latin America, although a few nations with no communist threat preferred to play a "see

no evil, hear no evil" attitude that was shortsighted. Both communism in general and Castro in particular have been a stone around Cuba's neck for 40 years.

A costly adventure in air piracy from the late 1960s through the 1970s gave Cuba (and its Soviet patron) an unnecessary and unprofitable black eye. It led to sharply increased security measures, with attendant inconveniences and delays at most U.S. airports, and left a sour taste in the perceptions of many potential friends that exists to this day and will continue into the foreseen future, even if things ultimately improve on the island.

In 1993, Caribbean tourist trade totaled more than $60 billion annually. Cuba's share: a paltry 2%. Even much smaller Jamaica earned twice as much from tourist visits as does Cuba. This limitation in tourist income was largely the product of the U.S. embargo, which prohibits Americans from spending dollars in Cuba except under very tight conditions. This effectively halted tourist trade, although there are loopholes available by traveling through the Dominican Republic, Mexico and Canada. But the bottom line is punitive: the United States will not guarantee the safety of its citizens who venture onto the island, although there is a United States interests section attached to the Swiss Embassy in Havana.

Fall of the Soviet Benefactor

The ascension to power of Mikhail Gorbachëv in the Soviet Union marked the beginning of the end for communist Cuba. Things began to deteriorate in 1986, as Soviet trade terms became tougher, and subsidies started to shrink. Soviet aid to Cuba had been as much as $6 billion a year. But in 1989, Gorbachëv visited the island. He had already concluded that overlaying the Castro regime with Soviet technicians and

advisers simply had not been working and would not work in the future. More important, the Soviets were by that time having to borrow money from Western banks and import food from the United States. The Soviets sought additional sugar, which was by then rationed in Moscow. No increase could be delivered—crop production was down in Cuba because of corruption and inefficiency. The deterioration accelerated rapidly and by 1991–1992 Cuba was in the grip of economic disaster.

Castro's response was to get rid of all elements of dissent, particularly Carlos Aldana, formerly No. 3 in the Cuban hierarchy, who represented a moderate trend corresponding to the Soviet Union's *glasnost* and *perestroika*.

Between 1989 and 1992, Cuba's annual purchasing power had descended from $8.1 billion a year to $2.2 billion. Sugar production descended to 7 million tons even with rationing and dispatching urban workers to harvest the cane by hand (there was no fuel). The 1992 harvest was 4.2 million tons and less was produced in 1993–4.

The administration of President George Bush decided to tighten the 1960 embargo in late 1992 with the Torricelli Law. No U.S. company, affiliate or subsidiary in this country or abroad, may trade with Cuba in any form. All U.S. ports are closed to any ship of any nation or registry that has, within the previous six months, called at a Cuban port. These tightened screws, together with the disappearance of $300 million a year in Soviet aid, has left the Cuban people in near destitution. The average Cuban is estimated to consume only 1,900 calories a day, compared with the 2,600 minimum recommended by the World Health Organization (the Castro regime claims the country's calorie consumption is 3,500, about that of the normal obese American). The result has been that increasing numbers of Cubans have attempted to flee the island in flimsy boats or inner–tube rafts. There may never be an accurate accounting of how many have drowned, died of dehydration or been eaten by sharks in a desperate attempt to escape their misery.

The last few years have seen some basic changes, brought on by the economic prostration of Cuba. Possession of the U.S. dollar was legalized in August 1993 and has since that time become virtually the only hard currency on the island. The peso officially trades at 1 = 1 with the dollar, but it takes more than 100 pesos to buy a dollar on the open market. With the advent of the dollar came a system of black markets that pervade everything. Few people bother with the lines and empty shelves of state stores now, even though the black market means paying two to 10 times more for an article.

Persons in certain trades and professions were allowed to become "self–employed" in a variety of enterprises, but only if they first secured a government permit from an inefficient bureaucracy. Of course, a permit that is granted can be revoked. Small enterprises have bloomed, particularly in urban areas. A large number of "Mom and Pop" restaurants are known for delicious food in Havana, for fees payable in U.S. dollars. Bicycle repair, plumbing, and all similar services are by contract with one of the entrepreneurs. Physicians are not allowed the same freedom.

Several events occurred in 1994 that suggested, falsely, that basic change was on the horizon. Cuba decided to use the threat of a renewed flood of refugees to lessen or abate the U.S. embargo. Severe shortages of just about everything led to increased pressures to migrate to the United States. When these were resisted, there was an anti-government riot in and near Havana. The Clinton administration, dealing with a flood of Haitian refugees, tried to discourage the Cubans, but refused to budge on removal of the tight embargo. A stop–gap "solution" of interning refugees in the territory of Guantanamo Bay was devised, but failed; conditions in the camps set up there were *worse* than in Cuba. The attempts to leave Cuba for Florida resulted in the loss of many lives. Castro threatened to unleash another wave of boat people in the summer of 1995; this was averted by a U.S. plan to gradually admit the Cubans remaining at Guantanamo.

Both Mexico and Canada, following the example set by the UN in 1993, urged that the U.S. embargo of Cuba be abandoned. It has been revealed that Cuba was sustained in large part during 1994 by funds arriving from Mexico (drug money, top level government personnel and banking investment) and from Spain (hotel construction). With the Salinas government of Mexico a thing of the past and the economic collapse of Mexico in late 1994, receipts dropped considerably.

On February 24, 1996, in an unexplainable and stupid act, Cuban air force jets shot down two unarmed small aircraft that were patrolling the waters off the coast of Cuba to protect the "boat people" from mishap. Three men, who were members of the Miami-based exile organization Brothers to the Rescue, were killed. There was an immediate outcry in the U.S. Congress; the result was the Helms–Burton Act, strengthening the already-existing embargo. Now, any foreign firm doing business with Cuba can be penalized in the United States. The avowed purpose is to stifle even minuscule investment and loans to Cuba.

In some respects, the Helms–Burton Act has backfired on the United States in that it appears to have done more to anger

traditional U.S. allies, Canada in particular, than to genuinely punish Cuba economically.

Both Castro and his revolution marked a milestone in August 1996 when the dictator, his beard now fully gray, observed his 70th birthday. It was a reminder that both the revolution and its leader now are living on borrowed time. Almost as though to demonstrate that age has mellowed him, the once–flamboyant revolutionary made a number of state visits, including a tour of Europe and to the Latin American summit in Chile, dressed in stylish business suits rather than the fatigue uniform of old. While in Rome, the avowed athiest visited Pope John Paul II, and the two announced that the pontiff would visit Cuba for the first time in 1998.

A visit to Havana in 1996 by Democratic U.S. Representative Bill Richardson of New Mexico succeeded in winning release of a number of political prisoners. As a further sign of an easing of tensions, the White House approved a request by 10 U.S. news organizations to establish bureaus in Cuba, but in early 1997 Castro had approved only one: the Cable News Network, which he praised for its "objectivity."

No foreign media, however, were allowed to cover Castro's seven–hour speech on October 8, 1997, before the Fifth Communist Party Congress, the first in six years. In that speech, the aging dictator squelched any hopes that Cuba would deviate any further from its dogmatically Marxist course. He also placed the blame squarely on the United States for a series of terrorist bombings at Cuba's tourist-oriented hotels in September, accusing the Clinton administration of trying to undermine the Revolution by frightening away badly needed foreign tourists (see Economy). Castro tied the congress to a public relations stunt that brought Cuba renewed international attention: the week-long ceremony to rebury the skeletal remains of Che Guevara that had been recovered from the Bolivian jungle after 30 years. On the eve of the congress, however, four dissidents, among them Vladimoro Roca, a former air force pilot and son of revolutionary hero Blas Roca, attempted to rain on Castro's parade by issuing a document titled "Homeland for Us All," which ridiculed the congress for focusing on the past glories of the revolution without offering solutions for the problems of the present. All four were arrested and subsequently sentenced to prison terms.

The Papal Visit of 1998

Another public relations gimmick was even more stunning: Castro's invitation to Pope John Paul II to visit Cuba, which the Pope accepted. This was a major gamble for Castro, because he would not be able to censor this strong–willed pope the way he controls his own people's thinking. On the other hand, he apparently reasoned, the gesture might bring a relaxing of the U.S. trade embargo. Enigmatic as ever, Castro declared in November 1997 at the Ibero-American Summit in Venezuela that Cuba would never deviate from its revolutionary course, rejecting calls from Argentina's Carlos Menem and Nicaragua's Arnoldo Alemán for more respect for human rights. Yet, in December, as a gesture to the Pope, Castro permitted the first Christmas holiday Cubans had had since

Varadero Beach—a protected area which the Cuban government would like all to believe is "typical."

Photo by Sheila Curtin

116

1969 (the declaration of atheism as official state doctrine had been rescinded in 1992). Even more unthinkable, he eased the restrictions on religious worship, and suddenly the Catholic churches were filled for Mass; other sects began receiving increased interest as well from a people starved for spirituality, including young people born after the Revolution.

Between Christmas and the Pope's arrival in January, however, Cuba suffered another public relations disaster with the defection of the talented pitcher Orlando "El Duque" Hernández, half-brother of the Florida Marlins' Livan Hernández, who had just been named the most valuable player of the 1997 World Series. Livan Hernández himself had defected in Mexico in 1995, and in 1996, his half-brother was banned from playing baseball when it was feared he, too, would leave to, quite literally, seek his fortune in the United States. "El Duque" and seven others left the island in a tiny boat and turned up a few days later in the Bahamas, where they sought political asylum. From there they went to Costa Rica, where the pitcher was eventually given a U.S. visa and was immediately recruited into the majors. It was yet another humiliation for the baseball–loving Castro. So was the much–publicized request of his 41–year–old daughter, Alina Fernández Revuelta, for political asylum in Spain during the papal visit.

The pope's four–day visit to Cuba from January 21–25, 1998 was truly historic, with hundreds of thousands of Cubans attending open–air masses. Castro, true to his word, welcomed the pontiff at the airport and even attended a Mass; he also addressed John Paul as "holy father" and recalled that he had been schooled by Jesuits. Hundreds of Cuban exiles were granted special permission to enter the country for the event, many of whom were reunited with loved ones they had not seen for nearly 40 years. The pope's public declarations must have made Castro cringe at times. He denounced human rights violations and the denial of religious freedom, and called for the release of political prisoners. At the same time, he noted that the Vatican and the Cuban Revolution find common ground in their concern for the poor. More importantly for Fidel, he lamented the human suffering on the island and called for a lifting of the U.S. embargo. The pope privately presented Castro with the names of 270 jailed dissidents and requested their release (some human rights groups claim there are as many as 500 "prisoners of conscience"). In February, all were released but 70, who remained jailed for "security reasons." At the same time, the government reiterated that the laws against political dissent remain in effect, raising doubts as to whether there has been any meaningful move toward greater freedom of expression.

The bicycle is the only sure method of transportation in this gas–and–car starved nation. Photo by Sheila Curtin

Nonetheless, Castro's gamble at least partly paid off. After the dissidents were freed, President Clinton announced a resumption of sales of medical goods and of airline service that had been severed after the 1995 downing of the two unarmed planes flown by Cuban exiles. He also renewed permission for dollars to be sent to Cuba. Since then, however, U.S.–Cuban relations resumed their usual roller coaster course, while continued repression on the island brought even more international condemnation.

Dissent and Baseball Diplomacy

The government implemented a new sedition law in 1998, aimed primarily at independent journalists and political dissidents. One of its first victims was journalist Mario Viera, who sent abroad a column, "Morals in Underwear," that lampooned the Cuban justice system and poked fun at Foreign Minister José Peraza Chapeau's participation in a meeting in Rome dealing with the establishment of an international criminal court. Viera was jailed for "defaming" Peraza Chapeau, and his trial in November 1998 drew about a dozen courageous protesters. Still another independent journalist, Jesús Joel Díaz Hernández, was jailed in January 1999 and sentenced the following day to four years for "dangerous social behavior." The New York–based Committee to Protect Journalists has named Castro as one of the world's 10 "enemies of the press." Unfortunately, a less scrupulous independent journalist gave the government the excuse it needed for a propaganda counterattack

in 1998. An unnamed Cuban correspondent for the Madrid daily *ABC* dispatched an ostensible interview with Cuban Cardinal Jaime Ortega that turned out to be phony; the cardinal himself denied giving the interview. The official daily mouthpiece *Granma*—itself hardly a paragon of truth—denounced the "falsehoods" of the independent journalists and branded them as "mercenaries."

The so-called "Group of Four," meanwhile, was sentenced on March 25, 1999, to jail terms ranging from three and a half to five years for issuing the 1997 document criticizing the party congress. The sentences sparked protests on the island and brought denunciations from human rights groups abroad. National Assembly President Ricardo Alarcón defended the harsh sentences, calling the dissidents "subversives" and saying that the sentences were "not that severe."

Cuban dissidents continued their courageous activities, which are reminiscent of the non-violent movements of Gandhi and Martin Luther King Jr. In September 1999, they opened a "school" for teaching the tactics of civil disobedience. Later that month, two opposition movements, the Socialist Democratic Current and Democratic Solidarity, boldly delivered to the Council of State a document that detailed plans for a peaceful transition to a democratic Cuba. That December, about 30 dissidents staged a protest march in Havana and, remarkably, none was arrested. It soon became apparent that this seeming tolerance did not represent a change in policy, however, for only a week later about a dozen leading dissidents were arrested and held for several days to discourage a planned demonstration marking the 51st anniversary of the Universal Declaration of Human Rights. Meanwhile, international pressure against Castro's repression continued. The Inter American Press Association, the Committee to Protect Journalists and Reporters Sans Frontieres in France all sent notes to Castro demanding he release jailed independent journalists and stop harassing others. One such independent journalist, Raúl Rivero, was named the recipient of the prestigious Maria Moors Cabot Award by Columbia University in September 1999, but of course the Cuban government refused to grant him a visa; his daughter, who lives in Miami, accepted the award for him. Another leading dissident, Elizardo Sánchez, formed the Commission for Human Rights and National Reconciliation, which monitors dissidents' arrests and reports them to the outside world.

The dissidents finally received some encouraging news in May 2000 when the government suddenly and unexpectedly granted an early release to three of four dissidents who were imprisoned in July 1997 for criticizing a Communist Party document to foreign journalists, among

From a street scene in the small town of Artemisa, Havana Province, to . . .

other alleged sins. The sentences ranged from three and a half to five years, and the case had sparked international condemnation, even from Castro's friend, the Colombian Nobel Laureate Garbriel García Márquez. One of those released, Marta Beatríz Roque, had staged a two-month hunger strike in 1999. No reason was given for the early releases. It was not a harbinger of a Cuban *glasnost,* as it turned out. On February 24, 2001—the fifth anniversary of the shootdown of the two Cuban exile planes—Cuban security forces rounded up about 40 known dissidents at various locations around the island to ensure there were no demonstrations marking the event. They were released a few hours later.

Not so with José González Bridón, leader of the dissident labor group Confederation of Democratic Workers. In 2000, he wrote an article reporting that a dissident had been killed by her ex-husband, which was published on the Web site of the Miami-based Cuba Free Press. He was jailed in December and tried in May 2001 for reporting "false news" about Cuba. In June he was sentenced to two years.

On a happier note, the baseball-loving Castro finally approved an exhibition game in Havana between the Baltimore Orioles and the Cuban All-Stars that had been in the works for three years. Castro attended the historic, invitation-only game on March 28, 1999, the first time a U.S. major league team had played in Cuba since 1959. Some observers compared the initiative with the "ping-pong diplomacy" in the early 1970s that presaged U.S. recognition of the People's Republic of China. Much to Castro's chagrin, the Orioles won the game in the 11th inning, 3–2. The All-Stars redeemed themselves in a second game in Baltimore on May 3, defeating the Orioles 12–6. The victory was muted, however, by yet another embarrassing defection; a 54-year-old pitching coach went to a Baltimore police station and requested political asylum. The Cuban team was abruptly ordered

home, canceling a planned reception and tour of Baltimore.

Cuba has continued to experience a mix of triumph and embarrassment with its sports program, which, of course, is merely an appendage of the government-party apparatus. The Cuban baseball team won the championship at the 1999 Pan American Games in Winnipeg, Canada, but soon after the games ended three Cuban athletes were stripped of the medals they won at the games for alleged drug use. A high jumper reportedly tested positive for cocaine, while two weightlifters tested positive for anabolic steroids. Castro bitterly denounced the decision, using a typical argument that someone had put cocaine in the athlete's food to discredit the Cuban program. He said Cuban tests showed no steroids in the systems of the weightlifters—tests that could hardly be accepted as objective. Then, in May 2000, Castro's baseball diplomacy led to another defection. A U.S. team from the University of St. Thomas in Minnesota had played an exhibition game in Cuba during the winter, and a team made up of University of Havana players flew to Minneapolis for a second game in May. Moments after the

team arrived at the airport, one of the players, Mario Miguel Chaoui, hurriedly left with a Cuban-American uncle and asked for political asylum. He told journalists he hopes to play for the Florida Marlins.

The Elián González Controversy

In late 1999 and through the first half of 2000, the attention of the entire world was focused on U.S.-Cuban relations because of an incident that demonstrated the passions that Castro excites among his adherents at home and his detractors among the exile community in Florida. On November 25, a five-year-old Cuban boy, Elián González, was found clinging to an innertube off the east coast of Florida. In the ensuing days, the boy was turned over to an uncle who lives in Miami, and it was learned that he was one of just three survivors of a raft that left Cuba with 11 people on board. Among those lost were the boy's mother and her boyfriend, who had organized the ill-fated venture.

The case immediately became a media sensation in the United States, while Castro quickly and predictably exploited the incident for its propaganda value. He declared that the boy, who turned six on December 6, had been "kidnapped" by his mother and demanded that he be returned immediately to his father in Cuba. He organized mass demonstrations to focus world attention on the case. Counterdemonstrations soon occurred in the exile community in Miami to demand that the boy be granted political asylum and be allowed to stay with his Miami relatives. (The difference between the mass demonstrations, of course, was that participation at the ones in Miami were purely voluntary.) Castro also paraded the boy's tearful father, Juan Miguel González, before television cameras, to plead for his son's return.

Legally, Castro had a strong case. Under U.S. and international laws, a surviving parent is the presumptive custodian.

. . . the lush Cuban countryside

Photos by Sheila Curtin

In January 2000 there began a tortuous legal battle, after the Immigration and Naturalization Service declared that the boy should be returned to his father. Attorney General Janet Reno supported that position a few days later, whereupon the Miami relatives filed suit in federal court seeking an immigration hearing.

Meanwhile, passions continued to rise, and the case became a political football in the United States. The Republican-controlled Congress suggested either granting the boy U.S. citizenship so he could not be deported to Cuba or granting resident alien status to the father if he chose to live with his son in the United States. Juan Miguel González, a Castro loyalist, indignantly refused, and Castro gleefully milked his refusal for its propaganda value. The case even became an issue in the U.S. presidential campaign when Vice President Al Gore, sensing an opportunity to carry Florida, dramatically broke with the position of the Clinton administration and advocated giving the boy resident alien status. Opinion polls, however, showed that a majority of Americans nationwide favored returning the boy to his father in Cuba.

Tensions increased after a U.S. district judge rejected the family's suit on March 21, 2000. The United States granted a visa to Juan Miguel González, who arrived in Washington on April 5 believing he would soon be reunited with his son. But his Miami relatives and their attorneys continued to file legal motions to delay surrendering Elián. Her patience wearing thin, Reno demanded that they surrender the boy so he could be reunited with his father, but still they stonewalled. Finally, in the pre-dawn hours of April 22, INS agents in SWAT gear stormed into the González house in Miami and hustled the terrified child into a waiting van. Cuba's totalitarian leader praised Reno for the forcible seizure, praise that must have made the attorney general squirm a bit. Elián was flown to Washington, where father and son finally were reunited. They took up residence in a government-leased estate in Maryland, while waiting on the Miami relatives' appeal to be heard by the U.S. circuit court in Atlanta. On June 1, that court ruled that the INS had acted properly when it had rejected an asylum hearing for Elián and that only a parent should have the right to make such a decision for a child that age. Although the decision was what Elián's father (and Castro) wanted, Castro nonetheless summoned more mass demonstrations in Cuba to protest it. Why? Because Elián and his father could not return immediately but had to wait until the Miami relatives exhausted their appeals. On June 28, after the U.S. Supreme Court rejected the Miami relatives' appeal, Juan Miguel and Elián returned to Cuba to a heroes' welcome.

Cuba's Isolation Worsens

U.S.-Cuban relations turned decidedly chillier with the election of the new U.S. president, George W. Bush in 2000. The fact that Bush owed his razor-thin election victory to the overwhelming vote he received from the Cuban exile community in Florida, thus giving him Florida's 25 electoral votes, was not lost on the Castro brothers.

On April 15, 2001, in an appearance commemorating the 40th anniversary of the Bay of Bigs invasion, Raúl Castro issued uncharacteristically strident remarks, accusing Bush of planning a new invasion of Cuba and vowing that it would be repulsed. Such paranoia seemed to dissipate somewhat later that month when Secretary of State Colin Powell stated publicly that Fidel Castro "had done good things for his people." That prompted Castro to compliment Powell for his audacity.

In May 2001, Senators Jesse Helms—co-author of the Helms-Burton Act—and Joseph Lieberman—the losing Democratic vice presidential candidate in 2000—co-sponsored a bill that would allocate $100 million to dissidents in Cuba over four years. It was unclear how they would receive the money or how it would be protected from seizure by the dollar-hungry Cuban government. In an apparent case of reverse psychology, Cuban Foreign Minister Felipe Pérez Roque endorsed the measure, saying it would demonstrate to the world that the United States is seeking to subvert Cuba.

Meanwhile, Cuba continued to experience triumphs and embarrassments in the diplomatic sphere. In November 1999, Castro proudly played host for the first time to the Ibero-American Summit. But the host soon became annoyed when some of the participants, including the king of Spain and the leaders of Portugal, Panama and even onetime defender Mexico, called for greater democratization on the island. Several leaders held meetings with leading dissidents, and Castro, accustomed to a controlled, obedient media, lashed out at the international media for what he termed disproportionate coverage of the dissidents. Whatever public relations value Castro may have gleaned from the summit was effectively nullified on April 18, 2000, however, when the U.N. Commission on Human Rights in Geneva approved a censure motion against Cuba for its repression of political dissent and religious freedom. The vote was 21-18, with 14 abstentions. Especially galling for Castro was the fact that two of Cuba's erstwhile allies, Poland and the Czech Republic, had sponsored the motion. Castro held a live, televised discussion the day after the vote that droned on for five hours, during which Castro vilified the countries that supported the censure as well as the dissidents at home.

Despite the perceived harder line toward Cuba of the Bush administration, on July 16, 2001, the new president angered Cuban exiles by doing the same thing that President Clinton had done every six months for four years: He exercised the executive prerogative granted under the Helms-Burton Act to block lawsuits against foreign companies occupying expropriated U.S. property in Cuba. Nonetheless, the Bush administration continued to tighten the screws in other areas, including stricter enforcement of the trade embargo and greater support for internal dissenters. Under a new initiative, the United States is offering scholarships to Cuban prisoners of conscience, and the U.S. Interests Section in Havana has been distributing radios and information about free-market capitalism. Castro, of course, has bitterly denounced such activities as interference in Cuba's internal affairs and threatened to expel the U.S. diplomats. One explanation for the harsher U.S. stance: Bush has appointed Otto Reich, a Cuban exile and hard-line opponent of Castro, as assistant secretary of state for Western Hemisphere affairs. Still another: The president's brother, Jeb, is

View of Havana

running for reelection as governor of Florida in 2002.

Surprisingly, despite souring bilateral relations, Castro was quick to condemn the September 11, 2001, terrorist attacks on the United States, and even more surprisingly, he was conciliatory toward the imprisonment of al-Qaeda and Taliban prisoners at Guantanamo Bay. Castro even offered to provide medical and sanitary support, and pledged to return any prisoners who escaped; it was a far cry from his attitude toward the detention there of Haitian and Cuban refugees. Perhaps in response to Castro's gesture, the Bush administration permitted the historic sale of food to Cuba in November 2001 as a humanitarian gesture in the wake of Hurricane Michelle, which caused widespread suffering. Cuba purchased a total of $30 million forth of food, which was delivered in December. Both governments, however, noted that the sale did not herald a change in policy by either side. In January 2002, about 500 U.S. business leaders visited Cuba under the auspices of the Treasury Department.

Recent Developments

In early 2002, Castro stunned the world, as he had with the invitation to the pope in 1998, by inviting former U.S. President Jimmy Carter to Cuba; Carter, long a champion of Latin American democracy, accepted. On the very eve of the historic Carter visit, however, a State Department official generated news by adding Cuba to the list of "rogue" countries, such as Iraq and Iran, that are believed to be working on biological weapons for purposes of terrorism. Castro issued the usual indignant denials, but then Secretary of State Powell himself modified the accusation, saying it was believed only that Cuba had such a "research capability."

Carter spent five days in Cuba in May, the highest-ranking American to visit Cuba since 1959. To his credit, Castro kept his word to allow Carter to address the Cuban people in his unpracticed Spanish without censorship. In his live address on radio and television, which was reported verbatim in the next day's issue of *Granma*, Carter denounced Cuba's restrictions on human rights, and he endorsed the "Varela Project," a petition drive recently initiated by dissidents and signed by 11,000 Cubans, for a referendum on free elections and free expression. Of course, his puzzled listeners had read or heard nothing about the Varela Project through the Cuban media. At the same time, Carter called for an end to the U.S. economic embargo. After Carter's departure, Castro trumpeted Carter's call for an end to the embargo, while ignoring his calls for democratization.

Carter met with President Bush at the White House after his Cuban visit. Almost as if in response to Carter's call for an end to the embargo, however, Bush flew to Miami to deliver a policy address on the 100th anniversary of Cuban independence. In the address, Bush flatly rejected any notion of rescinding the embargo, and called on Castro to impose long-overdue reforms.

In a seeming response of his own to Bush's address, to Carter's calls for democratic reforms and to the Varela Project, Castro cynically launched a petition drive of his own, one calling for a constitutional amendment declaring the principles of the Cuban Revolution "untouchable." In effect, it was like calling for a constitutional amendment forbidding constitutional amendments. By late June, the government was claiming that 8.2 million of the country's 11 million people—statistically, virtually everyone of voting age and then some—had signed the petition, which was placed before the National Assembly. On June 27, to no one's surprise, the 557 deputies present approved the amendment unanimously, without discussion.

A bizarre spectacle occurred on July 4. As the head of the U.S. Interests Section hosted a Fourth of July party, at which she gave guests the small radios that have so annoyed the Castro government, the government itself was paying homage to the "noble" American people with a musical tribute at the Karl Marx Theater. Among the songs performed were Jerome Kern's "Old Man River" and George Gershwin's "I Got Rhythm."

As if Cuba did not have enough problems from his traditional nemesis, the United States, by 2002 Cuba was becoming increasingly isolated diplomatically and was encountering serious problems in its relations with two traditional friends, Russia and Mexico. In October 2001, Russian President Vladimir Putin announced that Russia was closing its electronic surveillance station it had operated at Lourdes, 13 miles south of Havana, since 1964, at the height of the Cold War. In undiplomatic language, Castro angrily denounced the decision, saying he had not been asked for his "permission" to close the base and arguing it would create security problems for Cuba. He accused Putin—probably correctly—of trying to curry favor with President Bush, whom Putin needs far more than he needs Castro. What Castro probably lamented the most, however, was the loss of the $200 million annual rent Russia paid for the station.

In early February 2002, Mexican President Vicente Fox, the first opposition president in 70 years and a conservative businessman who enjoys a warm working relationship with President Bush, made his first state visit to Cuba. Fox and Castro engaged in cordial talks, aimed primarily at trade. During the visit, Mexican Foreign Minister Jorge Castañeda assured the Cubans that Mexico would neither "sponsor nor co-sponsor" a resolution before the U.N. Human Rights Commission in Geneva in April, implying that Mexico would abstain as it had in previous years. The visit turned sour when Fox, unlike previous visiting Mexican presidents, agreed to meet with Cuban dissidents, a distinct slap to Castro's face. Later that month, Castañeda said during a visit to Miami that "the doors of the Mexican Embassy are open to all Cubans," a remark that was paraphrased by Radio Martí as an invitation to seek political asylum. On February 27, 25 young men crashed a bus through the embassy gates. Police moved in and forcibly prevented hundreds of others from entering the embassy compound; foreign journalists were pushed back, cursed or manhandled. The incident posed a ticklish diplomatic problem for Mexico and prompted a phone call from Fox to Castro. For one thing, some of the Cubans inside the compound yelled anti-Castro slogans from the roof. When the men did not seek asylum and refused to leave, Fox decided to allow Cuban security forces to enter the embassy grounds to arrest them.

Things grew worse in March when Fox hosted an international poverty summit in the city of Monterrey, which Castro decided at the last minute to attend, posing still another dilemma for Fox because Bush was scheduled to attend. Castro angrily left after his prepared speech to the conference on March 21, accusing Fox of asking him to leave; Fox denied the allegations.

But the final straw for Castro came on April 19, when Mexico joined eight other Latin American nations in voting for a resolution, proposed by Uruguay, calling on Castro to permit democratic reforms; the resolution passed 23-21, with nine abstentions. Castro angrily denounced Mexico for its "betrayal." For good measure, and in a stunning breach of diplomatic protocol, he called Fox a liar for denying Castro had been unwelcome at the Monterrey conference, and he played for international journalists a recording of his telephone conversation with Fox, which did imply that Fox was concerned about Castro's presence at the conference. Such a betrayal of confidence was grounds for Mexico to sever diplomatic relations, but it has not done so. (In fact, in May the two countries marked the 100th anniversary of their diplomatic relations.) Not so with Uruguay, which Castro also had denounced for its role in the U.N. resolution; he also called President Jorge Batlle a "lackey"of the United States. Batlle promptly responded by breaking diplomatic relations that had been reestablished in 1986 after a 25-year break, giving the Cuban ambassador 72 hours to leave the country.

Meanwhile, dissent to Castro continues to grow at home. In December 2001, about two dozen people belonging to a group called the Pro-Human Rights Party, staged a march in a Havana neighborhood without apparent incident. On February 24, 2002, police staged preemptive moves to thwart the usual protests marking the anniversary of the 1996 shootdown of two unarmed planes; 24 people were taken into custody. On May 5, 2002, Vladimoro Roca, the last of the "Group of Four" who had criticized the 1997 party congress to remain in prison, was released after four years and 10 months behind bars. However, the international watchdog group Human Rights Watch estimates that there are still 240 prisoners of conscience in Cuban jails. Then there is the Varela Project, organized by Oswaldo Payá and named for Félix Varela, a priest who was a hero of independence. The fact that Castro launched his own petition drive to make the revolution "untouchable" is an indication that the dissidents' efforts are striking a raw nerve.

Culture: Cuba is an ethnic peculiarity in Latin America. The Spaniards largely exterminated the native Carib Indians, but the influx of blacks from the British West Indies has given Cuba a distinctive Euro-African culture. About 62% of Cubans today are black or mulatto. Although Roman Catholicism took root in colonial times and has survived the repression of the communist government, thousands of Cubans of African descent, both before and after the Revolution, practice a hybrid religion called *santería* that blends elements of Catholicism with ancient African tribal rites.

Although independence came to Cuba eight decades later than it did to its sister republics, some Creole writers and poets gained recognition during the 19th century. Best known of these is the poet José Martí, a leader in Cuba's quest for independence, who was martyred in a battle against the Spanish in 1895. Cuba's best known 20th century poet was Nicolás Guillén, whose verse celebrated the island's African cultural heritage.

Cuba's leading cultural export has been its music. The African-based rhythms of the mambo, the rhumba and the cha-cha-cha were the rage in the United States and Europe during the 1940s and 1950s, and brought stardom to such bandleaders as Xavier Cugat and Desi Arnaz.

The Cuban Revolution has proved to be a cultural tradeoff. On the one hand, the repressiveness of the totalitarian system caused many of Cuba's most talented writers, artists, singers, musicians and actors to abandon Cuba for the United States, Spain or another Latin American country to more freely express themselves. On the other hand, previously banned leftist writers and other intellectuals were free to come to Cuba. The Castro regime has taken great pride in its commitment to fostering arts and preserving the indigenous culture, particularly art, music, literature, theater and cinema. Several Cuban films have achieved international recognition in high-brow circles, but naturally they convey subtle—or not so subtle—ideological messages.

Some outstanding talent remained in Cuba after the Revolution, including the composer José Ardévol and Latin America's prima ballerina, Alicia Alonso. But other creative minds felt the heavy hand of the communist system. At least two cases of repression brought international condemnation upon the regime even from its sympathizers. When the writer Herberto Padilla was jailed in 1971, there was an outcry from such leftist intellectuals as Jean-Paul Sartre, Colombian novelist Gabriel García Márquez and the Mexican poet Octavio Paz. Castro ordered Padilla released, but only after the writer signed a confession of his "errors against the Revolution," which he was obligated to read before the Cuban Congress on Education and Culture.

As an indicator of post-revolutionary culture, the congress passed a resolution that said, in part, that the mass media, writers and artists "are powerful instruments of ideological education whose utilization and development should not be left to spontaneity and improvisation." Padilla worked in obscurity as a translator before being allowed to emigrate to the United States in 1980. In 1981, the poet Armando Valladares was imprisoned, provoking more international pressure. He, too, was allowed to resettle in the United States. Several intellectuals remain imprisoned in Cuba, although a visiting U.S. congressional delegation won the release of a few in 1996.

Cuba's literary community had cause to celebrate in July 2002 when one of its own, writer and poet Cintio Vitier, 80, received Mexico's coveted Juan Rulfo Literature Prize. He had received Cuba's National Literature Prize in 1988.

The history of the Cuban press is not a happy one, either before or since the Revolution. There was an eight-year period of relative press freedom during the constitutional administrations of Ramón Grau San Martín and Carlos Prío Socarrás prior to Batista's imposition of dictatorship in 1952. The Cuban government subsidized the press, which placed an economic sword of Damocles over newspapers critical of Batista. There were several independent dailies before the Revolution, the most prestigious being *Diario de la Marina*. By 1962, Castro had expropriated all the independent newspapers and magazines, and only one daily newspaper remained: *Granma*, the official *Communist Party* and government mouthpiece, named for the boat that brought Castro and his revolutionaries from Mexico in 1956. *Granma*, of course, is more of a propaganda organ than a genuinely informative newspaper. The regime retained the name of one confiscated magazine, *Bohemia*, which is somewhat less propagandistic and more of a literary and artistic review.

All things considered, the term "revolutionary journalism" is an oxymoron, because everything that appears in print or is transmitted over the airwaves is tightly controlled by the regime. Meaningful intellectual freedom or pluralism of thought remains non-existent, and modern Cuban cultural expression has been rendered quadriplegic for nearly four decades.

Economy: Like so many Latin American countries, Cuba was condemned to a monocultural dependency on a given commodity, in Cuba's case, sugarcane. Nickel deposits and Cuba's famous black tobacco provided some economic diversity, but for the most part Cuba's prosperity or lack of it depended largely on the world market price for sugar. Even so, Cuba enjoyed a generally higher standard of living than did most of its sister republics, and it was somewhat ironic that Marxism took root here rather than in one of the more destitute nations.

The Marxist experiment has proved no more feasible in this tropical setting than it did in Eastern Europe. As industry minister in the early 1960s, the legendary Che Guevara set out to convert Cuba into an industrialized state, with disastrous results. What Cuba became, and what it still is today, is an illusion of self-sufficiency, with housing, education and medical care all provided "free." But it was the infusion of nearly $1 million a day worth of Soviet aid for 30 years that made this smoke-and-mirrors economy seem viable. The dependency on sugar continued, the difference being that with collectivized agriculture, crop yields dropped precipitously after the Revolution. On paper, the Cuban peso was proclaimed to be worth more than the U.S. dollar, while in reality it was worthless. Official per capita GDP figures were disregarded by international economists. The classic communist method of distribution of goods and services resulted in chronic food shortages, which the regime blamed solely on the U.S. embargo rather than face the reality of the system's design flaws. When the Soviet sugar daddy (no pun intended) died and the aid stopped pouring in, the plight of the people became increasingly desperate.

The unpredictable Castro suddenly decided to allow private agricultural plots, fruit markets and even some mom-and-pop restaurants in the late 1980s in a desperate bid to alleviate the destitution. The Cubans eagerly responded, but when many of them began showing signs of bourgeois prosperity, Castro just as unpredictably terminated the experiment in limited capitalism. At the

Fourth Communist Party Congress in 1991, again motivated by desperation to alleviate food shortages, he resumed limited private and cooperative cultivation. By 1997, the private plots and co-ops were providing more food than the state farms.

In another seemingly counterrevolutionary move in 1994 that stemmed from raw desperation, he ordered the old decadent hotels, casinos and night clubs to reopen under state tutelage. Cubans were not permitted to frequent such bourgeois establishments, of course, only to work there. The fun spots are reserved for foreign tourists, Canadians mostly, who are encouraged to pay with dollars. The gimmick to bring in desperately needed foreign exchange was successful, so much so that anti–Castro dissidents—whether from Florida or Cuba has not been determined—set off bombs in three of the hotels in September 1997, killing one tourist and injuring four, in an obvious attempt to frighten other tourists away.

Economy Minister José Luis Rodríguez claimed at the end of 1998 that the country showed a 1.2% increase in GDP, the slowest since 1994. That was still well short of the 7.8% claimed in 1996. Since then, growth has averaged a respectable 4.7% per year, thanks almost wholly to foreign capitalist investors who are theoretically anathema to the Marxist-Leninist model. Growth was estimated at 6.9% for 1999, 5.6% for 2000 and 5% for 2001. On paper, the country claimed a per capita income of $1,700, which is suspicious considering that the average monthly wage is only about $20.

Cuba remains the world's eighth-largest sugar producer, but the sugar industry has deteriorated dramatically in recent years, in part because of natural factors, but also because of outdated equipment and low world market prices. Hurricane Georges was a factor in the 24% drop in sugar production in 1998, from 4.2 to 3.4 million metric tons. The sugar crop was hit again in 2001 by Hurricane Michelle, which destroyed an estimated 35% of the crop. Nonetheless, official figures released in June 2002 put the harvest at 3.61 million tons, up slightly from the record low of 3.53 million in 2000-01, but a far cry from the record of 8.1 million in 1989. Because of lower market prices, the 2002 crop was expected to bring in about $120 million less in export earnings than the $561 million from the 2001 crop. In mid-2002, faced with grim economic realities, the government grudgingly and quietly closed 71 of the island's 156 sugar mills and said it plans to modernize the remaining ones. It also announced plans to replace about half of the 3.5 million acres devoted to sugar cultivation with crops that will help feed the Cuban people, such as rice. On the remaining land, using im-

proved techniques, the government hopes to increase the sugar yield from 16 tons per acre to 23.

Cuba had hoped tourism would be its economic savior. In April 1999, Vice President Carlos Lage stated officially that the country is relying increasingly on foreign tourism for development. He said that tourism brought in $1.7 billion in badly needed foreign exchange in 1998 and that it showed a 30% increase in the first quarter of 1999. Figures since then have been hard to come by, although an estimated 1.8 million tourists visited Cuba in 2000, bringing in $1.9 billion, dwarfing the amount from sugar exports. In 2001, the number of tourists dropped to 1.7 million, reflecting the global drop in tourism as a consequence of the September 11, 2001 terror attacks on the United States, and in the first quarter of 2002 it was down by 14%. During the winter of 2001-02, several Cuban hotels actually closed up for lack of business—temporarily, insisted the tourism minister—while prices at dollar stores skyrocketed. Most of Cuba's tourists are from Canada and Europe, and in response to that fact, Cuba officially began accepting the euro as well as the dollar at its main resort town of Varadero on June 1, 2002. Nonetheless, so desperate is Cuba for foreign exchange that Venezuela, about the best friend Cuba still has and the source of a third of its oil, was forced to suspend oil shipments in April 2002 when Cuba was unable to pay more than $63 million it owed for past shipments.

Also dwarfing sugar earnings as a source of foreign exchange in recent years, now second only to tourism, have been remittances from Cubans living abroad, primarily the United States, Mexico and Spain.

Since the collapse of the Soviet Union, Cuba has come to rely on foreign—i.e., capitalist—investors for economic development. By the end of 2001 there were nearly 400 joint ventures with the state, about 60% of them with Canadian, Spanish, French and Italian firms., specializing primarily in tourism, construction and biotechnology. Such investments have totaled an estimated $5 billion. But the drop in tourism, coupled with an unfavorable business climate, has led to a dramatic decline in foreign investments. From an annual average of $268 million from 1996–2000, including $488 million in 2000, it plummeted to only 38.9 million in 2001.

Thus, Cuba today remains an economic basket case, a destitute society with an economy propped up only by a flourishing black market for almost everything, including parts for the prerevolutionary Fords and Chevrolets that still chug along on Havana's streets as in a scene from a 1950s movie. Prostitution is rampant and uncontrollable despite revolutionary dis-

approval, and begging, something Castro once boasted he had eliminated, is back. A beggar, in fact, is what the entire country has become, totally reliant on pity from friendly countries, but even they are finding it increasingly difficult to ignore Castro's appalling abuse of human rights. Although the U.S. government is under increased pressure from its friends abroad and from some members of Congress and businessmen at home to lift the 1960 economic embargo—the argument being that it penalizes the average Cuban more than it does the Castro regime—an end to the embargo would not prove to be the panacea that many assume. Only through economic reform, such as occurred in Hungary and other former East Bloc nations, will bring significant improvement. But that will not happen as long as Castro is alive.

The Future: One of the world's great guessing games for years has been: How much longer can Castro last? With his people deserting the island like rats from a sinking ship, his Soviet benefactor consigned to the dustbin of history and his health evidently failing, he continues to amaze admirers and adversaries alike with his resilience. This author has given up predicting how much longer he will remain in power; I am now of the conviction that only death will end his rule. Still, time is not on the side of the leader of one of the world's few remaining Marxist-Leninist systems. Castro is a living relic, but he cannot live forever. A dramatic reminder of his mortality came on June 23, 2001, when he briefly fainted while giving a speech under a blazing sun, something the Cuban people had never seen happen to their loquacious leader. He turned 76 in August 2002. When he dies, there will be a monumental power vacuum, almost certainly filled in the short term by brother Raúl. But Raúl lacks the charisma and legendary aura of *el Comandante*, and it will be interesting to see how long he can stand up to the inevitable and irresistible pressure that will be brought to bear on him to bring Cuba into the fellowship of the democratic nations of the 21st century.

The dissident movement in Cuba encompasses some very courageous individuals, who may form a cadre from which post-Castro leadership may be drawn. Others may return from Miami. It is noteworthy that the Varela Project, which collected more than 11,000 signatures for a referendum on democratic reforms, sparked an immediate counteroffensive by the regime, which led to the collection of 8.2 million signatures in favor of making the revolution "untouchable." There was one major difference between the two petition drives, however; it did not require any courage to sign Castro's petition.

The Dominican Republic

Panorama of Santo Domingo with the Presidential Palace in the foreground

Area: 18,811 square miles **Population:** 8.7 million

Capital City: Santo Domingo (Pop. 2 million, estimated).

Climate: Tropical, tempered by sea breezes; moderate rainfall is heaviest from April to December.

Neighboring Countries: The Dominican Republic occupies the eastern two thirds of the island of Hispaniola, the second largest of the Greater Antilles; the Republic of Haiti occupies the western one-third of the island.

Official Language: Spanish.

Other Principal Tongues: There are small French and English–speaking groups.

Ethnic Background: Mixed European, African and Indian origin (73%), White (16%), Negro (11%).

Principal Religion: Roman Catholic Christianity.

Chief Commercial Products: Tourism, sugar, bananas, cocao, coffee, nickel, gold, textiles, clothing.

Currency: Peso.

Gross Domestic Product: U.S. $19.7 billion in 2000 ($2,304 per capita).

Former Colonial Status: Spanish Crown Colony (1492–1795); French Possession (1795–1808); Spanish Control (1808–1821); occupied by Haiti (1822–1844).

Independence Date: February 27, 1844.

Chief of State: Hipólito Mejía, President (since August 16, 2000).

National Flag: Blue and red, quartered by a white cross.

The Dominican Republic occupies the eastern two–thirds of the island of Hispaniola, also known by its Indian name, *Hayti*, which means place of mountains. Majestically cresting at 10,000 feet in the center of the island, mountain spurs run south to the Caribbean Sea and to the east, dropping to rolling hills before reaching the coast. A separate range, with peaks reaching 4,000 feet, runs along the north coast of the Dominican Republic. The Cibao Valley, lying between the central range and north coast hills, and the southern coastal plains, are the most productive agricultural lands of the island and the most heavily populated regions. The slopes of the mountains, green throughout the year, are forested and well–watered and are the locale of most of the country's coffee production.

The climate, while tropical, is moderated by invigorating sea breezes. During the dry season, December to March, the trade winds cool the air, making the southern coast beaches a major tourist attraction.

History: The island of Hispaniola was discovered by Columbus on his first voyage and selected as the site for his first colonization effort. The city of Santo Domingo, founded in 1496, is the oldest European–established city in the Americas. The native Indians were described as peaceful by Columbus and were absorbed into the Spanish population; they became virtually extinct as a race within 30 years of the Spanish discovery. Slaves from Africa were introduced in the 1520s. The discovery of more valuable domains on the mainland and the exhaustion of gold deposits on the island caused the Spanish to lose interest in Hispaniola at an early date after it was settled by them.

The island was frequently attacked by pirates and privateers—Santo Domingo was held for ransom by the English privateer Sir Francis Drake in 1585. Buccaneers took the western part of the island in 1630, and French settlers arrived shortly thereafter. The western portion of Hispaniola was ceded to France in 1697. With the outbreak of the French Revolution in 1789, a series of rebellions occurred on the island. The French section of the island, Haiti, was overrun by British and Spanish forces in 1791; they were expelled by the French in the same year and France was given possession of the entire island by treaty in 1795. Returned to Spain in 1806, the Spanish–speaking Dominicans declared themselves independent in 1821, but were conquered by the neighboring Haitians in the following year, and did not achieve final independence until 1844.

The independent history of the Dominican Republic has been a continuation of internal war, foreign intervention and misrule. From 1844 to 1861, the country was governed by a succession of military men who were put in office by various factions of the island's upper class. Constant unrest and invasions from Haiti caused General Pedro Santana to invite the Spanish to return in 1861; however, the Spanish discipline was no more welcome than it had been earlier, and the Spaniards were again ousted in 1865. The second republic was as restless as the first, and the government passed from one dictator to another in an unbroken series of corrupt administrations which had little or no governing ability.

By 1905, the Dominican Republic was largely bankrupt and threatened with occupation by European powers seeking to collect bad debts; the United States intervened under a 50–year treaty to administer the island's finances. There were more or less continuous revolts—in 1914 the United States landed Marines to bolster the government; nevertheless, the president was ousted in 1916. From 1916 to 1922, the country was administered by the U.S. Navy.

A provisional government was reestablished in 1922 and in 1924 U.S. troops were withdrawn. It soon became apparent that the Dominicans' political habits had not changed by the six years of military occupation; following a reasonably effective administration, revolt again broke out in 1930. General Rafael Leonidas Trujillo Molina, commandant of the military, seized power and brought a semblance of order to the country.

The Trujillo Era

The era of Trujillo provided a 31-year respite in a long history of violence and dissension. Ruthlessly suppressing all opposition, Trujillo dominated the island as its absolute ruler. Tyrannical as his rule was, no other dictator in Latin America approached his material benefits.

In 1930 he assumed control of a nation which had never known anything but lawlessness, banditry, bankruptcy and foreign intervention. With the treasury empty, the people poverty–stricken, the capital city destroyed by a hurricane and foreign debts almost three times the total annual income, Trujillo took on the herculean task of rebuilding his country. Twenty years later, internal and foreign debts had been paid; the national income had multiplied to 40 times the level of 1930 and the nation had a balanced budget for most of the period.

Schools, roads and numerous public buildings were constructed during the Trujillo years. *"El Benefactor"* also built a huge personal fortune, valued at an estimated $800 million and comprising 60% of all land in the nation. The cost of his rule was the total loss of personal liberty for the Dominican people, who were held in check by Trujillo's efficient and merciless secret police force. Trujillo's assassination in mid–1961 ended an era of one of Latin America's most brutal dictatorships. Attempts by his son to retain control of the country were unsuccessful and the family fled the island in late 1961.

The Balaguer 'Democracy'

Joaquín Balaguer, titular president at the time of the assassination, was able to maintain a semblance of order after the flight of the Trujillo family by promising to step down when provisions for elections could be made. Balaguer was overthrown by a military coup in early 1962 and a few days later, a counter–coup installed the vice president.

The first experiment in democratic government was undertaken in late 1962; Juan Bosch was chosen president in honest elections. He was inaugurated with feelings of optimism; honest, well–intentioned but politically inexperienced, he was overthrown by a military coup six months later as he attempted to limit the power of the armed forces.

A new regime was soon dominated by a former car salesman, but in April 1965 a civil war erupted when dissident elements in the armed forces sought to return Juan Bosch to office. As the toll in human lives quickly mounted (an estimated 2,000 were killed), fearing the imminent defeat of the conservative faction and creation of a new Castro–style government, the United States intervened with 22,000 combat troops.

Following considerable debate, the Organization of American States agreed to send in additional troops and take over the task of preserving order and conducting elections. Nevertheless, the fact that the United States intervened unilaterally—in apparent violation of existing inter–American agreements—caused widespread discontent among Latin American diplomats.

Carefully supervised by the OAS, free elections were held in mid–1966 and Balaguer, supported by a centrist coalition, won the presidency. He followed a moderate economic policy, satisfying few of the demands of the warring factions. The U.S. intervention solved none of the social or economic problems—it merely postponed the day when these questions would be resolved.

After amending the constitution so that he could succeed himself, President Balaguer was reelected to a second term in 1970. Unable to unite, the rival candidates provided only token resistance. Bosch boycotted the elections because he knew the military would overrule his liberal policies.

Under Balaguer, the economy achieved the most spectacular growth of any Latin America nation. Indeed, the gross national product rose by an impressive 12.5% in 1972–73—the world's highest rate in those years. Virtually every key sector of the economy set records in 1973, particularly agriculture, tourism and mining. Pacing the growth was the nation's revitalized sugar industry, where workers responded to a profit–sharing plan by increasing output.

The significant factor in the nation's economic boom was the political stability enforced by the soft–spoken Balaguer. The president's conservative Reformist Party pursued a policy called *continuísmo*, which meant a strong emphasis on law and order and economic development. To achieve political stability, opposition parties often received heavy–handed treatment. The all–important loyalty of the armed forces was obtained by granting the military special favors.

During 1971, the administration was linked to a right–wing vigilante group called "The Gang," which terrorized and murdered several hundred suspected and

General Rafael Leonidas Trujillo Molina, 1930

real leftists. When a tiny group of 10 Cuban–trained guerrillas entered the country in early 1973, they were quickly eliminated by the efficient Dominican forces. Balaguer then used the occasion to polish off the rest of his opposition; political opponents were jailed, the university was closed and opposition newspapers and media were seized. Major political leaders were forced into hiding or exile.

The repression of political opponents set the stage for the 1974 elections. Although the opposition was divided among about 20 small parties, the two major groups (one liberal, the other conservative) formed a coalition and nominated Silvestre Antonio Guzmán Fernández, a wealthy cattle rancher.

Although Balaguer was at first regarded as a shoo–in for reelection despite his promise during the 1970 campaign to seek a constitutional change banning the reelection of presidents, a sudden groundswell of support for Guzmán clearly alarmed the administration. When a new voting rule was hurriedly put into effect by Balaguer, the opposition responded by boycotting the election, charging that the new rules would permit administration supporters to vote more than once.

With the military openly supporting his reelection and the opposition boycotting the election, Balaguer coasted to an easy "victory."

Major problems facing him at the start of his third term were inflation, which had reached an annual rate of 20% by mid–1974 and high unemployment. A more fundamental problem was the fact that although the Dominican Republic was enjoying the most prosperous period in its history, the benefits of the boom were confined largely to the upper class, while fully 80% of the people remained trapped in poverty. The annual per capita income hovered at $350 while the population growth was increasing at a dangerous 3.6% (now down to 2.7%) a year.

Balaguer suffered a stunning upset in 1978 presidential elections when he was defeated by Guzmán of the Dominican Revolutionary Party (PRD). Tabulation of the votes was temporarily halted by Balaguer supporters in the army when early returns showed him losing. However, strong protests at home and abroad finally forced the military to allow the results to stand.

Guzmán's program to promote domestic peace and a strong economy was generally successful during the first three years of his term, with gains in health, education and rural development. However, a dramatic increase in the price of imported oil plus a sharp drop in sugar export earnings at the same time the United States and the Western Hemisphere were gripped by recession plunged the economy into a recession by late 1980. Guzmán announced he would not run for reelection in mid–1981—the first time in history that a Dominican chief of state had offered to step down *voluntarily*.

May 1982 elections saw the ruling PRD presidential candidate, moderate social democrat Salvador Jorge Blanco, win with 46% of the vote. His two main opponents, both former presidents, were Balaguer (39.14%) and Bosch (9.69%).

Blanco, a 55–year–old constitutional lawyer affiliated with the Socialist International, saw his PRD also win control of Congress and most local governments. Although 12 people died in campaign violence, the election was generally the most honest and peaceful in the nation's history. Unhappily, however, the last victim proved to be President Guzmán himself, who committed suicide the day before leaving office.

At the insistence of the International Monetary Fund and creditor banks the new president imposed a program of economic austerity, reducing luxury imports and limiting government expenditures. These measures contributed to a slow increase in the growth of domestic production. But as in Colombia and Ecuador, the growth rate of the economy was lower than that of the population, and the per capita income fell slightly in terms of purchasing power.

The situation became tense in May 1984 when a series of popular demonstrations against rising prices was dispersed by the police after bloody confrontations. Austerity was a national necessity, but it certainly paved a dangerous political path. Due to adverse economic conditions and inflation, Blanco's popularity sagged badly in 1985. He granted government workers a small raise in mid–1985 and the resident IMF agent threatened to withhold the next installment of a loan unless it was repealed. The legislature called for expulsion of the IMF representative on the ground that he was interfering with internal affairs.

The elections in both 1986 and 1990 pitted an elderly Balaguer against an energetic opponent. Both campaigns were heated, replete with personal insults and slanderous statements. Notwithstanding an attempt by the military to halt ballot counting in 1986, Balaguer won even though his opponent was considered a shoo–in and in spite of the fact that Balaguer was virtually blinded by glaucoma.

The contest in 1990 was between Balaguer and Bosch, only four years younger than the president; Balaguer won by a margin of 22,000 votes out of 1.9 million. The reason for the two victories of the aging president was simple: relative prosperity. To be sure, the Dominican Republic was and is afflicted with a substantial number who live in poverty, but they are unreliable voters.

Both elections were tainted with the usual irregularities. Balaguer carefully paved the way for yet another run for the presidency in 1994. This time, the favored opponent was José Francisco Peña Gómez, leader of the PRD and former Santo Domingo mayor. The campaign was extraordinarily dirty. Since Peña Gómez was black, and Dominicans harbor a deep fear–distrust of black Haitians, Balaguer successfully capitalized on these emotions.

Haitians are not only feared by Dominicans, they are looked down upon. They work in menial jobs, sometimes being reduced to virtual slavery. A video was used allegedly showing Peña Gómez practicing voodoo in Haitian style. Balaguer won by an estimated 30,000 votes amid charges of fraud. Many supporters of Peña Gómez somehow hadn't been registered even though they had gone to register.

The Clinton administration, backing an embargo of Haiti and needing Dominican help, chose to virtually ignore it. Balaguer cooperated with the embargo, with the tacit understanding that the Clinton administration would not protest the 1994 election results. The matter quietly faded, and the 87–year–old Balaguer was inaugurated in August; by then he was totally blind.

Balaguer steps down

Tacitly acknowledging irregularities, Balaguer, then 89, agreed to step down and new elections were held in 1996. In the first round of voting in May, Peña Gómez of the PRD led with 46% of the vote to 39% for Leonel Fernández Reyna of the PLD, founded by Bosch in 1973. Balaguer, though the longtime rival of Bosch, disliked Peña Gómez even more, and threw his support behind Fernández, a 42–year–old lawyer who grew up in New York City. In the runoff election July 1, Fernández edged out Peña Gómez with 51.25% of the vote in a contest that international observers proclaimed fair and

Former President Leonel Fernández

untainted by the traditional Balaguer trickery. The new president promised to take the Dominican Republic down a "new road."

Fernández found that "new road" a bumpy one. In the 1996 elections, his party won only one seat in the 30–member Senate and 12 of 120 seats in the lower house. In the May 1998 congressional elections, the *PRD* swept all but five seats in the Senate and won an absolute majority in the Chamber of Deputies. Peña Gómez, however, died before he could savor his party's triumph.

Tension among the political parties took a violent turn in January 1999. At issue was the election of a new secretary–"general of the Dominican Municipal League, the organization that distributes revenues totaling 4% of the national budget to the local governments. The *PLD* and Balaguer's Social Christian Reform Party (*PRSC*) joined forces once again to elect a secretary–"general, prompting the dominant *PRD* to meet separately and "elect" its own candidate. Pro–*PRD* demonstrators surrounded the headquarters of the municipal league and soon clashed with police. In the ensuing melee, several demonstrators were injured by police shotgun pellets, including two *PRD* senators. Soldiers also surrounded the Congress building in a show of force, prompting the *PRD* to denounce Fernández as a would–be dictator.

A truly historic event occurred in August 1998 when Fidel Castro visited the Dominican Republic for the first time, shortly after Fernández reestablished diplomatic relations. Officially, Castro's visit was to attend the 14–nation Caribbean Forum summit, but he took advantage of the opportunity to lay a wreath at the birthplace of Cuban revolutionary hero Máximo Gómez. Few were surprised when Castro paid a call on his old ally, Juan Bosch, then 89. But Castro astonished everyone by also paying a visit to the 92–year–old Balaguer at his home. The two aging Cold War antagonists sat side–by–side on a sofa for nearly an hour and engaged in a cordial, even jocular conversation.

The Election of 2000

By 1999, as political parties began gearing up for the 2000 election, the Fernández administration could boast a 40% increase in economic growth in its four years and Latin America's second-highest growth rate of 7% per year (see Economy). Such booms usually favor the party in power, but Fernández could not run for reelection himself, barred by the law aimed at Balaguer. Thus, he engineered the nomination of an economic adviser, Danilo Medina, 47, as the *PLD's* standard bearer. Within the *PRD*, meanwhile, a 59-year-old agricultural economist, Hipólito

Mejía, had assumed the mantle of the deceased Peña and became the party's nominee. Then, in January 2000, the venerable and resilient Balaguer, by then 93, once again became the nominee of the *PRSC*. "Let's go forward!" he shouted to convention delegates in a still-robust voice.

In the end, the quixotic Balaguer candidacy proved to be a spoiler for the *PLD*, as it divided the conservative vote. Mejía, meanwhile, preached a populist message, vowing that the poor would begin enjoying the fruits of the burgeoning economy through expanded public works and improved education, a persuasive message to those who felt left out of the growing prosperity evident all around them. He fostered his image as a simple farmer, and charmed voters with Lincolnian folk wisdom and humor.

Polls consistently showed Mejía with a strong lead for the first round of the election scheduled for May 16 of between 40% and 50%, but short of the majority needed to avoid a runoff in June. Medina and Balaguer were virtually tied at 25% each, meaning the real suspense in the first round would be which of them would face Mejía in the runoff. The campaign experienced an ugly incident on April 30 in the town of Moca. As Mejía's car passed the house of a local *PLD* official, gunfire erupted, and Mejía's bodyguards shot and killed the *PLD* official and another man, claiming an assassination attempt. The *PLD* maintained that the bodyguards had fired first.

The vote results of May 16, certified as fair by more than 100 international observers, were as predicted—but the aftermath was not. Mejía received 49.87% of the vote—tantalizingly close to a first-round victory. As the polls had predicted, Medina and Balaguer finished in a dead heat for second place—but with Medina slightly ahead, 24.94% to 24.61%. On May 18, Balaguer announced he was accepting Mejía's election, meaning he would not endorse Medina in a runoff. Medina, faced with the near-impossibility of closing a 25-point gap with Mejía, then pragmatically withdrew, handing the presidency to Mejía. That same day, Balaguer graciously congratulated the president-elect when Mejía made a courtesy call at the novegenarian's home. Scattered gunfire that night marred the celebrations of Mejía's victory.

Mejía was inaugurated on August 16, 2000.

Recent Developments

Continued economic growth, the strongest in Latin America, benefited Mejía's *PRD* in the mid-term congressional elections of May 16, 2002. The party swept 29 of the 32 Senate seats, a gain of 10; strengthened its lead in the 150-member Chamber of Deputies; and won con-

trol of 104 of the 125 municipalities. Election-related violence was minimal by Dominican standards; "only" one person was killed and seven injured.

On February 7, 2002, the *PLD* lost its patriarch when Bosch died at the age of 92. He was buried with full military honors, and diplomatic representatives of six countries and Puerto Rico—but not the United States—attended the funeral, as did thousands of Dominicans.

Bosch was followed in death five months later by his arch-rival, Balaguer, who died on July 14 at the age of 95.

Culture: The succession of lengthy dictatorships since independence has not proven conducive to the development of Dominican culture. Ethnically, the island is a mix of European, Indian and African, and the domestic culture is a hybridization that has influenced its music. A dance that has won popular acceptance abroad is the *meringue*, with its contagious Caribbean rhythm.

The absence of educational reform and the resulting low literacy rate crippled the Dominican Republic's literary growth. The prose fiction writer Juan Bosch, who served briefly as president in the 1960s and remains influential in Dominican politics, is one of only a handful of Dominicans who have obtained international recognition in literature or the arts. Perhaps the country's most notable cultural contribution has been the fashion designer, Oscar de la Renta.

The independent Dominican press often has felt the pressure of dictators. The dean of the press is the daily *Listín Diario*, founded in 1889, which flourished until shut down by the Trujillo dictatorship. It resumed publication in 1963 and has followed a left–of–center editorial line, counterbalanced by the country's other "respectable" newspaper, *El Caribe*.

Sports is a national obsession, particularly soccer and baseball. Numerous Dominican baseball players have gone on to play in the U.S. major leagues, most notably Sammy Sosa of the Chicago Cubs, a source of great national pride, who along with Mark McGuire broke Roger Maris' single-season home run record of 61 in 1997; McGuire hit 70, Sosa hit 66.

Economy: The Dominican economy has been traditionally based on agriculture, with sugar being the main cash crop. However, now tourism produces more income than sugar as sugar prices fell and the U.S. reduced the Dominican quota allowed for importation. New hotels and tourist facilities have been springing up throughout the nation. In 2002, tourism revenue amounted to $2 billion. An aggressive government program to place unused farmland into production has increased the output of other cash products such as meat, coffee, tobacco and cacao.

Thanks to an ambitious irrigation program centering around a four–dam system on the Nizao River, some farm regions are now producing up to three crops a year in contrast to a single crop in previous years.

Also gaining in importance is the nation's mining industry. A Canadian-based consortium has started exporting Dominican ferro–nickel ingots worth $75 million a year; other important exports include bauxite, salt and gypsum. Production of gold and silver has begun at newly developed mines. Three huge new oil refineries have also boosted the economy. Intensive efforts are being made to increase the output from the nation's own small oil fields. The Dominican Republic continues to attract record amounts of investment, partly because of the comparatively stable (at least on the surface) political conditions enforced by the government.

Foreign investment in luxury hotels and resorts, as well as textiles and clothing have added countless new jobs—more than 100,000 in garment factories alone—during the last several years.

The result is what can only be called a boom. Even as some of the major economies of the region slipped into recession after the Brazilian market meltdowns of 1998 and 1999, the Dominican Republic has continued to maintain the highest sustained GDP growth in Latin America: 7.3% in 1996, 8.2% in 1997, 7.3% in 1998, 8.0% in 1999 and 7.8% in 2000. Real GDP has increased over those years from $13.5 billion in 1996 to $19.7 billion in 2000, and per capita GDP has risen from $1,572 in 1996 to $2,303 in 2000. Surprisingly, however, unemployment has remained stubbornly in the double digits, and in 2000 was 13.9%. The inflation rate in 2000 was 9.0%. Figures for 2001 and 2002 will probably reflect a 20% drop in tourism in the wake of the September 11, 2001 terrorist attacks in the United States.

The Future: Hipólito Mejía is the Dominican Republic's first social democratic president since Blanco, and his election ironically came at a time of unprecedented prosperity for the country. *PLD* officials delivered dire post-electoral predictions that Mejía would derail the economic boom that privatization and foreign investments had brought. Mejía, however, has indicated that he will increase taxes from 8% to 10%, less than the 12% Medina had advocated. If he is as wise as the country philosopher image he sought to project suggests, he will follow the lead of the center-left, post-Pinochet presidents in Chile who, inheriting an economic boom, opted not to try to fix something that wasn't broke. If, however, he does succeed in channeling some of the country's wealth into public works and better schools as he promised, without upsetting the breathtaking growth rate, that would be an enviable—and long overdue—achievement.

Partial view of the port of Santo Domingo

The Republic of Ecuador

Fishermen out from Guayaquil, Ecuador

Area: 104,749 square miles.

Population: 12.8 million.

Capital City: Quito (Pop. 1.5 million estimated).

Climate: The eastern lowlands are hot and wet; the coastal plains receive seasonally heavy rainfall; the highland climate becomes increasingly temperate with altitude.

Neighboring Countries: Colombia (north); Peru (east and south).

Official Language: Spanish

Other Principal Tongues: Quechua and Jívaro.

Ethnic Background: Predominantly Indian, with small groups of European and African origin.

128

Principal Religion: Roman Catholic Christianity.

Chief Commercial Products: Petroleum, coffee, bananas, cacao, shrimp, sardines.

Currency: U.S. Dollar (formerly the *sucre*).

Gross Domestic Product: U.S. $17.424 billion in 2001 ($1,353 per capita).

Former Colonial Status: Spanish Crown Colony (1532–1821); a state of *Gran Colombia* (1822–1830).

Independence Date: May 13, 1830.

Chief of State: Gustavo Noboa, president (since January 23, 2000).

National Flag: A top yellow stripe, center blue stripe and a lower red stripe.

Because of disputes with Peru over boundaries, and territorial losses in the 1942 settlement of a war with Peru, no definite statement of Ecuador's area can be given with certainty. It has three distinct zones: the vast Andean highland, with lofty, snow–capped peaks and green valleys; the narrow coastal plain between the Andes and the Pacific, from 50 to 100 miles wide; and the *Oriente* (East), consisting of tropical jungles in the upper Amazon Basin. The high mountain valleys have a temperate climate, rich soils and moderate rainfall suitable for dairy farming and the production of cereals and vegetables. The Pacific coastal plains are tropical and devoted to plantation farming of bananas, cotton, sugar and cocoa. The *Oriente* is more than one third of the agricultural land of Ecuador and is a thick, virgin forest and jungle land containing valuable timber, although much of it cannot be transported to market at a profit.

Lying about 650 miles off the coastline are the Galapagos Islands, an archipelago situated on the Equator. Consisting of 14 islands and numerous islets, it is a haven for many species of waterfowl and giant turtles. With a population of 650, it is regularly visited by tour groups interested in its unspoiled setting.

History: Shortly before Spanish penetration of Ecuador, the ancient Inca Empire had been united under a single chief, Huayna Cápac, in 1526. Francisco Pizarro, the Spanish *conquistador*, touched along the coastline in 1528 at about the time Cápac died.

After returning temporarily to Spain, Pizarro came back to Ecuador with a larger force seeking the treasures he believed were in the interior. Huayna Cápac had divided his empire between two sons—Huáscar, who ruled the Cuzco area, and Atahualpa, who ruled over Quito.

After holding him for a huge ransom of gold and silver, Pizarro executed Atahualpa and mercilessly started the suppression of the Incas.

The invasion of Ecuador followed the pattern of other Spanish conquests. As the Incas and their subject tribes were defeat-ed, the land was awarded in large grants to the successful leaders; the Indians were enslaved to work the estates and the Spaniards built strategically located cities to administer the territory. The low, unhealthy coastal plains had been shunned by the Incas, who lived in the temperate highland and valleys. The Spanish followed the same pattern building their cities of Quito, Ona, Cuenca and Loja above the 5,000-foot level.

The Spanish made little effort to improve the port of Guayaquil or to farm its valley, leaving the fever–ridden region to later arrivals and outcasts from the highlands. Thus, the colonial period continued a regionalism well established in the Inca period and which still divides the highlander from the coastal dweller.

Spanish rule was not challenged for several harsh, uneventful centuries. Antonio José de Sucre, a brilliant military leader under Simón Bolívar, united Ecuador with neighboring Colombia and Venezuela from 1822 to 1830. This union dissolved when Ecuador and Venezuela withdrew. Bolívar died at the age of 47 shortly thereafter.

Ecuador's history as an independent state has been an alternating swing from near anarchy under weak governments to the enforced peace established by dictators. The first president of Ecuador, Juan José Flores, a brave soldier but an indifferent governor, appealed to the Conservatives in Quito and aroused the opposition of the Liberals in Guayaquil. However, he worked out a scheme to alternate as president with Vicente Rocafuerte, a Guayaquil Liberal—a device which remained in effect until 1845.

In the next 15 years, Ecuador had 11 changes of administration, most of which carried the Liberal Party label; there were three constitutions and sporadic civil wars as well as border wars with Peru and Colombia. By 1860 there was little semblance of a central government—local strongmen ruled the communities with the support of their gunmen. Popular opposition to the cession of Guayaquil and the southern provinces to Peru in 1860 brought a Conservative to power, who established a theocratic Catholic dictatorship which lasted until his assassination in 1875. However, he did more for the unification of the country and for its economy than any other 19th century leader.

For twenty years, Ecuador returned to civil war and anarchy, banditry, and economic deterioration. Conservatives regularly won the elections and were regularly ousted by Liberals from Guayaquil until the revolution of 1895; this brought 50 years of Liberal rule to Ecuador, highlighted by three more constitutions, the passage of 28 presidents and uninterrupted political, social and economic crises. While the power of the Conservatives and the church were curtailed, the Liberal promises of free elections and honest government had little meaning, by and large. Galo Plaza Lasso (1948–1952) was a notable exception to this pattern; he was installed as secretary general of the Organization of American States in 1968.

From 1952 to 1963, Conservatives alternated in power with Liberal José María Velasco Ibarra until a reform military government seized power; it was promptly overthrown by the liberals it sought to assist.

A constituent assembly elected an interim president in 1966; he was succeeded by Velasco, aging and cranky, who was elected president for a fifth time. Always controversial, he soon grew restless with his inability to win congressional approval for his economic policies. With the approval of the armed forces, he seized dictatorial power in mid–1970, dismissing the Congress and replacing the moderate constitution (Ecuador's 16th) with a more conservative 1946 version.

To the surprise of many, Velasco later vowed to surrender power to his legally elected successor by June 1972. But, fearing a free election would be won by Assad Bucaram, a left–leaning former mayor of Guayaquil, the armed forces seized power in early 1972 and installed General Guillermo Rodríguez Lara as president. Modeling itself after the reformist Peruvian military government, the new regime pledged its policies would be "revolutionary and nationalistic."

The regime concentrated on how best to spend the huge tax royalties pouring into the treasury from Ecuador's newly developed oil fields; most funds were spent on public works (education, highways and hospitals) and fancy military hardware.

Despite the oil boom, dissatisfaction arose against the center–right regime. Leftists denounced inaction of promised social and economic reforms, while Conservatives condemned swollen civil service rolls (one in every 10 workers) and new taxes on luxury imports. And everyone seemed annoyed by the oil revenue-fed inflation, high unemployment and continuing government corruption and repression.

Democracy

An unsuccessful attempt by 150 soldiers to oust Rodríguez Lara in 1975 left 22 dead and 100 injured. But after widespread student and labor unrest in early 1976, the strongman was finally toppled by a three–man military *junta* headed by Admiral Alfredo Poveda. The new rulers moved promptly to restore civilian rule. In January 1978, voters approved still a new constitution; elections were held six months later, followed by a run–off vote in April 1979.

Jaime Roldós Aguilera, a mild–mannered populist attorney from Guayaquil was elected president by an amazing 59% of the vote. At 38, he was the youngest chief executive in Latin America. Although his own Concentration of Popular Forces party and the allied Democratic Left party won 45 of the 69 seats in the unicameral national legislature, the new president was unable to build a ruling coalition. Ironically, his most bitter foe was Assad Bucaram, his father–in–law and leader of Congress. Because Roldós rejected Bucaram's populist program in favor of a more conservative approach, the two quickly became enemies and the president's proposals in Congress were virtually all blocked.

Austerity measures further damaged Roldós' effectiveness; food and fuel prices rose, leading to widespread disorders and the threat of another military coup. A timely border clash with Peru in early 1981 temporarily diverted attention from Ecuador's economic problems. Although the basic dispute dates back to 1830, the latest crisis centered around the 1942 border treaty between the two nations, the settlement of which Ecuador later disavowed.

Roldós, his wife and seven others were killed in a plane crash while on a trip to the troubled border region. He was succeeded by the vice president, Osvaldo Hurtado, who maintained continuity in government by retaining most of the cabinet. Further, the late president's brother, León, was named vice president.

As in the rest of Latin America, the austere economic program demanded by the International Monetary Fund forced the government to take measures that not only affected its popularity, but threatened the social stability of the country. In May 1984, León Febres Cordero, of the Social Christian Party, a businessman and candidate of the Front for National Reconstruction, was elected president.

The first year of Febres Cordero's presidency was characterized by a modest economic growth, but accompanied by workers' unrest and often bitter friction between the president and Congress. By mid–1985 the political situation remained tense, but was resolved when seven deputies changed their party allegiance to support the government of the president. Febres Cordero, an energetic, free–"market capitalist, provided Ecuador with strong if heavy–handed leadership. He packed a .45 automatic pistol. When the choice of 18 members of the judiciary by the opposition legislature didn't suit him, he had the Supreme Court surrounded by tanks so they could not take the oath of office. Eighteen others, more to his liking, were chosen. Dramatic efforts were taken to restrict the leftist revolutionary group, *Alfaro Vive, Carajo!* (Alfaro Lives—F—k It!), 3,000 strong. The death of its leader was reported in late 1986. Its specialty was the sabotage and destruction of installations vital to the government and people; the government responded firmly—with torture and executions.

Opposition members were fired from government positions and critical newspapers had a drop in advertising income. Difficulties with the military, punctuated by two attempts at mutiny, ultimately led to an effort to impeach Febres Cordero for "disgracing the national honor." Although dramatic, the whole affair was overrated. Adverse economic conditions led Ecuadorians to turn to two leftists in 1988 elections. The contest was hot, with charges such as "alcoholic atheist" and "drug-trafficking fascist" commonplace. Rodrigo Borja ultimately won the contest.

Political bickering and infighting, corruption and a stale economy were the main features of the Borja years. Apparently tired of the "same old thing," the people turned to a conservative in the 1992 elections. Sixto Durán Ballén, a 71–year–old architect born in Boston, was elected after a campaign in which he promised basic reforms. After his election, he wasted no time in putting them into effect.

The currency was devalued by 27.5%, and state–owned enterprises, inefficient money–losers, were put on the auction block. Subsidies on commodities were sharply reduced or eliminated, but to prevent hardships caused by this measure, Durán raised wages modestly. Ecuador dropped its membership in OPEC and announced it would establish its own quotas to market its petroleum. Production rose 18% in 1993 over the previous year, but lower international oil prices meant decreased income from this source.

Higher fuel and electricity prices, reduced state spending and a freeze on government employment combined to create serious unrest by the end of 1992. Payment on the $13 billion external debt was suspended, freezing international credit. Strikes and bomb attacks by terrorist groups added to Ecuador's difficulties.

There was a marked shift to the left in mid–1994 congressional elections; the president's party retained only 9 of 65 locally elected seats. Payment of interest on the external debt was resumed, making IMF and private sector loans again possible.

Ecuadorians were abruptly distracted from their domestic economic woes on January 29, 1995, when the long–simmering border dispute with Peru finally erupted into open warfare in an isolated, mountainous area. Several times before there had been minor border clashes close to the anniversary of the January 29, 1942, Rio Accords by which Ecuador had been forced to cede nearly half its territory. This time, however, the incident quickly escalated into full–scale war with mortar attacks on the ground and air attacks from above. Ecuadorian gunners shot down a Peruvian helicopter and three jet fighter-bombers. Frightened civilians fled their villages. Two tentative cease–fires in February failed to hold. The four guarantor countries—Argentina, Brazil, Chile and the United States—finally succeeded in effecting a definite cease–fire on July 25. In the three weeks of heavy fighting at the outset of the hostilities, 73 people were killed and at least 200 wounded; each side took a number of prisoners, later expatriated.

The economy became generally better–organized during the Durán years, but scandal detracted from its successes and little attention was paid to the poor. This neglect was to have an impact on the 1996 election.

Quito—the modern and the colonial

130

In the first round of voting in May, Jaime Nebot of the Social Christian Party led Abdalá Bucaram of the *Roldosista* Party, 30% to 26%. The runoff on July 7 thus presented voters with a clear choice: Nebot, a conservative who favored continuation of privatization of key economic sectors, and Bucaram, a populist who opposed privatization or reform of the cumbersome social security system. Bucaram also displayed a flamboyance on the campaign trail that startled, and apparently amused, voters. He unabashedly proclaimed himself *"El Loco."* The unorthodox appeal to the unsophisticated masses for support worked: Bucaram defeated Nebot 54.1% to 45.9%.

What followed in the six months after Bucaram's inauguration in August marked the most bizarre episode in modern Ecuadorian political history, as the unpredictable Bucaram shocked Ecuadorians almost daily with his strange public antics and his even stranger governmental measures. He made international headlines when he invited Lorena Bobbitt, the Ecuadorian–born woman infamous for severing her husband's penis in the United States, to the presidential palace for lunch. He took to singing in a rock band, and the Associated Press distributed a photo of the president, clutching a microphone and flanked by buxom, scantily–clad beauties, that was published all over the world. When a presidential helicopter crashed and burned in November, Bucaram denounced it as an assassination attempt.

On a governmental level, he shocked almost everyone by hiring Argentina's recently sacked economy minister, Domingo Cavallo, to be his economic adviser. More shocking still, he discarded his populist campaign promises and imposed an austerity program that included geometric price increases for public services, such as public transport (200%), electricity (more than 100%) and natural gas (250%). Bucaram's draconian measures sparked widespread protests, some of them violent, by teachers, students and labor unions. The approval rating of the president who once amused the masses dropped out of sight.

In February 1997, as Bucaram came under intense pressure to resign, Ecuador plunged into semi–chaos. The beleaguered president attempted to salvage his presidency by imposing a state of emergency that allowed him to take extra–constitutional measures, such as banning demonstrations and imposing press censorship. In a move that delighted the public but which totally disregarded the constitution, Congress removed Bucaram from office on February 6 on the grounds of "mental incapacity," despite the absence of any authoritative medical or psychiatric testimony.

Bucaram's peculiar behavior proved to be the least of his transgressions, however. He went into self–imposed exile in Panama (long a dumping ground for deposed and disgraced presidents), denouncing Congress for its unconstitutional actions. In March, evidence surfaced that he may have absconded with as much as $26 million from the treasury. Some estimates placed the total that Bucaram and his entourage withdrew illegally from the treasury during his six months in power at $80 million. The Supreme Court formally charged Bucaram and four of his aides with corruption, influence peddling, embezzlement and nepotism, and the former president's extradition is being sought. (Guatemala, it should be noted, has tried unsuccessfully since 1993 years to extradite former President Jorge Serrano from Panama, who also allegedly stole millions from the treasury.) One of the aides was arrested in Peru, carrying $3.4 million. The full extent of the corruption of the ill–fated Bucaram administration is still under investigation.

The post–Bucaram transition also proved chaotic—and probably unconstitutional as well. At first, Vice President Rosalia Arteaga was duly sworn in as president, with the tacit blessing of the armed forces. But within days Congress "elected" one of its leaders, Fabián Alarcón, to serve as interim president until a new presidential election could be called, supposedly within a year. In a special referendum on May 25, 74% of Ecuadorian voters "ratified" Alarcón's interim presidency until August 1998. On another of the 14 referendum issues, 65% of voters indicated that they approved of Bucaram's removal from office. Interviewed by CNN in Panama, Bucaram ridiculed the plebiscite as a "political show."

Meanwhile, Ecuadorians once again were distracted from domestic concerns by renewed tensions along the border with Peru, which in July 1997 had begun acquiring advanced Russian MiGs. Unlike 1995, however, sanity prevailed this time and the two countries sent representatives to Brasilia to negotiate a timetable for demarcation of the 50–mile stretch of disputed frontier. On January 19, 1998, the representatives signed an accord that set a deadline of May 30 for reaching a final agreement. Also signing were representatives of the four peace guarantors—Brazil, Argentina, Chile and the United States.

Ecuadorians went to the polls on November 30, 1997 to elect a constituent assembly charged with overhauling the 1978 organic law in the wake of the Bucaram fiasco and to prepare for the election of a new president. In the balloting, the conservative Social Christian Party of former President Febres won a convincing plurality of 24 of the 70 seats. Former President Hurtado's Popular Christian Party was a distant second with nine seats, while 11 other parties split the remainder, ensuring

Former President Jamil Mahuad Witt

that whatever emerged from the assembly would be by broad consensus. The assembly convened in December. Consensus was evident on at least one issue; on February 21, 1998, the assembly voted 60–7 to preclude anyone convicted of corruption, embezzlement or other misuse of public funds, from running for public office, a move aimed squarely at Bucaram, who already had announced from his refuge in Panama that he planned to run in the presidential election scheduled for May 31.

From Panama, Bucaram at first defiantly threatened to campaign from abroad. But in March, he announced he was relinquishing his presidential bid and endorsed the country's leading banana exporter, Alvaro Noboa, as the *Roldosista* candidate. As in 1996, the first round of voting became a free–for–all, with five other candidates vying with Noboa. The clear frontrunner was Quito Mayor Jamil Mahuad of the Popular Democracy movement. Surprisingly, the Social Christians, who did so well in the balloting for the constituent assembly and who narrowly lost the 1996 presidential election to Bucaram, opted not to field a candidate. Its losing candidate in 1996, Jaime Nebot, heads the party's delegation in Congress and announced he preferred to wield power from within the legislative branch.

In the first round of balloting on May 31, Mahuad placed first with 36.6% and Noboa came in second with 29.7%. In the July 12 runoff election, Mahuad pulled off a harrowingly narrow victory over the Bucaram stand–in, receiving 51% of the valid votes, or 2,242,836 to Noboa's 2,140,628. Noboa at first refused to concede defeat, but the 48–year–old Mahuad took office on schedule on August 10.

Ecuador's new president presented a sobering change from the last popularly

The main marketplace in Guayaquil

elected chief executive; apparently the only thing he has in common with Bucaram is a Lebanese ancestry. He was well prepared professionally, having served as labor minister under President Roldós, then as a member of Congress before being elected mayor of Quito in 1992 and re-elected in 1996. In between, he managed to earn a master's degree in public administration from Harvard in 1989. His personal life was somewhat cloudier. He was the divorced father of a 20–year–old daughter, and acknowledged fathering a son out of wedlock while he was married.

In his first months in office, Mahuad could claim a major diplomatic achievement in reaching a peace agreement with Peru, but in coming to grips with the country's nagging economic woes he was faced with the same sort of public protests that had plagued Bucaram.

On the diplomatic front, Mahuad and Peruvian President Alberto Fujimori signed the peace accord in Brasilia on October 26, 1998, that definitively delineated the disputed 48–mile stretch of frontier that led to the 1995 war. The agreement was almost entirely along the lines Peru had demanded, that the border would follow the divide of the Cordillera del Condor range. As a gesture to Ecuador, however, Peru acquiesced Tiwintza Hill, which Ecuadorian soldiers had successfully defended against the Peruvians in 1995. As his own gesture of conciliation, Mahuad gave Fujimori a canteen used by an Ecuadorian soldier in the 1941 border war. The next step of the peace process came on January 18, 1999, when Mahuad and Fujimori met again along the border to dedicate the first border post at Lagartococha. The two leaders met again in

Washington on February 4, where they worked out the final details of the peace agreement and of a $3 billion cross–border international loan package. Fujimori pledged not to buy any new weapons, while Mahuad announced he was cutting the draft by 60% and converting 8,000 soldiers—a fourth of the army—into policemen. Under the 10–year border development plan, the two countries will make the border region accessible by new roads, integrate their electrical grids and embark on joint irrigation and resource–exploitation projects. Moreover, Peru will allow Ecuador to use its oil pipeline. President Bill Clinton hosted the two presidents at the White House to toast them on their achievement, the peaceful resolution of the last major border conflict in Latin America.

Back at home, however, Mahuad was forced to face the ever–present economic crisis (see Economy). No longer a member of OPEC, Ecuador could only watch helplessly as the price of oil on the world market plummeted in 1998, at one point diving to just over $11 a barrel. The price of Ecuador's other major export, bananas, also remained depressed. Compounding this already bleak picture, Ecuador sustained $2.6 billion in damage from the floods of the 1997–98 *El Niño* and suffered financial fallout from Brazil's economic meltdown in late 1998. The day after his triumphant meeting along the border with Fujimori in January, Mahuad delivered grim economic news to his countrymen: a $1.5 billion budget deficit and a projected growth rate of 1.7 percent for 1999, with inflation estimated at a more merciful but still formidable 22%. Meanwhile, public discontent over the inevitable austerity

measures erupted once again into street demonstrations.

By the first week of March 1999, the crisis deepened as several banks foundered. On March 8, Mahuad declared a week-long bank holiday and the following day imposed a 60–day state of emergency. The value of the *sucre* went into a free-fall, losing 60% of its value at one point. As part of a new austerity plan, Mahuad decreed a price increase for gasoline from 89 cents to $2.33 a gallon and raised the value–added tax from 10% to 15%. Transit workers immediately went on strike, virtually paralyzing the country for five days. Street demonstrations led to 235 arrests. The Social Christian Party, the coalition partner of Mahuad's Popular Democracy party, denounced the austerity plan as "inhuman." Mahuad's public approval rating fell to 16% in one poll.

On March 19, Mahuad caved in to the public outcry and struck a deal with the left–of–center parties in Congress for a watered–down austerity plan. The price of gasoline, for example, was rolled back to $1.20 a gallon, and in place of the VAT increase the Congress reinstated the income tax, with a 15% ceiling. This new coalition comprised 70 of the 121 seats in Congress but was shaky.

At the height of the crisis, there was another startling development in March: Former President Alarcón was arrested on charges that while president of the Congress he had padded congressional payrolls.

Over the next 10 months, the political and economic situations deteriorated from bad to worse to impossible. Every time Mahuad sought to impose austerity measures to win IMF approval for desperately needed capital, he would be faced with more public protests that forced him to back down. He sought a $1.2 billion bailout of 18 defunct banks, but then the head of one of the banks, who had been arrested for fraud, revealed he had donated more than $3 million to Mahuad's 1998 campaign.

In August, Mahuad announced that it could not make the $98 million interest payment on its $6 billion in Brady bonds, which the U.S. Treasury had extended to 18 countries to help them restructure their debts (Ecuador's total foreign debt by then was a ponderous $13.6 billion). A month later, Ecuador suffered the ignominy of becoming the first nation to default on its Brady bonds. By the end of the year, the *sucre* had fallen from 7,000 to 25,000 to the dollar; inflation had hit 61% for 1999; foreign creditors were pounding on the door; and military officers were publicly criticizing the civilian government's inaction, prompting rumors of an imminent coup. Moreover, a poll showed that 91% disapproved of Mahuad's performance and that 53% wanted him to resign.

Dollarization and Downfall

On January 9, 2000, the desperate president unveiled a desperate plan: He would replace the *sucre* with the U.S. dollar—not merely peg the *sucre* to the dollar as the Argentines had done, but make the dollar the official currency, as it is in Panama. For a few fleeting days, the dramatic proposal seemed to have a popular consensus. The Social Christian Party, *Roldosista* Party and Mahuad's own Popular Democracy party reached a rare agreement in support of dollarization, while one of the ubiquitous opinion polls showed that 59% of the public supported the idea.

Apparently that survey neglected to poll the rural Indians who make up 40% of the population. Within days, the Ecuadorian Confederation of Indigenous Communities (*CONAIE*), which reportedly is the most powerful Indian-rights group in the Americas, not only declared its opposition to dollarization but demanded that Mahuad resign and mobilized thousands of peasants to march on Quito. Violence appeared imminent.

Matters came to a head on January 21. The *CONAIE* protesters actually stormed and occupied the Congress building. More dramatic still, they were joined by about 150 field-grade military officers who echoed the Indians' demand that the president resign. Faced with open rebellion, Mahuad fled the presidential palace and took refuge at a military base in Quito, but he steadfastly refused to resign. It didn't matter whether he did or not, however. His newly appointed defense minister, General Carlos Mendoza, announced that he was assuming power at the head of a three-man junta, which also included *CONAIE* leader Antonio Vargas and former Supreme Court Justice Carlos Solorzano. With the backing of the military, the ouster of Mahuad became a *fait accompli*; it was Latin America's first military *coup d'etat* since the overthrow of Jean-Bertrand Aristide in Haiti in 1991. After 22 years of tenuous democracy, Ecuador's constitutional system finally had broken down, a victim of mob rule.

For 24 tense hours, the rebel junta came under intense diplomatic pressure from the United States, Canada, the Organization of American States, the European Union, U.N. Secretary-General Kofi Annan and most of the Latin American presidents. Even the enigmatic Bucaram, who had long denounced Mahuad as a usurper, nonetheless condemned his rival's overthrow from his exile in Panama. The following day, in a stunning turnabout, General Mendoza declared that he would yield power to the constitutional vice president, Gustavo Noboa, apparently to maintain some semblance of constitutional niceties; Vargas and Solorzano had little choice but to go along. Mendoza later would claim that he "tricked" Vargas and Solorzano and that agreeing to form a junta was merely a means of defusing a potentially explosive situation.

Though the transfer of power was in no way democratic, the new president was at least a respectable figure. Noboa, then 62, is a lawyer and former dean of Catholic University, who gained fame as one of the negotiators of the border settlement with Peru. The hapless Mahuad, who still refused to resign, lamely expressed his backing for Noboa. "A deposed president doesn't resign," he said wanly , "he's just deposed." Congress, in an equally lame show of legitimacy, duly confirmed Noboa to fill out the remainder of Mahuad's term, to 2003.

Ironically, Noboa almost immediately announced that he would push forward with the plan to replace the *sucre* with the dollar, the very proposal that sparked Mahuad's downfall. In March, under pressure from the IMF and other international lending institutions, which had promised $2 billion in loans.

Congress approved the dollarization plan. The IMF approved the first $304 million loan package on April 19, with the remainder contingent upon further concessions (see Economy). Noboa announced the following day that Ecuador would resume payments on its Brady bonds.

In another transparent and hypocritical attempt at constitutional window-dressing, the government moved quickly to "punish" the people who had brought about Mahuad's overthrow. Just six days after the coup, the defense ministry arrested four colonels and 12 lieutenant colonels for their roles in the event and began investigating the roles of hundreds more junior officers. The ministry narrowed the number to be court-martialed to 16 officers and one sergeant. The Supreme Court, meanwhile, brought charges against Vargas and Solorzano, together with two members of the Democratic Left party whom Congress had expelled for their involvement in the coup, for "attempts against the security of the state." To bring this farce to an end, Noboa asked Congress to declare an amnesty to those who participated in the coup. The head of the Joint Chiefs of Staff and the commanders of the navy and the air force (but not the army) resigned their posts to protest the president's recommendation for amnesty for the rebellious soldiers. Nonetheless, Congress approved the amnesty for all 117 military. Public opinion polls, which seem to govern Ecuador, showed that 67% of the public supported the amnesty.

Not so with the dollarization plan. A majority, according to the polls, opposed it. *CONAIE*, labor unions and students called a one-day strike to demand that the government revoke its agreement with the IMF, and the usual 10,000 demonstrators peacefully turned out in the streets of the capital. Teachers, hospital workers and other groups called for another, "indefinite," strike in May, which closed schools and created some inconveniences before sputtering out after a few days.

The dollarization went into effect as planned in September 2000, and by year's end, the stability of the currency, coupled with the rising international price of petroleum and a $2 billion international loan package arranged by the IMF, led to a surprisingly rosy economic picture by the end of the year. Noboa consequently began enjoying a relative popularity few of his recent predecessors knew.

Recent Developments

Nonetheless, he has had his problems. In August 2000, defections gave a center-left bloc a majority in Congress, which has continued to resist Noboa's privatization plans for electricity, petroleum and telecommunications that the IMF—and foreign investors—expect. Moreover, the constitutional tribunal ruled 44 points of the privatization program unconstitutional. Then, in February 2001, when Noboa acceded to IMF demands and doubled the price of cooking gas and raised the price of gasoline by 22% to offset the reduction of subsidies, *CONAIE* and other groups took to the streets and roads again after months of dormancy, blocking the roads around the capital. Noboa declared a state of emergency, and in the ensuing violence four protesters were killed. To defuse the crisis, Noboa caved in to demands to scale back the increases. The IMF reluctantly agreed.

In March 2001, Congress capriciously —and overwhelmingly—thumbed its nose again at the IMF by rejecting an increase in the value-added tax from 12%

President Gustavo Noboa

to 15%. It also rejected other revenue-raising measures, virtually assuring a crushing budget deficit that would not please the IMF. In August 2001, the Constitutional Tribunal got into the act of hamstringing the president's efforts at fiscal reform by declaring unconstitutional a tax he had proposed to satisfy IMF demands; international financial markets reacted negatively. That same month, Noboa submitted to Congress a dramatic governmental overhaul that would have created a bicameral Congress and allowed the president to dissolve Congress once per term. The proposal met with the usual congressional indifference.

To compound Noboa's domestic problems, in May 2000 members of a dissident faction of the Revolutionary Armed Forces of Colombia (FARC) encroached into Ecuadorian territory. Two of the rebels were killed in a firefight with the Ecuadorian army. Since then, drug-related violence has continued to spill over from Colombia. In February 2001, the army beefed up its 1,500-man border forces with an additional 2,000 troops. The border situation remains tense.

On the positive side, the dismal economic picture improved dramatically in 2001, although the improvement was in part illusionary (see Economy).

Presidential and congressional elections have been scheduled for October 20, 2002.

Culture: Ecuador is the quintessential *mestizo* country, with pure European and Indian descendants being heavily outnumbered by their ethnic hybrid. Of the two cultures, it is the Indian that has had the greater influence on the country's cultural identity. Ecuador is a remnant of the Inca Empire, and Quéchua is still widely spoken. The 200–odd Quéchua–based dialects serve as a unifying thread among the rural people. The Indian roots are visible and audible in the country's art and traditional folk music and dances.

Like other Bolivarian countries of northern South America, Ecuador has been whipsawed by dictatorship and political instability that has had a negative impact on cultural growth. Ecuadorian culture attracted little attention outside its borders until the 20th century. Its outstanding literary figure remains Jorge Icaza, whose 1934 novel, *Huasipungo*, is a Latin American classic and has been translated into at least 17 languages. Another prominent novelist was José de la Cuadra.

Ecuador's principal cultural contribution has come from its many talented artists, the best known of whom have been Oswaldo Guayasamín, a revolutionary painter in the style of Mexico's Diego Rivera, and Kingman Riofrío, whose works stress indigenous subjects.

The high illiteracy rate has hampered development of the printed media. There are a number of mid–sized dailies, centered in Quito and Guayaquil. The oldest is the elite *El Telégrafo*, founded in 1884 and located in Guayaquil. The nation's circulation leader with about 200,000 daily is *El Universo*, which dates to 1921 and also is published in the port city. The capital's leading paper is *El Comercio*. There also are a number of magazines.

Economy: Ecuador's economy was always dependent upon the sale of agricultural products (bananas) and minerals abroad to pay for needed imports. It now is dominated by oil exportation (more than 385,000 barrels per day).

The agricultural/mineral exports are produced by illiterate, poorly paid labor in economic bondage to the land, who live on a per capita income of about $500 a year. Substantial resources in the form of fertile soils, valuable forests and mineral wealth have not been seriously exploited.

Ecuador's economic future improved dramatically with the discovery of rich oil deposits, estimated to total 5 billion barrels of high–grade petroleum, in the jungles east of the Andes. Oil income quadrupled government revenues with royalties reaching about $500 million by 1975. Nationalistic oil policies later forced most private firms to leave the country—thereby reducing exploration for new oil deposits. As a result, production declined; domestic oil consumption came close to outstripping production.

Although the government announced with much fanfare in 1981 that important new deposits were located, some observers feel that these would not greatly increase Ecuador's oil reserves. During 1981, oil output rose 27% to a total of 77 million barrels. However, the country's unfriendly attitude toward foreign oil companies prior to 1984 made it difficult to obtain foreign expertise needed to develop Ecuador's resources. This was remedied, however, by the administration of Febres Cordero and as a result, additional exploration was underway in 1986.

But in 1985 another oil–related problem raised its ugly head: Saudi Arabia announced a rise in its production because other OPEC nations were cheating on their oil quotas. This allowed the price for the product to "float," and the worldwide market thus headed into a steep decline. The price descended to one-third of its 1980 level in 1986 (less than $10 a barrel), but rebounded to $17 by 1995. Production in existing fields was sufficient to last until 2000, but new discoveries have extended this. Plans to exploit deposits in the Amazon basin have been opposed by environmentalists and local Indian tribes; they have progressed unevenly.

A major earthquake in 1987 caused a severe economic setback. Remedial measures were not well coordinated.

During the 1990s, prices generally have been depressed for bananas, cacao and coffee, but the price for the coffee doubled at the start of 1995 when killing frosts destroyed half of Brazil's trees. Ecuador, together with Peru and Bolivia, is a major producer of raw cocaine paste, which is processed into powder in Colombia. Numerous "factories" are located within Ecuador (owned by the Colombian cartels) where the paste is processed because of control measures within Colombia. Ecuador now imports four to five times as much of the chemicals needed to process cocaine than it would be able to use in the absence of that drug's production. Distribution is still via Colombia, equally to Europe and the United States.

The devastating effects of *El Niño* in 1997, the drastic drop in world oil prices in 1998 and the simultaneous meltdown of the Asian and Brazilian financial markets all have contributed to an economic crisis that President Mahuad declared to be the worst in 70 years. The president told Congress in his state of the nation address in January 1999 that the country recorded real economic growth of only 0.8% in 1998, while inflation soared to 43.4%, the highest in Latin America.

Meanwhile, the Ecuadorian economy received some heartening news from two other international organizations: OPEC and the World Trade Organization. OPEC's decision in March 1999 to boost the depressed price of oil augured well for Ecuador. In April, a panel of WTO experts meeting in Panama sided with the United States, Ecuador, Guatemala, Honduras and Panama in their complaint that the European Union's banana import policy was discriminatory. The five plaintiff countries had charged that the EU showed favoritism to bananas imported from former Caribbean colonies and against Latin American producers and U.S. distributors, in violation of international trading regulations. Ecuador exports 16% of its bananas to the EU, or $238 million of its $1.05 billion 1998 production, amounting to more than 650,000 tons.

But the bad news still outweighed the good. In March 1999, Mahuad and the Congress reached an accord on a watered-down austerity plan that called for an income tax, a luxury tax on cars, more efficient collection of existing taxes and $100 million in spending cuts in an effort to cut the brutal budget deficit by $520 million. The plan also severely limited withdrawals from bank accounts. The IMF gave its approval to the plan, although Mahuad, faced with the opposition of the left-wing parties in his new coalition, was forced to abandon his privatization plan.

These painful measures deepened the recession, and the year-end figures for 1999 reflected the severity of the crisis that led a desperate Mahuad to recommend replacing the *sucre* with the dollar. Real GDP declined by a devastating 7.5%, unemployment jumped from 11.5% in 1998 to 16.9%, per capita income fell from $1,619 to $1,164, and inflation was officially the highest in Latin America: 50.4%.

The dollarization scheme led to massive public protests that led to Mahuad's ouster in January 2000, but his vice president and successor, Gustavo Noboa, somehow managed to embrace dollarization, to put it into effect and to survive. The dollar replaced the *sucre* as Ecuador's legal tender in September. The resulting currency stabilization, coupled with the fortuitous rise in international oil prices, led to a much healthier than expected growth rate for 2000 of 2.0%. Inflation, however, nearly doubled to a crippling 96.6%, again the highest in Latin America, but unemployment dropped slightly to 14.7%.

The figures for 2001 were dramatically better, although deceptive. The good news was that real GDP increased by 5.4%, the fastest growth in all of Latin America, and it was expected to grow another 4.2% in 2002. In reality, of course, this only recovers the ground lost in 1999. Inflation, meanwhile, plummeted to "only" 22.4%.

There are two factors responsible for the improvement. In February 2001, Noboa signed a $1.3 billion contract for an oil pipeline that is expected to create 50,000 jobs and, when completed, boost petroleum exports by 50%. But a more important factor is a peculiar demographic phenomenon. Since the 1999 economic meltdown, Ecuadorians have been abandoning the country in droves, legally and illegally, seeking work abroad in the United States, Spain, Italy and other countries. In 2001, the government actually created a program to expedite the exit visas of its citizens to work abroad; in March 2002 alone, 30,000 Ecuadorians signed up! Year-end figures for 2001 showed that this has both cut domestic unemployment almost by half to 8.8% (although 40% are still considered underemployed) and generated $1.4 billion in remittances from abroad, accounting for an astonishing 8% of GDP, second only to oil exports.

The Future: The elections scheduled for October 20, 2002 will be a crucial test of Ecuadorian democracy—if it may be called that. However justifiable the January 2000 ouster of the unpopular Mahuad may have seemed to those who effected it, the fact remains that the Ecuadorian constitution does not contain a clause stipulating that the military may remove a president when (1) his approval rating in the opinion polls falls to single digits and (2) when at least 5,000 demonstrators congregate in front of the presidential palace to demand his resignation. The argument could be made that Mahuad's overthrow prevented a social explosion, but it established a precedent for future mobs to depose a duly elected president once he demonstrates he is not Superman. The same phenomenon occurred in Argentina in December 2001 and almost occurred in Venezuela in April 2002. Political scientists have a term for this: anarchy.

Noboa, admittedly a decent fellow who enjoyed a honeymoon with the public in the wake of the early success of the dollarization plan, nonetheless is an illegitimate president. Moreover, he has faced the same daunting economic and political tasks that faced his three immediate predecessors, and has met with the same congressional recalcitrance. Unfortunately for him, he is the president of a nation of spoiled, willful crybabies, who will turn on any president when he attempts to make the hard, painful decisions that he must inevitably make if Ecuador's economic house is ever to be put in order. There is no reason to suspect this will be any different with the new president elected in October. Ecuadorians must be willing to make some sacrifices; they are not.

Giant tortoises of the Galápagos Islands

135

The Republic of El Salvador

Street scene in San Salvador

Area: 8,260 square miles.
Population: 6.26 million (2000 estimate), including refugees living elsewhere).
Capital City: San Salvador (Pop. 1.75 million, estimated).
Climate: Tropical in the coastal plain, becoming temperate at higher altitudes.
Neighboring Countries: Honduras (North and East); Guatemala (West).
Official Language: Spanish.
Ethnic Background: *Mestizo* (mixed Spanish and Indian).
Principal Religion: Roman Catholic Christianity.
Chief Commercial Products: Coffee, Cotton, Sugar.
Currency: U.S. Dollar (formerly the Colón).
Gross Domestic Product: U.S. $13.217 billion in 2001 ($2,100 per capita).
Former Colonial Status: Spanish Crown Colony (1524–1821).
Independence Date: September 15, 1821
Chief of State: Francisco Flores, President (since June 1, 1999).
National Flag: Blue, white and blue horizontal stripes with the national coat of arms on the white stripe.

El Salvador is the smallest and most densely populated of the Central American republics. Most of the country is a volcanic upland with two parallel rows of volcanos running east to west. Fourteen of the cones exceed 3,000 feet and three reach more than 7,000 feet. Lowlands lie north and south of the volcanic ranges. El Salvador's principal river, the Lempa, drains the northern lowlands by cutting through the volcanic region to reach the Pacific.

El Salvador's soils are rich and easily accessible from the Pacific coast; thus it is one of the few Latin American countries in which the whole of the national territory is settled. Various estimates are given for the percentages of European, Indian and African ancestry in the national population, but the most obvious facts are that there are no tribal Indians and few blacks, and that the white minority claiming pure European origins is indistinguishable from the admittedly *mestizo*, a mixture of Spanish and Indian. Cotton and sugar are raised on the coastal plains and the Lempa River valley, while the slopes of the

volcanoes produce coffee. The climate is healthful and the rainfall abundant, with the rainy season running from May through October.

History: El Salvador was conquered by Pedro de Alvarado with a force from Mexico in 1524. Defeating the Indians and capturing their capital, Cuscutlán, he joined the region to the Captaincy–General of Guatemala. The small number of Spanish settlers intermarried with the Indians and established large agricultural and cattle-raising estates in the fertile valleys of the volcanic uplands, a pattern of land holding which exists today, and the root of most of El Salvador's present–day problems. The remnants of the Indian population still farm village–owned lands in the mountains.

El Salvador declared its independence from Spain on September 15, 1821, with the other countries of Central America. Joining in a short-lived federation until its breakup in 1838, El Salvador was a center for the liberal republican opposition to the conservatives of Guatemala. It sought admission to the United States at one time and participated in several attempts to unite with Honduras and Nicaragua. As was true in most of the Central American republics, the political history of El Salvador during the 19th century after independence was one of turbulence, revolution, dictators, military governments and civil strife. Added to the internal difficulties of the nation were frequent periods of conflict with neighboring states.

The first quarter of the 20th century was relatively peaceful in El Salvador, but this was followed by virtual anarchy which did not end until the seizure of power by an absolute ruler, Hernández Martínez, from 1931 to 1944. The low point of his years in power came in 1932, when a peasant uprising in protest against the landed elite cost 20,000 lives, almost all of them peasants, an event remembered today as "*La Matanza*" (the slaughter).

Various factions have been labeled conservative (favoring central government and close church–state relations) and liberal (anti–clerical federalists); however, those represented only blocs within the elite landowning class and were not truly different political entities. A degree of political stability was evidenced by regimes in power from 1948 to 1960, but popular opposition to the elite domination of politics and continuing economic problems continued to center around a small number of wealthy and a comparatively huge number of poor. This led to minor change in October 1960.

A provisional military–civilian *junta* took power, promising to reform the nation's political structure and hold elections. A new constitution was adopted in 1962 and in presidential elections held the same year there was but one candidate, Adalberto Rivera of the *Partido de Conciliación Nacional (PCN)*, a movement controlled by the oligarchy and the military. Although he and his party were supposed to be "middle–of–"the–road," there was no such thing in El Salvador. There were right–wing, elitist elements and communist–leftist rebels, with little in between. Providing capable and honest leadership, Rivera encouraged the development of light industry and supported the nation's participation in the Central American Common Market.

Starting about 1960, a culture of violence gripped the country. Right–wing vigilante groups, such as the White Warrior's Union, and other murky names often joined with government forces—including rightist members of the army, the National Guard and the Treasury Police—to torture and execute peasant leaders and other advocates of social reform. Leftist groups—including Marxist–led guerrilla units such as the People's Revolutionary Army, the Popular Forces of Liberation, and the Armed Forces of National Resis-

tance—responded in kind with attacks against military forces and their conservative supporters. Generally, leftist groups tended to pinpoint specific targets, while right–wing terrorists appeared less discriminatory. As a result, a large percentage of the political deaths in El Salvador have been linked to conservative forces.

Another *PCN* "moderate" candidate, Colonel Fidel Sánchez Hernández, won the 1967 election; his policies included an unheard–of land ownership reform proposal that infuriated conservatives, businessmen and wealthy landowners. A brief—but bitter—open war with Honduras was fought in 1969 (see Honduras).

Great controversy surrounded the presidential elections of 1972. Christian Democrat José Napoleón Duarte, a nominal moderate, apparently outpolled *PCN* candidate Colonel Arturo Armando Molina. However, a subsequent "official" government count gave the ruling *PCN* party a 22,000 vote victory; Molina's "election" was confirmed by Congress, where the *PCN* enjoyed a two–thirds majority. The military used a similar tactic for the presidential elections of 1977 when the ruling *PCN* candidate, General Carlos Humberto Romero, was declared the winner by a two–to–one margin over his opponent, another right–wing officer. When riots broke out against the rigged elections, the government imposed martial law. Before order was restored, an estimated 100 protesters were killed.

A staunch conservative, Romero was involuntarily faced immediately with urgent problems of land reform, human rights and the Catholic Church, which had become reformist. He equated change from the old order with communism. Most of the fertile farmland in the valleys and lowlands (about 60% of the total) continued to be owned by a handful of families who were closely allied to the ruling armed forces. In contrast, more than 65% of the population lived in abject poverty. Backed by the military, the conservative aristocracy had traditionally blocked disorganized peasant demands for land and reform. Wealthy landowners (including military officers who owned large estates) feared a repetition of the unsuccessful peasant uprisings against the landed elite of 1932.

The pace of fighting between rightists and leftists rose dramatically after Romero became president. Hoping to wipe out all opposition, he launched a bitter campaign against leftists and their sympathizers.

Coup and Civil War

As the nation moved toward complete chaos, a group of liberal army officers led by Colonel Adolfo Arnoldo Majano ousted Romero in a bloodless coup in November 1979. Power then shifted to a progressive five–man *junta* that included Majano and two members of the "centrist" Christian Democratic Party. The new rulers promised sweeping economic and social reforms that provided: (1) nationalization of key parts of foreign trade industries, including coffee marketing, (2) nationalization of many banks (which traditionally provided loans only to the upper class, and (3) land reform.

On paper, the land reform proposal was comparable in scope to those of Mexico, Bolivia and Peru. The first phase, affecting 400 estates containing more than 1,235 acres each, would have redistributed about 600,000 acres of land (about 25% of

the nation's arable land) to peasants. A second phase, planned for 1981, was to involve all farms larger than 370 acres.

A major catalyst for reform was the Carter administration in Washington, which supplied El Salvador with economic and military assistance. Washington feared that unless fundamental reforms were enacted, El Salvador would slide into a disastrous class war. Such a conflict might well be won by leftists, who could then be expected to combine with radicals in Nicaragua to force Marxist governments onto neighboring Honduras and Guatemala.

Conservative opposition to the *junta's* reforms proved overwhelming, however, and right-wing violence rose dramatically. The assassination of Archbishop Oscar Romero in 1980 shocked the nation, and in 1980 conservatives murdered the head of the country's Human Rights Commission (its report had embarrassed the government). The top six leaders of a "centrist" political front which included the Christian Democratic Party were killed in late 1980, and the following month four U.S. women missionaries were murdered. Early January was marked by the murder of two U.S. agricultural agents associated with the nation's land reform program.

Appalled by this violence, President Carter halted all aid to El Salvador in late 1980. The Salvadoran military responded by taking aim at the *junta,* but the result was unexpected. Majano was replaced by a new four–member *junta* under the leadership of José Napoleón Duarte of the Christian Democratic Party. A graduate of Notre Dame University, the 55–year–old civil engineer pledged to move forward with social reform while taking steps to control right-wing terrorism. Duarte qui-

José Napoleón Duarte

etly retired some right-wing military leaders while others were reassigned to isolated posts.

Convinced that the time was ripe for revolution, the guerrillas launched a full–scale "final assault" against government forces in January 1981. Although supplied with Nicaraguan and Cuban arms, the rebels found no popular support in the countryside, and the offensive soon foundered.

In Washington, the new Reagan administration issued in February 1981 a hastily prepared report claiming to have "concrete" evidence that the Salvadoran guerrilla front was a part of a "worldwide

communist conspiracy" masterminded by the Soviet Union. Insisting that it was necessary to "draw the line" against communism, President Reagan soon ordered a resumption of large–scale military and economic assistance to El Salvador. He also fired the Carter-appointed ambassador.

Despite such aid, Duarte's regime found itself increasingly dependent on the military for survival. To placate powerful right-wing critics in the country, Duarte predictably shelved many of his promised reforms. Hoping to increase domestic support for the government and to improve El Salvador's international image, Washington pressured Duarte to hold elections for a Constituent Assembly in March 1982 as the first step toward a return to constitutional government. While almost all leftists boycotted the elections—and the guerrillas sought to disrupt the balloting—voter turnout was heavy. Official returns showed 1.3 million votes cast.

Duarte's centrist-left Christian Democratic Party won 40% of the vote and 24 seats in the 60–seat Constituent Assembly, the largest total of any single party. But right-wing tickets led by the National Republican Alliance (*ARENA*) and the National Conciliation Party (*PCN*) gained nearly 60% of the vote and 34 seats in the Assembly.

Much to the chagrin of Duarte and his supporters in Washington, the rightists promptly formed a coalition and voted to exclude the Christian Democrats from participation in the new government. Named president of the Assembly was arch–conservative Roberto D'Aubuisson, an ex–army intelligence officer allegedly linked with the right-wing death squads. In 1980 he had been arrested for plotting a coup against the government.

Under strong pressure from the army's influential defense minister, General José Guillermo García, the Assembly elected a moderate U.S.–educated economist and banker as provisional president: Alvaro Alfredo Magaña, 56. The Assembly also named three vice presidents, one each for *ARENA, PCN,* and the Christian Democrats.

As the first democratically elected president in 50 years, Magaña was expected to have only a limited impact on the country's destiny. The rightist–controlled Assembly sought to strip the president of any real power while Assembly President D'Aubuisson tried to repeal many of the reforms planned by the previous Duarte regime. In one of its first acts, the Assembly voted to dismantle Phases II and III of the land reform program longed for by the poor. (By mid–1982, provisional land titles had been given to more than 7,000 peasants under the program.) D'Aubuisson boasted he would wipe out the nation's guerrilla movement "in no more than six months."

Although weakened by the failures of its 1981 "final assault," the guerrillas were

Salvadoran guerrillas, Usulatan Province

A young rural mother does the family wash

not dislodged. The insurgents controlled most of Chalatenango and Morazán provinces in the mountainous north part of the country near the Honduran border.

The nation's five major Marxist groups continued to quarrel among themselves, although their activities became coordinated under a single umbrella organization, the Farabundo Martí National Liberation Front *(FMLN)*. Most of the groups, which trace their common roots to the communist–inspired peasant uprising in 1932, became active in the late 1960s and early 1970s. Both France and Mexico recognized the rebels in August 1981 as a "representative political force"—a move which could only alienate the United States.

Finding itself in the midst of a civil war, the Salvadoran government also began to improve its own military capabilities. Especially effective were the U.S.–trained battalions which used new tactics and sophisticated equipment provided by the United States.

The United States was drawn into an anti–communist war in El Salvador. A blank check was written to those in charge, a military establishment whose loyalty was consistently identified with the elite of the country. They faced an insurgency initially of poor guerrillas, who rapidly came to be supported by Soviet–via–Cuba resources, military and financial. A heavy infusion of U.S. aid was furnished during the Reagan years with a single instruction: win. American advisers took their place alongside the Salvadoran military, quickly training and developing rapid–response battalions that were virtually invincible, and which soon acquired the dubious label of "death squads."

Alongside the government forces, including these deadly battalions, there were private forces, capable of the worst atrocities to accomplish the desired goal: win. But it was not one–sided by any means; the communists also had a single goal: win. Both sides resorted to the worst sort of warfare, using any tactic or method necessary to instill total fear in innocent bystanders so they would apparently support, out of fear, the military effort immediately controlling their destiny. Public torture, mutilation and murder of innocents, all became acceptable tools used by both sides.

With the heavy infusion of American aid, the Salvadoran military increasingly resembled the U.S. Army; troops armed with highly sophisticated equipment that were sometimes plagued with mobility, maintenance and cost problems, together with 55 U.S. military advisers (a number limited by the U.S. Congress) plus support personnel, government forces became more and more effective.

The U.S. Senate Foreign Relations Committee voted to cut $100 million from the Reagan administration's $226 million aid package in mid–1982. The U.S. House of Representatives passed a resolution requiring the president to certify that the Salvadoran government was making "good faith efforts" to prosecute five National Guard personnel accused of the 1980 murder of three American nuns and a lay worker.

El Salvador's civil war increasingly spilled over into other parts of Central America. Thousands of Salvadoran peasants fled to Honduras to escape the terror from the guerrillas and the right–wing death squads, including *ORDEN*, a rural civil defense force feared even more than the regular army. An estimated 2 million Salvadorans lived outside the country; 1 million of them, mostly illegal immigrants, were in the United States.

Guatemala, Honduras, Costa Rica and El Salvador formed a common front to exchange intelligence and coordinate strategy against Nicaraguan and Salvadoran guerrillas. Both Honduras and Guatemala maintained large troop concentrations along their common borders with El Salvador. Honduran troops controlled a contested zone along the border of the two countries, partly to prevent the communist rebellion from spreading into its territory.

The *FMLN* sought to disrupt elections in 1984, but Salvadorans went to the polls under the eyes of scores of international observers. Duarte ultimately defeated D'Aubuisson for president, and immediately traveled to Washington to ask for more economic aid for social programs and military assistance. In 1985 legislative and municipal elections, the Christian Democratic Party, in an upset, captured a majority of seats in the National Assembly and municipal councils. The rightists hatched a scheme to list a single candidate as the choice of two parties, but the effort was voided by the Supreme Court.

An announcement by a Catholic Church official that it would try to mediate in the civil war eased the cautious attitude of the U.S. Congress, which in 1984 appropriated additional emergency and military aid to El Salvador. But in 1985, the communists kidnapped the daughter of Duarte as she was leaving the San Salvador University. The president had to agree to the release of 22 rebels and safe passage for 96 wounded guerrillas to Cuba (and then to Eastern Europe for medical treatment) before his daughter could be released. He sent his family to the United States to

Former President Armando Calderón Sol

avoid further kidnappings. The military and rightists were furious at his apparent weakness, but talk about a coup rapidly faded. He was, after all, necessary for continued U.S. military aid.

The years 1986–87 saw a beefed up military achieve greater successes. Ultimately the conflict cost $6 billion in U.S. aid. Periodic negotiations failed, as both sides negotiated with ultimatums. In 1988 the *FMLN* flatly rejected a proposal that the organization participate in municipal and legislative elections. When it finally tried this in 1991, in spite of successfully blocking observation at 30 polling places it controlled, only one of its candidates was sent to the National Assembly.

But in 1989 the communists agreed to take part in and respect the outcome of presidential elections *if* they were postponed for six months. They demanded a multitude of other conditions that made the offer impossible. They resorted to terrorism to disrupt the electoral process, and the right–wing death squads retaliated, committing their own atrocities. As usual, the innocent suffered.

The Christian Democrats had unwisely divided into two factions. *ARENA*, well unified under D'Aubuisson, was able to mount an unexpected upset in local and legislative elections, and was the decisive victor in a contest marred by charges of ballot box stuffing.

Six candidates vied for office in 1989 presidential elections. The *FMLN* nominally supported one, but did its best to keep voters away from the polls. *ARENA* candidate Alfredo Cristiani won with almost 54% of the votes.

By late 1989 it was apparent that Soviet–Cuban aid was going to dry up. Deciding that negotiations were the best course, the *FMLN* tried two super–offensives—last–ditch efforts in 1989–90 to win as much territory as possible and thereby be in a better negotiating position. The guerrillas held parts of San Salvador for several days, but could not consolidate their gains. Nine members of a death squad murdered seven pro-guerrilla Jesuit priests in cold blood, together with their servant and her daughter in the melee. Two of the soldiers later were sentenced to 30 years imprisonment for following orders.

Peace at Last

After the last–gasp rebel offensive of 1989, both sides were forced to acknowledge a stalemate. Neither could achieve full victory, and each side was willing to make peace; all that was needed was an appropriate broker. In September 1991, the U.S. ambassador and his military group commander seized that initiative by traveling boldly into guerrilla territory in a four–wheel-drive vehicle to confront an astonished *FMLN* leadership. Essen-

tially, the two U.S. officials asked what it would take for the *FMLN* to make peace. It turned out that two of the rebels' key expectations for a post–war El Salvador were relatively reasonable ones: rural electrification and an end to death–squad atrocities. The ambassador brought these and other bargaining points back to the capital. On December 31, the two sides signed a truce that ended 12 years of slaughter that had claimed an estimated 75,000 lives, a grim toll in a country of only 6 million people.

The formal signing of the peace accords followed on January 16, 1992. Under the terms of the peace agreement, guaranteed by the United Nations, the *FMLN* laid down their arms and agreed to participate in the democratic process. The army ceased its sponsorship of death–squad activities. Despite an occasional low–level violation, the desire for peace superseded the deep–seated class hatreds that had led to the bloodbath. Less realistic was the establishment of a "truth commission" to investigate the atrocities committed during the war. Among the recommendations in its 211–page report was that the entire Supreme Court be sacked. President Cristiani chose to ignore these and other recommendations, but the mood of the country was one of forgive and forget. Despite some pessimism and a few setbacks, the tenuous armistice took hold.

The first postwar elections revealed a great deal about the conflict in El Salvador. Both Duarte and D'Aubuisson had died of cancer since 1989. Armando Calderón Sol was the candidate of *ARENA* in the March–April 1994 contest; Rubén Zamora was the choice of a leftist coalition which included the *FMLN*. Campaigning was vigorous by all candidates. Calderón appeared as a mild–mannered moderate, although he had been a close adherent of D'Aubuisson. But Zamora, appearing with a narrow black beard and moustache, closely resembled the evil Mephistopheles; the comparative appearance of the two was not lost on the public.

The war had been fought largely on a local and regional basis, so the candidates of the left were immediately recognized even though their dress had been totally altered. The people were incredulous at the idea of seeing people capable of killing them for a dozen years suddenly soliciting their votes. In the first round Calderón scored not quite 50% of the vote in balloting which was free of irregularities; Zamora received 25%. *ARENA* sailed to an easy victory in the runoff held in April.

ARENA and an allied party took 43 seats, a bare majority in the 84-seat Assembly, while the *FMLN* won 21 and the Christian Democrats fell to 18. In December 1994, the Christian Democrats fragmented, with nine of their deputies bolting to the Renewal Social Christian Movement and one becoming an independent.

Making *pupusas* (a *tortilla* made of cornmeal, onion, pork rinds, and shortening) at a sidewalk restaurant in San Salvador.

Photo by the author

While the elections were underway, the Clinton administration sliced the aid appropriation for El Salvador to 40% of what it received in 1993.

It would be pleasant to report that all is well (at last) in El Salvador. It isn't. The fighters of the *FMLN* were promised jobs and stipends to enable them to live decently. But no one planned where the funds for this would come from. They have split into numerous factions and groups, many of which practice thievery, kidnapping and demolition of homes to obtain and extort money from small villages and the countryside. This illustrates an age-old problem: what is done with the revolutionaries when the revolution is over?

The lower echelon army troops went frequently unpaid, but were promised tracts in the rich, upper highlands, to be taken from the land barons. Anticipating this, many squatted on the large *estancias*, but have been driven from them. They are embittered and restive.

These developments show the elite have not learned an important lesson: the wealth of El Salvador must be shared, otherwise they, sooner or later, will lose all of what they have.

The political and economic elites thus received a well–deserved scare in the municipal and congressional elections of 1997. *ARENA* lost its absolute majority in the National Assembly, winning just 28 of the 84 seats, while the *FMLN* shocked the country—and the world—by winning 27. *ARENA* was forced to govern in coalition with small conservative parties. Moreover, the *FMLN* won the mayoralties of

most of the major cities, including San Salvador. The winner in the capital was Hector Silva, a Boston–born gynecologist, who has become highly popular for his public works improvements and who at one point seemed the logical *FMLN* candidate for president in 1999. The *FMLN* also had an unlikely ally in President Calderón, who by 1998 had become highly disliked because of a stagnant economy, allegations of corruption within his administration and an alarming increase in violent crime that he seemed impotent to control. By mid–1998, it seemed inevitable that the former guerrillas would win through the ballot box what they had failed for 12 years to win on the battlefield. But two things happened to blunt the pro–*FMLN* trend.

First, in March 1998, *ARENA* wisely decided to clean up its act by nominating as its presidential candidate Francisco "Paco" Flores, an innocuous, 39–year–old former philosophy professor who had no link to the dark days of D'Aubuisson's death squads. In fact, he was an undergraduate at Amherst College in Massachusetts when the civil war erupted in 1979, then stayed in the United States to study for a year at Harvard before traveling to India to study Hindu philosophy. At the height of the civil war, he was studying Eastern philosophies at an obscure, unaccredited university in Ojai, California, from which he claims a master's degree. After returning to El Salvador, he taught at Central American University, where he became friends with the Jesuit priests later slain by the army during the 1989 guer-

rilla offensive. He taught philosophy at a small college in the capital before becoming an adviser to President Cristiani. He was then elected to the National Assembly, where he became the chamber's president after the 1997 elections.

Second, the *FMLN* began disemboweling itself with nasty intra–party bickering between Marxist hardliners and moderates. In a party caucus in July 1998, the popular Silva, a moderate, deadlocked with another popular moderate, Victoria Aviles, who had served as U.N. human rights ombudsman. They deadlocked again in a second round of voting in October. Finally, they both acquiesced in favor of yet another moderate, Facundo Guardado, 44, a former commander–in–chief of the rebel army, who was best remembered for his seizure of the Sheraton Hotel during the 1989 offensive on the capital. But the public squabble within the *FMLN* ranks, which at times resembled a barroom brawl, was shown to the country on television, creating grave doubts about the party's ability to govern the country. Five other candidates entered the race, including Rubén Zamora again, and Rodolfo Parker for the Christian Democrats, which further fragmented the vote of the left. Polls showed the race would boil down to Flores and Guardado.

The Election of 1999

This author spent six days observing the election campaign in January 1999, interviewing both the major candidates and other Salvadorans, from cab drivers to

President Francisco Flores

journalists to the dean of the law school. I found the campaign low–key, even dull. The consensus among the people I interviewed on both right and left was that Guardado was handicapped by his image as a guerrilla commander, which stood out in especially sharp contrast with the intellectual and urbane Flores, as well as by the infighting within the *FMLN* ranks. Guardado did not help matters by choosing as his running mate Nidia Díaz, the *nom de guerre* for María Marta Valladares, whom the U.S. Justice Department still wants in connection with the killing of four U.S. Marines in a San Salvador restaurant in 1985. She has insisted that she was a prisoner of war at the time. As René Perla, the dean of the law school, put it, "It wasn't that many years ago that we were told that if the communists came to power they would eat our children. That may make us laugh today, but these ideas die hard."

Flores was forthright about *ARENA*'s own image problem, and insisted to me that he had turned it around in 10 months of campaigning. "People understand that there has been a deep change within *ARENA*," he said in English. "It's not only a generational change, but it's a change in the way we do things and the way we relate to other politicians, to other political parties and to the Salvadoran people." He predicted that, as a result, he would enjoy better relations with the United States than had his two *ARENA* predecessors. "There is a very large door of opportunity in the relationship with the United States," he said. "In the United States there is this idea that *ARENA* is involved with this or that negative aspect. This is an opportunity to establish a new relationship based on trust and on the fact that there are many things that we have to do together. For example, all this drug smuggling that is going on through Central America to the United States is something we have to (solve) together. There is this immigration problem that has to be faced together. There is this issue of environmental protection that we have to do together."

Asked about the lackluster campaign, Flores said, "There are people who like to see conflict during a campaign, to see candidates taking potshots at each other and insulting each other, but in El Salvador it's important to show that we're capable of conducting a responsible, respectful campaign, because this is a step forward in the peace process. The *FMLN* candidate and I don't insult each other or trample on each other. This represents something important for the country."

In a separate interview in Spanish, Guardado agreed that the campaign has been respectful, but insisted that *ARENA* has not changed its spots and that the *FMLN* better represents the middle class.

"The danger of our losing is that the country will be prostrate for another decade," he said. "In five more years, *ARENA* will concentrate even more economic power in its hands, and use the power of the state to commit more abuses. El Salvador can't have development because the majority are excluded from the system. It's a heavy weight. Fifty percent don't have the power to acquire things. They don't have access to basic services. They live in a subsistence economy. We're going to have to renovate and modernize our capitalism, but the capitalists were against that. The rich have a lot to lose under our government—all their privileges." Asked why *ARENA* is so successful if it represents only the upper class, Guardado replied, "*ARENA* has much greater access to information and they can manipulate it. The lower classes are much more easily manipulated. Also, (*ARENA* has) a lot of money for buying votes."

Guardado acknowledged that internal strife had damaged the *FMLN*. "It's a party in transition," he said, "and the conflicts are indicative of that transition. By allying itself with other forces, the Front can present an option for governing. To do this we had to pass through an internal convulsion. It was inevitable."

While Guardado was handicapped by his image as a guerrilla, Flores' own glowing academic credentials came under scrutiny. His résumé claims he did "postgraduate studies" in economics and philosophy at Harvard. But I called Harvard's Graduate School of Arts and Sciences, whose registrar told me there is no record of that. Flores then conceded to me in a subsequent telephone interview that he was enrolled in a "special student program" that was not degree–conferring. The registrar at Harvard's GSAS acknowledged that many Latin American students are admitted to such programs but that those records are kept separately, that it is not considered "post–graduate study" and that "his résumé should not state that." Flores also stated that he had studied at Oxford's Trinity College in the summer of 1980 as part of Amherst's honors program, but the Amherst registrar's office told me there was no record of his having received credit for going to Oxford. Flores then told me he attended Trinity College as part of the summer program of the University of Massachusetts at Amherst. As for his "master's degree" from World University of America in California, which in 1999 had only 78 students, Flores admitted the school lacks prestige. "I won't say I got took, but it wasn't what I expected," he said. His flirtation with Oriental religions became a campaign issue in Catholic El Salvador, to the point that Flores ran a campaign ad showing him attending Mass.

In the end, the polls and the pundits proved correct in their forecasts of the outcome. In the March 7 balloting, Flores avoided a runoff by receiving just under 52% of the vote, to 29% for Guardado; Zamora ran a distant third. Flores was inaugurated on June 1, 1999.

Recent Developments

The *FMLN* soon rebounded from its electoral loss. In the March 2000 congressional elections, they shocked the establishment once again by winning 31 seats in the National Assembly, while *ARENA*'s seats remained unchanged at 29. The *FMLN* is now the largest bloc in the legislature, although *ARENA* still enjoys a small majority through a coalition with smaller conservative parties.

Two major but unrelated events occurred in January 2001. On January 1, El Salvador joined Panama and Ecuador in abandoning its currency and embracing the dollar. On January 13, the country was hit by a devastating earthquake that killed 1,200 people and caused an estimated $1 billion in damage—about half the national budget. A second quake struck exactly a month later, on February 13, which added to the damage but mercifully claimed far fewer lives.

A potentially significant political event occurred in November 2001. Salvador Sánchez Cerén, who under the *nom de guerre* Leonel González had commanded the largest of the *FMLN*'s guerrilla factions during the civil war and who adheres to the party's traditional socialist roots, scored a decisive victory, 45% to 22%, over a reformist candidate to lead the *FMLN*. A third candidate, who had attempted to steer a middle course between the two factions, was second with 31%.

On January 16, 2002, Salvadorans marked the 10th anniversary of the signing of the peace accords that ended the civil war. Symbolically, President Flores attended a ceremony in the mountain village of Perquín, a former guerrilla stronghold. Although most Salvadorans still applaud the decade of peace, the hard-line Sánchez rained on the parade by complaining that peace had not eased the plight of the poor.

In March 2002, U.S. President George W. Bush included El Salvador on his itinerary for a three-nation visit to Latin America. His visit became the occasion for a summit with the other presidents of Central America, at which Bush preached his gospel of free trade. He also promised to increase U.S. aid for the 2001 earthquake from $67 million to $100 million.

Culture: The people of El Salvador are friendly, agricultural, Christian people. They have adopted European customs for the most part—pure Indians are hard to find in the Republic. Independent and fun–loving, their life revolves around the family as the primary social, economic and political unit.

El Salvador (The Saviour) has perhaps some of the most beautiful churches found in Latin America—the people devote a full 12 days of the year to a festival in honor of their Christian namesake.

Ancient ruins of Mayan civilization have yielded treasures from the countryside which are being intensely studied, and there are explorations in progress for traces of even earlier inhabitants. One invaluable site near San Salvador has been bulldozed for a housing development and a brand–"new (bulletproof) American embassy.

Economy: Agriculture is the dominant factor, with the major cash crops being coffee, sugar and cotton. Despite its small size, El Salvador ranks among the top five coffee producers in the world. Farming remains largely under the control of a small group of wealthy landowners; the large peasant population lives in virtual serfdom. Serious overcrowding and limited economic opportunities in rural regions have caused many peasants to migrate to the already congested cities.

Since World War II, light industry has gained steadily, making El Salvador the most industrialized nation in Central America. The civil war was costly in spite of U.S. assistance and seriously undermined economic growth. Since 1982 the government has had serious cash flow problems. U.S. aid in 1992 was $82 million and $230 million in 1993. That was reduced to $94 million in 1994. The state banking industry has been privatized. A major portion of the federal budget formerly devoted the military is now being used for health and welfare.

Salvadorans love to grumble about the state of their economy and to frighten the governing elite by voting for *FMLN* candidates for the National Assembly, but in relative terms, their lot is not that bad. While El Salvador is plagued by widespread poverty, and although its economy is far from booming, it is certainly nowhere near the basket cases of neighboring Honduras, which has about one third the per capita income of El Salvador, or Nicaragua, where it is one fifth as much. In reality, peace has brought greater foreign investment in the form of *maquiladora* assembly plants for textile products, which in turn have created jobs. Tourism has risen modestly since the killing stopped. Moreover, Salvadoran expatriates still living in the United States send home an estimated $1.3 billion a year to their families back home, not an insignificant contribution to the economy.

Real GDP growth has been sluggish for years and has grown steadily worse, declining from 2.1% in 1997 to 1.4% in 1998, 1.3% in 1999 and .5% in 2000. Some of the blame can be attributed to the damage wrought by Hurricane Mitch in October 1998 and the twin earthquakes of January and February 2001. Preliminary figures suggest that growth for 2001 will still be less than 2%.

Unemployment, conversely, has declined somewhat, from 7.6% in 1998 to 6.9% in 1999 to 6.7% in 2000. Inflation in 2000 was a manageable 3.0%, and prices may become even more stabilized as a result of replacing the *Colon* with the dollar on January 1, 2001. The dollarization makes sound economic sense; tens of thousands of Salvadorans live and work in the United States, and the tens of millions of dollars they send home to their families annually have become an important pillar of the economy since the exodus of refugees during the civil war. The dollarization also has stabilized inflation, which was only 3.5% in 2001.

The Future: President Flores' first three years in office have been marked by neither spectacular initiatives nor incredible blunders. He inherited a so-so economy from Calderón, although he must come to grips with a wave of violent gang-related crime perpetrated from Salvadoran thugs who have repatriated from the *barrios* of Los Angeles. Such crime is an impediment to the tourism industry, now in its infancy but which has great potential. nor incredible blunders. He inherited a so-so economy from Calderón, and he must come to grips with a wave of violent gang-related crime perpetrated by Salvadoran thugs who have repatriated from the *barrios* of Los Angeles, California. Such crime is an impediment to the nascent tourism industry, which has great potential.

But such problems seem trivial when one remembers the wholesale slaughter that gripped the country for 12 years.

The harmonious ceremonies marking the 10th anniversary of the 1992 peace accords were a healthy sign that the armistice has indeed taken hold and that Salvadoran democracy is showing signs of, if not maturity, at least of pubescence. The election of an unreconstructed socialist, Salvador Sánchez Cerén, to lead the FMLN just as it is emerging as a viable political force, probably will backfire on the party, as did the nomination of Guardado to be its presidential candidate in 1999. Experience should have demonstrated that even poor Salvadorans reject a Marxist formula, and if the *FMLN* goes into the 2004 election with a fire-breathing socialist instead of a more pragmatic reformer, the party will probably continue to control municipal governments but not the presidency.

Children in an alleyway in San Salvador

The Republic of Guatemala

Guatemala City in the late evening

Area: 42,031 square miles.

Population: 11.5 million.

Capital City: Guatemala City (Pop. 2.4 million, including surrounding areas).

Climate: Tropical on the coastal plains, temperate at the higher altitudes; heaviest rainfall is from May to October.

Neighboring Countries: Mexico (north and west); Belize (northeast); Honduras, El Salvador (east).

Official Language: Spanish.

Other Principal Tongues: Twenty distinct dialects based on either Maya or Quiché.

Ethnic Background: Maya–Quiché (55%), *mestizo or Ladino* (mixed Spanish and Indian, (42%) European or African (3%).

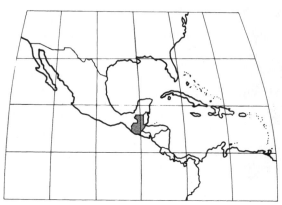

144

Principal Religion: Roman Catholic Christianity. A substantial number of people have converted to evangelical Protestantism (about 35%).

Chief Commercial Products: Coffee, cotton, bananas, corn and other agricultural products.

Currency: *Quetzal.*

Gross Domestic Product: U.S.$20.2 billion in 2001 ($1,729 per capita, about $300 among those of Mayan descent).

Former Colonial Status: Spanish Crown Colony (1524–1821).

Independence Date: September 15, 1821.

Chief of State: Alfonso Portillo, president (since January 14, 2000).

National Flag: Blue, white and blue vertical stripes with national crest in the center white stripe.

Guatemala, the most populous of the Central American republics, is a mountainous highland bordered by coastal plains in the North and South. The southern Pacific coast plain is a 200-mile ribbon of land reaching a maximum of 30 miles in width. The highland rises abruptly from this plain to an elevation of 8,000 to 10,000 feet with a string of volcanos on the southern rim. Three of these volcanoes are above 13,000 feet and three of them are still quite active.

The highland is broken by inter–mountain basins ranging from 5,000 to 8,000 feet which are the most heavily populated regions of Guatemala. The northeastern lowlands are more extensive than the southern, and include the valleys of the Motagua River, which originates in the southern volcanoes and flows 185 miles into the Gulf of Honduras; the Polochic River drains the more westerly mountains along a 200–mile course into Lake Izabal, a salty lagoon extending some 50 miles west from the Gulf of Honduras.

The Petén, a low, poorly drained plain, extending north 100 miles into the Yucatán Peninsula, is heavily forested and sparsely populated.

History: Guatemala was conquered by Spanish forces from Mexico in 1523. Finding little precious metal and a land peopled by a sedentary agricultural folk, the Spanish governor rapidly lost interest in the region. Left to their own devices, the Spanish settlers intermarried with the Indians, and the missionaries sought to Christianize the Maya–Quiché people, whose culture began many centuries before the birth of Christ. The fertile mountain valleys were developed into semi–independent estates worked by virtually enslaved Indians. The majority of the Maya–Quiché people simply withdrew from the Spanish–speaking community and maintained their traditional way of life. The efforts of the missionaries to Christianize the Indians did not fully displace their pagan gods—rather, the Indians tended to add the Christian God to their own deities.

Before independence, the Captaincy–General of Guatemala included the modern Central American states and the southern provinces of present–day Mexico. Sparsely settled by the Spanish, the region contained subdued tribes in the highlands and poor settlements on the Pacific coast, while the Caribbean coast was in the hands of buccaneers, native Indians who had retained their independence and a few illegal British settlers.

Augustín de Iturbide, emperor of Mexico, invited the patriot committee of Guatemala to join Mexico in 1821. Despite considerable opposition, the Central American states were annexed in 1822; with Iturbide's abdication in 1823 they declared themselves independent. The northern state of Chiapas elected to remain with Mexico and Soconusco later joined that nation in 1842.

The independent states formed a federation known as the United Provinces of Central America. Two parties appeared in the formation of a government—the *Serviles* (conservatives) who wanted a strong central government and close ties with the Church, and the *Radicales*, who favored a federal republic and curtailment of the privileges of the landowners and the clergy. A constitution based on that of the United States was adopted and a liberal president was installed. The liberal–conservative conflict resulted in a series of wars, and the confederation collapsed in 1838.

Independence and Dictatorship

From the time of dissolution of the union to 1944, Guatemala was ruled by four dictators. The first was Rafael Carrera (1838–1865), who was an illiterate but popular *mestizo* leader, beloved of the Indians, but a religious fanatic of conservative persuasion. Hating liberals, he intervened in neighboring countries, seeking the overthrow of liberal presidents. After his death, another conservative was elected, but liberal Justo Rufino Barrios gained control of the government in 1871 and ruled until his death in 1885.

A man of progressive ideas, he fostered public education, built railroads and achieved a measure of economic development. He also curtailed the privileges of the landowners and destroyed the political power of the clergy. Manuel Estrada Cabrera (1897–1920), a cultured and ruthless man, ruled as a despot with no effort to conceal his absolute power. Jorge Ubico came to power in 1931 and ruled until 1944. Honest and hard–working, he suppressed the previous corruption in government, bolstered the economy and carried out many social reforms of benefit to the laboring classes.

Opposition to Ubico's strict discipline resulted in public disorder and he ultimately resigned in mid–1944.

Following two short–lived military governments, liberal Juan José Arévalo was elected president, taking office in 1945. In the elections of 1950, Jacobo Arbenz Guzmán won as the as candidate for the Revolutionary Action and National Regeneration parties. Inexperienced, with a government infiltrated by communists, he was overthrown in 1954 by Colonel Carlos Castillo Armas in a coup promoted by the U.S. CIA. Basically corrupt and ineffective, the latter was assassinated in 1957.

Following inconclusive elections, Miguel Idigoras Fuentes was appointed president; also corrupt and arrogant, he was in turn overthrown by a military coup in 1963. Colonel Enrique Peralta Azúrdia,

Panorama of Guatemala City with the civic center in the foreground

who assumed the power of chief of state, suspended the constitution, dismissed Congress and ruled by decree until 1966 when in free and apparently honest elections, Julio César Méndez Montenegro, a liberal, was elected. This was an effort to return constitutional government to Guatemala. In reality, it was the beginning of 20 years of military-dominated governments. It was also in the 1960s that a guerrilla insurgency began.

The single most impressive accomplishment of President Méndez Montenegro was his ability to stay in office until the end of his term. Beset by radicals and powerful conservatives, Méndez was forced to abandon reform programs and concentrate instead on pleasing traditionally powerful elements.

With virtual civil war between right–wing and leftist extremists continuing unabated, voters turned to conservative Colonel Carlos Arana in the 1970 presidential elections. Promising "bread

General Jorge Ubico

and peace," the noted counter–insurgency expert nearly wiped out the leftist guerrilla movement by indiscriminately repressing all opposition political groups. His term was marked by a reduction in political violence and improved economic conditions.

As the 1974 presidential elections approached, the military stipulated that any candidate would be acceptable—so long as he was in the armed forces. The ruling coalition thus nominated as its candidate the moderate former defense minister, General Kjell (pronounced "shell") Eugenio Laugerud García of the *Partido Institucional Democrático (PID)*. But when the early election returns gave National Opposition Front candidate Brigadier General Efraín Ríos Montt a formidable lead, the government suddenly halted the tabulation. Several days later the regime announced that its own candidate, Laugurud, had won with 41% of the vote. Although such blatant fraud caused an up-

roar, the military refused to permit a recount.

The election also catapulted Ríos Montt into national prominence, where he remains to this day.

Relations between the new president and ultra–conservative elements in the ruling coalition—led by former President Arana and the right–wing *Movimiento de Liberación Nacional (MLN)*—soon began to sour when Laugerud suggested mild reforms to ease the plight of the impoverished highland Indians. The *MLN*, representing the wealthy landowners, bitterly accused the president of being a communist when he encouraged the formation of rural peasant cooperatives to increase production from inefficient, small peasant plots.

Guatemala was devastated in early 1976 by one of the worst natural disasters of the 20th century when a violent earthquake in 17 of the nation's 22 provinces killed 24,000 people. In addition, 76,000 were injured and 1.5 million left homeless. Worst hit were provincial towns and highland Indian settlements, where peasant dwellings were not built to withstand an earthquake. Although large amounts of foreign aid quickly poured into the country, little of it filtered down to the peasants because of bureaucratic bungling and political corruption.

None of the presidential candidates received a majority of votes in the 1978 general elections. The government–supported candidate, General Fernando Romeo Lucas García, was later named the winner by Congress. The outcome was no monument to the democratic process: (1) the race was limited to military candidates, (2) fully 60% of the electorate ignored or boycotted the balloting and (3) only 35 of the eligible lawmakers participated in the congressional runoff vote. The new president promptly ordered an about–face on the previous administration's policy of supporting limited reforms. Thus began an all–out campaign against both moderates and leftists—a strategy that had failed ousted, ultra-conservative regimes in neighboring El Salvador.

Right-wing paramilitary "death squads" such as the Secret Anti–Communist Army—which drew most of their support from army and police units—systematically wiped out thousands of government opponents. Key targets included student, labor, peasant and political leaders. During its four years in office, Lucas García's regime was widely regarded as the most repressive and corrupt in Latin America. London–based Amnesty International even accused the regime of operating "murder and torture" chambers in an annex of the Presidential Palace!

A report released in 1981 by the Human Rights Commission of the Organization of American States found that the Lucas García regime was responsible for the "great

majority" of political murders in the country at the time. Evangelical Church officials estimated in Guatemala that at least 11,000 civilians died from political violence in 1981. The Catholic Church there reported that 200,000 Guatemalan peasants fled to neighboring Central American countries to escape the violence.

Many of the country's human rights violations were linked to the government's counter–insurgency program. In an attempt to halt rural support for the guerrillas, Lucas García sought to wipe out key segments of the Indian population. Such repression, however, induced many peasants to join the insurgents. As a result, warfare spread to seven provinces and the number of guerrillas increased from 1,500 in 1980 to about 4,000 in 1982.

Because of Guatemala's dismal human rights record, the Carter administration in Washington halted most military and economic aid to the country in 1977. Lucas García angrily responded by rejecting all U.S. military assistance. The subsequent election of Ronald Reagan in the United States was warmly applauded by the supporters of the Guatemalan president, who hoped that Washington would resume assistance to their country. Yet, the Reagan administration also kept its distance, although $3.2 million in military aid was provided in 1981.

Unbridled repression by the regime was not limited to its battle against peasants and leftists. When moderate Christian Democracy *(DC)* party members urged in late _1980 that all political groups be allowed to participate in upcoming March 1982 elections, right-wing terrorists responded by assassinating 76 *DC* party members.

General Fernando Romeo Lucas García

Not surprisingly, only conservatives dared to run for president in the March 7, 1982 elections, which liberals and leftists. When the balloting failed to produce a winner with a majority, Congress voted to elect the government–supported candidate, General Angel Aníbal Guevara—who had received a bare 16% of the popular vote. The three losing candidates were arrested when they protested that the election was a fraud.

The 1982 Coup

On March 23, 1982, as the political crisis escalated, a core group of 20 junior officers in the barracks decided to vote with their guns. Early in the morning, they surrounded the Presidential Palace, forcing Lucas García to flee from a side door.

The bloodless coup was attributed to a variety of factors: (1) the administration's heavy–handed treatment of opponents had offended nearly all segments of the population, (2) the president–elect was seen as a clone of the unpopular Lucas García and (3) the rising dissatisfaction of junior officers in the army. Indeed, while these men were being sent to the field to fight against the guerrillas, senior officers were frequently given cushy jobs away from battle zones. The widespread corruption that permeated the regime and the military high command was galling, even by Guatemalan standards. Vast public works projects initiated by the regime seemed to have been created for the sole purpose of providing a source of graft for top government officials. The military was also top–heavy with *chiefs,* with seemingly few *Indians* left to do any fighting. Of the 900 or so officers in the Guatemalan army, fully 240 were colonels or generals!

The sudden ouster of the president created a temporary political vacuum; on the day of the coup three different *juntas* were proclaimed before the military finally settled on one led by retired Brigadier General Ríos Montt, then 55. The general's participation tended to give the *junta* some legitimacy, since Ríos Montt had probably won the 1974 elections, only to see the prize stolen from him.

Within hours of assuming power, the new *junta* annulled the March elections, abolished Congress, suspended the 1965 constitution, barred activities by political parties, reaffirmed Guatemala's age–old claim to Belize, arrested various civilians for corruption, ruled out elections in the near future and announced that the new government would rule by decree. In the hope of dealing with the country's insurgency problems, the *junta* proposed an amnesty plan to leftist guerrillas. When the offer was rejected, Ríos Montt ordered an all–out "final assault" against the guerrillas in mid–1982, wiping out about 400 villages in the process.

Finding the three–member *junta* cumbersome, Ríos Montt fired his partners in mid–1982 and proclaimed himself president—breaking his pledge not to do so when he first joined with his cohorts.

The new president was a curiosity. A "born–again" evangelical Christian, he loved to quote the Bible to friends and foes alike when enunciating government policy. Thus, when asked about the nation's civil strife, he answered that the best way to combat it was with "love." On Sundays he gave spiritual pep–talks on national television. He was fond of saying that he "had lunch with God today."

His moralistic approach produced some positive results. He ordered a rare public campaign against corruption and cracked down on right-wing paramilitary vigilante groups. As a result, urban terrorism subsided somewhat, although political violence continued unabated in the countryside. Impressed by his efforts to reduce human rights violations, the Reagan administration offered Guatemala $4.5 million in military aid and $50 million in economic assistance in 1982.

Ríos Montt's grip on the presidency was tenuous. Some powerful elements in the military opposed his anti–corruption campaign which reduced lucrative supplementary income sources for high–ranking officials. Others disliked his moralistic approach, dubbing him "Ayatollah." His anti–Catholic stand made him extremely unpopular among members of that religion. General Oscar Humberto Mejía Victores overthrew the Ríos Montt regime in mid-1983 and proclaimed himself president.

Democracy Returns

The new leader promised a return to democracy. Elections for a constituent assembly were held in mid–1984; 71% of the

General Oscar Humberto Mejía Victores

electorate voted, which remains the record voter turnout. The *DC* appeared to be the most popular, although by a slim margin. By the middle of 1985, all political parties were deeply involved in preparing for congressional and presidential elections held in November.

In honest elections, Vinicio Cerezo, a Christian Democrat who proclaimed himself "left of center", won the presidency—a dubious honor. During the military years, immense debts were run up and the treasury was empty. The International Monetary Fund suspended loan agreements. Military and state police death squads had caused the disappearance of about 100,000 people. Victorious leftists insisted on punishing the military, but Cerezo wisely established firm control and announced that although investigations would be conducted into violations of human rights, no punishments would result, infuriating many of his supporters. Mejía Victores had decreed a general amnesty for the military during his final days in office. Underlining this, during the first three weeks of civilian government, five dozen bodies, some mutilated, were scattered throughout the country. More selective killings followed.

But "Vinicio," as the then-popular young president was known, carefully planned and executed a single raid and mass arrest of the Department of Technical Investigation, a military unit devoted to "counter–insurgency." Two hundred agents were fired and 400 were dispatched for "additional training." The message: the military was not always sacred. Substantial changes in military leadership were made in 1986–87.

A committee on human rights was formed. But the civilian government had the same problems experienced in Argentina and most lately in El Salvador: self–protection by the military. The matter was "resolved" when the Supreme Court issued more than a thousand writs of habeas corpus. As might have been expected, no one had any genuine desire to go around digging up dead bodies.

General José Efraín Ríos Montt

The right–wing military, police and vigilante groups did not have a monopoly on cruel violence. Three left–wing guerrilla groups joined into the Guatemalan National Revolutionary Union *(URNG)*; as of 1990 they moved their operations from remote, rural areas and were operating in the more populous regions around Guatemala City. They were bold enough to stop traffic on the Pan-American Highway to collect "taxes."

Talks were held in Madrid in 1987 between the government and rebel representatives. The rebels were down to 1,000 men (vs. a high of 10,000) and only operated in remote, rural areas where they were equally despised by local Indian inhabitants, who just wanted to be left alone by everyone. The talks lasted through 1988 and were inconclusive.

Military coups were aborted without violence in 1988 and 1989. But murders and disappearances at the hand of right–wing groups continued at the rate of more than 1,000 a year. Cerezo's popularity dwindled as his inability to control the military became increasingly apparent; further, he justifiably acquired the reputation of being a playboy, spending much of his time during the week away from the capital.

The country was in a state of near–anarchy by 1990. Countless paramilitary groups and the army operated freely, murdering at will virtually anyone suspected of being a leftist, the definition of which sometimes included anyone found outside after dark at night. In this setting, Ríos Montt campaigned in the 1990 elections on a "no–nonsense" platform; he was ruled ineligible under the 1986 constitution in a provision probably directed against him.

Jorge Serrano Elías, a fellow evangelical Protestant, was elected president in a January 1991. About one third bothered to vote, losing faith in the idea that things could be changed by the ballot box. He pledged to end the 30–year–old civil war. This proved to be impossible.

Moreover, while Cerezo had proved inept, Serrano proved venal and power-hungry. In late May 1993, he attempted to effect a Fujimori–style "self coup" that initially had the backing of the armed forces. Serrano announced that he was dissolving Congress and ruling by decree on the familiar pretext that only in this way could he come to grips with the serious socioeconomic problems facing the country. To make sure the Guatemalan people received only the information he wanted them to, he imposed prior censorship on the print and broadcast media, which immediately began collaborating with one another to outwit the censors and get information to the public.

For a week, it appeared that Guatemala would experience a throwback to the bad old days of strongman rule. But thousands of demonstrators flooded the streets of the capital to protest Serrano's power grab, among them such eminent figures as 1992 Nobel Peace Prize Laureate Rigoberta Minchú and UN Human Rights Ombudsman Ramiro de León Carpio. Moreover, the U.S. State Department hinted not very subtly that aid to Guatemala would likely evaporate. Simultaneously, the Constitutional Court declared Serrano's actions illegal. The armed forces quickly realized that they were backing the wrong side and refused further to support the coup attempt. For a change, the military found itself hailed as a champion of democracy! Serrano, already a wealthy man, fled the country to a life of luxurious exile in Panama with an estimated $20 million in "retirement funds" from the treasury. (Guatemala is still trying unsuccessfully to have Serrano extradited.) The Congress then named de León Carpio interim president, which proved to be a sound choice. As was the case with the interim presidency of Gerald Ford after the power abuses of Richard Nixon, de León Carpio proved fair and just, albeit a bit lackluster.

Legislative elections in mid–1994 (14% voted) resulted in a plurality for the Guatemalan Republican Front *(FRG)* led by Ríos Montt, who became president of the Congress. Four other parties split the remainder of the 80–seat body. But the *FRG* repeatedly found itself outmaneuvered by the other parties in Congress.

Most of the next two years in Guatemala were even more turbulent than ever. The president turned to the army for support, which may, itself, have tried to oust him in 1994. General fighting continued in spite of an agreement ending it—an agreement to keep on negotiating, in reality. The U.S. State Department warned tourists to avoid Guatemala; about 400 Peace Corps volunteers took shelter in Guatemala City. Torture and murder remained commonplace.

In November 1995, 12 candidates vied for president, whose term had been reduced from five to four years. The top two vote–getters were former Guatemala City Mayor Alvaro Arzú of the Party of National Advancement *(PAN)*, and Alfonso Portillo of the *FRG*, the political vehicle of the still–popular Ríos Montt, whom the Constitutional Court again had ruled could not run. The court also prohibited the former strongman's wife from running, leaving Portillo as the stand–in candidate. Portillo unabashedly declared that Ríos Montt would serve in a high–level advisory capacity if he were elected.

Polls indicated that Arzú would win the January 1996 runoff in a landslide, but he squeaked into office with only 52% of the vote; he lost 18 of the 21 departments outside his power base in the capital, an indicator of the lingering popular appeal of Ríos Montt. Arzú's *PAN* won 43 of the 80 seats in the unicameral Congress, though Ríos Montt's *FRG* remained a potent opposition. The *URNG*, in its first test at the polls, elected two deputies.

The Arzú Presidency—and Peace

The new president pledged to respect human rights and insisted, not altogether convincingly, that the armed forces would be subordinate to the civilian authority. However, Arzú was mainstream enough, coming from a wealthy and prominent

Woman picking corn

WORLD BANK Photo

Former President Ramiro de León Carpio

business family, that he posed no threat to the generals and seemed adept at working with them.

Above all else, Arzú pledged to continue the peace talks and see them through to fruition. The two sides met throughout 1996 in Mexico City and finally reached an historic truce, though some grumbled over the amnesty given to members of the security forces for past human rights abuses. On December 27, 1996, several Latin American presidents and UN Secretary–General Boutros Boutros–Ghali came to Guatemala City to witness the momentous signing of the accords that ended Central America's longest civil war. The peace seems to have taken hold, with no serious violations by either side. The war–weary country at last had reason for some optimism regarding its future.

Arzú, who was smooth and charming when he was courting votes, proved ornery and arrogant as president. Days after his inauguration in January 1996, an incident occurred that began to sour his already stormy relationship with the press. While Arzú was horseback riding near the colonial city of Antigua, a milk truck suddenly headed toward the chief executive. Halted by the president's bodyguards, the driver fled from the vehicle. The bodyguards then opened fire, killing him. The presidential palace described the incident as an assassination attempt. But when the media looked deeper, they concluded that the driver was a drunken milkman who had panicked. A furious Arzú accused the media, most of which are not supportive of him, of attempting to discredit him.

The incident could have been dismissed as the tragi–comic case of a thin–skinned president, except that Arzú began taking measures clearly aimed at curtailing the independent press. He used the government–subsidized television program,

Avances, as a vehicle to vilify his editorial critics in the press and investigative reporting that had proved embarrassing to the administration. Not content with rebutting criticism, which it could be argued was his right in a democratic society, Arzú resorted to a more sinister method to silence his critics. According to evidence obtained by the Inter American Press Association, Arzú cajoled wealthy friends to stop advertising in specified print media, particularly the country's leading daily, *Prensa Libre*, and the weekly newsmagazine *Crónica*. For business people who were not his friends, he extended a God-father–like offer: Stop advertising, or face tax audits. For a time, he apparently succeeded in driving away about 80 advertisers. *Prensa Libre* was too economically viable to have been seriously hurt by the campaign, but *Crónica* was driven to the point of bankruptcy. In November 1998, *Crónica* was bought out by a group of businessmen loyal to Arzú; its editorial staff was fired and its editorial tone, not surprisingly, changed overnight.

On the positive side, the peace process took hold during the Arzú administration, although the public found itself polarized between those who demanded justice for past atrocities and those who preferred to forget the horrors of the past. Unfortunately, horrors kept occurring.

The Gerardi Murder

In April 1998, a Roman Catholic bishop, Juan José Gerardi Conedera, head of the church's human rights office, released a controversial report that laid the blame for most of the human rights abuses squarely at the feet of the army. Days later, on April 26, Gerardi was found bludgeoned to death in his quarters; the crime stunned the country and reverberated abroad. The official, secular investigation into the murder has resembled a Keystone Kops farce. First, a local drunk who had been a laborer of the slain bishop was arrested, but eventually he was released for lack of evidence. Then authorities arrested a priest and accused him of killing Gerardi in a homosexual crime of passion. At the same time, police arrested the bishop's cook and accused her of complicity in the crime. After five days, both were released. To make this comic–"opera spectacle complete, the suspect priest's dog was "arrested" on suspicion of mauling Gerardi to death. However, Gerardi's body was exhumed for a second autopsy, which ruled out the canine theory. In a touch of irony worthy of a Greek comedy, Gerardi's successor as head of the church's human rights office is none other than Bishop Mario Ríos Montt, brother of the former strongman.

The Gerardi investigation ground on throughout 1999, largely because of intense public and media pressure, both

**Former President
Alvaro Enrique Arzú Irigoyen**

domestic and international, to find the respected cleric's killer. In August, authorities announced a break in the case, stating that DNA from blood samples taken at the scene matched one of the suspects. Still, there were no arrests. Guatemalan public opinion already had indicted the same culprit that Gerardi had named: the army. These suspicions were intensified in October, when the prosecutor in the case, who had been following the military lead, fled to the United States because of death threats. It wasn't until January 2000, days after the change of presidential administrations, that the priest and the cook were arrested again, along with three army. In January 2001, police arrested army Captain Byron Lima Oliva and his father, retired Colonel Disrael Lima Estrada, in connection with the Gerardi murder. Police also re-arrested Gerardi's cook and issued a warrant for a priest, Mario Orantes, both of whom had been arrested and released in 1998. An intelligence officer with the presidential guard, José Obdulio Villanueva, was arrested the next day. It was Villanueva who had killed the milkman in 1996. He had been sentenced to five years in prison, but he arranged to pay a $1,500 fine instead. Orantes was arrested on February 9 when he returned from the United States to face the charges. A judge subsequently freed Villanueva on February 28 because of an apparently iron-clad alibi. He was later rearrested, but another year passed before the four accused men went on trial in March 2001. The trial absorbed Guatemala's attention—and that of human rights activists around the world—before the historic verdicts were handed down on June 8: guilty!

The author interviews Nobel Laureate Rigoberta Menchú in Guatemala City, December 1999.

Photo by Mario Antonio Sandoval

The judge sentenced the two Limas and Villanueva to 30 years and Orantes to 20; the cook was acquitted. Six weeks later, the judge fled the country because of death threats.

Quest for Justice

Some measure of justice for past atrocities also was meted out in November 1998, when three former members of an army–organized civilian militia force were convicted and sentenced to death by lethal injection for their roles in the so–called Rio Negro Massacre in March 1982—during the first days of the Ríos Montt regime—in which 130 Indian peasants were slain. The death sentences were overturned by an appeals court, but they were reinstated in October 1999.

Guatemala moved even closer to its long–sought catharsis on February 26, 1999, when the three–member Historical Clarification Commission issued its report after 18 months of investigation into the human rights abuses committed during the civil war. The panel was headed by a German judge, Christian Tomuschat, and included a Guatemalan lawyer, Edgar Balsells, and a Mayan teacher, Otilia Lux Coti. Among its more controversial findings, the commission concluded that more than 200,000 people had been killed during the course of the civil war; that there had been 42,000 individual human rights violations, 29,000 of them fatal; that 92% of these violations had been committed by

the army; and that U.S. businesses and the CIA had pressured the successive Guatemalan governments into suppressing the guerrilla movement by ruthless means, particularly when Ríos Montt was in power. When the commission presented its report at the National Theater before a crowd of about 2,000 people, mostly relatives of victims, the crowd chanted, *"justicia! justicia!"* President Arzú dutifully attended the ceremony and shook hands with the commission members, but studiously avoided accepting a copy of the report, citing "protocol." This led to catcalls from the crowd for him to accept the report. Some observers concluded that Arzú's actions were intended to distance the government from the report. Just days later, President Clinton visited Guatemala during his tour of countries affected by Hurricane Mitch and, while stopping short of a formal apology, expressed "regret" for the United States' role in the human rights abuses.

The quest for justice became an international issue in December 1999 when Guatemala's most illustrious human rights champion, 1992 Nobel Peace Laureate Rigoberta Menchú, flew to Madrid to file a lawsuit before the SPANish Supreme Court against eight past military and civilian figures, including former military strongmen Ríos Montt, Lucas García and Mejía Victores. It was the same court that had requested the extradition of former Chilean dictator Augusto Pinochet from Britain for alleged human rights abuses.

This author interviewed Menchú in Guatemala that December shortly before she returned to Spain to testify. She explained that she chose Spain because it had shown its commitment to human rights in the Pinochet case and others. (Ironically, Ríos Montt had served as Guatemala's military attaché to Spain during the 1970s, a consolation prize for having been cheated out of the presidency in the fraudulent 1974 election.) Asked whether her action prevents Ríos Montt from traveling abroad without facing arrest, she replied, "Well, Guatemala is a beautiful country. It's not a terrible punishment never being able to leave."

Among Menchú's complaints is the assault by security forces on the Spanish Embassy in Guatemala on January 31, 1980 after it was seized by guerrillas. In the ensuing fire, 39 Spanish diplomats and guerrillas perished, including Menchú's father. She also cites the deaths of her mother and two brothers between 1980 and 1982, and for the deaths of four Spanish priests during the same period. Menchú's eyes filled with tears as she explained that her mother's remains were never found. "I just want to recover my mother's bones and give her a decent burial," she said.

Asked if a dialogue between her and Ríos Montt were possible, she said bitterly, "I'd have to wait 2,000 years." The Spanish court has not taken action on her lawsuit.

The Elections of 1999

In politics, the country's attention was focused in 1999 on both a referendum, called the "Consulta Popular," held on May 16 to ratify the constitutional changes agreed upon in the peace agreement between the government and the guerrillas, and on the upcoming presidential election. In the *Consulta Popular*, there was an almost unprecedented consensus reached among the *PAN*, the *FRG* and the *URNG*. About 50 complex issues were boiled down to four separate referendum items, including a restructuring of the role of the armed forces in society and the granting of far greater cultural and political autonomy to the indigenous Mayas. Voters were asked to vote *sí o no*, and the results stunned the country's political establishment. Only about 18% of the electorate bothered to vote, and those who did rejected all the initiatives by more than a 2–1 margin. The initiatives were approved only in some scattered Mayan communities. Despite the broad consensus of the political parties, the voters seemed to be saying they were not quite ready for their society to be overhauled by politicians. But with a turnout of 18%, most Guatemalans clearly didn't care one way or the other.

In the presidential race, Alfonso Portillo, the Ríos Montt stand–in who almost

Alfonso Portillo addresses an *FRG* rally a week before the December 26, 1999, runoff.

Photo by the author

spectable record in two terms as mayor of the capital, but who was handicapped by scandals within the *PAN*-controlled national government. The worst of these was the sale of the state-owned telecommunications company for far below market value to a consortium that included friends of the president. There also were numerous examples of government contracts being awarded to Arzú's relatives and friends instead of advertising for bids. In my interview with him, Berger (pronounced bear-ZHAY) was obviously frustrated with the fact that the public seemed unconcerned about the Mexico killings. "I'd be depressed about it, but he seems upbeat," he said of his opponent. Of the economic crisis, he said, "If the price of gas goes up, everyone blames the government. We've committed errors, but you can't blame us for the fall in prices (of export products)." Citing the positive achievements of the *PAN*, he warned, "We've started a process of change that will be set back 20 years (if Portillo wins)."

"Not everything they did was bad; the way they did it was bad," responded Portillo in my interview with him in his law office, which had portraits of Emiliano Zapata and Martin Luther King Jr. on the wall. "We're going to govern in a different way. Above all, we're going to investigate the awarding of contracts, and we're going to have clear regulations." He also pledged to crack down on common crime, another major issue concerning voters. Of the Mexico incident, he said, "I take responsibility for my errors, like a man. At least I'm not a coward like Arzú, whose

Too young to vote, two children attend a campaign rally with their father

Photo by the author

upset Arzú in the 1996 runoff, was renominated early–on as the *FRG*'s candidate. He had been campaigning for three years, as has Ríos Montt on his behalf. The aging strongman has demonstrated that he still has a charismatic appeal with the masses, albeit not among the rural Mayans against whom he had waged genocide.

The *PAN*, meanwhile, had a rougher time fielding its candidate. The party dutifully nominated Arzú's hand–picked choice, Guatemala City Mayor Oscar Berger, who quickly had a falling–out with the president when he demonstrated he intended to be his own man, not a puppet as Portillo is to Ríos Montt. Berger then withdrew his candidacy, declaring that his decision was "irreversible." Arzú huffily responded that he had plenty of candidates to choose from, but, in fact, he didn't, at least not one with any chance of winning. A feeling of defeatism began to descend upon the party regulars, and they prevailed upon Berger to reconsider. He did, but in so doing damaging his own credibility and making himself the butt of jokes.

For its part, the *URNG* experienced the same sort of intra–party bickering between moderates and hardliners that doomed the chances of victory for the *FMLN* in neighboring El Salvador in 1999. It eventually nominated a moderate, Alvaro Colom, an Indian rights advocate and nephew of a well–known leftist politician and mayor of Guatemala City who was assassinated during the presidency of Lucas García. The *URNG* became part of a left–wing coalition called the New Nation Alliance (*ANN*).

The campaign for the round of voting on November 7, 1999, took an interesting twist in July when Portillo was asked during a television interview about rumors that he had killed a man when he was living in exile in Mexico during the military regime. "That isn't true," he replied; "I killed two." He explained that while teaching at a school in the state of Guerrero in 1982 he had become involved in a local political dispute and that when two members of the rival faction attacked him with firearms, he killed them both with a pistol. The Mexican authorities eventually dropped the charges against Portillo. Berger was quick to try to make political capital out of this confession, but the polls showed that it had no effect on public opinion. If anything, in fact, Portillo's candor (and perhaps the obvious *macho* factor of an outnumbered man killing two assailants) may have helped him, because he began to pull increasingly ahead of Berger in the polls. Berger then began to use the Ríos Montt bogeyman, as Arzú had successfully in the last election, warning that Ríos Montt would become the *de facto* president if Portillo were elected and that foreign aid could evaporate if Ríos Montt, an international human rights pariah, assumed an influential role in the government.

This author spent 10 days in Guatemala during August observing the campaign and interviewing all three of the major candidates, as well as people from all social classes, as a free-lance journalist. It became obvious to me that voters were more concerned about the blatant corruption and cronyism of the Arzú administration and about the sour economy than they were about a 17-year-old incident in Mexico or the possible influence of Ríos Montt.

By all accounts, Berger himself was an honorable man who had compiled a re-

Ficha técnica
La empresa Borge & Asociados efectuó la séptima encuesta de opinión política, a solicitud de los diarios Prensa Libre, elperiódico y Nuestro Diario.

1,200 empadronados se tomaron como muestra para el estudio a nivel nacional.

95% es el nivel de confianza de la encuesta, con error de estimación de + - 5%.

Portillo, favorito para ganar

A cuatro días de las elecciones, Alfonso Portillo, del Frente Republicano Guatemalteco, FRG, luce como claro favorito para ganar la Presidencia de la República, con superioridad de 3-1 en la intención de voto sobre Oscar Berger, del Partido de Avanzada Nacional, PAN.

La Encuesta, efectuada por la firma Borge & Asociados –que pronosticó con bastante exactitud el triunfo del FRG en la primera vuelta– confirma que Portillo ha sacado amplia ventaja y se proyecta como el primer presidente guatemalteco para el nuevo milenio.

Tras una segunda campaña electoral sin impacto por parte de ambos candidatos presidenciales, parece poco probable que la tendencia que se muestra en La Encuesta pueda cambiar en pocos días, sobre todo, por el dominante ambiente navideño que ha superado a los mensajes políticos.

La ventaja de Portillo, con algunas variantes, se observa en todas las regiones del interior, incluyendo el departamento de Guatemala, aunque no se hizo una medición especial de la capital, considerada en el pasado como bastión del PAN y del propio Berger.

● **Hubo interés en campaña**

De acuerdo con el estudio de opinión, se pudo comprobar que los guatemaltecos participaron mayoritariamente de una u otra manera en la campaña electoral, la cual prácticamente ha terminado.

Un 59% dice que participó en algún mitin o concentración de alguno de los candidatos presidenciales, y la misma cantidad reconoce que puso en su casa o carro algún símbolo del partido de su preferencia.

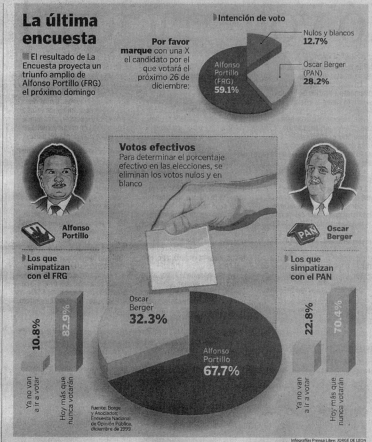

La última encuesta

■ El resultado de La Encuesta proyecta un triunfo amplio de Alfonso Portillo (FRG) el próximo domingo

Por favor marque con una X el candidato por el que votará el próximo 26 de diciembre:

▶ **Intención de voto**

Nulos y blancos **12.7%**

Alfonso Portillo (FRG) **59.1%**

Oscar Berger (PAN) **28.2%**

Votos efectivos
Para determinar el porcentaje efectivo en las elecciones, se eliminan los votos nulos y en blanco

Alfonso Portillo

Oscar Berger

▶ Los que simpatizan con el FRG

Ya no van a ir a votar **10.8%**

Hoy más que nunca votarán **82.9%**

Oscar Berger **32.3%**

Alfonso Portillo **67.7%**

▶ Los que simpatizan con el PAN

Ya no van a ir a votar **22.8%**

Hoy más que nunca votarán **70.4%**

Fuente: Borge y Asociados; Encuesta Nacional de Opinión Pública, diciembre de 1999

Infografías Prensa Libre: JORGE DE LEON

Solamente 54% dijo que vio personalmente a alguno de los candidatos, y la cifra baja a 28% cuando se pregunta si hubo participación directa de ayuda en las actividades de campaña.

● **La solidez del voto**

El triunfalismo del FRG, tras la victoria en la primera vuel-

ta, le concede también ventaja en cuanto a la solidez de su voto, ya que 83% de sus simpatizantes dice que acudirá a las urnas "hoy más que nunca", mientras que esa misma frase únicamente la pronuncia 70% de simpatizantes del PAN y Berger.

De acuerdo con el análisis de los resultados, con las respues-

tas y la posibilidad de que el abstencionismo alcance –según observadores– entre 60% y 65%, es difícil pensar que Alfonso Portillo pueda alcanzar el próximo domingo los 1.5 millones de votos que pretende, a pesar del amplio margen a su favor en la intención de voto, de acuerdo con La Encuesta.

● **Las ofertas que se hicieron**

El electorado escuchó durante varios meses los discursos de ambos candidatos y sus respectivos partidos políticos.

El FRG impactó en primer lugar por su promesa de "seguridad" –31.2% del electorado– seguida por "beneficios a los pobres", con 14%, arriba de otras como "hacer cambios", "aplicar justicia" y "mejorar la economía" o "dar educación para todos".

El PAN y Berger, por su parte, son recordados por las promesas de "aumento de salarios", 30%; continuar con obras, 10%; "trabajar para la gente", "educación" y "bienestar".

● **Partidos violentos**

Después de los disturbios posteriores a las elecciones de noviembre, personas vinculadas al FRG fueron señaladas como responsables de la mayoría de hechos, a pesar de lo cual 16% considera que el PAN es el responsable, y únicamente 11% concede esa responsabilidad a los republicanos.

A la pregunta de ¿cuál de los dos partidos considera más violento?, la respuesta resultó bastante dividida: 44% que considera así al FRG contra 36% que le concede ese calificativo al partido oficial.

● **TSE y anteriores comicios**

El estudio midió, también, el nivel de calificación por parte de la población hacia el Tribunal Supremo Electoral, TSE, tras las críticas formuladas después de las elecciones del 7 de noviembre último.

Un 35% de los electores considerados en la muestra calificó de "bueno" el desempeño de los magistrados del TSE, mientras que 53% opinó que fue "regular", y apenas 8% dijo que fue malo. El resto no opinó.

Sin embargo, un elevado 21% considera que la primera vuelta fue "fraudulenta", aunque 40% de los consultados las calificó de "limpias", y 34%, "más o menos limpias".

El voto por región

■ Las preferencias del electorado varían, según la región.

Porcentajes por regiones					
	Central	Sur	Norte	Oriente	Occidente
Partido de Avanzada Nacional	30.2	32.6	18.6	28.6	27.7
Frente Republicano Guatemalteco	57.8	56.0	51.3	57.9	64.4
Nulos y blancos	12.0	11.4	30.1	13.6	8.0

Fuente: Borge y Asociados; Encuesta Nacional de Opinión Pública, diciembre de 1999

The daily newspaper Prensa Libre carries its last poll on December 22, 1999, four days before the presidential runoff. The election results were almost precisely what the poll predicted.

men killed a milkman and then he tried to say it was an assassination attempt." He added that Berger's brother once killed two men in a botched kidnapping attempt. Asked the degree of influence Ríos Montt would have in his government, Portillo replied that his mentor was heading the list of the *FRG* candidates for Congress and that if the party received a majority, Ríos Montt would become president of that body, as he had been from 1994-96. "The general is aware that it would be a great risk for him to take an administrative post," he insisted. "He's 74 years old. These are different times. It would be a political waste for him to hold an administrative post different from that which he once held." He conceded, however, that if he won, Ríos Montt "will be part of a group of advisers" in his government. (A political joke during the campaign was that Portillo intended to appoint Ríos Montt ambassador to Britain, a reference to the arrest of Chile's Pinochet.)

For his part, Colom, a 48-year-old engineer and an honorary shaman in a Maya tribe, admitted to me that he was unlikely to make the runoff but said "we will be negotiating" before deciding whom he would endorse. (In the end, he endorsed no one.) He also predicted the *URNG* would greatly increase its number of seats in Congress through the *ANN* alliance. Asked if there were a danger the former guerrillas becoming disenchanted with the peace process, Colom said, "I haven't heard anyone say we ought to return to the battlefield." Like Berger, who is of Belgian descent, Colom conceded he is of pure European ancestry, while Portillo claims only a grandmother who had "some indigenous blood." Asked why the *ANN* nominated a Caucasian as its candidate, Colom replied, "One person can serve as a bridge."

Portillo, already on the ascendancy in the polls, received a stunning endorsement in August when former President de León Carpio declared his support for him and said he would be a candidate for Congress on the *FRG*'s proportional representation list. In an interview at his home, de León conceded to me that the *FRG* is blemished by its association with Ríos Montt, "but above all I believe in Portillo's capacity to deal with the economic and social crisis. I am more for Alfonso Portillo than for the *FRG*. He has opened the doors of the party program and agenda, and he has a very sound policy." Of de León's endorsement of Portillo, Berger told me, "I think he has damaged himself more than us. I think it's a serious wound for him, a stain to his reputation."

Apart from the polls, I could sense unscientifically the shift in public opinion since the last election toward Portillo, whom the public called *"Pollo Ronco,"* or "Hoarse Chicken," because of his raspy, Godfather-like voice. When I asked people on the street in poor towns who they would vote for, most were too frightened to answer, but others replied simply, *"la manita,"* or the little hand, referring to the *FRG*'s blue party symbol of a hand with the thumb and first two fingers extended, representing "welfare, security and justice." Others responded by holding up a hand with the thumb and two fingers extended. (Party symbols appear on the ballot because of the high illiteracy rate.) Of all the interviews I conducted, however, it was a conversation with a humble 29-year-old taxi driver named Edgar that seemed most to typify the electorate's mood. He explained that he voted for Arzú in 1996 because he feared Ríos Montt. This time, he said, he would vote for Portillo. *"PAN* has built a lot of things like highways and bridges, but it doesn't have any humanitarianism," he complained. "They haven't spent enough on education and health." He said he is certified to be a teacher, but that the $20 he makes in the 18 hours a day he drives a cab is more than he could make teaching. *"PAN* doesn't believe in people and the people don't believe in them," he continued. "Portillo grew up on a farm and knows how to milk a cow. He is used to eating *frijoles*; Arzú is used to eating caviar."

The scientific and unscientific indicators both proved correct on November 7, when an unexpectedly high 53% turned out to vote. Portillo almost won an outright victory, receiving 48% of the vote to 30% for Berger and 12% for Colom; nine lesser candidates split the remainder. The *FRG* complained bitterly, with some justification, that Portillo would have won without a runoff but that the *PAN* had monopolized the municpal buses in the capital to transport their voters to the polls, while *FRG* voters were left without transportation. Despite this apparent dirty trick, the *FRG* won an absolute majority in the newly expanded Congress, winning 63 of the 113 seats and ensuring Ríos Montt's return to the president's chair. (His daughter, Zury, was No. 2 on the party's proportional representation list of deputies.) The *PAN* won 37 seats, the *ANN* but nine. In addition to former presidents Ríos Montt and de León Carpio, former President Vinicio Cerezo was elected to Congress as one of the *DC*'s two deputies.

The campaign for the *segunda vuelta* on December 26 seemed almost anticlimactic, as a Portillo victory was all but inevitable. It drew international attention, however, because of Menchú's lawsuit against Ríos Montt and others. This author spent eight days in Guatemala in December and again interviewed the two candidates. Surprisingly, even Berger downplayed the lawsuit, saying it "hasn't even made an echo here. There's a lot of interest in it internationally, but here everything is calm. They voted for him (Ríos Montt) anyway," referring to the *FRG*'s congressional victory. Meanwhile, when I asked Portillo about what impact the lawsuit would have, he said, "None. None. It's a show. There's not a country in the world that can judge something that happened in Guatemala. Rigoberta Menchú doesn't even have followers in her home town so she's looking for some in Europe. It's a show. Ask her people why I got 48 percent of the vote." Portillo acknowledged candidly, however, that he is seen internationally as the surrogate of a former dictator. "The people in human rights circles don't believe my speeches," he said. "All I ask is, give me the benefit of the doubt. Judge me by my actions." He also assured me in the taped interview that he would "not tolerate harsassment of the press" by members of his government, something for which Arzú was notorious.

Ríos Montt himself refused me an interview, but he told the Guatemalan press, "My conscience is clean, because one should abide by the law. However, I do not know the foundation for Mrs. Menchú's denunciation. That girl (*esta chica*) has the right to open all the doors she wants. I remain within the law and I have moral authority, which was ratified on November 7."

Although Berger, whose own sobriquet was *"El Conejo"* ("the Rabbit"), spoke valiantly in public of scoring an upset victory, in the interview with me he appeared resigned to defeat. "We're going to be a constructive opposition," he said, adding tartly, "not the kind of opposition they were. Anyway, it's only for four years, then the voters will do the same thing to them they did to us."

Because the runoff was held the day after Christmas, voter turnout was predictably much lower than it had been on November 7, 40.9% of the 4,458,744 registered voters. Nonetheless, Portillo won by the anticipated landslide: 1,184,932 of the valid votes, or 68.32%, to 549,407 votes, or 31.68% for Berger. A total of 4.79% of the votes cast had been blank or were voided. Portillo thus became the first Guatemalan presidential candidate to poll more than 1 million votes.

The Portillo Presidency

The 48-year-old Portillo was inaugurated on January 14, 2000, joining a growing list of Latin American presidents who won on their second attempts: José Miguel Rodríguez of Costa Rica, Mireya Moscoso of Panama, Andrés Pastrana of Colombia and Fernando de la Rua of Argentina. In his address, he vowed to fulfill reforms promised in the peace accords which the Arzú goverment had failed to implement, and he pledged to bring the killers of Bishop Juan Gerardi to justice, whoever they may be, calling the failure to do so after two years a "disgrace."

President Alfonso Portillo

He then moved quickly to make good on his promise to "govern in a different way" and on his challenge to human rights advocates to "judge me by my actions." Just four days after his inauguration, Portillo stunned both the Guatemalan political and military establishments as well as the international community by appointing as defense minister a mere colonel, Juan de Dios Estrada, who had participated in the peace negotiations with the guerrillas, replacing General Marcu Tulio Espinosa, a hardliner who was himself suspected of human rights abuses. In naming Estrada, Portillo had bypassed 19 generals and one admiral. The significance of the appointment was that, under military regulations, a lower-ranking officer cannot give orders to a superior officer, meaning that the 20 officers of star rank on active service were forced to retire or to be placed on leave. Simultaneously, and equally as significantly, Portillo announced that Estrada's appointment was only temporary, until Congress acted on a military reform package he had introduced that would allow him to appoint a civilian as defense minister. The reforms also would abolish the elite presidential guard, which had been blamed for numerous human rights abuses, including the shooting of the unfortunate milkman in 1996; it was also the prime suspect in Gerardi's murder. The reforms were assured of approval when Ríos Montt agreed to support them.

In March 2000, in another apparent effort to assert his sincerity on the human rights issue and to distance himself from Ríos Montt, Portillo proposed that Congress establish April 22—the anniversary of the Gerardi murder—as the National Day of Dignity for Victims of Violence.

However, not only did this proposal meet immediate resistance from many *FRG* congressional deputies whose first loyalty was to Ríos Montt rather than to Portillo, but also from human rights groups. The Rigoberta Menchú Foundation ridiculed the proposal as a "political ploy."

Even as Portillo was exerting great effort to portray himself as a human rights champion, however, an incident occurred that tarnished this image and acutely embarrassed the president. Not only did Portillo assure this author in a private interview seven days before the runoff that he would respect freedom of the press, he made the same promise at a news conference the day after his landslide election. Then, two weeks after his inauguration, a popular investigative television program on Channel 7, *Temas de noche*, which had been highly critical of Portillo during the campaign, was abruptly canceled. It was the program's host, the respected journalist José Eduardo Zarco, to whom Portillo had admitted that he had killed not one but two men in Mexico. Channel 7, and the other privately owned channels in Guatemala, are owned by a Mexican national, Angel González, who has enjoyed this illegal monopoly for years by ingratiating himself to a series of winning presidential candidates by providing them free air time. In 1999, González had played both sides, providing Berger free air time on his television stations and Portillo free time on the radio stations he owned. The obvious impression was that Portillo had used his leverage with González to pull the plug on the nettlesome Zarco. To increase the appearance of complicity, Portillo had appointed González's brother-in-law as minister of information. From what this author has learned from reliable contacts in the Guatemalan media, however,

González canceled Zarco's program unilaterally, thinking it would please Portillo, who instead was furious about it because of the damage it caused to his image. He apparently even urged González to reconsider, and then offered Zarco air time on the government-owned channel.

As many had expected, President Portillo and his mentor, Ríos Montt, soon became tangled in a struggle for power and influence within the ruling *FRG*, in both the executive and legislative branches. In September 2000, Ríos Montt and 22 other *FRG* deputies were caught up in a scandal, gleefully reported in the press, involving the illegal altering of the percentage on a revenue bill on liquor from 20% to 10%—after it had passed. When the press reported the discrepancy, Ríos Montt and the other deputies vehemently denied they had changed the figure, but a reporter for the daily *Prensa Libre* produced an audio tape of a committee meeting in which the amount had been set at 10%. The press immediately dubbed the scandal "Boozegate." Portillo apparently was not involved, but the allegations against the members of his party embarrassed him. Ríos Montt and the others faced possible expulsion, which has not happened. The power struggle continued into 2001. Portillo vetoed five bills supported by Ríos Montt; in apparent retribution, Congress slashed the appropriations for the ministries headed by members of the Portillo faction of the party.

Recent Developments

Portillo's image was further tarnished in March 2002 when the daily newspaper *Siglo Veintiuno* and the Panamanian daily *La Prensa*, reported they had documentation that the president and Vice President

Guatemalans queue up to vote in the town of Livingston on the Caribbean coast.
Photo by the author

154

Francisco Reyes had used dummy companies to open Panamanian bank accounts in 2001 designed to receive $1.5 million monthly in deposits. Days later, 3,000 protesters banging pots and pans demonstrated in front of the government palace demanding that Portillo and Reyes resign. Portillo has denied the allegations, maintaining they are a smear campaign by members of the oligarchy. Indeed, *Siglo Veintiuno* is owned by interests friendly to former President Arzú, but the same cannot be said of *La Prensa*, which has an impeccable reputation for accuracy.

Human rights advocates also have questioned whether Portillo is softening his commitment to civilian control over the military. The presidential guard has not been abolished, merely embellished with 70 trained civilians. Moreover, in June 2001, the human rights group Amnesty International told the Reuters wire service that threats against human rights workers in Guatemala had increased on Portillo's watch. As if to confirm this assertion, a member of Amnesty International was attacked the day after the interview with Reuters when she answered a knock on her hotel room door. She was left gagged and drugged on a fire escape. On April 29, 2002, Guillermo Ovalle, an administrator of the Rigoberta Menchú Foundation, was slain in a hail of automatic weapons fire in broad daylight at a takeout restaurant in the capital. Authorities maintained—as they had in the Gerardi murder almost four years to the day earlier—that it was a common crime, an apparent robbery attempt. Human rights groups remain skeptical. Also in April, human rights workers excavating the mass graves of victims of army massacres in the 1980s began receiving death threats. In 1999, Portillo had told this author that human rights groups should "judge me by my actions." Apparently, they are.

By mid-2002, the country already was gearing up for the November 2003 presidential and congressional elections. The first aspirant to announce for president has a name from the past—Jacobo Arbenz Villanova, son of the late Jacobo Arbenz Guzmán, the president overthrown in the 1954 coup. The younger Arbenz, 56, is a resident of Costa Rica and a "born-again" evangelical. He will be the candidate of the newly organized United Guatemala Party. Berger appears poised to be the *PAN* candidate again, with the business sector uniting behind him to try to stave off another *FRG* victory. Meanwhile, the *URNG* appears to be fragmenting into disparate factions.

On April 16, 2002, former President de León Carpio died at an apartment he owned in Miami, apparently of a heart attack after he lapsed into a diabetic coma. He had created controversy in the 1999 election by being elected to Congress as a deputy of Ríos Montt's *FRG*. Just three weeks before his death, de León resigned from the *FRG* and publicly declared his affiliation to have been "a mistake."

Culture: The culture of modern Guatemala represents a compost of traditional Mayan and colonial Spanish. Although the mixing of the two bloods has produced a *mestizo* element called by the locals *"Ladino,"* the majority of the population remains unassimilated, pure–blood Indians of Mayan descent who speak a number of dialects, the most widely spoken being Quiché. The Mayan heritage has largely shaped the country's rich folklore in art and music, much to the benefit of the country's tourist industry. Guatemalans take special pride in their *marimba* bands, which often greet arriving visitors at the capital's airport.

Guatemala's religious practices are among the most curious in Latin America. Roman Catholicism never firmly took root, despite efforts by zealous colonial–era priests to force or entice the Indians away from their pagan practices. Eventually, the Church came to realize that it would have better results with a little more tolerance. Today, in towns such as Chichicastenango, visitors can see Indians practicing their tribal rites inside the Catholic cathedral. The shallow roots of Catholicism also made Guatemala a promising target for the proselytizing of U.S.–based evangelical Protestantism. Today an estimated one third of the population are zealous, "born–again" fundamentalists; among the converts were former strongman Efraín Ríos Montt and former President Jorge Serrano.

An abysmally low literacy rate, combined with chronic dictatorship and political violence, forced many of Guatemala's talented writers, artists and musicians to work abroad. But the cultural glass is far from empty. The country's most eminent writer was Miguel Angel Asturias, probably best remembered for his novel, *El presidente.* In 1967, Asturias became only the second Latin American to receive the Nobel Prize for Literature. Former President Juan José Arévalo was a noted literary figure as well, though he later became more identified with Cuba than with Guatemala.

Illiteracy and political violence also took its toll on the development of the Guatemalan press. Dozens of journalists, from newspaper publishers to reporters, were murdered by one side or the other during the 36–year civil war that ended in December 1996. There are only a handful of daily newspapers, all of them relatively young and all published in the capital, and even fewer magazines. The oldest, most prestigious newspaper, and the circulation leader, is *Prensa Libre,* founded in 1952. *Siglo Veintiuno* began publishing in 1991 and has become the country's second–ranking daily, winning high marks for its quality and reliability. Both papers now publish sensational, working-class tabloids as well.

Radio is a popular, and influential, medium in Guatemala because of the poverty and illiteracy. The three privately owned televisions stations are monopolized by a Mexican, Angel González, who is married to a Guatemalan; critics charge that his ownership, and the monopoly, are illegal, but he has managed to remain friendly with all the powers that be, no matter what their political leanings.

Economy: Guatemala's economy is based almost entirely on agriculture. Major cash crops include coffee, bananas, beef and cotton. Most farmland is controlled by huge estates—the top 2% of the population owns more than 60% of the farmland. The large Indian population lives outside the money economy on small plots in the highlands. The average per capita income is about $1,500 U.S., but among rural Mayans it is only about $300.

Light industry has grown in recent years, but economic development remains handicapped by the traditional, largely feudal economic system. Also impeding development are communications problems caused by the large number of Indian dialects used in Guatemala.

Although the devastating earthquake of early 1976 destroyed much of the nation's productivity by damaging roads, water facilities, power supplies, communications and the like, economic output survived largely intact. Major cash crops, produced mostly along the coastal regions, were unaffected by the quake. Light industries such as textiles, food processing and pharmaceuticals, located around the capital, also suffered only minor damage.

Like nearly all its neighbors in Central America, Guatemala has suffered from the high cost of foreign credit and from low export earnings from sugar and cotton. The economy went into a tailspin in 1981. Poor world prices and a low demand for Guatemalan products threaten economic gains, with the exception of coffee.

Efforts to root out corruption, a national pastime in Guatemala, accomplish very little, if anything. Tax evasion, also another pastime, costs the government at least 50% of its intended revenue each year.

Although not as seriously affected by Hurricane Mitch in 1998 as were Honduras and Nicaragua, Guatemala was far from unscathed. The human toll was 268 dead, 121 missing and 734,198 adversely affected. Ninety–eight bridges were destroyed, 60% of the roads were damaged and 45–60% of the corn crop, so vital for domestic consumption, was destroyed.

The hurricane could be only partially blamed for the grave downturn in the economy in 1999. Real GDP dropped from $19 billion in 1998 to $17.8 billion, a decline of 6.2%. Urban unemployment remained unchanged at 5.2%, while inflation was a merciful 5%. Figures do not reveal everything, however. During both of this author's visits to Guatemala in 1999, I heard several knowledgeable people discuss a financial crisis caused by the exodus of hard cash from the country as the victory of Alfonso Portillo appeared more certain. The wealthy elite, who control the now-opposition *PAN,* feared the populist economic policies of Portillo and his mentor, Ríos Montt, and began stashing their money in foreign banks for the duration.

GDP has since shown a healthy and steady growth of 3.3% in 2000 and 3.0% in 2001, which just recovers the ground lost in 1999. Inflation in 2001 was a modest 6.0%. The government has been contemplating the possibility of following the lead of Ecuador and of neighboring El Salvador in adopting the dollar as the official unit of currency and abandoning the *quetzal.*

The Future: It is ironic that Portillo's winning percentage in the December runoff (68%) was identical to those of Vinicio Cerezo in 1986 and Jorge Serrano in 1991; both are now pariahs, having disillusioned the people who had elected them overwhelmingly. Portillo is fast following in their footsteps as a result of allegations of corruption. Since the restoration of democracy in 1986, Guatemalan voters have never returned a party to power. Portillo did not deliver on his promises before the weather vane of public opinion, as Berger had predicted to me, turned against him.

Portillo's approval rating in the public opinion polls is abysmal. This author's friend, Mario Antonio Sandoval, the in-tune political columnist with *Prensa Libre,* predicted shortly before the 1999 runoff that the 2003 election could see the *URNG* win "because that's the only thing the voters haven't tried yet." Indeed, the *FMLN* in neighboring El Salvador controls the capital and is the largest bloc in Congress,

and has proven it is not the bogeyman it was portrayed to be. Sandoval also predicted that if Guatemalans do begin to drift toward the left, the *PAN* and the *FRG* may be forced to form an unholy alliance to stop the left from coming to power. His prediction seemed to be coming true in 2001, as several left-leaning deputies of the *PAN* abandoned the party, leaving it in the hands of the oligarchy, and began allying themselves with moderates within the *URNG.* Since then, however, the *URNG* has begun to splinter, and there could be several new parties, hopelessly splitting the votes of the left. One is the newly formed United Guatemala Party and its candidate, Jacobo Arbenz Villanova, son and namesake of a man who is still an icon of the Guatemalan left. If the next president also proves a disappointment, there is a real danger that Guatemalans may conclude that democracy is simply not all that it's cracked up to be and start searching for alternatives that work better.

A street vendor hawks copies of 6 different daily newspapers.   *Photo by author*

The Cooperative Republic of Guyana

A diver prepares to look for diamonds in the Essequibo River

Area: 82,978 square miles.

Population: 772,000 (2000 estimate).

Capital City: Georgetown (Pop. 210,000, estimated).

Climate: Tropically hot and humid; there are heavy rains from April to August and from November to January.

Neighboring Countries: Suriname (East); Brazil (South and West); Venezuela (West).

Official Language: English.

Other Principal Tongues: Various East Indian dialects.

Ethnic Background: East Indian (about 52%), African and mulatto (about 41%), European and mixed (about 7%).

Principal Religion: Christianity (Anglican Protestant).

Other Principal Religions: Roman Catholic Christianity, Hinduism, Islam.

Chief Commercial Products: Bauxite, sugar, rice, aluminum, shrimp, molasses, timber, rum.

Currency: Guyana Dollar.

Gross Domestic Product: U.S. $577 million in 1999 ($824 per capita).

Former Colonial Status: Colony of the Dutch West India Company (1616–1796); British Colony (1796–1966).

Independence Date: May 26, 1966.

Chief of State: Bharrat Jagdeo, president (since August 11, 1999).

National Flag: A yellow field bordered in green with black, red and white triangles from top to bottom along the staff.

Guyana lies on the northeast coast of South America. A narrow (5 to 10 miles wide) ribbon of swampy plain extends along the 200–mile length of the coastline. Much of this land lies below sea level and is intersected by large rivers requiring a complex system of dikes and canals to protect it from both floods and drought. Annual rainfall averages 80 to 100 inches and the country is hot the year round; the daily temperature variation of 10° F is greater than the seasonal changes. This coastal region is the country's principal agricultural area and contains some 90% of the population.

Inland from the coastal plains, the land rises to natural grassy plains with poor soils and scrub bush. It is here that gold, diamonds and bauxite are found. Further inland, heavily forested hills rise to the base of the Guiana Highlands, with elevations of over 8,000 feet on the Guyana-Venezuela border, rising out of the forests in vertical red cliffs of 2,000 feet. Rivers flowing out of the highland produce spectacular falls as they drop to the lowlands.

Guyana's principal rivers, the Corantijn on the Suriname frontier, the Berbice and the Essequibo, which flow into the Atlantic at Georgetown, are navigable for only short distances because of falls and rapids—yet they are of major importance as means of communication in the roadless interior.

History: The Dutch first settled on the banks of the Essequibo River as early as 1596, but permanent settlements were not established until the Dutch West India Company started its operations about 1620. The Dutch drained the swamps and lagoons and initiated the system of dikes and canals which make the coastal plain habitable. The Spaniards and Portuguese conquerors of the lands to the west and south saw no apparent value in the Guianas and did not molest the British, French and Dutch settlers of the region. British forces captured the Dutch settlement in 1796, and the territory now incorporated into Guyana was ceded to the British in 1814. In 1831, the colony was officially named British Guiana. The British confined themselves to plantation operations along the coast and some lumbering along the rivers. Sugar, rice and cotton were the principal crops.

The population arrived in two different groups. The Africans came in the 17th and 18th centuries to work the plantations. With the abolition of slavery in 1830, Asiatic peoples migrated from India, China and southeast Asia, and they now account for the largest element in the population. During the 19th century, the British further developed the drainage system and built roads and railroads in an effort to open the interior for settlement and exploitation of the mineral wealth. However, few people moved to that area. Descendants of the African people have tended to gather in the urban areas as mechanics and tradesmen; the Asiatics have remained on the farms and plantations along the coast. Despite Guyana's size, the habitable land is overcrowded and the interior is uninhabited except for a few aboriginal Indians.

Politically, the British started tutoring the people of Guyana for independence after World War II. Self–government which was planned for 1962 had to be postponed until 1966 because of bitter racial controversy between the Asiatic and African sectors of the population. Cheddi Jagan, leftist leader of the Asiatic people, was premier during most of these four years. His open sympathy with world communism and policies directed against those of African descent led to his defeat, and Forbes Burnham, of African descent, became prime minister. A constitutional change of 1965 provided for proportional representation of the two communities in the national legislature, and the election of moderate leaders in the 1964 elections made possible the granting of independence in 1966.

Under the leadership of Burnham, racial tensions were eased, although scattered disturbances surfaced from time to time. Burnham was reelected in 1968, easily defeating Cheddi Jagan. During his second term, he emphasized broadening the base of the economy and a neutral foreign policy. To reduce dependence on sugar exports, more attention was given to the development of other crops.

Burnham started moving toward the political left in 1970—he declared Guyana to be a "cooperative republic" whereby 1,200 small worker cooperatives were established. The government began taking over the nation's foreign–owned bauxite mining operations in 1971. Burnham was elected in 1973 to a third term, defeating Jagan. His People's National Congress (PNC) won 37 seats in the 57–member Parliament; the People's Progressive Party (PPP) of Jagan was reduced by five to a total of 14 members.

Burnham's main strength came from blacks who live in the cities, while Jagan traditionally has dominated the East Indian vote in the more rural areas. Although Asiatics comprise 52% of the population compared to 40% who are black, Burnham skillfully garnered his winning margins through political patronage and by espousing ideas originally proposed by his opponent.

Both Burnham and Jagan were dedicated Marxists. In May 1976, the government nationalized the huge British–owned sugar industry—the last remaining major foreign investment in Guyana. Steps were taken to control the insurance, banking and rum industries, so that the state ultimately owned 85% of the economy.

With Burnham continuing his swing to the left, he gained the endorsement of Jagan, who in an unexpected move, pledged his support to Burnham's economic programs. This political accommodation brought an unfamiliar tranquility to Guyana, which was short–lived.

World attention focused on Guyana in late 1978 when 913 members of a bizarre religious cult from California living in the isolated new jungle settlement of Jonestown committed suicide after drinking a concoction laced with cyanide.

Burnham decreed a new constitution in 1980 that gave him increased control over opposition political parties and the nation's judicial system. Three months later, he won another five–year term in office.

The 140–year–old border dispute with Venezuela erupted anew in 1982 with territorial incursions into Guyana. This latest dispute had been smoldering since 1962, when Venezuela suddenly declared

the 1899 accords (which the United States helped to arrange between Britain and Venezuela) void. The dispute has quietly faded into the background since 1988, which marked state visits by the heads of the respective nations to each other.

Burnham died of heart failure in 1985 after minor throat surgery in Moscow. Although he had made plans for his family to take over Guyana, surprisingly the party endorsed his vice president, Desmond Hoyte. Balloting in a subsequent election gave the PNC 42 of the 53 seats in the National Assembly; Cheddi Jagan claimed the contest was rigged.

President Hoyte, realizing that the Soviet Union offered no economic hope for Guyana, dropped all pro–Soviet rhetoric and traditional communist pronouncements and actively sought closer ties with Western nations. He personally visited the United States to encourage investment (without results). Energetic plans were put into execution to get the state out of business, of which it controlled 85%, and to drastically cut government personnel. Credit became available from the International Monetary Fund and the United States as a result. Hoyte wisely included talented Asiatics at top levels within his administration.

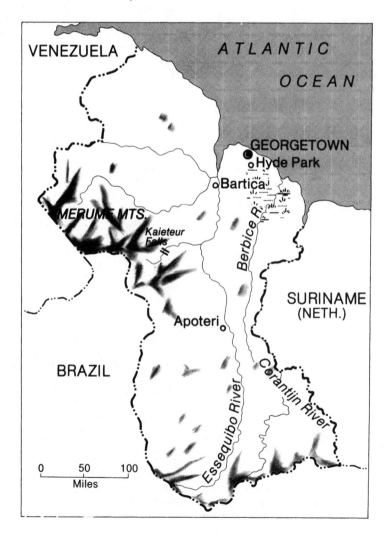

158

Elections, considered the fairest ever held in Guyana, in October 1992 ended the 28 years of PNC power. The outcome was totally unexpected—in 1991–92 Guyana's economy hummed along well, and conditions had improved considerably. Usually in times of prosperity voters settle for what they have. Cheddi Jagan led the PPP to victory, gaining a working majority of 35 seats in the Assembly. But this was *not* the old Cheddi Jagan. He also had dropped all illusions of Marxism and was able to portray himself as a moderate progressive rather than as a radical leftist.

With the typical zeal of the newly converted Jagan implemented sweeping economic changes. From its high of 105% in 1989, inflation was reduced to 4.5% in 1996. That same year, he signed an agreement to reduce Guyana's debt to the Paris Club of creditor nations by two thirds. The erstwhile Marxist also opened Guyana's agricultural, mining and forestry sectors to foreign investors. Foreign economists praised Guyana's example as one of the most successful adjustments from a state–controlled to a free market system. That legacy proved to be Jagan's requiem. On February 16, 1997, the 78–year–old president suffered a serious heart attack. He was taken to Walter Reed Hospital in Washington, where he died on March 6. Prime Minister Samuel Hinds was sworn in to succeed Jagan. Hinds then named Jagan's widow, Chicago–born Janet Rosenberg Jagan, as Guyana's first woman prime minister.

For the presidential and parliamentary elections of December 15, 1997, Hoyte again stood as presidential candidate for the PNC, but President Hinds stood aside to allow Mrs. Jagan to stand as the standard–bearer of the PPP. Mrs. Jagan insisted she was running reluctantly to fulfill a deathbed wish of her husband. But Hoyte accused her of nepotism and of seeking to establish a nation of "Jagana." Race also played a role in the campaign, with Hoyte supporters denouncing her as "that Caucasian old lady" and alleging that she still carries a U.S. passport. In reality, Mrs. Jagan's Guyanese credentials were impeccable. She had lived there for 54 years and had lost her U.S. citizenship when she voted in British Guiana in 1947. She served time in jail with her husband during the independence struggle in the 1950s.

In balloting that the PNC immediately denounced as rigged, Mrs. Jagan unofficially received 191,332 votes to 144,359 for Hoyte. She was hastily inaugurated just four days later, publicly defying a court injunction the PNC had obtained to block the ceremony. Hinds became prime minister. Although observers from the Organization of American States pronounced the elections fair, PNC loyalists embarked on a month of street protests, some quelled by army troops and police using tear gas. To help defuse the volatile situation, a negotiating team from the Caribbean Community (Caricom), headed by former Barbados Prime Minister Henry Forde, brokered an agreement between Mrs. Jagan and Hoyte that called for an end to street demonstrations and the institution of constitutional reforms. The deal was a remarkable concession for Mrs. Jagan's government, because it calls for new elections within three years, two years short of her constitutional mandate. Under the agreement, the constitutional reforms would be worked out within 18 months, and the elections would come within 18 months after that. Although the unrest has quieted down, the personal animosity between Jagan and Hoyte lingered.

Hoyte and other critics of Jagan blamed her unreconstructed Marxism for discouraging badly needed foreign investments; her government, they note, steadfastly refused to consider tax incentives, which drove potential investors to other, more inviting countries. Despite her life–long devotion to Marxism, however, Jagan pragmatically but grudgingly moved to privatize some cumbersome state–controlled enterprises, including the airline and a bauxite operation. Such economic reforms paid dividends in May 1999, when the World Bank and the IMF granted Guyana $256 million in relief for its $1.09 billion national debt under the Heavily Indebted Poor Countries initiative that rewards countries that implement painful but needed reforms. Guyana was only the third country to receive such debt relief under this program.

A chronic heart condition forced Jagan to undergo treatment in the United States, as had her husband, but on August 11, 1999, she yielded to the weight of her age and health and resigned. Although Prime Minister Hinds was in line to succeed her, he deferred in favor of the finance minister, Bharrat Jagdeo, a Hindu who, at 35, became the youngest head of state in the hemisphere. The departure of Jagan has done little to defuse the tense political rivalry between the PNP and the PPP, however, as Hoyte has refused to recognize Jagdeo's government either.

Hugh Desmond Hoyte

President Bharrat Jagdeo

But in 2000, Jagdeo's main preoccupation was the long-simmering border disputes with both Venezuela to the west and Suriname to the east. In May, Venezuela issued a formal protest over a concession that Guyana had granted to a Texas company to construct a $100 million satellite launching facility in the disputed Essequibo region. In a strongly worded note to Foreign Minister Clement Rohee, Venezuelan Foreign Minister José Vicente Rangel called the concession an "unfriendly act" and called on the Guyanese government to "review" it. The site was chosen because of its proximity to the Equator, which makes it easier to launch heavy payloads into geosyncronous orbits. The European Space Agency has a similar facility in nearby French Guiana.

Then, on June 2, Suriname ordered a Canadian oil drilling company to tow its offshore platform from what it claimed was Surinamese territorial waters in the Atlantic Ocean. Like the Essequibo dispute with Venezuela, this dispute dates to colonial times. At issue is which bank of the Corantijn River forms the boundary between the two countries. The river empties into a V-shaped gulf, and the border is extended into the Atlantic Ocean. It was in that narrow disputed corridor that Guyana had granted a drilling concession to the Toronto-based company, which reluctantly towed its expensive platform into undisputed Guyanese waters and waited for the two countries to resolve the matter diplomatically. For a time, it seemed the matter would not be settled in a gentlemanly fashion, as each country accused the other of moving troops up to their common land border. The two governments then agreed to a series of talks, first in Georgetown, then in Paramaribo, June 13–18, which ended in failure. Another round of talks in July also failed, and further talks were put on hold because of the campaign for the March 19, 2001 election in Guyana. Meanwhile, each country made tragicomic attempts to build up its minuscule military force. Guyana, which has no navy, purchased two aging British and three U.S. warships, while Suriname beefed up its existing navy. There is far more at stake in the

7,700 square-mile disputed zone than water and fish; it sits atop an estimated 15 billion barrels of oil which, at a time of rising oil prices, could prove a jackpot for both of these impoverished nations—if they are willing to strike a deal.

The Elections of 2001

The general elections originally had been scheduled for January 2001, but an independent electoral commision, headed by the highly respected retired Major General Joseph Singh, concluded they could not be held before March. On December 8, Jagdeo, after consulting with Hoyte, moved them back to March 19. Because of the ugliness of the disputed 1997 elections, the contest of March 19, 2001, drew an unusual amount of international scrutiny: 170 observers from six separate organizations and 45 nationalities. For a time it appeared that the voter ID cards would not be ready in time, but the election was carried out with a minimum of discord.

The results were a resounding victory for the incumbent Jagdeo and his PPP, which had an electoral alliance with the small Civic Party: 209,031 votes, or 53% to 164,074, or 42%, for Hoyte's PNC. In the 65-seat Parliament, the PPP-C won an outright majority of 35 seats, the PPP won 27 and minor parties took the remaining three. Despite the clear-cut results, which the international observers termed fair and honest, the PNC filed a formal complaint with the electoral commision, claiming thousands of opposition voters had been turned away at the polls. Meanwhile, disgruntled PNC supporters vinted some sour grapes on March 26 by going on a rampage in Georgetown, looting shops and torching a gas station. Police used tear gas to restore order. It was politics as usual in Guyana.

Not long after the election violence, the international human rights group Amnesty International accused Guyanese police of operating death squads that had allegedly summarily executed as many as 15 criminal suspects. The government denied the allegations. A few days after that negative international publicity, the United States ceased issuing visas to Guyanese citizens in reprisal for Guyana's refusal to repatriate 100 Guyanese nationals who had been arrested in the United States for various felonies.

Political violence erupted once again in July 2002 when pro-PNC demonstrators staged protests outside Jagdeo's office, apparently in an effort to embarrass the president, who was hosting a summit of leaders of the 14 Caribbean Community countries. In the ensuing violence, two protesters were killed and six wounded.

Jagdeo called the incident an assassination attempt.

Culture: The people of Guyana have adopted the culture of the British ruling elite of the past century. Schooled through the elementary grades, their literacy rate is higher than those in neighboring nations. There are few cultural traits reflecting the origin of the African community; the Asiatic community still retains some of its original customs, especially in marriage and family relations.

Economy: Despite large mineral and forest resources, Guyana's economy is agricultural and severely limited to foreign markets. Much of the nation's sparsely settled but potentially rich interior is also claimed by Venezuela. Efforts to populate this inhospitable region have been unsuccessful.

Although the ambitious Burnham sought to convert Guyana into a Marxist state, change was initially gradual in an attempt to avoid the disruptions that occurred in Cuba and in Chile during the communist interlude of the latter. But after 1982, all curbs in the march toward socialism disappeared—and Guyana commenced a more rapid disappearance down the economic drain. The result was disastrous. The purchasing power of the average citizen declined by 40% compared to 1976 figures.

The state–owned bauxite operation, called *Guybau*, showed a profit largely because of comparatively inflated world prices, which have since declined. Before the romance with communism, farm output was constant; rice and sugar export initially rose after independence. Guyana reported a favorable balance of trade by 1975. In early 1977 Guyana applied for formal association with *Comecon*, the communist bloc's common market. Perhaps in order to emphasize its interest in trade rather than ideology, Guyana also became a member of the Inter–American Development Bank, a Washington-based organization of the OAS.

Critical of Guyana's close ties with Cuba, and adhering to its policy of encouraging the private sector, the United States in late 1983 vetoed a $40 million Inter–American Development Bank loan to increase Guyana's rice production because that plan actually would have created a lack of incentive for farm production; the loan was later approved. Workers' strikes in late 1983 and 1984 resulted in a sharp decline in bauxite production. Guyana's economic situation deteriorated dreadfully in 1984–86. Negotiations with the International Monetary Fund were suspended and the IMF

declared Guyana ineligible for further assistance. There initially was no improvement under Hoyte, but rather, further decline; he inherited an economy that had descended to primitive agriculture.

A substantial part of the Essequibo River had to be closed for a week in the summer of 1995 because of a leak of cyanide–contaminated slurry from the Omai gold mine. The huge mine is Guyana's largest enterprise, and is 95% owned by two Canadian firms.

The Hoyte administration brought about a slowly rising prosperity that quickly gained momentum in Guyana. Although strict conditions imposed by the IMF were resented, they were successful.

Throughout most of the 1990s, Guyana experienced extraordinary GDP growth averaging 7% a year. Unlike many of its Latin American neighbors that were cursed by dependence on one export commodity, Guyana was blessed with diversified exports, including bauxite (aluminum ore), gold, timber, sugar and rice. But the robust growth halted abruptly in 1998, when the Asian financial crisis and *El Niño* both hit Guyana. World market prices for timber, gold, bauxite and sugar all fell; timber exports alone dropped 35% because of the crisis in Asia, the major consumer of Guyanese wood. Only rice exports showed an increase. As a result, GDP growth for 1998 was a meager 1.1%. It declined by 1.8% in 1999 and another .8% in 2000. Unemployment in 1999 was 11.9%; more recent figures are unavailable. Inflation in 2000 was a modest 5.9%.

The Future: Guyana may at last have passed the torch, in President Kennedy's words, to a new generation of leaders. The two men who dominated the country since even before independence, Forbes Burnham and Cheddi Jagan, are dead. Janet Jagan retired at 79, and the PNC's Hoyte is 72. The youthful President Jagdeo, despite some skepticism that he could fend off challenges from within his own party as well as from the PNC, emerged from the March 2001 election with a convincing mandate. But will it prove to be a Pyrrhic victory? He now must resume battles on four fronts. He must try to resolve peacefully border disputes with neighboring Venezuela and Suriname. He must try to salvage a faltering economy. But most importantly, he must reach out to the Afro-Guyanese and assure him that the PPP represents their interests as well as those of its Indo-Guyanese constituency. Only until he begins to erase the boundaries that have polarized Guyana along ethnic lines will political violence cease.

The Republic of Haiti

Emperor Henri Christophe's *La Citadelle*, the mountaintop fortress in the north which took 13 years and the labor of 200,000 men to build.

Area: 10,711 square miles.

Population: 8 million (estimated).

Capital City: Port–au–Prince (Pop. 1.2 million, estimated).

Climate: Tropical, moderate at higher elevations; rainy season from May to December.

Neighboring Countries: Haiti occupies the western third of Hispaniola, the second-largest of the Greater Antilles; the Dominican Republic occupies the eastern two thirds of the island.

Official Languages: French and Creole, a mixture of French and African origin spoken by almost all Haitians.

Other Principal Tongues: Creole, a dialect of French and African origin spoken by a majority of the rural Haitians.

Ethnic Background: African Negro (90%), mixed African and European (10%).

Principal Religion: Officially Roman Catholic Christianity, but a majority of Haitians practice *voodoo*, a variety of animism similar to African native religions, but with a greater emphasis on mysticism.

Chief Commercial Products: Coffee, light industrial products, sisal, sugar and textiles.

Currency: Gourde.

Gross Domestic Product: U.S. $4.3 billion in 2001 ($520 per capita).

Former Colonial Status: Spanish Colony (1492–1697); French Colony (1697–1804).

Independence Date: January 1, 1804.

Chief of State: Jean-Bertrand Aristide, president (since February 7, 2001).

National Flag: Blue and red vertical stripes, coat of arms on white square in center.

The Haitian western one third of the island of Hispaniola is covered by tropically green mountains rising to heights of 9,000 feet. The narrow coastal plains and river valleys, one fifth of the total territory of the nation, are arable, but irrigation is necessary in many of the fields. Of these areas, the Artibonne River valley and the north coastal plains are most suited to agriculture. The mountains that divide Haiti and the Dominican Republic prevent the moisture–laden trade winds from reaching Haiti, thus its lands are generally drier than those of its neighbor.

History: Haiti was discovered by Columbus in 1492 and remained under Spanish control for the following 200 years. Because of the limited number of settlers, the Spanish exploited the eastern part of Hispaniola, neglecting the western portion, which became a popular base for French–speaking pirates. The western portion of the island was ceded to France in 1697, and ultimately became one of that country's most profitable colonies. African slaves had been brought in by the Spanish and their numbers increased during French rule. The slaves obtained their freedom during the period of the French Revolution in a confusion of slave rebellions and civil wars that involved blacks, mulattos, French, Spanish and English on the island of Hispaniola.

Toussaint L'Ouverture, a former slave, rose rapidly to the rank of general during this period. He fought with the Spanish against the French, later joined the French against the English, and ultimately forced them from the island. Napoleon sent a large force under his brother–in–law, General Victor–Emmanuel Leclerc, which captured L'Ouverture and attempted to restore slavery. Independence was finally achieved in 1804 after a dozen years of bitter bloodshed when the French forces were defeated and expelled by the Haitians.

General Jean Jacques Dessalines, commander of the black army, was named governor–general for life. An ex–slave, illiterate, brutal and arrogant, he lacked the qualifications for ruling his newborn nation and was unable to secure aides capable of compensating for his ignorance. The few whites left in Haiti were slaughtered by Dessalines' order—the war had been fought not only to obtain freedom, but also to destroy anything that would remind the blacks of serfdom and forced labor.

Drafting a constitution abolishing slavery, prohibiting land ownership by whites and making the term *Negro* synonymous with Haitian, Dessalines was enthroned as Emperor Jacques I. By use of conscripted labor and enforced discipline, he made some progress in restoring order and in rebuilding the economy until he was assassinated in 1806 by his two trusted military commanders, Henri Christophe and Alexandre Pétion. Haiti then split into two states—the north ruled from Cap–Haitien by Henri Christophe and the south ruled as a republic by Alexandre Pétion. Christophe styled himself emperor; he constructed a massive castle and established an elaborate circle of courtiers, dukes, duchesses and barons who were former slaves. In contrast, Pétion governed the south as an independent republic, and his rule was relatively moderate and progressive. He was at war with Henri Christophe from 1811–1818, when the latter, faced with rebellion caused by his cruelty, shot himself with a silver bullet.

Haiti was reunited between 1818 and 1820 by Jean Pierre Boyer, a French–educated mulatto who was able to dominate the entire island by 1822. Initially of moderate outlook, the declining economy and disruption of society induced Boyer to resort to harsh tactics to till the land and restore governmental authority. When he was overthrown in 1844, the Spanish–_speaking eastern portion of the island regained its independence and Haiti again fell into the hands of illiterate leaders.

The period from 1843 to 1915 was one of disorder, tyranny and bloodshed under 22 dictators. It was a period of economic and social deterioration. The only occupants of the presidential palace who accomplished any beneficial acts were Fabre Geffrard (1859–1867), who cut the army in half, built a few schools and signed a concordat with the Vatican to revitalize the church. Lysius Salomon (1879–1888) created a national bank, built rural schools and imported French school teachers. The last, Florvil Hyppolite (1889–1896), built bridges, docks and public buildings and opened telephone and telegraph services.

U.S. Intervention, 1915–34

The country degenerated into anarchy in 1908, culminating in the killing and dismemberment of President Guillaume Sam by an angry mob on July 28, 1915. Sailors and Marines on a U.S. naval vessel offshore promptly seized Port–au–Prince to restore order. The occupation was to last for 19 years under five U.S. presidents of both parties, during which the military high commissioner, Marine Brigadier General John H. Russell, oversaw the successive "elections" of puppet presidents. The president from 1922–1930 was Louis Borno, who collaborated so well with

Russell that a U.S. financial adviser to Haiti called the arrangement a "joint dictatorship." The United States also imposed a new constitution on Haiti in 1918, written by the assistant secretary of the Navy—Franklin Delano Roosevelt. FDR later was to boast of its authorship. Under Russell's tutelage, there was no freedom of the press or other basic civil liberties. Several newspaper editors, in fact, were jailed in the name of establishing democracy, something that Thomas Jefferson would have frowned upon.

In 1919, the *cacos*, or peasants, under the leadership of the charismatic Charlamagne Peralte, revolted against U.S. rule. In an operation that has become part of Marine Corps folklore, Major Smedley Butler disguised himself, infiltrated Peralte's camp, killed him with his revolver and forced the other *cacos* to flee. The revolt was crushed, with more than 3,000 Haitians killed in the process.

On the positive side, the Marines greatly improved Haiti's infrastructure. From 1919 to 1922 they built 365 miles of roads and improved 200 miles of existing road. Irrigation systems were repaired and experimental farms set up. The Marines also established the *Garde d'Haiti*, a constabulary that had American officers, to maintain law and order. This force, however, later would become little more than the personal goon squad for a succession of

dictators. Moreover, the Americans made no effort to diversify the coffee–dependent economy or to train schoolteachers, with the result that Haiti remained the poorest and least literate nation of the Americas.

When a strike led to another outbreak of violence in 1929 that the Marines ruthlessly crushed, President Herbert Hoover dispatched an investigative commission to inspect the U.S. role in Haiti. In its report, the commission concluded: "The failure of the occupation to understand the social problems of Haiti, its brusque attempt to plant democracy there by drill and harrow, its determination to set up a middle class—however wise and necessary it may seem to Americans—all these explain why, in part, the high hopes of our good works in this land have not been realized."

A new legislative assembly was elected on October 14, 1930, General Russell resigned on November 1, and on the 19th legislators chose an opposition newspaper editor, Stenio Vincent, as president. Haitians reassumed control of key public agencies a year later. On August 15, 1934, President Roosevelt, who had once boasted of writing Haiti's constitution, withdrew the Marines. It would be 60 years, one month and four days before the next U.S. military intervention.

The departure of the U.S. Marines in 1934 was hailed as Haiti's second emancipation. Haitian politicians and military officers were restored to their former privileges, and the following three decades revealed that Haiti had profited little from U.S. military rule. The Marines had sought to place the educated *mulatto* minority in power, but the *Garde d'Haiti*, consisting principally of mulattos, emerged as the dominant force.

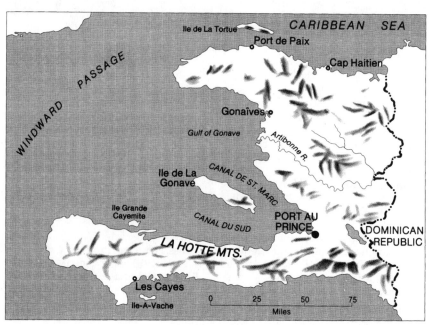

The Duvalier Era

The election of Dr. Francois "Papa Doc" Duvalier as president in 1957 began a new era of dictatorial rule. A devoted voodoo practitioner, Duvalier ruled Haiti by a combination of superstition and brutality. He created an incredibly cruel and imaginative force known as the *Tonton Macoutes* (rough translation: "Uncle's Boogeymen"), which had the capability of appearing out of nowhere to dispense instant justice (usually death or unbelievable torture). This force became an all–pervasive instrument of Haiti's "government." The single most significant accomplishment of his administration was his durability and longevity—he died apparently of natural causes in April 1971. Before his death, Duvalier named his portly, naïve, childish, fun–loving son, Jean–Claude ("Baby Doc") as Haiti's next president for life. Assuming a serious attitude not considered possible, the youthful ruler immediately proceeded to reshape Haiti's horror–filled image with a semblance of political stability and programmed economic growth under the tutelage of his older sister Simone and his mother. New foreign investments created more than 80,000 low–paying jobs.

Although Haiti received more per capita foreign aid than any other Western Hemisphere nation, most benefits were diluted by corruption. Half of all foreign loans and grants were funneled into secret accounts controlled by government leaders. The nation's stagnant economy prompted thousands to flee—often in unsafe boats—to the Bahamas and the United States in search of work. At one time, one out of every 10 persons in the Bahamas was said to be an illegal alien from Haiti.

To improve its international image, Haiti permitted limited free elections in 1979. The so–called "liberalization program" was short–lived; in November 1980 opposition political and intellectual leaders were arrested and deported in the worst government purge since 1963. Although it was not initially apparent to the outside world, "Baby Doc" apparently had become estranged from his mother and "divorced" his sister as the "first lady" of Haiti in favor of a very light–skinned charmer, Michèle Bennett. Her father, on the verge of bankruptcy, quickly became the coffee export baron on Haiti and the family attached itself firmly to the inner circles of government. Michèle tried to emulate the late Evita Perón of Argentina.

To outward appearances, Michèle Duvalier was the soul of charity and kindness, opening orphanages, providing relief for the poor and tirelessly working against injustice. But the palace life she created was another story. Luxuries piled upon luxuries and she "ran" Jean–Claude with an iron fist. Worst of all, she had television sets placed in every small town and settlement to (1) show all of her charitable works and, foolishly, (2) to broadcast the festivities from the marble palace. Her father and family graduated from the edge of bankruptcy to rich, elite exporters and businessmen. Goose liver paté contrasted sharply with garbage—anger started to smolder.

The Revolt of 1986

Perhaps the straw that broke Haiti's back occurred when Michèle went on a Paris shopping spree that cost more than $1 million! Among the items purchased in profusion were fur coats to be given as gifts to close friends. But alas, the palace was too hot for fur coats! The solution: install coolers. When this appeared on rural television (a charity ball!) it proved too much, and further, the beginning of the end.

The final insult came with the arrival of 1,200 money–laden passengers for the inauguration of a much celebrated and criticized new tourist haven on the island of Labadie at a resort developed under questionable financial circumstances. They were not to be exposed to Haiti's "backward" atmosphere, but rather, to luxury.

Rioting erupted in late January 1986. Duvalier made tentative efforts to disband the *Tonton Macoutes* and undertook some other reforms—all too late. The rioting continued and intensified. Amid chaos, "Baby Doc" and his wife were flown out of Haiti in a U.S. plane for France ("to spend eight days") in early February. Since no other country would receive him, he is still there. "Papa Doc's" tomb was raided (his body wasn't there) and others were broken open; skulls were paraded through the streets. The Bennett family was all but wiped out. Shopkeepers had closed their shops, frozen with fear, in spite of governmental threats. One of the prime movers behind the revolt was the "liberation theology" priests of the Roman Catholic Church who from the pulpit regularly condemned the government.

A military regime under General Henri Namphy literally emerged from the dust to lead Haiti. Assets of the Duvaliers in various parts of the world, including the United States, France and Switzerland were frozen. However, enough remained untouched to apparently enable "Baby Doc" to live in comfort during his lifetime.

The ouster of Duvalier did not end violence in Haiti. Mobs sought out the members of the *Tonton Macoutes* and brutally murdered them. There were riots when the head of that organization was allowed to leave for Brazil instead of facing trial.

After a new constitution was adopted in 1987 there followed a procession of presidents averaging eight months in office before being overthrown. They all had initial approval of the military and the elite Haitians which quickly soured as they tried to expand the base of their popularity. The last one in early 1990 took the offensive: he had all significant rivals for power seized and repeatedly beaten; they were exiled to Florida. He also went after the American ambassador persuaded him that there was no choice—either he left or Haiti faced unbridled violence.

Elections were again attempted in late December 1990. Jean-Bertrand Aristide, a "liberation theology" priest who had been thundering anti–Duvalier, anti–elite rhetoric from his pulpit (defrocked by the Catholic Church for meddling in politics) was elected president. This was by a majority of 70%, despite the opposition of the army, the elite, the Catholic Church and what was left of the *Tonton Macoutes*. But he was revered by the poor. The army commander was able to coerce his men into inaction and silence to ensure free elections.

Lacking military support, President Aristide imported 60 Swiss officers to train a new palace guard loyal to him. Fearing loss of power, the military ousted him on September 30, 1991, and only the intervention of the United States, Canada, France and Venezuela prevented his assassination. He went initially to Venezuela, later entering the United States in early 1992, where he spent large sums of money from frozen Haitian assets without accounting for them.

French, EC and U.S. aid to Haiti was immediately suspended. An uneven trade embargo was imposed, dampened by President Bush and Europeans eager to make dollars from Haitian misfortune. Acting in spite of the embargo, they shipped petroleum to Haiti, which was immediately snapped up by the military and the elite. The poor of the island became even more desperate, and began leaving by home–made boats for Florida and Guantanamo Bay, Cuba. The United States immediately blocked this with its Coast Guard, even though their activities were not within the coastal limits of the United States.

Of the Haitians who made it to the United States or Guantanamo, only one out of nine were admitted as political refugees. Incredibly poor, diseased and uneducated, they were undesirables. Even the most ardent U.S. black advocates, including the Black Caucus of the U.S. Congress, shuddered at the thought of an impoverished Haitian family moving in next door. But at the same time, they participated in a chorus of black U.S. voices demanding that Aristide be returned and installed in office by U.S. troops, if necessary.

One of the cruelest hoaxes occurred during the U.S. presidential campaign of 1992. Democrat candidate Clinton flatly promised that, if elected president, he would immediately admit refugee Haitians to the United States without limit. When Clinton was elected in November, countless numbers of Haitians began building boats, using any materials they could find, legally or illegally, awaiting the day of Clinton's inaugural so they could set sail from misery to hope. Literally within hours of taking the oath of office, he decided that it was "wise" to continue the policies of his predecessor in office whom he had defeated.

A substantial number of Haitians were quarantined at Guantanamo Bay because they were carriers of the HIV virus which develops into AIDS. A U.S. district judge ordered their release to the United States in mid–1993 because they had been in quarantine "too long"

Although thousands of Haitians were returned to their country by the United States, there was no evidence that they were mistreated by the military led by General Raoul Cedras.

The question of Haiti appeared to have been solved in mid–1993 when an agreement was signed in New York by Aristide, Cedras and Police Chief François that the president would return by October 31. Training officers for the Haitian police appeared at Port–au–Prince aboard U.S. and Canadian vessels, but were prevented from landing by Haiti's informal military. The agreement was not followed by Cedras.

When President Clinton received black support in Congress on the NAFTA treaty and other measures, he was called upon to respond with more energetic action to remove the military from power in Haiti and reinstall Aristide. On the refugee problem, the United Nations adopted directives that they be received by all nations (actually meaning the United States).

To try to lower the pressures concerning Haiti, the U.S. Central Intelligence Agency was clumsily used in 1994 to float rumors that Aristide in his earlier life had experienced bouts of insanity. There was no proof of such a charge; what seemed to be a good reason to dump him became an acute embarrassment.

Pressures for action mounted after mid-1994 and there was increased talk from Clinton threatening invasion of the island. Such a move was authorized by the U.N. Security Council in July. Troops were readied in September, and in a last–ditch effort, the president dispatched former president Jimmy Carter, Senator Sam Nunn and retired General Colin Powell to Haiti. They persuaded the military leadership to stand down and leave Haiti, most probably with promises of money. Within days the military leadership departed the island.

U.S. Intervention, 1994

At a tremendous cost, a force overwhelmingly of U.S. troops entered the island peacefully on September 19 and took up a triple role: janitors, policemen and, later, presidential guard after Aristide returned to the island. Little in their combat training prepared them for such roles. Both before and after his return on October 15, the Haitian president modified his former radical positions so as to become acceptable to the "movers and doers" and the military of Haiti which had supported his 1991 ouster. Although a disarmament program was immediately organized, for every weapon obtained under it, at least 10 were hidden by their owners. Almost 4,000 Haitian refugees were repatriated from Guantanamo Bay to their native country.

Aristide appointed Smarck Michel as prime minister; together they devised plans for election of a new legislature in mid-1995. There were plans to withdraw U.S. forces by the fall of 1995, which proved impossible. Aristide's supporters started behaving as goons, not as saviours of their nation. A well–known opponent of Aristide was mercilessly gunned down in March 1995. This was one of the first in an incalculable number of murders of anti–Aristide Haitians; his personal involvement was suspected.

He tried to float the idea of canceling presidential elections scheduled for the fall of 1995 so he could remain in office—a proposition that even liberals in the U.S. Congress shrank from in horror. René Préval won in an election with a light turnout; although Aristide hates him, he embraced him at his inauguration in February 1996.

Préval undertook the unenviable task of trying to govern a country still beset by economic, political and social conditions that have made it the basket case of the Western Hemisphere. As if he didn't have problems enough, he inherited a literal palace guard that was loyal to Aristide and whom he did not trust. The United States dispatched a special security team to guard the president during the second half of the year.

Like so many other recent Latin American leaders, Préval faced economic reality and launched a program aimed at privatizing the inefficient state–owned enterprises. He had the added incentive of meeting requirements of the International Monetary Fund to qualify for additional loans, which account for 60 percent of Haiti's budget. Part of the painful austerity program is the elimination of 7,000 of 43,000 public employees. As usually happens, the austerity measures sparked a series of protest demonstrations early in 1997. Préval also undertook an effort to distribute parcels of land to peasants, but the tracts are so tiny—1.2 acres—that they cannot be commercially viable, and while he may have won meager appreciation from the recipients of the parcels, he was condemned by those who have been left out.

More serious even than public discontent was a wave of political violence in 1997 that claimed the lives of about 50 people between February and March. Préval attributed the killings to remnants of the *Tonton Macoutes,* the paramilitary gang of thugs that enforced the will of the two Duvaliers.

The democratic process came close to total breakdown following Senate elections in April 1997. Aristide had established an offshoot of his *Lavalas* (Avalanche) Political Organization, or *OPL,* called the *Fanmi* (Family) *Lavalas,* apparently designed as a vehicle for his reelection in 2000. The Aristide faction was accused of rigging the April election, which would have given *Fanmi* a majority in the Senate. Préval indefinitely postponed the runoff elections until the matter could be resolved. Prime Minister Rosny Smarth

A wedding near Port–au–Prince

Panoramic view of Port–au–Prince

resigned in June to protest Aristide's alleged power play, but agreed to remain until Parliament confirmed a successor. In August, however, the 83–member Chamber of Deputies, in which the *OPL* is the largest bloc with 33, rejected Préval's nominee, Ericq Pierre, the Haitian representative on the Inter–American Development Bank Board. In October, Smarth finally abandoned his post, and Préval nominated Hervé Denis, a 58–year–old economist committed to privatization of nine state–owned companies. In December, the Chamber voted 34–33 to confirm Denis, but abstentions left him short of the needed majority. Préval stubbornly re–nominated Denis in March 1998, and the *OPL* just as stubbornly vowed not to confirm any nominee until the president dismissed the nine members of the electoral council and had the election results revised. Préval refused, and while this petty contest of wills continued, as much as $300 million in foreign aid packages were tied up because there was no one to negotiate them. It also frightened away whatever foreign investors who may be bold enough to do business in Haiti. U.S. Secretary of State Madeleine Albright visited Haiti in March and chided both sides for their failure to resolve the impasse. It seemed the logjam may have been broken in April when the Chamber finally confirmed Denis. But on April 15, the nomination was blocked in the Senate when it received approval of eight of the 16 senators—but not an absolute majority.

While the domestic crisis was unfolding, the three–year mandate of the U.N. peacekeeping force, composed of Canadians and Pakistanis, expired on November 30, 1997, and the foreign troops withdrew the next day. It was the worst possible timing, as political violence and common street crime were engulfing the country and drug traffickers were swarming into Haiti like cockroaches into a dark, filthy kitchen. Not only was the 5,200–member police force established under U.S. and U.N. auspices proving incapable of maintaining order, but the new police force had killed about 100 people, roughly half of them without any apparent justification. Two of Préval's bodyguards and two of his chauffeurs were gunned down (even his dog was stabbed to death), and he asked the United Nations to protect the presidential palace. Two days before the peacekeeping force left, the U.N. Security Council voted to establish a 290–member civilian police force with a one–year mandate. There also were 500 U.S. military "engineers" still in Haiti engaged in public works projects. They left in early 2000.

With the Denis nomination twice rebuffed by Parliament, Préval staged a strategic withdrawal in July 1998 and nominated as prime minister his minister of education, Jacques Edouard Alexis. For

months, Parliament took no action, and the crisis rumbled on without resolution. Meanwhile, the Senate, facing the imminent expiration in January of the terms of eight of its remaining 16 elected members, simply voted in November to extend those terms until November 1999, apparently hoping that the impasse would be resolved and new elections called before then. It was an act of dubious constitutionality, and the Chamber of Deputies took no similar action to extend its own expiring mandate.

It suddenly seemed the logjam would be broken when, on December 15, the Senate unexpectedly ratified Alexis with 12 votes for, one against and three abstentions. Two days later, the lower chamber followed suit, with 46 of the 78 remaining deputies voting to ratify Alexis. All that remained was for Parliament to approve a cabinet for Alexis to take office. The president then promised to appoint a new electoral council by the end of December, and the country—as well as the United Nations and the U.S. government—breathed a collective sigh of relief.

Alas, Préval ignored his own deadline and failed to appoint the electoral council. The crisis flared up anew on January 11, 1999, the date of the expiration of parliamentary mandates. Declaring that in the absence of new elections there was no longer a parliamentary quorum, Préval announced that he would begin ruling by decree. The reaction was immediate and violent, as pro-*OPL* demonstrators, denouncing the move as a ploy by Préval to assume dictatorial powers, took to the streets. So did pro-Préval demonstrators, who blockaded local municipal councils on the pretext that their terms, too, had expired. Members of Parliament showed up for work in what was a largely symbolic gesture, because they found only one functioning telephone and the Finance Ministry had severed their operating funds.

The day after Préval's announcement, his sister was critically wounded in an ambush that killed her driver, and she was evacuated to Cuba for treatment. Alexis, meanwhile, announced that he was assuming the post of prime minister and naming a cabinet in the absence of Parliament. Once again, Préval set a deadline of February 2 to name a new electoral council that would call new elections, and once again he let his own deadline pass, claiming he needed more time to choose a suitable council. Denying he was setting himself up as Haiti's latest dictator, he insisted, "It is democracy we are building."

The Electoral Farces of 2000

If so, the architect and carpenters should have been fired. Twice in mid-1999 the Provisional Electoral Council *(CEP)* set election dates, first for November 28, then

Former President René Préval

President Jean-Bertrand Aristide

for December 19. Both were canceled. On September 29, a third date was set for March 19, 2000, and insisted that this date was firm, but just two weeks before the elections the *CEP* declared a third postponement, which Préval ratified on March 15. The *CEP* then set April 9 and May 21 as the new dates for the first and second rounds, but Préval declared those dates did not have his approval. At that point, the United States and the European Union impatiently reminded Préval that $500 million in aid that Haiti desperately needed was contingent upon his calling the long-overdue parliamentary elections. The Haitian people began showing their impatience as well with mass demonstrations on March 27 that left four people dead. According to the Organization of American States, there had been at least 50 separate incidents of politically related violence since the previous October. In a case of unfortunate timing, the last of the U.N. forces had withdrawn from Haiti just nine days before.

On April 11, the *CEP* and Préval agreed on a fourth date: May 21, with runoffs on June 25, later moved to July 8. At stake were 19 of the 27 Senate seats and all 83 members of the Chamber of Deputies, plus about 7,500 local offices. During the six-week campaign that followed, at least 15 candidates or campaign workers for various parties were murdered, some hacked to death with machetes in traditional fashion. Another casualty, on April 11, was Jean Dominique, the country's most prominent radio commentator, who was gunned down as he arrived at work. Dominique had made enemies on both the far right and the far left, and the killing remains unsolved. Just two days before the voting, six opposition groups hastily formed an alliance in a last-ditch effort to prevent a predicted landslide by Aristide's *Lavalas* movement.

It did not appear to have worked, although it was hard to tell. The election was marred from start to finish by poor

organization and outright manipulation. Many polling places opened late, and at others, the ballots had not yet arrived; they were still being printed. In the department of Grand Anse, the election was postponed altogether because inter-party bickering had prevented voter registration. In some cases, workers refused to deliver election material unless they were paid in advance. OAS observers reported cases of vote fraud and intimidation of voters by pro-Aristide militants, which the U.N.-trained police force seemed uninterested in stopping. A policeman was killed, however, as was a gunman at one polling place. An opposition candidate for a local office was stoned to death. Some opposition pollwatchers reported they were denied entry by *Lavalas* partisans. Finally, as polls closed, armed goons, presumably from *Lavalas,* stormed several polling places and made off with the ballot boxes. Marked ballots, representing about 10% of those cast, were found lying in the street in front of the vote-counting center in the capital; workers swept up about 90% of them.

The OAS official in charge of the 200 international observers, speaking with considerable understatement, termed the irregularities "most unfortunate." Former U.S. President Jimmy Carter, whose Atlanta-based Carter Center also participated in observing the election, told this author in Caracas, Venezuela, six days later: "It is obvious to me that the election in Haiti was seriously flawed." About the only thing to cheer was the record voter turnout: an estimated 60% of the 4 million eligible voters—a far cry from the 5% who voted in the annulled 1997 elections. Unfortunately, not all their votes were counted.

According to the "results" released by the *CEP* days after the election, *Lavalas*

won 16 of the 19 Senate seats and 23 deputy seats without a runoff. But on June 2, the deputy chief of the OAS observation mission reported that the *CEP* apparently had miscalculated the final percentages for the Senate by counting only the votes for the top four candidates for each seat. Eliminating the votes for lesser candidates gave several *Lavalas* candidates outright majorities that they did not actually have. The opposition and the observers claimed that 10 "winning" *Lavalas* Senate candidates should have faced a runoff. When the official results were finally announced, *Lavalas* held all but one of the 27 Senate seats and more than 80% of the seats in the Chamber of Deputies; it also controls almost all the municipal governments.

This creative tabulating brought international demands that the *CEP* count the votes properly. In June, even U.N. Secretary-General Kofi Annan lent his weight to calls for a clean vote count. But the government refused to budge. In fact, on June 18, two weeks before the runoff elections, the president of the *CEP* fled to the Dominican Republic and then to the United States, saying that government officials had threatened him with death if he did not certify the flawed results. He had refused to do so. The following day, Aristide supporters took to the streets to set tires on fire and to demand that the government release the results. It did—the flawed ones.

This farce was continued into the presidential election of November 26, which the major opposition parties boycotted to protest the parliamentary elections. (In a peripheral farce, two days before the election Parliament finally confirmed Alexis in the office he had held for 20 months.) Aristide, who almost certainly would have won anyway, was thus opposed only

Palm trees along the northern coast of Haiti

166

by six unknown candidates, and even they did not campaign because of threats of violence against them. In the usual pre-election violence, nine pipe bombings killed two people and injured at least 16. The United States, Canada and the European Union withdrew their observers rather than participate in a sham. In the balloting, Aristide predictably received 92 percent of the vote. The government declared that the turnout had been 60.5%, but more objective assessments put it at between 15% and 20%, depriving Aristide of a thumping mandate.

Three weeks later, 15 opposition parties, calling themselves the Democratic Convergence, declared they would form an "alternative government" and even brashly called on *Lavalas* to join them. Certain of his position, however, Aristide brushed aside their call, and he was sworn in on February 7, 2001. Just as the opposition parties had boycotted the election, the international community largely snubbed the inauguration to protest the pitiful parody of democracy; the United States was represented only by its ambassador.

Recent Developments

Since Aristide's inauguration, political tension and violence have continued. The opposition rebuffed Aristide's invitation to join his government, saying his election is illegitimate. It has demanded new elections, and suggested Gerard Gourgue as an interim president. On March 14, 2001, an opposition demonstration in front of the local headquarters of the Organization of American States, which has sought to broker a truce between the government and the opposition, was broken up by Aristide supporters. The ensuing violence left three people dead. In early April, OAS Assistant Secretary-General Luigi Einaudi arrived in Haiti to attempt to jumpstart talks. Aristide supporters staged a tire-burning demonstration and blocked traffic, apparently to impress the OAS team that while Aristide is open to new talks with the opposition, they will be on his terms.

The talks dragged on until July, when they broke down. Under pressure from the United States and the OAS, *Lavalas* and the Convergence agreed to renew talks on October 13. They agreed in principle for a new parliamentary election to be held in November, but the opposition rejected Aristide's "nonnegotiable" demand that the incumbent lawmakers be allowed to serve out their terms, which made new elections pointless. The talks collapsed after one day.

On December 17, 2001, a band of about 30 armed men stormed the National Palace in an attempted *coup d'etat,* killing two guards and two bystanders; they had first attacked the national penitentiary but were repulsed. Forces loyal to Aristide quickly recaptured the palace, killing one of the gunmen and capturing seven; another was apprehended as he attempted to cross the Dominican border. In the days that followed, two other men were arrested, and Haiti demanded that the Dominican Republic extradite a former police captain believed to be hiding there; there also was evidence of involvement by Dominican soldiers in the attack.

Although the attackers appeared to be disgruntled former soldiers from the army that Aristide had disbanded in 1994, rather than Convergence activists, Aristide supporters around the country used the palace attack as a pretext to go on a rampage against the opposition, wielding machetes, erecting barricades and burning tires. A Convergence party headquarters and the homes of three Convergence leaders were burned; four people were burned alive by mobs. Fearing for his life, Gourgue went into hiding. Pro-Convergence radio stations received threats. Much of the violence was believed linked to Aristide's personal good squads, called the *chimère.*

The violence has continued on into 2002. In February, a *Lavalas* member of Parliament was assassinated in his car by two men on motorbikes. In May, a peasant demonstration against the government near the northern town of Ouanaminthe erupted into violence that left two peasants dead.

In March 2002, Prime Minister Jean-Marie Cherestal resigned amid mounting public pressure from Aristide supporters, who faulted him for not doing enough for the economy, which shrank by 1.2% in 2001. As his replacement, Aristide nominated, and Parliament approved, Senate President Yvon Neptune, who said his first priority would be to promote a dialogue between the government and the opposition. On June 15, Aristide met with Convergence leaders for the first time in two years. The president assured the opposition that he would move to satisfy their demands, including reparations for the property destroyed by mobs in December. When this book went to press, however, the stalemate continued, and each side blamed the other for the continued freeze on $500 million in desperately needed international aid.

Culture: Haiti's culture is a singular blend of African and European influences. A minority, the mulattos, relatively better educated in the French language schools, boast of their European culture and superiority. Educated in medicine and law, they patronize the arts and disdain most manual work. Most are Christian.

The Haitians are, for the most part, an illiterate peasant society. Poor and neglected, they practice *voodoo,* a type of animism with African roots with many spirits and deities, and great emphasis on the powers of evil and good spirits. Their singular beliefs are also a source of pride. Their language is a dramatic indication of their culture—called *Creole,* it is a blend of French, Spanish, English and Dutch, the foreign influences to which Haiti has been exposed, with a distinct basis in African dialects and tongues.

Creole is the basic language of the country; in addition to their French, the mulattos also speak this tongue. Some of its terms baffled troops sent by the United States to help Haiti. An important, wealthy person in Creole is a *gros neg—* "big nigger"—and a foreigner, regardless of race, is a *blanc—* "white." Most artistic expression has *voodoo* overtones. Traditional African designs blend with imaginative contemporary motifs in cloth, wood carving and basketry. Such crafts are valued internationally.

Economy: Haiti's economy, based on peasant survival at unbelievably low levels, is almost nonexistent. Deforestation, soil erosion and overpopulation all combine to limit agricultural production. The leading cash crops are coffee, cotton, sisal, cacao and sugar. Low wage scales are attracting foreign investment in light industry such as electronic assembly, finished leather goods and tourism. A new industry centered around clothes assembly is booming. Precut materials are sent from the United States and sewn into garments in Haiti. This substantially lowers import duties when the finished product is shipped to the United States.

When former President Bush watered down the embargo on Haiti, he did so not out of consideration of Haitians, but because of extreme pressure from the U.S. garment makers and merchants.

During the 1980s the economy suffered from expensive fuel imports, low prices for coffee exports and hurricane damage to crops. Continued U.S. assistance kept the nation economically afloat—barely—before 1987. The already prostrate economy was further stricken by Hurricane Georges in 1998. Aid in future years will depend on what shape the government takes under the new constitution. But the old system of granting monopolies in various imported articles to political favorites can hopefully be buried. It results in artificially high prices paid for goods by an impoverished people.

Beginning in the 1980s, the desperate economic conditions led to a massive exodus of economic refugees by boat, bound for Florida, the Bahamas, or anywhere they might find a better life; untold numbers died at sea. About the only cause for grim cheer in recent years was that in 1997 Haiti's per capita income of $458 exceeded that of Nicaragua by a few dollars, meaning Haiti was no longer officially the poorest country of the hemisphere. In 2001, the per capita figure had risen to $520, but unemployment remains an estimated 70%—by far the highest of the hemisphere. Economic growth declined by 1.2% in 2001.

The Future: The Haitian people have discovered the cruel fact that political democracy is not a panacea for two centuries of tenacious poverty and political misrule. Haiti remains the Western Hemisphere's basket case: destitute, illiterate, lawless and virtually ungovernable. There is little room for optimism that this dismal picture will change in this generation. Haiti desperately needs an enlightened leader, and Aristide has demonstrated, both in the way he governed in his first term and in the electoral farce of 2000, that he is anything but enlightened. He is a pariah to the international community, but he may very well succeed in pulling off what Peruvian President Alberto Fujimori failed to do–thumbing his nose at both the opposition and the international community and staying in power under a mandate of questionable legitimacy. Meanwhile, it is widely believed that what public finances the bankrupt government enjoys are coming from payoffs from drug traffickers who use Haiti as a way station. God save Haiti.

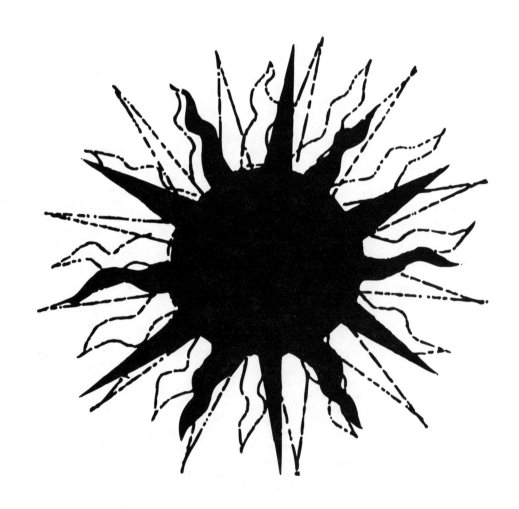

The Republic of Honduras

Detail from a carved stone pillar at the Mayan ruins of Copán in western Honduras

Area: 43,266 square miles.

Population: 5.6 million (estimated).

Capital City: Tegucigalpa (Pop. 725,000, estimated).

Climate: Tropical, with clearly marked wet and dry seasons. Heaviest rains occur from May to December.

Neighboring Countries: Nicaragua (Southeast); El Salvador (South); Guatemala (West).

Official Language: Spanish.

Other Principal Tongues: Various Indian dialects.

Ethnic Background: *Mestizo* (Mixed Spanish and Indian, 90%) African (5%), Indian (4%) European (1%).

Principal Religion: Roman Catholic Christianity.

Chief Commercial Products: Coffee, bananas, lumber, meats, petroleum products.

Currency: Lempira.

Gross Domestic Product: U.S. $6.318 billion in 2001 ($720 per capita).

Former Colonial Status: Spanish Colony (1524–1821).

Independence Date: September 14, 1821.

Chief of State: Ricardo Maduro, president (since January 27, 2002).

National Flag: Blue, white and blue horizontal stripes, 5 blue stars in a cluster on the center stripe.

Honduras is the second largest of the Central American republics and one of the most thinly populated. Much of the country is mountainous; an irregular plateau in the southwest has peaks approaching 8,000 feet near Tegucigalpa and La Esperanza. The plateau drops to a narrow plain on the Pacific Coast (Gulf of Fonseca). To the north there also is a narrow coastal plain broadening to the east. The valleys of the Ulúa (N.W.) and Aguán (N.E.) rivers extending south from the Atlantic coast (Gulf of Honduras), are important agricultural regions. Running south from the Ulúa to the Gulf of Fonseca is an intermountain valley which is the principal route of communications from the Atlantic to the Pacific oceans. The eastern plains along the Patuca River are covered with jungle and only partially explored.

The central plateau descends into several basins at 2,000 to 4,000 feet, in which are located the principal urban centers. The southern and western highlands contain the majority of the native Indian societies. The black population is found in the banana–raising section along the Atlantic coast. Prevailing winds are from the east, and the Atlantic coastal plain, receiving heavy rainfall, is covered with forests that are also found on the eastern slopes of the plateau and mountains.

History: Honduras was settled by Spanish treasure seekers from Guatemala in 1524. The mainstream of movement and settlement was along the Guatemala trail, a pattern that today governs the population distribution. The Spaniards ignored the Atlantic coast and the region was untouched until the U.S. fruit companies set up banana plantations in the late 19th century.

Honduras achieved independence from Spain with the other Central American states in 1821, and joined with them in a short–lived federation. Going its own way as a separate state in 1838, Honduras has been subjected to interference from Guatemala, El Salvador and Nicaragua as these countries sought Honduran support in conflicts among and between them. Honduran politics has followed the Central American pattern—two-party conflict between liberal and conservative factions of the elite, little popular participation in the political process and a long list of ever–_changing dictatorial regimes. However, Honduras' dictatorships have been somewhat more benign than those of its neighbors, and several governments have been committed to social and economic reform. Less inclined toward revolution than its neighbors, sparsely populated and with few roads, Honduras has been able to avoid the large–scale bloodshed of its neighbors. Still, during its first 161 years of independence, Honduras witnessed 385 armed rebellions, 126 governments and 16 constitutions. The most capable presidents were Policarpo Bonilla (1894–1899) and Tiburcio Carías Andino (1932–1948). Neither made any pretense of democratic rule, governing instead as benevolent despots.

During his 16 years, Carías did more to advance the social and economic well–_being of the country than any of his predecessors. Some roads and a few schools were built, and modern agricultural methods were introduced. His regime was maintained by jailing or exiling his critics.

After peacefully surrendering power following 1948 elections, Carías was followed by a series of mediocre presidents. The military seized power in 1963, led by

General Oswaldo López; Honduras joined the Central American Common Market, trade was improved and an industrial development program was initiated in the northern plains region around San Pedro and Puerto Cortés. Presidential balloting held in 1965 resulted in his election at the head of the National Party to a six–year term.

A long–simmering dispute between Honduras and El Salvador, stemming from the fact that tiny El Salvador is badly overpopulated, erupted into a brief, but bloody clash in 1969. Since the 1940s, some 300,000 landless peasants have settled illegally on vacant land near the border inside underpopulated Honduras. Some Salvadorans fled their homeland to escape the horrors of prolonged civil strife. Others came to Honduras in search of a better life. In time, these highly industrious people were living better than many native Hondurans in the region.

Alarmed by what it viewed as a growing flood of "squatters," Honduras enacted a new land reform law which, among other things, distributed to native Hondurans plots that had been cleared and brought under cultivation by the Salvadorans. All too often, the immigrants would be evicted just before their crops were ready for harvest. The mass deportation of 17,000 Salvadorans created such tension between the two countries that a disputed soccer game between them was all that was needed to cause a war in 1969.

Although the North American press tended to joke about the "soccer war" between the two "banana republics," the conflict claimed more than 2,000 lives and devastated the economies of both countries. Because of the strife, Honduras withdrew from the Central American Common Market, causing further economic damage to both nations.

Capitalizing on his role as a "wartime" leader, President López sought to remain in office by amending the constitution to permit his reelection in 1971. When that effort failed, López persuaded the Liberal and National parties to divide equally most national offices. Under this "Pact of National Unity," Ramon Ernesto Cruz was elected president.

Unable to cope with the nation's growing economic and political problems, the elderly Cruz was ousted in a coup led by López in 1972. To gain popular support, he promised a major land reform program. The plan was opposed by both the landowners, who rejected any change in the tenure system, and by peasants, who felt the concept was too little too late. López was ousted in a coup in 1975 as a result of a "bananagate" scandal in which high government officials were accused of accepting a $1.25 million bribe from the U.S.–owned United Brands Company to lower taxes on banana exports.

The new chief of state, Colonel Juan Alberto Melgar Castro, sought to implement various social and economic development projects. Partly as a result of these efforts, the country enjoyed a healthy gross national product growth rate of 6%–8% annually until 1980. Pledging to enact the land reform program promised earlier by López, Melgar also soon found himself in a deadly crossfire between wealthy farmers and landless peasants.

The heart of the dispute is land. Much of Honduras is extremely mountainous; only 22% of the land is arable. A lion's share has traditionally been controlled by just 667 families (0.3% of the population) and by two U.S. banana firms. In contrast, the peasants (87% of the people) live as peons on small, difficult–to–till plots. The end result is often widespread malnutrition, particularly among the young. Still, the recent land reform program, while not meeting all expectations, has permitted a larger number of peasants to be resettled on their own property.

President Melgar was replaced in 1978 by a three–member *junta* headed by General Policarpo Paz García. Yielding to pressure from the Carter administration, Paz appointed a civilian–dominated cabinet to direct the transition to civilian government. Elections in April 1980 for the 71–seat constituent assembly gave the reform–minded Liberal Party 35 seats while the conservative Nationalists took 33 seats.

The Return to Democracy

General elections in 1981 marked the return of democracy to Honduras, resulting in the presidency of the Liberal Party's Roberto Suazo Córdova. A country doctor, he tried to revive a patient that was suffering from backwardness, a declining economy and growing security problems caused by events in neighboring countries. More than 25,000 Salvadoran refugees flooded into Honduras to escape that nation's war. Many were relocated away from the border and were placed under the U.N. High Commissioner for Refugees.

When the Marxist *Sandinista* movement took over the revolution in Nicaragua, Honduras became a sanctuary for the Nicaraguan *Contra* forces opposed to the communists. During the 1980s there were repeated raids into Honduras from Nicaragua as the *Sandinista* forces periodically tried to destroy *Contra* encampments. The losses in coffee production in areas abandoned by farmers because of the conflict was substantial.

The United States in 1984–86 stepped up its military aid commitment to Honduras in response to the communist threat from Nicaragua. In addition to weaponry, military personnel were sent. Economic aid in large amounts was insufficient to alleviate economic woes, however, associated with fluctuations in the prices of bananas and coffee. The Reagan administration initially insisted that aid come from the private sector. Such a "solution" might well have impoverished the civilian government at a time when the military was growing, leading in turn to a military seizure of power.

Cuba used Honduras as a transport route to dispatch Soviet–bloc arms and munitions to communists in El Salvador, and to a lesser extent, Guatemala. By 1983, U.S. military advisers were training Salvadoran troops within Honduras. Friction

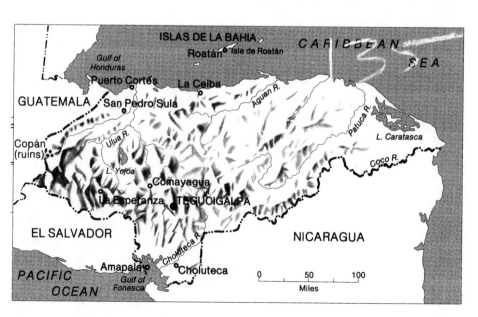

with Nicaragua increased because of the *Contra* presence. In an effort to control the situation, a combined U.S.–Honduran military force established permanent American military bases close to the Nicaraguan border. Some thought this was an effort by President Reagan to provoke the *Sandinistas,* justifying direct intervention in Nicaragua.

An incident did occur—*Sandinista* troops entered Honduras in 1988 to wipe out a *Contra* base after a cease–fire had been negotiated between the warring parties. When 3,000 additional U.S. troops were sent into the country, the *Sandinistas* beat a hasty retreat.

President Arias of Costa Rica devised a peace plan for Central America which, although widely hailed, was impractical as long as the Soviets continued their support of the *Sandinistas.* The plan was also undermined by an on-again-off–again vacillation in the U.S. House of Representatives on the issue of granting support to the *Contras* in a transparent effort to embarrass President Reagan. With the breaking up of the Soviet Union and the end of its support in 1989, a semblance of peace finally came to Central America.

But this left a burgeoning, expensive military in Honduras with little purpose since the end of the conflicts. Releasing them would not help in a country where the unemployment–underemployment rate has been close to 50% for more than a generation.

In spite of financial and security woes, democracy has proceeded well in Honduras with the elections of José Azcona (1985), Rafael Leonardo Callejas (1989) and Carlos Roberto Reina (1993). All has not been tranquil, however. Ethnic Indians, largely ignored by the government, have become more politically aware and have been expressing their dissatisfaction with their status. Vague guerrilla groups periodically appear and disappear, and there was an assassination threat against the president in early 1994 by a killer hired by a drug trafficker.

As U.S. aid dwindled (now less than $100 million annually) other sources of funding have been sought. The International Monetary Fund agreed to loans, but attached a host of conditions that were difficult, including reduction of the size of the legislature and military.

President Reina raised eyebrows in 1994 when he launched an anticorruption campaign that saw charges brought against 18 former officials, including none other than former President Callejas, who was immune from prosecution as a member of the Central American Parliament. But it was the paring of the once–omnipotent military that may be regarded as Reina's enduring legacy. He ended the draft, obtained executive control over the armed forces' budget, removed the national po-

Former President Carlos Flores Facussé

lice from military control and reduced troop strength; some units are only 20% of their former size. Moreover, there were Argentine–style efforts to hold the military accountable for human rights abuses during the 1970s and 1980s. In January 1998, days before Reina left office, a civilian judge ordered an investigation into the possible role of Armed Forces Commander General Mario Hung in the disappearance in 1988 of Roger González, a left–wing student leader. At the time, Hung was a lieutenant colonel in a special forces battalion.

The armed forces have complained that the downsizing has emasculated their ability to defend Honduras, but to defend Honduras against whom? The guerrilla wars in neighboring Nicaragua and El Salvador, which once threatened to embroil Honduras, have ended. More significantly, on January 18, 1998, nine days before leaving office, Reina signed a long–sought border agreement with Salvadoran President Armando Calderón Sol that formally delineated the disputed frontier areas that led the two countries to war in 1969.

The presidential and congressional elections of November 30, 1997, proved to be the most colorful yet for this fledgling democracy. To succeed the 71-year-old Reina, the Liberal Party made a generational leap to the president of the Congress, 47-year-old Carlos Flores Facussé, who lost an earlier bid to Callejas. The National Party, meanwhile, nominated Alba Nora de Melgar, widow of erstwhile military strongman Juan Alberto Melgar Castro and a former mayor of Tegucigalpa. Her link to the days of dictatorship, plus her decision to hire as her campaign adviser Dick Morris, President Bill Clinton's onetime aide who resigned in disgrace in 1996 after admitting frequenting prostitutes, brought the campaign international attention. Three minor parties also fielded candidates. Flores sought to distance himself from Reina and from the party's traditional middle–class base and to reach

out to the country's impoverished masses, although he has little in common with them. The scion of two of the country's wealthiest families, Flores is the son of journalist and Liberal activist Carlos David Flores, who in 1976 founded the daily newspaper *La Tribuna,* now the country's largest. His mother, Margarita Facussé, is the sister of Miguel Facussé, a Palestinian immigrant who amassed a fortune in food processing and textiles. The younger Flores received a degree in industrial engineering from Louisiana State University and holds a master's degree in international economics and finance. His wife, Mary Flakes, still holds U.S. citizenship. He held a cabinet post in the civilian government of Suazo Córdova.

While Mrs. Melgar pledged to promote economic growth by making Honduras a free–trade zone and by reducing illiteracy from 30% to 5% by 2001, Flores issued a 10–point New Agenda that stressed women's rights, child care and health improvement. A near–fatal helicopter crash during the campaign sidelined Flores for several weeks. Ultimately, his populist approach and youthful appeal proved successful, as he won a decisive victory over Mrs. Melgar, 53% to 42.4%. It was almost an exact replay of the two parties' results in the 1993 race. Flores was inaugurated on January 27, 1998, some five weeks before his 48th birthday on March 1.

Like his predecessors since the restoration of democracy, Flores found his will tested by the military. The armed forces commander promoted a list of officers without clearing them with the president—who objected to the men chosen and who nullified the promotions.

That problem, however, was trivial compared with the blow dealt to poverty-plagued and debt–ridden Honduras in late October 1998 by Hurricane Mitch, one of the most powerful storms in recorded history. Entire villages on the Caribbean coast were swept away by the winds and floods. The local governor compounded an already tragic situation by inflating the death toll to 9,000, for which the president fired her. In human terms, 5,657 Hondurans were confirmed dead, another 8,058 missing and uncounted thousands more left homeless. In terms of economic damage, the storm destroyed 170 bridges and damaged 70% of the country's roads; property losses were in the billions of dollars, and 90% of the vital banana crop was destroyed. International relief efforts to alleviate the immediate human misery were quick in coming, although an aid package for Honduras and neighboring countries affected by Mitch became a political football in the U.S. Congress. In December, the World Bank approved a $200 million loan, and in March 1999 the IMF extended a $215 million credit. But these were little more than band–aids, and a bewildered President Flores declared to the world that

Honduras's debt was "unpayable." The government announced in April 1999 that it would attend a meeting of donor nations in Stockholm in May and request $4 billion in aid for 2,462 separate rebuilding projects.

The Elections of 2001

Hondurans were in the mood for change as they prepared to elect their sixth president since the establishment of democracy. The dominant Liberal Party nominated a party insider, Rafael Piñeda, 71, the president of the Congress, who had served as a deputy for 20 years. The opposition Nationalists, however, gambled on a 55-year-old businessman, Ricardo Maduro, whose only political office had been head of the Central Bank under the 1990-94 Nationalist administration of President Callejas. There was a handful of minor party candidates

As both major parties are center-right, the campaign focused on personalities and the issues of who could better combat crime and promote foreign investment. Maduro, whose own son had been killed in a kidnap attempt in 1997, made a crackdown on crime the centerpiece of his platform. He visited New York City and came home promising the "zero-tolerance" approach of then-Mayor Rudolph Giuliani, not only against violent crime but against such petty offenses as littering, vagrancy and defacing public property, all of which, Maduro argued, discourage tourism and foreign investment. Piñeda, a former elementary schoolteacher, countered that enhanced education was the solution to the crime problem, which had become exacerbated by violent gangs known as *"maras."* In a country plagued by more than 2,000 murders a year, a staggering figure for a nation of only 6.2 million,

President Ricardo Maduro

Maduro's proposal enjoyed widespread support. The violence issue was underscored just two days before the election when a Nationalist candidate for Congress was assassinated; police later arrested three employees of a Liberal deputy.

On election day, November 25, voters gave Maduro a convincing mandate of 53% to Piñeda's 44%. It was only the second Nationalist victory since democracy was implemented in 1982. The Nationalists also won the mayoralty of Tegucigalpa, but minor parties kept either of the two major parties from gaining a majority in the 128-seat Congress.

That night, Maduro told his cheering supporters from the balcony of the party headquarters, "We are not just going to administer the country; we are going to effect significant reform." He also vowed "to enforce the laws as never before." In the days that followed, he also promised

to reduce the bloated government payroll, to streamline the bureaucracy and to make it more efficient, and to crack down on abuses of privileges by government officials. For one thing, he said he would forbid public servants from flying first-class at taxpayer expense.

The gangs evidently took Maduro's promises seriously. In January, police foiled a plot by one gang to assassinate the president-elect two days before his inauguration. He was duly sworn in on January 27, 2002.

Culture: Honduran culture is almost entirely based on that of its colonial conquerors. The ancient Mayan civilization, the subject of intensive research and archaeological exploration for more than 100 years, had declined many centuries prior to the arrival of the Spaniards. An isolated burial site with Spanish artifacts was supposed to belie this well–known fact, but it is most likely an isolated discovery of a burial site, not a civilization.

Moorish–Spanish architecture prevails throughout most of the nation, particularly in the beautiful churches built during the centuries since the arrival of Roman Catholicism. Education is compulsory through the age of 15, but there is a serious shortage of trained teachers, a lack of schools and little effort to enforce the educational law. Higher education is available, including that offered by the National University of Honduras, established in the capital city in 1847. Only a small percentage of Hondurans engage in such studies.

The folklore and music of Honduras are not distinctive, bearing a close resemblance to those of the other Central American nations. Culture division exists between the bustling cities and the isolated, mountainous rural areas—the people of the lonely countryside have been almost completely bypassed by the civilization of the more mundane city people.

Economy: Honduras is a classic example of a "banana republic," with a small aristocracy, almost no middle class and a large peasant population that lives on a per capita income of less than $800 per year. Most of the nation's farmland is controlled by U.S.–owned banana firms and by a few huge cattle ranches. Mountainous terrain and periodic droughts limit farm output and methods are primitive. Most industry is foreign–owned. Coffee production has recently replaced bananas as the chief source of foreign exchange, followed by lumber, meat, sugar, cotton and tobacco. Continued balance–of–payments problems left the treasury nearly bankrupt by mid–1987 while the nation's debt has grown to $3 billion—the size of the annual gross national product. This is the highest ratio in Central America and indicates that substantial credit and borrowing will be required for years.

In this mountainous nation, passengers and freight share a flight

Honduras remains one of the three poorest countries of Latin America, along with Haiti and neighboring Nicaragua, and all three were buffeted by powerful hurricanes in 1998—Haiti by Georges and Honduras and Nicaragua by Mitch.

Largely because of the devastation caused to the banana crop, real GDP growth declined from 4.5% in 1997 to 3% in 1998, and for 1999 it was –3%. It rebounded to 6.3% in 2000 and tapered off to 4.0% in 2001. Per capita income has been stagnant for years—$643 in 1998, $650 in 1999, $698 in 2000 and $720 in 2001. The external debt leaped from an already burdensome $3.5 billion in 1998 to $4.4 billion in 1999. Unemployment doubled, from 6.3% to 12%. Inflation, mercifully, declined from 15.7% to 11.6%. Mitch was a disaster from which it will take this already prostrate economy years—perhaps decades—to recover.

The Future: Although the Liberal Party retained control of Honduras in the 1997 elections, when the septuagenerian Reina placed the presidential sash on the young shoulders of Flores it marked as symbolic a shift from one generation to another as when John Kennedy succeeded Dwight Eisenhower. With the 2001 election, the peaceful transition from the long-dominant Liberal Party to the opposition National Party augured well for Honduras' still-struggling democracy. Even though the two parties are so similar in outlook that the transition represents little in the way of policy change, and although the young Flores has been succeeded by an older man, the business-like Maduro has the opportunity to make some significant and long-needed changes in the administration of the country if he takes his reform promises seriously.

Waiting to go into a stadium for a soccer game

Jamaica

Dunn's River Falls near Ocho Rios on the north–central coast, a 600–foot stairstep waterfall which is one of the island's favorite attractions.

Area: 4,470 square miles.

Population: 2.6 million (estimated).

Capital City: Kingston (Pop. 710,000, estimated).

Climate: The coastal climate is hot and humid; the uplands are moderate, variable and pleasant.

Neighboring Countries: This island state, the third largest of the Greater Antilles, lies about 100 miles south of Cuba and 100 miles west of the southwestern tip of Haiti.

Official Language: English.

Other Principal Tongues: A distinct variety of English spoken with a very rhythmic pattern.

Ethnic Background: African Negro and mulatto, with a very small European minority. There are prominent Chinese and East Indian minorities.

Principal Religion: Protestant Christianity (Anglican); the Roman Catholic Church and other Protestant sects are very active, as is Rastafarianism, which holds that former Ethiopian Emperor Haile Selassie was the reincarnation of Jesus Christ.

Chief Commercial Products: Alumina (partially refined bauxite), bauxite, sugar, bananas and other tropical fruits, rum. Tourism is a very important source of income

Currency: Jamaica Dollar.

Gross Domestic Product: U.S. $7.0 billion in 2001 ($2,683 per capita).

Former Colonial Status: Spanish Colony (1494–1655); British Colony (1655–1962).

Independence Date: August 6, 1962.

Chief of State: Queen Elizabeth II of Great Britain, represented by Howard Cooke, governor–general.

Head of Government: Rt. Hon. Percival James "P.J." Patterson, prime minister.

National Flag: Gold diagonal stripes, with black triangles at either side and green triangles at the top and bottom.

Jamaica is a picturesque, mountainous island about 145 miles long by 50 miles in width. The mountains run east and west, with spurs to the north and south reaching 7,420 feet in the east and descending in the west. The coastal plains are intensively cultivated and are the most densely populated. The Jamaican people are descendants of African slaves imported by Spanish and English planters. Rich soils and adequate rainfall encouraged sugar and cotton production during the colonial period, while the small valleys provided fruits and vegetables for local consumption. Jamaica possesses large deposits of bauxite and gypsum which are commercially exploited.

History: Jamaica's history is inextricably interwoven with the struggle between Spain and England for domination of

Atlantic trade in the 16th and 17th centuries. The island was discovered by Columbus in 1494 during his second voyage to the New World; the Spanish adventurer, Juan de Esquivel, settled the island in 1509, calling it Santiago. Villa de la Vega, (later, Spanish Town) was founded in 1523 and served as the capital until 1872. The native Arawak people were rapidly exterminated and Negro slaves were imported to provide labor. When Jamaica was taken by the British in 1655, the total population was about 3,000. The Spanish were completely expelled by 1660, at which time their slaves fled to the mountains. These people, known as *Maroons,* resisted all efforts to recapture them, and maintained a state of guerrilla warfare against the British through the 18th century. British title to Jamaica was confirmed in 1670, and from 1672 on, the island became one of the world's largest slave markets. By the end of the 18th century, Jamaica had a slave population in excess of 3 million, working 70 sugar, 60 indigo and 60 cacao plantations. With a profitable trade with London and an equally great illegal trade with Spanish America, the Jamaican planters were extremely wealthy. The prohibition of slave trade in 1807, freedom of the Spanish colonies by 1821 and the abolition of slavery in 1833–38, ended the plantation economy as the freed slaves took to the hills, occupying small plots of land, where their descendants are found today.

The 19th century was marked by increasing resistance to colonial rule as the economic situation deteriorated. Riots in 1865 brought about changes in the government, while disturbances in 1938 led to the establishment of dominion status in 1944 and an advance preparation for independence, granted in 1962.

Jamaica's history has also been influenced by natural disasters. A violent earthquake in 1692 destroyed Port Royal and led to the founding of Kingston. It in turn was destroyed by a 1907 earthquake, but was rebuilt. Hurricanes have also exacted their toll and revised the island's agricultural patterns. The island nation has a parliamentary system of government with a two–chamber legislature consisting of 21 senators and 60–member House of Representatives. The prime minister, selected from the majority party, chooses 13 senators and the remaining _8 are selected by the governor general with advice from the leader of the opposition party. Technically, Jamaica is still _a member of the British Commonwealth and a constitutional monarchy with the queen of Great Britain as the titular head of state. The queen appoints a governor general (a Jamaican recommended by _the prime minister) as her local representative.

By law, elections must be held every five years, but can be called by the party in power sooner. The two major political parties in Jamaica are the Jamaica Labour Party (JLP) and the People's National Party (PNP).

The Manley–Seaga Years

The ensuing two decades after 1972 were dominated by Michael Manley, whose father, Norman Manley, founded the PNP and played a key role in the independence movement, and Edward _P.G. Seaga of the JLP. Both were Caucasian. Their policies were energetically directed toward improving Jamaica, and both tried a number of ideas to accomplish this, Manley from the left and Seaga from the right. Both, however, were hamstrung by the deep–seated problem of managing a poor country in deep economic water.

Manley, who won the 1972 elections, was at the time left–of–center. He swung all the way left quickly, and by 1976 had established a centrally planned economy and forged close ties with the Soviet Union via Castro's Cuba. Government spending increased tremendously and production fell sharply. By 1980, the prime minister's spending habits had all but bankrupted the country, and his popularity, even among the poor, plummeted. Although he counted on subsidies from the Soviet Union in the same manner that Cuba was receiving funds, the money and goods never seemed to make it beyond Cuba if, indeed, it had been sent at all by an overextended Soviet Union.

With political violence rampant, Manley scheduled elections for late 1982. A violent campaign took the lives of an estimated 650 people. Manley was opposed by the leader of the Jamaica Labour Party (JLP), Edward P.G. Seaga, which, in spite of its liberal–sounding name, was right of center. Impoverished Jamaicans listened to his message and gave the JLP 51 of the 60 House seats—a landslide.

Nine years of financial caution followed, coupled with slowly established close ties to the U.S. Slow financial growth resumed, but there was criticism of Seaga because of a devaluation of currency in

Rt. Hon. Michael Manley   Errol Harvey

late 1983. He called elections abruptly, catching the PNP off balance. It boycotted the contest and the JLP won all seats in the House. Another devaluation of the currency followed, but the Jamaican economy continued to falter. Export prices for bauxite (aluminum ore) dropped in large part because of widespread recycling of the metal. Discontent over the lack of progress led to a resurgence of Manley's party in 1986, when it captured all but one of the municipal elections.

Seaga was battling a new edition of Manley, who had the foresight to realize the imminent worldwide collapse of communism. He had discarded all the old rhetoric and concentrated on attacking Seaga's record, which actually was a by-product of the miserable state of the Jamaican economy. In national elections, Manley's party captured 44 seats in 1988. But discontent again swelled when there were two currency devaluations, rising unemployment and prices and a roaring hurricane in 1988 that left a half million homeless.

Faced with growing discontent, and in failing health, the then 67–year–old

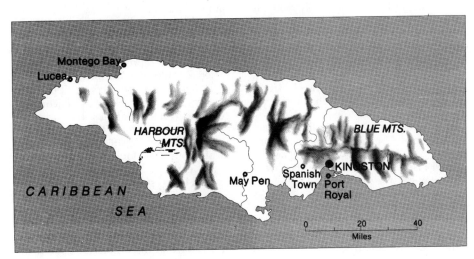

175

Rt. Hon. Edward P.G. Seaga

Manley announced his imminent retirement. In spite of allegations of earlier questionable dealing, his deputy prime minister, Percival James "P.J." Patterson succeeded. Patterson, soft–spoken and well–educated, is the first post–independence black prime minister of Jamaica.

Elections were called for March 1993. Patterson and the PNP waged an openly racist campaign ("He is one of us"), appealing to the 75% black population of the island. He and his party won in a landslide, but the PLP charged that there was wholesale fraud in the contest. It initially boycotted the legislature, but returned to claim the eight seats it won.

Recent Developments

The JLP fared little better in the general elections of December 19, 1997, in which it raised its number of seats only to 10. Overall, the PNP polled 56% of the vote to 39% for the JLP and 5% for the National Democratic Movement, which won no seats. Turnout was lower than usual, but so was the traditional politically motivated violence that in 1980 claimed 800 lives. A 60–member team of international observers, headed by former U.S. President Jimmy Carter, declared the elections generally fair, although Carter admitted there had been "serious problems." Chief among these was the peculiar Jamaican tradition of "garrison constituencies" controlled by one party or the other, a practice Carter said he had never seen in monitoring 22 elections in 15 countries. In several cases, all the ballots in a box were cast for one party.

A political era, and a dynasty, ended when Manley died of prostate cancer on March 6, 1997. Fidel Castro was among those attending his funeral. Manley was buried next to his father.

In July 2001, Patterson was forced to mobilize the entire 3,000-man army to quell violence between gangs suspected of ties to the two major parties that left 28 dead in and around Kingston. He and Seaga held an unusual three-hour meeting in August aimed at reducing the partisan violence, but there were new outbreaks in September and October 2001 and in January 2002 that left scores dead, including several children. There was a total of 1,140 murders in Jamaica in 2001, a 28% increase over 2000, and the violence has begun affecting the all-important tourism industry as hotels report a wave of cancellations.

A special commission investigating the July 2001 outbreak concluded its work in March 2002, but the report was criticized by Amnesty International as one-sided because it relied solely on the testimony of the police and military forces. Not surprisingly, the report concluded that the security forces had acted properly. For his part, Seaga was called to testify before the commission but he refused.

Parliamentary elections must be held by December 2002.

Culture: The Jamaican people have inherited a vibrant culture. Their musical expression is found in the hypnotic rhythms of "reggae," a style popularized by Bob Marley, Jimmy Cliff and Peter Tosh. Reggae, grounded in the Rastafarian religion, is the basis of a thriving recording industry in Jamaica and has achieved international acclaim.

Rastafarianism, or "Rasta," as its adherents call it, is a Christian cult with African roots. Its central tenet is that Haile Selassie, the late emperor of Ethiopia, was the reincarnation of Jesus Christ. The "dreadlock" hair style is a distinctive feature of this faith.

Performing arts have been exemplified by such groups as the National Dance Theatre and the Jamaica Folk Singers, which take the country's dance and song abroad. Kingston and almost all of the larger resort towns have excellent theatrical presentations.

The National Gallery of Art, established in 1974, houses a collection of priceless works executed by Jamaican artists, but also contains representative works centuries old and new ones from many nations. Local artists, potters, sculptors and weavers produce works which encompass all schools and techniques. They range in price from $10 into the thousands. Many art galleries and craft shops are found throughout this lovely island with its broad expanse of palm–lined beaches washed by crystal–clear waters.

Tourist guides advise strongly against thieves and pickpockets and warn one never to wander around alone. Some areas of Kingston are off limits to any sensible visitor, and further advice is not to get

Rt. Hon. P. J. Patterson, Prime Minister

involved in local night life unless you have a Jamaican friend. However, more than 1 million visitors a year have been traveling to Jamaica's structured resorts without risk—access to them is limited.

Handguns abound in Jamaica and are the favored means of "settling" all disputes. A "Gun Court" was established more than a decade ago to hand down stiff sentences for illegal firearm activity. Capital punishment was abated after 1988, but it was reinstituted in 1999. All appeals must be completed within six months; execution will again be by hanging.

Economy: Rich bauxite deposits, tourism and agriculture have dominated Jamaica's economy, and the financial conditions of the nation have been traditionally closely tied to these assets. The long–range outlook for the island's economy is linked to diversification and expansion. The Seaga government focused upon agricultural development. The goal was to become self–sufficient in food production as well as to capture a share in the lucrative U.S. market for winter vegetables. However, a winter vegetable plantation developed with Israeli cooperation was shut down because of lack of profits.

Although Jamaica's business community was buoyed by the election of pro–business Seaga and private investment did rise somewhat, foreign capital for economic development continues to be slow in responding. A lowered annual inflation rate (5%) of the 1980s climbed back to 22% in the 1990s. Tourism is centered around all–inclusive resorts (definitely "code" words, meaning native Jamaicans are excluded) in which people from the United States and Europe bask in the sun.

Marijuana is plentiful in Jamaica and is exported to the United States informally.

Its availability is a large factor in the Jamaican crime rate, which is unacceptable by any standard.

An economic dilemma that has no immediate solution is the crushing external debt, which in 2000 stood at $3.1 billion, almost half of GDP. The per capita GDP of $2,683 is deceptively high, because it is inequitably distributed. Moreover, unemployment was 15.5% in both 2000 and 2001, which is at least partially responsible for the alarming increase in crime; culture is another factor. GDP growth has been dismal for years: –1.8% in 1996, –2.4% in 1997, 0.5% in 1998, -0.4% in 1999, 0.8% in 2000 and 2.0% in 2001.

The Future: What future, a cynic might well ask. Jamaica is plagued by a moribund economy based on market-sensitive commodities such as bauxite ore and sugar, and a culture of political violence and common crime that is threatening the only other potential source of foreign exchange: tourism. Jamaica needs visionary leadership but doesn't have it. And even if it did, how can one leader transform an entire culture? It cannot happen under even the imperfect democracy that Jamaica has. Parliamentary elections must be held by December 2002, and with the current wave of violence, they are likely to be the bloodiest since 1980.

Netting a catch, Jamaica

Mexico City in 1962 . . .

. . . and on the worst days of pollution

The United Mexican States

STATES OF MEXICO

BAJA CALIFORNIA NORTE

SONORA

CHIHUAHUA

COAHUILA

BAJA CALIFORNIA SUR

DURANGO

SINALOA

ZACATECAS

NUEVO LEON

TAMAULIPAS

SAN LUIS POTOSI

GULF OF MEXICO

QUINTANA ROO

NAYARIT

AGUASCALIENTES

GUANAJUATO

QUERETARO

HIDALGO

DISTRITO FEDERAL

Mexico City

YUCATAN

JALISCO

TLAXCALA

CAMPECHE

PACIFIC OCEAN

COLIMA

MICHOACAN

VERA CRUZ

TABASCO

MEXICO

GUERRERO

OAXACA

CHIAPAS

MORELOS

PUEBLA

Area: 767,919 square miles.

Population: 97.4 million (growth, 1.8% per year).

Capital City: Mexico City (Pop. 20 million, estimated).

Climate: Hot, wet on the coast; milder winters, hot summers in the dry north; mild, dry winters in the central highlands.

Neighboring Countries: United States (North); Guatemala and Belize (South).

Official Language: Spanish.

Other Principal Tongues: Various Indian dialects (the census of 1960 identified 52 non–Spanish–speaking groups); English.

Ethnic Background: *Mestizo*, (mixed Spanish and Indian, 60%); Indian and predominantly Indian, (30%); White or predominantly white (9%); other (1%).

Principal Religion: Roman Catholic Christianity.

Chief Commercial Products: Petroleum, petroleum products, border assembly plants, tourism, cotton, coffee, non–ferrous metals, shrimp, sulfur, fresh fruit and vegetables, clothing.

Currency: Peso.

Gross Domestic Product: U.S. $540 billion in 2001 ($5,460 per capita).

Former Colonial Status: Spanish Colony (1510–1821).

Independence Date: September 16, 1810 (observed); September 27, 1821 (achieved).

Chief of State: Vicente Fox Quesada (b. July 2, 1942), president (since December 1, 2000).

National Flag: Green, white and red vertical stripes with the national coat of arms (an eagle strangling a snake) in the white stripe.

Mexico is a vast upland plateau lying between the two branches of the Sierra Madre Mountains plus the low–lying Yucatán Peninsula. The Sierra Madre range enters Mexico in the south from Guatemala at elevations from 6,000 to 8,000 feet, then dips to low hills in the Isthmus of Tehuantepec and then rises abruptly to a jumble of scenic high peaks and inter–mountain basins. Mexico City is located in one of the most beautiful of these. From this point northward, the Sierra Madre Occidental (west) runs to Arizona in the U.S. and the Sierra Madre Oriental (east) proceedsnortheast to the border of Texas. The eastern mountains are not as high as their counterpart in the west.

Mountains and their plateaus occupy two thirds of the land area of Mexico. The highest elevations are found south of Mexico City, where Citlaltepetl (the highest 18,696 feet) with an almost perfect conical shape, is reminiscent of Fujiyama in Japan. Mountains and plateaus drop gradually toward the north. The western range descends steeply to the Pacific Ocean with few passes, while the eastern range is more gentle, with gaps to the Gulf of Mexico at Tampico and Veracruz.

The western mountain slopes, the northern plateau and the peninsula of Lower California (*Baja California*) are arid; the southern inter–mountain valleys receive moderate rainfall; the eastern slopes and the Gulf of Mexico coast receive up to 100 inches of rainfall between the months of June and December.

The whole of Mexico lies in the tropical and subtropical zones; however, climatically, altitude is a more important influence than latitude. Temperatures are hot between sea level and 3,000 feet, temperate between 3,000 feet and 6,000 feet and cold above the latter height. The majority of Mexico's population is found in the southern part of the plateau at elevations between 3,000 and 7,000 feet.

History: Mexico has a rich, dramatic and colorful history that for the purposes of this chapter can be divided roughly into four periods: pre-Conquest, colonial, post-independence and post-revolutionary. Modern Mexico remains heavily influenced by its past, which must be explored if the current realities and dynamics there are to be understood.

The Pre–Conquest Period

A number of succeeding civilizations thrived in the land area that is now Mexico south of the Tropic of Cancer for more than a millennium before the arrival of the Spanish, among them the Toltecs, Mixtecs, Zapotecs and Olmecs. The Toltecs, who flourished on the central plateau in about the ninth and 10th centuries of the Christian era, are remembered for their development of metallurgy as well as for worshiping a deity known as Quetzalcoatl, or the feathered serpent. When the Toltec civilization collapsed, it was attributed to the departure of Quetzalcoatl to the lands beyond the eastern sea, though he promised to return one day to reclaim his dominions. Six centuries later, it was to become a self–fulfilling prophecy.

Perhaps the greatest of these early peoples, however, were the Mayas, whose empire extended from central Mexico as far south as modern–day Honduras. They were an advanced, if somewhat barbaric, people, paradoxically developing remarkable mathematical, astronomical, engineering, agricultural and medical knowledge even as they practiced rituals that included human sacrifice. The ruins of some of their greatest cities lie in present-day Mexico, such as Chichén Itzá on the Yucatán Peninsula and Palenque in the state of Oaxaca. This great empire suddenly and mysteriously disappeared in about the 15th century.

To the north, even before the decline of the Mayas, another great civilization began to flower: the Aztecs. They, too, devel-

The ruins of the Maya civilization's temple of Chichen–Itza near Mérida, Yucatán.

oped advanced knowledge in the sciences and medicine, but also practiced a barbaric cruelty to vassal tribes that eventually would lead to their undoing. According to legend, the Aztec god Huitzilopochtli instructed the tribal priests that their capital should be established where they found an eagle perched upon a cactus devouring a serpent. This omen was seen on an island in Lake Texcoco in the great central valley of Mexico in the early 14th century, and consequently the Aztecs began building their great city, Tenochtitlán, upon man–made islands in the lake connected by causeways to the mainland. With its network of canals for streets, the Spanish later dubbed Tenochtitlán, the "Venice of the New World," but the venue also explains why parts of modern–day Mexico City are sinking. The omen, of course, later became the basis for the modern–day symbol of the Mexican Republic, which graces the national flag.

The Aztec empire had reached its zenith by the end of the 15th century, and Tenochtitlán was as resplendent as any city of the Old World. In 1503, Moctezuma II ascended the throne, destined to be the last of the Aztec emperors. In February 1519, a force of 500 Spaniards landed first in Yucatán, then in Tabasco, and finally at Vera Cruz, on the Gulf coast. In command was a young nobleman and soldier–of–fortune determined to make himself rich and famous in this new, unexplored land—Hernán Cortés. Unlike earlier Spanish freebooters who had robbed the coastal Indians, Cortés treated them benevolently and soon found in them willing allies against their oppressors, the Aztecs. Unknown to Cortés, he also had another ally in the legendary

Quetzalcoatl. When this bearded, fair-skinned stranger from across the eastern sea landed in Mexico, the superstitious Indians immediately assumed that he was the reincarnation of the feathered serpent, returning as promised to reclaim his land.

Cortés and his band marched to Tenochtitlán, where Moctezuma, also influenced by the legendary prophecy, greeted him almost as a deity. The wily Cortés, sensing an incredible opportunity, seized the emperor and, through him, issued orders to the Aztecs. The plan unraveled, however, when the Aztecs revolted against these uninvited "gods," and in

Moctezuma II

Route of the Spanish on *"la noche triste."*

the resulting melée Moctezuma was hit in the head by a rock and killed. On the night of June 30, 1520—remembered in Spanish and Mexican history as *la noche triste*—Cortés and his men had to fight their way across the narrow causeway to the mainland, suffering heavy losses. Reinforced by later arrivals from Cuba, however, he again marched on the Aztec capital with 900 men in early 1521. Meanwhile, Moctezuma had been succeeded by his 20–year–old nephew, Cuauhtémoc, who was to prove less amenable to the invaders than was his uncle. Cortés besieged the capital for three months, but despite starvation and disease, Cuauhtémoc refused to surrender. The Spaniards finally took Tenochtitlán by storm on August 13, 1521, and set it ablaze; Cortés reportedly wept at the destruction of such a beautiful city. Cuauhtémoc was captured trying to escape by canoe and brought before Cortés, who angrily blamed him for the capital's destruction. Cuauhtémoc requested that Cortés kill him, and the conqueror complied. The remainder of Mexico was subdued quickly, and the Spanish would remain for precisely 300 years.

The Colonial Period

The viceroyalty of New Spain was a vast territory extending from Central America to modern–day California, Colorado and Texas. As was true in Spain's other American colonies, the colonial experience in Mexico differed sharply from that in England's colonies farther north. For example, the wealth of the English colonies lay primarily in their fertile agricultural land, which gave rise to a class of independent small–scale farmers. Mexico, too, had rich farmland in the central plateau, which attracted Spanish fortune-seekers willing to work it. These were not small–scale farmers, however; they were the first of the *hacendados,* who ruled over vast estates like feudal lords.

Moreover, Mexico, like Peru, was blessed—or cursed, depending on one's standing in colonial society—with fabulously wealthy deposits of gold and silver, which filled the coffers of the royal treasury in Madrid and gave rise to a class of idle rich who occupied the top 1% of the social pyramid. Unlike their English counterparts, however, the Spanish did not

drive the indigenous peoples from their lands and either exile or exterminate them and import African slaves or indentured servants to perform the heavy labor. Instead, the Spanish drove the Indians from their lands and enslaved them for labor on the *haciendas* and in the mines.

Besides the soldiers and the fortune-hunters, the Spanish Crown had another ally in its quest to establish its dominion over this new territory: the Catholic Church. The first priests arrived in tandem with Cortés and set about converting the pagan inhabitants to Christianity. At first, the Indians were loathe to abandon their tribal gods in favor of the one worshiped by their oppressors, and they resented the destruction of their idols. At the same time, the veneration of saints and relics was not terribly unlike their pagan idolatry.

But in 1531, just 10 years after the Conquest, an event occurred that was to accelerate dramatically the conversion of the aborigines and would provide Mexico with an institution that remains part of its national identity. An Indian peasant named Juan Diego reported to the bishop that the Virgin Mary had appeared to him on a hillside outside the City of Mexico and had instructed him to return to gather the roses he would find there. Diego did as he was bidden and found roses lying among the cactus. He gathered them in his cloak and carried them to the bishop, but when the cloak was opened, the roses had disappeared and on the cloak was an image of the Virgin. At first skeptical, the church authorities accepted this version, which the Vatican later recognized as a bonafide miracle. The news that the Mother of God had appeared to a humble Indian peasant electrified the Indians and greatly facilitated the priests' job of bringing them into the bosom of the church. Below the hill where the roses were found was constructed the Shrine of Our Lady of Guadalupe, and over its altar still hangs the cloak of Juan Diego with the mysterious image that modern-day art experts have pronounced unexplainable. In December 2002, the Vatican canonized Juan Diego as a saint, which was a cause for national celebration.

Apart from the conversion of the Indians, there would be few changes in Mexico during the three centuries of Spanish colonial rule. There was, however, a gradual demographic change that was to have a major impact on the subsequent history of the country. Slowly, the Spanish conquerors began to pass their seed to their Indian subjects, and within a few generations a new, *mestizo* race began to grow and which would constitute a majority by the end of the colonial period. Yet, they were to be a race without any real identity, relegated by the Spanish to second-class citizenship, while resented by the Indians for their mixed ancestry. Although amorous dalliances with Indian women and the spawning of bastard children were commonly accepted, the Spanish men married women of their own race and social position, producing yet another class, the *criollos*, or creoles, people of pure European ancestry born in the New World.

The Spanish colonial experience in Mexico can only be described as exploitative. Her land and peoples were seen to exist only for the enrichment of the Crown. While England experienced the Renaissance, the Protestant Reformation, the Enlightenment and the Glorious Revolution, whose ideals were exported to its American colonies, Spain wallowed in the fear, tyranny and superstition of the Inquisition, which also was exported to America. Unlike the English colonies, there was no large middle class of well educated planters, merchants, craftsmen and intellectuals. Eventually the ideas of Locke, Rousseau and Voltaire did trickle into Mexico via a most unlikely source— the king himself. The sole exception to the succession of reactionary, divine-right monarchs was Carlos III, a reasonably en-

lightened sovereign who reigned from 1758–1788. Appalled when he learned of the abuses of power that characterized colonial rule in Mexico, Carlos instituted a number of reforms that improved local administration and facilitated trade. He also encouraged science and the arts, expanded education and appointed competent viceroys to carry out his ideas. At the same time, his French-inspired anticlericalism, exemplified by his expulsion of the Jesuits from Mexico, caused alarm within the church, which had heretofore enjoyed great wealth and privileges in the colony. As often happens when reforms are undertaken, there can be no turning back the clock. When Carlos died—on the eve of the French Revolution—he was succeeded by his pathetic son, Carlos IV, who was dominated by his wife who, in turn, was dominated by her unscrupulous paramour, Manuel de Godoy.

The misrule of Carlos IV contrasted so sharply with the enlightened rule of his father that resentment soon set in. Mexico already had enough reason for resentment by the end of the 18th century. The *criollos* resented the social superiority of the

Father Miguel de Hidalgo

Spanish-born elite, whom they referred to disparagingly as *gachupines,* or the ones with spurs. The *mestizos* and the Indians, meanwhile, chafed under the oppression

This cathedral was erected on the site of the humble church in the town of Dolores— now Dolores Hidalgo, Guanajuato—where on September 16, 1810, Father Miguel Hidalgo rang the bell to summon the peasants to take up arms against their Spanish oppressors.

Photo by the author.

of their Spanish masters. For 20 years after Carlos III's death, these resentments continued to ferment, while news of the American and French revolutions gave rise to talk of independence. Ironically, it was the French themselves, in the form of Napoleon Bonaparte, who were to become the catalysts for Mexican independence.

In 1808, the detested Carlos IV abdicated and was succeeded by his son, Fernando VII. Lured to Paris by Napoleon, both were imprisoned and replaced on the Spanish throne by Napoleon's brother, Joseph, whose "reign" was supported only by French bayonets. The resulting power vacuum in Madrid threw Mexico and all of Spain's American colonies into turmoil. For two years the various factions—the *gachupines* and the *criollos*, the liberals and conservatives, debated whether to maintain their allegiance to an imprisoned king or to rule themselves in his stead. Cells of independence–minded creoles sprang up in the major towns, and the one in the city of Querétaro included a liberal priest from the town of Dolores who had endeared himself to his Indian and *mestizo* parishoners—Miguel de Hidalgo. On September 16, 1810, as a Spanish force moved toward Querétaro to arrest Father Hidalgo and other conspirators, the priest rang the bells of the church in Dolores to assemble his parishoners and declared that the moment had come to take up arms against their oppressors. The date of the famous *Grito*, or cry, of Dolores, has been observed ever since as Mexico's independence day.

As with the U.S. War of Independence, the struggle in Mexico was to be long, bloody, tedious and marked by discouraging reverses that would continue for 11 years. Father Hidalgo quickly assembled a rag–tag "army" of peasants who, motivated by a quest for social liberation as much as for independence, eagerly followed their creole leader. The rebels marched inexorably southward, gaining momentum, defeating the better–armed and trained but hopelessly outnumbered Spaniards. Yet, on the very threshhold of Mexico City, Hidalgo lost his nerve and retreated. He would never regain the momentum. The Spanish counterattacked and defeated the rebel army at the Battle of Calderón, and Hidalgo fled to the northern mountains. There a trusted comrade betrayed him and other rebel leaders to the Spanish, who captured them. On July 31, 1811, the father of Mexican independence was defrocked and executed by firing squad in Chihuahua, and his head was sent to Guanajuato, where it remained on public display until independence was achieved.

However, the Spanish soon learned that the cause of independence did not die with Hidalgo. Another creole priest, José María Morelos, a man with more military skills than Hidalgo, raised a guerrilla army and took the offensive. Like Hidalgo before him, Morelos enjoyed the initiative for a time, scoring a succession of victories before he, too, was betrayed, captured and shot in 1815. Yet, still more leaders arose to take up the cause.

Meanwhile, the fall of Napoleon and the restoration of Fernando VII to the throne eliminated the issue of who was in charge in Madrid, but by then the movement for independence had taken on a life of its own. Fernando VII dispatched more troops to quell the uprising and, in a byzantine maneuver, even negotiated with Mexican conservatives a scheme by which Fernando would leave Madrid and become the king of an independent Mexico. This occurred after Spanish liberals had forced him to swear to a constitution he abhorred. A pivotal moment in the war came when Agustín Iturbide, a competent officer in the Spanish army, defected and took up the cause of independence. He issued a decree, called the *Plan de Iguala,* under which an independent Mexico would be governed either by Fernando or another European monarch, the *gachupines* and *criollos* would become social equals, and the church would retain its privileges. The two principal rebel generals, Vicente Guerrero and Guadalupe Victoria, embraced the plan, and one by one the major cities fell in behind. Finally, faced with the inevitable, the newly arrived Spanish viceroy also accepted the *Plan de Iguala,* and on September 27, 1821, the Spanish abandoned Mexico City to Iturbide's army—300 years and one month after Cortés had taken it from Cuauhtémoc.

The Post–Independence Period

Just as the colonial period lasted exactly 300 years, the post–independence period would span 99, from 1821, when Iturbide triumphantly entered Mexico City, until 1920, when another military hero, Alvaro Obregón, would assume the presidency and begin to consolidate the gains of the Revolution. Those 99 years would prove to be the bloodiest and most contentious in the country's history, being marked by intrigue, betrayal, dictatorships and civil war. Few of the key players of this period would die quietly in their beds of old age.

The struggle for independence had found the various segments of Mexican society—the privileged creoles, the *mestizos* and the Indians—fighting together in a peculiar alliance against a common enemy. With the departure of the Spaniards, however, the alliance became unraveled and friction inevitably developed among the classes. Moreover, as they fled, the *gachupines* took with them what little treasure remained, leaving the new country virtually bankrupt. Compounding Mexico's travails, the Spanish did not bequeath

General Agustín Iturbide

a strong governmental infrastructure the Mexicans could build upon for self–rule. As was the case in other emerging Latin American republics, such as Chile and Colombia, Mexico's first century and beyond would be marked by a struggle between the forces of conservativism—the landed gentry and the clergy—and liberalism patterned after the ideals of the French and American revolutions.

The Liberals, understandably in the majority, counted on the support of the *mestizo* and Indian masses, whose cause they ostensibly championed. Fiercely anticlerical, the Liberals nonetheless were pragmatic enough to recognize that the devoutly Catholic masses would never accept such a radical concept as Protestantism. The Liberals' opposition to the properties and privileges of the church led to the embrace of Freemasonry, a secret society with ancient roots in Europe and the Near East that remains influential among the governing elite to this day.

Unfortunately for the Liberals, the concept of Jeffersonian democracy was to prove unfeasible in a land where the vast majority of the population was illiterate, where there was no democratic tradition to build upon and where the lines of communication were too primitive for effective centralized government. That situation suited the outnumbered Conservatives just fine, many of them being local *caciques*, or strongmen, who wanted no interference from Mexico City. Also unfortunately for the Liberals, the generals who held the genuine power, backed by the cannon, the musket and the bayonet,

Mexico City street scene in the early 19th century

opted to side with the Conservatives because it was they who possessed what wealth the country still had. The generals, quite simply, were bought off, rewarded for their services with land and treasure. As many a Mexican leader would discover over the next century, the lifespan of the generals' loyalty coincided with that of the payroll.

Iturbide, the conquering hero of the moment but also a man of unbridled ambition and pretentiousness, soon "amended" the *Plan de Iguala*. Instead of a European monarch, he himself would become emperor of Mexico, and he had the military forces to enforce that decision. The country was to witness the tragicomic spectacle of a woefully expensive coronation that the country could ill afford. Iturbide proved a less able administrator than he had a military commander, however. After a little more than a year, his governmental ineptitude, coupled with his profligate spending on the ridiculous trappings of monarchy, left the government bankrupt. That meant, of course, that he couldn't pay the army, which

quickly overthrew him and sent the hemisphere's first "emperor" into exile. When he returned uninvited in 1823, he was arrested and shot.

With the fall of Iturbide, Mexico at last became a republic, the Liberals came to power, and in 1824 they promulgated the first of Mexico's three reasonably enlightened constitutions. Guadalupe Victoria (the inspirational *nom de guerre* of Félix Fernández) became the first president, and he was succeeded in 1828 by the third great military hero of independence, Vicente Guerrero. Alas, as was the case with Iturbide before them, their proficiency on the battlefield proved of little value in the halls of government. Both were crude, abrasive men who alienated their own congress as well as the Conservatives. Mexico dissolved into chaos and in 1830 the Conservatives seized power in a *coup d'etat*. When Guerrero fled and took to the field to combat the usurpers, the deposed president was betrayed, captured and shot, like Hidalgo and Morelos before him. Also like Morelos, a southern state later was named in his honor.

Into this volatile situation was to stride a charismatic figure who was to dominate the country off and on for the next 30 years: Antonio López de Santa Anna. A former Spanish officer who, like Iturbide, had joined the independence movement, Santa Anna was the quintessential Latin American *caudillo*, the charismatic man on horseback who rules with an iron fist to maintain order. At the time of the Conservative coup, he was the commander of the garrison in Vera Cruz (today spelled Veracruz) where the all–important customs house was located. Santa Anna rebelled against the Conservative government in 1832. By the end of the year the grateful Liberals ill–advisedly made him president and Valentín Gómez Farías, a Zacatecan who would be the guiding force of Mexican Liberalism for 30 years, vice president. On the four occasions he would enjoy the supreme power of the republic, Santa Anna followed a curious practice of retiring to his *hacienda* in Vera Cruz and leaving the day–to–day responsibilities of governing the country to surrogates until such time as the situation demanded his strong hand.

Betraying the Liberals who had mistakenly hailed him as their champion, Santa Anna dissolved the Constitution of 1824, assumed dictatorial powers, and began calling himself the "Napoleon of the West." Liberals in the state of Zacatecas rose in revolt, and Santa Anna mercilessly suppressed them. Then the Anglo–American settlers of the far northern province of Texas, unaccustomed to being ruled by despots, also rebelled. In what is now a legendary epic in Texas history, Santa Anna marched into Texas in 1836 with an army of 6,000 men, killed the 187–man garrison at the mission fortress of the Alamo in San Antonio de Bexar after a

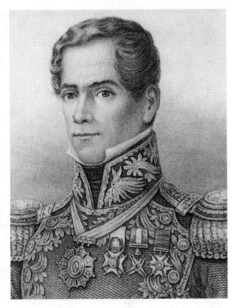

General Antonio López de Santa Anna

desperate and bloody battle, ordered the execution of the 300 Texans who had surrendered the fort at Goliad, then swept eastward almost to the border of Louisiana. There he was defeated and captured by the army of General Sam Houston at the Battle of San Jacinto.

Houston, himself as skilled at politics as he was at war, bartered Santa Anna for Texan independence rather than hanging him, then sent the defeated dictator to Washington to meet with President Andrew Jackson. Santa Anna returned to Mexico in disgrace, retired again to his *hacienda*, and waited patiently for his country's call. It came in 1838, when the French landed an invasion force to impose collection of debts. In the ensuing battle, Santa Anna's leg was shot off by a French cannon ball, and again he became a national hero. His leg was ceremoniously buried in the cathedral in Mexico City and in 1841, at the height of the latest Liberal–Conservative power struggle, he again became dictator. An efficient tax–collector, he was an equally extravagant spender. As had happened to Iturbide, the army deposed

him in 1844 when he was unable to meet its payroll and sent him into exile in Cuba.

Meanwhile, a border dispute with the United States erupted into full–scale war in 1846, and Santa Anna was recalled from exile to take the field against the invaders from the north. Cunning as ever, Santa Anna slipped through the U.S. naval blockade by convincing American agents that he would make peace if he returned to Mexico. Instead, he was named acting president and took up arms against the Americans. Defeated by General Zachary Taylor at the Battle of Buena Vista near the city of Saltillo in February 1847, Santa Anna nonetheless sent back dispatches to Mexico City declaring that he had won a resounding victory. Returning to the capital a hero, he again assumed dictatorial powers. He next opposed General Winfield Scott's army, which had landed in Vera Cruz and was marching on Mexico City. Again Santa Anna was ignominiously defeated, and the capital fell to the Americans. Under the resulting Treaty of Guadalupe–Hidalgo, Mexico ceded nearly half its territory, from Texas to California. In return, the United States paid Mexico $15 million—a welcome deposit for the bankrupt treasury. Santa Anna again went into exile, this time to Venezuela.

There followed a few years of stable and efficient Liberal civilian governments, but in 1853 Santa Anna, this time the champion of the Conservatives, again was placed in power by *coup d'etat*. To raise money, he sold off another tract of land to the United States—the Gadsden Purchase, in what is today southern Arizona and New Mexico—for $10 million.

Of course, he quickly and frivolously squandered the money. The Liberals, under the leadership of Ignacio Comonfort, rebelled against the dictator and published the *Plan de Ayutla*, which called for the drafting of a new constitution. Santa Anna fell from power for the fourth and final time in 1855 and spent most of the rest of his life in Cuba. Eventually allowed to return, he died in poverty and obscurity in 1876.

Mexico's second Liberal constitution was promulgated in 1857 under the presidency of Comonfort, but it was so anticlerical that the archbishop threatened anyone who took the required oath with excommunication. By January 1858, the Conservatives had again overthrown the government, but this time the two sides found themselves in full–scale civil war, which was to last for three years and leave the country torn apart. Two Liberal champions emerged during the conflict who would later play decisive roles in Mexican history.

One was a full–blooded Zapotec Indian who was governor of Oaxaca: Benito Juárez. It was he who would become the moral and spiritual guardian of Liberalism and social justice and become revered

as the greatest of Mexico's leaders. The other was a *mestizo* guerrilla leader who would betray the cause of reform and become one of Mexico's most reviled villains: Porfirio Díaz.

After Comonfort was deposed, Juárez was named president and removed the constitutionalist government to the north, where it enjoyed the support of the United States. The Liberals won the civil war, and on January 11, 1861, Juárez became the newest hero to triumphantly enter Mexico City, but in keeping with his humble image he did so in a plain black carriage. He was reelected president, but the Conservatives were not yet ready to admit defeat. They resurrected the old idea of installing a European monarch on a Mexican throne, and they found a willing ally in France's Emperor Napoleon III.

Emboldened by the Americans' distraction with their own civil war, Napoleon

Benito Juárez

landed an army at Vera Cruz and began the traditional march of conquerors to Mexico City. But at Puebla, the stubborn Mexican defenders dealt the French a stinging defeat on May 5, 1862, still commemorated as a national holiday—*el Cinco de Mayo*. The victory was fleeting, however, and the French soon captured the capital. Juárez again fled to the north with his government. In his place the Conservatives invited Archduke Maximilian, brother of the Hapsburg emperor of Austria, to reign as Mexico's second emperor.

Maximilian and his wife, Carlotta, a member of the Belgian royal family, are two of history's truly tragic figures. The Conservatives duped Maximilian into believing that he had been elected emperor in a plebiscite, and he and Carlotta arrived in Mexico expecting to be treated as beloved sovereigns. Instead, they found the country at civil war over his intervention. Ironically, Maximilian was himself something of a liberal, and he shocked the Conservatives by implementing some of the very reforms the Liberals had advocated. The Conservatives soon cooled toward their new emperor, and the *Juarista* army began scoring victories over the French and Conservative forces. With the end of the U.S. Civil War, the U.S. government warned Napoleon III to remove its forces from Mexico or the United States would intervene to enforce the Monroe Doctrine. To compound the woes of the beleaguered Maximilian, Carlotta began showing signs of mental instability. She was evacuated to Europe, where she sought unsuccessfully to win an audience with Napoleon III. Faced with the threat of war with the United States and lack of success on the battlefield, Napoleon III abandoned Maximilian to his fate. After a final defeat at Querétaro, the emperor and his army surrendered. Maximilian and two of his generals were executed by firing squad atop the Hill of Bells, today a

Emperor Maximilian of Mexico

national landmark, a few days later on June 19, 1867. Carlotta spent the remaining 60 years of her life in insanity.

Once again, Juárez triumphantly entered Mexico City and was soon reelected to a third term. By most accounts, the Juárez presidency was the most honorable and enlightened in Mexico's troubled history, before or since. There was no shameless self–enrichment such as Santa Anna and others had engaged in. The industrial base began to grow, and railroads were built. Juárez also began to implement the reforms of the Constitution of 1857, and he devoted special attention to secular education, particularly for the hapless Indians who had long been treated as third–class citizens. This, of course, alienated Juárez from even the Liberal creoles. Moreover, in the name of economy and to guard against the praetorianism that had been the bane of Mexico since independence, Juárez had brusquely cashiered most of the officers and soldiers from the army with scant compensation for their services during 10 years of civil war. There were the inevitable military rebellions, which Juárez crushed as ruthlessly as his predecessors had. In the 1867 election, Juárez was opposed by one of his own generals, Porfirio Díaz.

Juárez was elected to a fourth term in 1871, which raised accusations that he hoped to become merely another dictator. In reality, the 1871 election was quite fair by Mexican standards, and Juárez failed to receive a majority, so his election was decided by Congress. Alas, Juárez died suddenly of a heart attack on July 18, 1872, and with him died Mexico's greatest hope for democracy with social reform. Vice President Sebastián Lerdo de Tejada, a respected and honest intellectual, succeeded him and was elected to a full term that fall, but when he chose to run again in 1876 Díaz issued a *pronunciamiento* that cynically purported to uphold the Liberal cause of "effective suffrage, no reelection." After a brief military struggle, the *Porfirista* forces captured the capital and forced Lerdo into exile. Díaz became provisional president, ushering in the longest dictatorship in Mexican history.

The Díaz dictatorship was a veritable yin–yang dichotomy of good and evil, darkness and light. On the one hand, Mexico was to experience unprecedented modernization and economic development during the 35 years he would control the country. On the other, Díaz ruled in the style of the classic Latin American *caudillo*, enjoying absolute power through a principle called *pan o palo* (bread or club). Díaz could be exceedingly generous in return for whole–hearted support, but those who refused his good offices faced imprisonment, economic deprivation, or worse. Turning his back on the Liberal principle of nationalism, he opened the doors to massive foreign investment,

General Porfirio Díaz

chiefly U.S. and British, which capitalized the country and expanded the middle class but left much of Mexico's land and wealth in foreign hands. Himself a *mestizo*, Díaz nonetheless abandoned Juárez's goal of improving the lot of the Indians, who were to continue to languish in the feudalism to which they had been consigned since the Conquest. Díaz surrounded himself with a cadre of creole technocrats, called *científicos*, who managed the economy *so* efficiently that in 1894 Mexico recorded the first budget surplus in its history. The dictator poured much of this revenue into much–needed public works projects and into the beautification of Mexico City, which he wanted to rival the grand capitals of Europe.

Because he had come to power on a platform opposing reelection, Díaz cleverly chose one of his sycophants, Manuel González, to be "elected" in 1880. During his single term, which of course was overshadowed by Díaz, González engaged in corruption on an unprecedented scale, even for Mexico. By 1884, the public was only too happy to forget about Díaz's supposed opposition to reelection and clamored for him to retake the presidency. He maintained himself in power thereafter through six rigged elections, in some of which he awarded himself a unanimous vote! In 1904, he also extended the presidential term to six years. He concentrated all the patronage in his own hands, and enjoyed such power that he literally designated every state governor and member of Congress. Employing a system of divide–and–conquer, he pitted various factions against each other, and if one faction became too strong for his liking, he would undermine it by throwing his support to another. He did much the same thing with the officials in his government, so great was his fear of possible usurpation. So jealous was he of possible rivals, he made absolutely no preparations for an eventual successor. By the time of his last "election" in 1910, he was 80 years old and showing signs of senility, raising concerns among the ruling elite. But there also was a restiveness among the lower classes who had been bypassed in the economic development of the Díaz years. Mexico was a social powder keg.

The spark that was to set off the inevitable explosion came from an unlikely source, a short, unassuming young man from a wealthy creole ranching family in the state of Coahuila: Francisco I. Madero. Díaz had indicated in an interview with a U.S. correspondent that he would not seek reelection in 1910, a statement that had been intended to mollify the democratic sensibilities of the U.S. government but which soon became reported in Mexico. Díaz then reneged on his promise not to stand again, and the idealistic Madero announced his own candidacy against him. Díaz at first tolerated the opposition of this seemingly insignificant upstart in order to perpetuate the myth of Porfirian democracy, but Madero's campaign appearances began attracting large, enthusiastic audiences. Madero was arrested on a trumped-up charge that he was conspiring to overthrow the regime, and he was kept behind bars until after Díaz had safely "reelected" himself. Symbolically, Díaz's latest power play had coincided with his grandiose centennial celebration of Father Hidalgo's *Grito de Dolores*.

Released from jail, Madero fled to the United States and issued a *pronunciamiento*. Suddenly there were spontaneous demonstrations against the dictatorship. Reentering Mexico, Madero found influential people flocking to his standard, but he also found himself the champion of the lower classses. Among his most important supporters was a legendary bandit from Chihuahua who had become a revolution-

ary: Francisco "Pancho" Villa. Meanwhile, in the southern state of Morelos, Emiliano Zapata organized a peasant army that seized the lands of the *hacendados* and engaged in battle with Díaz's federal army. The Mexican Revolution had begun.

Within months, the 35-year-old dictatorship began collapsing like the house of cards it was. When Villa's forces captured the border city of Ciudad Juárez in May 1911, Díaz made the traditional "withdrawal" from the treasury, fled to Vera Cruz and took ship to France. He died in Paris four years later. Madero, meanwhile, became the latest hero to enter the capital to the cheers of the masses.

Unfortunately, for all his noble ideals, Madero was no Benito Juárez. He proved an inept administrator and was easily manipulated by his family and their friends, some of whom had been among Díaz's *científicos*. The masses who had joined his movement expecting genuine social revolution were soon disillusioned. But a graver threat came in the traditional form of military uprisings, this time by counterrevolutionary *Porfiristas*. The Revolution took on the aspect of a free-for-all, with Villa and Zapata battling the counterrevolutionaries in the name of social justice and Madero's creole generals fighting essentially for themselves. The U.S. ambasador, meanwhile, angered by Madero's reversal of Díaz's *carte blanche* to foreign business interests, threw his support behind the counterrevolutionaries. Faced with the possibility of military defeat, Madero entrusted the defense of his government to a general he believed to be loyal: Victoriano Huerta. But in February 1913, with the complicity of the U.S. ambassador, Huerta arrested Madero and Vice President Pino Suárez and ordered them shot, allegedly while trying to escape. Huerta then seized the presidency for himself through a Machiavellian manipulation of the constitution.

Huerta, an alcoholic and drug addict and one of the most treacherous and repugnant figures in Latin American history, immediately found himself faced with formidable opposition. He had arrested Villa shortly before Madero's death, but the wily bandit bribed his way free and fled to the north. After Madero's murder became common knowledge, both Villa and Zapata took to the field against Huerta. In Coahuila, Governor Venustiano Carranza refused to recognize Huerta's regime and in time became the acknowledged leader of the constitutionalist forces. In Sonora, a laborer–turned–businessman–turned–general, Alvaro Obregón, raised yet another army to oppose the usurper. Meanwhile, Woodrow Wilson became the U.S. president, and Huerta's naked power grab offended Wilson's democratic principles. He replaced the U.S. ambassador with one who applied pressure on the dictator. When

Francisco "Pancho" Villa

Emiliano Zapata

Francisco I. Madero

Wilson learned a shipment of German arms was en route to Mexico, he ordered the Marines to seize the port of Vera Cruz in April 1914 to prevent the guns from reaching Huerta. This intervention backfired, however, causing the various warring factions to unite temporarily in their denunciation of this new *gringo* invasion, even as the constitutionalists accepted shipments of U.S. arms. In one of the most glorious and celebrated periods of Mexican history, the twin northern armies of Villa and Obregón literally raced each other southward, taking city after city from Huerta's forces, while Zapata's revolutionaries fought their way north toward the capital. In August 1914—the very month that Europe exploded into full-scale war—Huerta fled Mexico City and made his way to Texas, where he drank himself to death a year later.

All three revolutionary armies converged on the capital, and for a few days there was near-anarchy. Order was restored as the various leaders met to discuss how Mexico was to be ruled, but peace was not yet at hand. Much to the displeasure of Villa and Zapata, Carranza was elected provisional president, and the two revolutionaries took to the field once again. This time, however, Villa met his match in Obregón, who employed modern concepts from the battlefields of Europe, such as massed machine guns and barbed wire, to decimate Villa's once-_invincible cavalry at Celaya. Driven farther north, Villa was outflanked when President Wilson allowed constitutionalist forces to use Texas railroads for troop movements. Enraged, Villa captured some American engineers and had them shot, and in March 1916 he sacked the border town of Columbus, New Mexico, killing about 40 Americans. Wilson ordered General John J. Pershing into Chihuahua in pursuit of Villa, a hopeless mission which, once again, served only to unite the warring factions against the invading *gringos*.

Even as the bloodshed droned on, Carranza summoned a constitutional convention that assembled in Querétaro in December 1916 and early the next year finalized the country's third liberal constitution. Unlike the earlier organic laws, this one guaranteed the rights of labor and decreed that property rights were secondary to the public good. The Constitution of 1917, which has decidedly socialist overtones, remains the oldest basic law in effect in Latin America. The constitution should be Carranza's legacy, but he is remembered as much for the rampant corruption that went on during his administration as for his role in the creation of a new Mexico.

The Mexican Revolution, which by most estimates claimed about 1 million lives, slowly wound down. A Carranza officer betrayed and assassinated Zapata in 1919. His armed struggle died with him,

Venustiano Carranza

although the Morelos peasants were permitted to retain the lands they had seized from the *hacendados*. Villa, meanwhile, was bribed into passivity with an amnesty and a huge *hacienda* in Durango. Though he never took up arms again, he remained such a threatening force that he, too, was assassinated in 1923. In 1920, when Carranza sought to circumvent his own constitution's ban on reelection by hand-picking a puppet successor, Obregón and others turned against him. He was forced to abandon the capital and, a few days later, was murdered in his sleep by a trusted lieutenant. Obregón's army became the latest to enter Mexico City in triumph, and Obregón was duly elected president and took office in November 1920. After 10 years of Revolution, Mexico was at peace.

Alvaro Obregón

The Post–Revolutionary Period

Obregón, unlike earlier conquering generals who became president, proved both an able and enlightened leader, the best since Juárez. There was some of the inevitable corruption, but nothing on the scale of Díaz. Himself a former laborer who became a businessman before the call to arms, Obregón was friendly to labor but chose not to enforce some of the more radical aspects of the new constitution. He did, however, begin a modest land–redistribution program, primarily to the Indian communal plots, called *ejidos*. He also allowed unprecedented press freedom and adhered to the constitution by stepping aside at the end of his term in 1924—although he essentially dictated who his successor would be. Largely because of Obregón's guidance during those first critical post–revolutionary years, Mexico embarked on a nominally democratic path with guarantees of civil liberties, rather than embracing the totalitarian experiment of the Bolsheviks who had seized power in Russia the same year the Mexican constitution was drafted. And in 1924, the very year Lenin died and was succeeded by Stalin, Obregón duly relinquished power to another revolutionary general, Plutarco Elías Calles. Although this new president was to succumb to the temptations of near–absolute power, he was certainly no Stalin.

Calles served only one term, but he was destined to wield the actual power for 10 years. His administration basically was a continuation of Obregón's, with whom he maintained a close, harmonious personal relationship. It was suggested that the two men essentially were co–presidents. Calles, however, was even less committed to the social goals of the Revolution than was Obregón, and he slowed even the modest land distribution program. On the subject of the church, however, Calles was deeply committed to the anticlerical principles that had been embodied in all three liberal constitutions. Both he and Obregón were practicing Freemasons, who are decidedly anti–Catholic and whose influence was believed to be even stronger after the Revolution. When the church opposed Calles' programs, he began enforcing all the radical anticlerical provisions of the constitution. The church's property, even the actual church buildings, were expropriated; priests were forbidden from engaging in political activity or even from wearing clerical garb on the street; foreign priests were expelled, and members of the clergy were required to register with the government. The clergy literally went on strike in 1926, refusing to say Mass for three years. Some fanatical Catholic laymen, called *cristeros*, engaged in acts of terrorism. Church-state relations remained hostile for decades. Not until 1993 did Mexico establish diplomatic relations with the Vatican.

As the election of 1928 approached, Calles and Obregón found themselves unwilling to turn over power to a third man, so the constitution was amended to allow Obregón to run for a second term. Another amendment lengthened the presidential term, as Díaz had done, from four to six years. Obregón was elected over token opposition, but just three weeks later, on July 17, he was shot to death while dining in a restaurant by a young artist who apparently was a *cristero* acting on his own initiative. An eminent intellectual, Emilio Portes Gil, was named interim president until another election could be held in 1929, although it was Calles who actually held the power. During this brief interregnum, however, an institution was established that was to be the dominant force in Mexican political life for the next 71 years. Calles and Portes Gil organized a new political party, the National Revolutionary Party, or *PNR*, that incorporated the revolutionary sectors of *campesinos*, or peasants, and organized labor under its umbrella. Its name would be changed in 1938 to the Party of the Mexican Revolution and yet again in 1946 to its current name, the Institutional Revolutionary Party, or *PRI*. Its candidate in 1929, Pascual Ortiz Rubio, won a suspiciously lopsided victory, a phenomenon that would be repeated over and over again.

Ortiz Rubio's three–year presidency is remembered as little more than a footnote because it was Calles who was really in charge. His control was so complete that when, in 1932, the president fired some officials who enjoyed Calles' support, Calles merely summoned a news conference to announce that Ortiz Rubio had resigned. The hapless president had no choice but to comply. Calles hand–picked Abelardo Rodríguez to fill out the last two years of what was to have been Obregón's term, then likewise designated a well–respected, 39–year–old former revolutionary general, Lázaro Cárdenas, as the official party's candidate for the 1934 election.

Cárdenas won by the predictable landslide, but before long the left–leaning president and the quasi–fascist Calles clashed over policy. A bloodless power struggle ensued, but this time it was Cárdenas who prevailed. The Cárdenas administration is generally regarded as the most honest and socially conscious of the post–revolutionary period. During his six years in power, Cárdenas redistributed 45 million acres of land to the peasants, compared with 19 million that had been distributed from 1920–1934. He also gave unprecedented moral and official support to organized labor. He refused to recognize the government of the victorious Generalissimo Francisco Franco at the end of the Spanish Civil War and gave refuge to thousands of defeated Republicans. But the act for which Cárdenas is best remembered was the nationalization of foreign oil companies in 1937 after the companies refused the government's terms for settling a prolonged strike. Today, despite the privatization trend sweeping Latin America, oil drilling, refining and fuel retailing remain in the hands of the state monopoly, *Petroleos Mexicanos*, or *Pemex*.

Despite the near–absolute power Mexican presidents enjoy, there was less abuse under Cárdenas than under many of his predecessors or successors. Press freedom continued to grow, and Cárdenas tolerated the establishment of a conservative opposition movement, the National Action Party, or *PAN*, in 1939. It also was Cárdenas who finally and irrevocably established the revolutionary principle of "no reelection" by stepping aside at the end of

Lázaro Cárdenas

his *sexenio*, or six–year term. Although he was to remain a respected and influential voice in Mexican politics until his death in 1970, Cárdenas made no effort to remain the power behind the throne as Calles and others had done.

However, Cárdenas chose to continue, and thus perpetuate, the decidedly undemocratic practice of Obregón and Calles of hand–picking his successor. Referred to in Mexico as *el dedazo*, or the tap of the finger, this practice was followed by all of Cárdenas' successors until Ernesto Zedillo disavowed it in 1999. By tradition, the incumbent conferred in secret about a year before the election with former presidents and a handful of top party leaders to discuss a list of possible candidates. At this stage, the heir apparent was referred to as *el tapado*, or the hidden one, whose identity became the focus of intense speculation by the public and the press. When the president announced his decision, the designated candidate was hailed by all sectors of the party and pro–*PRI* newspapers as a near–messiah and acclaimed as the greatest possible choice. The process more closely resembled the selection of a new pope by the College of Cardinals than the nomination of a presidential candidate in a supposedly democratic system; all that was missing was the emission of white smoke from the presidential palace to announce that a choice had been made. Some scholars have suggested the *PRI*'s selection process was based upon Masonic rites.

Cárdenas' choice was yet another revolutionary general, Manuel Avila Camacho, who had served as Cárdenas' defense secretary. This surprised many, because Avila Camacho was far to the right of Cárdenas. Moreover, he was a devout Catholic, which represented a sharp break with the anti–clericalism of the past. This transition established a precedent that would be seen again in the ensuing decades of alternating between presidents that were leftist and centrist, also between presidents who were dynamic and passive. Under Avila Camacho, land redistribution slowed to a glacial pace. On the other hand, World War II was to result in an economic boom for Mexico, which joined the Allies and declared war on Germany and Japan. Mexican industries churned out war supplies that were exported to the United States; relations in general between the United States and Mexico, strained since the beginning of the Revolution, finally began to improve. Avila Camacho hosted President Franklin D. Roosevelt at a meeting in Monterrey in 1943, the first time a sitting U.S. president had crossed the southern border.

As his successor in 1946 Avila Camacho picked Miguel Alemán, his *secretario de gobernación*, usually translated as interior minister, the most powerful post in the cabinet, one that is roughly the combined equivalent of the secretary of the interior and White House chief of staff in the U.S. system. Whoever holds it is automatically placed on the "short list" to be nominated for president. Unlike earlier elections, however, this time there was a serious opposition candidate in the form of Foreign Minister Ezequiel Padilla, who was disgruntled over not being selected himself. Alemán, of course, was declared the winner with 80% of the vote. How honest that vote count was remains questionable, but for Mexico even 20% for an opposition candidate was extraordinary. The transition was a watershed in modern Mexican history because Avila Camacho was to be the last general to serve as president.

Like Avila Camacho, however, Alemán was a centrist who did little more than give lip service to the socialist principles of the Revolution, but he was more dynamic and more of a visionary than his predecessor. The Mexican economy was still growing, and Alemán chose to devote much of the increased revenues to mammoth public works projects like highways and dams. He also embarked on the greatest building program since the days of Díaz, and one of the chief beneficiaries of this program was the National Autonomous University of Mexico, or *UNAM.* Moreover, Alemán greatly improved the efficiency of state–owned enterprises like *Pemex.* On the negative side, corruption reappeared on a scale reminiscent of the days of Carranza and Díaz. The president himself escaped scandal, but it was noted that he and many of his appointees left office far wealthier than they had been before.

Apparently in response to the public discontent over the corruption, Alemán chose his interior secretary, Adolfo Ruíz Cortines, as the *PRI* presidential candidate in 1952. Once again, however, a *PRI* defector, a wealthy businessman and former general named Miguel Henríquez Guzmán, launched a serious independent candidacy. Ruíz Cortines supposedly defeated the popular Henríquez and minor candidates with 77% of the vote—still questionable, but it would be the smallest percentage the *PRI* would admit to for 36 years.

Ruíz Cortines restored an atmosphere of integrity to the presidency. Lacking Alemán's flamboyance and charisma, he often was derided as colorless. But he proved an aggressive, if not demonstrative, reformer. While Alemán had constructed grand projects, Ruíz Cortines focused on roads, irrigation, schools and hospitals. Among his lasting achievements was extending the suffrage to women in 1953, and in his last year in office Mexico became for the first time a net exporter of food.

Ruíz Cortines selected his young labor secretary, Adolfo López Mateos, as the *PRI* candidate in 1958. The *PAN* for the first time mounted a reasonably serious challenge, but López Mateos won by the usual landslide, about 90%. López Mateos swung the pendulum back to the left and toward more dynamic leadership. As labor minister he had earned the respect of the unions, and there were fewer strikes during his *sexenio* than in the previous three. Land distribution, which had tapered off steadily under his three predecessors, picked up dramatically. López Mateos parceled out about 22 million acres, making him second only to Cárdenas.

The pendulum then swung sharply back toward conservatism and drabness. As his successor, López Mateos picked his interior secretary, Gustavo Díaz Ordáz, a homely, most unpresidential–looking

choice. For the first time, the *PAN* garnered more than 1 million votes in the 1964 election, and its percentage rose to just above 10%. There was nothing particularly breathtaking in the achievements of Díaz Ordáz other than the sports complex that was built for the 1968 Olympic Games. On the very eve of the games, however, something occurred that was to haunt the president until his death. The student unrest that had spread across Europe and the United States in 1968 arrived in Mexico that summer. Federal troops occupied the *UNAM* to quell a lengthy student strike. On the night of October 2, when students staged a peaceful demonstration in the Plaza de Tlatelolco in Mexico City, troops opened fire on the pretext

Manuel Avila Camacho

that snipers had fired on them. Little or no evidence supports this, but as many as 300 people were killed, hundreds more wounded and more than 1,000 arrested. It was the greatest outbreak of violence since the *cristero* revolt of the 1920s. More than 30 years later, the "Tlatelolco Massacre" remains a national controversy, with questions still unanswered.

Ironically, the man who was responsible for crushing the protests, Interior Secretary Luis Echeverría, was the man Díaz Ordáz selected to succeed him in 1970. This time the *PAN*'s percentage of the vote edged up to 13%. As if to atone for his role in the Tlatelolco incident, Echeverría swung the pendulum dramatically back to the left. Early in his term he freed hundreds of students who had been jailed for two years. He angered the United States by establishing diplomatic relations with the People's Republic of China and by speaking out against the war in Vietnam. He made a point of expressing support for Cuba's Fidel Castro and welcomed Castro on a state visit to Mexico. He refused to recognize the government of General Au-

gusto Pinochet after the 1973 coup that overthrew and killed Marxist President Salvador Allende in Chile, and he granted asylum to thousands of Chilean leftists. He ordered his U.N. delegate to support a resolution condemning Zionism as racism, but when U.S. Jews launched a boycott of Mexican resorts, he abruptly reversed course. He made pretentions about being a leader of the so–called "Nonaligned Movement" and even sought to become U.N. secretary–general upon his retirement.

On the whole, Echeverría can be described as a fountain of hollow rhetoric. He denounced capitalism, and increased the number of state–owned enterprises from 50 to 750, but pragmatically did little to interfere with free enterprise in Mexico. He talked about democratizing the *PRI,* but didn't follow through. He encouraged the creation of left–wing publications, but when the leftist editor of the daily *Excélsior,* Julio Scherer García, became too critical for his taste, Echeverría used his influence to have him fired. Scherer then launched a weekly newsmagazine, *Proceso,* which the president tried to strangle at birth by refusing to sell Scherer government–subsidized newsprint. *Proceso* survived, however, and today is the leading news weekly. Four months before he left office in 1976, Echeverría set a precedent for future presidents by making a dramatic economic move and leaving the consequences to his successor: he devalued the peso, from 12.5 to 20 to the dollar. He also bequeathed a 50% unemployment/underemployment rate and a 22% inflation rate.

That successor would be Echeverría's finance secretary, José López Portillo, who was elected without any meaningful opposition when the *PAN* refused to field a candidate in 1976 to protest what it called, not incorrectly, *PRI* electoral manipulations. In keeping with tradition, López Portillo swung the pendulum back to the right. The major departure from his predecessor's policy was to stop baiting big business, international lending institutions and the United States. He met with President Jimmy Carter, who was sworn in six weeks after himself, in Washington early in their terms and agreed to an emergency sale of Mexican natural gas to help the United States cope with the brutally cold winter of 1977. He also became the first Mexican president to address the U.S. Congress, to which he delivered a fatherly lecture about being good neighbors. Carter would later reciprocate the visit and become the first U.S. president to address the Mexican Congress—in Spanish. López Portillo later would exchange visits with Carter's successor, Ronald Reagan. López Portillo did not, however, distance himself from Fidel Castro. He also lent moral and financial support to the *Sandinista* regime in Nicaragua, which

A panoramic view of the beautiful colonial city on Guanajuato, still a center of silver mining and a popular tourist destination. The triangular park in the right foreground is the Jardín de la Unión; the University of Guanajuato, one of the oldest and most prestigious learning institutions in Mexico, is the large white building on the hill at upper left. *Photo by the author.*

came to power on his watch in 1979, and opposed Reagan's support for right–wing regimes in El Salvador and Guatemala.

Still, he wisely mended fences with the International Monetary Fund and major foreign banks and succeeded in reassuring them that Mexico was a sound credit risk again. In this he was aided by the discovery in the early 1970s of vast deposits of petroleum, by some estimates rivaling the reserves of Saudi Arabia, in the southern states of Tabasco and Chiapas. *Pemex* brought the fields on line just in time to take full advantage of OPEC's quadrupling of the world market price for oil. Mexico opted not to join OPEC, but the revenue from petroleum sales began to fill government coffers. López Portillo, like a poor man who has suddenly won the lottery, went on a wild spending spree. When the money ran out, he merely borrowed more from abroad on the assumption that the petroleum gravy train would rumble on indefinitely. He would leave office before the full weight of his folly came crashing down upon his successor.

So, too, would the massive corruption committed by López Portillo and his top officials on a scale unseen since the time

of Alemán. He became the embodiment of an old Mexican quip about the president: "The first two years he talks about corruption, the next two years he does nothing and the last two years he takes all he can." In López Portillo's case, he acquired a palatial estate called Dog Hill, with five mansions, swimming pools, stables, tennis courts and a gymnasium. On the positive side, he finally moved to give opposition parties a somewhat greater voice, while, of course, not actually jeopardizing the *PRI*'s grip on power. In the 1960s, the opposition had been reserved a maximum of 20 seats in the 197–seat Chamber of Deputies, the lower house of Congress, distributed by proportional representation. López Portillo enlarged the chamber

Former President López Portillo and family

Former President de la Madrid and family

to 400 seats, of which up to 100 could go to the opposition.

In 1982, López Portillo's final year in office, the world price of oil took a downturn and Mexico found itself in deep financial trouble. López Portillo was forced to implement a drastic—and exceedingly unpopular—austerity program that threw about 1 million bureaucrats out of work. He also was forced to devalue the peso again. In the midst of this crisis, he broke with convention by selecting as his successor his secretary of planning and budget, Miguel de la Madrid. Among other things, this shattered the long–accepted tradition of never picking a *PRI* candidate who speaks English. Not only that, but de la Madrid had earned a master's degree in public administration from Harvard University. It was, moreover, to establish a new trend of selecting presidents who are technocrats who have never held elective office, reminiscent of Díaz's *científicos*, except that these new ones received their training in the United States. In the July 1982 election, de la Madrid reportedly received 74.4% to 14% for the *PAN* candidate and 5.8% for the candidate of a coalition of left–wing parties. Just two weeks before he left office, López Portillo did something that not even the leftist Echeverría had dared to do—he nationalized the banks. On December 1, 1982, he turned over the mess he had created to de la Madrid and retired to Dog Hill.

De la Madrid was left to cope with the country's gravest economic crisis since the Depression of the 1930s. In 1983 the inflation rate was 60%, and the foreign debt continued to mushroom, from $65 billion in 1983 to $105 billion in 1988—among the greatest per capita debts in the world. Even as the president struggled to cope with this daunting challenge, the country was hammered by a dual blow in 1985. OPEC slashed the price for a barrel of petroleum by about two thirds, from roughly $30 to $10, a move that completely pulled the rug out from under the debt–ridden economy. Even nature seemed to

be against Mexico; a disastrous earthquake struck Mexico City that year, killing an estimated 10,000 people and causing $3.5 billion in property damage—much of which was attributed to shoddy construction of government–sponsored projects. The peso began to plummet against the dollar, and the country faced the kind of hyperinflation that had once plagued Argentina, Brazil and Peru. Inflation soared to more than 100% on de la Madrid's watch, and the peso dropped from 24.5 to the dollar to 2,800 by 1990. Compounding the dilemma was Mexico's burgeoning birthrate of 3.2% annually. Even in the boom times the economy had barely been able to absorb the young new workers flooding the labor market, but in these lean times the situation became especially desperate. The cardboard shanty towns on the outskirts of Mexico City grew larger and larger, and more Mexicans than ever were seeking the traditional escape route from their misery—illegal entry into the United States. This, of course, served to strain bilateral relations.

Desperate times do indeed call for desperate measures, and de la Madrid employed them. He allowed the price of Mexican crude oil to "float" instead of pegging it at an artificial price. He also began to sell off some of the government–owned enterprises whose payrolls had become bloated from *PRI* patronage. Attempts to renegotiate the foreign debt satisfied neither Mexico nor its creditors. Finally, de la Madrid succeeded in obtaining a $3.5 billion "bridging" loan from the Reagan administration in 1988.

As if de la Madrid did not have enough problems, early in his administration he was faced with still another—a scandal that erupted over the corruption committed under his predecessor. Among the high–level López Portillo officials accused of financial wrongdoing were the head of *Pemex*, who could not account for a missing 300,000 barrels of oil. Perhaps the most egregious case, one which especially outraged the public, was that of the Mexico

City police chief, who had built himself an unbelievably ostentatious estate complete with air–conditioned doghouses! The chief was prosecuted and his property was expropriated and opened to the public as a "museum of corruption." López Portillo himself managed to escape prosecution (no such action has ever been taken against a former head of state since the Revolution), but the damage to his reputation wrought by his shameless nest–feathering was irreparable and today he remains a political outcaste even within the ranks of the *PRI*.

The lean economic times and the publicizing of outrageous cases of corruption took a serious toll on the *PRI*. Up to that point, the *PRI* not only had won every presidential election since 1929, but it had never lost an election for a state governorship or a federal Senate seat and rarely lost at any level. Now, for the first time, the *PAN* began winning municipal elections and even won some directly elected seats in the Chamber of Deputies, not merely the scraps the *PRI* reserved for the opposition under proportional representation. In the 1988 presidential election, the *PRI* was to face the greatest threat to its power in its 60–year history, not from the right, but from the left. Cuauhtémoc Cárdenas, son of the revered former president and himself a member of the *PRI*, abandoned the party to organize a new left–wing movement—the Party of the Democratic Revolution, or *PRD*. To succeed him, de la Madrid selected another technocrat who, like himself, spoke fluent English, was schooled at Harvard and had never held an elective office: Carlos Salinas de Gortari. The *PAN*, meanwhile, launched its most determined effort to date with the candidacy of Manuel Clouthier, a wealthy landowner from Sinaloa. Polls showed that Salinas not only might fail to win an absolute majority, but even more unthinkable, might actually lose to Cárdenas. The campaign was the most contentious in living memory, and the actual election on July 6 remains the most controversial. As the polls had indicated, on election night early returns showed Cárdenas closing on Salinas. Then, suddenly, it was reported that the vote count had been delayed by a computer breakdown. Federal troops seized the ballot boxes. The results weren't announced until September 10, and it was reported that Salinas had neatly received a bare majority of 50.36% to 31.06% for Cárdenas and 16.81% for Clouthier. Both opposition parties cried foul, but Salinas was duly sworn in on December 1 under a cloud of suspicion and illegitimacy that haunts him to this day.

Just as Echeverría had sought to atone for the Tlatelolco Massacre by tilting heavily to the left, so Salinas attempted to neutralize the outrage over his suspicious election victory by portraying himself as a political reformer. The timing of the Salinas reforms, beginning in 1989, was especially symbolic. *Perestroika* and *glasnost* were in full flower in the Soviet Union; the democracy movement was underway in China, although it was to be crushed that June; the Berlin Wall came tumbling down in November, and the autocratic regime of Romania's Nicolae Ceaucescu came to a bloody end in December. Moreover, one Latin American dictatorship after another had given way to multi–party democracy. With the temper of these times, Mexico's monopolistic political system suddenly looked like a man with his fly open at an elegant dinner party. Salinas put out the word that at least some elections must be fair and clean, if only to keep up appearances. As a result, the *PAN* began winning state governorships, first Guanajuato, then Baja California Norte, Jalisco, and Chihuahua. Both the *PAN* and the *PRD* began winning more directly elected seats in the Chamber of Deputies, and even the *PRI*'s monopoly in the 64–member Senate was finally broken.

Perhaps just as important as the electoral reforms, however, was the relaxation of controls on the media. Salinas abolished *Pipsa*, the government newsprint monopoly that offered paper at subsidized prices but which often had withheld it from overly critical publications. The virtual monopoly enjoyed by the giant pro–*PRI* television network *Televisa* also came to an end as rival network *TV Azteca* went on the air although it, too, had pro–*PRI* owners. As a consequence, reporting became both more aggressive and more critical. Salinas, and the so–called "dinosaurs," or traditionalists within the *PRI*, soon discovered what Mikhail Gorbachev was to learn: that reforms after decades of repression gain momentum and take on a life of their own; once the forces of openness are placed in motion, they cannot be reversed without a violent reaction.

Meanwhile, Salinas sought to cope with the economic crisis he had inherited from his predecessor. He negotiated another "bailout" loan in 1990 from President George Bush, with whom he met several times and enjoyed a satisfactory working relationship. In addition, Salinas embraced the Latin American trend toward privatization of state–owned enterprises. The Mexican Revolution was essentially dead. In its place was a stampede toward free–market capitalism. No longer were foreign, particularly U.S., businessmen viewed as bogeymen. Assembly plants, called *maquiladoras*, sprang up along the northern border. Hundreds of thousands of Mexicans found jobs in them, at wages well below U.S. levels but far above what they had before—nothing.

Slowly the economy began to improve, and Bush and Salinas discussed a grand scheme designed to benefit both economies—a North American Free Trade Agreement (NAFTA) that would encompass Canada, the United States and Mexico. NAFTA became a hot political issue in the U.S. presidential election of 1992, with organized labor vehemently opposed to it. But after some vacilation, Democratic candidate Bill Clinton also endorsed the concept. The independent candidate that year, tycoon H. Ross Perot, warned that NAFTA would create "a giant sucking sound" as U.S. jobs disappeared south of the border. After Clinton's victory, the U.S. Senate ratified the treaty in late 1993—after the Canadian Parliament and Mexican Congress already had done so—and it took effect on January 1, 1994. Modeled loosely after the European Common Market, in theory it benefits all three countries by eliminating tariffs, thereby stimulating trade and, indirectly, production. There has, indeed, been an explosion of trade. Tractor trailers flow in an endless stream across the Rio Grande in both directions, although in those heading north illegal drugs frequently ride piggy–back with legitimate cargo. The boom in northern Mexico was to be cut short, however, by yet another disastrous peso devaluation.

By the 1994 elections, Salinas' reforms had ricocheted on him, and the *PRI* was split more than ever between the reformers and the "dinosaurs." The traditionalists contemptuously regarded the reformers, most of whom had held only appointed offices by virtue of their advanced degrees, many of them from the United States, as upstarts who had not paid the necessary dues by coming up through party ranks. Despite his reforms, Salinas was not about to abandon the practice of the *dedazo*. According to tradition, he met privately in September 1993 with a handful of influential party leaders before announcing he had selected yet another technocrat with a U.S. doctorate, Luis Donaldo Colosio, as the *PRI* candidate. Though he was a technocrat, the party elders regarded him as harmless and pledged to support him.

But Colosio soon demonstrated that he was his own man, not Salinas'. He campaigned as a populist and drew large, enthusiastic crowds, which led to a falling out with Salinas. The rift may have been Colosio's doom. On March 23, 1994, while pressing the flesh with a crowd of cheering supporters in Tijuana, Baja California Norte, Colosio was shot in the head by a man wielding a pistol and died on the spot. The killing sent shock waves through Mexico, because although violence is relatively commonplace in local politics, this was the highest–level assassination since the murder of President-elect Obregón in 1928. The lone gunman was apprehended, convicted and sentenced to 45 years in prison (Mexico does not have the death penalty), and although he never implicated anyone else in the assassination, there remains a widespread public belief that the killing was the result of a conspiracy.

Stunned, *PRI* officials met again with Salinas, who chose yet another technocrat, the Yale–educated Ernesto Zedillo Ponce de León. While Colosio had been perceived as shy, Zedillo was seen as colorless and reclusive. He had a flat, uninspiring speaking voice and initially showed no talent for leadership. He had spent his 21 years with the party hidden away from the public in various bureaucratic assignments. He received coaching to improve his style, but with dire results. In the spirit of Salinas' reforms, he agreed to meet the *PRD*'s Cárdenas and the *PAN* candidate, Diego Fernández de Cevallos, in a televisied debate; his performance was disastrous. Polls after the event showed Fernández leading by 20%.

The well–oiled *PRI* machinery rushed to Zedillo's rescue. Although the "dinosaurs" were lukewarm about having a *fourth* Ivy League–trained bureaucrat as the party nominee, they rallied behind him to ensure victory through the *PRI*'s time–honored methods. Zedillo likely would have won the August 21 vote even without creative vote counting, but like

Former President Salinas de Gortari and family

193

Salinas, he reportedly—and suspiciously—received the magic 50% majority. Fernández supposedly received 26%, while Cárdenas dropped to 17%. The PAN and the PRD made significant gains in the Congress. The PRI won an even 300 of the 500 seats in the Chamber of Deputies, while the PAN total rose to 119, the Workers Party (PT) had 10 and the PRD 7. In the expanded Senate, the PRI had 95 of the 128 seats, the PAN 25 and the PRD 8.

Like Echeverría before him, Salinas decided in the waning days of his administration to devalue the peso and let Zedillo deal with the consequences. The consequences were terrible; the economic recovery collapsed virtually overnight and the country plunged once again into recession. The trauma of this latest downturn on the newly emerging middle class was to have long–lasting political fallout for the PRI. Even today, young urban professionals from different states tell this author that they vote for the PAN because of Carlos Salinas.

Even before Zedillo could take office on December 1, 1994, the country would be shocked by yet another assassination, one that shook the government and the PRI to their very foundations. On September 28, PRI Secretary General José Francisco Ruíz Massieu, the No. 2 man in the party and a leader in the reform faction, was gunned down. Salinas, whose sister was once married to the slain politician, appointed Ruíz Massieu's brother Mario to investigate the murder. A few months later, after Zedillo had taken office, Ruíz Massieu resigned, alleging that the PRI was obstructing the investigation. Ostensibly to ensure a non–partisan investigation, Zedillo appointed as attorney general a PAN loyalist, Antonio Lozano. In February 1995, Lozano stunned the nation again by ordering the arrest of former President Salinas' brother, Raúl, on charges of masterminding the Ruíz Massieu murder. A month later, Carlos Salinas—disgraced as much by his brother's arrest as by the recession already being blamed on him—absconded from the country, first to the United States, then to Canada, and finally to Ireland, which has no extradition treaty with Mexico. He remains there to this day, while back home he remains a pariah. The Ruíz Massieu assassination and the Salinas brothers' alleged links to it, as well as revelations they may have been linked to drug traffickers, remain almost daily grist for the Mexican media. In January 1999, Raúl Salinas was convicted of the murder and sentenced to 50 years' imprisonment.

The Political Earthquake of 1997

Mexico embarked on an uncharted political course with the mid–term elections of July 6, 1997. At stake were all 500 deputies in the lower house of Congress,

**Former President
Ernesto Zedillo Ponce de León**

300 of them elected directly by district and 200 by proportional representation, and 32 of the 128 senators, allocated by proportional representation. The ruling PRI would have had to poll at least 42.2% to retain its absolute majority in the Chamber of Deputies, but it received only 39%.

Of the 300 deputies elected directly, the PRI won 164, the PRD won 70, the PAN took 65, and the PT had one. Proportionally, the PRI received 39% of the vote, PAN 27% and the PRD 25.5%. When the complicated formula is put into effect, the PRI fell about 10 seats short of a majority. Its majority in the Senate remained secure.

Buffeted by opposition from right and left, the PRI took an unprecedented drubbing in local races. In Mexico City, where the mayor was elected directly for the first time rather than appointed by the president, Cuauhtémoc Cárdenas, the PRD presidential candidate in 1988 and 1994, received a landslide victory, polling 47.1% of the vote to 25.6% for the PRI's candidate and 15.3% for PAN's. The PRD also captured 38 of the 66 seats in the Federal District's legislative assembly.

Of the six governorships at stake in the election, the PAN won decisive majority victories in both Nuevo León (Monterrey) and Querétaro. Those triumphs brought to six the number of states PAN had wrested from the PRI since 1989, after President Salinas' electoral reforms were implemented. In Nuevo León, PAN also swept 19 of the 26 seats in the state legislature, nine of the 11 seats for national deputy and held onto the mayoralties of Monterrey and four of its suburbs, which it had won in 1994. The PRI scored undisputed wins in San Luis Potosí and Colima states, but PAN claimed vote fraud cost it the governorship of Sonora, which borders Arizona, while the PRD made the same claim in Campeche, in the southeast.

Apart from these charges, the election, which this author observed in Monterrey, apparently was carried out with unprecedented rectitude. Elections are now conducted under the auspices of the Federal Electoral Institute (IFE), an independent, non–partisan entity, not a creature of PRI patronage as was the case in the past; each state has a similar body. Since 1994, each voter has a plastic ID card with photo and thumb print, which is matched against a master list in each polling

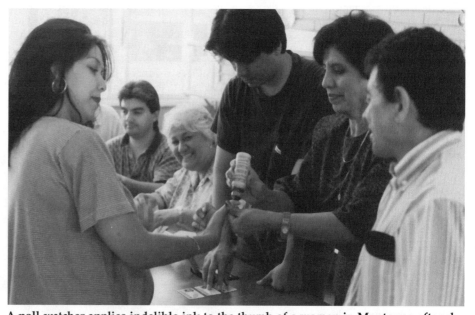

A poll-watcher applies indelible ink to the thumb of a woman in Monterrey after she cast her ballots in the historic 1997 congressional elections, one of the many safeguards now in effect to prevent electoral fraud. The ruling PRI lost its majority in the lower house of Congress for the first time.
Photo by the author

194

station. Each party is entitled to five accredited poll watchers at each station. Voters mark their ballots in secret, free from intimidation by *PRI* operatives. After a voter casts his ballot, his thumb is marked with indelible ink to thwart Chicago-style multiple voting. Alcohol sales are banned not only on election day but on election eve.

An incident in Monterrey underscored how seriously the sanctity of the electoral process was being taken. Members of the communication faculty of the University of Nuevo León were caught printing anti–*PAN* satirical pamphlets on departmental equipment early on the morning of July 3, in violation of the ban on political activity after midnight July 2. A university disciplinary committee promptly fired four of them, and the state electoral commission filed criminal charges against two.

The business newspaper *El Financiero* had perhaps the most succinct headline the morning after the election: "END TO 70 YEARS OF HEGEMONY." Julio Castrillón, one of the victorious *PAN* candidates for national deputy from Nuevo León, had what the author regards as an accurate assessment. "This is the death of the one–party system," he proclaimed during an interview. "This is an historic turnover. The decisions in the Congress will have to be by consensus. The president will lose his absolute power."

The effect of this election went beyond Mexico finding itself in a U.S.–style situation of an opposition–controlled Congress, however. An examination of Mexico's electoral map shows a troubling polarization of the country between north and south, rich and poor, right and left. The *PAN* clearly is on the ascendancy in the northern half of the country, where proximity to the U.S. border has a positive correlation to the number of jobs generated by ubiquitous *maquiladora* assembly plants. The author was stunned by the increased affluence he found in Monterrey since his last visit 14 years earlier. With prosperity, it seems, has come political conservatism. In those states where *PAN* now controls the governorships, it scored lopsided victories in the races for federal deputies. In Baja California Norte, for example, the *PAN* won all six, in Chihuahua eight of nine, in Jalisco 18 of 19, in Guanajuato 11 of 14. The farther south one goes, however, the worse the poverty and the greater the voting strength of the *PRD*.

A learning process got underway in Mexico in the wake of the historic 1997 elections, as the *PRI*, the opposition parties, the media, the business community and the public in general all came to terms with the new political realities. For the first year, the *PAN* and the *PRD* were able to put aside their obvious ideological differences in order to join forces to wrest control of key committees in the Chamber of Deputies from the *PRI*. Cárdenas took of-

Headlines in the Monterrey newspaper *El Norte* the morning of July 7, 1997, declare the opposition *PAN* candidate, Fernando Canales, the winner of the Nuevo León governor's race, as well as announcing that the opposition parties have broken the *PRI*'s domination of Congress and that the *PRD*'s Cuauhtémoc Cárdenas has won the mayor's race in Mexico City.

fice as mayor of Mexico City in December 1997, vowing in his inaugural address to combat the city's three major ills: crime, corruption and pollution. But the euphoria of victory abruptly gave way to the grim realities of governing the world's most populous city. For one thing, the extent of *PRI* patronage and corruption proved to be even more mind-boggling than had been imagined. When Cárdenas' team took over city offices, it discovered that the outgoing *PRI* officials had erased the hard drives of all the computers—all, that is, except for the computers that had mysteriously vanished. The erasures apparently were less an act of sour-grapes sabotage by the losers against the winners than a matter of destroying evidence of criminal malfeasance. Meanwhile, scandal after scandal dominated newscasts and the front pages of newspapers throughout the country in 1998, most of them involving *PRI* officials or wealthy patrons.

Two months after the July election, Zedillo sacked the *PRI* president, Humberto Roque Villanueva, apparently because of his vituperation against the opposition parties. In his place, Zedillo appointed the far more conciliatory Mariano Palacios Alcocer. Zedillo's action, seen as a pragmatic gesture to rule by consensus with the opposition, nonetheless contradicted his vow not to interfere in internal party affairs. Palacios told the party bluntly, "We must learn to be a party of opposition," and that "we have to recognize the rest of the political parties as our equals." He also called for a "redefinition" of the party's ideology, although in reality the *PRI* has never been based on ideology but rather on the power and patronage that comes with it.

The aftershocks of the political earthquake of 1997 continued to be felt through 1998 and 1999, when Mexico elected most of its governors. These races were closely watched bellwethers of the three major parties' electoral muscle heading into the crucial 2000 presidential election. Even before the campaigning got underway, however, the *PRI* was tarnished by yet another scandal.

In March 1998, President Zedillo startled the Chamber of Deputies with a cavalier proposal for the government to assume $65 billion in bad debts from the 1994-95 economic crisis. The debts were held by the Bank Savings Protection Fund, the equivalent of the U.S. Federal Deposit Insurance Corporation, known by the acronym *Fobaproa*. Zedillo's plan amounted to a massive bailout of banks that went under during the crisis, with the taxpayers footing the bill. Soon, however, investigative journalists and opposition congressmen began disclosing that many of the bad debts resulted from incredibly stupid loans to multi-millionaires for high-risk ventures. Many of those businessmen, it turned out, had contributed millions of dollars to the *PRI*'s 1994 campaign chest. The public outrage was immediate and intense. For months, the oppositiion *PAN* and *PRD* deputies joined forces to keep Zedillo's bailout bill hostage in the lower house, while the government made lame efforts to assuage public opinion by arresting more than 180 businessmen for fraudulent loans. That December, the logjam was broken when the *PAN* struck a compromise with the *PRI* on the 1999 budget, by which $55 billion of the *Fobaproa* debt would be converted into public debt. The *PRD* denounced the bailout as a travesty, signaling an end to the era of cooperation between the two opposition parties.

Prelude to 2000

With the *Fobaproa* scandal reverberating in the background, Mexicans proceeded to elect 17 of their 31 governors in 1998 and 1999. The first major tri-cornered showdown came on July 5, 1998, in the contiguous north-central states of Chihuahua, Durango and Zacatecas. This author drove to Zacatecas to cover that election, considered the most newsworthy of the three, as a free-lance journalist. There, a former *PRI* whip in the Chamber of Deputies, Ricardo Monreal, had bolted the party when its kingpins refused to endorse his candidacy for governor. He then stood as the candidate for the *PRD*, while the *PRI* nominated a longtime party hack. The race was considered symbolic both because of Monreal's defection and because Zacatecas had long been a faithful *PRI* stronghold and had given President Zedillo the largest percentage of the vote of any state in 1994. Moreover, Zacatecans boasted a long tradition of rebelliousness—against the Spanish, against Santa Anna, against the French, against Díaz and Huerta. Now, after decades of unkept promises and abuse of power by the *PRI*, they were restive again.

The evening I arrived in the beautiful colonial-era capital city, also named Zacatecas, thousands of Monreal supporters filled the Plaza de Armas for his closing rally. Hundreds of the enthusiastic and humbly dressed *PRD* partisans carried lighted candles. "We're burying the *PRI*," an elderly woman explained. "These are for its wake." Monreal told the cheering crowd, "We're about to witness the second taking of Zacatecas," alluding to the city's capture by Pancho Villa's rebel army in

1914. Pointing to the adjacent government palace, he declared, "That house is going to get a cleaning!" The same plaza was filled again a few nights later with even more euphoric Monreal supporters as election results confirmed his decisive victory, 43% to 36%, despite evidence of *PRI* vote tampering.

That same day, the *PRI* easily held onto the governorship of neighboring Durango, 40% to 28% for the *PAN* and 22.5% for the *PT*. But the *PRI* made history in Chihuahua with the first *recapturing* of a governorship from the *PAN*, which had won there in 1992. Local issues, particularly an alarming increase of drug-related violence in Ciudad Juárez, the state's largest city, appeared to have been the decisive factor in the *PRI* 's 48%-43% victory. But there may have been another: Chihuahua was the first state where the *PRI* adopted a U.S.-style direct party primary for choosing its candidate, Patricio Martínez.

The *PRI* seemingly had had a good day, but the defeat in Zacatecas was devastating. Raúl Delgado, a political scientist at the University of Zacatecas, told me why: "It's much more important, first, because of the *PRD*'s campaign slogan, 'Sí, se puede' ('Yes, we can'); second, because it's the most *Prista* state in Mexico; third, because of the symbolism of the *PRI* losing a rural state, which it always said was its base of support; and fourth, because Zacatecas has been the cradle of historic changes for the country. Even though the *PRI* won two of the three states, the atmosphere is one of defeat." Moreover, the victory in Zacatecas marked the first time the *PRD* had won a key election outside its power base in the south.

Thousands packed the Plaza de Armas in Zacatecas for the closing rally of the *PRD* gubernatorial candidate, Ricardo Monreal, in July 1998. *Photo by the author*

196

From Zacatecas I drove 70 miles south to Aguascalientes, capital city of the like-named state, which was to elect its governor on August 2. The contrast between quaint, poverty-stricken Zacatecas and modern, affluent Aguascalientes was striking. Heavily industrialized, with a burgeoning middle class, Aguascalientes was as fertile a ground for the *PAN* as Zacatecas was for the *PRD*. The *PAN* had won control of the state legislature and the municipal government of the capital three years before. Polls showed the *PAN* candidate, Felipe González, in a dead heat with the *PRI*'s Hector Hugo. In a different way, a defeat in this Delaware-sized but economically significant state would be as symbolic for the *PRI* as its loss in Zacatecas. "Look," the managing editor of one of the daily newspapers explained to me, "Aguascalientes is one of four states, along with Jalisco, Guanajuato and Querétaro, that make up the Bojío region, which is the industrial heart of Mexico. The *PAN* already has the governorships of the other three, and the *PRD* controls Mexico City. If the *PAN* wins here, the *PRI* will be left with nothing but insignificant states. It's a matter of power. A defeat here would be a debacle for the *PRI*." Yet, the *PAN*'s González won by about 10 percentage points.

The same day, the *PRI*'s Miguel Alemán, son and namesake of the former president, won by an even greater margin in Veracruz, while the *PRI* held onto the governorship of Oaxaca against a determined *PRD* challenge. The *PRD* cited incidents of vote fraud. Once again, the *PRI* had won two of three contests, but there still was a malaise of defeat.

On October 25, 1998, the *PRI* easily won in Tamaulipas with 58% of the vote; the *PAN* was second with 25% and the *PRD* third with 14%. On November 8, the *PRI* withstood stronger challenges from the *PAN* in Puebla, winning 51% to 34%, and in Sinaloa, where the margin was 47% to 32%. But in tiny Tlaxcala, as had been the case in Zacatecas, a former *PRI* loyalist, Alfonso Sánchez Anaya, ran as the *PRD* candidate in that long-time *PRI* stronghold state. Sánchez pulled off a narrow upset victory, 45% to 43%.

Guerrero and Baja California Sur voted on February 7, 1999, in what were essentially two-way contests between the *PRI* and the ascendant *PRD*. In the former, a poor southern state where there had been guerrilla insurgency and where the *PRD* has a natural constituency, the *PRI* candidate was declared the winner by 49% to 47%. The *PRD* immediately cried foul, alleging that the *PRI* had swapped votes for groceries. But in Baja California Sur, once again the *PRD* had nominated a *PRI* renegade, Leonel Cota Montana, who won by a landslide 55% to the *PRI* candidate's 36%.

Two weeks later, the *PRI* won in Hidalgo and even in Quintana Roo, where the

incumbent *PRI* governor, Mario Villanueva Madrid, was under federal investigation for drug trafficking. In both states, the two opposition parties had failed to present a united front, thus dividing the opposition vote and assuring the *PRI* easy wins. In Hidalgo, the *PRI* received an absolute majority of 53%, the *PAN* received 32% and the *PRD* 15%. But in Quintana Roo the *PRI* obtained a mere plurality of 43%, to 34% for the *PRD* and the remainder for the *PAN*. As a bizarre anticlimax to the Quintana Roo election, Governor Villanueva absconded the day before the inauguration of his successor and disappeared. For two years he was an international fugitive before being arrested in Cancún in his home state on May 24, 2001.

On July 4, 1999, the nation's attention was riveted on two governor's races: in Mexico, the most populous state with 12 million people, which borders the Federal District, and in Nayarit, a small, impoverished state of 1 million on the Pacific coast. In Mexico, the *PAN* and a *PRD-PT* coalition both mounted strong candidates to face the *PRI*, thus dividing the opposition vote. But in Nayarit, to which this author drove to report on the campaign, the *PAN*, *PRD*, *PT* and the minuscule Socialist Revolutionary Party (which uses a hammer and sickle in its logo!) put aside their obvious ideological differences to field a single candidate, Antonio Echevarría, a *PRI* defector. These two races underscored what a united opposition could achieve. In Mexico, the *PRI*'s Arturo Montiel won with a 41% plurality, to 31% for the *PAN* candidate and 21% for the *PRD-PT* candidate. But in Nayarit, Echevarría defeated the *PRI* candidate 50% to 44%, despite frantic *PRI* attempts to bribe opposition voters into surrendering their voter ID cards in return for a *dispensa*, or welfare package of groceries. "Remember," Echevarría had said when the bribe scheme became public, "a *dispensa* lasts for three days, but a bad government lasts for six years!" Similar charges surfaced in the Mexico election.

The same tricks also came into play before the gubernatorial election in the border state of Coahuila on September 26, 1999. While this author was in Saltillo to write about the campaign, one of the local newspapers carried a front-page photo montage of trucks carrying *dispensas* from a government warehouse to *PRI* precinct headquarters. Four parties—the *PAN*, the *PRD*, the *PT* and the small Environmental Green Party of Mexico (*PVEM*) had forged an alliance similar to the one in Nayarit. In Coahuila, however, the *PRI* candidate, Enrique Martínez y Martínez, a popular former mayor of Saltillo, was elected with 58% of the vote.

Thus, voters sent mixed signals in the governorship races of 1998–99. The major psychological winner was the *PRD*, which went into the races with no state governorships and emerged with three, Zacatecas,

Tlaxcala and Baja California Sur. It also ran a strong second to the *PRI* in Oaxaca, Guerrero and Quintana Roo, and may have won in Guerrero except for possible *PRI* electoral trickery. The *PAN*, meanwhile, didn't quite break even, losing a large, powerful state (Chihuahua) while picking up a smaller, but still influential one (Aguascalientes); it still held six states. In Puebla, Sinaloa, Hidalgo and Mexico, it ran a strong second, garnering a third of the vote in all four, and received about a fourth of the vote in Durango and Tamaulipas, but second place just doesn't translate into power. An opposition alliance won the governorship of Nayarit but lost in Coahuila. The *PRI* could console itself that it won 13 of the 17 governorships, including the recapturing of Chihuahua, and that it still controlled 21 of the 31, but there was no escaping the mathematics that it suffered a net loss of four states and saw its electoral strength eroded in several more. Of the three parties, it clearly was the major loser.

The Elections of 2000

One of the potentially most important events in 20th century Mexico occurred in October 1998 when President Zedillo stated uniquivocally in a press interview that he was disavowing the *dedazo*, or tap, by which for 65 years the incumbent president had personally designated the next *PRI* candidate.

Seven candidates expressed interest in the *PRI* nomination. The earliest to enter the race, months even before Zedillo had disavowed the *dedazo*, was Manuel Bartlett, former governor of Puebla and interior secretary under de la Madrid. Bartlett was closely identified with the party's "dinosaur" faction, and his critics constantly badgered him by recalling that he was interior secretary during the infamous 1988 presidential election that Salinas allegedly stole at the expense of Cárdenas. Also declared was Humberto Roque Villanueva, Palacios' sacked predecessor as *PRI* chief. A late entry was Interior Secretary Francisco Labastida, a former governor of Sinaloa, considered a reformist and unquestionably Zedillo's preferred choice. Tabasco Governor Roberto Madrazo, a dinosaur, also formally announced, and new Veracruz Governor Miguel Alemán, son and namesake of the former president, coyly expressed an interest without formally declaring his candidacy. Rounding out the field of likely precandidates were Foreign Secretary Rosario Green, who would have been the party's first female candidate and Mexico's first woman president; Social Development Secretary Esteban Moctezuma, and Génaro Borrego, director of the Social Security Institute. Meanwhile, party chief Palacios resigned on March 18, reportedly to give the party a fresh face going into the selection process. Two weeks later, party leaders (not Zedillo) chose José Antonio González to succeed him.

Both the other major parties switched leaders in March 1999 as well. Felipe Calderón, stinging from the *PAN*'s lackluster showing in the governor's races, had resigned in December and was replaced in March by Senator Felipe Bravo, seen as a bridge between the conservative ideologues (the *PAN*'s equivalent of the *PRI*'s "dinosaurs") and the pragmatic, business-oriented faction represented by Guanajuato Governor Vicente Fox, a rancher and former Coca-Cola executive, who was spending large sums of his own money on a quest for the presidential nomination without the blessing of party regulars.

Meanwhile, the *PRD*'s presumed candidate, Mexico City Mayor Cárdenas, who had been the frontrunner for president in most opinion polls throughout 1998, began to suffer a decline in public esteem. Some of the complaints were normal for Latin American countries, such as the discovery that he was not Superman and could not resolve all of Mexico City's problems in his first year in office. But his prestige suffered a greater blow in April 1999 when the eminent political scientist Jorge Castañeda published a new book in which he alleged that Cárdenas had met secretly with Carlos Salinas shortly after the highly suspect 1988 election and agreed not to challenge Salinas' stolen victory. A prominent *PRD* leader, Porfirio Muñoz Ledo, harshly attacked Cárdenas and voiced his intention to challenge him for the presidential nomination. About the same time, Cárdenas publicly advocated a joint *PRD-PAN* candidate to overcome the *PRI*'s mathematical advantage in a country that does not have runoff elections but where a plurality wins. Some within the *PAN* publicly embraced the idea of an alliance, but Fox dismissed the suggestion as "a joke."

In an historic eight-hour meeting on May 17, 1999, 328 members of the *PRI*'s 335-member National Political Council (*CNP*) approved the primary election process over a party convention by a vote of 307–21 and set November 7 as the date for the primary; the winner would be formally nominated on November 20. The nominee would not be elected directly however; the nomination would go to the candidate who polled a plurality of the vote in the largest number of the country's 300 districts for the Chamber of Deputies. This was seen as an effort to ensure that the candidates do not neglect the rural areas. Interestingly, the primary was opened to all voters regardless of party affiliation, apparently because the *PRI* does not have party membership cards. The *CNP* also set strict rules for campaigning: Public officials had to resign their posts by June 15, an obvious dilemma for newly installed Governor Alemán; the candidates were to present their platforms between June 15

A newly paved stretch of Highway 59 vaults through La Muralla, a notch-shaped pass through the rugged volcanic mountains north of Saltillo, Coahuila. *Photo by the author*

and July 10; formal registration was to take place between July 15 and July 25; and the official campaign period was to be August 1–November 3.

The new rules winnowed the number of contenders to four: Labastida, Madrazo, Bartlett and Roque Villanueva. Labastida resigned his cabinet post, Madrazo went "on leave" as governor of Tabasco, and the *PRI*'s first-ever presidential primary was underway. It was a classic contest between the factions of traditionalists and reformers, with Labastida emerging as the champion of the latter. Nonetheless, despite President Zedillo's public avowals of neutrality, Labastida's three opponents began grumbling that the *PRI* machinery and patronage power were being subtly used on Labastida's behalf. There was probably an element of truth to the charges. On election day, Zedillo declared that he had voted for all four candidates, thus nullifying his ballot, to demonstrate his neutrality. (No one was with the president in the voting booth to verify that claim, however.)

True or not, Labastida scored a landslide victory in the historic November 7 showdown, which attracted worldwide media attention. Labastida received an outright majority of 5.3 million votes, or 55% of the 9.7 million votes cast, and in the vote that really mattered, carried 274 of the 300 districts for the Chamber of Deputies. Madrazo finished second with 2.7 million votes, or 27.8%, and 21 districts. He glumly congratulated Labastida and pledged to remain faithful to him during the coming campaign. Bartlett was third with 580,000

votes, or 6%, and five districts. He was not as gracious a loser as Madrazo. Roque Villanueva brought up the rear with 420,000 votes, or 4.3%; he carried no districts. The *dedazo*, it appeared, was not quite dead after all.

The campaign then began in earnest for the July 2, 2000 election. Mexico had never seen the likes of this race. Prior to the *PRI* primary, Fox had replaced Cárdenas as the frontrunner in all the major polls. But once Labastida's landslide primary victory was a fact, he quickly eclipsed Fox as the frontrunner, by varying margins. All attempts to forge an alliance between Fox, who had taken leave as governor of Guanajuato, and Cárdenas, who had resigned as mayor of Mexico City, ended in failure. Neither man, each known for an oversized ego, was willing to yield to the other.

In the first half of 2000, however, Fox continued to chisel away at Labastida's lead, and the race became essentially a contest between the two 57-year-old men. In December, the Green Party (*PVEM*) candidate withdrew from the race to endorse Fox and the two parties forged a coalition called the Alliance for Change. Later in the campaign, the candidate of the small but venerable Authentic Party of the Mexican Revolution (*PARM*) also withdrew and endorsed Fox. The *PRD*, meanwhile, formed its own coalition with the *PT* and two smaller left-wing parties, called the Alliance for Mexico.

Fox effectively closed the gap with the April 25 debate, in which the flamboyant Fox was widely seen as the victor over

Labastida and Cárdenas. His unorthodox campaign style, unknown to Mexicans, also seemed to strike a responsive chord, although his tendency to make outrageous statements against Labastida alienated some. For example, the six-foot, six-inch Fox, who enhances his image by wearing cowboy boots, took to deriding the five-foot-10 Labastida as "shorty;" once, he referred to him as "*La Vestida,*" the slang for cross-dresser, an unmistakable attack on his masculinity.

In June, Fox committed what once would have been considered heresy by advocating scrapping the 1917 Constitution and drafting one more in line with the times.

The candidates failed to agree on the groundrules for a second debate among the top three candidates, but in May they squared off on *Televisa* from separate locations. Fox and Labastida dominated the so-called "mini-debate" by accusing each other of lying and by attacking the other's record. In June, Labastida was embarrassed by the revelation that his brother had benefited from the *Fobaproa* bank bailout.

Never had a *PRI* candidate faced such a determined and aggressive challenger. The *PRI* counterattacked with some unorthodox tactics of its own, such as a male strip show in a Mexico City suburb designed to attract female voters. It responded to the "*La Vestida*" remark by reminding voters that Fox's four children are adopted, in effect, questioning *his* masculinity. The usual charges surfaced that the *PRI* was attempting to bribe voters with groceries and building materials and was leaning on government workers to vote for Labastida—or else. The Federal Electoral Institute (*IFE*) declined to take the charges seriously, however, stating that ballots are secret now and that even if charges of bribery were true the *PRI* would have no way of verifying how the "bribees" voted. Moreover, the opposition parties complained that Labastida was receiving a disproportionate amount of coverage in the media, especially television.

In June, Labastida (and Cárdenas) accused Fox of illegally accepting foreign campaign contributions, which Fox adamantly denied. Labastida even suggested that the devoutly Catholic Fox would impose his religious beliefs on the country.

As the campaign neared its climax, both Labastida and Fox issued sinister warnings of possible unrest if the election were decided by a narrow margin, in effect saying, "Better give me a landslide." Nonetheless, by June 22, the last day legally to publish opinion polls, all the leading surveys showed Labastida and Fox in a statistical tie with about 39%–42% each. Cárdenas languished far behind in all the polls at 16-17%; still, he would not consent to withdrawing and supporting Fox.

Five days before the showdown vote, this author drove to Mexico to cover the final days of the campaign for several newspapers. Convinced that Fox was where the story was, I arrived in León, in Fox's home state of Guanajuato, for his closing rally in a huge soccer stadium on Wednesday, June 28. Enthusiastic *Panistas* began lining up in the hot sun nearly three hours before the rally began at 7 p.m. By starting time, the stands of the 60,000-seat stadium were overflowing, the crowds filled the playing field, and hundreds more waited outside, unable to enter. I spoke to several people to get quotes for my newspaper article, and was invariably given two reasons why they were supporting Fox: His positive record as governor, especially in education and exports, and the corruption of the *PRI*. But when I asked whether they thought he would win, many of them hesitated, then expressed their belief that the *PRI* would

pull off a sneaky trick at the last minute to deprive Fox of victory, as it had Cárdenas in 1988.

In his speech, the candidate was surprisingly low-keyed, with none of the personal attacks on Labastida that had marked the campaign. Instead, he reiterated his goals for 7% annual economic growth that would generate 1.3 million new jobs a year, for an attack on corruption and narcotrafficking, for improvements in education, and for an elevation of the status of women. "If you are tired of the *PRI*, if you are sick of the corruption, if you want a government that is pluralist and inclusive, the only choice is to vote for the Alliance for Change!" he shouted. "Give me 10 seconds of your time, and I will give you six years working to give you a Mexico of grand opportunities. Vote for your children! Vote for Mexico! Don't hold back! With your vote you write your name in the

The pre-election issue of the weekly newsmagazine *Proceso* carries irreverent caricatures of the three major candidates. At left is Vicente Fox, a Coca-Cola in one hand and an obscene gesture in place of his trademark *"Ya"* sign in the other; around his neck is a cross, symbolizing his devout Catholicism. In the middle is Francisco Labastida, carrying an enormous forefinger representing *"el dedazo,"* meaning he was the favored candidate of President Ernesto Zedillo. On his lapel button is the unpopular former president, Carlos Salinas de Gortari. At right is Cuauhtémoc Cárdenas, portrayed as a moralistic reformer.

President Vicente Fox Quesada

book of history!" The crowd cheered as though Mexico had won the World Cup.

Labastida had closed his campaign that same day in his home state of Sinaloa, to a much smaller crowd, while Cárdenas chose to close his in the poor and troubled state of Chiapas. After more than a year of fevered campaigning, an eerie stillness settled over Mexico as her 60 million voters prepared to render their verdict.

If the mid-term elections of 1997 were a political earthquake, the elections of 2000 were a tidal wave. I observed some of the voting Sunday morning in the beautiful colonial-era state capital, also called Guanajuato, and was struck by a new feature I had not seen in the elections in 1997 and 1998: there were plastic curtains on the voting booths to ensure secrecy! On the booths were the words, "The vote is free and secret." Would it make a difference, I wondered.

From Guanajuato I drove north to Saltillo, Coahuila, arriving precisely as the polls closed at 8 p.m. On my car radio I heard the news that was once unimaginable: Exit polls showed Fox with 44%, Labastida with 38%, Cárdenas with 16%. Those figures fluctuated only slightly over the next two hours, as Fox's stunning and decisive victory became assured. The upset was of David-and-Goliath or hare-and-tortoise proportions.

Coahuila was a microcosm of the *PAN* victory. Not only did Fox carry the state with 55% of the vote, the *PAN* won two of the three irectly elected Senate seats and four of the seven seats in the Chamber of Deputies; in the outgoing Congress, the *PRI* had held two Senate seats and six of the seven deputies. Along Saltillo's Boulevard Venustiano Carranza, thousands of jubilant *Panistas* honked horns, waved banners and posters and flashed the two-fingered symbol for Fox's campaign

A women casts her ballot in the city of Guanajuato on July 2, 2000. The sign on the voting booth at rights says, "The vote is free and secret." In the past, that wasn't always the case. That night, after the results began coming in, jubilant young supporters of *PAN* candidate Vicente Fox congregate in Avenida Venustiana Carranza in Saltillo to celebrate his victory—and the *PRI*'s first presidential defeat in 71 years.

Photos by the author

The front page of the Saltillo, Coahuila, daily newspaper *Vanguardia* proclaiming the stunning and decisive victory of Vicente Fox in the July 2, 2000, presidential election.

smooth transition, but not as graciously spent considerably more time praising the losing Labastida, reminding his viewers what a positive force the *PRI* had been and pledging that the party would remain a vital force in the life of the nation. Soon thereafter, Fox appeared, and graciously praised Zedillo and Labastida. Ironically, July 2 also had been the victor's 58th birthday.

By morning, Mexico awoke not to a hangover but what seemed like another impossible dream. Not only had Fox carried 21 of the 31 states, but it appeared that the *PAN* would have near-parity with the *PRI* in the next Congress. Cárdenas carried only two states—Baja California Sur and his home state of Michoacán. To make the *PAN*'s night complete, it retained the governorship of Guanajuato, which Fox had relinquished, and picked up the governorship of the southern state of Morelos (the state of Emiliano Zapata) with an astounding 58% of the vote. It was the first time the *PAN* had won a governorship outside of its power base in the north. Meanwhile, the *PRD* candidate for mayor of Mexico City, Manuel López Obrador, narrowly won with 38% of the vote. What was surprising was that the *PAN* candidate finished a close second with 35%, while the *PRI* candidate was a distant third. Overnight, it seemed, Mexico had been turned upside down, and a shell-shocked *PRI* began taking stock of the situation and wondering, as were all Mexicans, what the future would bring. One of my final images before leaving Mexico was a car with a sign painted on its back window that largely summed up the feelings of a decisive plurality of Mexicans: "GANO PAN, GANO MEXICO" ("PAN WON, MEXICO WON").

Final official tabulations by the non-partisan *IFE* were: Fox, 15,988,740, or 42.52%; Labastida, 13,576,385, or 36.0%; Cárdenas, 6,259,048, or 16.64%. Fewer than 1 million votes were scattered among three minor candidates, and 789,838 ballots were nullified. A total of 37,603,924 Mexicans had voted, a respectable turnout of 63.97%. The breakdown in the lower house after the allocation of the 200 seats by proportional representation was as follows: The *PAN*, 208, and its partner, the *PVEM*, 15, for a total of 223 for the Alliance for Change, 27 seats short of a majority; the *PRI*, 209; the *PRD*, 52; the *PT*, 8; the Convergence for Democracy, 3; the Nationalist Society, 3; and the Social Alliance, 2. The breakdown of the 128 Senate seats was 58 for the *PRI*, 53 for the *PAN* and the *PVEM* and 17 for the *PRD*.

The new president was born on a ranch in Guanajuato on July 2, 1942, one of nine children of a Spanish mother and a father of U.S. descent. He received a Jesuit higher education at the Ibero-American Institute in Mexico City, then went into the family's business. He ran a boot manufacturing

slogan, *"Ya!"* ("Right now!") There was a far larger explosion of jubilation around the Angel of Independence monument along the Paseo de la Reforma in Mexico City, which I watched on television. It was a euphoria I had witnessed only once before—the night in 1989 that Patricio Aylwin was elected president of Chile to end the 16-year dictatorship of Augusto

Pinochet. For Mexico's opposition, the wait had been 71 years.

At midnight, a dour President Zedillo addressed his countrymen on television and acknowledged that "it appears unquestionable that the next president will be Licenciado Vicente Fox Quesada." He graciously congratulated Fox on his victory and pledged his cooperation for a

Mexico City's main thoroughfare, *Paseo de la Reforma*

company and a frozen fruit and vegetable firm as well as becoming chief of Coca-Cola's Latin American division. He was elected to the Chamber of Deputies in 1988, and it is illustrative of his persuasiveness that as a member of the opposition he was instrumental in passing a constitutional amendment to allow citizens with one foreign-born parent to be elected president; previously, both parents had to be born in Mexico. (I heard a rumor from a *PRI* candidate for the Chamber of Deputies in Guanajuato that Fox had covered up the fact that his father really was born in the United States, which would have disqualified Fox for the presidency, but apparently there is no evidence to support that.) Fox was elected governor in 1995 and won high marks for his honesty, his work ethic and his administration. Despite his devout Catholicism, Fox is Mexico's first divorced president.

The Fox Era Begins

It is not an exaggeration to state that a new era of Mexican history began when Vicente Fox was inaugurated as president on December 1, 2000. Not only was he the first president in 71 years who was not a member of the *PRI*, he was the first unapologetically devout Catholic since Avila Camacho. From the start, he has shown himself to be a master of symbolism, as if to underscore that the changes he represents are more than cosmetic. The morning of his inauguration, he literally rolled up his sleeves and, clad in his trademark cowboy boots, he mingled with the people in a poor neighborhood of the capital. The inaugural ceremony itself was attended by such ideologically diverse personalities as Cuban President Fidel Castro, Colombian Nobel Laureate Gabriel García Márquez, U.S. Secretary of State Madeleine Albright and Microsoft chairman Bill Gates.

After receiving the presidential sash from Zedillo before the Congress, still wearing cowboy boots, he kept a campaign promise by ordering an army withdrawal from Chiapas as his first official act. He has since exerted greater effort than his two predecessors to reach a peace accord with the *Zapatistas* (see Armed Rebellions). He then did something no *PRI* president could have done: He went to the Basilica of Our Lady of Guadalupe to offer thanks to Mexico's patron saint, then delivered speeches before throngs of supporters in a soccer stadium and in the Zócalo. He proposed a breathtaking list of reforms: amending the constitution to permit referenda; a crackdown on corruption; greater environmental protection; streamlining, but not privatizing, *Pemex*; strengthening U.S.-style judicial review over laws passed by Congress; a code of ethics for cabinet secretaries; increased availability to university scholarships; increased incentives for savings and investments; greater government support for small businesses; universal health care; greater autonomy for the states; and the Indian rights bill demanded by the *Zapatistas*.

Fox's cabinet appointments also were symbolic of the new order and diversity of representation. As foreign secretary he appointed Jorge Castañeda, the noted political scientist; as attorney general, General Rafael Macedo, the army's prosecutor, who has a reputation for incorruptibility and has cashiered officers for corruption and collusion with drug traffickers; as interior secretary, the *PAN's* leader in Congress, Santiago Creel. Fox stripped the interior and justice ministries of their domestic surveillance functions, concentrating them instead in a newly created law enforcement portfolio headed by the police chief in the *PRD* administration in Mexico City, Alejandro Gertz. As ambassador to the United States, Fox appointed veteran diplomat Juan José Bremer, a former ambassador to Spain, who is highly critical of the U.S. drug certification policy.

Mexican-U.S. relations began experiencing a dramatic improvement under Fox and the new U.S. president, George W. Bush, who is fluent in Spanish and who as governor of Texas became closely acquainted with Mexican affairs. It was historic that for the first time ever, a U.S. president opted to make his first foreign visit to Mexico. Fox hosted his counterpart on his Guanajuato ranch for a one-day summit on February 16, 2001, less than a month after Bush assumed office. The two businesslike conservatives with ranching backgrounds got along well and covered the usual agenda: trade, drugs, immigration and energy. Even before he became president, Fox made regular appearances on U.S. interview programs, and he raised eyebrows by proposing that the U.S.-Mexican border be as open as the U.S.-Canadian frontier.

It was to that border that the new president traveled at Christmas to welcome Mexicans returning home from the United States to spend the holidays with their families. He made another symbolic gesture in April by opening the presidential palace of Los Pinos for the first time to the

202

public. That gesture was to boomerang on him, however, when the media reported that the towels in the presidential bathrooms cost $400 and that the remote-controlled curtains cost $17,000. The media immediately labeled the first Fox mini-scandal "Towelgate."

In March, however, Mexicans learned that their new president was serious about cracking down on corruption. He fired 12 high-ranking government officials after they were caught taking bribes in a sting operation. Undercover agents offered them bribes to obtain drivers licenses without taking the necessary driving or medical tests. Fox warned that there would be more such sting operations.

Fox obtained congressional support for his Indian rights bill, but he found less enthusiasm when he introduced an ambitious tax reform plan in April. Fox argued that the plan would encourage investments, create jobs and help redistribute wealth. Especially unpopular with the *PRI* and *PRD* legislators—and with the public—was his proposal to eliminate the value-added, or sales, tax exemptions on groceries and medicine. Fox countered that the plan would give $11 monthly rebates to the 27 million Mexicans below the poverty line and would provide an income tax exemption for those making less than 50,000 pesos (about $5,300) annually. The Green Party, which had been part of Fox's election coalition, broke with him over the tax reform scheme. In December 2001, Congress finally passed a watered-down version that focused on luxury taxes.

Fox stunned the nation, and allayed a possible personal scandal, by marrying his press spokeswoman, Martha Sahagún, on July 2, 2001, his 59th birthday and the first anniversary of his election victory. The nature of their relationship had been the subject of gossip for years, and she was known to be living in Los Pinos. It was reportedly she who had ordered the controversial towels and curtains. In the year since, the press has not been kind to the first lady, criticizing her actions and her taste, much to the displeasure of her husband.

In politics, the *PRI* continued to be plagued with problems since its defeat at Fox's hands. As expected, an internecine battle for control of the party ensued between the reformers and the dinosaurs, and the party's separation from the reins of power has stripped it of its most powerful tool—patronage. Moreover, it has continued to lose governorships.

Just seven weeks after its presidential defeat, the *PRI* candidate for the governorship of troubled Chiapas was soundly defeated on August 20 by Pablo Salazar of the *PRD*, running as the candidate of a coalition of opposition parties. Salazar received 54% of the vote, and the *PRI* graciously conceded defeat.

Burros graze along a desert highway between Saltillo and Zacatecas.
Photo by the author.

The head of the *PRI*'s dinosaur faction, Tabasco Governor Roberto Madrazo, in true dinosaur fashion hand-picked the *PRI* candidate to succeed him as governor, Manuel Andrade. In the election on October 15, 2000, Andrade eventually was declared the winner, 44% to 43%, over the *PRD*'s Raúl Ojeda. The *PRD* appealed the decision to the Federal Electoral Institute *(IFE)*, citing the usual evidence of *PRI* vote-buying. On December 29, just three days before Andrade's inauguration, the *IFE* made the unprecedented decision to nullify the election results. The decision threw Tabasco into turmoil; at one point, the rival *PRI* factions in the state legislature chose two separate interim governors. Eventually, the new election was set for August 5, 2001. Andrade won narrowly, 50.5% to 46%, apparently fairly.

Another *PRI* dinosaur, Yucatán Governor Victor Cervera Pacheco, attempted to defy a federal court order that nullified his stacked state electoral commission, setting off a confrontation between the national and state executives. The *PAN* had challenged the state electoral commission as too partisan; the federal court agreed, and appointed its own commissioners. Heretofore, tradition had been to grant state governors virtual *carte blanche* over their fiefs. The crisis came to a head in April 2001. President Fox backed away from the confrontation, but the two parties eventually reached a compromise. In the election on May 27, the *PRI* suffered yet another humiliating setback when the *PAN*'s Patricio Patrón defeated the *PRI*'s Orlando Paredes 51% to 46%. It brought to eight the number of states controlled by the *PAN*.

On July 8, the *PAN* easily retained control of the governorship of Baja California Norte for a third straight term under the candidacy of Eugenio Elorduy, a former mayor of Mexicali, who received 50% of the vote to 36% for the *PRI* candidate.

On November 11, the *PRI* suffered another defeat, for the governorship of Michoacán. There, Lázaro Cárdenas, son of Cuauhtémoc and grandson and namesake of the illustrious former president, defeated *PRI* candidate Alfredo Anaya 41.8% ro 36.7%; the *PAN* candidate received 18.6%.The hotly contested campaign was marred by an assassination attempt on Anaya in October. The victory brought to five the number of states, plus the Federal District, that the *PRD* controls and immediately transformed the 37-year-old Cárdenas into one of the rising stars of the party. President Fox himself attended his inauguration on February 15, 2002.

Mexico 2002. . .

Fox's relationship with the Congress and the opposition parties has continued its roller-coaster course. On October 7, 2001, it seemed as though the eight ideologically disparate parties had achieved a harmonious meeting of the minds when they signed a national accord whereby they agreed to work together to combat organized crime, terrorism and poverty and to implement overhauls of the tax system and the energy sector. The first failure came with the gutting of Fox's tax overhaul; even his own *PAN* deserted him rather than risk voter retribution by taxing groceries and drugs.

The accord said nothing, however, about cooperating on uncovering corruption and human rights abuses. Fox had promised a fact-finding commission to investigate disappearances during the 1960s and 1970s, but took no action until the high-profile murder on October 19, 2001, of Digna Ortíz, a prominent human rights lawyer. He then commissioned the human rights ombudsman to prepare a report on past abuses, which could only prove an embarrassment to the *PRI*. The 3,000-page report, released on November 27, concluded that 532 people who disappeared during that period had been illegally detained by security forces, including the military, and that 275 were murdered and their bodies disposed of. Fox appointed an independent truth commission to investigate the abuses, ostensibly with the aim of bringing those responsible to justice. (In June 2002, he ordered the declassification and release of 80 million intelligence files from the *PRI* period).

Oddly, however, Fox opposed resuming an inquiry into the 1968 Tlatelolco Massacre (see page 190), saying it was time to focus on the future, not the past. The Supreme Court disagreed in January 2002 and upheld a lower court decision that overturned a decision by the justice department that the statute of limitations precluded an investigation. On July 2, former President Luis Echeverría (1970-76), now 80, was summoned before the commission and spent six hours being interrogated about Tlatelolco, which occurred while he was interior secretary, and about atrocities committed during his term as president. He refused to answer, saying he would give his responses in writing. Never before had a president or former president been held accountable for his actions.

Still smarting from the human rights report, the *PRI* was outraged in January 2002 when Fox's comptroller general and attorney general announced that an investigation produced evidence that *Pemex* sent $120 million to the oil workers' union, which in turn channeled the funds to Francisco Labastida's 2000 presidential campaign. The interim *PRI* president, Dulce María Sauri, denounced the charges as politically motivated. The *PRI* thirsted for revenge; it got it in April.

With the rightward, pro-U.S. shift in Mexican foreign policy under Fox, it was inevitable that the *PRI* and the parties of the far left sooner or later would find common cause. The left began coalescing over Fox's lovefest with President Bush. On September 8, 2001, just three days before the terrorist attacks on New York and Washington, Fox addressed a joint session of the U.S. Congress and stressed the need for mutual trust. He praised Bush effusively as a friend and ally. When ultra-conservative Senator Jesse Helms praised Fox as "a great leader," it did not go unreported in Mexico. After the terrorist attacks, Fox quickly pledged his cooperation with the United States in beefing up border security. Although the Mexican public was largely in agreement with Fox on the terrorism issue, the opposition parties favored a more neutral position. It was not to be; Fox delivered an address to the nation in which he denounced terrorism as a "war against humanity," and he made another visit to Washington in October. As a sop to the left, however, he made it his policy that no Mexican troops would be used in any U.N. action—not that the United States expected Mexican military cooperation.

As another sop to the left, Fox visited Cuba in February 2002, which seemingly continued Mexico's tradition of friendship with the Castro regime. Foreign Minister Castañeda clearly stated in Havana that Mexico, as before, would not support a perennial resolution brought before the U.N. Human Rights Commission in Geneva urging Cuba to allow greater freedom of expression. But Fox outraged Castro—and the Mexican left—by breaking with tradition and meeting with Cuban dissidents. Relations were strained further when more than 20 dissidents invaded the Mexican Embassy (see Cuba). But relations with Cuba came close to the breaking point in April. First, Fox hosted a U.N. conference on poverty in Monterrey, which Castro decided to attend at the last minute. Castro left in a huff on the first day of the conference after making his speech, accusing Fox of pressuring him into leaving before Bush arrived; Fox flatly denied he had pressured Castro. A few days later, in Geneva, Mexico not only voted for the resolution critical of Cuba's human rights record, it co-sponsored it! An outraged Castro then broke with diplomatic courtesy and released a secretly recorded tape of his conversation with Fox concerning the Monterrey poverty summit that corroborated Castro's contention that Fox had pressured him into leaving; basically, the Cuban president was calling the Mexican president a liar. The Mexican left rallied to Castro's side, and in an unprecedented action, the Mexican Senate denied Fox permission for a trip he had scheduled to the United States and Canada. Fox was humiliated, and argued that the Senate's action would damage Mexico's international prestige. But the *PRI* had its revenge for the corruption probe, petty as it was. (Fox later was given "permission" to attend the summit of Latin American and European Union leaders in Madrid in May.)

In politics, the power struggle between the dinosaurs and the reformers within the *PRI* erupted to the surface with a fury during the election for the new party president in February 2002. Tabasco's Roberto Madrazo, as expected, was the candidate of the dinosaurs (who, not surprisingly, prefer the term *"tradicionalistas,"*) while Beatríz Paredes, speaker of the Chamber of Deputies, was the choice of the reform wing. During and after the bitter campaign, the two rivals came close to disemboweling their party. In the balloting on February 24, 2002, about 3 million *Pristas* voted, and the count was so close the final results weren't announced until March 3. Madrazo was declared the winner by a slim 52,000-vote margin, or 1.7 percentage points. The rift in the party may not heal in time for the crucial mid-term elections in July 2003.

The *PRD* also elected a new leader in a campaign that also was rambunctious but mercifully less acrimonious. The contenders were former interim Mexico City Mayor Rosario Robles and Senator Jesús Ortega. The election on March 17 was marred from the start by poor organization and high abstention, and stained by such irregularities as stolen or stuffed ballot boxes and burned ballots. Fewer than 700,000 of the party's 4.2 million registered members participated. As with the *PRI* election, it took nearly a week to certify the results. In the end, Robles was declared the winner with 60.8% of the vote.

Other Current Problems
Drugs

Given the geographic reality of Mexico's 2,000–mile border with the United States, it was inevitable that Mexico would become a conduit in the traffic of illegal drugs from Colombia to the United States. It is estimated that 70%–80% of the cocaine and heroin entering the United States comes across that lightly guarded border. Apart from those two drugs of Colombian origin, vast quantities of Mexican–grown marijuana also stream across the border, as do methamphetamines. It was also inevitable that domestic drug cartels would arise in Mexico, further corrupting already corrupt governmental and law enforcement institutions.

Until 1997 there were three major drug cartels operating in northern Mexico: the Gulf Cartel on the eastern flank, based in Matamoros, Tamaulipas, and headed by Juan García Abregu; the Juárez Cartel, based in Ciudad Juárez in Chihuahua and headed by Amado Carrillo Fuentes; and the Tijuana Cartel in Baja California Norte, run by the Arellano Felix brothers, Ramón, Benjamín, Eduardo and Francisco Rafael. Of these four brothers—there were a total of 10 siblings—Benjamín was considered the brains behind the business, while Ramón was a bloodthirsty enforcer.

These three groups had unofficially "divided" the 1,200–mile frontier with the United States into operational zones. Occasionally, however, friction between them erupted into gangland–style violence. In one legendary case, a lieutenant of the Arellano Felixes infiltrated the Juárez Cartel in 1989, seduced the wife of a Carrillo Fuentes lieutenant, persuaded her to withdraw $7 million from her husband's account, then killed her and sent her head to her husband in a box. He also reportedly threw the couple's two children to their deaths from a bridge in Caracas, Venezuela. Another spectacular incident was a 1993 shootout in the Guadalajara airport in which Cardinal Juan Jesús Posadas Ocampo was accidentally killed in the crossfire. Francisco Rafael Arellano Félix was convicted of his role in the archbishop's death, as was Joaquín Guzmán of the rival gang. Guzmán escaped in early 2001; Arelllano Félix remains in prison.

In April 1996, the Gulf Cartel was beheaded when García Abregu was extradited to the United States and sentenced to 11 life terms by a federal court in Houston. García Abregu was known for his high–level influence, among others, it is reported, with Raúl Salinas, brother of the former president, and former federal prosecutor Mario Ruíz Massieu. On July 4, 1997, Carrillo Fuentes, nicknamed "Lord of the Skies" because of his use of aging jetliners to ferry massive amounts of cocaine from Colombia and believed to have the largest of the three cartels, died while undergoing clandestine plastic surgery to alter his appearance. Reports surfaced in some Mexican media that his death was a "hit" by a rival drug gang, probably the Tijuana Cartel. Although the report never was officially confirmed, two of his surgeons later were found tortured and killed; a third was granted protection in the United States, where he insisted to investigators that Carrillo Fuentes' death was, indeed, due to nothing more than a botched medical procedure.

Carrillo Fuentes' brother, Vicente, is believed to have moved into the power vacuum created by his death, although he is seen as lacking his brother's genius for organization, logistics and control. The dead kingpin was not even in his grave before a monumental turf war erupted between his cartel and that of the Arellano Felix brothers. Both Juárez and Tijuana became war zones, averaging a killing every two days. Most of them are in imaginatively gruesome gangland fashion by strangulation, suffocation with plastic bags or multiple gunshot wounds. The bodies frequently are burned, dismembered or beheaded and found stuffed into suitcases, oil drums or automobile trunks. The violence has proved beyond the capability of federal, state or local police to contend with.

For a time, the Tijuana Cartel gained the upper hand. It was the richest, most powerful, most feared and most bloodthirsty of the cartels. The brothers maintained their power over public officials with a Godfather–like carrot–or–stick tactic called *"plata o plomo"* ("silver or lead"). They were Mexico's most wanted criminals, and Ramón was on the FBI's 10 Most Wanted List. In one incident, which garnered international news coverage, the gang massacred 19 members of a family in Ensenada who allegedly were competing for the local marijuana market. One reason the heat on them became so intense was that they committed a serious tactical error: they began shooting crusading journalists.

Benjamín Flores, the young publisher of a small daily newspaper in Sonora along the border with Arizona, had regularly reported on alleged ties between drug traffickers and public officials or police. He was gunned down outside his office in July 1997. Four months later, Jesús Blancornelas, publisher of a weekly magazine in Tijuana that has been a nemesis of the Arellano Felix brothers, was critically wounded in an ambush on his car that killed his bodyguard; one of the gunmen also was slain, either by the bodyguard or in the crossfire, and was identified as a hit man for the Tijuana Cartel. Another journalist from Sonora, Luis Mario García, was gunned down on a street in Mexico City in February 1998 minutes after leaving the office of the federal attorney general *(PGR)*, where he had refused to divulge his sources for his story on police corruption. Since 1988, more journalists have been murdered in Mexico than in any other Latin American republic save Colombia, but the number of drug–related killings seems to be accelerating. The wounding of Blancornelas created a backlash against the Arellano Felixes, with other journalists vowing to create unbearable pressure on their cartel. As one of them told this writer, "They can't kill all of us."

The Arellano Félixes' reign of terror came to an end in 2002. First, Ramón was killed in a shootout with police in Mazatlán on February 10. He killed the policeman who killed him in the exchange of gunfire. Because the body was quickly cremated, there was speculation as to whether the corpse was actually that of the notorious drug kingpin or belonged to an imposter; it was reminiscent of the death of the Juárez Cartel's Carillo Fuentes in 1997. Then, on March 9, Benjamín was arrested in a raid on a house in the city of Puebla. Benjamín confirmed that it was Ramón who had been killed in Mazatlán, although his credibility was suspect at best. However, police took blood and saliva samples from Benjamín, and DNA samples taken from the clothes of the man killed on February 10 proved they were a match. Another brother, Eduardo, a surgeon, remains at large and could possibly be assuming a leadership role. Benjamín scored a courtroom victory a month after his arrest when a judge ruled that there was insufficient evidence to implicate him, along with his imprisoned brother Rafael, in Archbishop Posadas Ocampo's death in 1993. A day later, there also was a bizarre postscript to Ramón's death. The Associated Press, citing an anonymous "senior U.S. law enforcement official," reported that the police who killed Ramón were in fact part of a hit paid for by Ismael Zembrano, head of a rival drug cartel in Sinaloa state. Mexican officials declined to comment on the report—but did not deny it.

Because of the endemic corruption that riddles government at all levels and the parallel law enforcement agencies, efforts to combat drug trafficking have sometimes taken on the semblance of a comic opera. Frequent changes of top law enforcement officials, for example, hamstrung any serious attempt to combat the drug cartels prior to 2000. Mexico had seven attorneys general in eight years during the 1990s.

In 1994, then–President Salinas established the Institute to Combat Drugs *(INCD)*, the equivalent of the U.S. Drug Enforcement Administration, but it, too, has had a revolving door, with four directors in as many years. One, Army General Jesús Gutiérrez Rebollo, was fired in March 1997 and arrested, accused of having taken bribes from Carrillo Fuentes. In March 1998 he was sentenced to 13 years and nine months in prison. The Gutiérrez case proved highly embarrassing to the Zedillo administration, coming at a time when the president was trying to prove to the United States that it is serious about drug enforcement. Gutiérrez was replaced by a lawyer, Mario Herrán Salvatti, but in May 1997, on the very eve of President Clinton's first state visit to Mexico, Zedillo abolished the *INCD* and returned its functions to the attorney general's office.

Despite the Gutiérrez affair and the obvious continued influence of the drug cartels, the Clinton administration recertified Mexico as an ally in the war on drugs in February 1997, at the same time that it again decertified Colombia. *The accusation provoked accusations* of cynicism from the Republican majority in Congress; the House of Representatives passed a resolution opposing Mexico's recertification, but the Senate upheld Clinton's decision by a narrow margin.

Another battle between Clinton and Congress erupted in February 1998 when Clinton again recertified Mexico. This time, the head of Clinton's own Drug Enforcement Agency (DEA) publicly opposed recertification and became embroiled in a public dispute with retired General Barry McCaffrey, head of the White House Office of National Drug Control Policy, who supported it. There were leaks to the press that alleged even more high–level corruption than had been reported. The *Washington Times* in February cited a CIA report that Interior Minister Francisco Labastida had dealt with drug traffickers when he was governor of Sinaloa from 1987–93. The Mexicans and

McCaffrey disputed the report. A month later, the *New York Times* reported on a secret DEA document that said the Mexican army's links to drug traffickers were greater than had been previously known. The Mexicans grudgingly lobbied in favor of recertification, but they made it clear they regarded the recertification process as demeaning and insulting to Mexico's sovereignty. This time, despite the negative publicity, a resolution opposing decertification fell short in the House of Representatives.

Between these two certifications, President Clinton made a state visit to Mexico in May1997, his first to any Latin American country. The visit was largely cosmetic, with few tangible results, but Clinton did succeed in ameliorating anti–U.S. feeling by acknowledging that the root of the drug trade was not Mexican greed but the insatiable demand for drugs in the United States.

Whatever good will was gleaned from Clinton's visit evaporated in May 1998 as a result of a secret three–year–long sting operation by U.S. agents to nab Mexican bankers involved in money laundering. Called "Operation Casablanca," the sting involved U.S. agents acting clandestinely in Mexico without the knowledge or approval of Mexican authorities. The operation yielded 150 arrests and $110 million in laundered money, and three Mexican banks were indicted. The operation was hailed as a huge success north of the Rio Grande, but the Mexicans were outraged by what they regarded, with more than a little justification, as a violation of their sovereignty. Clinton and Secretary of State Madeleine Albright offered lukewarm apologies for the failure to consult the Mexicans, but apart from the violation

of the sovereignty issue there was the implicit unstated message: We don't trust you enough to tell you about undercover drug operations.

Bilateral relations appeared back on track when Clinton met with Zedillo in February 1999 for a one–day summit in Mérida, Yucatán, that focused mainly on drugs and trade. The two presidents worked out a new drug agreement that established performance measures of effectiveness (PMEs) for 16 areas of drug control—including reduction of demand in the United States. The United States also agreed to provide increased police training assistance in such areas as airport inspections. A few days after the summit, Clinton again recertified Mexico as an ally in the drug war. That June, 13 cabinet–level officials from the two countries, including U.S. Attorney General Janet Reno, met in Mexico City and reached agreement on such topics as airline fares, immigration and splitting seized drug money. The talks were overshadowed, however, by embarrassing reports in *The New York Times* and *The Washington Post* that Reno and other U.S. officials suspect high–level Mexican officials, including Zedillo's private secretary, of ties to drug traffickers.

In 2000, the newly inaugurated president, Vicente Fox, pledged a crackdown on corruption, which in Mexico is almost synonymous with drugs. In a one-day meeting with his new U.S. counterpart, George W. Bush, in early 2001, Fox pledged continued and even heightened cooperation in the war on drugs, although like his predecessors he voiced his disapproval of the U.S. drug certification policy.

In its first year, the Fox administration scored some significant victories in the drug war. One was the capture on May 24,

2001, of the fugitive former governor of Quintana Roo, Mario Villanueva, who allegedly aided the Juárez Cartel in smuggling 200 tons of cocaine into the United States; he reportedly once flew 440 pounds into the United States aboard his private jet. He had been on the run for two years. In April, a Mexico City judge convicted Juan José Quintero, believed to be one of the leaders of the Juárez Cartel since Carillo Fuentes' death, and sentenced him to 17 years. Another of Carillo's suspected heirs, Ramón Alcides Magaña, known by the sobriquet *"El Metro,"* was captured in Villahermosa, Tabasco, on June 13. It was he who was suspected of paying off Villanueva, $50,000 per shipment.

In April 2001, Mexican authorities arrested 21 alleged members of the Gulf Cartel, now headed by Ociel Cárdenas, among them one of the suspected kingpins, Gilberto García, known as *"El June."* Two months later, Juan Manuel Garza, another of the alleged leaders of the Gulf Cartel, crossed the border from Reynosa into McAllen, Texas, and surrendered to the FBI. That September, six soldiers in an elite anti-drug unit were arrested in Mexico City, accused of protecting Cárdenas, who remains at large.

With the seeming downfall of the Arellano Félix brothers, Mexican and U.S. officials are examining evidence that suggests that the center of gravity in the drug trade has shifted to the state of Sinaloa—the original home of the notorious brothers. At least two known rival cartels have been operating in Sinaloa. One is headed by the Guzmán brothers, Arturo, known as "the Chicken," and Joaquín, who was serving a 20-year sentence for the accidental shooting death of Archbishop Posadas Ocampo in 1993 before he escaped in February 2001. He remains at large, but Arturo was arrested in September 2001. Arturo is believed to be responsible for an elaborate 1,400-foot tunnel under the U.S. border.

The other cartel is headed by Ismael Zembrano, apparently the "rising star" in Mexican drug trafficking. He has been attempting to muscle in on the Arellano Félixes' Tijuana operations for at least a decade, and according to some sources was responsible for Ramón's "execution" in Mazatlán on February 10, 2002. An exceptionally violent turf battle has erupted between the two gangs. Within days of Ramón's death, a suspected Arellano Félix ally was gunned down, sparking a wave of gangland killings. The most spectacular was the abduction and subsequent execution-style slayings of 12 people on May 12 by suspected Arellano Félix operatives.

In mid-2002, the bad news was that an estimated 9,500 tons of marijuana and seven tons of heroin were still being smuggled annually into the United States from Mexico. The good news was that the

Mariachis **in full voice**   *Courtesy: Col. and Mrs. Martin Shuey*

National University of Mexico Library

cocaine traffic has been disrupted, although not stopped, and that there have been more than 10,000 drug-related arrests, including soldiers and policemen, since Fox became president. Probably the biggest haul was the arrests of dozens of policemen—reports vary from 50 to 200—in Tijuana during a federal-state sting operation in April 2002, which also uncovered another tunnel under the border. In June, U.S. drug czar John Walters visited Mexico and praised the crackdown, calling the decapitation of the Tijuana cartel the greatest victory in the drug war since the 1993 killing of Pablo Escobar in Colombia. But a few days earlier, Mexican Attorney General Rafael Macedo was more subdued in a speech to state attorneys general and prosecutors, warning that despite the arrests of 2,000 members of the cartel, it remains in business and its operations remain normal.

Pollution

Mexico City faces a growing air pollution crisis beyond that of any other city in the world. Located in a "bowl" surrounded by high mountains, with a population of 20 million and 3 million cars and trucks, there is literally no air circulation for about eight months a year. The output of *Pemex*, the state-controlled petroleum monopoly, is principally poorly refined, pollutant-laden (particularly sulfur) gasoline. Engine exhaust hangs in the air to the extent that it has been necessary to sometimes close the schools. The No. 1 diseases among the young are respiratory (chronic and debilitating). Government response has been inadequate. Factories have been suspended from operation, and autos (both domestic and foreign) are allotted certain days of the week on which they may be operated.

Typical of the shoddy operations of *Pemex* was a widespread explosion in Guadalajara which claimed 200 lives and injured 1,000. The cause: gasoline had entered the water and sewer lines from a *Pemex* conduit. People complained for two days about the vapors before the ignition, which caused tremendous structural damage and homelessness. *Pemex* denied responsibility.

Mexico City's pollution is made worse by hundreds of tons of human and animal waste which, untreated, is dumped outside the city. It dries, and when the wind blows, it is picked up as a fine dust, further choking the air. Because of this and other pollution problems, educated and wealthy people are leaving the city for places such as San Luís Potosí.

Armed Rebellions

For all its corruption and political violence, Mexico had not experienced actual armed insurrection since the Revolution. Thus, the country was shocked on New Year's Day 1994 when an organized band of rebels calling itself the *Zapatista* National Liberation Army *(EZLN)* launched a bloody offensive against federal institutions in Chiapas state. The group proclaimed itself the champion of the poor southern peasants, most of them full-blooded Indians, much like the revolutionary hero Emiliano Zapata after whom it is named. Disputes between the wealthy ranchers and the impoverished masses had been festering in Chiapas for 175 years. The *EZLN*, whose strength was variously estimated at 200 to 2,000, denounced alleged electoral fraud by which the *PRI* won the governorship of Chiapas. The army was sent in and for 10 days there was some skirmishing in which about 145 people were killed on both sides. Then the government and the rebels agreed to negotiate.

What followed was a media circus. The *EZLN* leader who emerged as its negotiator went by the *nom de guerre* "Subcomandante Marcos," who always appeared in ski mask and with bandoliers containing ammunition that was not compatible with the shotgun he brandished. This "guerrilla" subsequently was identified as Rafael Sebastián Guillén, son of a wealthy Caucasian family in Tampico in far-off northern Mexico and a former *Sandinista* activist. The unmasking of Subcomandante Marcos largely undermined the credibility of the *EZLN*. Nonetheless, they made up in media savvy what they lacked in military expertise and proved to be skilled public relations practitioners. At first, it aroused sympathy, especially because many of its grievances were well-founded. But support began to wane in 1995 after the government engaged in a public relations counteroffensive that cynically blamed the rebels for frightening off foreign investments and thus contributing to the crippling recession. For the most part, the *EZLN* has engaged in what one political scientist wryly labeled "guerrilla theater."

Not so with a second group that burst on the scene—also in the south—in 1996. On June 28, peasants in Guerrero state held a memorial service to commemorate the first anniversary of the massacre of 17 peasants by Guerrero police. Dozens of hooded men and women showed up at the service, calling themselves the Popular Revolutionary Army (ERP). Unlike the EZLN, this group appeared to be well armed with AK–47s and clad more like serious guerrillas, with boots instead of sandals, for example. Alarmed, President Zedillo dispatched thousands of troops to Guerrero, provoking the wrath of many local officials who said the president was "militarizing" the state. Like Chiapas, Guerrero is characterized by a sharp division between extreme wealth (Acapulco and other posh Pacific resorts are in Guerrero) and abject poverty. It was the site of a minor insurgency in the 1960s and 1970s, led by the legendary, Robin Hood–like outlaw, Lucio Cabañas, who in the end was slain by security forces. After the June 28 memorial service, the Organization of American States sent a team of human rights workers to investigate charges of rights abuses in the state.

In August the ERP stunned the country with a series of well–coordinated attacks against military garrisons and police stations, not only in Guerrero but in Chiapas and Oaxaca states as well. They killed at least 18 people, including two civilians, while suffering only two confirmed fatalities. The attacks led to unprecedented security for the annual Independence Day festivities in the capital on September 16, and President Zedillo vowed to suppress the "terrorists." Since their first spectacular military strike, however, the ERP seems to have faded into the background. Unlike the EZLN, the ERP is calling for a violent overthrow of the government and shows no appetite for negotiation. Also unlike _the EZLN, it has failed to win public support, judging from opinion polls that showed two thirds of the public believe the ERP's use of violence was unjusti- _fied. Subcomandante Marcos himself distanced the EZLN from the new group, saying in a public statement, "You fight for power. We fight for democracy, liberty and justice."

In February 1996, the government and the EZLN reached a tentative agreement in the town of San Andrés de Larrainzar, called the San Andrés accords, that would grant the Indians in the south greater autonomy from the institutionalized state and local governments, almost all of them controlled by the PRI. The Zapatistas broke off from talks with the government the following September, alleging the government was acting in bad faith by dragging its feet in implementing the accords. For 15 months the talks were in limbo; it took a shocking tragedy to get things moving again.

On December 22, 1997, about 70 armed members of a PRI–affiliated paramilitary group in Chiapas entered the village of Acteal, about 12 miles north of San Cristóbal de las Casas. Without provocation, they began shooting anyone who presented a target—men, women, children, even infants in their mothers' arms. People were gunned down as they desperately attempted to flee, others as they huddled in a church, an atrocity reminiscent of My Lai during the Vietnam War or the "ethnic cleansing" in the Balkans. When the firing stopped, 45 Indian peasants had been slain, all but nine of them women or children; four of the women were pregnant. At least 25 others were wounded.

The massacre made international headlines and presented President Zedillo with an instant public relations nightmare. Reacting with considerable understatement, the president denounced the massacre as a "cruel, absurd criminal act." In a clumsy effort at damage control, "investigators" from Mexico City hurried to Acteal and initially offered the lame explanation that the massacre had been motivated by a local family feud. There was a time, before the emergence of viable opposition parties and press reforms, that the PRI's version would have been accepted. Mexico's independent media and foreign journalists, however, interviewed survivors and reported that the gunmen, armed with AK–47s and dressed in blue paramilitary uniforms, were members of a PRI paramilitary group from the neighboring village of Chanalho. One survivor stated that the gunmen opened fire in the direction of crying children. Eventually more than 30 men either were arrested, including the PRI mayor of Chanalho, or surrendered. Like the victims, the killers were Indians. The motive for the killings, they explained, was that the villagers were Zapatista sympathizers—including, presumably, the slain babies and fetuses. The opposition PRD demanded the resignations of Interior Minister Emilio Chuayffet and the PRI governor of Chiapas, Julio César Ruíz Ferro. Chuayffet huffily refused to resign, but Zedillo soon sacrificed his number two man on the altar of public opinion and replaced him with Francisco Labastida. Ruíz Ferro yielded to public pressure and resigned in January 1998.

According to subsequent press reports, such killings of peasants by PRI–linked paramilitaries have been occurring regularly on a smaller scale in Chiapas, but the Acteal massacre shocked the nation and the world and forced Zedillo to take action. Among other things, he pledged to reduce the army presence in Chiapas (the army is suspected of providing sophisticated weapons to the paramilitaries) and to crack down on paramilitary groups. Most importantly, however, Zedillo introduced sweeping constitutional reforms to Congress in an effort to jump–start the San Andrés accords. His proposal would recognize the rights of Mexico's 9 million indigenous people and permit them greater autonomy in their local affairs. The rebels denounced the initiative as providing "the peace of tombs." Moreover, some lawmakers in the PRI and the PAN opposed the proposal as giving in too much to the rebels, while the PRD faulted it for not going far enough. To be enacted, the proposal would have to receive a two–thirds vote of Congress and ratification of all 31 of the state legislatures, a goal that seems all but unattainable. If it fails, of course, Zedillo at least will be able to say, "Well, I tried."

Apparently, he didn't try hard enough. A clash between army troops and a resur-

The "divers rocks" at Acapulco

Conch shells for sale

gent *EPR* in Guerrero on May 31, 1998, left 11 civilians dead. Three days later, in Chiapas, there occurred the worst violence since the so–called peace process began. The *EZLN* ambushed a combined army-police patrol and in the ensuing clash eight rebels and one policemen were killed. Soon thereafter, Mary Robinson, the U.N. commissioner for human rights, rebuked the Mexican government for its alleged rights abuses in Chiapas. U.N. Secretary–General Kofi Annan touched off a diplomatic furor in June when he suggested the United Nations should play a role in the peace process. Mexico swiftly and vigorously denounced any outside interference in its internal affairs. Annan just as quickly backed off, and he made a three–day visit to Mexico in July to meet with Zedillo and Mexican human rights groups. Although Chiapas was not on the formal agenda, the two leaders discussed it at length. In the end, Annan said the government could be exerting more effort, but he also urged the rebels to return to the negotiating table, invoking the chiché, "It takes two to tango."

It appeared the "tango" might resume in November 1998 when 29 *Zapatista* delegates showed up in their trademark ski masks for a government–initiated meeting in San Cristobal de las Casas; Subcomandante Marcos was not among them. The government delegation included six congressmen from all three major parties. The rebels soon dashed any hopes the

talks might resume in earnest. They accused the congressmen of being "racists" and refused to return to the bargaining table until the government met the five demands that led to the collapse of the talks two years earlier, including release of *EZLN* prisoners, democratic reforms, disbanding of paramilitary groups and demilitarization of much of southern Mexico. The rebels even complained about the accommodations the government had provided for them, saying they were being treated "like animals."

The *Zapatistas* attempted to regain the public relations initiative in March 1999 by staging a "national referendum" on their five demands. Of course, the wording of the referendum items was heavily slanted. It turned into a public relations debacle.

In April 1999, a potentially explosive incident ended peacefully. About 1,000 unarmed *Zapatistas* came down from the hills and "reoccupied" the city hall in San Andrés de Larrainzar, site of the first talks. The 150 outnumbered state policemen wisely fell back without opening fire. A few days later, 300 state policemen expelled the few remaining *Zapatistas* without violence or arrests.

For his part, Subcomandante Marcos finally came out of hiding on May 9, 1999 for the first time since November 1997, attending a meeting in the Chiapas village of La Realidad. There, he delivered the usual diatribe against the government, the *PAN*, the *PRD* and foreign investors.

The peace process remained moribund until after the 2000 presidential election, and it took the election of the conservative *PAN* candidate, Vicente Fox, followed a month later by the election of *PRD* candidate Pedro Salazar for governor of Chiapas, to get it moving again. Fox's first official act after being inaugurated on December 1, 2000, was to fulfill a campaign pledge to order the withdrawal of army troops from Chiapas as a sign of good faith. Fox also introduced a constitutional amendment to Congress in December that would accede to one of the *Zapatistas'* demands, to grant greater autonomy to Mexico's indigenous citizens. With the detested *PRI* out of power both in Mexico City and in Chiapas, and a president in power who seemed serious about peace, the ball was then in Subcomandante Marcos' court. He was now dealing with a president who was at least as astute a public relations practitioner as himself.

What occurred next was typical of Marcos' theatrics, and it garnered worldwide media attention. The *Zapatistas* staged a caravan to the capital in March 2001, reminiscent of the civil rights marches in the United States during the 1960s, which the media quickly labeled the *"Zapatour."* Their stated goal was to lobby Congress directly for the indigenous rights bill. Traveling in trucks and buses, and leaving their weapons at home, Marcos and 23 other *EZLN* members and their entourage traveled through 12 states, receiving tumultuous welcomes from the impoverished Indians along the way, before arriving in the capital on March 11. They asked for permission to lobby the Chamber of Deputies. Fox was agreeable, although legislators of his own party adamantly opposed the idea.

he Zapatistas remained in the capital for 18 days and were threatening to return to Chiapas empty-handed on March 23 when they suddenly received the invitation to address the lower house. The EZLN leaders delivered not strident demands, but respectful requests to the country's lawmakers on March 28 during a meeting of several hours that was broadcast on national television; the always unpredictable Marcos did not appear. That same week, the army undertook the dismantling of its bases in Chiapas. The last base was dismantled in April.

After the dramatic appearance of the masked Zapatistas, which had turned into the inevitable media circus, Congress took up debate on the indigenous rights bill in earnest. The original bill was based on the accords reached by the EZLN and the government in 1996 in San Andrés de Larrainzar. But there was grumbling by PRI legislators that the bill infringed on the traditional authority of state governors, and from Panistas that it conceded too much to the Zapatistas. The Senate unanimously approved an amended version on April 25. Three days later, the Chamber of Deputies passed it, 386-60. This time the opposition came from the PRD and the PT on the left, because of language that stresses the preeminence of national sovereignty over indigenous rights. The EZLN also opposed the watered-down version because it eliminated the guarantee of rights over land, water and natural resources.

The constitutional amendment then required ratification of a majority of the state legislatures, and the Zapatistas staged protests outside the various legislatures and blockaded highways—but did not shoot. Nonetheless, on July 12, Michoacán became the 16th state to ratify the amendment. It took effect on August 15, with the EZLN still complaining about "betrayal."In the year since, the situation has remained tense, but to date the hostility has been confined to rhetoric, not gunfire.

On June 15, 2001, Fox announced an ambitious economic development program for southeastern Mexico and Central America, called Plan Puebla-Panamá. But the Zapatistas also denounced this plan as a capitalist ploy to force the Indians from their lands.

Culture: Appropriately symbolizing Mexico's ethnic composition is a park in Mexico City called La Plaza de las Tres Culturas. In Mexico as much as anywhere in the New World, the blending of the Spanish and Indian produced a third, separate race, the mestizo, which predominates today.

The giant of Spanish America in more ways than population size, Mexico had a rich cultural heritage centuries before the Spanish Conquest. The Aztec, Mayan, Toltec, Mixtec and other indigenous civilizations all have contributed much to Mexican folklore. Just as the mixing of bloods created a new race, so did the infusion of Spanish art, music, literature, food, and architecture, give rise to a new, discrete culture. It is Mexico's culture that most North Americans erroneously associate with all of Latin America: mariachi music, a spicy rice, bean and tortilla diet, red–tiled roofs and white stuccoed walls.

After independence, cultural development was slow owing to political instability, the crippling civil war between Liberals and Conservatives from 1857–61, the subsequent French intervention and general inattention to public education. Despite the Porfirio Díaz dictatorship rather than because of it, the late 19th and early 20th centuries were marked by the emer-gence of a distinctly Mexican literature. The most prominent writers of this period were Amado Nervo, Ramón López Velarde and Manuel Gutiérrez Nájera.

The demarcation line of Mexican culture, however, was the Revolution of 1910–20. Besides forever changing the political fabric of the country, the Revolution gave birth to a movement in realist art, appropriately called "revolutionary art," music and literature. Two classic revolutionary novels are Mariano Azuela's Los de Abajo (1916), and Martín Luís Guzmán's El aguila y la serpiente ("The Eagle and the Serpent," 1928), both of which focus on social issues. The poetry of Alfonso Reyes, José Gorostiza and Jaime Torres Bodet and the novels of Agustín Yáñez also are identified with the post–revolutionary period.

Mexico's best–known novelists of the second half of the 20th century are Juan Rulfo (1917-1986), best remembered for Pedro Páramo, and Carlos Fuentes (1928-), whose classic remains El gringo viejo, adapted into the 1989 motion picture The Old Gringo with Gregory Peck and Jane Fonda. The acknowledged master of the short story was Juan José Arreola (1921-2001), a friend of Rulfo's, who developed a half-prose, half-poetry genre called varia invención, after the title of one of his stories. He published 16 books of stories, probably the most renowned being "La feria" and "Bestiario."

But the titan of modern Mexican literature was the poet Octavio Paz (1914-1998), who received the Nobel Prize in 1990, the fifth and most recent Latin American to be so honored. His verse was a critical, brutally honest examination of Mexico's hybrid Spanish–Indian culture, which alienated him from many of his leftist intellectual contemporaries. Yet, when he died at age 84 on April 19, 1998, his former detractors heaped praise on him, and the government accorded him a state funeral.

The premier figures of post–revolutionary art were Diego Rivera (1886-1957) and José Clemente Orozco (1883-1949), whose heroic murals epitomize the social struggle of the Revolution. Yet, both also were at home in the avant–garde art crowd of 1920s Paris, and both were friends of Pablo Picasso, the influence of whose abstractionism can be detected in the paintings of the two Mexicans. One of Rivera's four wives, Frida Kahlo (1907-1954), carved out an international reputation as an artist in her own right and has posthumously become a feminist cultural icon in Europe and the United States.

Mexican music of the post–revolutionary period was dominated by Carlos Chávez, who founded the national symphony orchestra in 1928 and whose classical compositions were drawn from Mexico's Indian heritage. Popular music is characterized both by the ranchero style, a guitar–based sound that celebrates

Cancún, on the northeastern tip of the Yucatán Peninsula *Courtesy: Ann and Martin Shuey*

Mexico's *vaqueros*, (cowboys), and the quintessentially Mexican *mariachis*.

Mexico City has a robust theatrical community, though the works of its playwrights to date have been primarily for domestic consumption.

Mexican cinema, on the other hand, developed parallel with that of the United States, and Mexican films have been exported for several decades now. Many Mexican film stars went on to successful careers in Hollywood, such as Dolores del Río, Ramón Navarro, Anthony Quinn and Ricardo Montalbán. But arguably Mexico's most revered film legend was María Félix (1914-2002), perhaps because she eschewed moving to Hollywood and devoted her career to her native country. Known as the "Marilyn Monroe of Mexico," she made 47 films between 1942 and 1970 and was a national icon. Her death in April 2002 brought thousands of mourners to the Palacio de Bellas Artes in Mexico City; President Vicente Fox extolled her as "a great shrine to our country." Mexican cinema continues to thrive with a new generation of actors, such as Salma Hayak. A recent example of a Mexican film that has received international acclaim is *"De la calle,"* ("On the street"), directed by newcomer Gerardo Tort and released domestically in 2001, which is a searing glimpse of the lives of Mexico's street urchins.

Mexico's television industry has been characterized by a mix of public–private cooperation. The privately owned *Televisa* network is today one of the world's largest, and Mexican programs, chiefly *telenovelas*, are the most popular in Latin America. By the mid–1990s, a new privately owned channel, *TV Azteca*, was making inroads with daring new *telenovelas* that dealt frankly with formerly taboo subjects, such as women's sexuality and official corruption. Some programs began eclipsing *Televisa's* in the ratings.

The Mexican press is nominally independent, but for more than 60 years the Mexican government controlled the supply of newsprint through a subsidized public entity called *Pipsa*. This allowed the *PRI* to wield a powerful cudgel against overly critical newspapers, which often would find their supply of paper cut off. Meaningful reform came with the Salinas administration of 1988–94, but intimidation of the press continues. Mexico is second only to Colombia in the number of journalists murdered each year in Latin America. The press remains largely unbowed, however. About 30 dailies are published in the capital. The paper once regarded as the most prestigious was *Excélsior*, a cooperative owned by its employees, but in recent years its ties to the *PRI* have hurt the paper's credibility and its bottom line. The workers voted in June 2002 to sell the paper because of declining revenues—and lost wages. Newspapers

with greater circulation and with better reputations of independence and aggressive reporting today are *El Universal* and *Reforma*.

Mexico has a more vigorous provincial press than do most Latin American countries; in fact, it is these smaller papers in the interior that frequently are the targets of violence by drug traffickers or corrupt local politicians or police officials who themselves have been targeted by aggressive reporters. Probably the most prestigious of these provincial papers is *El Norte* of Monterrey.

Mexico also has a sizable magazine industry, producing slick, high–quality, full–color magazines comparable with those in the United States or Europe. Probably the magazine most read abroad is the left–of–center *Proceso*, launched by Julio Scherer García in 1976 after the thin–skinned President Echeverría forced him from the editorship of *Excélsior* for his critical reporting and editorials.

The new role of the Mexican media in exposing corruption cannot be understated. Many, if not most, of the allegations of wrongdoing stem from journalistic rather than official investigations. A decade ago, this would have been unheard of. The government used the newsprint monopoly as a carrot and stick to keep the print media in line. The owners of the television giant *Televisa*, meanwhile, were loyal *PRI* partisans. The termination of the newsprint monopoly and the diversification of television with the new network, *TV Azteca*, with the resulting increase in aggressive, investigative journalism, has been as significant a factor in curtailing the power of the once–omnipotent *PRI* as has the rising electoral strength of the opposition parties. In fact, some have viewed the two parallel developments as a chicken–and–egg analogy—which led to what?

At the same time, investigative journalism in Mexico remains a notoriously high–risk endeavor. Journalists investigating links between drug traffickers and public officials have been murdered or intimidated at an alarming rate since 1997 (see Drugs). This is not to say that all Mexican journalists are martyrs and saints, however. For decades, government officials and *PRI* leaders routinely paid bribes to low–paid reporters to ensure favorable news coverage, or—even better—no news coverage. This tawdry practice has been reduced with the election of opposition governors and an opposition president in 2000.

In addition, it must be conceded that too many Mexican journalists are overly subjective in their reporting and are not above slanting or even distorting the facts to make a story fit into that medium's particular agenda. Still, the fearless reporting of such Mexico City newspapers as *Reforma* and *El Universal*, as well as that of

numerous feisty newspapers and magazines along the U.S. border, is a refreshing change from the old days when the press was either cowed or bought, and it has sent many a corrupt official scurrying for cover like cockroaches from a bright light.

Economy: The economy of Mexico is divided into three major sectors: agriculture (20%), industry (30%) and services (50%), a pattern generally associated with advanced nations.

The industrial sector, formerly centered around Mexico City and Monterrey, now is more clustered generally throughout the north, based on factories, called *maquiladoras*, that assemble finished products for export; most are owned by foreign interests, though joint ventures have become more common.

The quasi-socialist nature of the economy during the seven decades of domination of the *PRI*, and especially after the expropriation of foreign-owned oil companies in 1938, hung a "not welcome" sign for foreign investors. For decades, a foreign national or a foreign business could own only a 49% share of real estate or a business. After the 1960s, government participation in industry increased under the *PRI*, which viewed this as a means of extending party power, accompanied by inefficiency and corruption. In the 1990s this was reversed under former President Salinas. By 1993, more than 363 state–owned companies had been sold or shut down, bringing the government (and *PRI*) more than $22 billion.

The *maquiladora* movement greatly stimulated national development, at least in the north. Mexico's hourly wage was less than half that of the United States, and the workforce was literate. The lure of assembling finished goods just across the border at bargain-basement prices was irresistible to U.S. corporation. Of course, it was anathema to organized labor in the United States. The *maquiladoras* led to a veritable boom along the border, and stimulated growth of a middle class. (By 2000, *maquiladoras* accounted for about 48% of Mexico's exports. compared with 10% for oil exports). The North American Free Trade Agreement (NAFTA) of 1994 accelerated the boom and unquestionably helped the country emerge from a disastrous peso devaluation that year.

Petroleum remains the only major government monopoly remaining, but it was a hotbed of *PRI* labor and management corruption. Efforts are now underway to find a means of privatizing *Pemex*, which controls production from the well–head to distribution at the gasoline station. In the last two decades it was forced to depart from production of sulphur–laden, sub–quality gasoline to include gasoline that meets U.S. standards. This was done to accommodate a burgeoning tourist trade; there are now more than 1,200 stations that sell lead-free, low pollutant gas. But Mexican standards are lower, and pollution is therefore higher.

Mexico has the fourth–largest oil holdings in the world, more than 200 billion barrels, 10 times that of the United States. But since the oil resources are part of the "national patrimony" under the constitution, there was considerable grumbling at the idea of pledging money from oil production to secure loan guarantees from the United States and other nations.

Mexico has profited enormously from Cuba's economic isolation, especially in tourist income. Various resorts offer complete package vacations to winter–weary neighbors to the north seeking the warm sun. The popularity of these soared in the late 1980s and 1990s as the peso plummeted in value against the dollar. Agriculture is limited by a lack of arable land and division of what there is into small parcels. The official policy of the government after the Revolution favored redistribution of land, much of it into communal plots called *ejidos*, but the program moved forward at a glacial pace. In reality, the most intensive production can come from large holdings, or those that are members of farmers' cooperatives.

In 1993, Mexico's economy appeared to be blooming, but in reality it expanded by only 0.1% that year. Part of the illusion of growth was caused by increased U.S investment in anticipation of the results of the NAFTA treaty, part was the repeated reassurances of former President Salinas, and part was Mexico's claim that it possessed $30 billion in hard currency foreign reserves. The latter claim was by the central bank controlled by the *PRI*, not the government.

In order to support this image of expansion, Mexico began printing more pesos—too many pesos—in the latter half of 1993 and 1994, diluting their genuine worth. Foreign investors began to demand more and more interest, as high as 33% per annum to compensate for what they decided was greater risk, a correct conclusion. More conservative investors chose two other alternatives: withdrawing their investments from Mexico, or investing in *tesobonos*, short–term (90 days) bonds repayable in dollars at still exorbitant interest rates (20%). The return on these bonds, 80% per year, should have been a clue of what was coming, in view of a well-known principle: the greater the return, the greater the risk.

Mexican reserves were sapped by the need to pay these bonds, an increasing burden, and by the need to defend the value of the peso, then 3.5 to the U.S. dollar, by buying them with dollars formerly held in reserve. Further complicating the picture was the imagined southern revolution, and the colorless character of the *PRI* presidential candidate, Ernesto Zedillo. In desperation, huge amounts were pumped into the *PRI* political campaign in the summer of 1994, further depleting reserves.

The break came on December 20, 1994 when the peso was devalued by 20% and then allowed to "float" four days later, all of which led to its decline of 50% by early 1995. The stock and bond markets reacted as might be expected: Panic selling fanned the flames, contributing to the decline of the peso. The IMF revealed in 1995 that in the two weeks before the December 1994 devaluation of the peso, individuals and institutions quietly moved $6.7 billion out of Mexico.

The year 1995 was difficult for Mexicans. The peso, devalued by 50% in 1994 and floating in 1995, went down to 7.6 to the dollar (prior to the devaluation the rate was 3.5). President Clinton proposed massive bailout loans to Mexico totaling $13.5 billion, which he got despite widespread oppositioin in Congress. More than 16,000 businesses ceased operation and more than 2 million Mexicans lost their jobs in 1995. Banks foreclosed on mortgages and repossessed autos at a record rate; more than 12% of bank loans were in default (the rate is about 1.2% in the U.S.). The loans were guaranteed by the Mexican equivalent of the Federal Deposit Insurance Corporation, known as *Fobaproa*. An organization of creditors, *El Barzón*, entered the scene, correctly charging that the aid being received by Mexico is being used to help depositors, not debtors. *Fobaproa* became the focus of a major political scandal in 1998 when it was learned that many of the failed banks had made risky loans to *PRI* political cronies (see History).

In January 1997, amid much media hype, Mexico repaid the last installment of the $13.5 billion loan President Clinton had authorized to see Mexico through its financial crisis. Mexico proudly noted that the loan was repaid two years ahead of schedule, a rebuttal to those in the U.S. Congress who had predicted the American taxpayers would never see any of the loan repaid. What Mexico downplayed was the fact that the loan was repaid by borrowing the necessary amount from European sources. The repayment, however, was a needed public relations gesture, coming two months before Clinton was to decide whether or not to recertify Mexico as an ally in the drug war.

Since the 1994-95 crisis, the Mexican economy has rebounded into one of the healthiest in Latin America, weathering both the drop in oil prices in 1998 and the Brazilian market panic of January 1999. GDP growth since 1997 has averaged a respectable 4.3% per year. Mexico finished 2001 with a GDP of $590 billion, second only to Brazil, which was $5,840 per capita, third highest in Latin America after Argentina and Uruguay. The drop in oil prices was probably responsible for a decline in GDP growth from 7% in 1997 to 4.8% in 1998 to 3.4% in 1999. Growth shot back up to 7.2% for 2000, thanks largely to the continued high price of oil. But the U.S. recession in 2001 and the September 11 terrorist attacks that year proved a double whammy for the Mexican economy. The recession caused trade to plummet, and the terrorist attacks caused a general decrease in tourism, compounded in Mexico's case by the inconveniences caused by tightened security along the border. Consequently, GDP for 2001 declined by 0.3%. Economists were predicting positive growth of from 1.5-2% in 2002, not enough to keep up with the growth in the labor market.

The NAFTA-generated boom in the north shrank the unemployment rate, from 5.5% in 1996, 3.7% in 1997, 3.2% in 1998 to a mere 2.8% in 1999 and 2.3% in 2000, the lowest (officially) in Latin America. In 2001, it crept back up to 2.8%. Inflation, meanwhile, has declined gradually from 18.6% in 1998 to 13.7% in 2001.

The Future: This revision is being written, coincidentally, on July 2, 2002—President Fox's 60th birthday and the second anniversary of his historic election victory. He is now about a fourth of the way through a term that was to have proven transcendental. Has it?

Yes.

Wielding the significant power that rests within the executive branch, Fox has ushered in the anticipated new era. He has cracked down on official corruption and drug trafficking. He has held public officials accountable for their actions for the first time. He has diversified and decentralized his government. He has broadened Mexico's foreign policy. He has sought an accounting for past human rights abuses.

He has been far less successful in passing meaningful legislation through the Congress, with the exception of the constitutional amendment on Indian rights. Last year, this author correctly predicted that Fox's conservatism on economic and foreign policy issues would eventually lead the *PRI* and the *PRD* to form a majority center-left opposition bloc that could hamstring the president. The embarrassing vote to deny Fox permission to travel to Canada and the United States—something no Congress ever did to a *PRI* president, of course—in retribution for Mexico's vote for a U.N. resolution critical of Cuba's human rights record was probably the first of many such rebukes. But even Fox's own *PAN* deserted him on his tax restructuring plan.

Nonetheless, even Fox's failure to deal with Congress is historic and transcendental. Heretofore, the *PRI*-controlled Congress was merely a rubber stamp for the wishes of *PRI* presidents. Mexico at long last has an independent legislative branch, so vital for a true system of checks and balances.

The same is true of Fox's stormy relationship with the press. Criticism from the slavish pro-*PRI* media was anticipated, but Fox, and even his wife, have been stung by criticism, some of it personal and admittedly nit-picky, from crusading newspapers that had exposed *PRI* abuses and had supported his candidacy. However, that is what a free press is supposed to be able to do in a democratic society, and while Fox has lashed back angrily at the media at times, he has not resorted to legal or extralegal measures to intimidate them as his predecessors once did. That change, too, is transcendental.

Thus, something monumental *did* happen in Mexico on July 2, 2000, something that ranks with the collapse of the Soviet Union, the election of a black president of South Africa, and the handshake of Yasser Arafat and Yitzhak Rabin. This author's master's thesis in 1971 was a comparison of the Soviet and Mexican revolutionary party systems, which came to power almost simultaneously, and it analyzed why one became totalitarian and the other a peculiar form of authoritarian democracy. I suspected 31 years ago that I would never live to see the *PAN*, which then had but 15 gratuitous seats in the lower house of Congress, no senators, no governors and precious few mayoralties, defeat the monolithic *PRI*, any more than I would live to see the other three events mentioned above. It is intriguing that the *PRI* clung to power for nine years longer than the Soviet Communist Party I once compared it with.

It also is worth noting in the way of contrast that in 1900, Mexico entered the 20th century under the dictatorship of Porfirio Díaz. One of the victorious *PAN* senatorial candidates in Coahuila, told me on election night in 2000, "Throughout the 20th century we have been under one form of dictatorship or another." How symbolic that on December 1, 2000, Mexico entered the 21st century under its first opposition president.

Fox's first major vote of confidence or no confidence will come in the crucial mid-term elections on July 6, 2003. In mid-2002, Fox still enjoys wide public approval. A year from now, as in any democracy, how well he and the *PAN* do may depend on the vicissitudes of the economy, which has been sluggish.

But much also will depend on the *PRI* itself. A bloody, internecine struggle for control between the dinosaurs and the reformers came close to disemboweling the party earlier this year. If Roberto Madrazo, the winner from the dinosaur faction, attempts to turn back the clock, the *PRI* probably will continue to lose credibility and voter appeal, and the once-powerful party could dwindle away into oblivion or become a mere shadow of its former self, like the Liberal Party of Great Britain.

Demographics must be taken into account here. A growing percentage of voters is under the age of 35. In Saltillo on election night in 2000, I was struck that the crowd of revelers was composed overwhelmingly of young people (see photo). The following day I heard on the radio that exit polls showed that 57% of young people voted for Fox; if so, they unquestionably proved the decisive factor in his victory. It would be politically foolhardy for all parties to fail to recognize that. These young people are full of hope and expectations. They do not have a past to long for nostalgically; they are concerned with the future.

Regardless of whether or not Fox and the *PAN* suffer reverses at the polls in July 2003, regardless of whether or not the *PRI* recaptures the presidency in July 2006, one thing is certain: Mexico will never be the same again—thank God.

The Republic of Nicaragua

A Saturday afternoon native dance in the countryside

Area: 49,163 square miles.

Population: 4.2 million (estimated).

Capital City: Managua. (Pop. 1.2 million, estimated).

Climate: Tropical, with distinct wet and dry seasons. Rainfall is heavier on the Atlantic coast, with the heaviest downpours from May to December.

Neighboring Countries: Honduras (North); Costa Rica (South).

Official Language: Spanish.

Other Principal Tongues: English, Indian dialects.

Ethnic Background: *Mestizo* (A mixture of Spanish and Indian, 69%), White (17%), Negro (9%), Indian (5%).

Principal Religion: Roman Catholic Christianity.

Chief Commercial Products: Cotton, coffee, bananas, sugar.

Currency: Córdoba

Gross Domestic Product: US $2.4 billion in 2001 ($470 per capita).

Former Colonial Status: Spanish Colony (1519–1821).

Independence Date: September 15, 1821.

Chief of State: Enrique Bolaños (since January 10, 2002).

National Flag: Blue, white and blue horizontal stripes with a coat of arms on the white stripe.

Nicaragua is the largest and most sparsely settled of the Central American republics. It has three distinct geographic regions: a triangular mountain extension of the Honduran highlands, with its apex reaching to the San Juan River valley on the Costa Rican frontier; a narrow Pacific coastal plain containing two large lakes (Managua, 32 miles long and Nicaragua, 92 miles long); there is a wider Atlantic coastal plain.

The Pacific plain is part of a trough that runs from the Gulf of Fonseca in the northwest through the two scenic lakes and the San Juan River valley to the Atlantic. This is one of the most promising sites for a new interoceanic canal. There is considerable volcanic activity in the northwestern part of this region. Three volcanoes reaching to some 5,000 feet have emerged from Lake Nicaragua, another stands majestically on the north shore of Lake Managua and some 20 more

lie formidably between the lakes and the Gulf of Fonseca. The moist easterly winds from the Caribbean Sea drench the San Juan River valley and the Atlantic coastal plains, which are heavily forested.

The Pacific coastal plains receive less rainfall and in some parts require flood control and irrigation for agriculture. The majority of Nicaragua's population is found between the western slope of the highlands and the Pacific Ocean. The few settlements on the Atlantic coast were founded by the British and the population in this region is predominantly of African–West Indian origin, with a few pockets of native Miskito Indians.

History: The Spanish conquerors reached Nicaragua from Panama in 1519. They found a fairly dense population of agricultural Maya Indians on the shores of Lake Nicaragua, from whom gold ornaments were acquired. The Spaniards returned in 1524 and founded settlements at Granada and León. By 1570 the flow of gold had ceased, most of the settlers left and the two towns were put under the administration of the captaincy–general of Guatemala.

León, more accessible to the sea, was chosen as the administrative center rather than the larger and more wealthy Granada. The eastern coast was entirely neglected by the Spanish—the towns of Bluefields and Greytown (San Juan del Norte) were established by British loggers cutting mahogany and other valuable timber. By the time of independence, the Lake Nicaragua basin was the site of productive sugar and indigo plantations and the town of Granada was the center of political conservatism. León, the center of less valuable grain and food production and capital of the province, was the seat of anti–clerical political Liberalism.

Independence came to Nicaragua as a by–product of the movements in Mexico and in the South American states. Through the actions of Guatemala, Nicaragua joined Mexico under Iturbide and became a member of the Central American Confederation, but withdrew from it in 1838. The Liberal–Conservative conflict that marked the period was manifested in Nicaragua by an as-yet unsettled feud between the people of Granada and León. Other factors also entered into Nicaraguan problems. British interests established a protectorate over the Atlantic region, known as the Autonomous Kingdom of Miskitia, which was not incorporated into the national territory until 1860. During the 1850s and 1860s, Commodore Cornelius Vanderbilt's transit company became involved in ferrying California-bound gold prospectors across Nicaragua, and the Liberals of León invited William Walker, a U.S. soldier of fortune, to head up their army to crush the Granada Conservatives. At the same time, there were conflicts of British and North American interests who backed the various factions.

Walker's successes in León were such that Vanderbilt was induced to aid the Conservatives of Granada. Walker finally was captured and executed in 1860 and the Conservatives established their dominance, which would endure for 30 years. They quelled numerous uprisings, installed their presidents as became necessary and convenient and gave the country a semblance of stable government. During this period the cultivation of coffee and bananas was started, gold production was resumed and a few immigrants arrived from Europe. However, factional quarrels among the Conservatives made possible a Liberal coup in 1893 and the seizure of power by youthful José Santos Zelaya.

Sixteen years of tyrannical misrule by Santos Zelaya became notorious both at home and abroad. He persecuted his Conservative enemies, betrayed his Liberal supporters and systematically looted both public and private funds. He maintained his position with a ruthless system of spies and police, suppressing all critics.

Despite his misrule, the economy prospered, railroads were built and public schools were increased.

His execution of two U.S. adventurers aroused the government of the United States and the dictator fled into exile in 1909; this left the country in a state of near anarchy—the government was bankrupt and foreign creditors were threatening intervention. The Conservatives appealed to Washington to intervene while New York financiers bought up foreign bonds and installed economic supervisors to manage the Nicaraguan economy and insure repayment of their investments.

Liberals revolted against a situation in which their country was the ward of foreign banks in 1912. United States warships landed a few Marines, suppressed the revolt and became involved in a 20-year war for the elimination of banditry and the establishment of a stable government. While Washington supported Conservatives, Mexico supported Liberals in a see–saw contest. Larger forces of Marines were introduced in 1927 to con-

trol the country; the United States tried to resolve the internal Liberal–Conservative conflict through supposedly free and democratic elections. A guerrilla leader fighting against the Marines became a legendary figure in Nicaragua and most of Central America: Augusto César Sandino. A colorful character sporting a 10–gallon hat and six–shooter, he carried on lively correspondence with the commanders of his U.S. opponents.

The Somoza Dynasty

Hoping after six years that things were settled, the U.S. forces left Nicaragua in 1933, with the government in the hands of a Liberal president (Sacasa) and a peace guaranteed by a Marine–trained police force, the *Guardia Nacional*, under the command of Anastasio ("Tacho") Somoza. By 1934 it was obvious that true power lay with the *Guardia* and its commander. Sandino still maintained his guerrilla forces, but had agreed to a cease–fire once the Marines had gone. The government accepted a sweeping amnesty for Sandino's men, additionally offering them land and jobs.

Things might have settled down if the Nicaraguan Congress had not voted to raise the salary of Sandino's 100–man personal guard and shortly afterwards to reduce the pay of the military. Further, Sandino's followers had not turned in all of their arms. The *Guardia* decided that Sandino had to be eliminated. A suppos-

Augusto César Sandino

edly innocent President Sacasa invited Sandino to the presidential palace to discuss outstanding issues, where there were several meetings. But after a farewell following supper one evening, the *Guardia* met Sandino at the gate, took him and his men to the airfield, where they were executed and secretly buried.

Anastasio Somoza ruled until his assassination in 1955 and Congress named his son, Luis, to the presidency, which he occupied until 1963. The elections that year were relatively quiet and honest.

In 1967, Anastasio ("Tachito") Somoza Debayle became the third member of the family to occupy the presidency. Barred by law from succeeding himself, Somoza created a caretaker three–man *junta* in 1971 to rule until 1974, when he was elected to a second term with 91.7% of the vote. Somoza was a "Liberal" in name only. Nine small opposition parties were barred from the election.

Anastasio Somoza's second term would be his last. Resentment against the regime grew as increasing numbers of Nicaraguans objected to his heavy–handed tactics. His brutal treatment of political opponents convinced many that the regime would never tolerate democratic elections in the country. The business community was bitter and angry with Somoza's levying of kickbacks on the major commercial transactions conducted in the country. Residents of Managua were outraged by the *junta's* blatant misuse of international aid earmarked for the city's reconstruction following a disastrous 1972 earthquake. Most Liberals and leftists were offended by the strongman's ostentatious display of wealth: his family owned a half billion

dollars worth of investments and 8,260 square miles of Nicaragua, while 200,000 peasants were landless.

Revolution

For the first time, opponents of the regime began to unite—joined by one thing: *anti*–Somoza feelings (but little else). A broad–based coalition—ranging from Marxist guerrillas to conservative business leaders—was formed. While the business sector continued its strikes to dry up the economy, the guerrillas battled the National Guard.

Many groups which helped oust Somoza, wittingly or unwittingly, joined together with the Sandinista National Liberation Front *(FSLN)*, named after the legendary nationalist guerrilla leader of the 1930s.

Actually, the origin of the group carrying this name was in the early 1960s under the auspices of Cuba's Fidel Castro. The *FSLN* grew rapidly when Anastasio Somoza became president. His brutal and corrupt rule pumped new life into the guerrilla movement. As the *Sandinistas* gained strength from association by non–communist elements, Somoza retaliated with sweeping attacks against rural peasants suspected of aiding the guerrillas—ironically, a tactic that caused many peasants to join them. Mass support for the *FSLN* developed further following the violent earthquake that leveled Managua in December 1972 when it became known that Somoza was pocketing some of the international relief funds and buying up Managua real estate at fire–sale prices.

While the *Guardia* enjoyed a 4–to–1 manpower edge, the *Sandinistas* and associates boasted a force of 3,000 members by 1978. It was actually divided into three groups: two openly Marxist and a third— by far the largest—consisting of socialists and non–Marxist leftist trade unionists, Catholic Church members and a sprinkling of businessmen. Known as the

Anastasio Somoza Debayle

Terceristas (Insurrectionists), this last group is best remembered for its daring 1978 occupation of the National Palace in Managua.

Collapse of the Regime

The crucial jolt in the long train of events leading to the overthrow of the Somoza regime came in January 1978, when assassins gunned down Pedro Joaquín Chamorro, longtime Conservative Party critic and publisher of the nation's leading newspaper, *La Prensa*. Although the identity of the killers remains unknown, most Nicaraguans attributed the murder to Somoza. Chamorro was widely respected— 10,000 attended his funeral—and his death quickly touched off three days of bloody demonstrations throughout the nation. The *Guardia* responded in a heavy–handed manner; its ruthless mop–up operations in five major cities left 3,000 dead. The Chamorro murder, combined with the *Guardia's* indiscriminate killing of many innocent bystanders, cost the regime the vital support of business leaders who then called for a general strike to demand Somoza's resignation. The strike brought more government reprisals. As the death toll mounted, the United States proposed a referendum to test national support for the Somoza regime. The plan was quickly rejected by the strongman in early 1979 because he insisted "If they want me to leave Nicaragua, they'll only get me out by force."

The Sandinistas were only too willing to oblige him. During its final two years in power, the Somoza regime faced a basic military problem: it seemed to be under attack throughout the country. The only significant Nicaraguan sector that continued to support the dictatorship was, as always, the *Guardia*. Meanwhile, the guerrillas continued to score important victories in rural areas, while major power groups in the cities were becoming more militant in their opposition to the strongman. One by one, rural areas began to fall under rebel control and by the spring of 1979 it was clear that Somoza could not endure much longer.

The Nicaraguan leader refused to budge. Secluded in his Managua bunker— a grim reminder of the last days of World War II in Berlin—Somoza continued to direct the military activities of his *Guardia*. Curiously, Somoza made the same tactical error committed by Hitler during the battle for Stalingrad. Both men ordered heavy bombing of civilian areas in order to deny the enemy food and shelter. In both cases, however, the bombed–out buildings provided ideal concealment from which the defenders could fight back. In Nicaragua, the *Guardia's* bombing of populated areas killed virtually no guerrillas—but it did further solidify public opinion against Somoza.

216

Sandinistas **celebrate Somoza's overthrow, 1979**

Along with the heavy shelling of civilian areas, Somoza also ordered the summary execution of suspected opponents of his regime. Many of these were youths, whose blindfolded and bound bodies were often found strewn along the shores of Lake Managua. During the final two years of fighting, thousands were killed and left homeless.

By late May 1979, ranking members of the regime began to flee the country. Somoza himself finally abandoned his bunker and flew to the United States, where he boarded a luxury yacht for a leisurely trip to Paraguay, to be given refuge by the Stroessner regime of that country. Thus ended one of the most durable dictatorships—46 years—in Latin American history.

He lasted only 14 months in Paraguay, however, before he was gunned down by three persons reported to be Argentine guerrillas. He had become depressed, drank to excess and grew fat. Before his death, he was involved in a much-publicized love affair with a former Miss Paraguay—who also happened to be the mistress of Stroessner's son-in-law.

The Sandinista Era

On July 19, 1979, the *Sandinistas* took control of Managua—and a *new* revolution was about to start. Their non-communist allies in the revolution had little power within the new government.

After Somoza's ouster, the country was administered by a three-member *junta* called the Revolutionary Junta Government (*JRG*). One of the three was Violeta Barrios de Chamorro, widow of the assas-

sinated journalist. This group, in turn, followed policy directives established by a nine–member *Sandinista* National Directorate, controlled by the *FSLN*. Power was shared with a Council of State, a *Sandinista*–dominated legislative body of 47 members representing various political and economic groups as well as the armed forces and the *FSLN*.

Although the Marxist influence was clearly in evidence—especially in the schools, the armed forces and the media—the government was initially primarily nationalistic. But in international relations, Nicaragua quickly joined the non–aligned bloc of Third World nations while also establishing close ties with communist–bloc nations. The regime refused to condemn the Soviet invasion of Afghanistan and in 1982 supported Argentina's invasion of the British Falkland Islands. Trade pacts were signed with various communist nations, including Bulgaria, East Germany, the Soviet Union and Cuba.

Relations became particularly close with the Castro regime of Cuba. Almost all communist *Sandinista* leaders visited Havana and in mid–1980 Fidel Castro was guest of honor in Managua for the revolution's first anniversary celebration. As many as 6,000 Cuban "advisers" were stationed in Nicaragua; hundreds of Nicaraguan youths were sent to Cuba for educational programs that stressed Marxism.

Increased ties with communist nations led to strained relations with the United States. Some powerful members of the U.S. Congress regarded the *Sandinista* regime as a threat to Central America.

Although the Carter administration provided some financial aid to Nicaragua in the hope of strengthening the pro–democratic forces there, the Reagan administration responded with a tough stance against what it concluded was a Soviet-sponsored client state within the Central American area.

Thus, Washington suspended all aid to Nicaragua in the spring of 1981 after the State Department accused the *Sandinistas* of aiding leftist guerrillas in El Salvador. In late 1981, the Reagan administration again denounced Nicaragua for "arms trafficking to El Salvador," and for building the largest military force "in the history of Central America." In early 1982, Reagan lectured Nicaragua's new ambassador to the United States against "adopting alien influence and philosophies in the hemisphere."

The Pentagon unveiled huge CIA aerial photos in 1982 to prove that Cuba and the Soviet Union were providing sophisticated military equipment to Nicaragua. Newly enlarged Nicaraguan airfields could be used for bombing raids against the Panama Canal, according to some U.S. officials. Several days later, a badly informed U.S. State Department staged a highly publicized press conference to display a Nicaraguan guerrilla who had been captured in El Salvador. But when the cameras started rolling, the Nicaraguan coolly accused his captors of torture. State Department officials, highly embarrassed by the incident, promptly deported the man to Nicaragua (where he received a hero's welcome). Later, Nicaraguan strongman Daniel Ortega Saavedra called an urgent meeting of the U.N. Security

Council to protest "aggressive and destabilizing acts" by the United States against his country. In June 1982, Washington accused Nicaragua of firing on a U.S. helicopter over international waters near the Nicaraguan coast (The United States recognizes a 12–mile territorial limit; Nicaragua claims 200 miles).

Despite the running conflict, both countries made very unenthusiastic efforts to negotiate. In April 1982, Washington gave the *Sandinistas* a list of proposals for improved ties. When Managua promptly responded with its own set of counterproposals, the Reagan administration delayed two months before replying. The reason: Washington thought that deteriorating economic conditions at home and exile opposition from abroad might doom the *Sandinista* regime.

The "Stolen" Revolution

What had been envisioned by the U.S. as a pluralistic revolution in Nicaragua that ousted the Somoza regime was not correctly evaluated. There were many elements joined together in the anti–Somoza struggle, but only one had cohesiveness: the *FSLN*. It was natural that upon the departure of Somoza this organization would assume a position of power. At first, other groups were allowed to nominally participate, but in 1982–83 the true nature of the *FSLN* became quite apparent, although during the revolutionary struggles the Marxist nature of the movement had a very low profile. There was no difficulty in initially enlisting the support of *La Prensa* and the Roman Catholic Church. Thus, although Conservatives have charged that the *Sandinistas* "stole" the revolution, such an accusation was not accurate. They simply filled a political vacuum and then refused to share it with any other Nicaraguan element. They insisted, on the contrary, that all Nicaraguans accept the *Sandinistas* as the only political force in the country—a move that never succeeded. In 1984, Ortega was elected president by a predictably wide margin. The opposition was divided and denied access to the media.

During more than 10 years in power, the *Sandinista* regime succeeded in generating widespread disillusion and disappointment within Nicaragua. Conservative rallies and meetings were broken up in 1981 and were later totally prohibited. A prominent leftist within the regime resigned, accusing the *Sandinistas* of planting "a reign of terror . . . a Soviet style Stalinist regime in Nicaragua."

The press that was not directly seized by the government was regularly harassed; *La Prensa* soon became the only non–government newspaper which quickly came to face daily government inspection and approval. Mrs. Chamorro resigned from the *junta* as a result. International credit quickly evaporated as the United States withdrew loan promises and private foreign banks balked at extensions of credit. The treasury had been emptied by Somoza, compounding the problems of the fledgling government.

Human rights violations sharply increased. Ultimately, an estimated 10,000 people, including former Somoza supporters and former members of the *Guardia*, were jailed and other opponents were sent into exile. A dispute between the government and the Miskito Indians (who had been given a large measure of independence under Somoza) was needlessly provoked. They were accused of aiding counter–revolutionary Somoza exiles living in Honduras. When the government attempted to resettle about 10,000 tribe members away from border areas, an estimated 20,000 fled to Honduras from where they started to harass the *Sandinistas*. The government responded by raiding Miskito settlements along the border in early 1982, leaving an estimated 105 dead. This would lead in the future to an alliance between the Indians and the "Contras."

Following a visit by Pope John Paul II in 1982, the Vatican adopted firm policies and selected personnel opposed to the regime.

Faced with acute money problems, the government desperately sought aid in 1982 from Cuba, the Soviet Union and other sources. The only response was inconsequential—it came from Libya.

For four years Nicaragua faced charges from abroad that a repressive, non–democratic dictatorship had taken hold of the country. That judgment was correct; the *Sandinistas* arranged a decade of increasing political, economic and social misery for Nicaraguans in the name of communism, which existed only as a set of slogans repeated endlessly.

President Reagan requested in 1985 military aid for the *Contras* ("antis"), a loosely–organized but relatively effective opposition to the regime. It had been armed by the CIA. Congress refused, but did allow $14 million for "humanitarian" aid. Ortega received *pledges* of $200 million from Moscow, much to the embarrassment of Congress. President Reagan imposed a total economic embargo on Nicaragua as required by law.

The state–controlled economy ultimately shrank to about one–third of the level that existed before *Sandinista* power. Crops were not harvested because of military pressures and the unwillingness of farmers to accept artificially low prices. Foreign aid and assistance dried up by 1987 when the final stages of a precipitous decline was underway in the former Soviet Union and its client, Cuba. Shortages were rampant and housing was shabby and crumbling.

Between 1985 and 1989 the U.S. Congress did not distinguish itself in dealing with the question of Central American "communism" and Nicaragua in particular. Reasons for its vacillating attitude were fashionable, but evasive: (1) "no more Vietnams," (2) we must *force* the *Sandinistas* to negotiate and (3) lack of *Contra* unity. At election time, aid for the *Contras* was provided lest there be an accusation that members of Congress were "soft on communism."

A last–ditch effort was made to overcome the *Contras* located in neighboring

Daniel Ortega exhorts a group of students about the spirit of the *Sandinista* revolution

Signing of the Summit Agreement

Honduras in 1988; the *Sandinista* effort was repulsed when two battalions of highly trained U.S. troops were sent to that country.

The Arias Plan

Signed by the leaders of Costa Rica, El Salvador, Guatemala, Honduras and Nicaragua meeting at Guatemala City on August 7, 1987, the Arias peace plan obligated the *Sandinistas* to negotiate a cease–fire with the *Contras,* allow freedom of the press and other media, cease political repression and allow free, open and democratic elections. Support of rebel forces in adjoining nations would be banned. It further provided for monitoring of all requirements by National Conciliation Commissions which would include government opposition, Church officials and Inter–American Human Rights Commission representatives. It appeared doomed to failure, since such conditions, if allowed to exist in Nicaragua, would lead to the replacement of *Sandinista* control.

Ortega, who signed the agreement, is an educated, but intellectually dishonest person, as were his cohorts of the *Sandinista* junta. He probably viewed the instrument only as a means to indefinitely lure the U.S. House of Representatives into continuing denial of military aid to the *Contras,* and to postpone the day of reckoning. Negotiations with the *Contras* and internal opposition groups began in early October 1987. They broke down immediately—the *Sandinistas* announced that "there will never, at any time or any place, be any direct *political* dialogue with the *Contras.*" The impasse continued until Cardinal Obando y Bravo volunteered to mediate talks between the parties. His efforts were short-lived: the *Sandinistas* were firm in their ultimatum that they were present to receive a military surrender from the *Contras,* not to discuss politics. The Cardinal walked out in disgust in January 1988, ac-

cusing the *Sandinistas* of negotiating in bad faith.

La Prensa and *Radio Católico* were allowed to resume their activities during the first week in October 1987. But they were again shut down for 15 days in the spring of 1988.

The *Sandinistas* declared a unilateral cease–fire in early 1988, *not* because of the Arias peace plan, but because of dire economic conditions within Nicaragua and again, with the intent to lull the U.S. House of Representatives into inactivity. The cease–fire was extended repeatedly into 1990.

The Ortega strategy worked temporarily for the *Sandinistas.* When former President Reagan requested $37 million in aid for the *Contras,* 10% of which would be military, the House rejected it, voting in favor again of humanitarian aid. In 1989, the Bush administration didn't even bother to ask for military assistance for the *Contras,* but had to settle for more humanitarian aid. To counter this, the administration linked world-wide arms reduction sought by the Soviet Union to reduced arms supply for Nicaragua.

Faced with economic and political bankruptcy, the *Sandinistas* engaged in a transparent effort to rig elections set for February 25, 1990, particularly insofar as it tried to control the media.

Chamorro Upsets Ortega

As the elections approached, it was clear that the *Sandinistas* were uneasy about the outcome. A cease-fire with the *Contras* was canceled, but the half–hearted military effort which followed was ineffective. Ortega *et als* took to the campaign trail. He discarded his khakis and appeared in a variety of costumes and said anything to please everybody, swinging his hips to rock music. Television and newspapers were full of propaganda extolling the party, and political rallies were held at which balloons and other trinkets

were distributed. The *Sandinistas* outspent the opposition, the National Opposition Union *(UNO),* by at least 10–1.

The *UNO* candidate was Violeta Chamorro, widow of the publisher slain in 1978 under the Somoza regime. One observer labeled the *UNO* campaign as amateurish. *Sandinista* efforts were stepped up, including crude efforts such as bludgeoning those attending opposition rallies.

A Washington Post–ABC poll published on February 21, 1990 predicted a *Sandinista* triumph by a margin of 48% to 32%. Even though the headline read "Pre–Election Poll Shows Ortega Leads," there were, in the article, strong disclaimers as to its accuracy.

The pollsters might well have listened to a wizened farmer, who said "Only I know what I am going to do on my ballot." Violeta Chamorro and the *UNO* won by 55.2% to 40.8%! Even the White House was startled.

Chamorro was sworn in on April 25 in Managua. Her inaugural speech was inspiring and displayed signs of apparent astuteness. After her inaugural, Nicaragua's slim hope for improved conditions evaporated swiftly. Much to the dismay of most participants in *UNO,* she appointed Humberto Ortega, brother of Daniel, to continue as minister of defense. She did direct that the army be reduced from about 80,000 to zero on the ground that it was no longer needed. There also were shadowy, informal forces, used to protect property seized by the *Sandinistas* by "law" between the time of Chamorro's election and the time she took the oath of office.

Following her inauguration, the disbanding of the *Sandinistas* and the *Contras* added tremendously (almost 100,000) to the rolls of the unemployed, which have risen to more than 50% of the workforce. Few Nicaraguan exiles have returned; the wealthy ones in particular, who took their money with them insofar as possible, remain outside the country. Conditions on farms, prosperous in the 1970s, were—and are—dreadful. Many that were split up and given to peasants and *Sandinista* fighters now are idle, with no hope of restored production. Potential investment capital is being withheld from Nicaragua.

The *Sandinistas* were betrayed by Soviet–Cuban communism and voted out of office by the Nicaraguans. The lower-level *Sandinistas* have deserted their cause, as have former low–income supporters of the movement. The more wealthy *Sandinistas* cling tenaciously to that which they acquired during their years in power. The *UNO* coalition in the National Assembly turned on Mrs. Chamorro, claiming she betrayed the elections of 1990. All she was able to speak about (vaguely) was "reconciliation" of Nicaragua.

With the *Sandinistas* in charge of the army, the police and the judiciary,

Nicaragua was far from democratic. The president ignored the legislature and formed an "inner cabinet" to rule the nation. She particularly relied on her son-in-law, Antonio Lacayo, in making crucial decisions that favored the top–drawer *Sandinistas*. The *Sandinista* controlled Supreme Court purported to nullify all actions of the National Assembly after September 2, 1992, on the ground that on that date it lacked a quorum! Its ruling was ignored.

The U.S. Congress appropriated $104 million in aid for Nicaragua to be released to it in 1992. Citing a U.S. law that forbids foreign aid to be granted to a country that has confiscated the property of U.S. owners without compensation, a senator demanded that the money be held up in the spring of 1992; it was. A team dispatched by the United States demanded the firing of army commander Ortega, discharge of the police chief and judicial reform, in addition to compensation, as the price for the aid. Nicaragua did fire the police chief and said it would "discuss" compensation of U.S. owners, specifying no time limit for the latter. President Bush reluctantly released $50 million in December.

Following President Clinton's inaugural, Nicaraguan government officials intensely lobbied the U.S. Congress for release of the remainder. On April Fool's Day 1993 the Clinton administration sent the funds as requested, citing "important strides that have been made by the Nicaraguan government," and "they need our help to continue this process . . ." An offended senator charged that the money was sent to a "government of thugs" and the decision was a "bad April Fool's joke come true." The Chamorro government did promise that Humberto Ortega would leave as army commander . . . in late 1995, by retirement.

Continued U.S. pressure resulted in the announcement that Humberto Ortega would be removed in 1994 instead of 1995; he was put under house arrest in early 1994 because of alleged involvement in a 1990 crime.

Humberto Ortega finally retired in early 1995, but his chief of staff was named to succeed him, thus continuing *Sandinista* control of the military. Six years after being elected by hopeful Nicaraguans who had "voted with their stomachs," Chamorro had proven totally incapable of raising Nicaragua out of its abject poverty.

The Alemán Presidency

Sensing an opportunity for a comeback, Daniel Ortega announced his candidacy for the October 20, 1996, presidential election. He entered the race an underdog behind the popular and conservative former mayor of Managua, Arnoldo Alemán, the candidate of the Liberal Alliance, like Ortega, 50 years old. Gone were Ortega's *Sandinista* uniform and his Marxist rhetoric, which he realized had helped defeat him in 1990. Six weeks before the election, the *Sandinistas* even softened the lyrics of their truculent anthem, removing the reference to "the Yankees, enemies of mankind." Opinion polls indicated that the rehabilitated Ortega, preaching a more social democratic gospel, was running even with Alemán and might be given another chance to lead Nicaragua out of the mess he had helped to create. With 23 candidates on the ballot, there appeared little likelihood that any one of them could garner the necessary 45% to avoid a runoff. But once again, the Nicaraguan voters startled prognosticators by giving Alemán a decisive first–round victory of 48.4% to Ortega's 38.6%—even less than Ortega had obtained in 1990. Ortega immediately—and unconvincingly—cried fraud. A delegation of observers from the Organization of American States—including longtime *Sandinista* apologist Jimmy Carter and former Secretary of State James Baker—concluded there was no evidence of any major irregularities. Carter was instrumental in persuading his friend Ortega to accept the results rather than resorting to mass protests as he had threatened to do.

The 1997 transition was to prove far more tense than that of 1990. Where Chamorro had pragmatically and almost with flattery sought to placate the *Sandinistas* whom she knew could easily overthrow her, Alemán was confrontational. But then, he had a personal score to settle with the *Sandinistas*. A onetime supporter of Somoza, Alemán had five farms confiscated by the *Sandinistas* in the 1980s. In 1989, while he was under house arrest, the *Sandinistas* refused even to allow him to accompany his wife, who was dying of cancer, to a hospital. Nor are the *Sandinistas* fond of Alemán. A lawyer by profession, Alemán was elected mayor of Managua in the same 1990 election that brought Chamorro to power. Like Guatemala's President Alvaro Arzú, Alemán compiled an impressive record of achievement as mayor of the capital city, which still felt the effects of the 1972 earthquake. He greatly improved the traffic engineering system and beautified the city. He also removed the *Sandinistas'* revolutionary art from walls and billboards.

Alemán was inaugurated on January 10, 1997 for a term that had been reduced to five years, marking the first time in Nicaraguan history that one duly elected civilian president had succeeded another. Seven Latin American presidents attended the ceremony, which was marred by the arrest of a former *Sandinista* security officer and two other men who were carrying four sticks of dynamite. Nonetheless, Alemán delivered a conciliatory inaugural address, offering a dialogue with the arch–rival *Sandinistas*. At first, the *Sandinistas* appeared resistant to his overtures and continued their bombastic threats to take their opposition into the streets. Yet, perhaps faced with the reality that they could no longer marshal the kind of public support they once enjoyed, the Ortega brothers met privately with Alemán in late January to discuss dialogue and conciliation.

Alemán has displayed a take–charge attitude, promising to reverse the *Sandinistas'* hostility to free–market capitalism and to make Nicaragua more attractive to foreign investors in order to bring in desperately needed capital. He also proposed to greatly expand the free–trade zone Chamorro established in 1992, which attracted Mexican–style *maquiladora* assembly plants, mostly for apparel. The zone has doubled exports every year, but the total is still only a fraction of the exports from Honduras' *maquiladoras*. Alemán said he hoped to greatly expand the output and create thousands of jobs to alleviate the country's punishing 52% rate of unemployment and underemployment.

Alemán's most controversial and divisive proposal was the plan to return land expropriated by the *Sandinistas* to its former owners, compensating the new owners with government bonds. After months of bickering between the Liberals and the *FSLN*, the two major parties came to realize the delay in resolving the title issue was hurting Nicaragua economically by discouraging foreign investment. Moreover, the United States was leaning on Alemán to resolve the issue because of the thousands of Nicaraguans displaced by the Revolution who were residing in the United States. By an overwhelming 70–4, the National Assembly approved a com-

Former President Arnoldo Alemán

Street scene in Bluefields on the Caribbean Sea

promise measure that essentially verified the current ownership of most of the 1 million hectares the *Sandinistas* had seized. The new law grants title to those who received rural plots of less than 35 hectares or urban plots of less than 100 square meters. About 5,000 pre–revolutionary landowners thus were frustrated in their hopes of getting their property back.

In 1998, the *Sandinistas* continued to suffer reversals of fortune. On January 30, the official *FSLN* newspaper *Barricada*, which had been the pro–Somoza daily *Noticias* before it was expropriated in 1979, succumbed to the realities of the marketplace and the loss of government subsidies and ceased publication. Its editors accused the Alemán government of retribution through the withholding of government advertising, a time-honored practice of Latin American strongmen, but their protests carried a hollow ring given the *Sandinistas'* own intimidation and censorship of the independent media when they were in power. *Barricada* subsequently reopened in March 2000.

Another blow, which threatened the very unity of the *FSLN*, came as a bombshell. On March 3, 1998, Ortega's 30–year–old stepdaughter, Zoilamérica Narváez, publicly accused him in an interview in a daily newsletter of having sexually abused her for years, beginning when she was 11 and continuing into the years that he was president. Narvaez's estranged husband, Alejandro Bendaña, like her a committed *Sandinista* and Ortega's former deputy foreign minister, denounced his former boss' "abuse of power." Ortega immediately and adamantly denied the accusation, as did his common–law wife, Rosario Murillo, Narváez's mother. Ortega supporters inexplicably denounced the charges as

"politically motivated" and even accused Narváez of participating in a CIA plot to undermine Ortega. The leader of the Liberals in the Assembly, Eliseo Nuñez, accused Ortega of hiding behind his legislative immunity and called on him to resign. With the storm of controversy swirling around him, Ortega issued a plea for party unity. It appeared to have worked; in May, he was reelected as Sandinista leader. Almost simultaneously, however, Narváez filed a formal civil suit against her stepfather and also accused high–level Sandinistas of aiding and abetting in the sex abuse. Ortega claimed parliamentary immunity, and for weeks the Nicaraguan media reported almost daily "no–I–didn't–yes–you–did" exchanges between Ortega and Narváez.

In April, Ortega attempted to divert attention from the sex scandal. In a mass demonstration, he called Alemán a "dictator" because of his move to re–establish a state security agency similar to that of the Somoza period. Ortega hinted darkly that if the president threatens human rights—as though he himself hadn't—the *Sandinistas* may be called upon "to take up arms." Alemán responded to this sinister suggestion on radio, calling on Ortega to "bury forever the hatchet of war and the rifle of death and let Nicaragua emerge from the poverty in which he left it."

In late October and early November 1998, Alemán faced a far greater adversary even than Ortega: Hurricane Mitch. The storm killed 2,863 Nicaraguans, 948 were missing and more than 867,000 were affected. Seventy–one bridges were destroyed, 70% of the roads were damaged and 30% of the banana crop was wiped out; Mitch also wiped out any hopes of immediate economic recovery. Only Honduras suffered greater devastation. International relief aid poured in to alleviate the appalling human suffering, but unlike the case of Somoza after the 1972 Managua earthquake, this president was not accused of pocketing the money as Somoza did after the 1972 earthquake.

However, Alemán was accused of enriching himself while on the public payroll. In February 1999, Comptroller General Agustín Jarquín, a member of the Social Christian Party and a longtime political rival of Alemán's, issued a report alleging that the president had increased his personal wealth by 900% between 1990, when he was elected mayor of Managua, and 1997, his first full year as president. Alemán did not dispute the increase but maintained it had come from property in Nicaragua and Miami that he

Nicaraguan cowboy

had inherited from his parents and from his wife's family. He countered that Jarquín was merely out to get him. Alemán counterattacked in November 1999, when the national police chief, before a crowd of journalists, arrested Jarquín and a well-known television journalist on supposed fraud charges. Jarquín was accused of permitting the journalist, Danilo Lacayo, who previously had served as President Chamorro's press spokesman, of signing a contract under a bogus name. Jarquín called the charges retribution for his investigation of Alemán. An appeals court subsequently dismissed the charges.

The Power-Sharing Accord

A major political development occurred in June 1999 whose long-term implications are still uncertain. The long-antagonistic Liberals and *Sandinistas* suddenly concluded an agreement by which they would cooperate more in governing the country and would apportion seats on the Supreme Court and the electoral council between them. The agreement also would have the effect of reducing the number of frivolous individual presidential candidacies; 23 people had appeared on the 1996 ballot. On the surface, it seemed a welcome respite from the partisan bickering that had plagued the country. However, the minor parties charged—with some degree of justification—that the new pact was designed merely to divide the country's political spoils between them and exclude all others from a place at the public trough. Similar bipartisan pacts had existed in Colombia and Venezuela.

As Alemán entered the last year of his five-year term, he could point to a dramatically improving economy as foreign investment poured into the country and shopping malls began to spring up, a sign of a growing consumer economy. But the charges of corruption took a toll on the president's popularity and even his control over his party. A poll taken by a Swedish firm in April 2000 showed that 88% of Nicaraguans believed Alemán was corrupt. Moreover, members of the president's party, now called the Constitutionalist Liberal Party *(PLC)*, voiced displeasure over the president's autocratic method of hand-picking party candidates for the November 2000 municipal elections. They also alleged that his call for a constitutional convention was aimed at allowing him to run for reelection. In May, Defense Minister Antonio Alvarado resigned, citing his disagreement with Alemán on the selection of candidates and his call for a constitutional convention. He also hinted he might run for president in 2001, though it was unclear whether he would do so within the *PLC* or launch his own movement.

About the same time, Alemán's brother-in-law, Eddy Gomez, who reportedly was angered that he was not chosen as the Liberal candidate for mayor of Managua, resigned his seat in the Central American Parliament and joined the opposition Nationalist Liberal Party. The Nationalist Liberals are identified with the defunct Somoza dictatorship. In the end, there was no constitutional convention, so Alemán was barred from seeking reelection.

The effect of the unholy political pact between the *PLC* and the *FSLN*, two parties with decidedly undemocratic ancestries, was seen clearly in the November 2000 municipal elections. The two major parties, through questionable challenging of the signatures of voters on party registration petitions, disqualified all parties but themselves from participating. In the voting, the *FSLN* won 11 of the 17 departments, and captured the mayoralty of Managua under the candidacy of Herty Lewites, one of the party's moderates.

The Elections of 2001

The *PLC* and the *FSLN* continued their heavy-handed treatment of other parties in the 2001 presidential race as well. Through their control of the Electoral Council, they denied registration to Agustín Jarquín's Social Christian Party, the National Unity Movement of former army commander Joaquín Cuadra and the fledgling party organized by former Defense Minister Alvarado, among others. Only the venerable Conservative Party was allowed to compete with the two major parties.

Denied registration for his own party, Jarquín made a bid to challenge Ortega for the *FSLN* presidential nomination. But in June 2001, the *Sandinistas* decided to stick with Ortega. The *PLC*, meanwhile, had nominated former Vice President Enrique

The Metropolitan Cathedral of León, considered the finest examples of colonial architecture in Central America

Bolaños, who had resigned the previous October to make the run. The Conservatives' standard-bearer was Noel Vidaurre.

When Ortega formally began his fourth campaign for the presidency— symbolically on July 19, 2001, the 22nd anniversary of the Sandinistas' defeat of Somoza—polls showed that he had a much better than even chance to stage a dramatic political comeback. Bolaños, who himself enjoyed a reputation for personal honesty, was nonetheless tarnished by his association with the unpopular Alemán, who was stonewalling queries into how he had increased his personal wealth ninefold between 1990 and 1997.

To further enhance his chances, Ortega broadened his political base by enticing prominent former Sandinista opponents to join his new coalition, called the Convergence. Chief among them was Jarquín, whom Ortega persuaded to become his vice-presidential running mate. Ortega also sought to sanitize his former guerrilla image even more than he had in 1996, abandoning the familiar black and red Sandinista colors in favor of the less threatening pink, and as a campaign slo-

President Enrique Bolaños

gan he adopted, "The Path to Love." He embraced the Liberals' free-market policies, and he even pledged to continue the Liberals' close ties with the United States. His victory appeared all but certain.

But as the November 4 election drew ever nearer, Ortega's lead in the polls shrank steadily. One factor was the withdrawal from the race of the Conservative Party's Vidaurre, reportedly under U.S. pressure not to divide the anti-Sandinista vote. After the September 11 terrorist attacks on the United States, Ortega vowed, if elected, to cooperate in the war against terrorism. Bolaños, however, effectively countered him with embarrassing television ads that showed then-President Ortega embracing Libyan leader Muammar Qadhafi and Iraqi dictator Saddam Hussein, both suspected of supporting Islamic terrorism. Ortega was stung further in October when two of his erstwhile protégés, Sergio Ramirez, who had been his vice president, and Father Ernesto Cardenal, his foreign minister, announced that they would boycott the election because, they complained, neither Ortega nor Bolaños was "worthy." The U.S. ambassador, in a startling breach of protocol, appeared openly at Bolaños rallies and said in interviews that an Ortega victory could jeopardize the future of crucial U.S. aid. Even Florida Gov. Jeb Bush, brother of the U.S. president, got into the act by urging the thousands of resident Nicaraguans in Florida to vote for Bolaños.

On election day, Nicaraguan voters once again confounded the pollsters and handed Ortega his third successive humiliating defeat, 56% to 43.5%, prompting jubilant Liberals to take to the streets chanting, "Three strikes, you're out!" The sometimes acrimonious campaign ended on a positive note, however, with Ortega once again graciously conceding defeat in the best democratic tradition, and an equally magnanimous Bolaños praising the Sandinistas as "worthy opponents."

In the balloting for the 90-seat National Assembly, the Liberals retained their majority with 49 seats to 40 for the Sandinistas and one for the Conservatives. In addition, under the Liberal-Sandinista pact, the retiring president (Alemán) and the losing presidential candidate (Ortega) both received seats in the assembly—thus assuring Ortega continued immunity from his stepdaughter's molestation charges and Alemán from charges of illegal enrichment.

Bolaños was inaugurated on January 10, 2002. Almost immediately, he launched an anti-corruption campaign that soon had him at odds with his predecessor. Alemán was charged with involvement in a $1.5 million embezzlement scheme at the state-owned television station. Bolaños sought to have Alemán, the new president of the National Assembly, stripped of his legislative immunity. Shortly before this book went to press in July, Alemán lashed out at Bolaños as "inept." Alemán offered to make a deal, and warned that if Bolaños did not accept it

223

could plunge the country into an economic and political crisis like Argentina's. The schism between the two men threatened the unity of the *PLC*.

Culture: Though a substantial number of Nicaraguans lead a modern, urban life comparable to that of the large cities of Latin America, the majority live in rural simplicity. The culture closely resembles that of the rest of the Central American states. Upheavals associated with the post–revolutionary period have affected the lives of all, very adversely.

The music of the people, derived from their Spanish–Moorish conquerors, is used to accompany a wide variety of local dances and festivals. It was possible to see the latest dramatic and musical productions professionally performed in the busy capital of Managua, and after a short journey to also view a traditional *mestizo* comedy quaintly performed in a combination of *Hahuatl* (an Indian dialect), Spanish and *Mangue*, another Indian dialect.

Under the *Sandinistas*, most education heavily stressed communist principles and ideals—all alien to a basically politically unskilled people who are seldom politically intelligent and aware. Culturally, Nicaragua is currently (except in the rural countryside) a desert.

Nicaragua contributed one of the world's foremost poets, Rubén Dario (1867–1916).

Economy: Although Nicaragua is largely based on agriculture, which employed 65% of the work force, the increased development of light industry before the revolution gave Nicaragua's economy a degree of hope for a broader base than was found in most other Latin American countries. Underpopulated and with many unexploited natural resources, the nation has a substantial potential for tremendous economic growth with proper management.

Nicaragua's most important farm commodities are produced in the western region. Rich in volcanic soils, this section is the source of cotton, coffee and sugar. The cattle industry was also expanding in the western section. While the eastern region is largely devoted to banana production, some operations have been shifted to the west coast because of banana plant dis-

ease. Nationalization of large producing farms did not contribute to their efficiency, and the breakup of some into smaller peasant farms actually seriously lowered production.

The U.S. commercial embargo on Nicaragua was a serious long–range economic threat. Commercial relations between the two nations had been steadily declining since 1982. The 1985 total embargo had a devastating effect. The closing of U.S. ports and a ban on technological imports all but shut down the economy. As in Cuba, perhaps even *worse* than Cuba—Soviet economic difficulties and increasing limitations on its economic aid to socialist countries added a somber note to Nicaragua's possibilities for development. During 1986–90, virtually all that was exported was bananas, sold to the Soviet Union and Eastern Europe at inflated prices.

The Chamorro government, hamstrung by the ever–present threat of the *Sandinista* military, accomplished little at reducing unemployment and underemployment, which totaled more than 65%. Alemán, however, has moved more aggressively to bring Nicaragua in line with International Monetary Fund demands and to make the country more attractive to foreign investors. GDP growth was a respectable 5% in 1997. Meanwhile, the IMF extended Nicaragua a three–year, $136 million loan package and praised Alemán for stabilizing the currency and reducing the bloated, featherbedded bureaucracy. The World Bank also granted a $70 million loan to help transform the financial sector from the old Marxist system.

Hurricane Mitch caused billions of dollars in damage to the economic infrastructure in 1998, a blow the country could ill afford and which added another $300 million to the already oppressive $6.2 billion external debt. Surprisingly, however, Mitch did not derail the expanding economy. GDP growth was still 4% for 1998 and a respectable 6.2% for 1999. In 2000 it had tapered off slightly to 5.0%, still more to 3.5% in 2001.

On the down side, Nicaragua's per capita income fell lower than Haiti's in 1997, to $436, making it for the first time the poorest country in the Western Hemisphere. In 1998 it dropped even lower, to

$431, compared with $497 for Haiti. It has increased slightly since then, to $454 in 1999, $466 in 2000 and $470 in 2001—hardly cause for cheering. Unemployment has steadily declined, from 12.3% in 1998 to 11% in 1999 to 9% in 2000. It rose slightly in 2001 to 10.3%. Inflation has remained steady at about 10% in 2000 and 2001.

The Future: No sooner had Ortega been defeated for the third time than pundits began predicting he would be forced from his leadership role in the *FSLN*. However, they had made the same prediction after his second straight defeat in 1996, but despite that and a personal scandal, Ortega remained in charge. What was not clear from the 2001 elections was whether the vote was a repudiation of the Sandinistas or of Ortega personally. The Sandinistas remain a potent political opposition, with nearly half the Assembly seats, and Ortega did increase his percentage of the vote by 5 percentage points from 1996. He is a member of the National Assembly, and he probably will remain at least a power broker or kingmaker. Several Sandinistas already have expressed interest in challenging him for the leadership.

For his part, the new president, at 73, hardly represents a change of generations; he is 18 years older than Ortega. His greatest threat, however, comes not from the opposition Sandinistas but from Alemán cronies within the *PLC*. The two leaders were on an inevitable collision course, and within days of his election Bolaños declared that he did not want to see Alemán as president of the National Assembly. Nonetheless, shortly before the new Assembly was sworn in, the outgoing body blocked a measure that would have stripped the tarnished retiring president of his legislative immunity, and Alemán was elected president of the assembly. The embezzlement charges against Alemán may well destroy the *PLC*. Bolaños needs to build a bipartisan consensus to tackle the country's woeful economic problems, including an oppressive $4 billion foreign debt, and that will not be easy under the circumstances.

In short, Nicaraguan politics promise to remain as intriguing as ever, while the long-term prospects for Nicaraguan democracy and economic development remain as nebulous as ever.

The Republic of Panama

The almost completed Panama Canal—final blasting of a channel, October 1913

Area: 28,745 square miles.

Population: 2.89 million).

Capital City: Panama City (Pop. 1 million, estimated).

Climate: Tropical, with clearly marked wet and dry seasons. The heaviest rainfall is from May to December.

Neighboring Countries: Colombia (southeast); Costa Rica (northwest).

Official Language: Spanish.

Other Principal Tongue: English.

Ethnic Background: Mulatto (mixed African and European, 72%); African (14%); European (12%); Indians and other (2%).

Principal Religion: Roman Catholic Christianity.

Chief Commercial Products: Bananas, shrimp and apparel.

Currency: Balboa (in reality, the U.S. dollar is the legal tender).

Gross Domestic Product: U.S. $10.44 billion in 2001 ($3,663 per capita).

Former Colonial Status: Spanish Colony (1519–1821), Province of Colombia (1821–1903).

Independence Date: November 3, 1903.

Chief of State: Mireya Moscoso, president (since September 1, 1999).

National Flag: A rectangle of four quarters; white with a blue star, blue, white with a red star, red.

Panama is a very narrow isthmus, 480 miles long and varying in width from 37 to 110 miles, connecting North and South America. Mountainous throughout, the highest elevation is the volcano Baru (11,397 feet) near the Costa Rican border. The Talamanca range continues southeast at an average elevation of 3,000 feet until it drops into the sea just west of Panama City. The San Blas range, rising east of Colón, runs southeast into Colombia; again the average elevation is 3,000 feet. A third range appears along the Pacific coast east of Panama City and runs southeast into Colombia. Both coasts have narrow plains cut by numerous small rivers running into the sea.

Lying in the tropical rainbelt, Panama's Atlantic coast receives up to 150 inches of

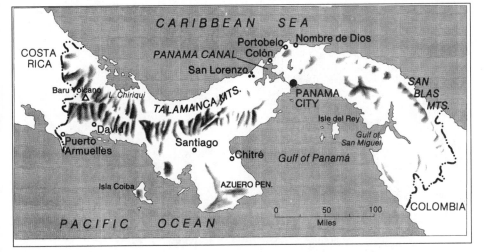

225

rainfall—the Pacific coast receives about 100 inches. The dry season, or "summer," runs from December to April. Four fifths of Panama's territory is covered with jungle and one half lies outside effective control by the Panamanian government. The principal reason for Panama's existence as a nation and the principal source of its earnings is the geographical accident of the north–south gap between the Talamanca and San Blas ranges, which permitted the construction of a canal between the Atlantic and Pacific oceans. Now the site of the Panama Canal and the nation's major cities, more than half the population is found in a narrow corridor and along the Pacific coast west of the gap.

History: Panama was discovered by Columbus in 1498–1500 and called Veraguas. It assumed importance in 1513 when Vasco Nuñez de Balboa discovered the Pacific. Panama City was established on the Pacific coast in 1518 and connected to three Caribbean ports by trails and rivers.

Nombre de Dios (Name of God) and Portobelo were the principal Atlantic ports maintained by the Spanish. Panama became the base for the outfitting of expeditions into Peru and Central America; it later was a major link in the route over which the wealth of the region was shipped to Spain. This wealth, and Panama's strategic importance, attracted pirates, buccaneers and foreign armies.

The British privateer Sir Francis Drake burned Nombre de Dios in 1573 and 1598; Henry Morgan raided the isthmus, looting and burning Panama City in 1617; British Admiral Edward Vernon captured Portobelo in 1739 and San Lorenzo in 1740. Spain abandoned the Panamanian route in 1746 in favor of the trip around Cape Horn at the tip of Argentina and Chile to reach its colonies in western Latin America.

For nearly 100 years Panama was bypassed by trade and ignored during the wars for independence fought on the southern continent. After independence, Panama was a province of Colombia. The discovery of gold in California brought renewed interest in quick transit from the Atlantic to the Pacific coast of the United States. A railroad was constructed between 1850 and 1853, and the De Lesseps Company of France started work on a canal in 1882. The work was abandoned in 1893, in part because of yellow fever epidemics, and in 1904 the United States acquired the assets of the bankrupt company.

There ensued three years of fruitless negotiations between the United States and Colombia. Colombia was gripped by civil war during the period. Philippe Jean Bunau-Varilla, the French agent of the defunct canal company, with the knowledge of the United States, engineered a revolution in Panama with the understanding that the United States would intervene to establish Panama as an independent state and that U.S. financial interests would acquire the right to complete the interoceanic canal across the isthmus. President Theodore Roosevelt recognized the independence of Panama three days after its proclamation on November 3, 1903.

Treaty negotiations between the United States and Panama were brief. Bunau-Varilla represented Panama, and the two sides quickly reached an agreement giving the United States virtually sovereign rights "in perpetuity" over the Canal Zone, a 10-mile-wide swath of Panamanian territory from coast to coast. Panamanians were horrified when confronted with Bunau-Varilla's *fait accompli*, but there was little they could do. Construction on the canal started shortly thereafter—as did 70 years of wrangling between the United States and the Republic of Panama over the sovereignty issue. In August 1914, the 400–year–old dream of Spanish, French, British and North American adventurers was accomplished when a vessel sailed through the completed canal from the Atlantic to the Pacific Ocean.

Panama's political history as an independent state was in keeping with the pattern of the Central American and Caribbean nations. Power lay in the hands of a small, elite Caucasian group that exploited the geographic situation for its personal benefit. The population at the time of independence was concentrated in the terminal cities of the trans–isthmian railroad and dependent upon commerce for its income. The influx of labor for the construction completely overwhelmed the administrative capabilities of the small nation. A

Panama's Declaration of Independence

The old part of Panama City

pattern ensued in which actual power was in the hands of the *Guardia Nacional*, whose head was infrequently the actual chief of state; more often he ruled through a figurehead president.

U.S. Patrimony

The United States took what measures it deemed necessary to achieve its purposes while Panama elected or appointed one ineffective government after another. The Panama Railroad, the United Fruit Company, which had established banana plantations during the late 1800s, and the Panama Canal Company, in consort with a small group of Panamanian families, exercised effective political and economic power in Panama. The steady influx of wealth supported a booming economy through the 1940s. Following World War II, the growing population exceeded the service demands of commerce and Panama began to feel the effects of 50 years of lack of direction and failure to invest its earnings in substantial industrial ventures.

Into this volatile political environment there appeared a charismatic and demagogic figure who was to dominate Panamanian politics for the next half–

century—and even beyond his death: Arnulfo Arias. The founder of the ultra–nationalist *Panameñista* Party, Arias exploited his people's near–xenophobic dislike of foreigners. He lashed out not only at the United States and the "Zonians" who enjoyed their suburban tropical paradise, but foreign immigrants as well, particularly those from Asia. On those rare occasions when the *Guardia Nacional* allowed Panamanians to vote in fair elections, Arias and his party did well—*too* well, for the *Guardia* and the elite. He was elected president in 1940 and in 1948, only to be deposed by the *Guardia* both times. He won again—and was deposed again—in 1968 and probably won two other elections, in 1964 and 1984, but was denied victory through creative vote–counting.

As the military, in league with the tiny clique of oligarchs, was the actual power in the country anyway, it "elected" one of its own, Police Chief José Antonio Remón, as president in 1952. Oddly enough, Remón was to prove one of Panama's more enlightened rulers, instituting long–overdue social reform, which estranged him from the oligarchy, and cracking down on some of the more overt corruption. He also was friendlier to the United States than many of his predecessors had

been, *too* friendly for some Panamanians,. Nonetheless, his more rational policy succeeded in obtaining an increase in the rent for the Canal Zone in 1955 from a paltry $430,000 (it had been only $250,000 until 1939!) to a still-ridiculous $1.9 million. Remón was assassinated that same year, but whether his killers were motivated by social reactionism or anti–Americanism never has been determined.

Remón's antithesis, Ernesto de la Guardia, was elected president in a reasonably fair count in 1956 and began making strident demands on the United States. The war over the Suez Canal that year helped further fan Panamanian passions. Some of the demands were quite legitimate, such as elimination of the inequitable wage scales between Zonian and Panamanian canal employees. President Eisenhower, who had served in Panama as a young Army officer in the early 1920s, acceded to the wage demands, as well as to a demand to allow the Panamanian flag to fly in the Zone. But it seemed the more the Americans conceded, the more antagonistic the de la *Guardia* government became. On Panamanian Independence Day in 1959, a well–orchestrated mob sought to "invade" the Zone, forcing U.S. troops to deter them with fixed bayonets. Ultra–nationalists and pro–Castro students exploited the incident for propaganda purposes. If nothing else, de la *Guardia* earned one important distinction for a Panamanian president: he served out his elected four–year term.

A far more moderate figure (and a member of the oligarchy), Roberto Chiari, was elected president in 1960 in what probably was the cleanest election Panama would ever have until 1994. Chiari enjoyed an amicable relationship with President Kennedy, who agreed to allow the Panamanian flag to fly alongside the U.S. flag in the Zone. Chiari also followed an anti–Castro line pleasing to Washington.

Nonetheless, toward the end of Chiari's term there occurred the worst incident of violence yet between Americans and Panamanians. In January 1964, foolhardy Zonian students at Balboa High School tore down the Panamanian flag flying next to the U.S. flag in front of the school and desecrated it. As word got out, Panamanians exploded in fury, and rioters flooded into the Zone, separated from Panama City only by the broad Fourth of July Avenue. In the resulting violence, 23 Panamanians and six Americans, most of them soldiers, were killed. Chiari broke diplomatic relations with the United States, and President Lyndon B. Johnson was faced with his first foreign policy crisis since succeeding the assassinated Kennedy two months earlier. Panama renamed Fourth of July Avenue *Avenida de los Mártires* (Avenue of the Martyrs), and to this day there are ceremonies marking each anniversary of the deadly riots.

In the election of May 1964, Chiari's cousin and fellow oligarch, Marco Aurelio Robles, narrowly defeated the fiery Arias, though the vote counting remains suspect to this day. Robles reestablished relations with Washington which, still shaken by the riots, began negotiating seriously about changes to the 1903 canal treaty. Robles withdrew government sanctioning on anti–U.S. demonstrations, and relations gradually improved—for a time.

The 1968 Coup

In the May 1968 elections, the perennial Arias won by a convincing margin that could not be denied. He was duly inaugurated on September 1, but just 11 days into his term, the *Guardia* overthrew him for a third time, ushering in 21 years of despotic military rule as heavy–handed as any in Latin America. For the first 13 of those years, absolute power rested with Colonel Omar Torrijos, who later promoted himself to brigadier general, a flamboyant and charismatic figure in the classic style of the Latin American *caudillo*.

Torrijos became a hero to the long–suppressed lower class as he established what

President Jimmy Carter looks on as Panama's Omar Torrijos signs the 1977 Panama Canal Treaty

amounted to a Panamanian version of a dictatorship of the proletariat. Political activity ceased, and a puppet legislative assembly rubber–stamped Torrijos' dictates. The egomaniacal Torrijos even had his heroic image emblazoned in a new friezework on the legislative palace. Press freedom vanished as the government expropriated three newspapers owned by Arias' brother, Harmodio, and blackmailed the owner of the venerable and respected *La Estrella de Panama* into becoming a sycophantish parrot of the government line. Critics of the regime were tortured, and more than a few took a one-way helicopter ride over the Pacific Ocean. Those too prominent to kill were hustled off into exile, often after being beaten as a farewell gesture. Torrijos reestablished diplomatic relations with Cuba, and he engaged in *gringo*–baiting on a scale not seen since de la Guardia. He

Brigadier General Omar Torrijos

attacked traditional corruption long practiced by the elite, but a newer, more sinister version with ties to Colombian drug traffickers soon arose. Torrijos implemented lax banking regulations that attracted branches of major banks from every continent, while the drug traffickers found Panama a veritable paradise for money-laundering.

The New Canal Treaties

National politics was dominated in the 1970s by the lingering dispute with the United States over the canal. Most of this centered around the 1903 treaty which granted the United States virtual sovereignty "in perpetuity" over the 530–square–mile Canal Zone. Widespread resentment against what was regarded as an outdated treaty unified most Panamanian political factions in demanding a new treaty. Key changes sought by Panama included (1) increased rental payments, (2) a large–scale reduction of U.S. military presence in the zone, (3) a greater Panamanian role in operating the canal and (4) recognition of complete Panamanian sovereignty over the zone.

Although there was an effort to place some nationals in management positions within the Canal Company, Panamanians insisted they could, and should, be allowed an even greater role in running their nation's major industry. Panamanians employed in the Canal Zone were usually given menial tasks at low wages. Since its opening in 1914, the canal was operated almost entirely by U.S. staff and supervisors. The zone itself resembled a "company town" as residents were provided with cradle–to–grave programs such as free schooling and medical care.

228

Because the 1903 treaty granted the United States territorial supremacy over the zone, Panama said the corridor represented a virtual foreign nation in its midst. It was a valid point. Zonians paid U.S. taxes. The Zone had its own police force. It had a U.S. federal district court, which was part of the 5th Circuit. It had U.S. post offices, although the Zone actually had its own postage stamps. Democrats in the Zone elected delegates to their party's national conventions. Panamanians could even be "deported" from the zone. It contended that U.S. control was a form of colonialism and insisted the 1903 treaty had to be replaced since it was forced on the tiny nation by U.S. "big stick" gunboat diplomacy.

An eight–point agenda for negotiators was signed early in 1974, during the waning days of the Nixon administration, and talks began shortly thereafter. The negotiations were continued into the Ford administration, and while they were not exactly secret, the administration certainly kept them low–key. In 1976, the canal talks became a campaign issue when Ronald Reagan, running for the Republican nomination against President Ford, assailed Ford for negotiating to surrender the vital U.S.–controlled waterway to a "tinpot dictator." Ford clumsily denied that he intended to give up the canal, an assertion that immediately drew the ire of the Panamanians. Caught between a domestic political dilemma and an international powder keg, Ford then backtracked and acknowledged that canal negotiations were underway, but he denounced Reagan as "irresponsible" for opposing them. Ford narrowly defeated Reagan for the

nomination, but lost the general election to Democrat Jimmy Carter.

Shortly after his inauguration in 1977, incoming President Carter gave a high priority to a new canal treaty. Ambassador Sol M. Linowitz was appointed to join Ellsworth Bunker as chief U.S. negotiators, and talks resumed in February 1977.

Completed in August, the new accord consisted of two separate treaties. The first one would permanently guarantee the canal's neutrality and use by all nations. In case of emergency, however, U.S. warships would be given priority over commercial traffic.

The second accord detailed a timetable for gradual transfer of the canal and the Zone from the United States to Panama. At noon on December 31, 1999, Panama would gain control of the whole works. Annual payments to Panama would also be boosted at once from $2.3 million to an estimated $60 million.

Although the two treaties incorporated a number of Panamanian demands, they left unsettled the question of a larger, deeper sea–level canal which President Carter said would be needed before the year 2000. The present facility employs the use of time–consuming locks. The Navy's largest warships and the new generation of super–tankers are too large to pass through the canal's locks. The waterway is also subject to congestion. Both traffic and tonnage have been rising in recent years, placing additional burdens on the canal's facilities.

The new treaties were signed with a flourish when leaders from 23 Latin American nations gathered in Washington in September 1977 to witness the historic

event. Still, the festive occasion could not hide the fact that the treaties faced a tough fight—both in the U.S. Senate (where critics said Washington gave up too much) and in Panama (where critics said Washington gave up too *little*).

The first test came in Panama, where the treaties were submitted to a national referendum. Despite vocal protests from both leftists and conservatives—who insisted that Torrijos should have held out for more money plus an earlier U.S. withdrawal—the treaties were approved by a comfortable 2–1 margin.

Attention next turned to Washington; for ratification, the agreements needed support from two thirds of the Senate—a tall order for an accord that public opinion polls said was still opposed by a majority of Americans. A campaign by retired and active high government figures was mounted in favor of the treaties. Ten weeks of debate ensued. Seventy–nine amendments were offered. The first treaty was approved in March by 68–32—just a one–vote margin above the necessary minimum. To gain approval, however, the president had to agree to an amendment permitting U.S. military intervention in Panama should the canal be closed for any reason, including a strike or even technical problems. This amendment caused an immediate uproar in Panama. Nationalists protested that it was not only an affront to Panamanian dignity, but it would also violate previous U.S.–Latin American agreements that specifically prohibited the concept of unilateral intervention. As the Senate prepared to vote on the second treaty, Torrijos—subjected to a blast of pressure from critics at home—sent a mes-

The Panama Canal at Miraflores locks

sage to 115 world leaders saying Panama could not accept the amendment.

In an 11th–hour attempt to save 14 years of painful negotiations with Panama, the White House and Senate leaders agreed to a new provision for the second treaty which promised that the United States would not interfere with Panama's "internal affairs" or "political independence." The lawmakers, obviously tired of the whole matter, voted in April by the same 68–32 margin in favor of the second treaty.

Behind the scenes, Carter had persuaded Torrijos that U.S. Senate ratification of the treaties would be impossible unless he sanitized his odious dictatorship. Torrijos pragmatically agreed to permit competitive elections and to ease restrictions on freedom of expression and of the press, which Carter trumpeted as proof of Torrijos' commitment to democracy. The seemingly close relationship between the U.S. president, who assailed right–wing Latin American military strongmen for their human rights abuses, and the Panamanian dictator who ordered the murders of political dissidents and confiscated newspapers, was most peculiar. This author was in Panama in June 1978 when Carter visited Panama to sign the instruments of ratification. At the public ceremony, Carter thrilled the Panamanian crowd by delivering a conciliatory address in his broken Spanish, in which he promised "no intervención." Torrijos, by contrast, was a disgrace. On this highly significant occasion in the life of his country, the representative of Panama was so drunk that his speech was badly slurred and he had to brace himself against the podium to keep from falling.

On October 1, 1979, an enormous Panamanian flag was raised atop Ancon Hill, which looms above Panama City and was the site of the U.S. Southern Command headquarters, and titular Panamanian sovereignty over the Canal Zone became a *reality*. Meanwhile, as window dressing, exiles were allowed to return. A new, more liberal press law was enacted, though the confiscated newspapers remained in government hands *and La Estrella* remained a faithful mouthpiece underneath its Sword of Damocles. The military established the Revolutionary Democratic Party *(PRD)* as its civilian political façade. In 1980, an ostensible "election" was held in which numerous parties participated, but the winner was predictable: Arístedes Royo, candidate of the *PRD*.

That same year, a group of anti–Torrijos businessmen and intellectuals, headed by Roberto Eisenmann, who had been in exile for four years, put the new press law to the test by establishing a new daily newspaper, *La Prensa*, which soon became a constant irritant to the regime with its investigative reporting of government

Arístedes Royo

corruption, its biting editorials and its acidic satirical cartoons.

Numerous problems faced strongman Torrijos and his protege, President Royo. Many of the financial benefits expected to flow into Panama as a result of the new treaties were slow to materialize. In 1980 unemployment grew to 20% and growing inflation touched off two days of general strikes that crippled 80% of the country's industries.

The election of Ronald Reagan in 1980 caused shock waves in Panama, where Torrijos feared that the new President might try to sabotage the canal treaties. Given Reagan's long–standing opposition to the pacts, Panama felt it necessary to safeguard its position by obtaining (with the help of Cuba) a seat on the U.N. Security Council in 1980.

The Panamanian political landscape was altered abruptly and dramatically on July 31, 1981, when Torrijos was killed in a plane crash while on an inspection of *Guardia* units in western Panama. Bad weather was cited as the official cause of the crash, though persistent rumors began circulating almost immediately that it was no accident. Fidel Castro, of course, immediately accused the CIA, then headed by Reagan protege William Casey, of rubbing out his friend. Torrijos, or what little remained of him, was buried in an elaborate masoleum on the parade ground of the former U.S. Army installation of Fort Amador. There was a frenzied outpouring of grief for the man who, whatever his shortcomings, had succeeded in reasserting Panamanian sovereignty over the Canal Zone. Command of the *Guardia* passed initially to Brigadier General Rubén Paredes, and democratic forces held their breath to see what course post–Torrijos Panama would take. Almost a year to the day after Torrijos' death, they found out. On July 30, 1982, Panama experienced a veritable night of the long knives as the military launched a widespread crackdown on dissent. President

Royo was summoned to military headquarters and informed that he was resigning for "health reasons;" he readily complied. At the same time, a goon squad invaded the offices of *La Prensa*, vandalized it and beat several of its employees, including women. The paper was padlocked for several days; other independent publications and radio stations also were silenced.

Noriega Comes to Power

After two years of a behind–the–scenes power struggle, command of the *Guardia*, which had been renamed the Panama Defense Forces *(FDP)*, passed to one of the most sinister figures in recent Latin American history: Colonel Manuel Noriega. The longtime chief of the *Guardia's* G–2, or intelligence section, Noriega was no charismatic *caudillo* like Torrijos. He was squat and ugly, with a face heavily scarred by acne, which led his many detractors to give him the uncharitable sobriquet "Cara de Piña," or "Pineapple Face." Where Torrijos had enjoyed the popularity of the masses, Noriega would rule by raw fear. Noriega was an alumnus of the U.S. Army's School of the Americas, then located at Fort Gulick, Panama, and had become a paid CIA operative. But he also acted as a double agent, providing intelligence to the Soviets and Cubans. Even more sinister, he enriched himself by providing protection to the Medellín Cartel of Colombia, which used Panama as a safe haven for its cocaine trafficking and money laundering. When this author served Army Reserve tours at the Southern Command in the 1970s and 1980s, Noriega's activities were well known, and his ascension to power was seen as the worst possible scenario. As *La Prensa*'s Eisenmann later told me, the difference between Torrijos and Noriega was that Torrijos merely ordered people tortured and murdered; Noriega participated in the torturing and killing and enjoyed it.

Noriega soon demonstrated the extent of his commitment to Torrijos' promise to Carter to ease human rights restrictions. In 1984, he dutifully held open presidential elections for an expanded five–year term. As its candidate, the military–backed *PRD* selected Nicolás Ardito Barletta, a respected economist and graduate of the University of Chicago. The *Panameñistas* again nominated the resilient Arias, by then 83. When early tabulations, which were monitored by international observers, showed an unmistakable trend in favor of Arias, the *FDP* abruptly impounded the ballot boxes and continued the vote counting in secret. By independent estimates, Arias would have received a plurality of between 25,000 and 50,000 votes out of 900,000 cast, but through the *FDP*'s creative vote counting, Barletta was declared the winner by 1,700 votes.

Public opposition to Noriega's heavy-handed rule intensified. A curious coalition of the wealthy elite, leftist intellectuals and housewives took to the streets waving white handerkerchiefs. Some of the demonstrations were broken up by truncheon–wielding goon squads from FDP–backed groups euphemistically named "Dignity Battalions." Not all opponents of the regime fared that well, however.

One of the most prominent Noriega critics was Dr. Hugo Spadafora, a physician who once had served as Torrijos' vice minister of health. He had served both the Nicaraguan *Sandinistas* in their struggle against Somoza and then, when he became disillusioned with their human rights abuses once in power, he lent his support to the *Contras*. He contributed a regular column to *La Prensa*, in which he vilified the Noriega dictatorship, and he announced he would return to Panama from Costa Rica to lead an opposition movement. He never made it. In September 1985, his bus was stopped when it crossed the border and, according to witnesses, he was forcibly removed. Days later, his decapitated body was found stuffed in a mail bag in Costa Rica; the body bore unmistakable evidence of hideous torture.

This time Noriega had overplayed his hand, and the Spadafora murder would backfire on him the same way the murder of journalist Pedro Joaquín Chamorro had served as the catalyst for the downfall of Nicaragua's Somoza. News of this atrocious crime made headlines around the world, and domestic and international pressure mounted on the regime. A half–hearted investigation concluded that the murder had occurred in Costa Rica and that Panamanian authorities had no jurisdiction. The Costa Ricans disputed that claim, which only served to fuel the mounting public indignation in Panama. Trying to appease public opinion, President Barletta publicly vowed to bring the killers to justice, a declaration he had foolishly made without consulting with Noriega. Like so many of his predecessors, the president was summoned to military headquarters and was informed he would not leave the building unless he resigned; he did. He was succeeded by the vice president, Eric Arturo Delvalle.

This author was stationed in Panama during the first half of 1986, when the outcry over the Spadafora murder reached a crescendo. The regime's response to the increasing number of protests was to cow the opposition with death threats. Graffiti accusing Eisenmann of treason began appearing all over Panama City, and the editor fled again to Miami for his life. That June, Pulitzer Prize–winning reporter Seymour Hersh of the *New York Times* reported what insiders in Panama had known for years, that Noriega was involved in drug trafficking and that he was a double

agent. I watched with amazement as a State Department spokesman testified on television before a congressional committee that there was no evidence to support Hersh's charges; apparently they hadn't been reading their intelligence cables for the past 10 years! Eventually, the U.S. government acknowledged that Noriega had once been a paid informant and was heavily involved in drug trafficking.

Noriega, of course, played the nationalist card, accusing the *gringos* of trying to undermine him. But in June 1987, one of his own former minions, Colonel Roberto Díaz Herrera, told the press not only that Noriega was a drug trafficker but that he had ordered Torrijos' fatal plane crash.

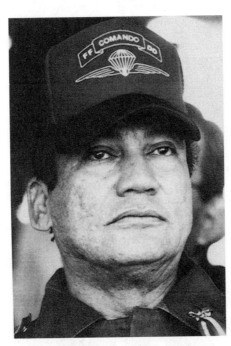

General Manuel Antonio Noriega

The opposition press gleefully published the charges. On July 26, 1987, Noriega cracked down hard. Díaz was arrested, and *La Prensa* and several other opposition papers and radio stations were shut down. The Reagan administration ostracized the Noriega regime economically. On February 25, 1988, President Delvalle attempted to salvage the country's devastated economy and to restore some degree of respect in the eyes of the world by firing Noriega as *FDP* commander. Noriega, of course, immediately fired Delvalle; Education Minister Manuel Solis Palma was installed to keep the president's chair warm until Barletta's term expired in 1989. That same year, a U.S. grand jury indicted Noriega on drug trafficking charges.

Incredibly, in May 1989, Noriega actually went ahead with yet another showcase election, as though anyone still believed Panama was a democracy. Arias had died in exile in Miami the previous

August, and the *Panameñistas*, now renamed *Arnulfistas*, nominated a portly and uninspiring doctor, Guillermo Endara, as the sacrificial lamb to head a coalition opposition ticket that included the Christian Democrats. The *PRD* nominated Carlos Duque, a member of the family that published the regime's faithful mascot newspaper, *La Estrella*. Perhaps the most enduring image of this sham campaign was the attack on an opposition rally by Dignity Battalion goons. Guillermo Ford, one of the opposition's two vice presidential candidates, was badly beaten, and international news photographers and cameramen recorded him fleeing for his life, his white *guayabera* shirt drenched bright red with his own blood; these images were carried around the world. International observers were present for election day on May 7. Nevertheless, in a replay of the 1984 electoral farce, early returns showed Endara winning by a landslide, and once again the *FDP* halted the vote counting. This time, however, the observers knew Endara had won, so instead of merely proclaiming Duque the winner, the government nullified the election results. The justification: "Foreign interference"! When the term to which Barletta had been "elected" in 1984 expired on September 1, the Council of State, composed entirely of *FDP* officers and their *PRD* lapdogs, designated a close associate of Noriega's, Francisco Rodríguez, as the newest figurehead president.

Operation 'Just Cause'

Relations between the United States and Panama continued to deteriorate after the 1989 "election." Noriega suppressed a coup attempt by a group of *FDP* officers on October 3 and ordered them summarily executed. The CIA made an abortive attempt to abduct Noriega, while President George Bush (who as CIA director in 1976 had been Noriega's "boss") issued an executive order banning Panamanian registered ships from entering U.S. ports. As Panama was second only to Liberia in the number of registries in world shipping, the order had potentially disastrous implications. But the bombastic Noriega soon proved to be his own worst enemy. Wielding a machete before a howling crowd of his adherents, he publicly "declared war" on the United States. In December, there were two separate incidents of off–duty U.S. service personnel—and one of their wives—being beaten by goons, and one U.S. serviceman was shot to death at a roadblock.

Faced with these provocations, Bush ordered the bombing of Noriega's headquarters on December 20, 1989, which was followed by an invasion by 9,500 U.S.–based paratroopers and Army Rangers in what was labeled Operation "Just Cause." Army forces stationed in Panama also moved to seize key installations. There were casualties on both sides as the *FDP* and the Dignity Battalions offered some futile resistance. Within days, order was restored, and for once, U.S. troops were actually cheered by the Panamanians, a stark contrast to the riots of 1964. The day after the invasion, Endara was inaugurated as president. Panamanians suddenly found themselves with more individual freedom than they ever had experienced. *La Prensa* and other closed media were reopened, the confiscated newspapers were returned to the widow and children of Harmodio Arias, the *FDP* was disbanded and replaced with a more benign civilian constabulary, and the country began building for the future.

Noriega went into hiding, changing his location every few hours. He sought and obtained refuge in the residence of the papal nuncio. A U.S. psychological warfare unit, in a move considered shrewd by some and crude by others, placed powerful loudspeakers outside the building and started broadcasting heavy metal rock at an overwhelming volume for the occupants of the building. The horrified nuncio told Noriega that the residence would be moved across the street and Noriega would not be welcome. Gloomily, the beaten man surrendered, to be taken to the United States with the assurance of no death penalty. He was sentenced to 40 years in 1992, but in 1999 a U.S. district judge ruled that he would be eligible for parole as early as 2000.

President Endara unsuccessfully tried to maintain a low profile to disguise his lack of talent. An opposition newspaper ridiculed him as "a non-musician leading an orchestra that does not play." Endara shrugged off chronic unemployment and rampant corruption as normal occurrences. By late 1993 his government became in fact a caretaker; influential cabinet members resigned to take part in 1994 presidential elections.

At the turn of the year, party reshuffling split Panamanian politics, enabling the organization that had supported Noriega, the *PRD*, to come to the fore. Its candidate was Ernesto Pérez Balladares, a former Citibank official with a U.S. education. He carefully distanced himself from Noriega, and won the election against an opposition that had split into numerous factions and parties. Running a strong second was Mireya Moscoso, the young widow of Arnulfo Arias, running as the *Arnulfista* candidate.

In June 1996, the *Miami Herald* and the *New York Times* carried reports linking top Panamanian government officials to an airline under indictment in the United States for its role in drug trafficking, including Panama City Mayor Alfredo Alemán, an adviser to the president; Foreign Minister Ricardo Alberto Arias, and intelligence chief Gabriel Castro. It also was reported that Pérez Balladares, like Colombia's Ernesto Samper, had received funds from drug traffickers for his presidential campaign. The president at first indignantly denied the allegations, and even threatened not to extend the work permit of Peruvian investigative journalist Gustavo Gorriti, recently named as editor of *La Prensa*. Pérez Balladares accused Gorriti of "masterminding a conspiracy" to undermine his government. A few days later, however, the president publicly made a contrite confession that the charges were true but insisted he had not known.

Gorriti continued to nettle the president. In 1997, *La Prensa* reported that Pérez Balladares had delayed passage of a new antitrust law to give his cousin time to acquire control of a second television station. This time the president followed through with his threat not to extend Gorriti's work permit, citing a provision in the labor law that media management positions must be held by Panamanians. The Interior Ministry ordered Gorriti to leave the country by August 28. The paper's lawyers went to court and succeeded in obtaining a delay of the deportation order. Meanwhile, Pérez Balladares became the center of a storm of international condemnation from journalism organizations and human rights groups; even Hillary Rodham Clinton discussed the Gorriti case during a state visit to Panama. Seeking to extricate himself from the tar baby he had struck, the president relented in October and agreed to extend Gorriti's work permit, while *La Prensa* agreed to the cosmetic change of giving the aggressive editor a different title. Panamanian press freedom

Far from the capital's cosmopolitan life: Cuna Indians of the San Blas Islands

thus survived a throwback to the days of Torrijos and Noriega.

Gorriti was not the only one who accused the president of nepotism and cronyism. International shipping companies expressed concerns that as the day inched ever closer for Panama to take over operation of the canal, Pérez Balladares was appointing friends and relatives to the Panama Canal Commission, now fully Panamanian. Even members of the president's own party criticized the appointments.

Although the effort to silence Gorriti failed, Panamanian officials resorted to yet another time–honored counterattack against media criticism: libel suits. Unlike the United States, Latin American countries have loosely defined defamation laws that allow public officials to sue for the expression of critical opinions, and Panamanian officials under both Endara and Pérez Balladares have resorted to it; Endara once sued a political cartoonist! By mid–1999, there were 85 such suits pending against the media in Panama, apparently more than in any Latin American country.

On the positive side, Pérez Balladares put the economy on a solid footing, nationally and internationally, through his program of privatization and fiscal discipline and pushed through a new bank law that should help crack down on the laundering of drug money, thus improving the country's image abroad.

Panama marked a major milestone in September 1997 when the U.S. Southern Command moved its headquarters from Quarry Heights to Miami, turning over the long–time U.S. nerve center atop Ancon Hill on the edge of Panama City to the Panamanians. Albrook Air Base also reverted to Panamanian control. It was something the Panamanians once dreamed of, but the Americans' departure also was a reminder that the payroll of the U.S. bases, which once pumped $370 million into the economy, was slowly drying up. Just three months after the Southern Command moved, Pérez Balladares announced that a multinational drug interdiction center would be established at Howard Air Force Base, one of the remaining bases under U.S. control. But in April 1998 the deal became unraveled when, in the view of the Panamanian public, it infringed too much on Panama's sovereignty.

The Elections of 1999

The transfer of U.S. bases to Panama continued on schedule during 1998 and 1999 as the election campaign heated up to select the president who would formally assume control of the canal on December 31, 1999. Pérez Balladares became the fourth Latin American president to seek to amend the constitution to permit him to run for immediate reelection. Constitutional amendments require only a majority vote in Congress, and the president had the votes needed for passage. But amendments then must be approved by the electorate. In a referendum on August 30, 1998, a resounding 64% voted "no" to Pérez Balladares' attempt to succeed himself, leaving the field wide open.

Even before the referendum, the opposition again coalesced around Mireya Moscoso of the *Arnulfista* Party, widow of Arnulfo Arias. After the referendum, the *PRD* decided to play the dynasty card as well by nominating Martín Torrijos, the

President Mireya Moscoso

35–year–old son of the former strongman, a businessman who once managed a McDonald's franchise in Chicago. Throughout most of the campaign, polls showed Torrijos leading by 10 to 15 percentage points. The two candidates differed little on major issues, with both pledging to maintain the canal efficiently and fairly, for the benefit of all nations. About the only issue that divided them was Moscoso's pledge to allay Pérez Balladares' moves to privatize utility companies. She also vowed to attack the rampant corruption that had been evident under Pérez Balladares; what could Torrijos say? Torrijos, meanwhile, scored points by chiding Moscoso for her lack of formal training; she had studied interior design at a junior college in Miami while married to the exiled Arias. Of course, there was another, unspoken handicap in a *macho* society: her gender.

Moscoso's chances definitely seemed doomed when a banker named Alberto Vallarino, disgruntled by Moscoso's nomination, defected from the opposition bloc and launched his own candidacy. But in the last two weeks of the campaign, the underdog woman suddenly pulled abreast of Torrijos in the polls. In a pathetic attempt to minimize a possible bandwagon effect, *PRD* loyalists bought up 20,000 copies of the newspaper *La Prensa,* which carried a poll showing Moscoso pulling ahead for the first time, and destroyed them.

On election day, May 2, 1999, Moscoso scored a stunning, Truman-like, come–" from–behind upset, receiving a clear plurality of 44% to Torrijos' 38% and Vallarino's 18%. With voter turnout a heavy 75%, her mandate was reasonably solid despite winning only a plurality. The combined anti-*PRD* vote represented a dramatic rebuke to the ruling party. Both Pérez Balladares and Torrijos graciously conceded defeat. Like the presidents of both neighboring countries—Miguel Angel Rodríguez in Costa Rica and Andrés Pastrana in Colombia—Moscoso had succeeded on her second try for the presidency.

Thus, from the grave, Arnulfo Arias finally achieved a sweet triumph, as his widow defeated the son of the man who had overthrown him in 1968. Moscoso, 52, had married Arias in exile in 1969, when he was 67 and she was 22, and was with him until his death in 1988. Very possibly it was his memory and his populist message, which she exploited, coupled with disturbingly high unemployment of 12.8%, that was responsible for her upset victory. If she serves out her term, she will have accomplished something vicariously for her late husband that he never could.

Recent Developments

Another milestone in the transfer of the former Canal Zone to Panama was observed on July 29, 1999, when the U.S. Army departed Fort Clayton for the last time, ending a U.S. military presence of 96 years.

Moscoso was sworn in as Panama's first woman president on September 1, 1999, the 31st anniversary of her late husband's ill-fated inauguration in 1968. Alas, the transition was not a pleasant one, as Pérez Balladares left office under an ethical cloud. Just two days before the ceremony, *La Prensa* reported that Pérez Balladares and his secretary had sold hundreds of illegal visas to Chinese immigrants in the waning days of his administration for up to $15,000 each. The president, through a statement released by his justice ministry, angrily denied involvement in the scheme and effectively left his secretary to take the fall.

To compound the ugliness of the transition, Pérez Balladares had packed the Supreme Court with last-minute appointees, denied public funds for the open-air inaugural ceremony Moscoso had requested at a stadium, and even ramrodded legislation through the lame-duck Congress that restricted presidential powers, including even spending emergency funds allocated to the president. Moreover, he ungraciously demanded that Moscoso reserve half the tickets to the inaugural ceremony for his *PRD* supporters, "so we can both be booed." She refused, and Pérez Balladares declined to attend the ceremony to place the presidential sash on his successor's shoulders. In her inaugural address, she insisted that she expected to enjoy harmonious relations with the United States, but that there would be no new U.S. bases in Panama unless approved in a popular referendum.

Moscoso received a sweet consolation for her predecessor's ungentlemanly actions when two small parties, Solidarity and National Liberal, withdrew from their coalition with the *PRD* and joined the *Panameñista Party* in a new coalition, giving it a one-seat majority in the 71-seat Congress.

Even before the inauguration, a controversy erupted in the United States and Panama when it was learned that a Hong Kong-based company, Hutchison Whampoa Ltd., had received a 20-year contract in 1997 to operate the port facilities at both entrances to the canal. This led U.S. Senate Majority Leader Trent Lott and other conservative Republicans in Congress to charge that the communist government in Beijing would be in a position to close the canal to U.S. shipping at will. Li Ka-shing, the billionaire owner of the company, denied any such intentions. The Clinton Administration also dismissed the idea of Chinese control as unfounded.

Because of fears of Y2K problems, the date for the ceremony transferring control of the canal was moved from December 31 to December 14. Representing the United States, appropriately enough, was former President Jimmy Carter, who had signed the new treaties in 1977. With his and Moscoso's signatures, Panama at last enjoyed full sovereignty over its territory and over the canal.

In November 2001, a two-year, $300 million project was completed that widened the Gaillard Cut, the "ditch" section of the canal, by 40 yards, increasing its traffic potential by 20 percent. But a far more ambitious $4.5 billion expansion project is expected to begin in 2004 and last eight years. A Belgian-French consortium has contracted to build a third lane of the canal, which will involve creating three more reservoirs.

In April 2002, the country experienced a catharsis of sorts when a special "truth commission" on disappearances and mysterious deaths during the 1968-1989 military regimes presented its report to President Moscoso. The commission investigated 168 cases and reached conclusions on 110. Of those, 70 were found to be assassinations of political dissidents, most of them during the Torrijos period. Another 40 remain unsolved.

Carlota—a Panamanian beauty in native costume

Culture: Panama's culture is a reflection of its unique geographical situation as a crossroads of both terrestrial and maritime traffic between two oceans and two continents. There is a polyglot of ethnic groups, not one of which predominates: the indigenous Indians, many of them unassimilated, such as the Cuna tribe of the San Blas Islands on the Caribbean coast that contributed the distinctive *mola* tapestries that have become so identifiable with Panamanian culture; the Caucasians, not merely Spanish descendants but the scions of latter–day European, Arab and Jewish immigrants who today account for a disproportionate share of the country's wealth and political power; *the mestizos,* who outnumber the first two groups; blacks and mulattos, who are about equal in number to the *mestizos,* descended not from slaves as in Brazil, but from workers imported from the British West Indies to help construct the canal; and the sizable community of Orientals, principally Chinese, who have filtered into the country in the decades since the completion of the canal.

Because of this, Panama boasts a distinctive culture, particularly in its folk music, dances and costumes that its tourist industry has helped to preserve. In popular music it also has made some contributions. Its best–known singer, Rubén Blades, won a following in Latin America before appearing in a number of U.S. movies. He ran for president of Panama in 1994 but made a poor showing.

Literacy is relatively high in Panama, but the small population has not been suf-

ficient to support much book or magazine publishing. Panama boasts one of Latin America's oldest daily newspapers, *La Estrella de Panamá,* founded in 1853. Unfortunately, *La Estrella's* owners were blackmailed into editorial support for dictators Torrijos and later Noriega, and the paper has never fully recovered from its reputation as a sycophant.

Until the U.S. invasion of 1989 that brought down the Noriega dictatorship, aggressive and critical journalism in Panama was a risky business. *El Panamá América,* expropriated from Harmodio Arias by Torrijos in 1968, was restored to his family and remains the second-leading daily. The country's leading daily today, *La Prensa,* was established in 1980 by Roberto Eisenmann and courageously stood up to both the Torrijos and Noriega dictatorships. For this it was repeatedly vandalized and finally closed in 1987. The month after the U.S. invasion, its repaired presses began rolling again.

Economy: Panama's economy is based on trade brought to it by an accident of geography. Farm output is unable to feed the population; the major source of income (about 20% of the gross national product) is tied to the Canal. The Torrijos regime sought to diversify the economy—in addition to stressing rural development and road construction, the government established incentives to make Panama an international banking center. Passage of the Panama Canal treaties has had the effect of stimulating new industrial investments.

An oil pipeline enables the transport of crude by supertankers ocean–to–ocean, compensating for their inability to fit through the narrow canal, providing substantial revenues to Panama.

In 1972 the government enacted a series of tariffs to protect local industries together with stringent worker protection laws at the request of the strong Panamanian labor movement. This had the effect of reducing competition from imports and raising the price of consumer goods. These moves were basically financed by foreign borrowing. By 1985 the International Monetary Fund insisted that these measures be sharply reduced as a condition to additional loans and assurances to private banks, a move which met with widespread disapproval.

Much of the impetus for Panama becoming a major international banking center in the 1970s and 1980s stemmed from

Washing clothes at an outdoor sluice

a Swiss–style banking law that made Panama a favored spot for the laundering of illegal drug money. Not until 1997 did Panama make a concerted effort to change the law and remove this stigma.

The prodigious economic spinoff from the canal, including the thousands of jobs generated by the canal itself and the numerous U.S. military bases, once gave Panama among the highest standards of living in Latin America, but per capital income remained static at $2,500 for more than a decade. In the 1980s, that figure was the fourth highest of the 20 Latin republics; today it is seventh. However, Panama has avoided the hyperinflation that has plagued so many of its neighbors. The reason: The official currency is called the Balboa, but in reality the U.S. dollar is the country's legal tender, which is a boon for international banking and provides monetary stability. (Panama has its own coins, which are identical in size and weight with U.S. denominations and thus are interchangeable in vending machines.) Largely because of the dollar-based economy, inflation has fluctuated between 1.7% and 1.0% for the past four years, remarkable for Latin America. For that reason, Ecuador emulated Panama by replacing its currency with the dollar in March 2000.

One of the country's greatest economic success stories is the Colón Free Zone, on the Caribbean side, which generates about $3 billion a year in exports. On the negative side, Panama has one of the most cumbersome national debts per capita in the world, at present about $5.6 billion.

Most experts concur that Panama should not consider its takeover of the canal on December 31, 1999, as an economic panacea. For one thing, there are serious concerns about Panama's ability to maintain the canal and keep it operational, worries that were generated in part by Panama's failure to maintain the transisthmian railroad it inherited from the United States in 1979. Moreover, there is increased talk of plans by other countries, such as Japan, to build a sea–level canal elsewhere, perhaps across Colombia or Nicaragua. Another concern is terrorism by narcotraffickers or Islamic extremists, which could close the canal with one blast.

Panama's GDP in 2001 was a respectable $10.44 billion, or $3,663 per capita, representing a 3.8% growth from 2000. Besides the long-term problem of the crushing per capita public debt, President Moscoso also inherited a high unemployment rate of 13.6%, which was still 13.3% in 2000. Thanks to using the U.S. dollar as its currency, Panama has enjoyed negligible inflation of less than 2% for several years; in 2001 it was 1.2%

The Future: Within the space of four months in late 1999, Panama witnessed two of the most dramatic events in its short history: the inauguration of its first woman president and the transfer of the canal to Panamanian control. The question the world must ask is, what now? President Moscoso acknowledged during the campaign that she lacked a university education, though she has some modest managerial experience as owner of a coffee company that employs 300 people. She has compared herself to Ronald Reagan, promising to surround herself with skilled advisers as he did.

Moscoso's major challenges are the canal and unemployment. The canal is a complex, expensive operation, requiring year–round maintenance. The unstable geology of the region demands constant dredging. The locks are intricate mechanisms requiring skilled technicians to keep them functional. An even greater threat, since September 11, 2001, is security. It would be relatively easy for al-Qaeda terrorists to cripple one of the locks or to sink a ship in the still-narrow Gaillard Cut, closing the canal. Although such an attack would be aimed at the United States, its effect on the Panamanian economy would be devastating. Panama's security forces are insufficient, either in manpower or intelligence capability, to effectively safeguard the vital waterway. It may be time to reconsider the U.S. pullout.

The Republic of Paraguay

The unspoiled beauty of a whitewater river in Paraguay

Area: 157,047 square miles.

Population: 5.6 million.

Capital City: Asunción (Pop. 750,000, estimated).

Climate: The eastern section *(Oriental)* lies in a temperate zone; the western *(Occidental)* section is hot and oppressive. Rainfall is heaviest from February to May; most of Paraguay receives adequate water except for the western plains.

Neighboring Countries: Brazil (East and Northeast); Argentina (South); Bolivia (West and Northwest).

Official Language: Spanish.

Other Principal Tongues: Guaraní, a native Indian dialect, spoken as a first language by half the population.

Ethnic Background: *Mestizo* (mixed Spanish and Guaraní ancestry).

Principal Religion: Roman Catholic Christianity.

Chief Commercial Products: Cotton, soybean, timber, vegetable oils, coffee, light manufactured goods.

Currency: Guaraní.

Gross Domestic Product: U.S. $7.741 billion in 1999 ($1,552 per capita).

Former Colonial Status: Spanish Crown Colony (1537–1811).

Independence Date: May 14, 1811.

Chief of State: Luis Angel González Macchi, President (since March 28, 1999).

National Flag: Red, white and blue horizontal stripes. The white stripe displays the national seal on one side and the words *Paz y Justicia* (Peace and Justice) on the opposite side. This is the only flag in the world having different sides.

Although Paraguay lies almost in the geographic center of the continent and is one of South America's two interior nations, it is not landlocked. The Paraná river forms part of the boundary with Argentina and Brazil and links Paraguay with the Atlantic. The north to south Paraguay River, a Paraná tributary, divides the country into two regions with very different characters. Paraguay's third important river, the Pilcomayo, forms the southwest frontier with Argentina and joins the Paraguay opposite Asunción.

The eastern *(Oriental)* region of Paraguay, between the Paraguay and the Paraná rivers, is referred to as Paraguay proper. Containing approximately 40% of the nation's territory, the *Oriental* has fertile rolling plains with scattered hills in the south central portion, rising to the Amabay Mountains (2,700 feet) in the northeast along the Brazilian border. This is the most densely populated region of Paraguay.

The western *(Occidental)* region of the nation, commonly called the *Chaco*, is a hot, grassy prairie, interspersed with stands of hardwood known as *quebracho* (axe–breaker). Crossed by numerous unnavigable streams, its underground water is too salty for irrigation or human consumption; until recently this region was largely uninhabited. Today, through the impounding of rainwater, the Chaco is dotted with cattle ranches and the *quebracho* is harvested for tannin.

History: The history of Paraguay centers on the capital, Asunción, and on the villages within a 60–mile radius around that city on the eastern side of the Paraguay River. To the primitive people who roamed the area prior to the Spanish conquest, the lush plains lying between the Paraguay and the Paraná rivers were their traditional Garden of Eden. Of the many tribes which resided here, most were of the Tupi–Guaraní linguistic group. An amiable people, living by trapping, fishing and simple plantings, they offered little opposition to the Spaniards who explored the Paraná valley and established a fort at Asunción on August 15, 1537, some 70 years prior to the first English settlement in North America.

Though neglected by the Spanish crown, the colony prospered and at the end of 20 years boasted 1,500 Spanish residents, a cathedral, a textile mill and a growing cattle industry. For two centuries, Asunción and its pleasant valley developed slowly while serving as the seat of Spanish authority in South America east of the Andes Mountains and south of the Portuguese colony in Brazil.

From Asunción, expeditions founded the cities of Santa Fé, Corrientes and Buenos Aires. Beginning in 1588, a company of Jesuit missionaries gathered some 100,000 Indians into mission villages and taught them better methods of farming, stock raising and handicrafts. The Jesuits protected their wards against enslavement by civil governors, settlers and Brazilian slave hunters; in the process, they helped to hold Paraguay and Uruguay for the Spanish. Unfortunately for the colony, the Jesuits were expelled in 1767.

Paraguay's transition from colonial status to independence was swift and unspectacular. In 1810, following the declaration of independence by Buenos Aires, Paraguay was invited to join with the Argentine ex–colony. The invitation was rejected and in 1811 Paraguay defeated a force sent from Buenos Aires to compel acceptance of Argentine leadership. A congress declared Paraguay to be a free and independent state and a five–man ruling council was established.

Dissension erupted; in 1814 a hopelessly deadlocked Congress voted full dictatorial powers to Dr. José Gaspar Rodríguez de Francia, who ruled until 1840. Austere, frugal, honest, dedicated and brutally cruel, he set the dictatorial pattern that persisted until 1989. Francia introduced improved methods in agriculture and in stock raising and was able to force the Paraguayan soil to produce more than ever before. Although dissent was ruthlessly suppressed, Paraguay was well ordered and well fed.

Francia's death created a power vacuum and a year of turmoil. The man who came to power, Carlos Antonio López, imposed a constitution, but one that let him rule with the same autocratic powers that Francia had. López established trade and diplomatic relations with other countries and groomed his son, Francisco Solano López, to succeed him. The son enjoyed playing soldier and built up Paraguay's army. After he succeeded his father, he gave himself the rank of *mariscal* (field marshal) and looked around for someone to fight. He foolishly declared war on Brazil, Argentina and Uruguay in 1865, a decision that was to decimate the country's male population. In the bloody, five–year War of the Triple Alliance, Paraguay's three enemies invaded the country and engaged in what today would be called genocide. Of a population of 520,000, at least 300,000 Paraguayans were slaughtered; only 28,746 males survived. It was a demographic cataclysm from which it took the country generations to recover. "Mariscal" López, for whom the main boulevard of Asunción is named today, was himself killed in a battle with the Brazilians in 1870, which ended the pointless struggle, the costliest in the history of post–colonial South America. It says something of the Paraguayan mentality that López still is revered as a national hero, as is Francia.

Between 1870 and 1928 Paraguay slowly recovered and remained at peace with its neighbors. However, internal turmoil persisted and presidents were put in office by gunplay rather than by elections. From 1870 until 1954, Paraguay had 39 presidents, most of whom were jailed, murdered or exiled before they completed their term. Economically, there was some progress. Immigrants from Italy, Spain, Germany and Argentina developed the agriculture, stock raising and forestry industries. Of the 800,000 population in 1928, the majority were illiterate and landless; profits from agriculture and industry went to foreign owners, mostly Argentine.

The Paraguay–Bolivia border remained unresolved after the war of 1870. A humiliated Paraguay sought to extend its *Chaco* territory. Bolivia sought access to the Atlantic via ports on the Paraguay River. War broke out in 1932, ending in a 1935 truce that awarded Paraguay about 20,000 square miles at a cost of 36,000 dead, and a seriously damaged economy. Six of the Chaco War's heroes later became president.

The Stroessner Era, 1954–89

Two of these proved to be unsatisfactory and a third was killed in an aircraft accident. Their successor, Alfredo Stroessner, came to power in a military coup in 1954; he was "re-elected" to the presidency by a large vote seven times, serving for more than 35 years. Although he initially allowed opposition elements to contest elections, they were subsequently eliminated by 1963. But later he allowed an opposition party, the Liberal Party, which participated in the elections in 1973 and 1978. Stroessner was able to arrange election victories by huge margins which made the very use of the term "election" a farce.

In the 1973 election, for example, Stroessner received 681,306 votes over his opponent, Gustavo Riart of the Liberal Party, who got 198,096. Abstentions and

blank ballots accounted for 35% of the vote. Elections for the new Senate and Chamber of Deputies were held at the same time. Since Stroessner's *Colorado* Party gained a majority in both houses, it was by law entitled to two thirds of the seats. The remaining one third was assigned to the opposition by a prescribed formula. The right–wing government party was the only well–organized one in the country. Two small opposition groups were actually similar in outlook to the *Colorados*. All three favored free enterprise with minimal state intervention into the economy. However, the Liberals favored a more democratic government. Whenever any individual appeared to gain *too much* popularity during Stroessner's years, he was either jailed, exiled or simply disappeared.

With solid military backing, Stroessner ruled Paraguay as his personal fiefdom. He stressed political stability in the nation, his strong stand against communism and the regime's emphasis of road construction. Living standards did rise slowly, but steadily, during his years of power.

Political stability did attract foreign investment. Relations with the Catholic church were generally poor, particularly when Stroessner sought to undermine the Marandú rural public housing program of the church. Supported with funds obtained in the United States, the effort attempted to provide the nation's impoverished Indian population with medical, legal and economic assistance. Nearly all of the 100,000+ Indians in Paraguay still live at the bottom of the nation's social and economic scales. The conservative elite viewed such attempts to help the Indians as a "communist conspiracy." Five Jesuit priests, leaders of the movement, were deported and others were jailed.

The country was governed under Stroessner by "state of siege" legislation that suspended constitutional guarantees. It was renewed every 90 days.

General Alfredo Stroessner

Predictably, Stroessner was "re-elected" in 1983 and again in 1988. Corruption within the ruling *Colorado* Party was reported by the independent newspaper *ABC Color,* on the radio and by the Paraguayan Episcopal Conference in late 1984. The first two were closed down and the latter was ignored.

Stroessner was elected to his eighth term by a majority of 89% in 1988. There were the usual irregularities and voter apathy. The *Colorado* Party became mildly divided over the issue of what should happen after the president left the scene—the *tradicionalistas* wanted the aging dictator to step aside, while the *oficialistas* thought Stroessner, barring ill health, should remain in office. The matter was postponed by Stroessner's candidacy for re-election. When opposition *Radio Ñanduti* became too vocal, it was jammed; the government claimed to know nothing about this.

When in late 1988 Stroessner disappeared for 10 days there were rumors he had died. He underwent prostate surgery at an undisclosed location; his recovery was very slow. Sensing the time was right, the Commander–in–Chief of the military, General Andrés Rodríguez, staged a coup in February 1989, exiling the now–feeble Stroessner to Brazil without opposition. Low estimates of deaths during the coup were 50, high ones 300. Thus ended the 35–year rule of the son of a German brewmaster and a Guaraní Indian woman.

Democracy?

Taking the opposition by surprise, Rodríguez announced elections for May 1, 1989; Rodríguez became the Colorado candidate, assuring his election. He projected the image of a populist in contrast to the aloof, distant Stroessner.

Things didn't really change in Paraguay. Rodríguez received more than 74% of the vote; the *Colorado* Party received two thirds of the seats in the Chamber of Deputies and in the Senate. Periodic power struggles within the party occurred after the election between the "democratic" faction and the slightly more conservative "traditionalists"; Rodríguez favored the former. His daughter married Stroessner's son. Under Stroessner and Rodríguez, Paraguay had become a giant fencing operation, the largest in Latin America. If one wanted to buy or sell anything that had been stolen, Paraguay was (and still is, to a large degree) the place to go.

But even this enterprise was shaken in 1992 when a "whistle blowing" colonel disclosed that the army had a virtual monopoly on fencing expensive, stolen cars—its specialty. Surprisingly, this led to Rodríguez's removal of four top military figures; this was probably done to avoid a charge that he was also involved in the operation, although there is no known evidence that he was.

In late 1992, preparing for primary and general elections, the *Colorado* Party again became badly divided. The "democratic" faction prevailed and nominated Juan Carlos Wasmosy, a civil engineer and businessman, and the conservatives ultimately joined to support him. He was opposed by two candidates in the May 1993 contest—Domingo Laino of the Authentic Radical Liberal Party and Guillermo Caballero Vargas of the National Encounter Party. Wasmosy won with more than 40% of the vote after campaigning on promises to improve the economy and employment.

The military had promised early in 1993 to continue "co–governing" with the *Colorado* Party. A charismatic officer emerged within the party, General Lino Oviedo. But the main political parties agreed upon a "governability pact" that excluded the police and military from party membership; the signing of it was postponed, however, after there were attacks by drunken *Colorado* Party supporters on opposition legislators.

A Liberal politician laid bare the existence of files of the secret police in December 1992 containing facts behind the disappearance of some 15,000 people during the Stroessner years. It also allegedly contained evidence supporting the existence of Operation Condor, a cooperative effort against leftists by Paraguay, Chile, Argentina and Uruguay during the 1980s that arranged disappearances of undesired people.

Democratic forces held their breath in late April 1996 when Oviedo publicly called for Wasmosy to resign. It amounted to an attempted coup, but the rest of the armed forces failed to move against the civilian president. Wasmosy then summoned Oviedo to his office and ordered him to retire, promising him the cabinet post of defense secretary. For 27 tense hours, Oviedo demurred, provoking fears of a throwback to Paraguay's bad old days of military strongmen. In the end, he relented and retired, but public protests against his accepting the cabinet post led Wasmosy to withdraw the offer. Paraguay, at least, appeared to have established civilian control over the military. Wasmosy went even further in December 1996 by cashiering 207 cavalry officers who he said had supported Oviedo's short–lived rebellion. A judge overturned Wasmosy's order in January 1997, citing insufficient evidence against the officers. A week later, however, an appeals court overturned the judge's decision and Wasmosy signed a decree dismissing the officers. Once again, civilian authority prevailed.

The Oviedo saga continued, however. In September 1997, the *Colorado* Party held its primary, in which Oviedo won the nomination for the May 10, 1998, presidential election. This infuriated Wasmosy, and relations between him and Oviedo went from poor to deplorable. In Novem-

Children celebrate Independence Day in a small town

ber, Oviedo publicly accused the president of incompetence and corruption; Wasmosy, falling back on his authority as commander–in–chief, ordered the general arrested for insubordination. Oviedo was a fugitive for 42 days before turning himself in. Wasmosy placed him under house arrest for 30 days.

There followed a series of legal battles between the two men in both civilian and military courts. In late December, the nation's top electoral court rejected a plea from Wasmosy to disqualify Oviedo as the *Colorado* candidate. There was another coup scare in late January 1998 when, after a judge indicated he might order Oviedo's release because he had never been formally charged, tanks began rumbling in the streets. The military claimed, unconvincingly, that it had merely been a practice for a ceremony. Meanwhile, a determined Wasmosy assembled a special military tribunal in February that dutifully ordered Oviedo jailed for an "indefinite" term for his abortive coup in 1996. On March 9, the tribunal formally sentenced Oviedo, still a presidential candidate, to 10 years.

When it became apparent that Wasmosy might not be able legally to strip Oviedo of the *Colorado* nomination, and faced with polls that showed the Guaraní-speaking Oviedo in the lead, the president briefly pondered a decidedly undemocratic move: to postpone the May 10 election. But Paraguay's *Mercosur* partners quickly reminded Wasmosy that democratic government was a condition of membership, and the United States also issued a warning against postponing the election. Wasmosy was saved from being cast in the role of antidemocrat by the Paraguayan Supreme Court, which on April 17 voted by a narrow 5–4 to uphold Oviedo's prison term, effectively disqualifying him as a presidential candidate. Oviedo vowed to campaign from jail, but the party, facing reality, nominated Oviedo's running mate, Raúl Cubas, a 54–year–old

businessman, to stand for president. The 11th–hour termination of Oviedo's candidacy gave a boost to the perennial standard–bearer of the Liberals, Domingo Laino, running this time as candidate of the Democratic Alliance coalition. Now it was the *Colorados* who called for a postponement of the May 10 vote.

It was just as well for them that the vote wasn't delayed. Cubas received 54% to Laino's 42%; the Democratic Alliance immediately claimed fraud, a charge that appeared to be largely unsubstantiated. Just days before the election, Cubas declared unabashedly that if the *Colorados* won, "Free, in jail, or wherever he is, Oviedo will have political power." He was to make good on that promise soon after he was inaugurated on August 15, 1998.

Assassination and Impeachment

Cubas' seven months in office were marked by byzantine political intrigues that culminated in a high–level assassination, the president's impeachment and then his resignation and the ignominious flights into exile of both Cubas and Oviedo. These events sorely tested whether this fledgling democracy would long endure. Just three days after his inauguration, Cubas pardoned Oviedo, which led to jubilant street demonstrations by the general's supporters, who chanted, *"Lino presidente!"* Cubas then appointed a new military tribunal, packed with Oviedo sympathizers, which quickly dismissed all charges against the general. This brash action was to plunge Paraguay into a constitutional crisis, pitting the executive branch against both the legislative and judicial branches; under Stroessner's rule, of course, it would have been a short–lived contest. Days after the tribunal cleared Oviedo, members of Congress began threatening the president with impeachment.

On December 2, 1998, the Supreme Court ruled Cubas' pardon and the mili-

tary tribunal unconstitutional and ordered Oviedo incarcerated again. Cubas merely ignored the order, which created a deep schism within the ranks of the *Colorado* Party. Heading the anti–Oviedo faction was Cubas' own vice president, Luis María Argaña, who prevailed in a vote by the *Colorado* leadership on December 5 to expel Oviedo from the party. Argaña had lost the *Colorado* nomination to Oviedo the year before, and when the courts blocked Oviedo's candidacy, Argaña became the running mate of an unwilling Cubas. The president and vice president had not even been on speaking terms since their inauguration. The crisis took an ugly turn on December 22, when Oviedo supporters demonstrated outside the Supreme Court; three shots were fired through the building's windows.

The constitutional impasse rumbled on into 1999. By February 9, there were rampant rumors that Cubas was planning a Fujimori–style military takeover, which he adamantly denied. His opponents, meanwhile, denounced him at a *Mercosur* summit, a reminder to Cubas that membership in the trade bloc requires a democratic form of government. It was not an idle threat; about two thirds of Paraguay's exports are to its *Mercosur* partners.

The threat of impeachment loomed larger on February 11, when the lower house voted 71–37 to charge the president with abuse of power for his actions the previous August—just two votes shy of the two–thirds–plus–one–vote majority needed for formal impeachment. Several *Colorado* deputies joined with the opposition Radical Liberals. To further complicate this byzantine spectacle, the armed forces high command—loyal to Oviedo— took action to dismiss the air force generals who had refused to participate in Oviedo's barracks revolt in 1996.

As this political drama reached a climax, Vice President Argaña was assassinated in broad daylight on March 23, 1999, as he arrived at work. A vehicle containing three or four men in camouflage fatigues curbed Argaña's jeep. One of the men threw a grenade, while others opened fire, hitting the vice president in the heart. He died at the scene. His driver also was killed and his bodyguard gravely wounded. The killing threw the country into even greater turmoil and brought international denunciations. Both Cubas and Oviedo issued statements denouncing their rival's murder, but not before thousands of Argaña's supporters took to the streets in protest; security forces opened fire, leaving seven people dead.

Events then began to tumble in rapid succession. The day after the assassination, the Chamber of Deputies overwhelmingly voted to impeach Cubas. The anti–Cubas *Colorados* and opposition Liberals did not come across as champions of democracy, however; at least one pro–Cubas *Colorado*

President Luis Angel González Macchi

A Paraguayan *alza prima* pulled by an ox.

deputy was roughed up when he arrived at the Congress and prevented from entering. The case then went before the Senate, which took it up immediately. Conviction and removal were certain.

On March 28, Cubas abruptly resigned and boarded a waiting Brazilian air force plane that flew him into a comfortable exile; he owns a beach house in southern Brazil. Almost simultaneously, Oviedo fled the country in a light plane and flew to Buenos Aires, where he was briefly detained for not having the necessary immigration papers. Within a day, however, Argentina granted him asylum, apparently giving him immunity from extradition. Nonetheless, the new government formally submitted an extradition request on March 31.

In accordance with the constitution, Senate President Luis Angel González Macchi, 52, next in the line of succession after the president and vice president, was sworn in as interim president hours after Cubas' resignation. The army dispelled any lingering doubts about a peaceful transition when it pledged him its support. The new president, a former professional basketball player who had an unspectacular career as a legislator, quickly cleaned house and appointed a new cabinet that included Argaña's brother and even some ministers from the opposition Liberal and National Encounter parties. Such power–sharing was unprecedented in the 52 years the *Colorado* Party has been entrenched in power. Moreover, the new government announced it would hold a new presidential election in six months and that a Liberal would be the running mate of the *Colorado* candidate. Later, however, the Supreme Court ruled that González Macchi could serve the remainder of Cubas' five-year term.

Paraguay angrily recalled its ambassador from Argentina in July 1999 after the government of President Carlos Menem refused to extradite Oviedo. Simultaneously, Paraguay recalled its envoy from Uruguay, which refused to extradite Cubas' defense minister, José Segovia Boltes, in connection with the Argaña assassination. The repeated failure to effect Oviedo's extradition led Foreign Minister Miguel Saguier to resign in September. In October, however, the election to succeed Menem in Argentina was won by Fernando de la Rua, who had pledged to extradite Oviedo. Sensing he had overstayed his welcome, the wily general literally vanished shortly before de la Rua's inauguration on December 10. Just after New Year's Day, 2000, Oviedo resurfaced, brazenly holding a news conference with a handful of reporters at an undisclosed location in rural Paraguay, which was reported by media throughout Latin America (this author read about it in the Chilean newspapers and saw it on television there). He continued to maintain his innocence and alleged that his enemies had murdered Argaña to discredit him. Cocky as ever, he boasted again that he would one day return to Asuncion as the people's champion.

Within the next few weeks, Argentine authorities arrested two Paraguayan fugitives suspected of being two of the gunmen in the Argaña assassination. They had been identified by a third suspected gunman, Pablo Vera Esteche, who had told Paraguayan authorities in October 1999 that Oviedo had paid the trio $300,000 to kill Argaña. Argentina extradited the two suspects in April.

Oviedo supporters in the military, the police and the Congress gave the country —and the world community—a scare on May 18, 2000, when three armored cars parked in front of the legislative palace and fired two shots at the building. A tense standoff ensued, as military unit commanders around the country publicly declared their support for González Macchi, who declared a 30-day state of siege. Denunciations of the revolt came pouring in from Argentina, Brazil, the United States and other democracies. At 2:45 a.m. the next day, about 25 soldiers, a few retired officers, 12 policemen and three pro-Oviedo congressmen surrendered. The president of the Congress claimed in a televised interview that documents found after the revolt indicated that the mutineers planned to assassinate several Colorado Party leaders, including González Macchi and vice-presidential candidate Felix Argaña, the 42-year-old son of the slain vice president, who was running to fill his father's vacant seat in an August election. González Macchi declared that the plotters would be duly punished. Oviedo, meanwhile, sent a communique from his hideout to the newspaper *ABC Color* denying he was involved in the short-lived revolt.

The whereabouts of the elusive general had become a national—and international—obsession even before the revolt. In late February 2000, a Bolivian newspaper reported that Oviedo was hiding out in that country, which was never confirmed. Just to be sure, the Bolivian government announced that it would not grant him asylum. Besides Paraguay, Oviedo sightings were reported in Brazil, which turned out to be correct. On June 12, 2000, acting on information from Paraguayan intelligence authorities who had been tapping and tracing Oviedo's numerous phone calls to supporters back home, Brazilian police arrested the fugitive in a posh apartment in Foz do Iguaçu, just across the border from Ciudad del Este. Oviedo had grown a mustache and long hair. Police found 10 cellular phones in the apartment and a .38 pistol, which allowed them to charge him with illegal weapons possession. He was hustled to Brasilia to await extradition, which his lawyers immediately began working to prevent. For 18 months he languished in jail, until December 17, 2001, when the 11 Brazilian Supreme Court justices unanimously rejected the extradition request as "politically motivated" and ordered Oviedo released. The Paraguayan government was highly displeased with the court's decision.

The following day, a jubilant Oviedo, boastful as ever, vowed to return to Paraguay and run for president again. His critics responded that they would welcome his return, so he could stand trial not only for the Argaña assassination but for the deaths of the bodyguards and the seven street protesters. They also pointed out that he still has to serve the remainder of his 10-year prison term for the 1996 coup attempt. Oviedo has since been living with a cousin in an affluent neighborhood of the capital city of Brasilia—a short distance from the home of the exiled strongman Alfredo Stroessner.

Recent Developments

In domestic politics, González Macchi's tenuous coalition with the Liberals fell apart in February 2000 after the Liberals voted overwhelmingly to return to their role as an opposition party to protest alleged political corruption. That left the *Colorados* with a minority in Congress. The bone of contention between the two parties was a reform bill that would have

streamlined and depoliticized Paraguay's cumbersome bureaucracy, which sucks up more than 80% of the national budget. Hard-line *Colorados* had resisted the reforms because patronage is a traditional tool by which the party had ensured support. The president also sought to privatize inefficient state-owned companies, which sparked a protest in front of the legislative palace on June 9 by state workers, who were joined by landless peasants demanding free land. The atmosphere was such that González Macchi canceled a trip to Colombia, just as he had been forced to cancel earlier trips to Spain and Germany.

After the Colorado-Liberal alliance fell apart, the two parties fielded separate candidates in the special election called for August 13, 2000, to fill the vacancy in the vice presidency caused by Argaña's assassination. The Colorados nominated Argaña's son, Felix, seemingly an unbeatable choice. But the political establishment was stunned when the Liberal candidate, Julio Cesar Franco, narrowly defeated Argaña. It was the Colorados' first national-level defeat, a political event virtually on a par with the defeat of the *PRI* in Mexico's presidential election the month before. With the opposition in the vice presidency, pressure has been increasing on the unpopular—and unelected—González Macchi to step aside. His position has not been helped by the continued deterioration of the already sour economy (see Economy). Nor was the president bolstered by the embarrassing revelations in the media in April 2001 that his personal BMW, which is worth about $130,000 and for which he reportedly paid only $80,000, apparently had been stolen in Brazil and smuggled into Paraguay in time-honored fashion.

For the second year in a row, the United States "decertified" Paraguay in February 2000 as an ally in the war on drugs, citing the government's inaction at countering rampant smuggling. Paraguay's remote Chaco region is an important way station in smuggling coca from neighboring Bolivia. The United States likely was displeased also when Paraguay re-established diplomatic relations with Cuba in November 1999 after a 38-year break, the last Latin American nation to do so. The United States recertified Paraguay in 2001.

Paraguay, which has a large Arab community, primarily Lebanese and Jordanians, was back in the international spotlight following the September 11, 2001 terrorist attacks in the United States. A month later, Paraguayan police raided several Arab-owned businesses in Ciudad del Este, notorious as a smuggling center because of the porous borders with Brazil and Argentina, and detained several people. Police seized evidence of links with the Palestinian terrorist group Hezbollah. Even before September 11, the U.S. State Department had identified the so-called "Tri-Border" area as a hotbed of Islamic extremists.

González Macchi, who already was being vilified for failing to improve the stagnant economy, managed to make himself even more unpopular on July 15, 2002, when he declared a state of emergency in the wake of anti-government demonstrations in three cities that left two people dead. Riot police apparently overreacted. Rioting and looting erupted the following day in Ciudad del Este. The president blamed the disturbances on Oviedo supporters and accused Vice President Franco of collaborating with them to bring down his government—an implausible scenario. Franco, however, has called for González Macchi's resignation, placing even greater stress on an already unpopular and crisis-wracked government.

Culture: It is no exaggeration to state that Paraguay's unique culture is a product of geography and politics. Landlocked and cut off from contact with the outside world by a series of 19th century strongmen, Paraguay developed differently from its sister republics. To begin with, the indigenous inhabitants, the Guaraní, were culturally different from tribes on the fringes of the continent. Just as it took a special breed of native to subsist in this hot, dry climate, so it took a special breed of Spaniard to eschew the relative comforts of either coast to pioneer this inhospitable land. Along with such pioneers came Jesuit priests, who effectively ran the colony in the 16th and 17th centuries, when the Spanish Crown expelled them. The ruins of their mini–civilization can be seen near modern–day Encarnación. Some scholars attribute the Paraguayan trait of obsequiousness to authority to this long–ago Jesuit influence, which inspired the motion picture, "The Mission."

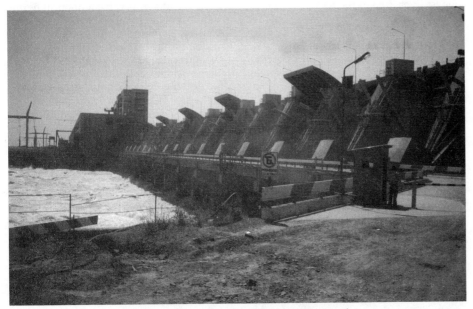

The water control spillways at Yacyretá

Because Paraguayan leaders placed little value on education, and in no small part because of the genocide committed during the War of the Triple Alliance of 1865–70, Paraguay never developed a European-based literary, artistic or musical tradition as did its neighbors. Paraguayan culture is derived almost wholly from the Guaraní, whose language still thrives; half the population learns Guaraní before Spanish. Several unassimilated Indian tribes still exist in Paraguay, providing tourists with cheap trinkets. But it is from the Guaranís that Paraguay developed the beautiful lacework that is so identified with the country.

Probably the most identifiable element of Paraguayan culture, however, is its lovely harp-based folk music. During the Stroessner regime, law dictated that 50 percent of the music played on radio had to be domestic. One Paraguayan folk song in particular, *Recuerdos de Ipacaraí*, is so well known that guitarists or pianists can play it from memory in restaurants or piano bars from Mexico City to Buenos Aires to Madrid.

As in many of the Latin American republics, dictatorship and illiteracy combined forces to stifle the development of viable independent newspapers. A few dailies are published, but only in Asunción. One is the official *Colorado Party* mouthpiece, but beginning in the late 1970s the others courageously exposed the endemic corruption of the Stroessner regime—although they wisely avoided mentioning the president by name. The country's leading daily is *ABC Color*, founded by businessman Aldo Zucolillo in 1967, which became more and more critical of the dictatorship, until Stroessner ordered it closed in 1984. It didn't reopen until immediately after Stroessner's overthrow five years later. Other leading dailies are *Hoy, El Diario* and *Ultima Hora*.

Economy: The eastern (*Oriental*) region of Paraguay, with its favorable climate, is the country's primary source of economic wealth. The western (*Occidental* or *Chaco*) region contributes far less, particularly because of adverse geography and climatic conditions. Approximately 40% of Paraguay's income is from agriculture, cattle raising and forestry in which half of the people are employed; industry and commerce account for the remainder. Farm output remains comparatively low due in part to feudal land practices under which 2.6% of the population owns 75% of the usable land, and partly because of an almost total lack of machinery in many rural regions. Paraguay's foreign trade is primarily with Argentina, the United States, the United Kingdom and Germany; principal exports are vegetable oils, grains, cotton, tannin, forest products, meat and tobacco.

Former President Raul Cubas

Paraguay has become a major banking center in recent years, partly because of political stability enforced by the Stroessner regime and partly because the nation is one of the few Latin American countries that places no exchange controls on the dollar. Because of liberal incentives to foreign investment, only 20% of the nation's industry is owned by Paraguayans. Explorations by three U.S.-owned firms in early 1975 in the bleak and desolate Chaco resulted in the discovery of modest amounts of petroleum.

The economy boomed in the 1970s and 1980s, bolstered by work on a huge hydroelectric dam: Itaipú (financed by Brazil). Paraguay is selling its share of electricity to Brazil. A contract was let for the construction of a second dam, Yacyretá, downstream on the Paraná River, to be financed by Argentina. This is the longest river dam in the world, extending 43 miles from the Paraguayan border to Argentina; it is now producing an abundance of electrical power.

Because of Paraguay's landlocked isolation, and its juxtaposition between two powerful neighbors, smuggling has traditionally been a major pillar of the economy. In recent years, traditional smuggling has been expanded to include drug trafficking, money laundering and copyright and trademark infringement. The United States at one point threatened Paraguay with economic sanctions because of the piracy of intellectual properties.

When Raúl Cubas assumed the presidency in 1998, he inherited a dismal economy and a budget deficit that totaled about 4% of the GDP of $10 billion. In his first month in office, he pledged to crack down on long-accepted tax evasion and black marketeering. He estimated that as much as 55% of taxes were not being paid.

The economy was imperiled even further by the market crisis in neighboring Brazil in late 1998. Paraguay finished 1998 with a 0.5% decline in real GDP. In 1999 it shrank another 1.0%, while unemployment increased from 15% to 17%. The economy finally showed some growth in 2000, but only an anemic 1.5%. Inflation fell from 14.6% in 1998 to 7.0% in 1999.

The Future: Paraguayan democracy remains among the most fragile in Latin America. The transition from Cubas to González Macchi in 1999, though marked by violence, at least adhered to the constitution. But this unpopular and unelected president is facing almost insurmountable pressure to step aside in favor of the elected Liberal vice president, Julio Cesar Franco, before his term expires in August 2003. Even if González Macchi should step aside—what then?

There are striking parallels between Venezuela's Hugo Chávez and Paraguay's Lino Oviedo. Both are charismatic speakers with a populist message that appeals to the poor masses in each country. Oviedo is fluent in Guaraní, still the predominant language among Paraguay's rural poor, a powerful political asset. In both Venezuela and Paraguay, the failure of elected civilian governments to come to grips with political corruption and sour economies has led to a flirtation with authoritarianism. A major difference between the two countries, however, is that only older Venezuelans can remember the Pérez Jiménez dictatorship, while in Paraguay memories of the Stroessner regime are still fresh after 13 years. Yet, a survey by a Latin American polling institution showed that the percentage of Paraguayans who would support an authoritarian form of government grew from 20% in 1995 to 42% in 1997, the period during which Oviedo staged his barracks revolt and became a political figure.

Like other peoples whose expectations for democracy after decades of dictatorship were unrealistically high, Paraguayans are growing disillusioned and impatient with their young democracy, not the least because of a stagnant economy. This author lived in Paraguay from 1977-79, and I was struck by the Paraguayans' traditional obsequiousness to authority and the reverence they still bestow upon their *caudillos* of yesteryear, like Francia and Francisco Solano López. It is not difficult for me to understand why Paraguayans would be seduced by a charismatic figure like Oviedo. It would be a mistake to dismiss lightly the enigmatic and bombastic general's vow to return and run for president again. The next year or two may well determine whether Paraguayan democracy begins to mature, or whether Paraguayans start to feel nostalgic even for Stroessner-style dictatorship.

The Republic of Peru

Peruvian school girls

Area: 482,122 square miles.
Population: 26.1 million .
Capital City: Lima (Pop. 8 million, esti- mated).
Climate: The eastern lowlands are hot and humid; the coast is arid and mild; the highlands are increasingly temperate as the altitude rises.
Neighboring Countries: Ecuador (north- west); Colombia (northeast); Brazil (east); Chile (south).
Official Language: Spanish.
Other Principal Tongues: Quechua and Aymara.
Ethnic Background: *Mestizo* (a mixture of Indian and Spanish ancestry) and pure Indian, 88%; European, mostly Spanish, 12%.

Principal Religion: Roman Catholic Christianity.
Chief Commercial Products: Fish, fish- meal, cotton, sugar, copper, silver, lead, crude petroleum.

Currency: Sol.
Gross Domestic Product: U.S. $54.1 bil- lion in 2001 ($2,074 per capita).
Former Colonial Status: Spanish Colony (1532–1821).
Independence Date: July 21, 1821.
Chief of State: Alejandro Toledo, presi- dent (since July 28, 2001).
National Flag: Red, white and red verti- cal stripes.

Peru sits astride the majestic Andes mountains. The Sierra (upland plateau) is at an average invigorating elevation of 13,000 feet from which ranges of high peaks emerge. The highest, Huascarán, is 22,334 feet; 10 others exceed 20,000 feet and there are many volcanoes in the southern region. The Sierra occupies about one fourth of Peru's surface and is home to more than 60% of the population.

The Sierra is cut and crisscrossed with rivers; those flowing to the west frequent- ly disappear in the desert before reaching the Pacific Ocean; rivers flowing to the east drop into the tropical jungles of the Amazon basin. Some of the eastern rivers have cut scenic gorges into the Sierra 5,000 feet in depth, with tropical climates and vegetation at the lower levels. The Pacific coastal shelf is a narrow ribbon of desert except for a few river valleys where there is sufficient water for irrigation.

The eastern slope of the Andes, known as the *selva* (jungle) contains over 60% of Peru's land and about 14% of the popula- tion. There are few roads into this region; travel is along the river valleys.

This area's resources are great, but inac- cessibility hampers their exploitation. Peru's climate varies with altitude—tropi- cal in the lowlands, it becomes temperate above the elevation of 3,000 feet and cold above 10,000–12,000 feet, with snow and bitter frost throughout the year on the high- est peaks of the Andes. People with respi- ratory or coronary difficulties dare not ven- ture into these heights—the air is too "thin" to support any but the hardiest of lives.

History: Peru has been host to civilized people from about the 3rd century A.D. Artistically sophisticated people have left pottery and textiles of excellent quality in the southern region which date from the 3rd to the 7th centuries. More primitive people lived in the vicinity of Lima, and a highly skilled culture existed in the north. The southern culture spread to the Sierra and gave rise to the Aymara society at Tiahuanaco, east of Lake Titicaca in the 10th to the 13th centuries. The Inca civi- lization began to develop in the Cuzco basin about the 11th century and by the end of the 15th century dominated the Andean Sierra and the Pacific shelf from Colombia to the Central Valley of Chile.

At the time of the Spanish invasion, a division had split the Inca rulers. The legitimate Inca Huáscar ruled the south from Cuzco while his half-brother, Atahualpa, ruled the northern provinces from Quito as a usurper challenging the legitimacy of Huáscar (see Ecuador).

When the explorers Francisco Pizarro and Diego de Almagro landed their small Spanish force in Ecuador in 1531, Atahualpa—apparently seeking allies to assist in his fight against his half–brother—allowed the Spaniards to reach the Sierra. The outnumbered Spanish tricked Atahualpa into an ambush, held him for ransom and killed him after it was paid. As Atahualpa had ordered the assassination of Huáscar, and his person was considered divine by the Incas, no one in the vast empire dared to raise a finger against the Spaniards as long as the emperor was a prisoner. Unopposed, the Spaniards moved into the interior of Peru, occupying the most strategic cities and, after the death of Atahualpa, ruled through puppet Incas until they felt strong enough to proclaim Spain's sovereignty.

Pizarro withdrew from Cuzco, the sacred capital of the Inca empire in 1535 and

Atahaulpa is ambushed by Spanish troops

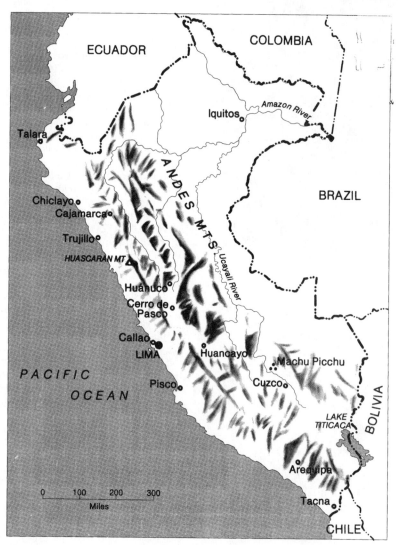

founded Lima near the coast. Almagro was sent to conquer Chile, but the arid territory and Indian hostility forced him to return to Lima. A brief struggle for power followed and first Almagro and then Pizarro were killed. Spanish authorities intervened, restored peace and began organizing the new rich colony. Francisco de Toledo, one of the best viceroys Spain ever had, established a firm basis for colonial power. He ruled from 1568 to 1582, adopted many Inca traditions like the "*mita*" (annually every male member of the Inca empires had to work free for the emperor during a few months) for Spain's benefit, and the colony prospered. By the middle of the 17th century, Lima was a splendid city with cathedrals, palaces and a university and the viceroyalty of Peru had become the political and strategic center of the Spanish empire in South America.

Exasperated by the exploitation of the Indians in the mining area, a descendant of the last Inca adopted the name of Tupac Amaru in 1780 and raised the banner of rebellion. Intelligently, he appealed to the creoles (people of Peruvian mixed Spanish–Indian blood), ratified his Catholic faith and proclaimed that he was not fighting against the king, but against his "corrupt officials." The rebellion spread rapidly, but Tupac's Indian followers killed Spaniards and creoles indiscriminately. The alliance of both, plus the condemnation of the Catholic Church, sealed his fate. Thousands of Indians rallied around Spanish authorities (a testimony to Spain's colonial policies) and Tupac was defeated, captured and publicly executed. The rebellion, however, left a lingering fear among the creoles. As in Mexico and Cuba, they remained lukewarm toward an anti–Spanish struggle that could trigger another Indian uprising. The initiative for independence had to come from *outside*.

The arrival of General José de San Martín and his small army of Argentinians and Chileans opened the period of armed insurrection. Unable to defeat the Spaniards, who were supported by many creoles, San Martín awaited the arrival of General Simón Bolívar, whose victorious army was marching south from Venezuela and Colombia. After meeting with *el*

Tupac Amaru

Libertador in Guayaquil and failing to reach an agreement on the impending campaign, a disillusioned San Martín retired to private life. Bolívar and his second–in–command, Antonio José de Sucre, opened the campaign against colonial authorities and in 1824 the battle of Ayacucho put an end to Spanish dominion in South America.

After the battle, Bolívar made an energetic attempt to organize the country. Taxes were cut, convents were turned into schools and the most glaring abuses against the Indians were suppressed. Elected president–for–life, Bolívar could have accomplished much more, but growing resistance on the part of alarmed and conservative Peruvian creoles, and the progressive disintegration of his "Great Colombia" (the union of Venezuela, Colombia, and Ecuador) forced him to leave Peru in 1826. A period of relative stability followed while most of the government and military forces concentrated on solidifying a union with Bolivia in a "Confederation of the North." Unfortunately, Chile considered that union as a threat to its future and invaded Bolivia. Chilean victory at the battle of Yungay forced the confederation to break up. The defeat plunged Peru into political turmoil until 1844, when a capable man, Ramón Castilla, seized power. President Castilla,

who served until 1850 and again from 1855-60, united the country, mediated differences between the pro–church Conservatives and the anti–clerical Liberals, established government services, abolished black slavery, ended forced tribute from the Indians and built a few schools.

The national economy, however, was restored by sea birds, whose mountains of dung (guano) on the offshore islands, were highly sought after in European fertilizer markets. The guano trade also led to the discovery of the nitrate deposits in the southern deserts; the extraction of the mineral was largely in British hands.

The period following Castilla's rule was one of tension and war. Nine presidents occupied the office between 1862 and 1885, of which only two completed their terms. The most competent of these was Manuel Pardo (1872–1876), Peru's first civilian president and founder of the *Civilista* Party. A war with Spain (1862–66) and the War of the Pacific (1879–83) were brought on by the prosperity which Peru was enjoying. Spain sought to recover its past grandeur and lost; Chile, with British connivance, sought the wealth of the desert nitrate fields and won.

The War of the Pacific was a disaster for Peru—thousands of lives were lost, much property was destroyed, some territory and the port of Arica were ceded to Chile, and the national economy was reduced to a shambles. Huge foreign debts were accumulated, the nitrate beds were lost and the guano deposits were almost exhausted.

British interests funded the foreign debt in exchange for the national railways, the steamers of scenic Lake Titicaca, the exploitation of remaining guano deposits, free use of ports and other trade privileges. Peru's recovery was slow, but a measure of peace and order was established and trade resumed under a succession of *Civilista* presidents.

The major event of the early 20th century was the rule of Augusto B. Leguía from 1919 until 1930. Energetic and able, he gave impetus to mining and agriculture and restored Peru's international credit. Leguía called his regime "A New Fatherland," adopted a modern constitution and freed the church from state patronage. Initially an honest administrator, he succumbed to graft and corruption under the temptation of loans proffered by the United States banks during the 1920s. When the inevitable protests arose, there was wholesale jailing of critics, restriction of the press and the closing of universities.

APRA is Founded

By 1930, the Peruvian people were fed up with Leguía's terrorism and the subsequent failure of business during the worldwide depression, which caused widespread unemployment. A revolt

caused him to flee; he was captured on the high seas and imprisoned on one of the offshore islands where he died.

During the last decade of the 19th century, there developed a movement for liberal reforms in Peru's higher society. Led by Manuel González Prada, a respected intellectual, demands were made to end feudalism, traditionalism and clericalism which González Prada declared enslaved the people to a handful of powerful men. Among the students attracted to González Prada was Victor Rául Haya de la Torre, a leader in the demand for educational reforms, who founded the American Popular Revolutionary Alliance (APRA) in 1924.

Anti–communist, with ideas borrowed from Russian, Mexican and European models, APRA sought to integrate the Indian into Peru's social and economic structure and to terminate the monopoly of political power which had been held by the landowners and the clergy for more than 400 years. During the dictatorship of Leguía, APRA grew and became the spokesman for the Indian in the Sierra as well as the urban worker.

APRA won the 1931 elections, but Haya de la Torre was jailed and the party outlawed. Revolts which resulted were savagely repressed, and Peru's second dictatorship of the 20th century was launched. Marshal Oscar Benavides ruled somewhat moderately until 1939.

Manuel Prado, a moderate, was president from 1939–45. He made progress in trade, public health, education and sanitation, but simultaneously firmly repressed all popular challengers to the landowner–clergy domination of political power. His successor came to office by a change of APRA tactics; reorganizing as the People's Party, APRA supported the most liberal of the candidates, hoping to secure congressional seats and cabinet positions.

The APRA success in this effort brought on a conservative coup headed by General Manuel Odría, who ruled from 1948–56. No pretense of democracy was maintained; restoring order and suppressing APRA, the army ruled with firmness. From a managerial standpoint, the regime gave a good account of itself, restoring confidence in Peruvian industry. Legal elections again returned Prado to leadership, but conditions did not remain stable.

When APRA won substantial gains in 1962 elections, the army again intervened by setting aside the results; in more carefully staged elections in 1963, Fernando Belaúnde Terry of the Popular Action Party (PAP) won a bare plurality and was named president.

Leftist Military Rule, 1968–80

Charging that the nation's political leaders were insensitive to the needs of

The Archbishop's Palace, Lima

the masses, a military *junta* again ousted the civilian president in 1968 and replaced him with General Juan Velasco Alvarado, who served as president for the next seven years. The new regime promised to end the traditional political and economic control of Peru by the "top 40 families" and foreign corporations through a program of "social democracy," patterned loosely on the Yugoslav model, which (they said) would guide the nation on a path between capitalism and communism.

The first phase of the program, largely achieved by 1975, called for state control of strategic sectors of the economy. Thus, the regime nationalized the fishing industry, banks, communications facilities, most of the news media and U.S.–owned mining operations. A unique feature of the Inca Plan required major industries to grant half–ownership to the workers.

A cornerstone of the economic plan was one of the most extensive land reform programs in Latin America. Before the military seized power, fully 90% of all farmland was owned by just 2% of the population. To break the power of the landed aristocracy, the military seized 25 million acres from large private estates and redistributed them to worker–owned cooperatives and to peasant families.

In foreign affairs, the military government was nationalistic and leftist. Diplomatic ties were extended to many non–aligned and communist nations and Peru became the second nation in the Western Hemisphere to import Soviet weapons and advisers. At international conferences, Peru was a major advocate of Third World causes as well as a frequent critic of U.S. economic power.

These policies naturally strained relations with the United States. Although Peru agreed to pay for some of the seized property, the prices were largely dictated by it. A low point in U.S.–Peruvian relations came in late 1974 when the *junta* ousted 137 members of the Peace Corps and several U.S. Embassy officials on charges of spying for the CIA.

By combining a nationalistic foreign policy with a state–controlled economy, the *junta* hoped to build what it described as a "new Peruvian man." To speed up the process, the government expanded education programs, increased per capita incomes (predominantly of coastal residents), promised to spend new oil revenues on social programs and to turn over farms and factories to workers. The expected popular support, however, failed to materialize. Farm workers who received land bitterly opposed sharing their gains with landless peasants. Factory workers continued to strike as often against state–owned industries as they had against the former owners. Part of the problem was rooted in the government's attempts to run Peru like a military barracks.

Congress was closed, most political parties were banned, and civilians were excluded from key government jobs. Professional organizations and free labor movements were suppressed and the press was censored. Compounding Peru's troubles were collapse of the fishmeal industry (the offshore anchovies disappeared), a plunge in world copper prices and the failure of new oil wells (in which the regime had gambled $1.5 billion) to produce as expected.

The government's economic program scared away badly needed foreign investment and poor management resulted in lowered production in nationalized industries. Benefits of the military revolution failed to filter down to the lower classes;

unemployment and inflation cut the living standards of the people.

Velasco Alvarado, partially disabled from circulatory problems and a mild stroke, increasingly ruled by decree, jailing or deporting his critics. When he turned his wrath against fellow military officers, the armed forced finally stepped in and deposed him in a bloodless coup in 1975.

Named as new president was General Francisco Morales Bermúdez, 54, a moderate and former prime minister. Although he pledged to follow the basic goals of the previous regime, he further stated that the revolution had entered a more conservative "consolidation phase." Faced with a bankrupt treasury, the regime turned away from a policy of rigid state control of industry. A number of major businesses (including the key fishing industry), nationalized by the previous administration, were returned to their former owners. At the same time, the role and power of labor unions were reduced.

Nevertheless, Peru's economy continued to decline during 1977. Hoping to prevent further labor unrest and related political violence, the *junta* announced in October 1977 that plans were being made to surrender power to constitutional government. The first election was set for June 4, 1978, when voters would name delegates to an assembly to rewrite the constitution. Under the plan, an elected president and congress would take control of the country by 1980. However, the military stipulated that the new constitution

General Francisco Morales Bermúdez

must embody basic nationalistic principles of the present government which had stressed social reforms and nationalization of major industries.

As an initial step toward the restoration of democracy, voters went to the polls in June 1978 for the first time in 11 years to elect representatives to a 100–seat Constituent Assembly, which would be given the task of drafting a new constitution. The biggest winner, with nearly 40% of the vote, was the *APRA* party, which campaigned on a slightly left-of-center plat-

form. In second place were the leftists representing six Marxist parties with nearly 28%. The conservatives and moderates, led by the Popular Christian Party, were a close third with nearly 27%.

Return to Democracy

When presidential elections were held in May 1980, former president Fernando Belaúnde Terry of the *PAP* was an easy winner over 11 other candidates with 43% of the vote. *APRA* was second with 26%, while extremist parties fared poorly. Five leftist presidential candidates received 17% of the total and the center–right Popular Christian Party *(PCP)* won 11%.

Belaúnde became Peru's 102nd president in mid–1980, ending 12 years of military rule. The generals refused to attend the inauguration. Because his *PAP* won only 27 of the 60 Senate seats and 95 of the 180 seats in the Chamber of Deputies, Belaúnde had to have the cooperation of the *APRA* and the *PCP*. The new administration promised to respect the new constitution, create an independent judiciary, promote human rights, ensure freedom of the press (including return of newspapers and TV stations taken over by the previous military regimes), and to encourage economic development. Programs for construction of roads, housing, increased farm production and water resources and nurturing foreign investments (especially in oil production) were given a high priority on the government's agenda.

Panoramic view of Lima with the broad Avenida Alfonso Ugarte in the foreground

The Belaúnde administration faced severe political and economic problems, the aftermath of the military regimes' wasteful spending (for failing social programs, an oil pipeline for nonexistent oil and for unneccessary exotic Soviet arms) which brought the nation to the brink of financial insolvency. To combat the crippling 80% inflation, a 40% unemployment rate, and almost defaulting on its international loans, Peru had acceded to the harsh terms for aid from the International Monetary Fund in late 1978. Austerity measures were taken to lower the inflation rate and to stimulate financial investments for economic growth.

As usual, the real burden for these reforms, however, fell most heavily on the poor and middle class as the cost of living rose sharply while real wages dropped. From August 1978 to mid–1980, strikes—particular and general—closed down mines, mills, oil installations and schools as workers protesting price rises for rice, gasoline and fertilizer, clamored for wage increases to catch up with galloping inflation.

There were more strikes during the summer of 1981—involving an unlikely combination: copper miners, doctors and bank employees, all demanding higher pay! The volatile atmosphere heated up in September when acts of terrorism became commonplace. Although it is still unclear what group was responsible for the surge of violence, far more than 1,000 acts were reported, among them a bomb attack on the U.S. Embassy and others directed at four private companies with ties to the United States. Guerrillas boldly attacked three police stations and a penitentiary in 1982; 247 prisoners were freed. The government was forced to crack down hard by suspending constitutional guarantees in five towns southwest of Lima after terrorists had killed three people.

An important diplomatic event occurred for beleaguered Peru in late 1981—Javier Pérez de Cuellar was named to a five–year term as secretary general of the United Nations.

Terrorism—Counter–Terrorism

Peru's democracy remained frail and much political squabbling in Congress slowed down the legislative process. But President Belaúnde assured the public that the military would not attempt another coup. This was put to a severe test, however, by the activities of Maoist guerrilla bands calling themselves *Sendero Luminoso* ("Shining Path"—curiously a Lenin expression).

The movement consisted of cells rather than organized larger forces, making it extremely hard to deal with. Founded about 1970 by Professor Abimael Guzmán (b. 1935) of the University of Huamanga, in Ayacucho State, it spread quickly to colleges and universities of the highlands, at-

High school girls

tracting many of Indian ancestry. Its actions, and the government's struggle against it, took the lives of more than 25,000 people.

Guzmán went into hiding in 1975 but remained active. From sketchy accounts of his rigid beliefs and behavior (traditionalist Stalinist, Maoist "communism") it was suspected that he was mentally deranged, becoming the leader of a mass cult which he mesmerized. One observer said he became "a Charlie Manson with an army to back him up."

Terrorism was committed not only by the *Sendero Luminoso* but also by elite military units sent to the impoverished region inhabited mostly by Indians. A group based in urban areas, the Tupac Amaru Revolutionary Movement, joined in the anti–government effort in 1984; it was named after the 18th century Peruvian Indian who revolted against Spanish rule. It knew how pipe bombs are made, and used them and heavier explosives to make life in Lima miserable. The city quickly came to be surrounded in the 1980s by "suburbs" of countless shacks and shanties where more than 8 million settled. It was easy in such a setting to bomb strategic locations—banks, businesses, embassies and the presidential palace—and disappear. The *Tupacs* shared their bomb talents with the *Senderistas*.

Further complicating life in Peru was the entry of coca production in the Upper Huallaga Valley which eventually became the source of 75% of coca used to produce illicit cocaine. The hirelings of drug traffickers were merciless and sometimes posed as revolutionaries to divert attention from their actual purposes.

Belaúnde rapidly declined in popularity (from 70% in 1980 to 20% in 1984). By mid–1984 the annual inflation rate reached 120% and Peru looked toward the presidential elections of 1985 with a mixture of hope and despair.

The contest was held April 14, 1985. *APRA* candidate Alan García received 46% of the votes, and the candidate of the United Left (which included communist elements), Alfonso Barrantes, popular mayor of Lima, got 21%. In order to discourage participation in the election, both the Shining Path and Tupac terrorists issued death threats and the Shining Path actually amputated the fingers of peasants to prevent them from voting. Police and military security at the polls was tight.

According to the Peruvian constitution, when none of the candidates obtains more than 50% of the votes, a second (runoff) election is obligatory. But before the date was legally determined, the president of the Electoral Tribunal was shot and gravely injured by members of the Shining Path. A few days later, Barrantes, probably trying to avoid a further decline of leftist votes, announced his withdrawal from the electoral contest.

García took the oath of office in July 1985. He immediately made dramatic and controversial promises. He stated that no more than an amount corresponding to 10% of Peru's export income would be used to "repay" a foreign debt of almost $16 billion, knowing that such an amount wouldn't even pay the interest on the indebtedness.

In order to deal with police and army corruption, García fired or retired many top figures in both organizations. He declared a state of emergency as lawlessness increased in Lima, ordering armored units from the military to patrol the streets. An American oil company was nationalized (assets: $400 million) without compensation. All U.S. aid was cut off as required by law. A new unit of currency, the *inti*, was introduced, which meant a devaluation of 64 to 1 in the national currency. It was later devalued several more times.

Peruvian conditions deteriorated severely after 1986. The Marxist–Maoist

Senderistas were very active, promoting simultaneous riots at three prisons, including Canto Grande in Lima (which later became a training and indoctrination center for the *Senderistas* into which the guards were scared to enter). The army responded by executing almost 200 prisoners after they had surrendered. A public pronouncement was made by the movement that 10 *APRA* leaders would be killed for each guerrilla who died. Three universities were raided by 4,000 government troops, who located *Senderista* propaganda, violating the traditional security of such institutions. Violence escalated rapidly, with extreme measures pursued by the guerrillas—tying bombs to small children and burros to carry them to their target. The army responded with equally horrible acts.

There would have been a military coup, but the military didn't want to inherit an ungovernable Peru. Much of the country came under martial law. The *Senderistas,* then went into the upper Huallaga Valley in northeast Peru where most of the coca is grown. They imposed a 10% "sales tax" on the farmers "for protection." Since they have no love for foreigners, the tourist trade all but dried up. The *Senderistas,* by then quite familiar with bomb fabrication and use, frequently disrupted the power supply of Lima, reducing it to three hours a day, if any.

People felt betrayed by García. More than half would have left the country if they could. He nationalized banks and insurance companies in 1987, creating economic havoc in Peru. Having defaulted on its external loans, Peru was on a cash–in–advance basis—as many as 50 ships at a time would lie in the harbor at Lima, laden with food, but awaiting payment in hard currency before unloading—while people in Peru were starving. Finally, after he left office, evidence surfaced that García had received a kickback for depositing Peru's reserves in BCCI, a shady bank that became the target of an international investigation, and from the construction of an Italian-built electric rail line. The charges were filed in 1992 but never were proved in court, because García fled into self-imposed exile in Colombia and stayed there for nine years—until the statute of limitations had expired.

The Fujimori Era

When 1990 elections approached, it was generally assumed that they would result in another *APRA* or traditional candidate victory. Polls showed the well-known novelist, Mario Vargas Llosa, the likely winner. But a surprise appeared on the horizon: Alberto Fujimori, soft–spoken son of Japanese immigrants, supported by a substantial number of Protestant evangelicals gathered into *Cambio 90* ("Change 90"), joined in the contest. His supporters,

going from door to door extolling his virtues, were persuasive. His popularity swelled from 3% in January to 60% in runoff elections a few months later.

A small element within the military, foreseeing the victory of Fujimori, attempted a coup just before the elections, replete with a plan to murder him. It failed—his intelligence received word of its time and place a week before it was attempted, and the candidate made himself unavailable for assassination.

Following his election, he immediately dismissed the chief officers of the navy and air force, and in December 1990, those of the army. He turned inward, trusting no one with basic decisions and policy. He ordered the reorganized military to commence a renewed campaign against the *Senderistas* and, showing imagination, he armed rural peasants, urging them to join the struggle against the terrorists.

The *Senderistas,* with their strength reaching about 15,000, launched a campaign in 1992 to gain control of Lima. Arms and munitions supplies via Colombia had become unreliable and they needed the support of the vast number of poor people surrounding the city in shacks. At the same time, it became evident to Presi-

Alberto Fujimori

dent Fujimori that the National Assembly, dominated by the traditional political elite, was obstructing him at every turn; he dismissed the body as well as members of the judiciary. He assumed personal control by decree in April. He had the backing of the military for this so-called "self-coup."

Faced with grumbling from Washington and the OAS, Fujimori called for elections to be held in late 1992. The *Senderistas* immediately launched a campaign to disrupt them, but two months before the contest, Guzmán was nabbed by the military and police, together with other key members. Having avoided publicity and pictures, little was known of Guzmán; he turned out to be an obese, ordinary-looking person with remarkable powers of persuasion, not unlike Charles Manson and David Koresh. Violence had become an end, not a means, for his followers, who engaged in the worst sort of torture, maiming, mutilation and murder of hapless victims. He was sentenced to a 40–year prison term within a month.

Fujimori and his supporters drafted a new constitution which was approved in late 1993 by a narrow margin.

Violence dwindled to less than 25% of what it had been in 1993. The *Senderistas* were reduced to a hard core of less than 1,000 who opposed Guzmán's surprising support from his jail cell of the new constitution.

Cambio 90 changed its name to *Nueva Majoría Cambio 90* ("New Majority for Change 90"). Political activity was on the rise in the latter half of 1994 in preparation for elections which were held in April 1995. Discord in the presidential mansion surfaced—Fujimori's wife, Susana Higuchi, had been seized by political fever and separated from her husband. Forming a new political party, Harmony 21st Century, she announced she would run for president. The National Election Board declared that most of the signatures on her application were invalid; she accused it of "techno– fraud."

Registration of 15 candidates included former U.N. Secretary-General Javier Pérez de Cuellar. A determined Higuchi aligned herself with the Police–Military Front. She was later excluded as a candidate. Fujimori won 64% of the vote, and his party was assured of a comfortable margin in the Congress. He acquired the nickname "Chinochet," a reference to his Asian heritage and the name of Chile's General Pinochet. He commented that Peru needed order, discipline, the principle of authority and leadership, administration, and honesty.

His magic has not always been transferred. He endorsed a candidate for mayor of Lima of Asian ancestry whom the voters rejected in 1995. Disgusted with his wife, he divorced her.

Because of severe unrest, Fujimori found it necessary to declare a state of emergency in Callao, the port city near Lima, in 1995. That same year, Peru fought a brief but bloody war with neighboring Ecuador over a border dispute that had simmered since 1942 (see Ecuador).

The Fujimori government barely had time to savor its triumph before it faced a new guerrilla threat in 1996 from its other active guerrilla group, the Tupac Amaru Revolutionary Movement *(MRTA)*. It differs from the *Senderistas* in that it is urban–based and far less bloodthirsty. Still, it demonstrated its ability to create mischief on December 17, 1996, when it raided a Christmas party at the Japanese ambassador's residence in Lima and took more than 400 diplomats and government officials hostage. The *MRTA* demanded release of prisoners, and gradually it released most of the hostages as tense negotiations unfolded with the Fujimori government. After four months, only 73 hostages remained in the compound, but the feisty Fujimori steadfastly refused to cave in to the demand to release prisoners. The standoff continued until April 22, 1997 when Peruvian commandos, acting on intelligence that the rebels were engaged in a soccer game, stormed the compound and killed all 14 of the remaining guerrillas, at a loss of only two commandos and one hostage, a Supreme Court justice. There was evidence that at least two women guerrillas attempted to surrender but were gunned down in cold blood, charges the government denied.

Meanwhile, Fujimori sent up a trial balloon on the possibility of his running for a third consecutive term, on the pretext that his first election in 1990 had predated the new constitution. But in January 1997 the Constitutional Tribunal rejected the idea. In a move that would have made Franklin Roosevelt envious, Fujimori cajoled Congress, controlled by his allies, to remove three of the tribunal's justices.

By July 1997, Fujimori's tendency to play fast and loose with the constitution and with basic civil liberties erupted into a major scandal, which the opposition and its media allies played up to the hilt. A female army sergeant assigned to intelligence went public in a televised interview to reveal she had been tortured and another woman sergeant, Mariela Barreto, murdered for leaking information that military intelligence was wiretapping Fujimori's opponents in the Congress and the media and threatening some with physical violence. When Barreto's dismembered body was found, confirming the report, the public outcry reached a crescendo against the president and the two men who it was widely believed were ruling Peru with him as a triumvirate: intelligence chief Vladimiro Montesinos and General Nicolás Hermoza, chairman of the joint chiefs of staff. Foreign Minister Francisco Tudela, who had been one of the

hostages held by the Tupac Amaru guerrillas, resigned to protest the government wiretapping campaign.

The embattled Fujimori, meanwhile, responded to the crisis by ordering the revocation of the Peruvian citizenship of Baruch Ivcher, the Israeli–born owner of *Frecuencia Latina* (Channel 2), the station that televised the interview, a move that flagrantly violated the constitution. Through a legal maneuver, control of the station passed to two pro–Fujimori minority shareholders. Fujimori pressured another station to fire a commentator who had been reporting on the alleged abuses of human rights. Spontaneous demonstrations erupted, and volunteers camped out at *Frecuencia Latina* to prevent an armed takeover by security forces. Fujimori's public approval rating nosedived to 19%, the lowest of his seven years in office.

There was more to come. For years, since Fujimori first ran in 1990, there had been rumors that he had been born in Japan and was thus constitutionally ineligible to serve as president. At the height of the crisis over the Ivcher case in 1997, the opposition weekly newsmagazine *Caretas*, the country's most respected, reported it had uncovered documents that raised further doubts about Fujimori's claim he had been born in Miraflores in 1938. The media began reprinting reproductions of the president's birth certificate, in which the place of birth obviously had been clumsily erased and the words "Miraflores, Lima" written over the erasure in a different handwriting. Other documents arose, such as Fujimori's mother claiming two children when she immigrated in 1934; Fujimori is her second son. Peruvian officials stood by the president's denial that the documents had been falsified, and it boiled down to Fujimori's word against the media's. In

that, of course, there was no contest as to who would prevail. The media also produced telephone records that suggest Fujimori had engaged in Watergate–style espionage of Pérez de Cuellar's 1995 campaign.

This tense situation took an even more bizarre twist in December 1997 with what was perceived as a showdown between Fujimori and the military. Fujimori published a book on the terrorist takeover of the Japanese ambassador's residence, in which he played up his own role and downplayed that of Hermoza. Relations between the two were reported to be strained because the reelection–minded president had begun to see Hermoza as a drain on his popularity; rumors began floating that Fujimori was on the verge of firing the general. In an apparent test of his authority, Hermoza summoned all the country's generals to Lima, ostensibly to attend his birthday party, but rumors of an imminent coup began to fly. Fujimori quickly ordered the generals back to their posts; just as quickly, they went. At year's end, Fujimori apparently had reached an accord with Hermoza: the general kept his job, but the president cashiered a regional commander who was seen as more loyal to Hermoza than to the president and he named Fujimori loyalists to command two key units. Once again, the feisty little president had prevailed in a test of wills.

Meanwhile, Fujimori began to recuperate some of the fading esteem of his people by once again doing battle with a common enemy, not terrorists this time, but Mother Nature. *El Niño*, the periodic weather phenomenon that affects climate worldwide but which invariably reserves its greatest fury for hapless Peru, returned with a vengeance in December 1997 and continued for months. Torrential rains brought massive flooding that destroyed

The Hitching Post of The Sun at Machu Picchu

whole villages and killed about 300 people. Fujimori, a professional engineer, went to the affected areas and took personal charge of the efforts to contain the flood waters. He mingled with distraught, homeless survivors and gave them personal assurances that relief would soon be forthcoming. To Fujimori's critics, this was micromanagement at best and shameless grandstanding and exploitation of a tragedy at worst, but it was a take-charge gesture that was typically Fujimori.

Dramatic events began unfolding in mid–1998. In May, apparently in an attempt to swing public opinion back in his favor, Fujimori replaced his loyal prime minister, Alberto Pandolfi, with Javier Valle Riestra, a Fujimori critic and opponent of the president's 2000 reelection bid. During his stormy three months in the post, Valle clashed repeatedly with his boss. Simultaneously, a popular movement called the Democratic Forum, backed by Fujimori's congressional opposition, collected 1.45 million signatures on a petition demanding a refererdum on the issue of whether Fujimori could run again.

Matters came to a head in August. The petition was presented to the electoral board, which voted 4–1 on August 20 that only the Congress—controlled, of course, by Fujimori allies—could approve a referendum.

Congress took up the referendum issue on August 27 and, not surprisingly, voted it down. Pro–Fujimori and opposition legislators almost came to blows twice during the acrimonious 13–hour debate. Police cordoned off the Congress building to repel demonstrators who chanted, "Death to the dictatorship." The vote effectively removed any remaining obstacle to a third–term bid except for one—the Peruvian voters themselves.

Perhaps one factor that improved Fujimori's popularity slightly in early 1999 was the signing of the long–sought peace agreement with Ecuador's President Jamil Mahuad in Brasilia in October, the dedication of the first border marker in January and the signing of bilateral economic development accords in Washington in February (see Ecuador).

On a darker note, Fujimori's government renewed its persecution of exiled television station owner Baruch Ivcher. In December 1998, a Lima court issued arrest warrants for Ivcher, his wife and daughter for allegedly altering the registration forms for his television station. Apparently stung by his growing image as a bully, Fujimori then shifted course and sought to reach an out–of–court settlement with Ivcher, arguing that the case was merely a legal battle between Ivcher and the pro–Fujimori shareholders who controlled the station. But the negotiations broke down when the two sides could not reach

an agreement before a March 31 deadline. Ivcher then took the case before the Inter–American Human Rights Commission, an organ of the Organization of American States. Fujimori said he "regretted" Ivcher's appeal to the OAS body. The commission forwarded the case to the Inter–American Court of Human Rights, which already had seven outstanding cases against Fujimori's government. On July 8, 1999, Fujimori resolved the matter in typical fashion: He simply withdrew Peru from the Court of Human Rights. At the same time, military intelligence officials adamantly opposed allowing Ivcher even to return to Peru, much less to resume control of *Frecuencia Latina*.

The "Elections" of 2000

The opposition to Fujimori grudgingly accepted the refusal of the Congress to call for a referendum on a third term and set out to defeat the president the only way left to them: at the ballot box. But three strong candidates emerged against him, thus dividing the opposition. The early favorite was Lima Mayor Alberto Andrade, of *APRA*, who won a landslide reelection victory of 65% in October 1998 against a Fujimori ally. Then a second candidate, Luis Casteñeda, who had earned high marks as head of the social security system, moved up in the polls even to Andrade by early 2000. Fujimori, meanwhile, as usually happens when there is fragmented opposition, held a strong first place in virtually all the polls, but not with the 50% needed to avoid a runoff. Suddenly, the fourth-ranking candidate, Alejandro Toledo, a 54-year-old economist of pure Indian descent, broke from the rear of the pack and moved up on the inside. In March, three weeks before the April 9 election, he jumped from 16% to 25% in a poll, emerging as the man for Fujimori to beat. The media made much of Toledo's humble farming background and how he had once shined shoes before going on the receive a doctorate at Stanford and to become an official at the World Bank.

Tension mounted as the election approached, as the opposition, the media and international election monitors began to uncover evidence that machinery was in place for possible vote-rigging. Fujimori adamantly insisted the vote would be clean. Nonetheless, the opposition was largely denied the access to the state-owned media that Fujimori enjoyed, and thugs suspected of being in the hire of security forces repeatedly pelted opposition rallies with rocks; no arrests were made. Moreover, the opposition candidates were the targets of scurrilous stories in tabloid newspapers.

The day after the election, it seemed that the worst fears would come to pass. Despite reliable exit polls that showed Fujimori well short of a majority, the first

"official" count—suspiciously delayed until midday on April 10—showed Fujimori a hair short of a majority, 49.6%; Toledo was a strong second with 40.6%. It was apparent that as the count progressed, the president would go over the 50% mark. As the tedious vote counting progressed over the next three days, however, reports began surfacing of serious irregularities, such as soldiers preventing people from voting, ballots with Toledo's name torn off the bottom, pre-filled ballots, and Fujimori campaign officials inserting votes into the electoral commission's computer via an Internet café. Domestic protests erupted, and the United States and other western democracies warned Fujimori that they would take a dim view of a fraudulent election. Then, as if by magic, election officials "revised" the final vote count, giving Fujimori 49.89%, just 20,000 short of a majority. Toledo obtained 40.15%.

The opposition took heart from Fujimori's failure to steal the election in the first round and even more from the results in the congressional election. Fujimori's *Perú 2000* party lost its absolute majority, dropping from 67 seats in the 120-member Congress to 51. Toledo's *Perú Posible* was second with 28 seats. The rest were scattered among smaller parties, but the opposition soon alleged that Fujimori loyalists were offering $50,000 bribes for legislators to join an alliance with *Perú 2000*.

The eyes of the world were focused on the May 28 runoff election, especially as it seemed obvious that Fujimori did not intend to allow a trifle like the will of the people to stand in the way of his retaining power. As election day neared, it became apparent to both the domestic watchdog *Transparencia* and to international observers from the Organization of American States and the Atlanta-based Carter Center, that it would be impossible to guarantee a fair and honest vote. Toledo proclaimed he would withdraw from the race unless the vote were postponed until June 18 to allow experts time to ensure there would not be the kinds of computer problems and irregularities that marred the first round. The international observers soon joined Toledo's call for a postponement. But Fujimori refused, countering that Toledo merely feared defeat.

The week before the election, Toledo kept his word and withdrew, saying he refused to lend the appearance of legitimacy to a fraudulent election. Then the OAS and the Carter Center pulled out their observers, saying they could not guarantee the integrity of the vote unless it were delayed as Toledo suggested. The OAS mission declared that the process "was far from free and fair." The day before the election, this author spoke with Jimmy Carter in Venezuela, which had just postponed its election because of technical problems. "In Venezuela, the election has been postponed, but with integrity," he said. "In Peru, the election has been allowed to proceed without postponement, but without integrity." The Clinton administration warned Fujimori that Peru could face economic sanctions. Street violence broke out as Toledo supporters attacked Fujimori campaign offices. Toledo at first called on his voters to boycott the election, but the $33 fine for failing to vote is too stiff for most impoverished Peruvians. He then called on them to deface their ballots by writing, "No to fraud!"

Days before the election, Fabián Salazar, a columnist for the newspaper *La República*, was given videotapes from contacts in the National Intelligence Service that reportedly showed the intelligence chief, Vladimiro Montesinos, giving instructions to the head of the electoral commission on rigging the congressional elections to deny seats to certain candidates. As Salazar was viewing the tapes in his office, security agents broke in, confiscated the tapes and sawed Salazar's arm to the bone. (Salazar is a former executive at Ivcher's *Frecuencia Latina*.)

The outcome on May 28 was a foregone conclusion. Fujimori received only a bare majority of 51.1%. Toledo received 17.4%, and 30.3% of the ballots were voided as Toledo had requested. The opposition could take some cheer from the fact that the pro-Fujimori bloc in Congress had lost its absolute majority, with newly elected independents holding the balance of power between the government and the opposition.

International reaction was immediate. The U.S. State Department quickly branded Fujimori's victory as "illegitimate," and the presidents of several Latin American countries expressed their concern. Toledo flew to Madrid to ask for support from Spanish Prime Minister José María Aznar for a new election. Toledo also called for a mass public protest two days before Fujimori's scheduled July 28 inauguration.

The tarnished election also headed the agenda of a meeting of OAS foreign ministers in Windsor, Ontario, June 4-6. But it soon became apparent that the Latin American representatives had no stomach for the U.S. position for strong hemispheric action. What emerged was a lukewarm Canadian resolution that called for former Colombian President César Gaviría and Canadian Foreign Minister Lloyd Axworthy to conduct a fact-finding mission to Peru to study ways to "strengthen democracy" there. There was no mention of sanctions or new elections. Axworthy, dashing any hopes among the Peruvian opposition, bluntly said that Fujimori's re-election was "reality." The Peruvian representative to the OAS meeting stated that Peru "welcomes" the mission's visit—so long as there is no discussion of a new election.

Fujimori Falls

Fujimori was inaugurated for his third term as scheduled on July 28, 2000, an event largely snubbed by the international community and vigorously protested in the streets of Lima. Only two presidents, from neighboring Ecuador and Bolivia, attended, compared with nine in 1995. On inauguration eve, Toledo marshaled 80,000 demonstrators for a non-violent protest. Inauguration day, however, was uglier, as riot police sought to disperse protesters with tear gas, which wafted toward the presidential palace and into the nostrils of the assembled dignitaries. Uglier still, a bank was torched, and six security guards died in the blaze; each side blamed the other for starting it. In his address, Fujimori ignored mention of the democratic reforms he had promised the OAS, focusing instead on economic growth. Meanwhile, as expected, several independent congressmen were "persuaded" to join the pro-Fujimori bloc, giving it a slim 63-57 majority.

If Fujimori believed that the protesters would eventually grow tired and gradually accept his stolen election as a *fait accompli*, he was soon disillusioned. For seven weeks, the protesters remained in the streets; usually the protests were non-violent, but occasionally there were clashes with riot police as tempers flared. Among the demonstrators' symbolic protests in front of the presidential palace: Washing the Peruvian flag in a tub of soap and water; using fumigation guns to spray the "rats" in the palace, and surrounding the palace with yellow police tape that bore the legend, "Caution! Mafia at work!" It was clever and effective non-violent protest in the best tradition of Gandhi and Martin Luther King.

The street protests proved little more than a minor annoyance for the thick-skinned and entrenched president. But in September, evidence became public that Montesinos may have been responsible for the transfer of arms through Peru to the *FARC* guerrillas in Colombia, which brought increased U.S. pressure on Fujimori. Then a television station broadcast a clandestine videotape that left little to the imagination: Montesinos was seen and heard attempting to bribe a congressman in the anti-Fujimori faction into switching sides. The resulting domestic and international pressure finally proved too much. On September 16, Fujimori stunned the nation in a televised address that he would order the disbanding of Montesinos' National Intelligence Service (whose Spanish acronym, *SIN*, is amusingly allegorical in English) and that he would call a new election—in which he would not be a candidate! He began talks with the opposition, brokered by the OAS, to effect a transition. Fujimori angered the opposition by agreeing to a new election

on April 8, 2001, with the new president to succeed him on July 28, but only if the Congress approved an expanded amnesty law to protect members of the armed forces from prosecution in other than human rights cases. The opposition refused to go along, and it prevailed. Many in the opposition preferred Fujimori's immediate resignation, which the president at first refused to do, and they made the resignation of Montesinos the *sine qua non* for continued dialogue.

On September 24, the nation was shocked again by the news that Montesinos had fled to Panama, Latin America's traditional dumping ground for unpopular and venal political figures. Fujimori had just "fired" his intelligence chief under mounting pressure, but his escape abroad smacked of collusion. Others, however, were relieved he was gone. Montesinos sought political asylum in Panama, which demurred, despite pressure from the United States and some Latin American countries to allow him to remain, thus removing the possibility of his continuing as a player in Peru's complex power game. Twenty-nine days later, his tourist visa expiring and no charges awaiting him yet in Peru in the bribery scandal, he returned to Peru on October 23 just as suddenly and as unexpectedly as he had left, precipitating an immediate domestic crisis. Rumors flew that the armed forces chiefs, known to owe their first loyalty to Montesinos rather than to Fujimori, were planning to stage a *coup d'etat*. Fujimori went on television to assure the country that he was in "total control" of the armed forces. Montesinos went into hiding, and Fujimori made a widely publicized effort to "find" his intelligence chief, although most Peruvians believed the president actually was harboring him. The opposition voiced its outrage over Montesinos' return and demanded Fujimori's resignation. Even First Vice President Francisco Tudela, long a Fujimori ally, resigned in protest—a decision he may have regretted a month later. Fujimori sought to mollify public opinion by firing the heads of the three armed forces, all Montesinos loyalists. But his new army commander also was a *montesinista*.

Over the next eight months, Montesinos' whereabouts became an international guessing game; eyewitnesses reported seeing him in the Galapagos Islands of Ecuador, then in Costa Rica, then in Aruba; in January 2001, he was believed to have returned to Peru. By November, reports circulated in the media that Montesinos and Fujimori had been involved in money laundering, arms dealing and drug trafficking. A federal prosecutor alleged that Montesinos had $48 million in Swiss bank accounts; his monthly salary was just $337. By early 2001, an investigation had raised that figure to $70 million, and further probing brought evidence that Montesinos may have amassed as much as $264 million. Evidence surfaced later that some of the money may have been laundered by two front companies that had been set up in Singapore—by Fujimori.

Events then began to unfold rapidly, as often occurs when the rule of a long-entrenched ruler begins to unravel. On November 13, Fujimori flew to Brunei for a meeting of the Asia-Pacific Economic Cooperation (APEC) conference. By then, defections from Fujimori's bloc in Congress had given the opposition control. Hours after Fujimori departed, Congress deposed his loyal speaker and replaced her with Valentín Paniagua, a respected but relatively obscure 64-year-old lawyer from the now-tiny Popular Action Party. The country was jolted yet again on November 17, when Fujimori absconded to Japan, his family's homeland. Three days later, he faxed his resignation to Congress—which rejected it. Instead, Congress voted by an overwhelming 62-9 to remove him from office as "permanently morally unfit." At first, Second Vice President Ricardo Márquez sought to exercise his constitutional right to succeed the ousted president, but Congress was in no mood to have the presidency go to a Fujimori minion. Márquez resigned, and Congress appointed Paniagua as interim president. He vowed a "total house-cleaning" and appointed the respected former U.N. Secretary-General Javier Pérez de Cuellar as prime minister. Another positive step: *Frecuencia Latina* was restored to its rightful owner, Baruch Ivcher, and the media were given free rein to report objectively on the upcoming election campaign, free of intimidation. Congress also restored the

Peru

three judges Fujimori had sacked from the Constitutional Tribunal for ruling against his bid to run for a third term.

Thus, one of the most intriguing eras of *personalismo* in 20th century Peruvian—and Latin American—history had come to an end. As this book went to press, Fujimori remained in Japan, as investigations in Peru uncovered more and more evidence that the man who had once vowed to vanquish corruption was himself rotten to the core. In February 2001, Congress brought formal criminal charges against him for dereliction of duty and other specifications. Although Japan seems unlikely to extradite him—it already has granted him Japanese citizenship—Fujimori was as much a fugitive as Montesinos, and will be unable to travel to countries that have extradition treaties with Peru. He may even face murder charges at home; according to a former Japanese hostage, three of the guerrillas slain in the commando raid on the Japanese ambassador's residence in 1997 were seen alive after the raid in commando custody. Fujimori had himself boasted of his micromanagement of that raid, making it unlikely that the prisoners could have been killed without his approval. It was a shabby end for a man once hailed as the country's savior.

Meanwhile, in early 2001, investigators seized from Montesinos' home about 2,400 videotapes on which the intelligence chief had unabashedly chronicled his bribes of a dazzling array of officials. Many of the so-called *"Vladivideos"* were released to the media, which kept the public spellbound—and further outraged. The public also learned that Montesinos had an escape tunnel under his bathtub.

Peruvian authorities then received word that Montesinos was in hiding in Venezuela, which the government of President Hugo Chávez denied for months. The Peruvians also learned that Montesinos had a secret bank account in Miami and asked the U.S. FBI to monitor it. Acting on irrefutable evidence from the FBI, the Peruvians confronted the Chávez government with the evidence of Montesinos' whereabouts, and on June 23, 2001, Venezuelan intelligence officials arrested Montesinos in a house in a seedy Caracas neighborhood. Reports that he had undergone plastic surgery the previous December turned out to be unfounded. Ironically, the Peruvian president-elect was in Caracas for the 13th Andean Summit, where Chávez announced that Montesinos was in custody. In just 24 hours, Montesinos was hustled back to Lima, not on an extradition request, but as an undocumented alien! His appearance in court the following day, in handcuffs and a bulletproof vest, was a hemispheric media event, and the Peruvian public began waiting expectantly for new revelations of Montesinos' perfidy like they would an unfolding *telenovela*. Besides the money

laundering, drug trafficking and arms smuggling charges, Montesinos also faces a possible murder charge in the death of the whistle-blowing female army sergeant in 1997. He is awaiting trial in a military prison. As this book went to press, he was reported on a hunger strike.

It was widely believed Chávez had harbored Montesinos, in theory because Montesinos had once granted refuge to some of Chávez's henchmen after the failed 1992 Venezuelan coup, and it has soured bilateral relations. (see Venezuela)

New Election, New President

In January 2001, even as the special prosecutor was making public some of the 700 videotapes seized in Montesinos' home that chronicled his bribery of various officials, no fewer than 10 candidates presented themselves for the April 8 election, including Toledo once again. Perhaps the most surprising postulant was former President García, who returned home that month after nine years of self-imposed exile in Colombia—just after the statute of limitations on his kickback charges had expired. At first, the García candidacy on the *APRA* ticket was dismissed as a joke, a relic of the dreadful days of guerrilla warfare and rampant hyperinflation. For two months, it seemed a foregone conclusion that the two candidates who would face each other in the runoff would be Toledo and Lourdes Flores, a veteran congresswoman from the conservative Popular Christian Party.

Toledo remained the favorite throughout the campaign with more than 30% in most polls, with Flores a strong second at 25%; García was a distant third. Toledo and Flores both sought to stake out the political center, with he slightly to the left, she slightly to the right, and García clearly to the left of Toledo. Suddenly, inexplicably, in March the polls began showing García moving up on the outside and closing in on Flores for the No. 2 spot. That sent a chill through domestic and international financial circles, which recalled that as president García had limited debt repayment to 10% of exports, thus sparking the hyperinflation that Fujimori was elected to combat. Nonetheless, García, an eloquent stump speaker, remained popular with the country's poor majority, who did not feel they had benefited appreciably from 10 years of *fujimorismo*. Still, he pragmatically toned down his fiery populist rhetoric so as not to frighten foreign investors and the ruling elite.

García also was aided by Toledo and Flores themselves, who began hurling mud at each other. Toledo was accused of fathering a child out of wedlock and refusing to take a paternity test. Also, *Caretas* magazine reproduced a medical report showing that he had tested positive for cocaine in 1998; Toledo countered that the *SIN* had abducted him and framed him. Race also became an issue. Toledo's Belgian-born wife, erroneously referred to by Peruvians as a *"gringa,"* ridiculed Peru's white ruling elite. Flores' father, meanwhile, used a racial epithet to refer to Toledo, which cost her votes among the indigenous majority.

Peruvians should have become inured to shocks by this time, but they received another on April 8. Toledo, as expected, led the field with 36.5%, less than he had received the year before in the first round against Fujimori. García won the coveted runoff spot with 26% to Flores' 24%.

The runoff was set for June 3. Again, Toledo was seen as an easy winner, as Flores' conservative voters obviously would prefer him to García. Both men frightened the moneychangers. Toledo was seen as unknown and unpredictable. García, however, was *known* all to well. Toledo, with his Stanford degree in economics, appeared less of a bogeyman. But again, the grassroots voters astonished the pollsters. On June 3, Toledo was elected by a slim 52% to 48%, making history as Peru's first full-blooded Indian president. García, at 52, is still young enough to try again—and probably will. He received a major boost in July 2001 when the Supreme Court dismissed all pending charges against him, citing the statute of limitation.

Recent Developments

Toledo was inaugurated on July 28, 2001. Eleven Latin American heads of state, plus Israeli Prime Minister Ariel Sharon and Spaion's Prince Felipe, attended the ceremony. In his address, Toledo pledged to combat the corruption left by Fujimori; to restructure the armed forces and police in the wake of Montesinos' departure; to create 400,000 jobs; and to continue cooperating with the United States in the war against drugs. The following day, in a symbolic demonstration of pride in his ethnic roots, Toledo participated in an Inca "inauguration" ceremony at the ruins of Machu Picchu. Fujimori's admirers had dubbed him *"El Chino;"* Toledo's have nicknamed him "Pachacutec," after a 15th-century Inca emperor.

The new president quickly surrounded himself with a kitchen cabinet of economic technocrats who, like himself, had been trained and had worked in the United States. As prime minister he named Roberto Danino, an international financial expert, and has finance minister he appointed a Wall Street investment banker, Pedro Pablo Kuczynski, who favors privatization and free trade.

Peru rapidly began moving toward a catharsis to cleanse itself of the Fujimori legacy, a legacy the disgraced former president continued to defend from his safe haven in Japan. A week before Toledo's inauguration and the installation of the new

President Alejandro Toledo

Congress, the imprisoned Montesinos began singing like the proverbial canary bird. He alleged that Fujimori had ordered him to pay hundreds of thousands of dollars in bribes to key members of Congress to secure his reelection in 2000. Montesinos even named the members who had accepted the bribes, including several who has just been elected again.

In August, Congress expelled two members of Fujimori's party for their role in his reelection maneuvers; they were seen plotting in a "Vladivideo." On August 27, Congress voted unanimously to strip Fujimori of his constitutional immunity from prosecution; 10 days later, Attorney General Nelly Calderón filed formal murder charges against the former president for his alleged knowledge and approval of two massacres of dissidents in 1991 and 1992 by a paramilitary group known as the "Colima Group," which left 25 people dead, and for complicity in the 1997 murder and dismemberment of Mariela Barreto, the whistle-blowing intelligence service sergeant. A few days later, a judge issued an international arrest warrant for Fujimori. Japan, however, continued to deny calls for Fujimori's extradition, which Justice Minister Fernando Olivera called "unacceptable."The Peruvian cabinet formally asked Japan to extradite Fujimori in June 2002 to stand trial for the massacres. Congress, meanwhile, voted unanimously again in October to strip Fujimori of immunity so he could be charged with embezzlement; Congress is investigating the disappearance of $372 million, $260 million of which apparently went into accounts controlled by Montesinos. Another international arrest warrant was issued against Fujimori

in January 2002 for an alleged $15 million payoff to Montesinos. In April 2002, Fujimori was formally charged with ordering the bribes of members of Congress to pave the way for his reelection.

Adding to Fujimori's woes, in May 2002 prosecutors cited forensic evidence that eight of the 14 guerrillas slain in the recapturing of the Japanese ambassador's residence in 1997 had been shot execution-style, not in combat as had been reported at the time.

In June, Montesinos was ordered to stand trial for his role in the killings, and investigators are still trying to determine whether Fujimori himself ordered them. (On July 1, Montesinos' first trial on other charges ended with his conviction; he was sentenced to nine years.) However, when police arrested a retired brigadier general, who was widely regarded as a hero in the hostage crisis, a public outcry quickly led to his release. A judge issued warrants for 11 other officers in the case, but none was detained.

Also in April 2002, the appointed Truth and Reconciliation Commission, which had been appointed the previous June by interim President Paniagua, began public hearings into human rights abuses committed during the 1980s and '90s. The investigations were continuing to unfold as this book went to press, as Peruvians were presented with horror stories of past atrocities. The commission was expected to interview 12,000 witnesses before releasing its report in June 2003. But Peruvians were abruptly reminded of another past horror that had led to the atrocities.

On March 21, 2002, a powerful car bomb exploded near the U.S. Embassy in Lima on the eve of a one-day visit by U.S. President George W. Bush, the first-ever visit by a U.S. president; 10 people were killed and 30 injured. Bush said that "no two-bit terrorists" would force him to cancel his visit, the purpose of which was a summit with the presidents of Peru, Colombia and Bolivia to discuss renewing the preferential U.S. tariff for Andean countries, the war on drugs and, ironically, the war on terrorism. More than 7,000 policemen were out in force to guarantee Bush's safety. The visit took place without further incident. (One result of the meeting was the decision of Bush and Toledo to resume drug interdiction flights by the Peruvian air force, which had been suspended in 2001 after an air force fighter pilot, armed with bad information from the CIA, mistakenly fired on a light plane, killing a female U.S. Baptist missionary and her baby.) In June 2002, police arrested three members of *Sendero Luminoso* in connection with the car bombing. The prospect of renewed violence by the once-feared group, which still has an estimated 400 adherents, sent a chill through the country.

By March 2002, it became apparent that Toledo's honeymoon with the Congress and the public was over. He is highly regarded in international circles as a darling of democracy, but as so often happens in Latin America's struggling democracies, presidents who promise a great deal and then are unable to deliver on them quickly enough are castigated by opposition legislators and media and by street protesters. Despite the fact that the economy was showing a brisk growth rate (see Economy), demonstrators took to the streets to denounce Toledo for failing to ease unemployment. In March his job approval rating in a major poll had plummeted to 25%, compared with 59% the previous August; 65% said they disapprove of him personally. The president himself has contributed to his image problem, coming across as inarticulate, unpunctual and indecisive. For example, he shelved a perfectly reasonable plan to purchase a helicopter to facilitate his travels around the mountainous country after critics complained loudly that the money would better be spent on alleviating poverty, as though one helicopter would make that much difference. When Toledo visited a garment market in a working-class Lima neighborhood, he was heckled and had to be protected by police shields from being pelted. Street protests in the capital were an almost daily occurrence, and unions organized strikes in Lima, Arequipa and Tacna. The protests forced Toledo to make a televised address to the nation to call for patience.

His efforts at privatization also have come under attack. In June, 700 soldiers and 1,000 riot police were dispatched to Arequipa to quell violent protests against plans to privatize two local electric companies; 20 people were injured in the disturbances the first day. Leaders of the protest alleged that Toledo had broken a promise not to privatize the companies. When the protests continued for a second day, Toledo declared a 30-day state of siege, which prompted his interior minister to resign in protest. By the time the rioting died down a week later, two people had been killed and 200 injured. On June 19, Toledo again backed down and called off the sale of the companies.

Peruvians took time from their grumbling to mourn the passing of former President Belaunde, the acknowledged patriarch of Peru's new democracy, who died June 4, 2002, at the age of 89. Toledo declared three days of national mourning and tearfully praised his predecessor as a "paradigm of democracy." June 6, the day of Belaunde's funeral, was a national holiday, and thousands filled the streets of the capital to honor him and to throw flower petals on his flag-draped casket as it was carried through the streets on a horse-drawn carriage. Former Chilean President Eduardo Frei, whose father had served as president in the 1960s during Belaunde's first term, was among the international dignitaries who attended.

Culture: The legacy of the Incas is evident in Peruvian folklore, art, music and architecture. Most of the population is full-blooded Indian today, and Quechua is the first language of millions of Peruvians. Still, the inevitable hybridization with Spanish culture produced something that is uniquely Peruvian.

Because Peru, like Mexico (New Spain), was a full-fledged viceroyalty that yielded dazzling amounts of gold and silver, the Spanish crown placed a higher value on this colony than on most. Consequently, a strong creole culture developed and along with it a literary tradition. Peruvian literary activity, however, never matched that of, say, Argentina or Chile. One of the most influential writers of the late 19th and early 20th centuries was Manuel González Prada, a journalist, poet and essayist who labored for reform and influenced later generations of idealistic Peruvian writers.

Many of Peru's best-known writers of the first half of the 20th century found their inspiration in politics, including the poet César Vallejo and the Marxist essayist José Carlos Mariátegui, who, like González Prada, was an major force in the *Aprista* movement. The most acclaimed novelists of that period and later years have all stressed indigenous themes, such as Ciro Alegría, Julio Ramón Ribeyra and José María Arguedas.

Without question Peru's most prominent contemporary writer is Mario Vargas Llosa. Born in 1936, he earned a doctorate in Madrid, and consequently his works are more cosmopolitan than those of his predecessors. His best-known novel, translated into several languages and the recipient of numerous international garlands, remains *La Guerra del fin del mundo*. One of his plays, *La señorita de Tacna*, also

has been translated into English and other languages and received favorable reviews when performed on Broadway. Vargas Llosa was Fujimori's opponent in the 1990 presidential election, and his electoral loss was seen as a victory for Peruvian literature. In November 2001, President Alejandro Toledo garlanded Vargas Llosa with the Order of the Sun, Peru's highest honor.

Peruvians are as fanatically devoted to their two native musical styles, *música criolla* and Peruvian waltzes, as Argentines are to the tango. The same is true of the national folk dance, the *marinera*, subject of an annual festival in Ayacucho. Until her death in 1983, the singer Chabuca Grande conveyed these distinctly Peruvian sounds to audiences throughout Latin America.

Peruvian theater, cinema and television are still in the developmental stage, though some works have achieved recognition abroad. Peru is now producing more of its own *telenovelas*.

Peru can claim to be one of the birthplaces of Latin American journalism. Even before independence, the literary journal *Mercurio Peruano* appeared in 1791. The leading contemporary daily, El *Comercio*, was founded in 1839, losing to Chile's El *Mercurio* by two years the distinction of being Latin America's oldest continuously published newspaper. For most of Peru's troubled history, press freedom either was nonexistent or severely limited. During the peculiar social experimentation of the 1968–80 military regime, the major dailies were expropriated and turned over to various "social organizations," such as teachers and labor unions. The result was a journalistic disaster, and the first act of President Belaúnde when he returned to power in 1980 was to re-

Peru

255

store the newspapers to their rightful owners. Numerous dailies of stature, plus the usual sleazy tabloids, are published in the capital. A relatively new one that has come to rival *El Comercio* in journalistic prestige is the pro–*Aprista La República*. Some dailies also are published in the major provincial capitals. There also is a thriving magazine industry, the highest quality probably being *Caretas* and *Oiga*.

Economy: Extraction and marketing of natural resources from mountain areas and the adjacent sea provides the basis of the Peruvian economy. Because the arid Pacific shelf and the high Andes restrict agricultural output, recent efforts have been made to open the eastern Andean slopes for farming. Water from the eastern slopes is also being used to irrigate former arid regions.

The ambitious land reform program implemented by the military government provided for the seizure of virtually all of the nation's large farms and their conversion into huge cooperatives rather than small, unproductive peasant plots. Relying on material incentives (profits were to go to the workers), the program was designed to increase farm output and bring—for the first time—larger numbers of peasants into the national money economy. However, because of poor management and a breakdown in the food distribution system, the land reform program fell far short of expectations. That failure, combined with a severe drought, caused widespread food shortages during 1979–80.

Abundant mineral resources provide the potential for sustained economic growth—with proper management. The prospect of finding large oil deposits in the Amazonian jungles proved to be over-optimistic—only one of 18 firms found oil during the 1960s and 1970s and most exploration was stopped.

However, in mid–1981 Occidental Petroleum reported that new oil fields had been discovered in Peru's Amazon basin. Peru then reported early in 1982 that its proven oil reserves have increased to 900 million barrels.

The inflation rate in 1989 was about 2,800%, creating a great deal of unrest among labor unions and an economically ruinous strike by the miners. The government began privatizing the nation's industry—the military had taken over more than 150 industries while in power. Peru's foreign debt is about $20 billion. To aid in its slow economic recovery, and under strict austerity requirements, the IMF in 1984 extended loans to the government; however, this was half as much as Peru hoped to receive. When President Alan García demurred on payment of Peru's debts in the late 1980s, the IMF declared Peru ineligible to receive further loans, and all other lenders followed suit. This meant that the nation was on a cash–in–advance status—an economic impossibility in a day and age when spare parts, machinery and manufacturing facilities are so vital to growth. It further meant that no government would honor Peruvian currency; the only substitute was foreign currency deposited in a foreign bank in advance to pay for imports.

All of this was reversed under President Alberto Fujimori. Peru again became credit–worthy and began receiving aid and investment from a number of sources. Approval of the constitution in late 1993 boosted available lending sources considerably.

Peru is the world's leading producer of raw coca leaf, from which refined cocaine is made. Chewed by the Indians for millennia as a mild anesthetic to allay hunger, coca thrives in the remote Andean valleys, where it is harvested and transshipped to neighboring Colombia for processing. The illegal coca exports once accounted for an estimated $1 billion a year. But in 1996, Fujimori ordered his air force to begin shooting down planes crossing the border that refused to identify themselves. Total coca acreage that year dropped 18% as peasants, finding it impossible to market that product, willingly accepted a government plan, backed by $45 million in U.S. aid, that provided them with incentives to switch to such alternative crops as coffee, cocoa, yucca and peanuts.

Fujimori's much–touted privatization plan, his conquest of hyperinflation and his successful campaign to lure more foreign investors to Peru, received high marks in international financial circles, but they did little to alleviate Peru's grinding poverty. With the modernization that inevitably comes with privatization, industrial jobs were cut by the thousands. The streamlining of the bloated bureaucracy threw middle–class Peruvians out of work as well. The construction boom was concentrated in affluent sections of Lima, with little or no trickle–down effect. Meanwhile, the elimination of government subsidies drove up utility prices, which hit the poor the hardest. In 1994, 46.5% of Peruvians lived below the poverty level; in 1996 the figure was 49%.

Figures for real GDP also have been discouraging in recent years. From a peak of $65.2 billion in 1997, which was a robust 7% growth from 1996, real GDP dropped to $51.6 billion in 1999. Per capita income also declined, from $2,675 in 1997 to $2,074 in 2001. Unemployment, which held steady at 7.7% in 1997 and 1998, jumped to 10% in1999. It fell to 7.4% in 2000 and remained steady at 7.5% in 2001. Inflation has dropped correspondingly, from 11.8% in 1996 to only 3.3% in 2001.

Despite the political uncertainty in 2000, real GDP grew by 3.1%, but it slowed to 0.6% in 2001, apparently because foreign investors held back to see what would happen when the dust from Fujimori's fall had settled. Fujimori's successor, Alejandro Toledo, has a doctorate in economics from Stanford and was once a World Bank official. He was elected on a moderately leftist platform, and was expected to be less enthusiastic about free-market economics and privatization than was Fujimori. However, he has surrounded himself with a retinue of U.S. trained economists like himself, not unlike the "Chicago Boys" in Chile during the Pinochet years. His finance minister, Pedro Pablo Kuczynski, is a former Wall Street banker and an advocate of free markets and privatization. The new team may be showing signs of success; the growth rate in January 2002 was a respectable 3.9% over January 2001. Despite this, and the encouraging decline in inflation, an impatient public has taken to the streets to demand more immediate improvements in the employment picture (see Recent Developments).

The Future: It appears that a new era is dawning in Peru, with Fujimori in Japan, Montesinos in jail, the first indigenous Indian in the presidential palace, the armed forces high command purged of their hand-picked loyalists, and the media given license to do what a free press is supposed to do—inform, enlighten and question. Ten years ago, Fujimori also represented the hope for a brighter future, and in many ways, he delivered. He tamed hyperinflation and crushed the *Sendero Luminoso*. Had he stepped down at the end of his second term as he should have, he probably would have been remembered as one of Peru's greatest presidents—perhaps even its greatest, as it has had a succession of dictators and fumblers. Clearly, when he dies, he will not receive a hero's burial as did Fernando Belaunde in June 2002—especially if he dies in Japan. But, as so often happens in Latin America, Fujimori came to regard himself as indispensable to the country's future and overstayed his welcome. If the embezzlement charges against him are true, and Japan continues to refuse to extradite him, he should live a very comfortable exile with the illegal fortune he amassed.

Toledo, meanwhile, has a Herculean task ahead of him in dealing with the political, social and economic problems facing the country. Events in early 2002 suggest that many of Toledo's impatient countrymen feel that he has already overstayed *his* welcome after less than a year on the job. It is an unfortunate and disappointing turn of events. One can only hope that Peru will not become a victim of the kind of mob rule that brought down duly elected presidents in Ecuador and Argentina, just because they did not prove to be Supermen. If mobs of howling protesters succeed in preventing Toledo from serving out his five-year term, then what—and who?

The Republic of Suriname

Street scene in the old section of Paramaribo

Area: 70,000 square miles +/–.

Population: 460,000 (2000 est.).

Capital City: Paramaribo (Pop. 190,000, estimated).

Climate: Very rainy, hot and humid.

Neighboring Countries: Guyana (West); French Guiana (Southeast); Brazil (South).

Official Language: Dutch

Other Principal Tongues: English, Spanish, Hindi, Javanese, Chinese and a local pidgin dialect called alternately *Sranan Tongo, Taki–Taki* or *Surinamese.*

Ethnic Background: Hindustani, 37%; creole (a person of mixed African and other ancestry) 31%; Asian, 15.3%; Bush Negro, 10.3%; Amerindian 2.6%; European and other, 3.8%. Figures are approximate.

Principal Religions: Hinduism, Roman Catholic Christianity, Islam, Protestant Christianity.

Chief Commercial Products: Refined aluminum ore, bauxite, aluminum, timber, rice, sugar, shrimp and citrus fruits.

Currency: Suriname Guilder.

Gross Domestic Product: U.S.\$843.8 million in 2000 (\$3,026 per capita).

Former Colonial Status: English Colony (1652–1667); Dutch Colony (1667–1799); English–controlled (1799–1815); colony of the Netherlands (1815–1948); self–governing component of the Dutch Realm (1948–1975).

Independence Date: November 25, 1975.

Chief of State: Ronald Venetiaan, president (since August 2000).

National Flag: Two green horizontal stripes, top and bottom, red horizontal stripe in the center, divided from the green by narrow white stripes; a gold five–pointed star is centered in the red stripe.

Separated from neighboring Guyana and French Guiana by large rivers, Suriname lies on the northeast coast of South America. Its 230–mile coastline is rather flat, a strip of marshy land lying mostly below sea level, which needs a series of dikes and canals to hold off the encroaching waters of the Atlantic Ocean. Along this fertile coast and stretching back about 50 of its 300 miles an inland extension is found where about 90% of the country's population lives.

Back from the coastal area, the land turns gradually into a grassland, becoming hilly and then densely forested with some 2,000 varieties of trees, 90% of the land area. This is a broad plateau land that reaches its highest point in the Wilhelmina Mountains. The land then dips down into the dense growth of the tropical rain forest where there are found hundreds of varieties of jungle birds, howler monkeys and all manner of wildlife typical to Brazil. In the interior is the 600–square–mile W.J. van Blommestein Meer (lake), which provides hydroelectric power for the bauxite industry located downriver.

History: Although in 1499 the Spanish touched along the coast of what is now Suriname, no attempt at colonization was made. European explorers generally ignored the entire region—the land was not inviting and there were not wealthy native empires to subjugate or loot for the motherlands. Toward the close of the 16th century, the Dutch appeared on the coast, but the first large–scale colonization efforts were made in the early 1650s by the English governor of Barbados, who became the region's first governor. These English colonists established successful sugarcane plantations.

In 1667 the Dutch received Suriname from the English in exchange for the colony of New Netherlands (now New York). Early in the 1680s, workers were brought from Africa to work in the fields since there were few local natives.

The territory again fell to the British during the period of the Napoleonic Wars (1799–1815); a series of agreements between the three powers established the whole of Guiana, as it was then called, into English Guiana (now Guyana), Dutch Guiana (now Suriname) and French Guiana. The latter of these later became infamous for its offshore penal colony, Devil's Island.

The Netherlands emancipated the slaves in 1863 and many of them settled on small farms to cultivate their own produce. This created an immediate and critical labor shortage, which caused the Dutch to import cheap labor from India in the 1870s and from Java in the 1880s.

The territory was slow to develop any political awareness, but since World War II, Far Eastern groups have become increasingly insistent on playing a greater role in the destiny of the land in which they live. This has created a bitter rivalry between the largely agricultural creoles and the prosperous, business–oriented East Indians. The colony became a self–governing component of the Netherlands in 1948 and adopted the name Suriname—it had been called either Netherlands or Dutch Guiana—and after 1950 controlled its affairs with the exception of defense and foreign relations.

Border clashes between Suriname and the soon–to–be independent British Guiana (Guyana) occurred in 1970. Early in 1973, serious unrest erupted when the government refused to pay increased wages to trade union members. A bloody strike lasted for more than a month before order was gradually restored.

Elections in November 1973 for the Legislative Assembly resulted in a victory for an alliance of parties favoring independence. Known as the National Party Coalition (of which the strongest force is the National Party), it gained 13 seats. The Progressive Reform Party won three seats; this victory by the black–dominated National Party ended a long period of political control by a coalition of East Indians and Chinese.

With the National Party Coalition victory, the colony moved a step closer to independence. Although the Dutch appeared anxious to leave, the large East Indian (Hindustani) population feared that independence would bring serious racial problems similar to those that erupted in neighboring Guyana. The spectre of violence soon sparked a mass migration to the Netherlands as independence day approached. All told, nearly a quarter of the population (140,000) fled Suriname.

Despite the damaging exodus, Suriname gained full independence after 308 years of colonial rule on November 25, 1975; the Netherlands agreed to help the new nation adjust to its status by giving it $100 million a year for the next decade—one of the most generous foreign aid programs on a per capita basis in history.

The new minister–president, Henck Arron, urged the nation's former residents to return. The appeal was indeed sincere since most of those who left were educated and skilled workers; their departure created a severe "brain–drain" for the new nation.

The principal political–economic controversy was the fate of the aluminum industry. Should it be nationalized, or should it remain in private hands, thus encouraging additional foreign investment? A decision was made to refrain from nationalization in spite of the fact that Arron's regime was initially leftist. Further complicating the political scene were ethnic differences and fears. The East Indian and Asiatic communities feared a black–dominated, oppressive regime.

Arron's policies gradually moderated and relative tranquility prevailed. But economic stability was in reality based on the $100 million annual Dutch subsidy; vital aluminum production was steadily declining. In 1980, however, non–commissioned officers ousted the government when it refused to allow them to form a Dutch–style military union. A nine–member National Revolutionary Council (RNC) was formed and backed the election of a government headed by Chin–A–Sen. The military, however, retained actual power; Lieutenant Colonel Desi Bouterse emerged as its leader. In December 1982 there was an attempted right–wing coup that led to assassinations of 22 military and civilian opponents of Bouterse.

The Dutch suspended aid and conditions rapidly worsened. Bouterse enlarged the military and conditions became extremely tense. Close relations with Cuba were established, to the extent that Cuba was viewed as a threat. The government was largely incompetent and inefficient. The "Cuban connection" was brief, ending after the United States invaded Grenada in 1983 (see Grenada).

Economically smarting because of the withdrawal of Dutch aid and lower world prices for aluminum products, Suriname announced a plan for "a return to democ-

racy" in late 1984. A 31–member National Assembly consisting of 14 military officers, 11 trade unionists and six from the private sector were to draft a new constitution. The move did not satisfy the Dutch. Bouterse launched a mass political movement, *Stanvaaste,* in a move apparently intended to dominate any future democratically elected administration.

A U.N. report released in early 1985 accused the military of involvement in political murders and "suicides."

In mid–1986, a Bush Negro (a descendant of escaped slaves) and former army sergeant, Ronnie Brunswijk (*Bruns*–veek) capitalized on the discontent of his people, about 50,000 strong, over the idea of being resettled in towns. They were used to living deep in the interior jungle, speaking their own language. The latter attempt is still underway; the government controls little else than the capital city. The United Nations condemned fighting tactics of both sides, but the response was "when you fight, there will be victims."

Beset with a small internal revolt in the interior and pressures from Washington, Bouterse called for elections to an Assembly to be held in November 1987. Balloting was enthusiastic and the National Front for Democracy and Development, a coalition of three ethnic groups, won 41 of the 51 seats in the Assembly. It elected

Lt. Col. Desi Bouterse

Ramsewak Shankar president for a five–year term in early 1988. Actual power, however, remained with Bouterse and the 7,000–man military until moves got underway to pass control to the civilian government. It was unable, however, to militarily best Brunswijk and his followers.

Dutch pressures, particularly in the form of denial of assistance under the 1975 treaty, continued to exert pressure on Suriname to settle its internal rivalries. Finally a vague, but written, agreement for a truce between the factions was reached in 1988. Bouterse alleged that the negotiations failed to end the rebellion. Many Bush Negroes *(Maroons)* had fled to French Guiana to escape the conflict.

The Dutch restored aid payments in generous amounts, but not enough to suit some Surinamese, particularly the military. Slow return of the Bush Negroes occurred after they were assured that the Suriname army would not occupy their traditional territories in the interior. Brunswijk, feeling safe, entered Paramaribo in March 1990 under a flag of truce. Feeling that at last his opportunity had arrived, Bouterse had the army arrest what he regarded as a criminal and fugitive. This was when the extent of Brunswijk's power (or lack thereof) was felt first–hand.

The following evening, all electrical power in Paramaribo was out; this included vitally needed sources to process aluminum. The Bush Negro force announced that power would stay out until their leader was set free. President Shankar *ordered* Bouterse to release Brunswijk. After a few hours, Bourtese did this, steaming with resentment. The lights were promptly turned on.

By 1990, an investigation revealed Suriname was an important link in the Colombia-to-Europe cocaine traffic; both Bouterse and Brunswijk were highly involved. When the drug started to reach the Netherlands, the Dutch brought pressure, but Bouterse simply threw the president out in a bloodless coup in late 1990. The Dutch *again* suspended their annual aid.

Elections in 1991 resulted in the coalition selection of Runaldo Venetiaan, former education minister, as president, after five months of wheeling and dealing. Continued Dutch pressure brought about the resignation of Bouterse as Commander–in–Chief in late 1992. As the government gained control over the military, it was also possible in 1992 to negotiate with the Surinamese Liberation Army (Bush Negro) and *Tucayana Amazonica* (native Indian) rebel movements, leading to a cease–fire.

Even though the coalition headed by President Venetiaan was successful in elections held in May 1996, Bouterse's National Democratic Party was the single most popular party.

Not unexpectedly, in elections held in September 1996, Jules Wijdenbosch of the National Democratic Party was elected as Suriname's new president. Outgoing President Venetiaan's New Front had won 24 out of the 51 seats in the National Assembly in May general elections, falling short of the two-thirds majority needed to form a government. Thus, the choice for president fell to the United People's Conference (comprising members of the National Assembly and regional and district councils). By a vote of 438 to 407, Wijdenbosch won the office.

Wijdenbosch's *NDP* and its coalition partner, the Movement of Freedom and Democracy *(BVD)*, initially held a majority of 29 seats in the National Assembly, but the coalition began showing signs of strain in August 1997 when the president fired Finance Minister Motilal Mungra of

Former President Jules Wijdenbosch

the *BVD* for criticizing government policy. The schism became more pronounced when Bouterse was charged *in absentia* in the Netherlands with drug smuggling and the Wijdenbosch government adopted an aggressive response toward the mother country, which still provided Suriname with $65 million a year in aid. In January 1998 four of the five members of the *BVD* abandoned the coalition to protest what they deemed the government's inclination toward dictatorship and for failing to consult with the *BVD* members on policy matters. The only *BVD* member who remained loyal to the coalition was the Assembly speaker, Indradevi Djwalapersad.

Bouterse, meanwhile, now a lumber executive, denied the Dutch charges that he had smuggled 1.3 tons of cocaine into Europe and had ties to Colombian cartels. He told the Associated Press in December 1997 that he was considering running for president in 2001 and that he wanted to wean Suriname away from Dutch aid.

Bouterse was placed on the Interpol wanted list, and he was arrested in Trinidad in July 1998. But that country rejected a Dutch extradition request, and Bouterse returned to Suriname, where he continued to serve in Wijdenbosch's government with the euphemistic title of "presidential aide." In February 1999, a court in The Hague issued a summons for Bouterse to appear for trial on March 22, but he ignored the order; not even his attorney appeared to offer a defense. Apparently to appease the Dutch, whose aid was still welcome, Wijdenbosch fired Bourtese on April 3. The Dutch court then began trying Bourtese *in absentia*, and in July he was convicted, sentenced to 16 years in prison and fined the equivalent of $2.17 million. To compound his legal problems, in November 1999 the families of 15 of the dissidents slain after the December 1982 coup attempt filed a complaint with an Amsterdam court because Dutch prosecutors had not investigated the deaths. In November 2000, a Dutch appeals court ruled that prosecutors do have jurisdiction to investigate on the grounds that the 1982 killings constitute crimes against humanity. Bourtese faced an international arrest warrant, much as does Chile's former strongman Augusto Pinochet, but in September 2001 the Netherlands High Court dismissed the suit on the grounds that Dutch courts have no jurisdiction over Suriname and because Bourtese is neither a Dutch citizen nor a resident of the Netherlands. The court also ruled that Bourtese could not be tried under a U.N. convention against torture that went into effect seven years after the 1981 incident.

In late May 1999, violent street protests erupted against Wijdenbosch's handling of the economy, especially drastic price increases and a precipitous drop in the exchange rate of the guilder. On June 1,

Boats tied up on the banks of the river at Paramaribo

Paramaribo's *De West*, March 28, 1990: "Military authority critizes Government's position." Insert shows Ronnie Brunswijk.

the opposition mustered 27 votes in the 51-seat National Assembly for a no-confidence motion against the president. Wijdenbosch refused to resign, and the constitution is ambiguous as to whether he can be removed. The consensus was that the National Assembly could call new elections by a two-thirds vote, or 34 members; Wijdenbosch's NDP has been reduced by defections to 16 seats, not quite enough to block the effort. In an attempt to defuse the move to unseat him, Wijdenbosch announced on June 14 that he would call for new elections no later than May 25, 2000, a year ahead of schedule.

Recent Developments

Efforts by the opposition to replace Wijdenbosch with an interim president failed, so Wijdenbosch limped along as a lameduck president for a full year. The May 25, 2000, election, in which 23 parties competed and 72% of the 265,000 registered voters participated, was a stinging rebuke both to him and to Bourtese. The New Front of former President Venetiaan won 33 of the 51 Assembly seats, one short of the two thirds needed to name a new president outright. Bourtese's Millennium Combination was second with 10 seats, while Wijdenbosch's Democratic National Platform 2000 won only three.

Venetiaan was inaugurated for a five-year term in August 2000. He immediately inherited an international crisis from Wijdenbosch. Just days after the election, the outgoing government ordered a Canadian offshore oil rig towed from the disputed zone with Guyana at the mouth of the Corantijn River. Both countries moved troops to the area, as diplomats began negotiating a peaceful solution. Two years later, no settlement has been achieved (see Guyana).

Culture: The majority of the people are found along the coastal, agricultural zone. Of this group, about a third live in the capital and chief port of Paramaribo, a picturesque city with palm–lined streets and colorful market areas. The creole population is well represented in the civil service and mining industries; the East Indians tend to concentrate in commerce and farming activities. Dutch is the official language, and there is a literacy rate of about 80%. Although most students of higher education go to the Netherlands, there are law and medical faculties in Paramaribo. Suriname boasts a cultural center, museums, active theatrical groups, a well known philharmonic orchestra and a modern sports stadium.

Economy: Alumina, aluminum and bauxite, the ore of aluminum, have accounted for as much as 85% of the country's exports and some 90% of its tax revenues. Production declined from 6.9 million tons in 1973 to 3.2 million tons in 1984 and only modest increases have occurred since then. The leading bauxite firm is U.S.–owned Suralco, a subsidiary of Alcoa. Although some bauxite is processed locally, aluminum is now shipped in a finished or semi–finished state to the United States. Panaram, the center of the vital industry, receives its hydroelectric power from Lake van Blommestein. Layoffs in the aluminum production facilities raised unemployment, already an estimated 35%.

The IMF requires removal of a substantial number of underused government employees as a condition for further loans. There are few roads; rivers and aircraft provide most of the transportation. The majority of the people are employed in agriculture. The major cash crops are timber, citrus fruits, sugarcane, bananas and corn. Rice is the chief crop and food staple, accounting for half of all land under cultivation and is the source of valuable export income. Major problems facing the economy are high inflation and unemployment. The government is increasing its economic ties with Colombia, Venezuela and Brazil; with the aid of Venezuela it is hoped that new bauxite mines can be developed in the southern part of the country.

President Ronald Venetiaan devalued the guilder in 1993 which brought needed monetary stability, and by the end of his term in 1996 he had brought rampant inflation down to single digits.

Inflation and unemployment in 1998 were both 20%, which helps explain the voters' overwheming decision to return Venetiaan to power in 2000. In 2001, the economy grew by a sluggish 1.9%.

The Future: Suriname, underpopulated and underdeveloped, is a land with great economic potential from natural resources and, recently, from ecotourism. But it must get a handle on its turbulent political situation. Bourtese is now an international pariah, although his party still emerged as the second-largest in the Assembly in May 2000. The five years under Venetiaan could prove decisive in the life of this still-fledgling nation.

Fishing off the coast of Suriname

The Republic of Trinidad and Tobago

Member of steel band beats his drums

Area: 1,864 square miles.

Population: 1.3 million.

Capital City: Port of Spain (Pop. 330,000, estimated).

Climate: Tropically hot and humid. The heaviest rainfall occurs from May to December.

Neighboring Countries: Trinidad forms the eastern edge of a shelf surrounding the Gulf of Paria on Venezuela's northeast coast, separated from the mainland by narrow channels. Tobago lies 18 miles north of Trinidad.

Official Language: English.

Other Principal Tongues: Hindi, French and Spanish.

Ethnic Background: African Negroid (43%), Asiatic (40%), European and other (17%).

Principal Religion: Protestant Christianity.

Chief Commercial Products: Petroleum, petroleum products, chemicals, tourism.

Currency: Trinidad Dollar.

Gross Domestic Product: U.S. $8.024 billion in 2000 ($6,202 per capita).

Former Colonial Status: Spanish Colony (1498–1797); British Colony (1797–1962).

Independence Date: August 31, 1962.

Chief of State: Arthur Robinson, president (since February 1997).

Head of Government: Patrick Manning, prime minister (since December 24, 2001).

National Flag: A diagonal black stripe bordered with white on a red field.

Trinidad and Tobago both have mountainous spines representing rounded extensions of the Venezuelan coastal ranges. Trinidad's mountains lie along the north coast. Plains extend to the south, rimmed with low, rolling hills. Petroleum and the famed asphalt lake are found in the south of the island. Tobago's mountains on the north are skirted with coral–dotted shelves. Trinidad's soils are rich and well suited to sugar and other crops. Sea breezes moderate the tropical climate and the annual rainfall of 65 inches is evenly distributed. Trinidad's asphalt has been of commercial significance since the colonial period. The more recent discovery of oil and gas has fostered industrial development. Trinidad and Tobago's population is primarily African and Asian, with smaller groups of cosmopolitan people of Spanish, French and English ancestry.

History: Trinidad was discovered by Columbus in 1498 and colonized by the Spanish in the early 1500s. During the French Revolution, a large number of French families were settled on the land that in 1797 was captured from Spain by British forces. Ceded to Britain in 1802, Trinidad was joined by Tobago as a colonial unit in 1889.

The history of the dual–island nation has been rather uneventful. Administered as a British Crown Colony until 1962, its early value was in asphalt and sugar. Slaves had been introduced by the Spanish to work sugar and indigo plantations, and the British continued to add slaves until 1834. With the abolition of slavery, indentured East Indians and Chinese laborers were imported to perform the manual labor. The decline of sugar markets hurt the island's economy, but the existence of asphalt and (later) petroleum cushioned the shock and led to a transformation of the economy.

The leasing of bases to the United States during World War II provided another source of income to bolster the economy. The transformation of Trinidad and Tobago from colonial dependency was relatively untroubled. Initially incorporated into the West Indian Federation, its reluctance to tie its healthy economy to the less well–endowed island dependencies was a major factor in the demise of the Federation.

The United States was drawn into the final phases of the negotiations for independence when Prime Minister Eric Williams sought to capitalize on the U.S. base at Chaguaramas as the site for a new capital city. The United States released part of the site in 1960, with the remainder reverting to Trinidad in 1977. Independence was attained in 1962.

When opposition parties boycotted the May 1971 elections to protest voting procedures, William's People's National Movement won all 36 seats in Parliament. Although generally a capable leader, Williams' popularity fell because of his heavy–handed methods. A major crisis developed in 1970 when labor unrest and rioting led to a mutiny by sections of the small army. Williams used government

President Arthur Robinson

forces in 1975 to quell violent strikes by petroleum and sugar workers.

The dispute soon erupted into a more general strike, joined by transport and electrical workers. The prime minister sought to disorganize the strikers by jailing key opposition leaders. Despite growing hostility by labor members and some sectors of the business community, Williams' political control seemed to remain firm, bolstered by the "mini–boom" caused by the enormous increases in oil prices.

The nation became a republic on August 1, 1976. Although the new constitution severed all ties to Great Britain, the country retains its membership in the British Commonwealth. Named as first president was Governor General Sir Ellis Clarke. In the general elections held in September, Prime Minister Eric Williams won a fifth five–year term while his People's National Movement (PNM) took 24 out of the 36 seats in the House of Representatives. The Democratic Action Congress, traditionally the main opposition party, won only two seats. In contrast, a new Marxist–Leninist labor–oriented United Labor Front (UPF) won 10 seats. Representing sugar, oil and transport unions, the ULF had criticized Williams for failure to provide more jobs and housing and to control inflation. The group also opposed sections of the new constitution that vastly increase the power of the prime minister to restrict personal and political rights during emergencies. Despite the steady flow of oil revenues, stubbornly high unemployment fueled social unrest and persistent criticism of Williams. He died in 1981 at the age of 69. George Chambers, the minister of agriculture, was immediately named interim

Prime Minister Patrick Manning

263

Carnival in Port of Spain

prime minister. Later, at the party convention, Chambers was designated Williams' successor.

In November 1981 elections, six political parties vied for the 36 parliamentary seats. Due to the splintered opposition, the PNM scored a major victory, winning 26 seats in the House by the largest margin of votes in the nation's history (219,000).

Relations with Jamaica and Barbados, which had deteriorated in 1982 because of a trade war within the Caribbean Community, became further strained in late 1983 when Trinidad and Tobago opposed the multinational invasion of Grenada. A multi-nation Caribbean organization to promote free trade was created in 1979 in which Trinidad and Tobago joined. At its meeting in mid–1986, Prime Minister Chambers joined with the other member chiefs of state in criticizing the United States' Caribbean Basin Initiative because of its import restrictions on Caribbean products, principally textiles, footwear and oil products.

The collapse of international petroleum prices presented severe economic problems during 1984–87. The sugar industry also became non-existent except for production to meet local needs. The government started importing crude oil for refining because of decreased local production. Sagging world prices from 1986–88 further cut income despite increased production after 1984. Despite this, in the 1980s Trinidad and Tobago had one of the higher per capita annual incomes in the area.

The National Alliance for Reconstruction (NAR) led by Arthur Robinson won 33 of 36 seats in 1986 elections, ending the PNM's grip on power. Austerity and high unemployment led to an attempted coup in mid–1990 by nominally Muslim blacks. The prime minister was shot and beaten before the loyal army ended the affair. The courts gave amnesty to the rebels, much to the government's displeasure.

In late 1991, the PNM returned to power with 21 seats in the Parliament. Patrick Manning, the new prime minister, stressed economic improvement and lowered black–Indian tensions.

The pendulum swung again in 1995, this time in favor of the Indian community, when the United National Congress (UNC) won a two–seat majority and elected Basdeo Panday as prime minister. He pledged to be "the leader of all the people," but blacks still feared Indian domination. Panday also was faced with a burgeoning crime rate, a divided judiciary and police corruption related to drug trafficking. Trinidad made international headlines, and brought condemnation from human rights groups, in 1999 when it hanged nine convicted murderers, justified as a deterrent to rising crime. The public seemed to approve of the hard-line policy.

Trinidadian courts have continued to hand down death sentences, although the crime wave has continued, as have inter-national protests. In July 2002, the Inter-American Court of Human Rights, an arm of the Organization of American States to which Trinidad and Tobago belongs, ordered the country not to carry out the executions of 31 men and one women on the grounds that their rights had been violated.

Panday's UNC was narrowly returned to power in general elections on December 11, 2000, winning 19 of the 36 seats in Parliament to 16 for the PNM, still led by Manning. The NAR won the remaining seat.

In his second term, Panday succeeded in creating a business-friendly environment that attracted new foreign investment. But critics, including three of his own cabinet ministers, complained that Panday was becoming *too* friendly with business. In September 2001, Attorney General Ramesh Maharaj and two other cabinet ministers publicly alleged corruption within the government. Panday fired Maharaj on October 1, precipitating a crisis that Panday unwisely sought to resolve by dissolving Parliament on October 9 and calling a new election for December 11, only a year after being returned to power. The election results led to a constitutional crisis when the UNC and the PNM each won 18 seats; the PAR was shut out.

A few days later, Panday and Manning struck a deal by which they would let President Robinson of the PAR, usually only a figurehead, to decide who would be prime minister, who would then head a unity government. On December 24, Robinson, who like Manning is black, chose Manning to head the government, giving only a vague explanation for his reasons. A miffed Panday then reneged on his promise to cooperate in a unity government.

The Parliament did not meet until the first week of April 2002, barely beating a six-month deadline that would have forced a new election. For two days, the Parliament deadlocked on the election of a speaker, and the tension between the two parties—and hence the two ethnic groups—threatened to turn ugly. The gridlock continued as this book went to press, but Parliament has a deadline of October 1 to approve a new budget. A new election may have to be called before then.

Culture: The people of Trinidad and Tobago, about 45% of black ancestry and 35% East Indian (Gujerat) have remained distinct ethnic groups, but have managed social and political integration during the period of British rule. Thus, people with many customs and origins live without restrictions of cultural variety. The Europeans find expression in sports clubs and in their business occupations. The African element has acquired renown for its *Calypso* music. The people learned that through hours of heating, tempering and pounding that the steel oil drums from World War II could be tuned into unique musical instruments that are world–familiar today. Although most speak English, it is with a unique lilt. Religious expression is unhampered, with popular participation in the *Carnival* of the Christians as well as the Islamic festival of Hosein.

Trinidadians felt a sense of pride in October 2001 when Vidiadhar Surajprasad (V.S.) Naipaul, a Trinidad-born novelist, was named recipient of the Nobel Prize for Literature, only the second West Indian to be so honored. Their pride was muted somewhat by the fact that Naipaul had spent 50 of his 69 years in Britain and has ridiculed his homeland as "primitive."Scion of a literary family, Naipaul attended Oxford and opted to stay in Britain, vowing to "beat them (the British) at their own language." Yet, he used Trinidad as the setting for some of his novels, which include *A House for Mr. Biswas, The Suffrage of Elvira, The Mimic Men, Guerrillas,* and *In a Free State;* his first published novel, *The Mystic Masseur,* was made into a movie in 2001 and the filming was in Trinidad. The Nobel committee praised the iconoclastic Naipaul for his "incorruptible scrutiny" of the post-colonial West Indes, but he also had attracted notoriety for his attacks on Islam and for ridiculing such literary greats as C.S. Forrester and James Joyce.

Economy: Although the nation contains rich soils and agriculture is important, the economy is based on oil and natural gas production. The only Caribbean country with oil deposits, Trinidad and Tobago was at one time the hemisphere's third–largest oil exporting nation. But this has been declining since 1982. Oil production rose for the first time in four years in 1984, allowing the government to purchase the assets of the Texaco-Trinidad, Inc. petroleum operation before the world price of oil plummeted in the mid-1980s.

The picture had brightened by 1996, when unemployment dropped from 21.5% to 16.5%, and inflation fell from 13% to 3.5%. The government has offered tax advantages to oil firms to encourage exploration. Natural gas is increasingly being exploited and exported in liquid form to the United States.

In July 2002, Prime Minister Patrick Manning announced plans for a gas pipeline under the Caribbean with branches to Cuba, Puerto Rico, Barbados, Guadaloupe, Martinique, Antigua and St. Kitts. The project was expected to take three years and cost $500 million.

During the days of the oil boom of the 1970s, per capita income was among the highest in the hemisphere, more than $7,000, but that plummeted to $3,800 at the depth of the recession of the late 1980s and early 1990s. By 2000 it had climbed back up to $6,202, although as is the case in many oil-rich countries, it is not equitably distributed. A serious problem is the external debt, which in 1999 stood at $1.42 billion, nearly 25% of GDP. Real GDP growth has been respectable, between 3% and 4% from 1996–98, and a healthy 7.1% in 1999 and 6.9% in 2000. Unemployment, however, has remained disturbingly high for the past three years, although it declined slightly from 13.1% in 1999 to 12% in 2000. Inflation in 2000 was a manageable 3.5%, down from 5.6% in 1998.

Tourism, now principally on Tobago, would provide more profits than drug trafficking and would help diversify the oil-and-gas-dependent economy, but as in Jamaica, tourists are shunning this would-be tropical paradise because of an alarmingly high crime rate.

The Future: Trinidad and Tobago offers the proverbial good news-bad news dichotomy. The bad news, of course, is the current 18-18 tie in Parliament that has pitted the African- and Indian-based parties against each other in a governmental gridlock. The good news is that unlike Guyana, where tension between the African and Indian communities has routinely erupted into political violence, Trinidadians have eschewed, thus far, the temptation to resort to violence. One can only hope that their traditional adherence to civilized norms of political behavior will continue.

Rural scene

The Oriental (Eastern) Republic of Uruguay

Gauchos enjoy folk music in the countryside

Area: 72,150 square miles.

Population: 4 million (estimated).

Capital City: Montevideo (Pop. 1.70 million, estimated. Pronounced Mon–tay–vee–*day–oh*).

Climate: Temperate throughout the year. There is a warm season from November to April and a milder season from May through October. Rainfall is moderate and evenly distributed.

Neighboring Countries: Brazil (North); Argentina (West).

Official Language: Spanish.

Other Principal Tongues: Portuguese and English.

Ethnic Background: European (90%), *mestizo* (a mixture of European and Indian ancestry, 10%).

Principal Religion: Roman Catholic Christianity.

Chief Commercial Products: Hides, leather products, beef and other meat, wool, fish, rice.

Currency: New Peso.

Gross Domestic Product: U.S. $19.8 billion in 2001 ($5,900 per capita).

Former Colonial Status: Spanish Colony (1624–1680); contested between Spain and Portugal (1680–1806); captured by Great Britain (1806–1807); War for Independence (1807–1820); Portuguese Brazilian Colony (1820–1825); contested between Brazil and Argentina (1825–1828).

Independence Date: Independence was proclaimed on August 25, 1825, but Uruguay did not actually become independent until August 27, 1828, when a treaty was signed with Brazil and Argentina as a result of British intervention in the dispute between Uruguay's two neighboring countries.

Chief of State: Jorge Batlle, president (since March 1, 2000).

National Flag: Four blue and five white horizontal stripes; a rising sun of 16 alternating straight and wavy rays on a white square is in the upper left hand part of the flag.

Uruguay, the second smallest of the South American countries, is a land of rolling hills covered with lush grasses and a few scattered forests. The highest elevation is about 2,000 feet; the country is crossed by numerous small streams and is bounded by the Atlantic and several large rivers. The estuary of the Río de la Plata and the Uruguay River, separating Uruguay from Argentina, are navigable and provide an important means of transportation. The River Negro, which arises in Brazil and crosses Uruguay from northeast to southwest is also navigable for some distance.

The rich, black soils produce a high quality of grasses which have encouraged cattle and sheep raising. Equally suited to agriculture, less than 10% of the land is used for farming. The climate is mild, though damp. Winter (June–August) temperatures average 57° to 60° F., with occasional frosts; summer (December–February) temperatures average 75° to 79° F. Rainfall is evenly distributed during the year, averaging 40 inches annually. Nature and history have caused Uruguay to become a pastoral country.

History: The Spanish explorers of the Río de la Plata in the 16th century passed up the hills of Uruguay as unlikely to have treasure in gold and precious stones. The warlike Charrúa Indians also discouraged invasion. Military expeditions against the Indians were uniformly unsuccessful, but Jesuit and Franciscan missionaries were able to establish missions in 1624. Cattle are supposed to have been introduced by Hernando Arias in 1580 during one of the unsuccessful military expeditions. A counter–invasion by the Portuguese from Brazil came in 1680, following slave raids on the missions and cattle roundups of the wild herds that roamed the grasslands.

The Portuguese founded Colonia as a rival to Spanish Buenos Aires. The remainder of Uruguay's colonial history is one of war between the Spanish and Portuguese contenders for control of the La Plata River. Montevideo was planned by the Portuguese, built by the Spanish and taken by the British in 1806, but abandoned in 1807 when an attack on Buenos Aires failed. A Brazilian attack in 1811 was resisted by the Uruguayan cattleman and patriot José Artigas, who declared Uruguay's independence.

The struggle continued until 1820 when Montevideo fell to the Brazilians, and Artigas fled to Paraguay where he died in a comfortable self-imposed exile. A group of 33 exiles returned from Buenos Aires to take up the cause in 1825, and with

Argentine assistance, they defeated the Brazilians at Ituzaingo in 1827 (the city of Treinte y Tres is named in honor of that band of exiles). At this point, Great Britain intervened. Both Brazil and Argentina renounced their claims and Uruguay became independent in fact on August 27, 1828.

The settlement of Uruguay proceeded slowly from the first missionary stations. The *gauchos* (cowboys) who hunted the cattle in the 17th and 18th centuries were nomads and not interested in the land. Slaughtering the cattle for hides, they sold their wares to merchants from Argentina. By the time of independence, the nomads had disappeared and large ranches had taken up the land. Farming was practiced only around Montevideo, where a market for produce was assured. Following independence, Italian and Spanish immigrants settled in the farming belt where their descendants still live today.

The early history of the republic was a chaotic period of civil war as the factions fought for power. Two parties emerged—the *Blanco* (White), representing conservative ranchers, and the *Colorado* (Red), favoring liberal reforms. The parties and politics established in the 1830s have been hardened in more than 150 years of combat and still persist today. A 10–year civil war was fought between the factions with support from other powers that intervened, including French, English and Italian. The foreign intervention terminated with the unseating of Argentine dictator Rosas in 1852; however, the Uruguayans continued the civil war for another 10 years.

Further strife in 1863 led to Brazilian support for a *Colorado* despot who unseated his *Blanco* opponent in 1865. The Paraguayan dictator Francisco Solano-Lopez came to the aid of the *Blancos*, precipitating the Triple Alliance (Argentina, Brazil and Uruguay) war against Paraguay. The defeat of Paraguay left the *Colorados* in power, which they retained for nearly a century except for the military period.

The year 1870 marks a turning point in Uruguayan history. The rancher with his *gaucho* army was out of place. The demand for better quality meat, hides and wool required more modern methods and business–like management of the huge estates. Railroads were built, European immigrants settled in the cities and a middle class mercantile society developed. Clashes continued between the two parties through the remainder of the 19th century, but a growing group of responsible citizens emerged. Three *Colorado* dictators ruled from 1875 to 1890 with some degree of moderation. Two more ruled from 1890 to 1896 with such disregard for the law that civil war again broke out, resulting in the division of the country into *Colorado* and *Blanco* provinces. This uneasy arrangement lasted until 1903 and the election of Uruguay's foremost statesman and leader, José Batlle y Ordóñez.

The Batlle Era

Uruguay's 20th century history has been dominated by Batlle—who assumed the leadership of a bankrupt, battle–torn and divided nation—even after his death. His first term, 1903–07, was spent in crushing civil war, uniting the country and securing popular support for sane, democratic government. From 1911-15 he campaigned for his plan, which included

replacing the powerful presidency with a council, an idea based loosely on the Swiss model but unheard of in Latin America. He encountered considerable opposition, but by 1917 a new constitution was adopted, and full franchise and progressive social legislation was enacted. Using the editorial pages of *El Día*, Montevideo's leading newspaper, Batlle pleaded his case and educated the people. By the time of his death in 1929, Uruguay was the most literate, democratic, well–fed state in Latin America. Batlle's unique plural executive system was in use until 1933.

Batlle's reforms did not, however, create the economic base needed to support the welfare state he had created. The next two presidents tried to carry out his programs, but they were restricted by the nine–member national council that wielded considerable power. Social and economic reforms were completely stopped when Uruguay went into an economic depression with the rest of the world in 1931.

Confusion, near-anarchy and no progress marked the years 1931 to 1951, replete with military dictators and corruption. Batlle's plural executive form of government was readopted as a result of a plebiscite in 1951 and its nine members functioned as the executive arm of govern-

ment until March 1967. The long–dominant *Colorados* again were returned to power, but high inflation and other economic woes led to disenchantment. In the 1958 elections, the *Blancos* won for the first time since 1865. They were reelected in 1962. However, they proved no more capable of dealing with the economic crisis than had the *Colorados,* in no small part because neither party had the courage to deal with the bloated bureaucracy and overly generous retirement system that the welfare state had wrought.

Bankrupt and in desperate need of dynamic leadership, Uruguayans voted overwhelmingly to return to a presidential executive in elections and a plebiscite in 1966. The *Colorados,* in the minority for eight years, elected a former air force general, Oscar D. Gestido, to the presidency, bypassing Jorge Batlle, grand–nephew of the reformer. When Gestido died in 1967, he was succeeded by the vice president, Jorge Pacheco Areco, a civilian. Encumbered by an inefficient bureaucracy and runaway inflation, and lacking forceful leadership abilities, Pacheco proved no more capable than his predecessor in solving Uruguay's monumental problems of economic stagnation, corruption and rising urban terrorism by the *Tupamaros*— Latin America's most infamous urban guerrilla force in the 1960s.

Promising law and order and economic reform, the *Colorados* received another mandate in the 1971 elections with the presidential candidacy of Juan María Bordaberry. Most of the president's program was soon blocked in the Congress, however, where his party lacked a majority.

The *Tupamaros* achieved international notoriety by kidnapping and murdering an agricultural official with the U.S. Embassy, Dan Mitrione, whom the Tupamaros alleged was a CIA agent who was training the Uruguayan security forces in torture techniques. As the *Tupamaros* increased their terrorism, and under U.S. pressure because of the Mitrione incident, Bordaberry turned to a new power source: the armed forces. With stunning efficiency, the military systematically routed some 2,000 guerrillas by early 1973. Then, instead of returning to the barracks, the military demanded major reforms in the nation's welfare programs, which it believed had been the basis for rampant political corruption and economic decay.

Military Rule, 1973–85

On February 8, 1973, the armed forces staged a coup d'etat. The generals agreed to allow Bordaberry to remain in office, provided he agree to governmental reform and a crackdown on the *Tupamaros.* Five days later, Bordaberry agreed. Backed by the armed forces, Bordaberry dissolved Congress, banned eight politi-

cal parties, closed the nation's only university, broke up labor unions, instituted strict press censorship and jailed 6,000 political opponents. Under the new order, all power was vested in the military-controlled Council of the Nation, which ruled by decree. The Mitrione incident and the subsequent coup inspired the Costa-Gavras film, "State of Siege."

Bordaberry decided he wanted to become president–for–life with the military backing him in 1977, but the military, favoring a gradual return to democracy, ousted him in a bloodless coup in mid–1976. An interim president was named, who was chief of a 27–member Council of State formed to replace the dissolved Congress.

Under the military's master plan, the new president was to have served for three years, at which time a president selected in controlled elections was to have remained in office for another five years. Full democracy would then be restored at the end of this eight–year period. Further, the military was prepared to purge top leaders from the *Colorado* and *Blanco* parties before these groups would be permitted to participate in free elections set for 1984. All other parties would be banned.

The master plan went awry, however, when the new president unexpectedly refused to issue a decree abolishing the nation's top political leadership. The military ousted *him* and, after consultation with top conservatives, the generals recruited a new civilian president, Dr. Aparicio Méndez, 72. Installed in September 1976, Méndez dutifully canceled the political rights of 1,000 leaders from all existing parties for a 15–year period.

In foreign affairs, Uruguay's military government received increased criticism for its violation of human rights. In 1980, the military *junta,* ruling through a civilian "front" administration, felt secure enough to submit a new constitution for popular approval. Although it provided for free congressional elections, it also established a National Security Council, empowered with final approval of almost all governmental activity and limited the presidential election to a *single* candidate approved by the military. On November 30, 1980, the voters rejected the constitution by a margin of 58% to 42%—to the utter amazement of the *junta.*

Rival factions divided the military: hardliners urged an end to the liberalization policy initiated in 1977; others focused on the power struggle to name the presidential candidate. Meanwhile, leaders of the *Blanco* and *Colorado* parties demanded immediate removal of a ban on political activity and restoration of a free press. Despite these appeals and the plebiscite, the military did not intend to surrender control, and as of January 1981, more than 1,200 political prisoners languished in Uruguayan jails.

After an investigation, without explanation, the *junta* announced the resignation of a group of senior officers in mid-1981. Included were those of the minister of the interior, commander of the Arms and Service School, the Montevideo police chief, the ambassador to Paraguay and several influential colonels. It was reported later that the officers had been involved in a get–rich–quick scheme with an unscrupulous broker, who used their money for loans to gamblers and for financing his own gambling. The broker disappeared, the officers lost hundreds of thousands of dollars and the *junta's* oft-proclaimed reputation for incorruptibility was tarnished. Ended, too, were the political careers of several generals.

General Gregorio Alvarez, former army commander, was appointed president and immediately began preliminary discussions with the political leaders of the two traditional parties for free general elections in 1984, that is, prior to March 1985 when his "term" expired. Negotiations stalled temporarily on the issue of membership of the commission to set rules for political activity and for framing a constitution to be submitted to a national referendum before the 1984 election.

By mid–1984, Uruguay's national attention was riveted on the dialogue between the government and the recognized political parties on the rules for the promised presidential election in November and several articles of a new constitution. The armed forces wanted guarantees that they would enjoy sufficient power under the new, legal regime, but the opposition insisted that the army's place is in the barracks.

On May 21, 1984, spokesmen for the armed forces hinted at the necessity of a "transitional period" between the military regime and return to democracy. Most political parties had either opposed the idea or stressed the brevity of such a "transitional period."

The tensions between the military and civilians reached their highest point when in June 1984 Wilson Ferreira Aldunate, leader of the *Blanco* Party, now generally known as the National Party, was imprisoned upon his return from exile. A wave of protests subsided as the elections approached; no group wanted to jeopardize Uruguay's return to democracy.

Return to Democracy

Held on November 25, 1984, the elections resulted in the victory of Julio María Sanguinetti, the *Colorado* candidate, who received 39% of the vote.; the Colorados also won a plurality in both houses of Congress. Democracy was restored officially when Congress convened on February 15, 1985, and Sanguinetti was inaugurated on March 1. As in most of Latin America, the new president, considered a centrist, had to face the rising expectations of a population free of military rule, the political inexperience of many of his advisers and a serious economic situation. By mid–1985 strikes had multiplied in Uruguay—including one which for weeks completely paralyzed the port facilities of Montevideo. The government had suspended the activities of the Bank of Italy and Rio de la Plata, and reassured the public that the "restlessness" of the armed forces, provoked by a cut in the military budget and investigations into the actions of the past military regime, would be peacefully solved.

A very delicate matter appeared to have been finally resolved in 1986: what to do with the military which, as in other Latin

American countries, had committed numerous human rights violations. To try them would be an invitation to a military takeover. An oral agreement had been reached prior to the return to civilian rule that there would be no trials of either *Tupamaros* or the military. A reluctant but very practical legislature passed a general amnesty measure at the request of President Sanguinetti. In consideration of this, the military publicly acknowledged that some officers had committed "transgressions of human rights."

This, however, enraged a substantial number of people, including survivors of 50,000 persons who were slain or disappeared, presumably murdered. The matter was settled in April 1989 when in a referendum the amnesty was upheld by a margin of 57% to 43%; there was no violence during the balloting.

A moderate *Colorado* candidate was expected to win 1989 elections, but Luis Lacalle of the *Blanco* Party captured a plurality of 37%. He had entered into a pre-election coalition with the leftist Broad Front, the candidate of which received 21% of the vote. Thus a loose combination of leftists, including communists, became a force to be reckoned with in Uruguayan politics, and it remains so today.

Although nominally leftist, President Lacalle followed a program of privatization of government enterprises, arousing substantial opposition generated by surplus employees of these industries. The program was largely halted by a 1992 referendum when 72% opposed the measure. A persistent, unacceptable rate of inflation plagued Uruguay in 1993–94, which led to a basic change in politics as shown by November 1994 elections in which Sanguinetti was returned to the presidency The Broad Front renamed itself Progres-

sive Encounter. The traditional two–party dominance of Uruguayan politics was effectively ended in the elections.

The Elections of 1999

The party primaries of April 25, 1999, provided an interesting dress rehearsal for the elections scheduled for October 31 and November 28. About half of the country's 2.4 million voters participated and a clear plurality, just over 37%, voted in the *Colorado* primary. The winner was Senator Jorge Batlle, grand-nephew of the party's illustrious founder and son of Luis Batlle Berres, who served twice as president, in 1947–51 and 1954–58. A former journalist, Batlle had failed in four earlier presidential bids. The primary of the left–wing Progressive Encounter movement drew slightly more participants than did the *Blanco* primary, 30.5% to 29%. Former Montevideo Mayor Tabare Vásquez received about 80% of the vote in the Progressive Encounter primary, while former President Lacalle was the easy winner in the *Blanco* primary.

Various left-wing groups, including the old Communist and Socialist parties, coalesced around the Progressive Encounter to form the Popular Front. In the first round of voting on October 31, Vásquez scored a convincing first-place finish, with 39% of the vote to 31.5% for Batlle and only 21.5% for Lacalle. Moreover, the Popular Front front stunned the two traditional parties by emerging as the largest force in the new Congress, winning 40 of 99 seats in the Chamber of Representatives and 12 of the 30 seats in the Senate. Vásquez also carried Montevideo.

Clearly, the Uruguayan left wing had come a long way since the 1973 coup, but the prospect of a Vásquez presidency

President Jorge Batlle

alarmed the political establishment. The defeated Lacalle swallowed his pride and endorsed the candidate of the *Blancos'* arch-rivals, the *Colorados*. Batlle pledged to continue Sanguinetti's moderate free-market reforms and derided the "crazy ideas" of his leftist opponent. In the November 28 runoff, on his fifth attempt for the job, the 72-year-old Batlle defeated Vásquez 51.6% to 44.1%. He was inaugurated on March 1, 2000.

The Popular Front holds 40% of the seats in both houses, which has forced the traditionally rival *Colorados* and *Blancos* to form a legislative marriage of convenience. The Batlle government at first resisted the hemispheric trend toward wholesale privatization, then reluctantly began making moves to reform the large public sector in order to appease the International Monetary Fund (see Economy).

Recent Developments

President Batlle found himself in the maelstrom of two international controversies in 2002. In April, Uruguay co-sponsored a resolution before the U.N. Human Rights Commission that called upon Cuba to democratize and to respect human rights. When Cuban President Fidel Castro angrily lashed out and called Batlle a "lackey" of the United States, Batlle broke diplomatic relations in 1986 after a 25-year break (see Cuba). In June, a television reporter asked Batlle at the end of an interview why he believed the Uruguayan economic situation was different from that of neighboring Argentina. Apparently thinking the formal interview had ended and the camera was turned off, Batlle replied that the Argentine government was "a band of thieves, from top to bottom." When he realized that his off-the-cuff remark would be broadcast, he shamefacedly rushed to Buenos Aires to personally apologize to President Eduardo Duhalde.

By early August, there were signs that Uruguay was facing the same type of socioeconomic crisis that led to the chaos in Argentina eight months before. On July 19, the government issued a surprise decision to let the peso float freely, and it plummeted in value from 17 to the dollar to 28. When Uruguayans began withdrawing their savings in a panic, and bank deposits dropped from $13 billion at the end of 2001 to just $8.8 billion, Batlle declared a "temporary" bank holiday on July 30. Newly appointed Economy Minister Alejandro Atchugarry announced the next day that the holiday would be extended until August 2, and violence and looting broke out on August 1 in a working-class neighborhood of Montevideo. The crisis was ongoing as this book went to press, as were negotiations in Washington with the IMF for an expedited transfer of the $1.5 billion loan.

Culture: <u>Almost entirely Caucasian, Uruguay in many ways resembles an extension of Europe</u>, and this certainly is true in its culture. Like Chile, highly literate and prosperous Uruguay has made cultural contributions far out of proportion to its small size. Also as in Chile, this cultural development was made possible by a climate of political stability and virtually unlimited freedom of expression.

Uruguay's contributions to art and music are not insignificant, but it is in the field of literature that the country has attained its greatest recognition beyond its borders. One of the most distinguished writers was José Enrique Rodó, whose 1900 essay, *Ariel*, extolled Latin American culture and denounced the United States as lacking in appreciation for cultural values. Needless to say, this essay was revered by latter–day Marxists and *dependentistas* throughout Latin America. Regarded as leading representatives of the romantic period in Uruguay were the novelists Eduardo Acevedo Díaz and Carlos Reyes; the poet Juan Zorilla de San Martín bridged the gap between romanticism and modernism. Two women of the post–modernist period, Delmira Agustini and Juana de Ibarbourou, also achieved international recognition. Some of Uruguay's leading contemporary writers abandoned the country during the military regime of 1973–86, the best known being the novelists Juan Carlos Onetti and Mario Benedetti.

Uruguayan journalism is highly developed but also highly politicized. The leading daily remains *El Día*, founded in 1886 by the future President of the Republic José Ordóñez y Batlle as a mouthpiece for his *Colorado* Party, which it still is today. Ordóñez's picture remains on the editorial page like the image of a patron saint. The *Blanco* Party has its own organ, *El País*, founded in 1918. The third major daily *is El Diario*, also pro–*Blanco*.

Economy: Uruguay's economy is almost totally dependent on its cattle- and sheep-raising industry, which accounts for more than 40% of all exports. Because of heavy taxation on farm products, as well as inefficient state management of the economy, the gross national product actually declined between 1955 and 1975. Inflation has also been a serious problem. Prices rose by an incredible 1,200% in the decade following 1968. To help control inflation, the government imposed new tax and credit policies. Steps were also taken to increase farm output, stimulate exports and begin offshore oil exploration.

Uruguay's seemingly enviable cradle-to-the-grave social welfare system and generous retirement benefits have helped to give Uruguay one of the hemisphere's best standards of living, and the per capita income of $5,900 is second only to Argentina's. But it has come at a high price; external debt in 1999 was $6.3 billion, about 30% of GDP, a heavy burden for such a small country, and by the end of 2002 it was expected to worsen to 60% of GDP.

Economic growth has been stagnant at best for several years. Real GDP shrank by an alarming 3.2% in 1999 and by another 1.3% in 2000; in 2001 growth "improved" to zero. Unemployment has remained stubbornly in the double-digits for several years and has grown increasingly worse: 11.3% in 1999, 13.4% in 2000 and 14.3% in 2001. One positive factor: inflation dropped from 5.1% in 2000 to 4.5% in 2001. The dismal economic picture for once-prosperous Uruguay was not likely to improve in 2002 as the dire economic situation in neighboring Argentina is destined to have an impact. It already has: Argentines who once crowded the beautiful beaches at Punta del Este stayed home in droves in the summer of 2002.

Uruguay received another economic blow in February 2002 when the international rating for its bonds was reduced, thus making it more costly to borrow money. The Batlle administration responded with an economic austerity plan, which included privatization of state-owned utilities, telecommunications, airports and even highways, and a cut in the bloated civil service pensions. He also promised to reduce the budget deficit, which was 4.2% of GDP in 2001, to 2.5% in 2002 and to balance the budget by 2004. The move was popular with the International Monetary Fund, which approved $743 million in loans in March and another for $1.5 billion in May, but highly unpopular with the left-wing opposition, the Popular Front, which has enough seats in Congress to force a referendum on the issues. The welfare system and the large public sector are sacred cows, and Batlle was forced to scale back his proposals shortly before this book went to press, but even the Popular Front was beginning to acknowledge that painful reforms would have to be made.

The Future: Uruguay has become the living proof of Churchill's comment that democracy is the worst possible form of government—except for all the others. Parties change in Uruguay, but little else seems to. Even faced with grim economic realities that threaten their once-enviable standard of living, Uruguayans, like Ecuadorians, are reluctant to abandon their cherished welfare state, which has become a luxury the economy cannot afford, and they will punish any party at the polls that seeks to do so. Still, Uruguay is a mature country, and it probably will grow old gracefully.

The Bolivarian Republic of Venezuela

Caracas and the mountains

Area: 352,150 square miles.
Population: 24.2 million.
Capital City: Caracas (Pop. 5 million, estimated).
Climate: Tropical in the coastal lowlands, increasingly temperate at higher elevations in the interior. Heaviest rainfall is from June to December.
Neighboring Countries: Guyana (East); Brazil (Southeast and South); Colombia (Southwest and West); Trinidad and Tobago are islands lying a short distance from the northeast coast.

271

Official Language: Spanish
Other Principal Tongue: English.
Ethnic Background: Mulatto–*mestizo* (mixed European, African and Indian ancestry, 83%); European (10%); African (5%); Indian (2%).
Principal Religion: Roman Catholic Christianity.
Chief Commercial Products: Petroleum and petroleum products, aluminum, alumina and bauxite, agricultural products, small manufactured products.
Currency: Bolívar.
Gross Domestic Product: U.S. $130 billion in 2001 ($5,283 per capita).
Former Colonial Status: Spanish Colony (1498–1811).
Independence Date: July 5, 1811. Venezuela seceded from *Gran Colombia,* also known as New Granada, on September 22, 1811.
Chief of State: Hugo Chávez Frías, president (since February 2, 1999).
National Flag: Yellow, blue and red horizontal stripes with seven yellow stars in a semi–circle on the red stripe.

Venezuela has four distinct geographic regions: the Venezuelan Highlands to the west and along the coast, the Maracaibo Lowlands around freshwater Lake Maracaibo, the *Llanos* or plains of the Orinoco River and the Guiana Highlands. The Venezuelan Highlands are an extension of the eastern mountains of Colombia and are Venezuela's most densely populated region, with Caracas, Maracay and Valencia located in the fertile inter–mountain basins. The northern slope of the Highlands is relatively arid, but the basins receive adequate rainfall and because of elevation, are temperate and suited to agriculture.

The Maracaibo Lowlands, encircled by mountains, are windless and one of the hottest regions in South America, famous for the great lake (129 miles long and 60 miles wide) under whose water are some of the most extensive oil deposits in the world. Rainfall in this region is heavy along the slopes of the highlands, gradually diminishing toward the coast.

The *Llanos* of the Orinoco are the great treeless plains of the Orinoco River valley, which run east and west between the Venezuelan Highlands and the Guiana Highlands. Extending some 600 miles in length and 200 miles across, these plains are low and wet; intersected with slow moving streams, this region has been plagued with periodic floods and drought, but the poor soil has supported cattle raising. Presently, the government is undertaking flood control and irrigation projects to make this land available for agriculture and to support the development of new breeds of cattle.

The Guiana Highlands, south of the Orinoco, comprise more than half of Venezuela's territory. Rising in steep cliffs from the *Llanos,* this area is a flat tableland that extends to the Brazilian border. Heavily forested in part, it contains vast deposits of iron ore and bauxite. Gold and diamonds also exist in this region, which has been explored only superficially.

History: At the time of the Spanish conquest, Venezuela was inhabited by war-like tribes of Carib and Arawak Indians who offered brave but ineffective resistance to the invaders; the first landing was in the Gulf of Paria, where pearls were discovered. Under Spanish direction, Indian divers soon stripped the beds of the Gulf. The first settlement was established at Cumaná in 1520, with additional settlements at Coro (1520), Barquismeto (1551), Valencia (1555) and Caracas (1567).

Indians were utilized to pan the rivers for gold, but the results were disappointing and the settlers turned to agriculture. The wealth found in Peru and Mexico caused the Spanish government to lose interest in Venezuela, and options to explore its potential were leased to Dutch and German adventurers. The Spanish settlers gradually consolidated their small holdings, but it was nearly a century later before a serious attempt was made to explore the interior. The enslaved Indian laborers perished on the coastal plantations, and Negroes from Africa were imported to work the sugar and indigo crops. The neglected planters, with little merchandise to ship to the Spanish markets and forbidden to trade with the growing American markets, revolted against Spanish authority in 1796.

Two additional abortive attempts to set up an independent government were made in 1806 and 1811 under the leadership of Francisco de Miranda. At his urging, a republican congress declared independence on July 5, 1811, but the so-called First Republic lasted only a year. Venezuela's national hero, Simón Bolívar, took up the struggle after 1811 and fought a limited, but deceptive, guerrilla war against local armies in the pay of Spain until his capture of Angostura in 1817. Here he was joined by British veterans of the Peninsular War in Spain and by cattlemen from the *Llanos* with whom he made a dramatic march on Bogotá. The Spanish were finally expelled from northern Latin America in 1819 and the country achieved full independence, becoming a part of the Republic of Gran Colombia, led by President Simón Bolívar and Vice President Francisco de Paula Santander, and including present–day Colombia and Ecuador. Dissension and the subsequent illness of Bolívar led to the dissolution of Gran Colombia; Venezuela withdrew from the Republic in 1830.

General José Antonio Páez, the country's first president and a hero of independence, dominated Venezuelan politics from 1830 to 1848. He later returned as a dictator from 1861 to 1863. A capable and popular leader, he was effective in restoring order to war–torn Venezuela and in the establishment of governmental services and control. He was followed in 1848 by 13 years of repressive dictatorship by the Monagas brothers, who forced him into exile.

Returning to the *Llanos* in 1861, Páez raised another force of cattlemen to regain liberty in Venezuela. He ruled for two years, but was less tolerant of opposition than he had been during his first tenure; he was ousted in 1863 and intermittent civil war wracked the country until 1870 as young liberals fought conservatives.

Antonio Guzmán Blanco emerged from the chaos of civil strife; as strongman, he served as president or ruled through puppets for 18 years. Well educated, arrogant and completely unscrupulous, he enforced honesty among his ministers while converting a substantial part of the national treasury to his personal use. A careless despot who enjoyed living in Paris, he left his office in the hands of a puppet once too often and was overthrown in 1888.

Eleven years of confusion ensued, punctuated by violence and short–term presidents. An illiterate soldier of fortune who had been exiled to Colombia, Cipriano Castro, captured the presidency with the help of a private army in 1899. His nine–year rule was certainly the most repressive in Venezuela's troubled history. His high–handed dealing with European powers resulted in a blockade of the Venezuelan coastline by British, German and Italian naval units. After intervention by President Theodore Roosevelt, the matter was settled by arbitration. Castro turned the government over in 1909 to Juan Vincente Gómez, who ruled until 1935.

Gómez gave Venezuela its most able and its most savage administration. Oil had been discovered and he arranged lucrative contracts with American, British and Dutch interests for its extraction and processing. Simultaneously, he fostered agriculture and public works, established sound foreign relations and paid off the national debt. He also mechanized the army to support his regime and built a personal fortune. By comparison with his predecessors, Gómez left Venezuela in a prosperous condition when he died, but totally bereft of qualified leaders to administer the wealth which he had accumulated or to control the army which he had enlarged and modernized.

From 1935 to 1948 a series of moderate, but ineffective presidents occupied the office; during this period, political parties were allowed to organize, the largest being the *Acción Democrática* (Democratic Action), a popular, leftist party which had attempted to consolidate rural labor into a mass organization. Fearful of a rigged election in 1945, the party revolted and named Rómulo Betancourt as provisional president.

Venezuelans were delighted with democratic government—action was taken to recover some of the wealth from Gómez's estate and from others who had privately benefited during his rule. In the first free and honest elections in its history, Rómulo Gallegos, a well–known novelist, was chosen as president in 1947. Moving too fast to accomplish his goals, he frightened the army, which feared loss of its power and position in the government; he was ousted by a coup within three months of his inauguration. The army declared that it would save the country from communism, and exiled Gallegos and Betancourt, establishing another dictatorship under General Marcos Pérez Jiménez. He loosed a reign of terror and with reckless abandon spent the income from oil on public works in the city of Caracas and on poorly planned industrial ventures, with a handsome cut to friends and to the army. By late 1957 Venezuelans had had enough—resistance increased to the point that even the pampered army refused to oppose the popular will. Pérez Jiménez fled in January 1958, and a combined military and civilian committee took over the government.

Democracy Takes Root

Three moderate parties vigorously competed for the presidency in free elections that December: Democratic Action, or *AD*; the Democratic Republican Union *(URD)*, and a social Christian movement with a cumbersome name that is better known by the acronym *COPEI*. The *AD*'s Betancourt was returned to the presidency with a 47% plurality and was sworn in for a five–year term on February 13, 1959, beginning an unbroken line of nine presidential administrations that has continued to the present, an enviable record of stability for Latin America.

An enlightened leader, Betancourt oversaw the adoption of a liberal constitution in 1961, but he also had to deal with a leftist insurgency incited by Cuba's Fidel Castro. Nonetheless, left–wing political parties such as the Movement to Socialism *(MAS)* were allowed to compete under Betancourt's tolerant constitution. One of the fundamental tenets of that document, designed to guard against another Gómez or Pérez Jiménez, was that no president could be reelected for 10 years after leaving office. Thus, the popular Betancourt was succeeded in 1964 by Raúl Leoni, also of *AD*, who received a 33% plurality. In the December 1968 election, *COPEI*'s Rafael Caldera was elected with only a 29% plurality. Caldera was instrumental in establishing the Organization of Petroleum Exporting Countries (OPEC).

AD was returned to power in 1973 elections in which Carlos Andrés Pérez won a landslide (by Venezuelan standards) 48% of the vote over his principal opponent. Both candidates had run on almost identical center–left platforms. Voters firmly rejected both the radical left and right—the Marxist–Socialist candidate received only 4.2% of the vote and the right–wing candidate, a former associate of former dictator Pérez Jiménez, got less than 1%. In congressional races, *AD* won 24 of 49 seats in the Senate and 102 out of 200 seats in the Chamber of Deputies. The new president launched new, ambitious programs in agriculture and education, which amazed even his own supporters.

Venezuela took charge of the U.S.–operated iron mines near Ciudad Guyana in 1975, offering $101.3 million in compensation rather than the $350 million sought by the companies. The most important nationalization occurred at the beginning of 1976 when control of the oil industry was assumed. The 40 private firms, most of them U.S.–based, were granted compensation of $1.2 billion, which Venezuela asserted was equal to the book value of their assets. The companies claimed the true value to be between $3.5 and $5 billion.

Although Pérez maintained that nationalization of the oil industry would now make Venezuelans "masters of their destiny," in actual fact the nation continued to depend heavily on the foreign oil companies to refine, transport and market the oil. In addition, the oil firms provide technical assistance to the state–owned oil organization, *Petroven*. Ironically, the fees charged by the private oil firms for these services are almost as high as the profits made by them before nationalization. Such a lucrative arrangement led to criticism of the Pérez administration by persons who claimed that "oil nationalization needed more nationalization."

In 1973, when it joined OPEC, in raising prices by more than 400%, Venezuela experienced windfall profits. With its oil income rising from $2 billion in 1972 to $10.4 billion in 1974 and $14.5 billion in 1983, Venezuela earned more from oil during the two years following the price hike than in the previous 56 years it had been exporting oil.

The gush of petrodollars swamped the nation with more money than could be realistically absorbed. To control the resulting inflation, which rose from the usual rate of 2–3% to 20% in 1974, the government channeled half the money out of the country. Some was invested in international lending agencies while other funds were loaned to developing nations, particularly in the Caribbean region. To further reduce the cash inflow, and to conserve the nation's dwindling oil reserves (now estimated at 12–15 billion barrels), Venezuela cut production from an average of 3.3 million barrels a day in 1973 to 2.2 million barrels in 1976.

The huge oil income vastly increased Venezuelan influence in Latin America. By raising contributions (and therefore voting power) in international lending organizations, it hoped to make these agencies less subject to "humiliating vetoes" of loans to nations out of favor with the

The house in Caracas where Simón Bolívar, "El Libertador," was born.

Photo by the author

273

Caracas boasts an ultra-modern skyline, but the makeshift vendors' stalls in the foreground are a reminder of the disparity between the elilte and the poor in Venezuela.

Photo by the author

United States. Venezuela has also helped to finance the establishment of cartels—such as in banana and coffee production and marketing—so that developing nations may charge more for raw materials sold to industrialized countries.

In foreign relations, Venezuela tried to become a leading advocate for the "Third World" causes and for Latin American economic independence. The Pérez administration played a major role in advocating greater respect for human rights in the region. Thus, it strongly condemned the use of torture by the military regime in Chile.

Relations with the United States have remained cordial. In late June 1977, President Pérez visited the United States, where he praised the Carter administration's campaign for greater respect for human rights in Latin America. Washington regarded Venezuela as a valuable bridge between North America and the Third World. Venezuela also was given high marks for its refusal to join a 1973 OPEC oil embargo against the United States arising out of the Arab–Israeli conflict, and for shipping extra quantities of oil to North America during the unusually cold winter of 1976–77.

Although the government tried to channel petrodollars into development projects, highly visible luxuries proved more tempting. Venezuela had one of the high-

est per capita incomes in Latin America, but most of that income was concentrated in the upper class (5%) and the middle class (15%), both of which literally went on a spending spree. Signs of the "good life" abounded—swimming pools, comfortable homes and beach villas. A 350% tax on new luxury cars didn't even slow demand. Although domestic car production reached record levels, there was a long waiting list for buyers. Further prestige was associated with the commencement of *Concorde* supersonic service in 1976.

In this jewel of opulence, fully 80% of the people lived in poverty (and still do), with attendant malnutrition afflicting half of the youth of the nation. Almost none of the oil money filtered down to the poor. Pérez warned, "Our country is rich, but our people are poor." Ironically, he at the time was one of the "fat cat" class engaged in open thievery.

The search for jobs and a better life lured 80% of the nation's population to urban areas, where they settled in filthy slums surrounding traditional city areas. This caused not only a costly drop in farm output and a jump in food prices, but created immense problems of how to provide basic services to this population encircling the cities. More than 70% of the population of Caracas lives in sordid *ranchos,* where even the police hesitate to go, in

sharp contrast to the gleaming skyscrapers of the city. Incentives encouraging slum dwellers to move back to the country failed.

Investment during the first Pérez administration centered on the oil, steel and electrical industries, traditional sources of income for the super–rich of Venezuela.

Such massive economic development projects also led to massive economic problems. In 1978, Venezuela suffered its largest balance of payments deficit in its history ($1.7 billion). Exports (mostly oil) were down 7.5% from the previous year. (During the five years that Pérez was in office, Venezuelan imports rose by more than 230%).

As is often common during periods of rapid economic expansion, there were also widespread reports of government fraud, inefficiency, administrative waste and a relative decrease in social services. The industrialization program seemed to benefit a fortunate few, while living standards actually declined for the lower–income masses. Although Pérez did boast that unemployment had been largely eliminated, the inflation rate ranged between 10% (officially) and 20% (more accurate). Urban residents also complained of inadequate basic services, including overcrowded schools, a shortage of water and electric power and declining health facilities.

Increased economic problems set the stage for late 1978 presidential elections when voters turned to Luis Herrera Campíns, candidate of the *COPEI*. He won with 46.6% of the 5.5 million votes cast. The ruling *AD's* candidate trailed with 43%. During the campaign, Herrera Campíns repeatedly charged that the nation's oil income had been squandered through government corruption, waste and deficit spending. All in all, the campaign was not an especially exciting one for the public, which found neither of the major candidates particularly inspiring.

The new president, a former journalist, was widely regarded as an intellectual. He promised in his inaugural speech in 1979 to emphasize state development of major industries while also encouraging greater private investments. He also pledged to pay more attention to the problems of the poor as well as to expand the nation's school system.

Like his predecessor, Herrera Campíns spent a considerable amount of time dealing with the country's economic development, and making efforts to diversify it from its great dependence on oil. He tried to steer Venezuela on a steady course, grappling with growing economic problems.

Herrera Campíns criticized the Reagan administration for its policies in Latin America—for its "treatment" of Nicaragua, its support of the appointed government in El Salvador and for its backing of Britain in the Falkland Islands invasion by Argentina. There was one matter brought out and set on the front burner: Venezuela's long–simmering border dispute with neighboring Guyana. Venezuela claimed a full 5/8 of Guyana's territory! There was strong anti–British feeling running deep in Venezuela—exacerbated by the Falklands dispute. Venezuelans have not forgotten that British warships shelled Venezuela's ports early in the 20th century when Venezuela failed to repay loans to British banks. Herrera Campíns wanted to settle the border dispute through negotiation. However, the amount of territory claimed makes a solution almost impossible to reach. The area claimed is rich in timber—and potentially rich in oil, minerals and precious gems.

Venezuela's oil wealth attracted a flood of immigrants from its poorer Latin American neighbors. Government efforts to register the newcomers were inadequate. The ethnic picture of the country was also changed by the presence of about 1 million Europeans who settled permanently, usually engaging in the higher technological aspects of petroleum production.

By 1981 it was clear that Venezuela's governments had not been able to follow the wise advice of Rómulo Betancourt "to sow the oil," which meant to diversify the economy and avoid the country's increasing dependence on oil exports. Limited industrialization, declining agricultural production and a lack of serious planning made the Venezuelan economy highly vulnerable to any change in the price of oil.

Consequently, the oil gluts of 1979–1980 and 1986 hit Venezuela immediately. In 1982 the country suffered from a severe cash crisis produced by falling oil revenues, a sharp decline in international reserves and a lack of confidence of potential investors. The government was forced to reevaluate its gold holdings and to place the state oil company under central bank jurisdiction, somewhat ameliorating the burden of a foreign debt that had swelled in a few short years to $18.5 billion. Unaccustomed to austerity, the Venezuelans reacted with mounting criticism to the erratic policies of the administration.

Presidential and congressional elections in late 1983 demonstrated the general discontent with *COPEI*, the ruling party. Jaime Lusinchi, the presidential candidate of *AD*, won easily, receiving more than 50% of the vote over ex–president and highly respected Rafael Caldera of *COPEI*. *AD* also received a majority in Congress.

Those who thought austerity measures would be eased were bitterly disappointed. The currency was devalued by almost one half, fuel prices were increased more than 100% to eliminate what amounted to an annual subsidy of $85 million and wage–price freezes were instituted in large sectors of the economy. An increase in the minimum wage was later allowed, unless an industry could show that paying the higher amount would result in a loss.

Venezuela had placed a moratorium on the repayment of its foreign debt in 1983, but under pressure from international banks, it renegotiated the obligation and agreed in February 1986 to resume payment. Although large reserves indicated the ability to maintain payments, at the same time the debt payment resumption was finally negotiated, Venezuelan oil was in the process of dropping from $28 per barrel to less than $10 in the face of increased Saudi Arabian and world production. The pressure was not direct—Venezuela and Mexico were competitors for the petroleum import needs of the United States. Mexico, too, was saddled with an immense foreign debt ($104 billion, Venezuela $30 billion; figures include public and private debt). Increases in the price of oil from $17 a barrel were beneficial, but the trade balance during 1986–88 was again in the red for the first time since 1982.

The 1988 campaign for the presidency was lively, but, as usual, centered around the two powerful political parties. The American expression "there's not a dime's worth of difference between them" applied to Venezuela much more than to the United States. *COPEI* was still dogged by popular association of it with the early 1980s sharp economic fall.

Pedestrians glance at the morning headlines at a news kiosk near Plaza de Bolívar in Caracas. Venezuela supports a multitude of newspapers and magazines, but press freedom has been under pressure under President Hugo Chávez. *Photo by the author*

Within *AD*, Lusinchi opposed the nomination of former president Pérez, but Pérez accurately accused the president of maintaining the illusion of prosperity by emptying out the treasury. Further, Lusinchi was involved in a divorce of his wife in order to marry his secretary, which did not endear him to the predominantly Roman Catholic population. Pérez had been convicted of theft during his first term, but departed for Spain to avoid going to prison. The voters' memory didn't reach back that far, and he received a majority of 53% over 40% for the *COPEI* candidate.

Rather than leave the task to his successor, President Lusinchi on the last day of the year announced yet another moratorium on debt principal repayment. Pérez at the same time negotiated additional aid from the International Monetary Fund, at the cost of imposing reforms on Venezuela. He waited a month before announcing them: an increase in gasoline by 90% (from 15¢ to 25¢ a gallon), doubled bus fares, unfroze prices on everything and ended numerous government subsidies.

Suddenly, the poor were faced with the brutal realization that the free lunch they had been enjoying was over. Riots broke out in Caracas during Pérez's inauguration in 1989 and quickly spread to other cities. Common criminals took advantage of the unrest to loot stores. The president declared martial law and ordered the army to crush the rioters. At least 300 people were killed and more than 2,000 injured in what came to be called the *"Caracazo."* It remains controversial to this day, just as the 1968 Tlatelolco Massacre is in Mexico.

In his first administration, Pérez was elitist, clumsy and dishonest. Conditions deteriorated swiftly in 1988 in spite of nominally improved economic conditions, and Caracas became a city owned by criminals, with homicides occurring at the rate of 1,500 and more per year. Drug trafficking became rampant, with associated criminal involvement. Wages for all but the elite were incredibly low. The mass of people enveloped by abject poverty began to fully realize who had benefited from more than a half century of oil exportation.

Crisis and Corruption

In 1992, Venezuela's once–admired democracy was shaken to its very foundations. There were two abortive military coups, one of which was nearly successful but collapsed when commanders of key units failed to join the effort to oust Pérez. The instigator, a charismatic paratrooper named Lieutenant Colonel Hugo Chávez, was sentenced to two years in prison. The same year, Pérez was accused of pilfering $17 million in public funds. He issued a clumsy, unconvincing, almost arrogant denial, and public opinion turned harshly against him.

Pérez's party, his majority in the legislature and his hand–picked Supreme Court, turned on him in 1993. The court voted to allow his impeachment if ordered by the upper house, which voted unanimously in favor of the measure. He was forced to step down; a 76–year–old centrist was named by the Senate in June 1993 to head an interim government for the rest of his term—until February 1994. For good measure, Pérez was convicted in a criminal court and served 28 months in prison, being released in September 1996. But in April 1998, now 74, Pérez was again placed under house arrest when he and his mistress

Former President Carlos Andrés Pérez

were charged with "illegal enrichment" for depositing large sums of undisclosed origin in U.S. banks.

In December 1993 elections the voters rejected the two principal political parties, voting for Caldera, now 80, who had ended his association with *COPEI*. He was the candidate of a 17–party coalition, the *Convergencia Nacional* (CN—"National Convergence"). His first term of office had been uncontroversial and somewhat uneventful during a period of relative Venezuelan wealth. This time, he inherited an absolute nightmare.

In spite of decades of oil money, Venezuela was in dire financial straits. A controversial value added tax (VAT) was intially extended, then canceled because of popular opposition in 1994. The second-largest bank collapsed in February, with fallout in the form of a run on all banks. The cause: massive thievery—83 were arrested.

Venezuela's years of drunken–sailor spending had given it a foreign debt in excess of $27 billion, more than half of GDP, which threatened the country with insolvency. The crisis was so severe that in 1996 Caldera was forced to eat crow and signed a reform package with the IMF, something he once vowed he would never do. Among other things, the package eliminated the gasoline subsidy and abolished price controls. The measures were annoying to Venezuela's small, crybaby middle class but were especially painful to Venezuela's poor, who account for 80% of the population.

The crisis lumbered on into 1997. The state–owned airline, *Viasa*, went bankrupt in February. At the end of the year, Caldera, the one–time populist, privatized the money–losing state–owned steel company, *Sidor*, and announced plans to sell off the state's aluminum company. In early 1998, the government was hit with a new fiscal blow when the price of oil, on which the government pegs its budget

A short-order cook prepares a batch of *cachapas*, a popular corn-based Venezuelan pancake, at one of Caracas' many sidewalk cafes. *Photo by the author*

The Cienpies Exchange, Caracas

estimates, suddenly dropped. The government had drawn up a $23 billion budget based on an estimate of $15.50 a barrel, but the price fell to $12.80. Moreover, despite efforts to reduce the size of the cumbersome bureaucracy (see Economy), the public payroll in 1997 actually *increased* by 4%! On a positive note, however, inflation was reduced to a still–high 38% in 1997, the highest in Latin America, due mostly to a 75% pay increase for public employees in February 1997.

The Elections of 1998

Like a retreaded tire, the second Caldera administration blew out and the country lumbered along for the last year of his term, as Venezuelans desperately searched for a mechanic. So eager were they for a fresh face offering dynamic new leadership that for a time it seemed they would entrust their future to Irene Sáez, the 1981 Miss Universe, who had compiled a respectable record as mayor of the Caracas suburb of Chacao. After she declared her independent candidacy in 1997, polls showed the 35–year–old Sáez with a commanding lead over any candidate from one of the traditional parties. After a few months, however, her poll figures began to drop when she failed to offer any substantive solutions for the country's ills; she was, it seemed, nothing more than a still–pretty face.

Not so Hugo Chávez, the leader of the abortive coup of 1992, who declared his own independent candidacy in early 1998 under the banner of the Fifth Republic Movement. His candidacy sent chills through the heavily entrenched political and economic establishments, but he soon gained a following among the downtrodden masses and by April polls showed him eclipsing Sáez. Unquestionably

homelier than the erstwhile beauty queen, Chávez nonetheless is a dynamic speaker, whose *macho*, charismatic mien and populist rhetoric are reminiscent of Latin American *caudillos* of old. Instead of a white horse and fringed epaulets, however, this 20th–century savior has his red paratrooper's beret. Born into the middle class in 1954, he is the son of two schoolteachers. As a boy, he sold fruit on a streetcorner, and the army recruited him because of his skill as a baseball pitcher. Besides the unquestionable appeal of his humble beginnings, his vow to clean up the country's cumbersome, corrupt political system, to wrest power away from the elite and to effect genuine socioeconomic reforms electrified Venezuela's destitute, long–suffering and resentful masses. As his bandwagon gained inertia, more alienated political groupings jumped aboard, forming an alliance called Patriotic Pole. At the same time, Chávez's open admiration for Fidel Castro alarmed the business and political elite, as well as foreign investors.

President Hugo Chávez Frías

The months leading up to the November congressional and regional elections and the December presidential election witnessed the most bizarre campaign in the history of Venezuela's 40–year–old democracy. As Chávez's lead in the polls widened, the two traditional parties panicked and began grasping for ways to stop this loose cannon. In May, adopting an if–you–can't–beat–'em–join–'em strategy, *COPEI* offered its nomination to Sáez, who foolishly accepted. Now identified with one of the establishment parties blamed for the country's woes, she began to fall even farther behind Chávez. *AD*, meanwhile, showed even less political sense, initially nominating Luis Alfaro, a 76–year–old party hack. Filling out the race was another independent, Henrique Salas, a respected 62–year–old businessman and Yale graduate, who formed a movement called Project Venezuela.

The first test of Chávez's Patriotic Pole came in the November 8 elections. His movement became the largest force in the new Congress, winning 34% of the seats in the 48–member Senate and 189–member Chamber of Deputies. *AD* was a distant second with 22%; Salas' Project Venezuela won 12% of the seats, and *COPEI* won a pitiful 11%. Patriotic Pole also won seven of the 23 governorships; Chávez's own father, also named Hugo, was elected governor of Barinas. *AD* fell from 11 governorships to eight.

Flushed with this triumph, the unpredictable but pragmatic Chávez surprised almost everyone by suddenly softening his fiery populist, anti–establishment rhetoric. Evidently aware that he was on the brink of full power, he now seemed to be reassuring the foreign investors and domestic financial kingpins on whose support he would depend to get the gravely ill economy off life support.

Meanwhile, the two traditional parties took heart from the fact that Patriotic Pole fell well short of a majority and clung to the hope that Chávez might still be defeated. In an unprecedented maneuver that can be described only as Machiavellian, *AD* and *COPEI* abruptly and unceremoniously jettisoned their own candidates on November 20 and rallied behind Salas, who by now was running second in all the polls. Sáez and Alfaro bitterly vowed to continue on their own. Chávez, meanwhile, sneered at this desperate move, saying it only proved that *AD* and *COPEI* had conspired all along to keep power between them.

But this last–ditch ploy failed. On December 6, an uncharacteristically high 65% of the electorate turned out to choose the new president. Chávez polled a landslide 56.5%, to 39.5% for Salas; Sáez was a microscopic third. Hours after his victory, the flamboyant Chávez appeared humble and conciliatory, insisting that neither he nor the Venezuelan people view him as a messiah, and reaching out to *AD* and *COPEI* for a consensus on how to solve the country's problems. Perhaps even more importantly, he reassured the business establishment that he did not seek to dismantle the capitalist system. Ironically, after all the fears Chávez had generated in financial circles, the Caracas stock market actually *rose* after Chávez's election victory, perhaps in acknowledgment that drastic reforms were indeed needed to save the terminally ill economy.

Chávez began acting like a president even before he took office, engaging in some free–lance diplomacy. Nine days after the election, he visited Brazil, where he met with President Fernando Henrique Cardoso and declared his intention to seek Venezuelan membership in the *Mercosur* trade bloc. From Brasilia he flew to Buenos Aires for talks with Argentine President Carlos Menem and Chilean President Eduardo Frei. In January 1999, he engaged in a tri–cornered meeting with Cuba's Fidel Castro and Colombian President Andrés Pastrana in an effort to jump-start stalled talks between the Colombian government and left–wing guerrilla groups.

Chávez also put his imprint on the new Congress that was installed on January 23. Elected president of the Senate was retired Colonel Luis Dávila of the Patriotic Pole, who participated with Chávez in the unsuccessful 1992 coup. *COPEI*'s Enrique Capriles, only 26, was elected president of the Chamber of Deputies, marking the first time in the 40 years of Venezuela's democracy that *AD* had been shut out of congressional leadership posts. Even before Congress was installed, however, the president–elect declared his intention to call for a referendum dissolving Congress and the judiciary and calling for the installation of a constituent assembly to rewrite the 1961 constitution. The traditional parties vowed to block Chávez's initiative, prompting Chávez to denounce what he called a "conspiracy" and to threaten to dissolve Congress and rule by decree. It was to be the first of many bombastic threats to circumvent democratic institutions.

New President, New Constitution

Chávez finally attained genuine power with his inauguration on February 2, 1999, just 11 days shy of the 40th anniversary of Rómulo Betancourt's inauguration, which ushered in Venezuela's new democratic era. Chávez, however, soon raised doubts about whether that democracy would long endure. From his first moments wearing the presidential sash, he has fanned the flames of controversy. He reiterated his plans to scrap the 1961 constitution he had just sworn to uphold, deriding the document as "moribund," and

proclaimed what he called the "Bolivarian revolution." He set April 25 as the date for the first of three referenda on constitutional reform. Among his proposals for the new basic law: removal of the ban against immediate reelection, proclaiming that he needs at least 10 years to put Venezuela's house in order.

He sent an even more ominous signal to the establishment when he postponed the traditional military parade for two days—to coincide with the seventh anniversary of his 1992 coup attempt. At that ceremony, he stirred still more controversy by reinstating the former coup leaders into the military, praising them as "anonymous heroes," and by promising to use the army as a social instrument to benefit society, an idea reminiscent of the Peruvian military government of the 1970s. On top of that, he appointed former coup participants as governor of the capital, as transportation minister and as head of the secret police. A few weeks later, this secret police chief arrested the son of a prominent *AD* leader on questionable drug charges, raising fears that Chávez would use his power to cow his opposition. Chávez did nothing to dispel such fears; on May 1, General Rubén Rojas Pérez, the son–in–law of former President Caldera, was indicted on corruption charges. Chávez's critics again accused him of seeking to imtimidate them; the president responded that it was merely part of his crackdown on corruption. Chávez also has resorted to blatant symbolism, eschewing his $1,200 monthly salary and wearing his fatigues and trademark red beret in public, an obvious emulation of his idol in Havana. On a more positive note, he appointed Atala Uriana Pocaterra as environment minister; she is

the first Indian to a hold a cabinet post in Venezuela.

On March 19, the Supreme Court boldly stood up to the brash new president and ruled that his referendum decree was unconstitutionally vague because it did not provide specific enough information on what the voters were being asked to approve. At first, the impulsive Chávez threatened to call his supporters into the streets and said he would ignore the court ruling. This time, however, Chávez cooled off and agreed to revisions to the decree so it would pass constitutional muster.

Like a weary parent trying to placate a willful child, Congress on March 27 acceded to Chávez's demands and approved an "enabling law" that would give the president the power to make sweeping economic decisions without congressional approval for six months. On April 7, Chávez announced he would veto the new law for not going far enough, and he threatened again to dissolve Congress and rule by decree. Once again, however, his emotions subsided and he signed the measure into law.

The April 25 referendum erased any doubt with whom the masses are siding. With a 60% turnout, a stunning 90% voted "*sí*" for a constituent assembly.

The next step was the election of the 131 members of the constituent assembly, which was scheduled for July 25. Even before that vote, Chávez found himself in another confrontation with the opposition-controlled Congress when the Senate refused to confirm 34 military promotions Chávez had recommended. Chávez angrily declared that Congress has no business second-guessing his actions as commander in chief and threatened to disband

Oil derricks, Lake Maracaibo

278

the Congress and replace it with the constituent assembly.

Predictably, in the July 25 election, 121 of the 131 members elected were members of Chávez's Patriotic Pole, including his wife, Marisabel, and his brother. A prominent loser for one of the seats from Tachira State: former President Pérez. The results were a dramatic rebuke of the *AD* and *COPEI* parties and an equally dramatic public ratification of Chávez's "Bolivarian revolution." Almost immediately, the assembly began moving to usurp the powers of the Congress and the judiciary, even though the Supreme Court had ruled in April that the assembly had to confine itself to drafting the new constitution. In late August, the assembly formally voted to strip the Congress of its remaining powers and sealed off the gold-domed capitol building, which sparked protests by Chávez opponents. Several opposition members of Congress scaled the fence around the *Capitolio* in defiance of the assembly's decision, while pro- and anti-Chávez factions clashed in the street outside. Violence appeared imminent. Surprisingly, and wisely, Chávez resisted the temptation to use force to evict the aggrieved lawmakers from the building, which the assembly also was using. The Catholic Church intervened to mediate a peaceful solution to the standoff between the rival powers on September 10, thus preventing what could have escalated into another bloody *Caracazo* that would have benefited neither side. Under the terms of the agreement, the Congress would continue to serve as the law-making body, including the power to approve the budget, until after the referendum on the new constitution (Chávez later broke that promise).

The Congress, meanwhile, pledged not to "sabotage" the work of the assembly.

The assembly soon renewed its attack on the judiciary, however. It appointed a special judicial investigative committee, which by October had summarily removed 130 judges who had been under investigation for taking bribes and other sins, some of them for years. Few had any sympathy for the sacked judges, as the judiciary had become notoriously corrupt, but the lack of due process was troubling. Nonetheless, the Supreme Court meekly upheld the committees' dismissal of the judges.

Meanwhile, the assembly moved like a steamroller on the new constitution, sometimes passing nearly 50 provisions a day. The final document had Chávez's fingerprints all over it. It renamed the country the Bolivarian Republic of Venezuela. It established a new 165-member unicameral National Assembly, abolishing the Senate. The presidential term was increased from five to six years, and immediate reelection was permitted. The president was to enjoy far greater authority than under the old constitution. The state and local governments were replaced by regional and municipal councils. Active-duty members of the military were given the right to vote for the first time. There was no prohibition against abortion, which drew fire from the Catholic Church. It reduced the work week from 48 to 40 hours, which upset businessmen. It declared that Venezuelans have a right to "free, truthful, uncensored information," but left unsaid who would determime what is "truthful," a clause seen as an attempt to silence Chávez's critics in the media. But, predictably, the cries of naysayers that the new organic law was

drafted too hastily and that it concentrates too much power in the president's hands were to be drowned out in an avalanche of public approval. On December 15, 1999, voters overwhelmingly ratified the new constitution.

It was not the only deluge to occur that day in Venezuela. Whether or not it was a sign of divine disapproval of the new constitution, the coast was pounded by cataclysmic rains that led to floods and mudslides that swept away entire communities. The death toll could only be estimated, but reports ranged from 5,000 to 30,000; if closer to the latter, it would be the worst natural disaster in terms of loss of life in recorded Latin American history. The monetary damage was estimated at $20 billion, dealing the already desperately ill economy a cruel relapse. International aid soon began pouring into the stricken country, but it could take years to overcome the disaster.

Renewed Mandate

Before Christmas, the constituent assembly, emboldened by the mandate given the new constitution, formally abolished the old Congress and the Supreme Court. It then created a 23-member standing committee, which came to be called the *"Congresillo,"* to act as the country's legislative authority pending the election of the new National Assembly. Elected president of the *Congresillo* was Luis Miquilena, a close Chávez ally who was widely regarded as the second most powerful man in the country.

Chávez then announced that he would subject himself to the will of the electorate under the new constitution to seek a renewed mandate. All other officials established under the new constitution would be selected in the same *"Megaelecciones,"* scheduled for May 28, 2000.

That February, the first schism appeared in Chávez's Bolivarian revolution. To mark the eighth anniversary of the 1992 coup attempt, three of Chávez's former comrades-in-arms in that attempt publicly broke with the president, accusing him of corruption and of betraying the goals of their revolutionary movement. They cited 46 specific cases of corruption, involving Chávez and Miquilena, among others. Stung, Chávez expressed his sadness on national television over the defection of his erstwhile comrades, expressed his continued affection for them and promised he would investigate their charges.

Among the three dissidents was Francisco Arias Cárdenas, governor of Zulia State, widely regarded as the intellectual author of the 1992 coup attempt. Though not as charismatic or brash as Chávez, Arias was widely respected for his more reasoned, moderate approach. To use a Steinbeckian metaphor, Arias played the role of George to Chávez's Lenny. An even

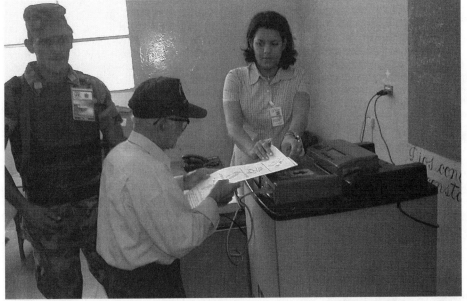

Under the watchful eye of a soldier assigned to maintain order, and with the assistance of a polling official, an elderly voter casts his ballot in a computerized tabulation machine in Caracas on July 30, 2000. Malfunctions in the machines delayed the voting for several hours past the scheduled time to close the polls. *Photo by the author*

Thousands of jubilant supporters of President Hugo Chávez crowd under the balcony of the Miraflores Place in Caracas late on July 30, 2000, to hear him proclaim his landslide reelection victory.

Photo by the author

unkinder cut for Chávez came, symbolically, on March 15—the Ides of March—when Arias declared that he would be a candidate for president against his former friend and chief. A former mayor of Caracas, Claudio Fermín, also declared his candidacy.

As the campaign progressed, polls showed Chávez with a commanding—but not insurmountable—lead over Arias. Chávez steadfastly—and wisely—eschewed the intellectually superior Arias' invitation to a debate. Capitalizing on what he termed Chávez's cowardice,

Arias then filmed a television commercial in which he "debated" a hen, which represented, of course, his "chicken" opponent. A white hen quickly became the unofficial symbol of the Arias campaign. Both major candidates crisscrossed the country, speaking to large, enthusiastic crowds.

But there was an ominous cloud over the campaign. The five-member National Electoral Council, or *CNE,* all of them Chávez appointees, began to complain that it was unsure it would be able to resolve computer problems in time for the election. The *CNE* blamed the problems on a U.S. firm that had the contract to tabulate the votes, while the company complained that the *CNE* had continued making last-minute changes to the database—11,000 changes in all—which prevented the company from having the flashcards, needed to program the computers that would be used in more than half the 8,400 polling stations, ready in time. Less than a week before the election, Chávez dispatched an air force jet to Omaha, Nebraska, to receive the necessary flashcards.

This was the milieu when this author flew to Caracas on May 24 to cover the elections the following Sunday as a freelance journalist. Arias had held his closing rally in the Avenida Bolívar the previous day, and Chávez's closing rally was in full sway that night, also in the Avenida Bolívar, as I checked into my hotel. The president's electrically charged voice was blaring from a radio in the lobby, sounding more like that of a soccer announcer than a politician. It was easy to understand from hearing him how he could so work up a crowd. I walked the four blocks to the rally just as it was breaking up. The atmosphere was more resemblant of a Louisiana Mardi Gras than a political rally. A majority of those in the almost entirely working-class multitude—many of them wearing Chávez's trademark red beret—showed signs of advanced inebriation, and crushed beer cans literally carpeted the streets.

At noon the following day, May 25, the bombshell struck. The *CNE* announced that it was postponing the election because of technical difficulties. Four hours later, the Supreme Tribunal of Justice appeared on national television to uphold the *CNE's* decision. The tribunal even declared a moratorium on further campaigning, which threw the electoral process into even greater turmoil. That night, Chávez met with journalists and expressed his support for the delay; from Maracaibo, Arias cautiously did the same thing, although he called for the dismissal of the *CNE* on grounds of incompetence. Reaction I heard on the street ran the gamut from anger to nonchalant acceptance. Within hours of the announcement, passionate Chávez supporters surrounded

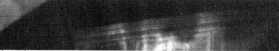

The Caracas daily *El Universal* reports the landslide reelection victory of President Chávez on July 30, 2000.

the *CNE* headquarters, already protected by a phalanx of police and national guardsmen in riot gear. The protesters chanted slogans and, ironically agreeing with Arias, demanded the resignations of the *CNE* members (apparently forgetting who had hand-picked them). The protests continued all the next day, despite Chávez's support for the postponement; evidently the Chávez backers felt cheated out of a victory they regarded as inevitable. For amusement, they decapitated a white hen.

On May 27, former U.S. President Jimmy Carter, who has become a sort of self-appointed guardian of Latin American democracy in recent years, held a news conference in Caracas to declare his support for the postponement which, he said, "was for a good reason." In response to my question, he drew a contrast with the obviously rigged election in Peru that would be held the following day and predicted that the Venezuelan election ultimately would be held and would "accurately reflect the will of the Venezuelan people."

On one point, there was almost universal agreement, among the Chávez supporters, Arias, the OAS observers and the U.S. election software company: The *CNE* had botched its job. On May 29, Chávez sacked the five members and replaced them, at Carter's suggestion, with a group that was less partisan and more representative of the discrete sectors of society. It contracted with a Spanish firm to conduct the election, and waited for computer experts to reach a consensus on how long it would take to resolve the glitches before announcing a new election date. That date was July 30, 2000.

Chávez was resoundingly reelected with 59.2% of the vote, a mandate even greater than his 1998 landslide. His Fifth Republic Movement *(MVR)* received 57.6% of the votes for the new National Assembly, which translated into 92 of the 165 seats. That fell short of the two-thirds majority needed for constitutional amendments and confirmation of judicial appointments, but it gives Chávez the three-fifths majority needed to pass emergency legislation that would allow him to rule by decree. Ironically, the much-maligned and discredited *AD* was second with 19.7%, giving it 35 seats. Arias' *Proyecto Venezuela* was a distant third with 4.9%, or eight seats, while *COPEI* was a poor fifth with a mere 2.4%, or four seats. The *MVR* and its ally, the Movement to Socialism *(MAS)*, won 15 of the 23 governorships, though there was compelling evidence of irregularities in a close race in Merida state, where an opposition governor was unseated and violent clashes occurred. The Carter Center criticized the apparent irregularities that occurred throughout the country and the failure of election officials to investigate them. But Chávez's mandate was unassailable.

An International Loose Cannon

Almost immediately after the overwhelming vote of confidence he received from voters, Chávez set out to make Venezuela—in reality, himself—a player on the world stage. Just 11 days after the election, Chávez raised diplomatic eyebrows around the world when he became the first head of state since the 1991 Gulf War to pay a state visit to Iraq's Saddam Hussein. Ostensibly, the visit was for bilateral talks between two OPEC members, but apparently the trip had no other purpose than for Chávez to poke his finger in the eye of the United States.

In late September 2000, Chávez enthusiastically hosted a meeting of OPEC heads of state in Caracas. There, his was the loudest voice in favor of curtailing production to drive up world oil prices. At the time, they were above $30 a barrel, the highest since the Gulf War. His motive may have been partially global, but more likely it was primarily domestic, as every $1 increase in the price of a barrel of oil adds $1 billion to his government's revenue over the span of a year. As 60% of his government's revenue comes from oil, he desperately needed the revenue to fund his "social revolution" and to bring the economy out of recession. Moreover, it was another way to irritate the United States, although high oil prices hurt poor countries the most. Chávez seemed to recognize that, too; Venezuela sells oil to Cuba and Central America at discount prices.

Chávez annoyed the United States again a month later by hosting a five-day state visit by Fidel Castro. The two long-winded orators spoke to Venezuelans on a live national broadcast from the Carabobo battlefield, site of one of Bolívar's victories. Chávez railed away against what he called a world market economy dominated by the United States, while Castro told Venezuelans that their country is considerably larger than Cuba and thus also could resist U.S. domination. Castro returned in August 2001 to celebrate his 75th birthday.

Meanwhile, Chávez also had strained relations with both Colombia and Peru. In March 2001, he met with a miffed President Andrés Pastrana of Colombia, after Venezuela had arrested, then released, a Colombian guerrilla wanted in an airplane hijacking (see Colombia). Chávez is known to be sympathetic to the guerrillas, which has strained bilateral relations. Nonetheless, Chávez and Pastrana announced that their intelligence services would begin exchanging information. That deal seemed ludicruous in November 2001 after Diego Serna, a member of the Revolutionary Armed Forces of Colombia *(FARC)*, admitted in a television interview in Colombia that he had helped provide security for Chávez during a re-

cent state visit to Colombia. Even more embarrassing, a captured video showed Chávez and Serna together.

During the first half of 2001, Chávez and then-Foreign Minister Rangel adamantly denied reports that the fugitive former Peruvian intelligence chief, Vladimiro Montesinos, was hiding in Venezuela (see Peru). In June, even as Chávez was hosting the 13th Andean Summit, Peruvian authorities presented him with conclusive evidence from the U.S. FBI that Montesinos was, in fact, in the country. Chávez's intelligence service then arrested Montesinos in a Caracas safe house without any apparent difficulty. Chávez had the audacity to boastfully announce the arrest during the summit; among those attending was Peruvian President-elect Alejandro Toledo. Chávez promised Toledo that Montesinos would be returned to Peru "faster than a rooster crows." He kept his word; Montesinos was flown back to Peru within 24 hours, not as an international fugitive, but as an undocumented alien! In the ensuing days, the opposition parties and media began asking pointed questions about how Montesinos could have entered Venezuela and remained there for several months without the knowledge of the intelligence agency—meaning, of course, of Chávez himself. The international wire services suggested that Chávez was beholden to Montesinos because the latter had provided refuge for some of the plotters of the failed 1992 coup. Chávez's response to these queries was an uncharacteristic and stony silence, and each country temporarily withdrew its ambassador from the other.

In April 2001, Chávez again relished being in the international spotlight at the third Summit of the Americas in Quebec. There, he was the only one of the 34 heads of state who opposed the idea of establishing a Free Trade Area of the Americas (FTAA) by the end of 2005. Chávez argued, with some validity, that little had been done to implement the lofty goals of alleviating poverty in Latin America that had been advanced during the second summit in Chile in 1998. He also argued that subregional integration should come before hemispheric integration, and he warned that the FTAA would be dominated by the United States. He also irked his fellow presidents by balking at the requirement that signatories to the FTAA be "representative democracies;" he said he preferred the term "participatory democracy," which apparently could be more loosely construed. The new U.S. president, George W. Bush, snubbed Chávez by avoiding a one-on-one meeting, as he held with most other presidents.

The deterioration in U.S.-Venezuelan relations further accelerated in August 2001 when the U.S. military mission was ordered to vacate its offices in the Venezuelan military headquarters and relocate elsewhere. The defense minister insisted that the Venezuelans needed the space.

Then came September 11. Chávez dutifully denounced the terrorist attacks on the United States as "abominable," but two weeks later, in a speech to Congress, Chávez defended his close ties with Iraq, Iran and Libya, calling them "our brothers and partners." He claimed there was insufficient proof to support U.S. assertions that they abetted international terrorists. Chávez made a point to make side trips to Iran and Libya again as part of a three-week tour of Europe and Algeria in October.

During his tour, he also managed to irritate the French by expressing, as he had in 1999, his concern over the welfare of the Venezuelan-born terrorist Ilyich Ramírez, better known by the sobriquet Carlos the Jackal, who was incarcerated in a French prison after two decades as an international fugitive.

Back home in Caracas on October 30, he criticized the U.S. bombing campaign in Afghanistan as "using terror to fight terror." The U.S. State Department responded that it was "surprised and deeply disappointed" by the remark, a diplomatic euphemism that meant the U.S. policymakers were mad as hell, and noted that his comments were not consistent with Venezuela's support for two U.N. resolutions recognizing the United States' right to self-defense. Three days later, the United States recalled Ambassador Donna Hrinak for consultation, a diplomatic move just short of breaking relations, which led the foreign minister to hurriedly reiterate Venezuela's support for the war on terrorism. The ambassador returned the following week, and Chávez insisted that Venezuela and the United States remain "allies and friends."

Nonetheless, Chávez's repeated kneejerk comments and actions have served to reinforce his international image as a rogue leader who is friendly to dictators and terrorists.

Dissent and Repression Grow

Chávez also has had to contend with pressing domestic issues, not the least of them declining living standards. One solution: Create a new labor organization to replace the Confederation of Venezuelan Workers (*CTV*), long affiliated with the discredited *AD*. The new organization would have the predictable name Bolivarian Workers' Force. As usual, confident of success, he put the idea up for a vote in yet another referendum, held on December 3, 2000, to coincide with some local elections. Critics warned that this was merely another attempt to concentrate more power in Chávez's own hands and to curtail, rather than enhance, the strength of organized labor. Chávez re-

ceived the expected lop-sided majority for his plan, but he reportedly was stunned by the anemic 25% voter turnout, a fraction of what he had grown accustomed to for his rubber-stamp plebiscites. Moreover, only two thirds of those who did vote cast ballots on the union issue, with the remaining third voting only in the municipal elections. In those contests, the *MVR* won 40% of the seats. It was a diluted victory for Chávez and, according to some observers, it was his first real electoral defeat, a sign that his honeymoon with the working class may be over.

That assessment was underscored in February 2001 when an apparently frustrated Chávez began shuffling his cabinet, something he has continued to do with bewildering regularity. Among the most controversial changes: Foreign Minister José Vicente Rangel, an erstwhile journalist and long-time leader of the *MAS*, became the first civilian defense minister in 70 years; the switch did not go over well with the corps of general officers. Miquilena, the former president of the *Congresillo*, at age 81 became interior minister.

In March 2001, school teachers, oil workers and university students staged a strike to protest the state of the economy. For the first time, the National Guard was sent into the streets to disperse the protesters, and Rangel warned that although the right of assembly was a constitutional one, henceforth demonstrators would have to "get permission" before using the streets. The next day, state employees and aging pensioners staged a peaceful protest outside the presidential palace to plead with their president for their overdue paychecks and pension payments; he did not appear.

There were other signs that Chávez was growing increasingly impatient with dissent, something he no doubt picked up from his friend in Havana. He long has assailed the Venezuelan press as controlled by the oligarchy. In one case of legalized suppression, Pablo López, editor of the gadfly Caracas weekly *La Razón*, went into hiding in August 2000 rather than face house arrest for charges he had defamed Tobías Carrero, a wealthy friend and financial benefactor of Chávez's. López already had been arrested once for refusing to testify in his defamation case. He went into hiding when he refused again to testify, after the judge had refused to allow López to introduce evidence that the articles published in *La Razón* about Carrero's influence peddling were true. In many countries with a Hispanic legal tradition, truth is not a defense in libel or defamation cases, as it is in the United States; all that must be proven is that the plaintiff was offended. López's lawyer took his case to the Inter-American Commission on Human Rights (ICHR) in Washington, an organ of the Organization of American States. In February 2001, the ICHR ruled

in López's favor and ordered the Venezuelan government to stop the persecution of López. Chávez has responded that the matter is a judicial one, and López remains in self-imposed exile in Costa Rica.

Even more chilling examples of Chávez's attitude toward democratic practices and freedom of expression came in June 2001. Addressing a meeting of the small Communist Party, Chávez renewed his commitment to an anti-imperialist revolution, threatened to confiscate the property of tax evaders and absentee landowners and threatened to declare a state of emergency and rule by decree if necessary. The next day, he stirred international condemnation when he addressed a seminar of ambassadors and foreign businessmen and declared he would expel any foreigner who "criticizes" Venezuela. He insisted that he had no objection to internal dissent, however. Such a threat contravenes the U.N. Declaration of Human Rights, to which Venezuela is a signatory. Just one day later, Rangel announced the establishment of pro-Chávez neighborhood groups called "Bolivarian Circles." Rangel denied that these circles were patterned after Cuba's Committees for the Defense of the Revolution, insisting, not terribly convincingly, that their purpose was for political association, not for internal intelligence. Another parallel with Cuba has been the application of a clause in the new constitution to teach "Bolivarian principles" in the public schools; critics contend that the nebulous term is a euphemism for pro-Chávez propaganda.

As if anyone needed another reminder of Chávez's feelings about pluralist democracy, Fidel Castro chose to celebrate his 75th birthday in August 2001 in Venezuela with *Compañero* Hugo.

In September 2001, in a move reminiscent of Salvador Allende's land reform program in Chile, Chávez presented the deeds to 105,000 acres of idle land to small farmers, and he warned large landowners that they should "donate" unused land to the state for redistribution or face confiscation. Chávez touted his agrarian reform plan as a means of relieving the crowded, squalid conditions in the slums around Caracas, something chillingly reminiscent of the Khmer Rouge in Cambodia. If what happened in Chile is any indication, it is doubtful that the "reform" will provide peasant homesteaders with plots large enough to be commercially viable, assuming they even have the necessary wherewithal to engage in agriculture.

On October 4, on the eve of his three-week tour of Europe and the Middle East, Chávez lashed out at the independent television station *Globovisión*, known for hard-hitting reporting that is often embarrassing to the government. He accused the station and its director of engaging in "terrorism" against the government, called them "enemies of the revolution" and threatened to revoke their license. Days later, the station was notified that it was being investigated under a broad provision of the new constitution that prohibits "false or misleading" information. The station was accused of inaccuracies in a news report on crimes against taxi drivers that supposedly led the drivers to strike.

Chávez threw even more fuel on the rapidly growing fire of public discontent on November 13, the eve of the expiration of his right to issue laws by decree. He stunned the nation with a list of 49 decrees affecting virtually all economic sectors, especially the all-important oil industry. Among the decrees was a doubling of royalties on foreign oil companies from 16.5% to 30%, a move that would drive away badly needed capital investment. His land-reform measure could only be described as draconian. The president's brash action had the unintended effect of forging an unlikely alliance between *Fedecamaras*, the country's main business lobby, led by Pedro Carmona; and the *CTV*, still smarting from Chávez's attempt to scuttle it the year before, whose president, Carlos Ortega, defeated Chávez's hand-picked candidate.

By December, Venezuela had become irrevocably polarized between two passionate camps, pro-Chávez and anti-Chávez. The president's approval ratings had slipped below 50% for the first time, and few Venezuelans remained ambivalent on the subject of Hugo Chávez and his revolution. Carmona's *Fedecamaras* called for a 12-hour general strike on December 10, and the *CTV* supported it. Ch#aavez foolishly ridiculed the strike and its organizers, saying "nothing can stop Venezuela." He had to eat his words; millions participated in the work stoppage, and the degree of its success surprised even its organizers. By the end of the year, there was growing dissent as well within the ranks of the military, which apparently had become riddled with corruption as the administrator of Chávez's $100 million social program, Plan Bolivar 2000. The president was acutely embarrassed by revelations that his hand-picked army commander, General Victor Cruz, had pocketed millions from the fund; Ch#aavez fired him on December 22, while refusing to give the reason. Yet, when the auditor-general uncovered still more examples of embezzlement of funds destined for the poor, Chávez responded by firing the auditor-general.

By early 2002, Chávez's popularity had dropped to 30%, in part because of his high-handed methods and in part because of the deteriorating economic situation (see Economy). His growing political isolation was demonstrated on January 5 by congressional defections from his *MVR*; his choice for speaker of the new Congress, William Lara, won by a surprisingly narrow margin, and the session was

marred by threats and rock-throwing against opposition lawmakers by pro-Chávez mobs outside. Far from condemning the behavior of his supporters, Chávez said the incident should serve as a warning to the opposition, and he called on *chavistas* to take to the streets when called upon "to defend the revolution." The president also managed to alienate the Catholic Church when he responded to its criticism of the leftward tilt of his revolution by calling the church a "tumor."

Emboldened by the success of the December 10 general strike and by the defections of Chávez loyalists, the opposition organized a demonstration scheduled, symbolically, for January 23, the anniversary of the fall of the Pérez Jiménez dictatorship in 1958. This time, Chávez confidently organized a counter-demonstration, but again was embarrassed when independent media reports showed that the anti-Chávez crowd, estimated at 200,000, was several times larger than his own.

Chávez was stunned even more in early February 2002 when two military officers, Air Force Colonel Pedro Soto and National Guard Captain Pedro Flores publicly called on Chávez to resign – just days before the 10th anniversary of his own coup attempt against President Pérez. Soto was forced to retire and Flores was jailed for 15 days. Other, higher-ranking officers would soon join the chorus for him to step down.

Suddenly, the always enigmatic Chávez began to sound conciliatory. In a televised address on February 13, he agreed to moderate some of his more radical economic decrees. He also announced budget cuts as a response to falling oil prices, and declared that the Bolivar, like the Argentine peso, would be allowed to float freely. He called for understanding from the opposition, and said he hoped he could "sheath my sword." For two weeks, Chávez toned down his harsh rhetoric against the opposition and the media. He met with a group of priests in an effort to mend fences with the church. He even condemned Colombia's *FARC* guerrillas and applauded President Pastrana's decision to suspend peace talks. But this era of good feeling proved fleeting.

During the last week of February, events began to unfold quickly and dramatically. It began when Chávez unexpectedly fired General Gauicaipuro Lameda as president of the state-owned oil company, Petroleos de Venezuela (*PDVSA*) and replaced him with a leftist economist, Gastón Parra. *PDVSA* white-collar workers protested the change by staging marches, but held off on calling a strike because of the damage it could cause the country by stopping oil exports. Chávez arrogantly refused to change his mind. At about the same time, two high-ranking officers, Vice Admiral Carlos Molina Tamayo and Air Force General Ro-

man Gómez Ruíz, publicly declared their opposition to their commander-in-chief for what they regarded as corruption and mismanagement of the armed forces; Gómez Ruíz called on Chávez to resign

Rumors of an imminent coup began to fly, and the media reported that dissident officers had approached U.S. diplomats to ask whether the United States would back such an effort. The State Department was compelled to issue a statement expressing its firm support for democratic institutions. The crisis escalated on March 5 when *Fedecamaras* and the *CTV* issued a plan for a post-Chávez Venezuela, without explaining how they planned to unseat the president. Meanwhile, the protests at *PDVSA* continued, threatening to upset the world oil market; production dropped by 450,000 barrels a day – about 20%. Venezuelans and the world watched anxiously to see what would happen next.

Coup and Counter-Coup

On Tuesday, April 9, 2002, *Fedecamaras* and the *CTV* declared a one-day general strike, which was successful. At the end of the day, *Fedecamaras* and the *CTV* extended the strike indefinitely—meaning, until Chávez resigned. On Thursday, April 11, about 150,000 people poured into the streets to demand Chávez's resignation, and pro-Chávez goons opened fire on them, killing 17 and wounding at least 100 more. The armed forces high command was to say later that Chávez had ordered them to implement "*Plan Avila*," the code name for the use of deadly force to protect the Miraflores Palace, but that they had refused to fire on unarmed civilians; a leaked audiotape corroborated their account.

After midnight on Friday, April 12, the generals acted, using the violence against the peaceful demonstrators as justification to restore order. The president was taken into "protective custody" and hustled off to the island of La Orchila; accounts leaked later to the media revealed that Chávez broke into tears when he surrendered. By Chávez's own account later, he was told to sign a resignation statement, but he refused. Nonetheless, General Efraín Vásquez, the army commander, announced to the nation and the world that Chávez had stepped down. As interim president, they named *Fedecamaras*' Pedro Carmona. Meanwhile, the U.S. State Department issued a statement, which would later backfire, suggesting that the forcible removal of the democratically elected president was the will of the Venezuelan people. The United States also sought to allay an OAS resolution denouncing "the alteration of the constitutional order," but in the end it grudgingly supported it.

Few anticipated what would happen next. First, Carmona unwisely announced that he was abrogating Chávez's 1999 constitution and dissolving the Congress and the Supreme Court; he called for new congressional elections in eight months. This was too much even for those delighted by Chávez's ouster, and it brought international rebuke—even from Otto Reich, President Bush's assistant secretary of state for hemispheric affairs, who directed the new U.S. ambassador, Charles Shapiro, to try to dissuade Carmona not to dissolve the institutions. Mexican President Vicente Fox, meanwhile, refused to recognize the interim government. To make matters worse, Carmona did not name any representatives of the *CTV* in his interim cabinet. Within hours, the new "government" began to unravel.

On Saturday, April 13, hundreds of thousands of furious *chavistas* poured into the streets around the country and rioted to demand Chávez's reinstatement. Fighting inevitably broke out, and at least 50 people were killed and hundreds injured in the ensuing violence. Some of the *chavistas'* rage was directed against the opposition media, and one of those killed was a news photographer. Suddenly, a schism appeared within the ranks of the armed forces, which had been thought to be almost solidly opposed to Chávez. Loyalist mid-ranking unit commanders rebelled against the rebellion and stormed the Miraflores Palace; among them were the paratroopers, from whence Chávez had sprung. On Saturday night, Carmona resigned; to fill the power vacuum, the high command agreed to allow Chávez's vice president, Diosdado Cabello, to take charge until Chávez returned. Carmona was placed under house arrest. An estimated 80 officers also were detained.

On Sunday, April 14, Chávez was back in power. Although brief, his forcible removal marked only the third military coup in more than 20 years of democratic reforms in the region, following that in Haiti in 1991 and Ecuador in 2000. In the days following the coup and countercoup, Chávez appeared chastened and, again, conciliatory toward his opponents.

"Let's put our house in order," Chávez said at a news conference, and promised not to seek revenge for his ouster. In an uncharacteristically contrite acknowledgment, he lamented that "We have sown hated." He also announced that he had accepted the resignations of Parra and the entire *PDVSA* board and that he was willing to compromise to settle the dispute with the protesting management at *PDVSA*. Oil production quickly returned to normal. On April 20, Chávez appointed Ali Rodríguez, the OPEC secretary-general and a former Venezuelan oil minister, as president of *PDVSA*. He also replaced Vice President Cabello with Defense Minister Rangel. Meanwhile, Chávez demoted Vásquez from command of the army and replaced him with General Julio García Montoya.

The U.S. government, meanwhile, denied, unconvincingly, that it had abetted the coup attempt. Presidential security adviser Condoleezza Rice did little to quell international suspicions when she stated in a televised interview that she hoped Chávez had received the "message" of the Venezuelan people and that he "takes advantage of this opportunity to right his own ship, which has been moving, frankly, in the wrong direction for quite a long time." Still, a State Department spokesman said he was "encouraged" by Chávez's new conciliatory tone.

In the ensuing days, OAS Secretary-General Cesar Gaviría, a former Colombian president, flew to Caracas to meet with Chávez and opposition leaders and urged the two sides to effect a reconciliation. But the opposition remained intransigent, arguing that Chávez was not a unifying leader. Admiral Molina called the government "illegitimate." The opposition party *AD* declared it did not recognize Chávez as president. Other opposition members of Congress called on Chávez to resign, or for a referendum on his remaining in power to be held by the end of the year.

On May Day, thousands of supporters of both sides took to the streets again, but this time there was no bloodshed. Meanwhile, an opinion poll suggested that the coup attempt had boosted Chávez's approval rating by 10 points, to 44% – still a far cry from the 90% he once enjoyed. Emboldened, he dropped the conciliatory tone and vilified those who instigated the coup as "Nazis." In a separate development, Carmona escaped from house arrest and sought asylum at the Colombian Embassy. Colombian President Pastrana, no doubt delighted to repay Chávez for his support of the *FARC*, granted it, and days later Carmona was allowed to leave for Bogotá.

As this book went to press, the situation in Venezuela remained volatile and unpredictable, and coup rumors were again circulating. On June 15, tens of thousands of anti-Chávez demonstrators filled the streets to demand he resign; at least this time, he didn't order the military to implement *Plan Avila*. As if he didn't have enough pressure from critics, his government was forced to admit it couldn't account for $2 billion that was supposed to have been deposited in a contingency fund to stabilize the economy. In an apparent effort to relieve some of the pressure, Chávez hinted that he may call yet another referendum on whether he should remain in office. He also invited former U.S. President Carter to Caracas to mediate a solution between him and his opponents, and Carter accepted.

Culture: Venezuela's ethnic makeup is an intriguing blend of European, Indian, mestizo, black and mulatto. The crippling

succession of dictatorships took a heavy toll on cultural development, however. Its two most distinguished men of letters both spent many of their most productive years abroad. The 19th century intellectual and writer Andrés Bello spent his last years in Chile, while in the 20th century Rómulo Gallegos spent two decades in Spain during the Gómez dictatorship. His best – known novel, Doña Bárbara, was first published in 1929 – in Madrid, not in Caracas.

In art, Venezuela has produced a few figures with a regional reputation, but in music and theater it still largely borrows from abroad. In popular music, however, Venezuela has produced one singer who is a Latin American mega star: José Luís Rodríguez, also known as El Puma. Venezuela's fledgling film industry continues to show promise, and a few Venezuelan telenovelas are marketed abroad.

The absence of free expression before the advent of democracy in 1958 also hamstrung the press. Since then, press freedom has caused the number of newspapers and magazines to mushroom. The capital's two prestigious dailies are the venerable El Universal, founded in 1909, and El Nacional, which dates to 1943. High-quality magazines include Resúmen, Momento, Bohemia, Elite, Auténtico and Zeta.

Economy: Venezuela's economy is completely dominated by petroleum production. Oil revenues account for more than two-thirds of all government income and more than 90% of the nation's exports; Venezuela is the world's fourth-largest oil producer. As a hedge against the day when oil reserves are depleted, recent governments sought to "sow the oil" – to invest oil revenues into other segments of the, with but limited success. To date, investments have increased output of industry and development of other mineral resources, including iron and aluminum. The program has produced two new cities: Ciudad Guyana (iron and hydroelectric power) and El Tablazo (a petrochemical center near Lake Maracaibo).

With the largest proven heavy oil reserves in the world, how to extract it from the tar-like deposits led to an $8 billion project to develop resources of the Orinoco oil belt. An even brighter note on the oil scene was the discovery of a large field in the eastern state of Monagas with an estimated 8.6 billion barrels in late 1987. Total reserves, including "heavy" oil, are about 300 billion barrels.

One bright spot on the economic horizon is renewed oil drilling in the Maracaibo area. Twenty-one years after Venezuela nationalized its oil industry, it began inviting oil companies to come back in 1996 to explore in promising areas. The contracts signed would give the government a generous 90 percent of the oil pumped, a veritable no-lose arrangement.

International experts agree that Venezuela will never put its economic house in order until it comes to grips with its most insidious problem: its bloated, featherbedded, indolent, inefficient and corrupt bureaucracy, which has become the horror story of Latin America. Of Venezuela's 24 million population, 1.35 million, or 6.1%, are government employees, compared with 4.5% in Brazil and 2.2% in Colombia. As just one anecdotal example, when the state-owned airline Viasa went bankrupt in 1997, it was learned that it had employed 291 pilots for its 12-plane fleet, or 24 pilots per plane! If society had received the benefits from such a huge public workforce, it would be one thing, but the bureaucracy was padded with phantom employees and real employees who are notoriously lazy and inefficient. The effect has been to discourage foreign investors and lenders and to drive up inflation. Despite President Caldera's effort to reduce the public sector, the workforce actually *increased* by 50,000 in 1997. Why? Because of decentralization, laid-off federal workers entered the payrolls of state and local governments. But another reason may be linked to that traditional dark side of democracy: spoils and patronage. To gain or keep power, politicians swap jobs for votes. It will not be easy to dismantle something so institutionalized, but until it is done, the bureaucracy, will remain, in the words of Caldera's own planning minister, "A huge leech sucking society dry."

In April 1999, Congress gave the new president, Hugo Chávez, virtual *carte blanche* for six months to remove that leech. Reducing the parasitic bureaucracy, in fact, is one of the demands the IMF has made for providing new credits to Venezuela, along with a tax increase to cope with a crushing fiscal deficit of $9 billion, about 9% of GDP. So far, it appears Chávez is engaging in smoke and mirrors. He announced plans for a 15.5% value added tax, but it is replacing a 16.5% wholesale tax, which means a net loss in revenues. And while Chávez has pledged to reduce the excess of government jobs, he has offset any significant savings by implementing a 20% increase in public sector wages.

Economic statistics confirmed the severity of the crisis. Real GDP growth in 1997 was an illusionarily rosy 5.1%, but that gain followed negative growth of –0.4% the year before. In 1998, the year of the free-fall in world oil prices, growth declined by –0.3%, and in 1999, respite skyrocketing oil prices, it plummeted by a devastating –6.1%. In 2000, Venezuela showed positive growth of only 3.2%, almost entirely the result of the continued high price of oil on the international markets, something Chávez had pushed at the September 2000 OPEC summit in Caracas, but it was not enough to overcome the losses of the previous three years. Growth in 2001 was 3.0%. Some economists were predicting the GDP could shrink by 2% in 2002 because of the ongoing political turmoil (see History).

Unemployment rose steadily from 10.6% in 1997 to 13% in 1998 to 14.5% in 1999. It then began to taper off, to 13.2% in 2000 and 13% in 2001, still almost the highest in Latin America after Colombia and Argentina. Inflation has declined from a paycheck-stealing 103.2% in 1996 to 12% in 2001.

Oil wealth once gave Venezuela among the highest standards of living in the region, but inflation and negative economic growth have steadily eroded it. In 2001 it still had a per capita income of $5,283, the fourth-highest of the 20 Latin American republics, but it is inequitably distributed; 80% of the population lives below the poverty line. The public debt, meanwhile, is a crushing $23 billion. It is small wonder that poverty-stricken Venezuelans, as well as a middle class that has seen its standard of living steadily erode, have turned in desperation to a charismatic demagogue who has promised to rescue them.

The Future: The dramatic events of 2002 have demonstrated that Venezuela has become sharply and hopelessly polarized into two passionate camps, one that desperately wants Hugo Chávez out of power and the other that still sees him as the champion of the underprivileged. The bizarre coup and counter-coup of April 11–14 was an incredible spectacle perhaps unprecedented in the annals of modern political science. This author is offering a new term, admittedly oxymoronic, to describe the situation in Venezuela: pluralist mob rule. In April, Chávez's mob won.

The socioeconomic upheaval currently underway in Venezuela is uncomfortably reminiscent of that which existed in Chile prior to the bloody 1973 coup that ended the three-year Marxist experiment of Salvador Allende. In both cases, a popularly elected leftist president sought to strip power and privileges from an oligarchical elite, creating a confrontation between social classes. Chile was on the brink of civil war when the military intervened. If passions continue to escalate and events continue to get out of hand, a civil war in Venezuela is not beyond the realm of possibility.

But there are two fundamental differences between the Allende's Chile and Chávez's Venezuela. First, Chávez has twice been elected with overwhelming majorities, whereas Allende squeaked into office as a constitutional fluke with a plurality of only 36% of the popular vote. If Chávez calls the bluff of his opponents and submits himself to a referendum, he may very well win. Second, the Chilean military was unified behind the decision to overthrow Allende, and the coup was supported by the preponderance of the civilian population. The events of April demonstrated that the Venezuelan military and population are both sharply divided. Mass anti-Chávez demonstrations and the stupid violent actions of Chávez supporters led to bloodshed, which led to the military coup, which led to violent counter-demonstrations by *chavistas*, which led to more bloodshed, which led to the counter-coup and his reinstatement. With the officer corps of the armed forces so divided, a civil war likely would see entire units, well armed and well trained, doing battle against each other; the bloodshed could become horrendous.

Despite the vocal opposition of half the population, Chávez is still idolized by the other half. This author covered the July 30, 2000, election as a free-lance journalist, and I was in the crowd outside the Miraflores Palace that night as Chávez claimed victory from the "Balcony of the People." I was struck by the expressions of reverence, adulation and hopefulness on the faces of his adherents, two of whom waved Cuban flags; one hoisted a poster of Che Guevara. It was eerily reminiscent of another famous balcony scene, that of the Casa Rosada in Buenos Aires, where Juan and Eva Perón used to exhort their "*descamisados*," or shirtless ones.

In fact, Perón is perhaps a better analogy to Chávez than is Allende; still another would be Louisiana's Huey P. Long. All three are, or were, populist demagogues who twice won overwhelming victories at the polls, which they then interpreted as mandates to abuse their constitutions in furtherance of their political agendas on behalf of the underprivileged and to run roughshod over their political opponents and media critics. Perón was overthrown by a military coup; Long was assassinated. Could one of these fates be awaiting Hugo Chávez?

Smaller Nations and Dependent Territories of Latin America

HAITI

DOMINICAN REPUBLIC

PUERTO RIC

CARIBBEAN SEA

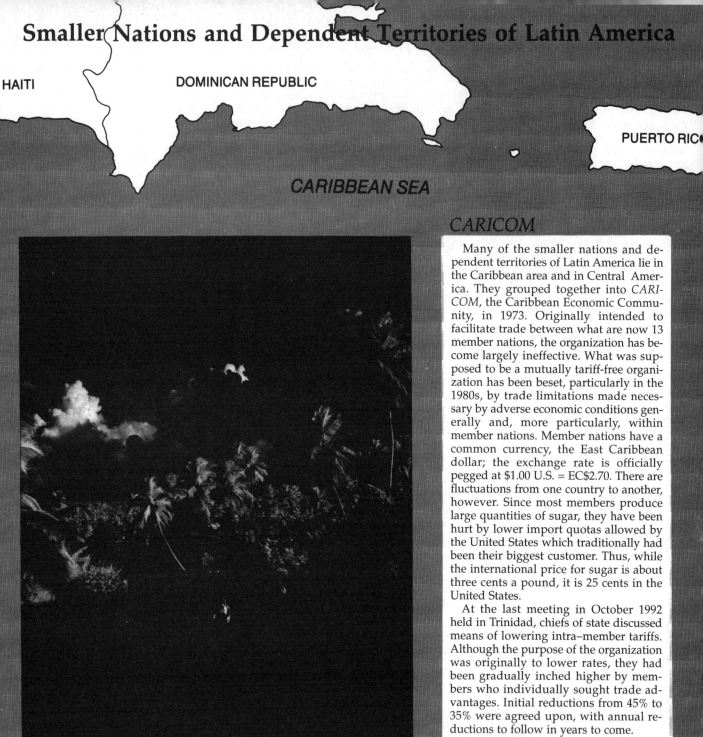

COLOMBIA

ARUBA (Neth.)

BONAIRE (Neth.)

CURACAO (Neth.)

0   100 Miles

VENEZUELA

CARICOM

Many of the smaller nations and dependent territories of Latin America lie in the Caribbean area and in Central America. They grouped together into *CARICOM*, the Caribbean Economic Community, in 1973. Originally intended to facilitate trade between what are now 13 member nations, the organization has become largely ineffective. What was supposed to be a mutually tariff-free organization has been beset, particularly in the 1980s, by trade limitations made necessary by adverse economic conditions generally and, more particularly, within member nations. Member nations have a common currency, the East Caribbean dollar; the exchange rate is officially pegged at $1.00 U.S. = EC$2.70. There are fluctuations from one country to another, however. Since most members produce large quantities of sugar, they have been hurt by lower import quotas allowed by the United States which traditionally had been their biggest customer. Thus, while the international price for sugar is about three cents a pound, it is 25 cents in the United States.

At the last meeting in October 1992 held in Trinidad, chiefs of state discussed means of lowering intra–member tariffs. Although the purpose of the organization was originally to lower rates, they had been gradually inched higher by members who individually sought trade advantages. Initial reductions from 45% to 35% were agreed upon, with annual reductions to follow in years to come.

Plans were made in 1993 for a pact between member nations that would provide for taxation of income at the place of its origin rather than the location where it is received; the agreement has not been

finalized. Further complicating the economic picture is the NAFTA treaty (Mexico, U.S., Canada) and the General Agreement on Tariffs and Trade (GATT), both lowering and/or abolishing tariffs.

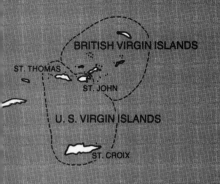

BRITISH VIRGIN ISLANDS

ST. THOMAS

ST. JOHN

U. S. VIRGIN ISLANDS

ST. CROIX

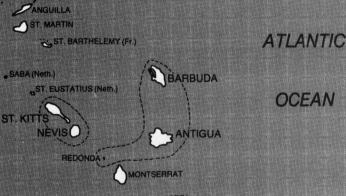

ANGUILLA

ST. MARTIN

ST. BARTHELEMY (Fr.)

SABA (Neth.)

ST. EUSTATIUS (Neth.)

ST. KITTS

NEVIS

REDONDA

BARBUDA

ANTIGUA

MONTSERRAT

ATLANTIC

OCEAN

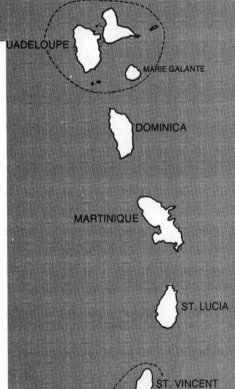

GUADELOUPE

MARIE GALANTE

DOMINICA

MARTINIQUE

ST. LUCIA

ST. VINCENT

BARBADOS

GRENADINES

GRENADA

British Virgin Islands (colony)

U.S. Virgin Islands (see page 277)

Anguilla (British Crown Colony)

St. Martin (see French and Netherlands dependencies)

St. Kitts and Nevis (Independent 9/19/83)

Antigua and Barbuda (Independent 11/1/82)

Montserrat (British Colony)

Guadeloupe (see French dependencies, page 271)

Dominica (Independent 11/3/78)

Martinique (see French dependencies, page 271)

St. Lucia (Independent 2/22/79)

St. Vincent and the Grenadines (Independent 10/27/79)

Barbados (see page 242)

Grenada (see page 243)

TOBAGO

TRINIDAD

The Commonwealth of the Bahamas

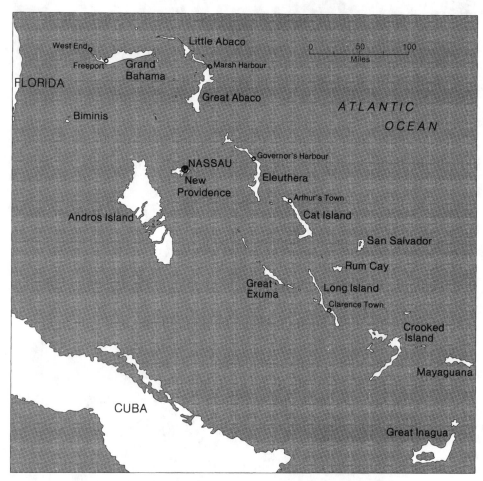

The Progressive Liberal Party (PLP) was formed in 1953 by Bahamians (pronounced Ba–*haim*–yans) who resisted rule by a small group of businessmen then in control of political and economic life on the islands ("The Bay Street Boys"). Continually gaining strength, the PLP was voted into office in 1967, and in 1972 it won 29 of 38 seats in the House of Assembly.

In July 1977, Bahamians voted in the island's first elections since independence in 1973. Although Prime Minister Lynden O. Pindling ("Black Moses") had been severely criticized for his economic policies, voters gave his PLP 31 of the 38 House seats. The government's "black power" image had hurt the all–important tourist industry.

Pindling followed a trend found throughout the Caribbean: increased state control over the economy. The government forced many businesses to hire local workers to replace foreigners. New taxes were placed on foreign workers and on the sale of property to non–Bahamians. The government claimed that these programs produced a black middle class.

One impact of these measures was an end to the Bahamas' former status as a tax–free haven for the rich. Many of the so–called suitcase companies moved from the Bahamas to the Cayman Islands, where taxes remain low.

General elections in mid–1982 saw Prime Minister Pindling's PLP win with 53% of the vote and a majority in the House of Assembly. A similar victory occurred in 1987, despite repeated accusa-

Area: 5,389 square miles, encompassing about 700 islands and islets only 35 of which are inhabited. In addition, there are over 2,000 cays which are low reefs of sand or coral.

Population: 305,000 in 2000.

Capital City: Nassau, on New Providence Island (Pop. 160,000, estimated).

Climate: Sunny and semi–tropical, with prevailing sea breezes; there is a hurricane season from June to October.

Official Language: English.

Ethnic Background: African (80%), White (10%), Mixed (10%).

Chief Commercial Ventures: Tourism, gambling, banking and drug smuggling.

Gross Domestic Product: U.S. $4.92 billion in 2000 ($15,850 per capita).

Chief of State: Queen Elizabeth II of Great Britain, represented by Governor–General Clifford Darling.

Head of Government: Hubert Alexander Ingraham, prime minister (b. 1947, since August 19, 1992).

Like the fragments of a broken piece of pottery, the Bahama Islands spread their natural beauty over about 100,000 square miles of ocean, making a gently curving

arc 700 miles long from a point off the Florida coast down to the islands of Cuba, Haiti and the Dominican Republic. Only 35 of the islands are inhabited, with New Providence Island having more than half of the nation's population.

History: In October 1492 Christopher Columbus first sighted his New World at the island he promptly named San Salvador—"the Savior"—lying on the eastern edge of the island group. The Arawak Indians who populated these islands were exterminated over a brief period of years by Spanish slave traders, who shipped them off to the large Spanish–owned islands to work on the sugarcane plantations.

Thinly populated, the islands were virtually ignored for a century and a half until 1647 when a former governor of the English island of Bermuda sailed south and landed on the long, narrow strip of land called Eleuthera. He and his party were seeking greater religious freedom than was found on Bermuda. In the late 1930s and early 1940s the tourist boom started; today the islands receive more than a million and a half vacationers annually.

Rt. Hon. Hubert A. Ingraham

tions that the prime inister was involved in drug trafficking, including eyewitness testimony linking him to Everette Bannister. The latter was known as "Mr. Fixit" of the Bahamas, and widely suspected as a drug smuggler.

In August 1992, elections resulted in victory for the opposition Free National Movement (FNM) and selection of Hubert Ingraham as prime minister, ending the 27–year rule of Pindling. An investigation of corruption in state owned enterprises during the Pindling years ensued. Ingraham's government also has stressed economic development through inviting foreign investment. The FNM was returned to power in general elections in March 1997, winning 35 seats to only four for the PLP.

Culture: The people of the Bahamas, approximately 90% of whom are of African ancestry, are good–humored and generally prosperous. Most derive their living from the tourist trade. Among their many festivals is a special holiday—*Junkanoo*—a carnival not unlike the New Orleans *Mardi Gras,* which takes place during Christmas week. A sportsman's paradise, the islands provide excellent fishing, first–rate golf courses, a lively night life, visiting ballet companies, concerts and other theatrical productions. *Goombay* is a musical sound which is exclusively Bahamian; it blends a combination of goatskin drums, maracas and saws scraped with nails. The rhythm is fast-paced, exciting and non-stop.

Economy: Tourism is the number one industry, accounting for 60% of GDP. Most visitors are from the United States on excursion cruises out of Miami who stay one or two days. Europeans, who stay for an average of two weeks, spend much more, and strong efforts are being made to cultivate this trade. New hotels and vacation facilities have been constructed in the "outer" islands.

Ranking second to tourism is the international banking industry (15% of GDP), with more than 350 banks located on the islands. Because there is no income tax and great secrecy of financial transactions, the Bahamas has traditionally been a major tax haven and scene of widespread "laundering" of money from illegal drugs. The government has attempted to broaden the base of the economy by lowering import duties and other attractive incentives. Production of bauxite is important. Oil refining and transshipment from large ships to smaller vessels at new terminals is a major source of income, together with cement production.

Another source of income is "dummy" registration of ships, which can be returned to U.S. registry in the event of a war. Better terms are being offered than those of Liberia; Bahamian registry includes huge supertankers. Commercial fishing is also being expanded. Lavish and lively gambling casinos, in operation around the clock, see millions of dollars changing hands each week, but they have felt the effect of U.S. state lotteries and legalized gambling.

Although new building developments are encroaching on the limited arable farmlands, "double cropping" each year in this warm climate makes most food plentiful, but imports have increased. Citrus fruit groves have replaced dairy farming as the most important sector of agriculture. Huge groves were planted to take advantage of severe frosts in Florida in the 1980s. Oranges, limes and other tropical fruit are plentiful and some are shipped to the United States. Other major exports include rum and salt.

Limitations on the economy include the presence of a large number of unskilled Haitians requiring high levels of social services.

The Bahamas posted a GDP in 2000 of $4.92 billion, a healthy growth rate of 5% over 1999.

The Future: Blessed with the highest annual per capita income in Latin America, the Bahamas is very prosperous; this does not include a considerable amount of money generated by illicit drug trafficking. This prosperity will continue despite a levelling off of tourist trade in 1993 from which there has yet to be recovery. As in most prosperous places of the world, prices are high, including items which attract tourists.

Flamingos at Nassau's Ardastra Gardens

Barbados

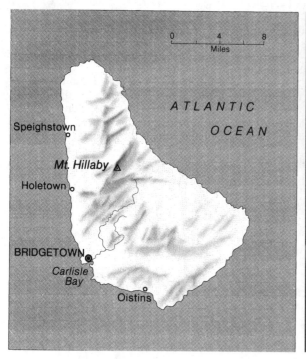

Rt. Hon. Owen Arthur

Area: 166 square miles.

Population: 268,000 in 2000.

Capital City: Bridgetown (Pop. 110,000, estimated).

Climate: Tropical, but pleasant, with moderate rainfall from June to December.

Ethnic Background: African (77%); mixed races (17%); European (6%).

Chief Commercial Products: Sugar, molasses, rum.

Gross Domestic Product: U.S.$2.549 billion in 2001 (about U.S. $9,444 per capita).

Chief of State: Queen Elizabeth II of Great Britain, represented by Governor General Sir Clifford Husbands.

Head of Government: Rt. Hon. Owen Arthur, Prime Minister (since September 1994).

Barbados is an island 21 miles in length and 14.5 miles at its greatest width, lying in the Atlantic Ocean 100 miles east of the Lesser Antilles. The island is surrounded by colorful coral reefs and has but one natural harbor, Carlisle Bay, on the southwestern coast; the island's high elevation is Mt. Hillaby (1,115 feet) on the northern part. The land slopes to the south in gentle terraces. Temperatures of the tropical climate are moderated by sea breezes. Fertile soils and adequate rainfall have favored sugar production.

History: Barbados was occupied by the British in 1625 and remained continuously in British control until its independence in 1966. Until the mid–19th century, sugar produced great wealth for the planters. The abolition of slavery in 1838 disturbed, but did not destroy, the island's economy. By comparison with other West Indian islands, Barbados' history has been tranquil. Riots occurred in 1876 and in 1937 because of efforts to federate the island with other British possessions. Ministerial government with partial self–rule was granted in 1954 by Britain. In 1961 Barbados became internally self–governing within the British Commonwealth. Full independence was achieved in 1966. The House of Assembly is the second–oldest legislative body in the Western Hemisphere, having first met in 1639.

Elections in 1971 were won by Prime Minister Errol Walton Barrow's Democratic Labor Party. Disturbed by the decline in the national economy, voters in 1976 turned to the Barbados Labor Party headed by Prime Minister J.M.G. (Tom) Adams. But in 1986 elections, in the presence of a declining economy, the people again turned to Barrow, who won a landslide victory in mid-1986, but died in June 1987. He was succeeded by his deputy, Erskine Sandiford.

Winning half the vote in January 1991, the DLP captured 18 of the 28 seats in the House of Assembly. Sandiford, who continued as prime minister, had promised to carry out the policies of his predecessor. The BLP had revitalized itself under the leadership of Owen Arthur since 1993 and promised competition based on the flagging economy in the next election.

Tax reforms, including a value–added tax, highlighted 1993, as did the development of tax reductions and incentives intended to boost export of small manufactured goods, including clothing.

In elections held in September 1994, the BLP ended the eight–year rule of the Democratic Labor Party winning 18 of the 28 seats in the House of Assembly, and Owen Arthur became prime minister. Arthur and the BLP won a landslide reelection victory in January 1999, winning 26 seats.

Crime has become such a serious problem, threatening the vital tourism industry, that the Arthur government has followed Trinidad and Tobago's lead in reinstating death by hanging. The last hanging was in 1984, but the British Privy Council has commuted recent sentences. Barbados may sever its judicial ties with Britain as a result.

Culture: The people of Barbados are descendants of British colonists and African slaves. They have a typically West Indian culture with a blend of English tradition. Their rhythmic dances and Calypso music, backed by steel drum bands (see Trinidad and Tobago), are in strange contrast to their love of cricket, always the joy of the British upper classes, but in Barbados the game of the people. African influence is as dominant as British, except in political and economic institutions, where the latter is maintained. Barbados is densely populated, with more than 1,500 people per square mile.

Economy: Sugar production and tourism account for a large percentage of the nation's foreign exchange earnings. Fish, fruit and beef output barely meet domestic needs of the nation, one of the world's most densely populated regions. In addition, a lack of mineral wealth hampers economic growth. To help reduce unemployment and racial tensions, the government has been making a concerted effort to involve its large, literate (97% adult literacy rate) black population in tourism to offset a decline in sugar production. Production of sugar has been steadily declining in the face of falling world prices.

The tourism boom of the 1990s has made Barbados a relatively prosperous little country, with an estimated per capita income in 2001 of $9,444, well above that of most of the 20 "Latin" republics. GDP grew by 3.7% in 2000, well above the 0.7% annual population growth rate. Nonetheless, unemployment remains stubbornly high: 12% in 1998, 10.6% in 1999, 9.3% in 2000. Inflation was only 1.6% in 1999 and 2.4% in 2000.

Tourism, which now accounts for three-fourths of GDP, has helped offset the serious balance of trade deficit. In 2000, Barbados imported $1.03 billion in goods and exported only $286 million.

The Future: Persistent unemployment led to an increase in crime in the 1990s. Tourism has not been growing as rapidly as might be expected because of this problem.

Grenada

Area: 133 square miles, including the islets of Carricou and Petit Martinique in the Grenadines.

Population: 100,700 in 2000.

Capital City: St. George's (Pop. 34,000, est.).

Climate: Tropically rainy and dry, hot, with prevailing ocean breezes.

Official Language: English.

Ethnic Background: African.

Chief Commercial Products: Nutmeg, tropical agricultural products.

Gross Domestic Product: US$366 million in 1999 ($3,080).

Independence Date: February 7, 1974.

Chief of State: Queen Elizabeth II of Great Britain, represented by Governor–General Sir Daniel C. Williams.

Head of Government: Rt. Hon. Keith Mitchell, Prime Minister (since June 1995).

Rt. Hon. Keith Mitchell

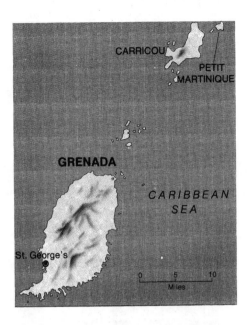

Like a large pearl, Grenada (pronounced Greh–NAY–dah) is the southernmost of the Windward Island chain, lying peacefully at the edge of the Caribbean Sea and the Atlantic Ocean. Blessed with beautiful beaches, clear water and a pleasant (but tropical) climate, the island is 21 miles long from north to south and only 12 miles horizontally at its widest point. Grenada has heavily wooded mountains watered by many streams that feed the quiet, lush valleys. There is the calm of smooth beaches and the rockbound coasts where the surf pounds and churns endlessly.

History: Discovered in 1498 by Columbus, Grenada was originally inhabited by the Carib Indians. In the 1650s the island was colonized by the French, who established large tobacco plantations. England acquired Grenada in 1763 by the Treaty of Paris, under which (among other exchanges of territory) France ceded Canada to the English. The new rulers of the island imported slaves from Africa to work the sugarcane plantations.

For over 200 years, Grenada basked peacefully in obscurity, harvesting its crops and almost oblivious to the rest of the world. During this period it was administered as a separate British Colony until its membership in the short–lived West Indian Federation (1958–1972). The federation collapsed partly because one key member, Trinidad, did not want to tie its own healthy economy to that of its poorer federation neighbors.

Elections held in 1972 brought an overwhelming victory to the Grenada United Labor Party of Premier Eric Gairy (13 out of 15 seats in the House of Representatives), whose major platform during the election was the complete independence of the island nation. As a result of talks in

London soon afterward, a constitutional conference was set for May 1973.

Grenada gained its independence in 1974. The most prominent figure in the nation's politics since 1962, Gairy continued to control Grenada through his domination of powerful labor unions. However, his corrupt and brutal rule generated widespread resentment. Opponents, led by the "new left" black–power New Jewel Movement, ousted him in 1979.

The new regime, headed by London–educated Maurice Bishop, 34, promptly dissolved Parliament and promised a new constitution that would make the island a "socialist democracy." Although it restricted personal liberties (no press freedom, no elections), the regime somewhat improved living conditions for the poor. Private enterprise remained largely intact.

In foreign affairs, Bishop embraced the Castro regime. Cuba responded with technical and military assistance for Grenada's new "People's Revolutionary Army."

The Reagan administration viewed the Grenada regime as a tool of Moscow via Cuba and imposed a blackout of the island. The government collapsed and anarchy ensued which was ended when a force of U.S. Marines and troops from other Caribbean nations and territories invaded. Several hundred Cuban troops were taken prisoner and returned to Cuba; vast amounts of Soviet and Cuban military equipment was found. The occupying force was withdrawn after elections were held in December 1984.

Herbert Blaize, leader of the New National Party, was selected prime minister over a coalition government that split in 1989; Blaize died shortly thereafter. Inconclusive elections in 1990 resulted in Nicholas Braithwaite being selected to lead yet another coalition government. He stumbled badly in 1993, failing to find economic measures acceptable to the media and people, and his resignation was

demanded. He vowed to stay until 1995 elections, but in 1994 resigned as head of the National Democratic Congress.

Contrary to his promise, Braithwaite resigned on February 1, 1995. In June elections, the New National Party (NNP) led by former Works and Communications Minister Keith Mitchell, defeated the NDC, taking eight of the 15 seats in the House of Representatives.

As prime minister, Mitchell embarked on a successful campaign to lure foreign investors to the island, but there were signs that his government corrupted itself in the awarding of public works contracts. When two of his ministers defected to the opposition in late 1998 over the allegations of corruption, Mitchell lost his one-seat majority and was forced to call general elections 18 months early. In the election held on January 18, 1999, voters resoundingly indicated they were more concerned about the jobs Mitchell had brought to the island than with the corruption charges: The NNP won all 15 seats in the House. Mitchell himself received 89% in his district. The leader of one opposition party complained that with the snap election and short six–week campaign, "We were caught with our pants down."

Culture: The people of Grenada, 95% of whom are black or mulatto, are a fun-loving and hard working group. Grenada's capital and main port, St. George's, rises steeply from the bay and the red–roofed houses are painted in pastel shades of pink and green. Night life in the city is often punctuated by continuous music from colorful Calypso bands.

Economy: Called the Isle of Spice, Grenada's economy has for centuries been based on its nutmeg. It is presently the world's second-largest exporter of this product. Other exports include bananas, sugar, cacao and mace. The tourist industry is vital to the island's economic health. Most exports go to EC countries. An annual U.S. assistance package will be necessary indefinitely. Grenada and the Windward Islands were greatly favored by EC import limitations on bananas from other Caribbean sources. GDP in 1999 was $366 million, or $3,080 per capita, a growth rate over 1998 of 8.16%

The Future: If the allegations of corruption within the NNP government were true when it had only a one–seat majority, one cannot help but speculate on what abuses—whether economic or political—could occur now that the government's legislative opposition has been wiped out. Legislative monopolies are not healthful for democratic governments.

THE DEPENDENT TERRITORIES

The dependencies in Latin America have a wide variety of relationships with the nations controlling them. Those of Great Britain have various degrees of internal self–government. In the Caribbean area, the British attempt to unite several territories into the West Indian Federation failed, and Barbados, Guyana and Jamaica became sovereign nations shortly thereafter.

The islands of Guadeloupe and Martinique, and mainland French Guiana, are governed as *departments* of France. The Netherlands Antilles are internally self–governing. Puerto Rico is a commonwealth within the United States that possesses internal autonomy, and the Virgin Islands are federally administered territories of the United States. The Falkland Islands, lying off the coast of Argentina, are governed by the British and claimed by the Argentines.

Fort-de-France, Martinique; Mt. Pelee looms behind the capital. Photo by Miller B. Spangler

British dependencies

CAYMAN, TURKS AND CAICOS ISLANDS

Area: 269 square miles.
Population: 28,000 (estimated).
Administrative Capital Georgetown (Pop. 4,700, estimated).
Heads of Government: Michael Gore (Caymans); Michael Bradley (Turks and Caicos), Governors.

These two groups of islands were administered by the Governor of Jamaica until 1962 when they were placed under the British Colonial Office. With the closing of the Colonial Office, administration passed to the Commonwealth Relations Office. The Cayman Islands lie midway between Jamaica and the western tip of Cuba. Turks and Caicos Islands are geographically a portion of the Bahamas. There are some 35 small islands in these groups, of which only eight are populated. The predominantly black and mulatto people eke a meager existence from fishing and the production of salt. Because of their limited resources, these islands cannot sustain themselves as independent nations. The Cayman Islands have become increasingly popular as a tax haven since the Bahamian government ended tax exempt status there for foreign corporations. There are numerous banks catering to "commerce," which means "laundering" money, the source of which is desired to be secret—usually narcotics. Crime associated with drug trade is increasing sharply. There are 532 banks, 80 of which actually have offices in the islands—one for every 53 people; more than 25,000 companies are registered to do business.

A five–member executive council is elected in the Caymans; political activity is minimal. Turks and Caicos Islands have a 20–member Legislative Council and an eight–member executive council.

FALKLAND ISLANDS

Area: 4,618 square miles.
Population: 2,600 (estimated).
Administrative Capital: Port Stanley
Head of Government: William H. Fullerton, Governor.

The Falkland Islands are made up of two large and 200 small islands, treeless, desolate and windswept, which lie off the southern tip of Argentina in the Atlantic Ocean.

The British discovered and named the islands in 1690; the French established a small colony on one of the larger islands in 1764 and the British started a settlement on the other large island in the following year. France gave up its possession to Spain in 1767 and the Spanish drove the British from the island they occupied. The territory was abandoned by the Spanish in 1811, and Argentina, after gaining independence, established a small colony on the islands in 1824. This settlement was destroyed by the U.S. Navy in 1831 in retaliation for Argentine harassment of whaling ships from Boston.

The British again gained possession of the islands in 1833 and have held them since that time. Argentina claims the islands based on its effort of 1824. Originally of strategic importance because of their closeness to the Atlantic–Pacific sea route around the Cape, with the opening of the Panama Canal their value greatly decreased. However, the British Navy successfully struck from the islands against the German Navy in both world wars.

The islands are an economic liability to Britain, but are still a symbol of its sovereignty, not to be relinquished. When Argentina suddenly invaded the Falklands in April 1982, Britain met the challenge head on . . . successfully. A later dispute was resolved when Britain and Argentina agreed upon a joint, 200–mile fishing boundary around the islands calculated to exclude Japan, Russia and Taiwan.

Development of oil deposits within the 200–mile radius, and a new Argentine constitution reaffirming sovereignty over what it calls the *Islas Malvinas*, have created problems that will be difficult to solve.

French dependencies

FRENCH GUIANA

Area: 34,740 square miles.
Population: 125,000 (estimated).
Administrative Capital: Cayenne (Pop. 32,000, estimated).
Head of Government: Jean–François Corden, Prefect.

French Guiana lies on the north coast of South America, north of Brazil and east of Suriname. The land consists of fertile, low plains along the coast, rising to the Tumuc–Humac Mountains on the Brazilian frontier. The Isles of Salut (Enfant Perdu, Remire and Ile du Diable—Devil's Island), lying off the coast, form part of the territory administered as a French *département*. The climate is tropical, with an average temperature of 80°F. The rainy season is from November to July, with the heaviest downfall in May.

Guiana was awarded to France in 1667, attacked by the British in the same year, taken by the Dutch in 1676 and retaken by France in the same year. In 1809 it was seized by a joint British–Portuguese effort based in Brazil, and remained under Brazilian occupation until 1817, when the French regained control. Gold was discovered in 1853, inspiring disputes with Brazil and Suriname which were not set-

tled until 1915. The colony is best known for its infamous prison colony, which was closed in 1945.

Guiana has fertile soils, 750,000 acres of land suitable for stock raising, vast resources of timber and coastal waters abounding in shrimp and fish. However, only some 12,000 acres are cultivated and most foodstuffs are imported. The population consists of creoles (descended from African black ancestors), Europeans, Chinese and a few native Indians. The principal products are shrimp, gold, hardwood and rum. French Guiana has adequate resources to support itself as an independent state, but little or no effort has been made to exploit these resources.

For a brief interval, French Guiana loomed in France as a 20th century *El Dorado*. During a three–day visit to Guiana in 1975, Olivier Stirn, minister of territories, announced a resettlement plan for the French colony, one part of which would initially require 10,000 settlers to develop a pulp and lumber industry. The plan was adversely received by Guiana local leadership and was condemned by 11 Caribbean chiefs of state. Nevertheless, French immigration to the territory proceeded. A satellite–launching base was

constructed at Kourou, and continental French now constitute about a third of the population of Guiana. They have gathered in an ultra-conservative political movement, the *Front National*, and, of course, oppose independence; the local movement for this faded quickly.

Political expression is mainly through the Guianese Socialist Party affiliated with the Socialist Party in France and the opposition Rally for the Republic, a Gaullist party affiliated with that of France. The prefect governs with the advice and consent of a General Council and a Regional Council.

Vast unused resources remain under the dense rain forest that covers more than 70% of the land area. Intense farming is done by the industrious Hmong people of Laos who were transplanted here more than three decades ago. Timber and fish are the most important exports. Hydro-electric installations completed in 1993 provide all electricity needed, albeit at a substantial cost in local animal and bird life. As in so many other tropical settings of the region, social and economic unrest is at a high level and probably has no "cure."

GUADELOUPE

Area: 657 square miles.
Population: 400,000 (estimated).
Administrative Capital: Basse–Terre (Pop. 21,000, estimated).
Head of Government: Franck Perriez, Prefect.

Guadeloupe consists of two islands separated by a narrow channel. Five small French islands in the Lesser Antilles are administered as a part of the Department of Guadeloupe (Marie Galante, Les Saintes, Desirade, St. Barthelemy and one–half of St. Martin).

Guadeloupe dependencies are occupied by the white descendants of Norman and Breton fishermen (and pirates) who settled there 300 years ago—the population is predominantly of mixed European and African derivation. The climate is tropical, with the rainy season extending from July to December.

Guadeloupe's principal products are bananas, sugar, rum, coffee, cocoa and tourism. Although this is an island of call for Caribbean cruises, it has excellent accommodations for extended vacations. The balance of trade is unfavorable and

the *département* has little hope for independence.

The people are apparently content with a Regional Council and a General Council, the latter of which exercises executive power. Elections are on a party basis and are spirited; the one in 1992 had to be voided because of "irregularities." The right wing prevailed in a re–run.

A new World Trade Center opened on Guadeloupe in 1994 and is the seat of numerous efforts to boost Euro–Caribbean trade.

MARTINIQUE

Area: 420 square miles.
Population: 380,000 (estimated).
Administrative Capital: Fort–de–France (Pop. 120,000, estimated).
Head of Government: Michel Morin, Prefect.

Martinique has been in French possession since 1635 except for two short peri-

ods of British occupation. Mountainous, with Mt. Pelee reaching 4,800 feet, its climate is tropical; the rainy season extends from July to December; violent hurricanes are frequent during this period. An eruption of Mt. Pelee in 1906 killed 10,000 people. The population is predominantly of mixed European and African origin.

Martinique's principal products are sugar, rum, bananas and other tropical fruits. This island also is an attractive tourist haven, with modern facilities available widely. Cattle raising is a steady industry, but presently produces enough for local consumption only. Politics in the 1990s have been dominated by conservatives.

Netherlands dependencies

NETHERLANDS ANTILLES

Area: 395 square miles.
Population: 260,000 (estimated).
Administrative Capital: Willemstad (Pop. 75,000, estimated).

The Netherlands Antilles consist of two groups of three islands each—one group lies off the north coast of Venezuela; the other lies just east of the Virgin Islands. Fully autonomous in internal affairs since 1954, the islands are organized into four self–governing communities—Aruba, Bonaire, Curaçao, and the Leeward Islands (southern portion of St. Martin, St. Eustatius and Saba). The population consists of about one third European ancestry and two thirds of mixed blood. Dutch is the official language. Spanish, English and a local *lingua franca* called Papamiento are also spoken. All of the islands are popular calls for cruise ships, and have, with the exception of St. Eustatius and Saba, have good facilities for extended vacations.

The economy of the Netherlands Antilles is based on the large oil refineries on Curaçao and Aruba. Almost all articles for consumption must be imported because fishing does not fill local needs and an arid climate coupled with poor soil do not support agriculture. The islands of Bonaire, St. Martin, St. Eustatius and Saba are of little economic importance. Despite some discontent among the non–European population, it is not likely that the islands will seek independence. Aruba was granted separate status from the other islands in 1986, with full independence set for 1996.

The lingering question of independence was probably laid to rest by balloting in 1993 on Curaçao and in 1994 on the remaining islands. Voters chose to remain a Dutch territory by a large majority, rejecting even the semi–independence that had been granted to Aruba. They undoubtedly wished a continuation of benefits derived from an annual Dutch subsidy of U.S. $160 million. Aruba, originally scheduled to become completely independent in 1996, instead continues in "special status."

The island of Curaçao has evidently been chosen as a drug outlet by Colombian, Surinamese and Dutch traffickers—rivals and their hired thugs fought pitched battles in late 1993.

Willemstad, Curaçao

United States dependencies

El Morro fortress for centuries guarded the entrance to the harbor at San Juan.

PUERTO RICO

Area: 3,423 square miles.
Population: 3,808,610 (2000 census).
Capital: San Juan (Pop. 2,450,292 in 2000, greater metropolitan area).
Per capita annual income: U.S. $8,000.
Head of Government: Governor Sila María Calderón, since January 2, 2001.

The easternmost and smallest island of the Greater Antilles, Puerto Rico is somewhat rectangular in shape, measuring 111 miles from east to west and about 36 miles north to south at its widest point; it includes four offshore islands, two of which are populated. Centrally located at almost the middle of approximately 7,000 tropical islands, most of them very tiny, hardly more than atolls, much of the island is mountainous or hilly—three quarters of the terrain is too steep for large–scale, mechanized cultivation. Puerto Rico is a *commonwealth* of the United States—while not a state, it is legally within the territorial jurisdiction of the U.S. The people are by language and culture part of the Caribbean and Latin America. Since it is not a state, Puerto Rico has no voting representation in Congress, but does have an elected resident commissioner with a four–year term who holds a seat, can speak out on issues, but does not have a vote. Otherwise, he enjoys the same privileges and immunities of other congressmen.

History: Puerto Rico was discovered by Christopher Columbus in 1493. There were at least three native cultures on the island, mostly of Arawak origin from the South American mainland. They were a peaceful group, quickly enslaved by the Spaniards and eventually died out as a race. The explorer claimed the island for Spain and named it San Juan Bautista (St. John the Baptist). After many years of colonization, the island was given the name Puerto Rico (Rich Port) and its capital city became San Juan.

Its first governor was Juan Ponce de León, who was later to discover Florida in his fabled search for the Fountain of Youth. Almost from the time of early colonization, Puerto Rico was a military target due to its strategic location. The French, British and Dutch were repelled

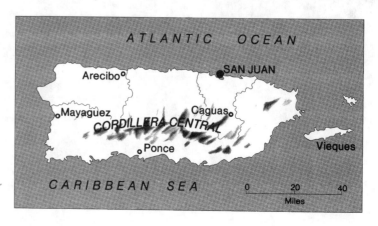

296

over the centuries and massive fortifications were erected by Spain to guard the harbor at San Juan. The 1700s up until the early 1800s were rather uneventful, and during Latin American wars for independence, Puerto Rico remained faithful to Spain. Sugar, tobacco and coffee produced on the island found a ready market in the United States, as did its flourishing rum industry. Toward the middle of the 1800s Puerto Rican social consciousness came slowly to life. In 1868 there was a revolution against Spain, which was quickly snuffed out.

Slavery was finally abolished in 1873. As the 19th century came to a close, Spain granted Puerto Rico broad powers of self–rule, but only days after the new government began to assume its duties the Spanish–American war broke out. The U.S. public had been appalled by the stories of harsh treatment of Cuban revolutionaries, which caused a growing anti–Spanish sentiment in the United States, carefully fed by the press, which printed sensational stories of supposed atrocities. After the battleship *U.S.S. Maine* was mysteriously blown up in Havana harbor on February 15, 1898, the United States declared war on Spain. One of the operations was the invasion of Puerto Rico by American forces under General Nelson A. Miles the following July.

The treaty of peace signed in Paris in December after the brief conflict forced Spain to withdraw from Cuba, and ceded to the United States were Puerto Rico, Guam and the Philippines. The Spanish-American war established the United States as a world power. A military government was set up in Puerto Rico, but in 1900 the first civil government was established. It gave the federal government full control over island affairs, with the president appointing the governor, the members of the Executive Council (legislature) and the island's Supreme Court. Members of the House of Delegates, which functioned as a second legislative branch, were popularly elected. All trade barriers with the United States were removed as Puerto Rico was placed within existing U.S. tariff walls. The island, the Philippines and Guam, were collectively designated an "unincorporated territory."

With the advent of civil government, men were again allowed the right to vote as they had under Spain. Also, the island was made exempt from paying federal taxes, duties and excise taxes collected in Puerto Rico on foreign products and on Puerto Rican products sold in the United States, all of which were handed over to the island treasury. Between 1900 and 1925, foreign trade increased from $16 million to $178 million annually; it now is a healthy $13.2 billion. A corresponding population increase occurred: from some 950,000 in 1905 to 1.3 million in 1921.

There was a rapid extension of the school system, accompanied by a reduction in illiteracy from about 90% to less than 50%. A more worrisome condition was the gradual concentration of wealth in fewer hands. Two half–mile tunnels were opened in 1909 through the mountains that provided irrigation for the south side of the island, very dry due to the constant trade winds. On the eve of World War I, Congress granted U.S. citizenship to Puerto Ricans and replaced the appointed Executive Council with a popularly elected Senate. However, the island remained exempt from federal taxes and was allowed to design its own tax system and raise its own revenues. Trade with the United States grew by leaps and bounds so that the island became one of the top consumers of U.S. goods in Latin America.

When the United States declared war on Germany in 1917, the Selective Service Act was extended to Puerto Rico by request of the island's government and some 18,000 men were inducted into service. As a result, Puerto Ricans were granted U.S. citizenship that same year. During the first decades of the 20th century, Puerto Rico developed its sugar production, but most of the profits went to the absentee landlords in the United States. By the time of the Great Depression of 1929, most Puerto Ricans were caught up in a web of poverty. There was mass unemployment, malnutrition and deteriorating health conditions. By 1930, unemployment stood at a frightening 60%. When the Roosevelt administration came into office in 1933, it began to extend a large measure of relief to the stricken land. Because of poor economic conditions, a strong nationalist movement emerged seeking complete independence from the United States. The movement reached its peak when in 1937 police fired on a nationalist demonstration in the southern city of Ponce, killing 20 people.

Commonwealth Status

Puerto Rico played an important defense role in the Caribbean region during World War II. President Truman finally in 1946 appointed a Puerto Rican governor for the island and one year later signed a law permitting it to elect its own governor, who in 1948 was Luis Muñoz–Marín of the Popular Democratic Party *(PDP)*. Further, in 1950 an act of the U.S. Congress allowed the island to draft its own constitution, which was approved with amendments by the Congress and then accepted in a plebiscite by the people in 1952. Governor Muñoz–Marín claimed the constitutional process and plebiscite were an act of self–determination of the Puerto Rican people, thus marking an end to American colonial rule. The Commonwealth was officially established on July

25, 1952, the 54th anniversary of the day the U.S. forces landed in 1898.

Despite the move toward self-determination, a small but aggressive minority of "nationalists" clamored for full independence, eventually resorting to terrorism. A band of nationalists attempted to assassinate President Truman in a bloody shoot- out in Washington in 1951. Three years later, nationalist terrorists opened fire from the gallery of the U.S. House of Representatives, wounding five congressmen. Militant nationalism resurfaced in the 1970s with the creation of the so-called Armed Forces of National Liberation, or *FALN*. Between 1974 and 1983, the *FALN* was believed responsible for 130 terrorist bombings in the continental United States that killed six people and wounded dozens of others. The worst bombing, on a tavern in New York's Greenwich Village in 1975, killed four.

The government of Muñoz–Marín laid the foundations for the industrial development of the island, aided by important incentives at home and aggressive promotion abroad. The program, called "Operation Bootstrap," was one of the 20th century's great success stories—Puerto Rico's economy was transformed from one based on a single crop (sugar) to a broadly–based manufacturing one, creating a strong middle class and one of the highest standards of living in all of Latin America. Per capita income has grown from about $120 per year in 1940 to more than $8,000 today. Further, university and college enrollment has soared from about 5,000 students in 1945 to about 150,000 by the mid–1980s.

In a 1967 plebiscite, 60% of the voters favored continuation and improvement of the commonwealth status with the United States, but there was strong opposition from pro–statehood supporters who received 38% of the vote. The major inde-

Former Governor Pedro J. Rosselló

Street scene in Ponce, Puerto Rico's second largest city.

Photo by Miller B. Spangler

pendence parties boycotted the plebiscite. The next year the pro-statehood New Progressive Party *(PNP)* won the governorship, winning again in 1976 and 1980. The pro-commonwealth *PDP* won in 1972, and 1988. These frequent changes in the political parties in power has produced a virtual stalemate on the future political status of the island. This still goes on; the effect is to discourage investment in job producing facilities in Puerto Rico that otherwise would occur.

In spite of President Bush's support for Puerto Rican statehood, the matter was bottled up in Congress in 1989–91; the Republicans did not wish to give Democrats an opportunity to tighten their hold on both houses of Congress. In a gesture of defiance, Puerto Rico enacted a measure providing that Spanish was the *only* official language. It since has been repealed by a measure in 1993 recognizing both Spanish and English. Only the wealthy and middle–class educated are genuinely bilingual.

In the 1992 elections, the *PNP* and its candidate for governor, Pedro J. Rosselló, again ran on a platform advocating statehood. The *PDP* favored continuing commonwealth status, and was soundly trounced in its worst defeat in its 54–year history. The victors promised and delivered another referendum (non-binding)

on statehood, which was held in November 1993. Fully 73% of the electorate participated and the result was 48.4% for commonwealth status and 46.2% for an application for statehood. Less than 5% favored independence. Rosselló, ignoring the result, warned that the struggle for statehood would go on.

The 1998 Referendum

Rosselló was reelected in November 1996, which he interpreted as a mandate to continue his quest for statehood. Responding to his persistent efforts, the U.S. House of Representatives voted in March 1998 for a *binding* referendum that ostensibly would decide the issue once and for all; the measure passed by only one vote, however, and the Senate failed to follow up.

Marking the 100th anniversary of U.S. occupation in July 1998, Rosselló then called for yet another non–binding referendum for December 13. Five options were listed on the complicated ballot: statehood, independence, an ambiguous "free association," continued commonwealth and "none of the above." The opposition *PDP,* however, advocated instead what it called an "enhanced commonwealth" by which Puerto Rico could enter into treaties with other nations and would

have the power to annul federal laws, definitely the best of both worlds but which likely would never win congressional approval. As its "enhanced commonwealth" was not on the ballot, the *PDP* campaigned vigorously for "none of the above." The 1998 referendum was a near-duplicate of the 1993 plebiscite, only this time "none of the above" won a slim but absolute majority of 50.2%, while the vote for statehood was virtually unchanged at 46.5%. Independence received 2.5%, "free association" 0.3% and commonwealth only 0.1%. This sent the ambiguous message that Puerto Ricans are ready to change their status, but don't yet know what that status should be.

Meanwhile, a corruption scandal exploded in March 1999 that tarnished Rosselló's reputation and credibility and was to prove a major political liability for the *PNP* in the elections of 2000. The former comptroller of the San Juan AIDS Institute—an entity Rosselló had approved in 1987 when he was health director of San Juan—pleaded guiltyto conspiracy and testified that $2.2 million in federal funds intended for AIDS victims had been diverted to the political campaigns of both *PNP* and *PDP,* including Rosselló, who allegedly received $250,000 for his 1992 campaign. Rosselló dismissed the allegations as a "character assassination." Although the governor himself was never indicted, he was forced to undergo the ignominy of appearing on the witness stand in the trials.which ended in 2000 with the convictions of two high-ranking officials. Then, in August 2000, *18 PNP officials*, including two mayors, were indicted on federal charges that they received $800,000 in campaign donations in exchange for $56 million in government contracts. Several of them also were convicted in 2001.

Rosselló also stood accused by pro–*PDP* newspapers of employing the time–honored cudgel of Latin American dictators of withholding government advertising from them. *El Nuevo Día*, which lost its government advertising after several investigative articles on corruption, sued the government in 1997. On May 12, 1999, the paper and the government reached a settlement by which the government restored the advertising, established a policy for distributing advertising fairly and expressed its respect for press freedom, but admitted no wrongdoing; the paper, meanwhile, agreed to offer the government discounted rates.

In September 1999, President Clinton sparked controversy with the unexpected announcement that he had offered clemency to 12 convicted members of the *FALN* and another militant group, the *Macheteros*, or machete wielders, in exchange for their promise to renounce terrorism. None had been convicted of any of the bombings of the 1970s and '80s, but on charges of seditious conspiracy and weapons possession. Nine of the prisoners accepted the clemency offer, and returned to heroes' welcomes in Puerto Rico. Even Governor Rosselló supported Clinton's offer. Not so the Republican-controlled Congress, which passed a stinging censure resolution against the president for his perceived softness on terrorists. Other critics alleged the president offered the clemency bid in order to help his wife, Hillary, win Puerto Rican votes in her successful campaign for the U.S. Senate from New York in 2000.

Independence activists seized the national spotlight again in 1999 and 2000 with their support for the 9,100 residents of the island of Vieques, who were protesting the island's use by the U.S. Navy as a bombing and gunnery range. The Navy had bombarded Vieques since 1941, but residents now complained that they were endangered by the exercises and by unexploded ordnance. Public protests began when a resident of the island was killed by a stray bomb in April 1999. In December, President Clinton announced a five-year withdrawal plan to placate the islanders. But they were not placated. In May 2000, 200 residents staged a nonviolent occupation of the range, forcing federal agents to take them into custody for trespassing on federal property. The occupation and arrests be-

Governor Sila María Calderón

came the focus of national and international media attention. Another 51 people were arrested 10 days later.

The Vieques controversy continued into 2001, with more protesters being arrested and others seeking redress in federal court to enjoin the Navy from using the range. But in May 2001, a federal court ruled in favor of the Navy, which resumed target practice. Even pro-commonwealth Puerto Ricans have been offended by the Navy's arrogance in disregarding the wishes of the island's residents. Also in May, the Rev. Al Sharpton, a controversial civil rights activist from New York City, who like Mrs. Clinton is believed to be currying favor among Puerto Rican voters there for a possible political bid, was among several protesters arrested on Vieques for trespassing on the range.

A referendum was held in July 2001, in which the island's residents voted 68% for the Navy to leave immediately. President George W. Bush announced that the Navy would abandon Vieques in 2003—not soon enough for many critics. As of mid-2002, however, the protests were continuing.

The Election of 2000

The corruption scandals of the Rosselló administration forced him to decide, wisely, not to seek a third term. Instead, the wounded *PNP* nominated Carlos Pesquera, a former secretary of transportation and public works, while the *PDP* nominated a woman, Sila María Calderón; the Puerto Rican Independence Party *(PIP)* nominated Rubén Berrios. Despite the corruption scandals, polls showed the race a dead heat between Pesquera and Calderón. The Vieques issue overshadowed the campaign, with Pesquera largely avoiding it, Berrios trumpeting it and Calderón making only vague statements in support of the island's residents.

An extraneous issue was interjected into the campaign in July when a pro-statehood federal judge in San Juan ruled in favor of 11 residents who demanded the right to vote in the U.S. presidential election between Al Gore and George W. Bush. The *PDP* and the *PIP* challenged the ruling, and in October the 1st U.S. Circuit Court of Appeals in Boston ruled that Puerto Ricans did not have that constitutional right.

The gubernatorial election was another reminder of how divided Puerto Ricans are on the statehood issue, and the results were almost a duplicate of the 1998 referendum: Calderón narrowly won with 48.5% of the vote to 46.1% for Pesquera and 4.9% for Berrios. The *PDP* also won clear majorities in the House and Senate. However, *the PNP*'s Jorge Santini recaptured the mayoralty of San Juan after 12 years of *PDP* control, making him a rising star in the party.

After her inauguration on January 2, 2001, as Puerto Rico's first woman governor, Calderón suddenly became far more strident in demanding that the Navy leave Vieques. She discussed the issue President Bush in Washington soon after his inauguration.

Political scandals have continued to stain both major parties. In October 2001, the FBI arrested the *PDP* mayor of the San Juan suburb of Vega Alta on charges of extortion, embezzlement and money laundering. But a far greater scandal tainted the *PNP* in January 2002, when the FBI arrested 17 people for money laundering and extortion in a $4.3 million kickback scheme involving private computer contractors and the department of education under the Roselló administration. Once again, federal funds destined for a worthy cause—the computer training of teachers—allegedly had gone into private pockets; $1 million reportedly went into the *PNP*'s 2000 campaign fund. Among those arrested were Victor Fajardo, Roselló's educaton secretary from 1994-2000; his deputy secretary; the former *PNP* speaker of the House of representatives; and the president of the Puerto Rico Chamber of Commerce.

The commonwealth-statehood-independence debate continues to raise controversy between elections and referenda; even license plates have become an issue. The new license plates issued under the Calderón administration contain the legend, "Free Associated State," and supposedly were issued to mark the 50th anniversary of the commonwealth's 1952 constitution. But both the *PNP* and the *PIP* denounced the plates as a *PDP* political statement.

Then, in June 2002, *PNP* president Carlos Pesquera sought to make a political statement of his own by forcing his way through a crowd to plant a U.S. flag alongside the Puerto Rican flag in the Office of

Women's Affairs, whose director had insisted on displaying only the Puerto Rican flag. Pesquera was arrested and charged with inciting to riot.

Culture: For centuries the Spanish presence in Puerto Rico left an indelible imprint on the island, but it also has been a true melting pot, a blend of the Spanish with Indians and Africans. Color lines are thus blurred and racial tensions hardly exist.

The abundant literature of Puerto Rico emphasizes its colonial past and the island's fight to retain its Hispanic identity. Leading authors include Luis Rafael Sánchez, Pedro Juan Soto, José Luis González and Enrique Laguerre. José Campeche (1752–1809) produced some magnificent portraits and points of historical and religious themes. Francisco Oller (1833–1917) was influenced by the great figures of French impressionism—two of his paintings hang in the Louvre Museum in Paris. Today the island is particularly strong in silk screening and plastic arts, with recognized masters such as Lorenzo Homar, Rafael Tufiño, Julio Rosado del Valle, Manuel Hernández Acevedo, Carlos Raquel Rivera and later, Antonio Martorell, Myrna Baez and Luis Hernández Cruz. Also, Francisco Rodón has emerged as one of Latin America's leading portrait artists.

In the mainland United States, Puerto Rican performers best known in the movies, music world, TV and legitimate theater include José Ferrer, Rita Moreno, Chita Rivera, Raúl Juliá, Erik Estrada, Justino Díaz and Pablo Elvira, to mention only a few. Puerto Rico's favorite sport is baseball, and it has contributed many dozens of players to the major leagues—in 1984 Willie Hernández of the Detroit Tigers was the American League's Most Valuable Player. The unforgettable Pittsburgh Pirate's Roberto Clemente shares company in Baseball's Hall of Fame with such greats as Babe Ruth and Hank Aaron.

On the bleak side, Puerto Rican slums and housing projects are comparable to the worst in the United States. The murder rate rose to more than any of the 50 states during the 1990s (but not as high as Washington, D.C.), forcing the governor in 1993 to call out the national guard with assault weapons to reduce street violence. Most of it is related to drug trafficking and use.

Economy: Although the Puerto Rican economy is reasonably strong, it has its problems. The main pillar of the economy is manufacturing. The island has nearly 2,000 plants, the majority of which are subsidiaries of U.S. companies attracted to Puerto Rico mainly because of tax advantages. The 1987 tax reforms, however, altered these incentives. These industries are geared to producing export items—the famous Bacardi Rum, for example, is produced on the island. Puerto Rico is a favorite location for U.S. pharmaceutical manufacturers because of particular tax advantages derived from locating on the island.

With industrialization, agricultural production, the dominant sector of the economy, commenced a decline starting in the 1950s. Agricultural workers first went to San Juan and then immigrated to the United States in search of jobs. As a result, about 3 million people of Puerto Rican heritage are now living in the United States.

Puerto Rico attracts tourists from all over the world; tourism, after manufacturing and agriculture, has been one of the mainstays of the economy. It now stands seriously threatened by crime directly connected to a burgeoning drug traffic from Colombia to the United States. It is relatively easy to get cocaine to the island and difficult to prevent it from entering the mainland United States since Puerto Ricans are citizens and need pass no more than the security check for weapons on flights to the United States, particularly New York. An area in which there could be much improvement is government employment: fully 28% of the people work for the government, a figure about 15% too high, at an enormous, unnecessary cost.

If Puerto Rico were independent, its 1998 per capita income of about $8,000 would be the second-highest in Latin America. In relative terms, that is only about one third the per capita income of the U.S. mainland, but it is four times as much as Puerto Rico's closest sovereign neighbor, the Dominican Republic. Because wages are so much higher than in other Caribbean countries, however, Puerto Rico is at a disadvantage in the competition for tourism.

Although Puerto Ricans pay no federal income tax, they qualify for welfare and unemployment benefits; unemployment at this writing was about 14%, compared with less than 5% on the U.S. mainland. Moreover, the island receives about $10 billion in aid from the mainland. In other words, the Puerto Ricans have the best of both worlds, which helps explain why a clear majority of them continues to eschew both statehood and independence.

The Future: Governor Calderón's narrow election victory will probably scuttle any further referendum on the statehood issue as long as she is in office. The burning issue now is the Navy's use of Vieques, which has strained the normal goodwill between the commonwealth and the mainland, and she has gone on record as demanding the Navy depart.

U.S. VIRGIN ISLANDS

Area: 132 square miles
Population: 140,000 (estimated).
Administrative Capital: Charlotte Amalie (Pop. 14,000, estimated).

The U.S Virgin Islands lie about 40 miles east of Puerto Rico and consist of three major islands (St. Croix, St. Johns and St. Thomas) and some 50 small islands and cays, mostly uninhabited. The islands were acquired by purchase from Denmark in 1917 and are administered as a Federal Territory by the U.S. Department of the Interior. Although voters turned down a proposed new constitution in 1978, attempts are being made to write a new charter. Most residents seem to prefer commonwealth status—rather than independence or statehood—with the United States.

The islands are hilly, with arable land given to small farms. The climate is tropical, with a May to November rainy season.

The population is about 20% North American and European descent; the remainder is of African and mixed heritage. The principal products for export are rum and bay rum, the fragrant distilled oil of the bayberry leaf. Cattle raising and truck farming are important for local consumption. The islands do not possess resources adequate for support as an independent entity.

Prosperity in the 1970s brought a tremendous influx of immigrants—now only about 40% of the islanders are natives. The ethnic derivation of these "newcomers" was about 75% black from neighboring Caribbean nations, including Haitians, and 25% white U.S. mainlanders. Because the Virgin Islands in the past relied principally on rum taxes for government expenses, tax changes have seriously undermined this scheme. The response was increased taxes on just about everything in the last several years—very unpopular to say the least. Tourism has been a mainstay of the economy and is being promoted. Unemployment remains very low by Caribbean standards—about 5%.

Charles W. Turnbull was elected governor in November 1998, succeeding Roy L. Schneider.

A referendum of the islands' future relationship with the United States was held in late 1993 after being postponed because of a hurricane. Ninety percent voted for continued or enhanced status—the *status quo*. But only 27% of the electorate bothered to participate in the balloting; it thus did not meet validation requirements.

Selected Bibliography of Key English Language Sources

General

Adelman, Jeremy, ed. *Colonial Legacies: the Problem of Persistence in Latin American History*. New York: Routledge, 1999.

Alvarez, Sonia E. *Cultures of Politics, Politics of Cultures: Revisioning Latin American Social Movements*. Boulder, CO: Westview Press, 1998.

Arnson, Cynthia. *Comparative Peace Processes in Latin America*. Stanford, CA: Stanford University Press, 1999.

Atkins, G. Pope. *Latin America and the Caribbean in the International System*. Boulder, CO: Westview Press, 1998.

Atkins, G. Pope. *Latin America in the International Political System*. Boulder, CO: Westview Press, 3rd. ed. 1995.

Barham, Bradford L. and Oliver T. Coomes. *Prosperity's Promise: the Amazon Rubber Boom and Distorted Economic Development*. Boulder, CO: Westview Press, 1996.

Beezley, William H. and Linda Curcio-Nagy, eds. *Latin American Popular Culture: an Introduction*. Wilmington, DE: Scholarly Resources, 2000.

Bethell, Leslie, ed. *A Cultural History of Latin America: Literature, Music and the Visual Arts in the 19th and 20th Century*. New York: Cambridge University Press, 1998.

Bethell, Leslie, ed. *Latin America since 1930*. New York: Cambridge University Press, 1994.

Bonilla, Frank, et al., eds. *Borderless Borders: U.S. Latinos, Latin Americans, and the Paradox of Interdependence*. Philadelphia, PA: Temple University Press, 1998.

Britton, John A. *The United States and Latin America: a Select Bibliography*. Langham, MD: Scarecrow Press, 1997.

Brysk, Alison. *From Tribal Village to Global Village: Indian Rights and International Relations in Latin America*. Stanford, CA: Stanford University Press, 2000.

Bulmer-Thomas, Victor. *The Economic History of Latin America since Independence*. New York: Cambridge University Press, 1994.

Burkholder, Mark A. and Lyman L. Johnson. *Colonial Latin America*. New York: Oxford University Press, 3rd ed. 1998.

Castañeda, Jorge G. *Utopia Unarmed: the Latin American Left after the Cold War*. New York: Random House, 1993.

Chasteen, John Charles. *Born in Blood and Fire: a Concise History of Latin America*. New York: W.W. Norton & Company, 2000.

Chomsky, Noam. *Latin America: from Colonization to Globalization*. Hoboken, NJ: Ocean Press, 1999.

Cockcroft, James D. *Latin America: History, Politics, and U.S. Policy*. Chicago, IL: Nelson-Hall, 2nd ed. 1996.

Craske, Nikki. *Women and Politics in Latin America*. Piscataway, NJ: Rutgers University Press, 1999.

Davis, Darien J. *Slavery and Beyond: the African Impact on Latin America and the Caribbean*. Wilmington, DE: SR Books, 1995.

De la Campa, Romban. *Latin Americanism*. Minneapolis, MN: University of Minnesota Press, 1999.

Dent, David W. *Monroe's Ghosts*. Westport, CT: Greenwood Publishing Group, 1999.

Dominguez, Jorge I. *Democratic Politics in Latin America and the Caribbean*. Baltimore, MD: Johns Hopkins University Press, 1998.

Dominguez, Jorge I., ed. *Latin America's International Relations and Their Domestic Consequences: War and Peace, Dependency and Autonomy, Integration and Disintegration*. New York: Garland Publishing, 1994.

Dominguez, Jorge I., ed. *Race and Ethnicity in Latin America*. New York: Garland Publishing, 1994.

Early, Edwin. *A History Atlas of South America*. Old Tappan, NJ: Macmillan Publishing Company, 1998.

Fagg, John E. *Latin America: a General History*. New York: Macmillan Publishing Company, 3rd ed 1977.

Fauriol, Georges A. *Fast Forward: Latin America on the Edge of the Twenty-First Century*. New Brunswick, NJ: 1997.

Ferman, Claudia, ed. *The Postmodern in Latin America Cultural Narratives: Collected Essays and Interviews*. New York: Garland Publishing, 1996.

Fitch, John S. *The Armed Forces and Democracy in Latin America*. Baltimore, MD: Johns Hopkins University Press, 1998.

Foders, Frederico and Manfred Feldsieper, eds. *The Transformation of Latin America*. Northampton, MA: Edward Elgar Publishing, 1999.

Fowler, Will, ed. *Ideologues and Ideologies in Latin America*. Westport, CT: Greenwood Publishing Group, 1997.

Franco, Jean, et al. *Profane Passions: Politics and Culture in the Americas*. Durham, NC: Duke University Press, 1999.

Gilderhus, Mark T., et al., eds. *The Second Century: U.S.-Latin American Relations since 1889*. Wilmington, DE: Scholarly Resources, 1999.

Green, Roy E., ed. *The Enterprise for the America's Initiative: Issues and Prospects for a Free Trade Agreement in the Western Hemisphere*. New York: Praeger, 1993.

Gutteridge, William F. *Latin America and the Caribbean: Prospects for Democracy*. Brookfield, VT: Ashgate Publishing Company, 1997.

Gwynne, Robert N. *Latin America Transformed: Globalization and Modernity*. New York: Oxford University Press, 1999.

Halebsky, Sandor and Richard L. Harris, eds. *Capital, Power, and Inequality in Latin America*. Boulder, CO: Westview Press, 1995.

Harvey, Robert. *Liberators: Latin America's Struggle for Independence*. New York: The Overlook Press, 2000.

Henderson, James D., et al. *A Reference Guide to Latin American History*. Armonk, NY: M.E. Sharpe, 2000.

Hillman, Richard S., ed. *Understanding Contemporary Latin America*. Boulder, CO: Lynne Rienner Publishers, 2001.

Hofman, André A. *The Economic Development of Latin America in the Twentieth Century*. Northampton, MA: Edward Elgar Publishing, 2000.

Jorge, Antonio, et al., eds. *Capital Markets, Growth and Economic Policy in Latin America*. Westport, CT: Greenwood Publishing Group, 2000.

Kanellos, Nicolas and Cristelia Perez. *Chronology of Hispanic-American History*. Detroit, MI: Gale Research, 1995.

Landau, Saul. *The Guerrilla Wars of Central America: Nicaragua, El Salvador, and Guatemala*. New York: Saint Martin's Press, 1993.

Langley, Lester D. *The Americas in the Age of Revolution: 1750-1850*. New Haven, CT: Yale University Press, 1996.

Loveman, Brian. *For la Patria: Politics and the Armed Forces in Latin America*. Scholarly Resources, 1999.

Lynch, John, ed. *Latin American Revolutions, 1808-1826: Old and New World Origins*. Norman, OK: University of Oklahoma Press, 1994.

MacDonald, Scott B. and Georges A. Fauriol. *Fast Forward: Latin America on the Edge of the Twenty-First Century*. Piscataway, NJ: Transaction Publishers, 1998.

Mainwaring, Scott, ed. *Presidentialism and Democracy in Latin America*. New York: Cambridge University Press, 1997.

Maldifassi, José and Pier A. Abetti. *Defense Industries in Latin American Countries: Argentina, Brazil, and Chile*. New York: Praeger, 1994.

Manzetti, Luigi. *Privatization South American Style*. New York: Oxford University Press, 2000.

Martz, John D., ed. *United States Policy in Latin America: a Decade of Crisis and Challenge*. Lincoln, NE: University of Nebraska Press, 1995.

Mendez, Juan E., et al., eds. *The (Un)Rule of Law and the Underprivileged in Latin America*. Notre Dame, IN: Notre Dame Press, 1999.

Mills, Kenneth and William B. Taylor, eds. *Colonial Spanish America: a Documentary History*. Wilmington, DE: Scholarly Resources, 1998.

Morales, Juan Antonio and Gary McMahon, eds. *Economic Policy and the Transition to Democracy: the Latin American Experience*. New York: Saint Martin's Press, 1996.

Morley, Samuel A. *Poverty and Inequality in Latin America: the Impact of Adjustment and Recovery in the 1980s*. Baltimore, MD: Johns Hopkins University Press, 1995.

O'Brien, Thomas F. *Century of U.S. Capitalism in Latin America*. Albuquerque, NM: University of New Mexico Press, 1999.-

Park, James William. *Latin American Underdevelopment: a History of Perspectives in the United States, 1870-1965*. Baton Rouge, LA: Louisiana State University Press, 1995.

Payne, Leigh A. *Uncivil Movements: the Armed Right Wing and Democracy in Latin America*. Baltimore, MD: Johns Hopkins University Press, 2000.

Peeler, John. *Building Democracy in Latin America*. Boulder, CO: Lynne Rienner Publishers, 1998.

Roberts, Paul. *The Capitalist Revolution in Latin America*. New York: Oxford University Press, 1997.

Roseberry, William, ed. *Coffee, Society, and Power in Latin America*. Baltimore, MD: Johns Hopkins University Press, 1995.

Schwaller, John F., et al., eds. *The Church in Colonial Latin America*. Wilmington, DE: Scholarly Resources, 2000.

Skidmore, Thomas E. *Modern Latin America*. New York: Oxford University Press, 2000.

Smith, Gaddis. *The Last Years of the Monroe Doctrine: 1945-1993*. New York: Hill & Wang/Farrar, Straus & Giroux, 1994.

Smith, Peter H. *Talons of the Eagle: Dynamics of U.S.-Latin America Relations*. New York: Oxford University Press, 1996.

Smith, William C., ed. *Politics, Social Change, and Economic Restructuring in Latin America*. Coral Gables, FL: University of Miami, North/South Center Press, 1997.

Stallings, Barbara and Wilson Peres. *Growth, Equity and Employment: the Impact of the Economic Reforms in Latin America and the Caribbean*. Washington, DC: Brookings Institution Press, 2000.

Taylor, Lance, ed. *After Neoliberalism: What Next for Latin America?* Ann Arbor, MI: University of Michigan Press, 1998.

Tenenbaum, Barbara A. *Encyclopedia of Latin American History and Culture*. New York: Scribner, 1996.

Thorp, Rosemary. *Progress, Exclusion and Poverty: an Economic History of Latin America in the 20th Century*. Washington, DC: Inter-American Development Bank, 1998.

Turner, Barry. *Latin America Profiled: Essential Facts on Society, Business and Politics in Latin America*. New York: Saint Martin's Press, 2000.

Valtmeyer, Henry and James F. Petras. *Dynamics of Social Change in Latin America*. New York: Saint Martin's Press, 2000.

Vera, Leonardo. *Stabilization and Growth in Latin America: a Critique and Reconciliation*. New York: Saint Martin's Press, 2000.

Von Mettenheim, Kurt and James M. Malloy. *Deepening Democracy in Latin America*. Pittsburgh, PA: University of Pittsburgh Press, 1998.

Caribbean

Beckles, Hilary M. and Verene Shepherd, eds. *Caribbean Freedom: Economy and Society from Emancipation to the Present*. Princeton, NJ: Markus Wiener Publishers, 1998.

Braveboy-Wagner, Jacqueline and Dennis J. Gayle, eds. *Caribbean Public Policy Issues of the 1990s*. Boulder, CO: Westview Press, 1997.

Braveboy-Wagner, Jacqueline, et al. *The Caribbean in the Pacific Century: Prospects for Caribbean-Pacific Cooperation*. Boulder, CO: Lynne Rienner Publishers, 1993.

Braveboy-Wagner, Jacqueline A. *The Caribbean in World Affairs: the Foreign Policies of the English-Speaking States*. Boulder, CO: Westview Press, 2000.

Carvajal, Manuel J. *The Caribbean, 1975-1980: a Bibliography of Economic and Rural Development*. Lanham, MD: Scarecrow Press, 1993.

Craton, Michael. *Empire, Enslavement and Freedom in the Caribbean*. Princeton, NJ: Markus Wiener Publishers, 1997.

Desch, Michael C., et al., eds. *From Pirates to Drug Lords: the Post-Cold War Caribbean Security Environment*. Albany, NY: State University of New York Press, 1998.

Dominguez, Jorge I., ed. *Democracy in the Caribbean: Political, Economic, and Social Perspectives*. Baltimore, MD: Johns Hopkins University Press, 1993.

Dominguez, Jorge I. *Democratic Politics in Latin America and the Caribbean*. Baltimore, MD: Johns Hopkins University Press, 1998.

Granberry, Julian, ed. *An Encyclopaedia Caribbeana: a Research Guide*. Detroit, MI: Omnigraphics, 2000.

Griffith, Ivelaw L. *The Political Economy of Drugs in the Caribbean*. New York: Saint Martin's Press, 2000.

Griffith, Ivelaw L. *The Quest for Security in the Caribbean: Problems and Promises in Subordinate States*. Armonk, NY: M.E. Sharpe, 1993.

Grugel, Jean. *Politics and Development in the Caribbean Basin: Central America and the Caribbean in the New World Order*. Bloomington, IN: Indiana University Press, 1995.

Maingot, Anthony P. *The United States and the Caribbean: Challenges of an Asymmetrical Relationship*. Boulder, CO: Westview Press, 1994.

Marshall, Don D. *Caribbean Political Economy at the Crossroads: NAFTA and Regional Developmentalism*. New York: Saint Martin's Press, 1998.

Meditz, Sandra W. and Dennis M. Hanratty. *Islands of the Commonwealth of the Caribbean: a Regional Study*. Washington, DC: U.S. GPO, 1989.

Palmer, Ransford W., ed. *U.S.-Caribbean Relations: Their Impact on Peoples and Cultures*. Westport, CT: Greenwood Publishing Group, 1998.

Payne, Anthony and Paul Sutton, eds. *Modern Caribbean Politics*. Baltimore, MD: Johns Hopkins University Press, 1993.

Portes, Alejandro, ed. *The Urban Caribbean: Transition to the New Global Economy*. Baltimore, MD: Johns Hopkins University Press, 1997.

Sheperd, Verene, ed. *Women in Caribbean History*. Princeton, NJ: Markus Wiener Publishers, 1999.

Smith, Robert Freeman. *The Caribbean World and the United States: Mixing Rum and Coca-Cola*. Boston, MA: Twayne Publishers, 1994.

Stallings, Barbara and Wilson Peres. *Growth, Equity and Employment: the Impact of the Economic Reforms in Latin America and the Caribbean*. Washington, DC: Brookings Institution Press, 2000.

Taylor, Patrick. *Nation Dance: Religion, Identity and Cultural Difference in the Caribbean*. Bloomington, IN: Indiana University Press, 2000.

Tulchin, Joseph S. and Ralph H. Espach, eds. *Security in the Caribbean Basin: the Challenge of Regional Cooperation*. Boulder, CO: Lynne Rienner Publishers, 2000.

Central America

Alexander, Robert J. *Presidents of Central America, Mexico, Cuba and Hispaniola: Conversations and Correspondence*. New York: Praeger, 1995.

Brockett, Charles D. *Land, Power and Poverty: Agrarian Transformation and Political Conflict in Central America*. Boulder, CO: Westview Press, 1998.

Coatsworth, John H. *Central America and the United States: the Clients and the Colossus*. Boston, MA: Twayne Publishers, 1994.

Dominguez, Jorge I., ed. *Democratic Transitions in Central America*. Gainesville, FL: University Press of Florida, 1997.

Foster, Lynn V. *A Brief History of Central America*. New York: Facts on File, 2000.

Krenn, Michael L. *The Chains of Interdependence: U.S. Policy toward Central America, 1945-1954*. Armonk, NY: M.E. Sharpe, 1996.

Langley, Lester D. and Thomas Schoonover. *The Banana Men: American Mercenaries and Entrepreneurs in Central America, 1880-1930*. Lexington, KY: University Press of Kentucky, 1995.

Lentner, Howard H. *State Formation in Central America: the Struggle for Autonomy, Development, and Democracy.* Westport, CT: Greenwood Publishing Publishing, 1993.

LeoGrande, William M. *Our Own Backyard: the United Stated in Central America, 1977-1992.* Chapel Hill, NC: University of North Carolina Press, 1998.

Moreno, Dario. *The Struggle for Peace in Central America.* Gainesville, FL: University Press of Florida, 1994.

Paige, Jeffery M. *Coffee and Power: Revolution and the Rise of Democracy in Central America.* Cambridge, MA: Harvard University Press, 1997.

Scott, Peter D. *Cocaine Politics: Drugs, Armies and the CIA in Central America.* Berkeley, CA: University of California Press, 1998.

Torres-Rivas, Edelberto. *History and Society in Central America.* Austin, TX: University of Texas Press, 1993.

Walker, Thomas W. and Ariel C. Armony, eds. *Repression, Resistance and Democratic Transition in Central America.* Wilmington, DE: Scholarly Resources, 2000.

Weaver, Frederick Stirton. *Inside the Volcano: the History and Political Economy of Central America.* Boulder, CO: Westview Press, 1994.

Woodward, Ralph L. Jr. *Central America: a Nation Divided.* New York: Oxford University Press, 1999.

Argentina

Adelman, Jeremy. *Republic of Capital: Buenos Aires and the Legal Transformation of the Atlantic World.* Stanford, CA: Stanford University Press, 1999.

Alonso, Paula. *Between Revolution and the Ballot Box: the Origins of the Argentine Radical Party.* New York: Cambridge University Press, 2000.

Armory, Ariel C. *Argentina, the United States, and the Anti-Communist Crusade in Central America.* Athens, OH: Ohio University Press, 1997.

Balze, Felipe A.M. de la. *Remaking the Argentine Economy.* New York: Council on Foreign Relations, 1995.

Biggins, Alan. *Argentina.* Santa Barbara, CA: ABC-CLIO, 1991.

Cavarozzi, Marcelo. *Argentina.* Boulder, CO: Westview Press, 1999.

Deutsch, Sandra McGee and Ronald H. Dolkart, eds. *The Argentine Right: Its History and Intellectual Origins, 1910 to the Present.* Wilmington, DE: Scholarly Resources, 1993.

Erro, Davide G. *Resolving the Argentine Paradox: Politics and Development, 1966-1992.* Boulder, CO: Lynne Rienner Publishers, 1993.

Escude, Carlos. *Foreign Policy Theory in Menem's Argentina.* Gainesville, FL: University Press of Florida, 1997.

Feitlowitz, Marguerite. *A Lexicon of Terror: Argentina and the Legacies of Torture.* New York: Oxford University Press, 1998.

Foster, David W. and Melissa F. Lockhart. *Culture and Customs of Argentina.* Westport, CT: Greenwood Publishing Group, 1998.

Horvath, Laszlo. *A Half Century of Peronism, 1943-1993: an International Bibliography.* Stanford, CA: Hoover Institution Press, 1993.

Ivereigh, Austen. *Catholicism and Politics in Argentina, 1810-1960.* New York: Saint Martin's Press, 1995.

Keeling, David J. *Contemporary Argentina: a Geographical Perspective.* Boulder, CO: Westview Press, 1997.

Manzetti, Luigi. *Institutions, Parties, and Coalitions in Argentine Politics.* Pittsburgh, PA: University of Pittsburgh Press, 1993.

Munck, Gerardo L. *Authoritarianism and Democratization: Soldiers and Workers in Argentina, 1976-1983.* University Park, PA: Pennsylvania State University Press, 1998.

Rein, Monica. Translated by Martha Grenzeback. *Politics and Education in Argentina, 1946-1962.* Armonk, NY: M.E. Sharpe, 1998.

Rock, David. *Authoritarian Argentina: the Nationalist Movement, Its History and Its Impact.* Berkeley, CA: University of California Press, 1993.

Sawers, Larry. *The Other Argentina: the Interior and National Development.* Boulder, CO: Westview Press, 1996.

Shumway, Nicolas. *The Invention of Argentina.* Berkeley, CA: University of California Press, 1996.

Tulchin, Joseph S., ed. *Argentina: the Challenge of Modernization.* Wilmington, DE: Scholarly Resources, 1998.

Barbados

Beckles, Hilary McD. *A History of Barbados: from Amerindian Settlement to Nation-State.* New York: Cambridge University Press, 1990.

Belize

Merrill, Tim L., ed. *Guyana and Belize: Country Studies.* Washington, DC: U.S. GPO, 2nd ed. 1993.

Sutherland, Anne. *The Making of Belize: Globalization in the Margins.* Westport, CT: Greenwood Publishing Group, 1998.

Wright, Peggy and Brian E. Coutts. *Belize.* Santa Barbara, CA: ABC-CLIO, 2nd ed. 1993.

Bolivia

Gallo, Carmenza. *Taxes and State Power: Political Instability in Bolivia, 1900-1950.* Philadelphia, PA: Temple University Press, 1991.

Gill, Lesley. *Teetering on the Rim: Global Restructuring, Daily Life and the Armed Retreat of the Bolivian State.* New York: Columbia University Press, 2000.

Hudson, Rex A. and Dennis M. Hanratty, eds. *Bolivia: a Country Study.* Washington, DC: U.S. GPO, 3rd ed. 1991.

Lehman, Kenneth D. *Bolivia and the United States: a Limited Partnership.* Athens, GA: University of Georgia Press, 1999.

Leons, Madeline B. and Harry Sanabria, eds. *Coca, Cocaine, and the Bolivian Reality.* Albany, NY: State University of New York Press, 1997.

Morales, Waltraud. *Bolivia: Land of Struggle.* Boulder, CO: Westview Press, 1992.

Brazil

Baronov, David. *The Abolition of Slavery in Brazil: the "Liberation" of Africans through the Emancipation of Capital.* Westport, CT: Greenwood Publishing Group, 2000.

Boxer, C.R. *The Golden Age of Brazil: Growing Pains of a Colonial Society.* New York: Saint Martin's Press, 1995.

Bresser Pereira, Luiz Carlos. *Economic Crisis and State Reform in Brazil: toward a New Interpretation of Latin America.* Boulder, CO: Lynne Rienner Publishers, 1996.

Burns, E. Bradford. *A History of Brazil.* New York: Columbia University Press, 3rd ed. 1993.

Capistrano de Abreu, João. *Chapters in Brazil's Colonial History, 1500-1800.* New York: Oxford University Press, 1997.

Cavalcanti, Clovis de Vasconcelos, ed. *The Environment, Sustainable Development and Public Policies: Building Sustainability in Brazil.* Northampton, MA: Edward Elgar Publishing, 2000.

Cavaliero, Roderick. *The Independence of Brazil.* New York: Saint Martin's Press, 1993.

Chaffee, Wilber A. *Desenvolvimento: Politics and Economy in Brazil.* Boulder, CO: Lynne Rienner Publishers, 1997.

Eakin, Marshall C. *Brazil: Once and Future Country.* New York: Saint Martin's Press, 1997.

Fausto, Boris. *A Concise History of Brazil.* New York: Cambridge University Press, 1999.

Goertzel, Ted G. *Fernando Henrique Cardoso: Reinventing Democracy in Brazil.* Boulder, CO: Lynne Rienner Publishers, 1999.

Hanchard, Michael. *Racial Politics in Contemporary Brazil.* Durham, NC: Duke University Press, 1999.

Hecht, Tobias. *At Home in the Street: Street Children in Northeast Brazil.* New York: Cambridge University Press, 1998.

Hudson, Rex A., ed. *Brazil: a Country Study.* Washington, DC: U.S. GPO, 5th ed. 1998.

Hunter, Wendy. *Eroding Military Influence in Brazil: Politicians against Soldiers.* Chapel Hill, NC: University of North Carolina Press, 1997.

Kingstone, Peter R. and Timothy J. Powers, eds. *Democratic Brazil: Actors, Institutions and Processes.* Pittsburgh, PA: University of Pittsburgh Press, 2000.

Lesser, Jeff. *Negotiating National Identity: Immigrants, Minorities, and the Struggle* for Ethnicity in Brazil. Durham, NC: Duke University Press, 1999.

Levine, Robert M. Brazilian Legacies. Armonk, NY: M.E. Sharpe, 1997.

Levine, Robert M. and John J. Crocitti, eds. The Brazil Reader: History, Culture, Politics. Durham, NC: Duke University Press, 1999.

Levine, Robert M. Father of the Poor? Vargas and His Era. New York: Cambridge University Press, 1998.

Mainwaring, Scott. Rethinking Party Systems in the Third Wave of Democratization: the Case of Brazil. Stanford, CA: Stanford University Press, 1999.

Page, Joseph A. The Brazilians. Reading, MA: Addison-Wesley, 1995.

Power, Timothy J. The Political Right in Postauthoritarian Brazil: Elites, Institutions and Democratization. University Park, PA: Pennsylvania State University Press, 2000.

Purcell, Susan K. Brazil under Cardoso. Boulder, CO: Lynne Rienner Publishers, 1997.

Ribeiro, Darcy and Gregory Rabassa. The Brazilian People: the Formation and Meaning of Brazil. Gainesville, FL: University Press of Florida, 2000.

Robinson, Roger. Brazil. Des Plaines, IL: Heinemann Library, 1999.

Skidmore, Thomas E. Brazil: Five Centuries of Change. New York: Oxford University Press, 1999.

Topik, Steven C. Trade and Gunboats: the United States and Brazil in the Age of Empire. Stanford, CA: Stanford University Press, 2000.

Von Mettenheim, Kurt. The Brazilian Voter: Mass Politics in Democratic Transition. Pittsburgh, PA: University of Pittsburgh Press, 1995.

Weyland, Kurt Gerhard. Democracy without Equity: Failures of Reform in Brazil. Pittsburgh, PA: University of Pittsburgh Press, 1996.

Willumsen, Maria J., ed. The Brazilian Economy: Structure and Performance. Coral Gables, FL: University of Miami, North/South Center Press, 1997.

Chile

Bosworth, Barry P., ed. The Chilean Economy: Policy and Challenges. Washington, DC: Brookings Institution Press, 1994.

Collier, Simon and William F. Sater. A History of Chile, 1808-1994. New York: Cambridge University Press, 1996

Constanble, Pamela and Arturo Valenzuela. A Nation of Enemies: Chile under Pinochet. New York: W.W. Norton, 1993.

Hachette, Dominique and Rolf Luders. Privatization in Chile: an Economic Appraisal. San Francisco, CA: ICS Press, 1993.

Hojman, David E. Chile: the Political Economy of Development and Democracy in the 1990s. Pittsburgh, PA: University of Pittsburgh Press, 1993.

Hudson, Rex A., ed. Chile: a Country Study. Washington, DC: U.S. GPO, 3rd ed. 1994.

Lomnitz, Larissa Adler and Ana Melnick. Chile's Political Culture and Parties: an Anthropological Explanation. Notre Dame, IN: University of Notre Dame Press, 2000.

Lonregan, John B. Legislative Institutions and Ideology in Chile. New York: Cambridge University Press, 2000.

Monteon, Michael. Chile and the Great Depression: the Politics of Underdevelopment, 1927-1948. Tempe, AZ: Arizona State University, Center for Latin American Studies, 1998.

Oppenheim, Lois Hecht. Politics in Chile: Democracy, Authoritarianism, and the Search for Development. Boulder, CO: Westview Press, 2nd ed. 1998.

Oxhorn, Philip. Organizing Civil Society: the Popular Sectors and the Struggle for Democracy in Chile. University Park, PA: Pennsylvania State University Press, 1995.

Petras, James, et. al. Democracy and Poverty in Chile: the Limits to Electoral Politics. Boulder, CO: Westview Press, 1994.

Pietrobelli, Carlo. Industry, Competitiveness and Technological Capabilities in Chile: a New Tiger from Latin America. New York: Saint Martin's Press, 1998.

Puryear, Jeffrey. Thinking Politics: Intellectuals and Democracy in Chile, 1973-1988. Baltimore, MD: Johns Hopkins University Press, 1994.

Roberts, Kenneth M. Deepening Democracy? The Modern Left and Social Movements in Chile and Peru. Stanford, CA: Stanford University Press, 1999.

Siavelis, Peter. The President and Congress in Post-Authoritarian Chile: Institutional Constraints to Democratic Consolidation. University Park, PA: Pennsylvania State University Press, 1999.

Sigmund, Paul E. The United States and Democracy in Chile. Baltimore, MD: Johns Hopkins University Press, 1993.

Silva, Eduardo. The State and Capital in Chile: Business Elites, Technocrats, and Market Economics. Boulder, CO: Westview Press, 1996.

Solimano, Andres. Distributive Justice and Economic Development: the Case of Chile and Developing Countries. Ann Arbor, MI: University of Michigan Press, 2000.

Spooner, Mary Helen. Soldiers in a Narrow Land: the Pinochet Regime in Chile. Berkeley, CA: University of California Press, 1994.

Valdes, Juan Gabriel. Pinochet's Economists: the Chicago School in Chile. New York: Cambridge University Press, 1995.

Colombia

Davis, Robert H. Historical Dictionary of Colombia. Lanham, MD: Scarecrow Press, 2nd ed. 1993.

Drexler, Robert W. Colombia and the United States: Narcotics Traffic and a Failed Foreign Policy. Jefferson, NC: McFarland & Company, 1997.

Duzan, Maria Jimena. Translated and edited by Peter Eisner. Death Beat: a Colombian Journalist's Life inside the Cocaine Wars. New York: HarperCollins, 1994.

Hanratty, Dennis M. and Sandra W. Meditz, eds. Colombia: a Country Study. Washington, DC: U.S. GPO, 4th ed. 1990.

Kline, Harvey F. Colombia: Democracy under Assault. Boulder, CO: Westview Press, 2nd ed. 1995.

Kline, Harvey F. State Building and Conflict Resolution in Colombia, 1986-1994. Tuscaloosa, AL: University of Alabama Press, 1999.

McFarlane, Anthony. Colombia before Independence: Economy, Society, and Politics under Bourbon Rule. New York: Cambridge University Press, 1993.

Menzel, Sewall H. Cocaine Quagmire: Implementing the U.S. Anti-Drug Policy in the North Andes-Colombia. Lanham, MD: University Press of America, 1997.

Mohan, Rakesh. Understanding the Developing Metropolis: Lessons from the Study of Bogota and Cali, Colombia. New York: Oxford University Press, 1994.

Posada-Carbo, Eduardo. Colombia. New York: Saint Martin's Press, 1997.

Rausch, Jane M. The Llanos Frontier in Colombian History, 1830-1930. Albuquerque, NM: University of New Mexico Press, 1993.

Thorpe, Rosemary. Economic Management and Economic Development in Peru and Colombia. Pittsburgh, PA: University of Press, 1991.

Thoumi, Francisco E. Political Economy and Illegal Drugs in Colombia. Boulder, CO: Lynne Rienner Publishers, 1995.

Wade, Peter. Blackness and Race Mixture: the Dynamics of Racial Identity in Colombia. Baltimore, MD: Johns Hopkins University Press, 1993.

Costa Rica

Basok, Tanya. Keeping Heads above Water: Salvadorean Refuges in Costa Rica. Toronto: University of Toronto Press, 1993.

Booth, John A. Costa Rica: Quest for Democracy. Boulder, CO: Westview Press, 1998.

Colesberry, Adrian and Brass McLean. Costa Rica: the Last Country the Gods Made. Helena, MT: Falcon Press, 1993.

Creedman, Theodore S. Historical Dictionary of Costa Rica. Lanham, MD: Scarecrow Press, 2nd ed. 1991.

Edelman, Marc. Peasants against Globalization: Rural Social Movements in Costa Rica. Stanford, CA: Stanford University Press, 2000.

Helmuth, Chalene. Culture and Customs of Costa Rica. Westport, CT: Greenwood Publishing Group, 2000.

Honey, Martha. Hostile Acts: U.S. Policy in Costa Rica in the 1980s. Gainesville, FL: University of Florida Press, 1994.

Miller, Eugene D. *A Holy Alliance? The Church and the Left in Costa Rica, 1932-1948*. Armonk, NY: M.E. Sharpe, 1996.

Rottenberg, Simon, ed. *Costa Rica and Uruguay*. New York: Oxford University Press, 1993.

Stansifer, Charles L. *Costa Rica*. Santa Barbara, CA: ABC-CLIO, 1991.

Wilson, Bruce M. *Costa Rica: Politics, Economics, and Democracy*. Boulder, CO: Lynne Rienner Publishers, 1998.

Yashar, Deborah J. *Demanding Democracy: Reform and Reaction in Costa Rica and Guatemala, 1870s-1950s*. Stanford, CA: Stanford University Press, 1997.

Cuba

Arbdeya, Jesus. Translated by Rafael Betancourt. *The Cuban Counterrevolution*. Athens, OH: Ohio University Press, 2000.

Baloyara, Enrique and James A. Morris. *Conflict and Change in Cuba*. Albuquerque, NM: University of New Mexico Press, 1993.

Benjamin-Alvarado, Jonathan. *Power to the People: Energy and the Cuban Nuclear Program*. New York: Routledge, 2000.

Blight, James G, et al. *Cuba on the Brink: Castro, the Missile Crisis, and the Soviet Collapse*. New York: Pantheon Books, 1993.

Bunck, Julie Marie. *Fidel Castro and the Quest for a Revolutionary Culture in Cuba*. University Park, PA: Pennsylvania State University, 1994.

Diaz-Briquets, Sergio and Jorge Perez-Lopez. *Conquering Nature: the Environmental Legacy of Socialism in Cuba*. Pittsburgh, PA: University of Pittsburgh Press, 2000.

Fernandez, Damian J. *Cuba and the Politics of Passion*. Austin, TX: University of Texas Press, 2000.

Fursenko, Alexandr and Timothy J. Naftali. *"One Hell of a Gamble": Khrushchev, Castro and Kennedy, 1958-1964*. New York: W.W. Norton & Company, 1997.

Halperin, Maurice. *Return to Havana: the Decline of Cuban Society under Castro*. Nashville, TN: Vanderbilt University Press, 1994.

Hernandez, José M. *Cuba and the United States: Intervention and Militarism, 1868-1933*. Austin, TX: University of Texas Press, 1993.

Ibarra, Jorge. *Prologue to Revolution: Cuba, 1898-1958*. Boulder, CO: Lynne Rienner Publishers, 1998.

Jordan, David C. *Revolutionary Cuba and the End of the Cold War*. Lanham, MD: University Press of America, 1993.

Kirk, John M. *Canada-Cuba Relations: the Other Good Neighbor Policy*. Gainesville, FL: University Press of Florida, 1997.

Kornbluh, Peter, ed. *Bay of Pigs Declassified: the Secret CIA Report*. New York: New Press, 1998.

Leonard, Thomas M. *Castro and the Cuban Revolution*. Westport, CT: Greenwood Publishing Group, 1999.

Luis, Julio Garcia. *Cuban Revolution Reader: a Documented History of 40 Years of the Cuban Revolution*. Hoboken, NJ: Ocean Press, 2000.

Mesa-Largo, Carmelo, ed. *Cuba after the Cold War*. Pittsburgh, PA: University of Pittsburgh Press, 1993.

Moses, Catherine. *Real Life in Castro's Cuba*. Wilmington, DE: Scholarly Resources, 1999.

Paterson, Thomas G. *Contesting Castro: the United States and the Triumph of the Cuban Revolution*. New York: Oxford University Press, 1994.

Perez, Louis A., Jr. *On Becoming Cuban: Identity, Nationality and Culture*. Chapel Hill, NC: University of North Carolina Press, 1999.

Perez-Lopez, Jorge F. *Cuba at a Crossroads: Politics and Economics after the Fourth Party Congress*. Gainesville, FL: University of Florida Press, 1994.

Perez-Lopez, Jorge F. *Cuba's Second Economy: from behind the Scenes to Center State*. New Brunswick, NJ: Transaction Publishers, 1995.

Perez-Stable, Marifeli. *The Cuban Revolution: Origins, Course, and Legacy*. New York: Oxford University Press, 2nd ed. 1999.

Purcell, Susan Kaufman and David Rothkopf, eds. *Cuba: the Contours of Change*. Boulder, CO: Lynne Rienner Publishers, 2000.

Quirk, Robert E. *Fidel Castro*. New York: W.W. Norton, 1993.

Ritter, Archibald R.M. and John M. Kirk, eds. *Cuba in the International System: Normalization and Integration*. New York: Saint Martin's Press, 1995.

Roy, Joaquín. *Cuba, the United States, and the Helms-Burton Doctrine: International Reactions*. Gainesville, FL: University Press of Florida, 2000.

Santi, Enrico Mario, ed. *Cuban Studies XXIV*. Pittsburgh, PA: University of Pittsburgh Press, 1994.

Schwab, Peter. *Cuba: Confronting the U.S. Embargo*. New York: Saint Martin's Press, 2000.

Schulz, Donald E. *Cuba and the Future*. Westport, CT: Greenwood Press, 1994.

Skoug, Kenneth N. *The United States and Cuba under Reagan and Shultz: a Foreign Service Officer Reports*. New York: Praeger, 1996.

Stubbs, Jean, et al. *Cuba*. Santa Barbara, CA: ABC-CLIO, 1996.

Suchlicki, Jaime. *Cuba: from Columbus to Castro and Beyond*. McLean, VA: Brassey's, Inc.: 4th ed. 1997.

Tulchin, Joseph S., et al., eds. *Cuba and the Caribbean: Regional Issues and Trends in the Post-Cold War Era*. Wilmington, DE: Scholarly Resources, 1997.

Dominican Republic

Atkins, G. Pope. *The Dominican Republic and the United States: from Imperialism to Transnationalism*. Athens, GA: University of Georgia Press, 1998.

Baud, Michiel. *Peasants and Tobacco in the Dominican Republic, 1870-1930*. Knoxville, TN: University of Tennessee Press, 1995.

Haggerty, Richard A., ed. *Dominican Republic and Haiti: Country Studies*. Washington, DC: U.S. GPO, 2nd ed. 1991.

Hall, Michael R. *Sugar and Power in the Dominican Republic: Eisenhower, Kennedy and the Trujillos*. Westport, CT: Greenwood Publishing Group, 2000.

Hartlyn, Jonathan. *The Struggle for Democratic Politics in the Dominican Republic, 1961-1996*. Chapel Hill, NC: University of North Carolina Press, 1998.

Howard, David. *Dominican Republic: a Guide to the People, Politics and Culture*. Northampton, MA: Interlink Publishing Group, 1999.

Roorda, Eric. *The Dictator Next Door: the Good Neighbor Policy and the Trujillo Regime in the Dominican Republic, 1930-1945*. Durham, NC: Duke University Press, 1998.

Sagás, Ernesto. *Race and Politics in the Dominican Republic*. Gainesville, FL: University Press of Florida, 2000.

Ecuador

Alchon, Suzanne Austin. *Native Society and Disease in Colonial Ecuador*. New York: Cambridge University Press, 1991.

de la Torre, Carlos. *Populist Seduction in Latin America: the Ecuadorian Experience*. Athens, OH: Ohio University Press, 2000.

Goffin, Alvin M. *The Rise of Protestant Evangelism in Ecuador, 1895-1990*. Gainesville, FL: University Press of Florida, 1994.

Hanratty, Dennis M., ed. *Ecuador: a Country Study*. Washington, DC: U.S. GPO, 3rd ed. 1991.

Hey, Jeanne A.K. *Theories of Dependent Foreign Policy and the Case of Ecuador in the 1980s*. Athens, OH: Ohio University Press, 1995.

Isaacs, Anita. *The Politics of Military Rule and Transition in Ecuador, 1972-92*. Pittsburgh, PA: University of Pittsburgh Press, 1993.

Muratorio, Blanca. *The Life and Times of Grandfather Alonso: Culture and History in the Upper Amazon*. New Brunswick, NJ: Rutgers University Press, 1991.

El Salvador

Angel, José, et al. *Strategy and Tactics of the Salvadoran FMLN Guerrillas: Last Battle of the Cold War, Blueprint for Future Conflicts*. New York: Praeger, 1995.

Beirne, Charles Joseph. *Jesuit Education and Social Change in El Salvador*. New York: Garland Publishing, 1996.

Didion, Joan. *Salvador*. New York: Vintage, 1994.

Doggett, Martha. *Death Foretold: the Jesuit Murders in El Salvador*. Washington, DC: Georgetown University Press, 1993.

Grenier, Yvon. *The Emergence of Insurgency in El Salvador: Ideology and Political Will.* Pittsburgh, PA: University of Pittsburgh Press, 1999.

Haggerty, Richard A., ed. *El Salvador: a Country Study.* Washington, DC: U.S. GPO, 2nd ed. 1990.

Hammond, John L. *Fighting to Learn: Popular Education and Guerrilla War in El Salvador.* New Brunswick, NJ: Rutgers University Press, 1998.

Hassett, John and Hugh Lacey, eds. *Toward a Society that Serves Its People: the Intellectual Contribution of El Salvador's Murdered Jesuits.* Washington, DC: Georgetown University Press, 1991.

Marenn, M.J. *Salvador's Children: a Song for Survival.* Columbus, OH: Ohio State University, 1993.

Pelupessy, Wim. *The Limits of Economic Reform in El Salvador.* New York: Saint Martin's Press, 1997.

Popkin, Margaret L. *Peace without Justice: Obstacles to Building the Rule of Law in El Salvador.* University Park, PA: Pennsylvania State University, 2000.

Quizar, Robin O. *My Turn to Weep: Salvadoran Women in Costa Rica.* Westport, CT: Greenwood Publishing Group, 1998.

Ucles, Mario L. Translated by Amelia F. Shogun. *El Salvador in the 1980's: Counterinsurgency and Revolution.* Philadelphia, PA: Temple University Press, 1996.

Williams, Philip J. *Militarization and Demilitarization in El Salvador's Transition to Democracy.* Pittsburgh, PA: University of Pittsburgh Press, 1998.

Grenada

Heine, Jorge, ed. *A Revolution Aborted: the Lessons of Grenada.* Pittsburgh, PA: University of Pittsburgh Press, 1990.

Guatemala

Benz, Stephen Connely. *Guatemalan Journey.* Austin, TX: University of Texas Press, 1996.

Dosal, Paul J. *Doing Business with the Dictators: a Political History of the United Fruit in Guatemala, 1899-1944.* Wilmington, DE: Scholarly Resources, 1993.

Dosal, Paul J. *Power in Transition: the Rise of Guatemala's Industrial Oligarchy, 1871-1994.* New York: Praeger, 1995.

Grandin, Greg. *The Blood of Guatemala: a History of Race and Nation.* Durham, NC: Duke University Press, 2000.

Handy, Jim. *Revolution in the Countryside: Rural Conflict and Agrarian Reform in Guatemala, 1944-1954.* Chapel Hill, NC: University of North Carolina Press, 1994.

Hendrickson, Carol. *Weaving Identities: Construction of Dress and Self in a Highland Guatemalan Town.* Austin, TX: University of Texas Press, 1995.

Jonas, Susanne. *Of Centaurs and Doves: Guatemala's Peace Process.* Boulder, CO: Westview Press, 2000

Jones, Oakah L. *Guatemala in the Spanish Colonial Period.* Norman, OK: University of Oklahoma Press, 1994.

Levenson-Estrada, Deborah. *Trade Unionists against Terror: Guatemala City, 1954-1985.* Chapel Hill, NC: University of North Carolina Press, 1994.

Lovell, George W. *A Beauty That Hurts: Life and Death in Guatemala.* Austin, TX: University of Texas Press, rev. ed 2000.

McCleary, Rachel M. *Dictating Democracy: Guatemala and the End of Violent Revolution.* Gainesville, FL: University Press of Florida, 1999.

McCreery, David. *Rural Guatemala, 1760-1940.* Stanford, CA: Stanford University Press, 1994.

Nelson, Diane M. *A Finger in the Wound: Body Politics in Quincentennial Guatemala.* Berkeley, CA: University of California Press, 1999.

Perera, Victor. *Unfinished Conquest: the Guatemalan Tragedy.* Berkeley, CA: University of California Press, 1993.

Schirmer, Jennifer. *The Guatemalan Military Project: a Violence Called Democracy.* Philadelphia, PA: University of Pennsylvania Press, 1998.

Shea, Maureen E. *Culture and Customs of Guatemala.* Westport, CT: Greenwood Publishing Group, 2000.

Stoll, David. *Between Two Armies: in the Ixil Towns of Guatemala.* New York: Columbia University Press, 1993.

Stoll, David. *Rigoberta Menchu and the Story of All Poor Guatemalans.* Boulder, CO: Westview Press, 1998.

Trudeau, Robert H. *Guatemalan Politics: the Popular Struggle for Democracy.* Boulder, CO: Lynne Rienner Publishers, 1993.

Woodward, Ralph Lee. *Guatemala.* Santa Barbara, CA: ABC-CLIO, rev. ed. 1992.

Woodward, Ralph Lee. *Rafael Carrera and the Emergence of the Republic of Guatemala.* Athens, GA: University of Georgia Press, 1993.

Yashar, Deborah J. *Demanding Democracy: Reform and Reaction in Costa Rica and Guatemala., 1850s-1950s.* Stanford, CA: Stanford University Press, 1997.

Zimmerman, Marc. *Literature and Resistance in Guatemala: Textual Modes and Cultural Politics from El Señor Presidente to Rigoberta Menchu.* Athens, OH: Ohio University Press, 1995.

Guyana

Da Costa, Emilia Viotti. *Crowns of Glory, Tears of Blood: the Demerara Slave Rebellion of 1823.* New York: Oxford University Press, 1994.

Merrill, Tim L., ed. *Guyana and Belize: Country Studies.* Washington, DC: U.S. GPO, 2nd ed. 1993.

Williams, Brackette F. *Stains on My Name, War in My Veins: Guyana and the Politics of Struggle.* Durham, NC: Duke University Press, 1991.

Williams, David P., et al., eds. *Privatiza-*

tion vs. Community: the Rise and Fall of Industrial Welfare in Guyana. Lanham, MD: Rowman & Littlefield, 1998.

Haiti

Chambers, Frances, ed. *Haiti.* Santa Barbara, CA: ABC-CLIO, 2nd ed. 1994.

Gibbons, Elizabeth D. *Sanctions in Haiti: Human Rights and Democracy under Assault.* Westport, CT: Greenwood Publishing Group, 1999.

Haggerty, Richard A., ed. *Dominican Republic and Haiti: Country Studies.* Washington, DC: U.S. GPO, 2nd ed, 1991.

Kumar, Chetan. *Building Peace in Haiti.* Boulder, CO: Lynne Rienner Publishers, 1998.

Laguerre, Michel S. *The Military Society in Haiti.* Knoxville, TN: University of Tennessee Press, 1993.

Langley, Lester D. *The Americas in the Age of Revolution, 1750-1850.* New Haven, CT: Yale University Press, 1996.

Perusse, Roland I. *Haitian Democracy Restored, 1991-1995.* Lanham, MD: University Press of America, 1995.

Rotberg, Robert I., ed. *Haiti Renewed: Political and Economic Prospects.* Washington, DC: Brookings Institution Press, 1997.

Stotzky, Irwin P. *Silencing Guns in Haiti: the Promise of Deliberative Democracy.* Chicago: University of Chicago Press, 1997.

Weinstein, Brian and Aaron Segal. *Haiti: the Failure of Politics.* New York: Praeger, 1992.

Zephir, Flore. *Haitian Immigrants in Black America: a Sociological and Sociolinguistic Portrait.* Westport, CT: Bergin & Garvey, 1996.

Honduras

Euraque, Dario A. *Region and State in Honduras, 1870-1972: Reinterpreting the "Banana Republic."* Chapel Hill, NC: University of North Carolina Press, 1996.

Merrill, Tim L. *Honduras: a Country Study.* Washington, DC: U.S. GPO, 3rd ed. 1995.

Meyer, Harvey Kessler and Jessie H. Meyer. *Historical Dictionary of Honduras.* Lanham, MD: Scarecrow Press, 2nd ed. 1994.

Jamaica

Butler, Kathleen Mary. *The Economics of Emancipation: Jamaica and Barbados, 1823-1843.* Chapel Hill, NC: University of North Carolina Press, 1995.

Gray, Obika. *Radicalism and Social Change in Jamaica, 1960-1972.* Knoxville, TN: University of Tennessee Press, 1991.

Heuman, Gad. *The Killing Time: the Morant Bay Rebellion in Jamaica.* Knoxville, TN: University of Tennessee Press, 1994.

Hewan, Clinton G. *Jamaica and the United States Caribbean Basin Initiative: Showpiece or Failure?* New York: Peter Lang Publishing, 1994.

Ingram, K.E. *Jamaica.* Santa Barbara, CA: ABC-CLIO, Inc., revised ed. 1997.

Keith, Nelson W. and Novella Z. Keith. *The Social Origins of Democratic Socialism in Jamaica.* Philadelphia, PA: Temple University Press, 1992.

Lundy, Patricia. *Debt and Adjustment: Social and Environmental Consequences in Jamaica.* Brookfield, VT: Ashgate, 1999.

Mordecai, Martin and Pamela Mordecai. *Culture and Customs of Jamaica.* Westport, CT: Greenwood Publishing Group, 2000.

Moser, Caroline and Jeremy Holland. *Urban Poverty and Violence in Jamaica.* Washington, DC: The World Bank, 1997.

Payne, Anthony J. *Politics in Jamaica.* New York: Saint Martin's Press, rev. ed. 1994.

Zips, Werner. Translated by Shelley L. Frisch. *Black Rebels: African-Caribbean Freedom Fighters in Jamaica.* Princeton, NJ: Markus Wiener Publishers, 1999.

Mexico

Alonso, Ana Maria. *Thread of Blood: Colonialism, Revolution, and Gender on Mexico's Northern Frontier.* Tucson, AZ: University of Arizona Press, 1995.

Aspe, Pedro. *Economic Transformation in the Mexican Way.* Cambridge, MA: MIT Press, 1993.

Bosworth, Barry P., et al., eds. *Coming Together? Mexico-U.S. Relations.* Washington, DC: Brookings Institution Press, 1997.

Britton, John A. *Revolution and Ideology: Images of the Mexican Revolution and the United States.* Lexington, KY: University Press of Kentucky, 1995.

Brunk, Samuel. *Emiliano Zapata: Revolution and Betrayal in Mexico.* Albuquerque, NW: University of New Mexico Press, 1995.

Bulmer-Thomas, Victor, et al., eds. *Mexico and the North American Free Trade Agreement: Who Will Benefit?* New York: Saint Martin's Press, 1994.

Butler, Edgar. *Mexico and Mexico City in the World Economy.* Boulder, CO: Westview Press, 2000.

Castañeda, Jorge G. *The Mexican Shock: Its Meaning for the U.S.* New York: New Press, 1995.

Chand, Vikram K. *Mexico's Political Awakening.* Notre Dame, IN: University of Notre Dame Press, 2000.

Cope, R. Douglas. *The Limits of Racial Domination: Plebeian Society in Colonial Mexico City, 1660-1720.* Madison, WI: University of Wisconsin Press, 1994.

Davis, Diane E. *Urban Leviathan: Mexico City in the Twentieth Century.* Philadelphia, PA: Temple University Press, 1994.

Dominguez, Jorge I. and James A. McCann. *Democratizating Mexico: Public Opinion and Electoral Choices.* Baltimore, MD: Johns Hopkins University Press, 1996.

Dominguez, Jorge I. and Alejandro Poire, eds. *Toward Mexico's Democratization: Parties, Campaigns, Elections and Public Opinion.* New York: Routledge, 1999.

Eisenhower, John S.D. *Intervention! The United Stated and the Mexican Revolution, 1913-1917.* New York: W.W. Norton, 1993.

Erfani, Julie A. *The Paradox of the Mexican State: Rereading Sovereignty from Independence to NAFTA.* Boulder, CO: Lynne Rienner Publishers, 1995.

Fehrenbach, T.R. *Fire and Blood: a History of Mexico.* New York: Da Capo Press, 1995.

Foster, Lynn V. *A Brief History of Mexico.* New York: Facts on File, 1997.

Garber, Peter M., ed. *The Mexico-U.S. Free Trade Agreement.* Cambridge, MA: MIT Press, 1994.

Gledhill, John. *Neoliberalism, Transnationalism and Rural Poverty: a Case Study of Michoacan, Mexico.* Boulder, CO: Westview Press, 1995.

Hamnett, Brian. *Juarez.* White Plains, NY: Longman Publishing, 1994.

Harvey, Neil, ed. *Mexico: Dilemmas of Transition.* London: British Academic Press, 1993.

Johns, Christina Jacqueline. *The Origins of Violence in Mexican Society.* New York: Praeger, 1995.

Jones, Richard C. *Ambivalent Journey: U.S. Migration and Economic Mobility in North-Central Mexico.* Tucson, AZ: University of Arizona Press, 1995.

Katz, Friedrich. *The Life and Times of Pancho Villa.* Stanford, CA: Stanford University Press, 1998.

Krauze, Enrique. *Mexico—Biography of Power: a History of Modern Mexico, 1810-1996.* New York: HarperCollins Publishers, 1997.

Krooth, Richard. *Mexico, NAFTA and the Hardships of Progress: Historical Patterns and Shifting Methods of Oppression.* Jefferson, NC: McFarland & Company, 1995.

Markiewicz, Dana. *The Mexican Revolution and the Limits of Agrarian Reform, 1915-1946.* Boulder, CO: Lynne Rienner Publishers, 1993.

Merrill, Tim L. and Ramon Miro, eds. *Mexico: a Country Study.* Washington, DC: U.S. GPO, 4th ed. 1997.

Meyer, Michael C., et al. *The Course of Mexican History.* New York: Oxford University Press, 1998.

Oppenheimer, Andres. *Bordering on Chaos: Guerrillas, Stockbrokers, Politicians and Mexico's Violent Struggle.* New York: Little, Brown, 1996.

Peters, Enrique Dussel. *Polarizing Mexico: the Impact of Liberalization Strategy.* Boulder, CO: Lynne Rienner Publishers, 2000.

Purcell, Susan K. and Luis Rubio, eds. *Mexico under Zedillo.* Boulder, CO: Lynne Rienner Publishers, 1998.

Rodriguez, Victoria E. and Peter M. Ward. *Opposition Government in Mexico.* Albuquerque, NM: University of New Mexico Press, 1995.

Roett, Riordan, ed. *Political and Economic Liberalization in Mexico: at a Critical Juncture?* Boulder, CO: Lynne Rienner Publishers, 1993.

Ruiz, Ramon E. *On the Rim of Mexico: Encounters of the Rich and Poor.* Boulder, CO: Westview Press, 1998.

Schulz, Donald E. and Edward J. Williams, eds. *Mexico Faces the 21st Century.* Westport, CT: Greenwood Publishing Group, 1995.

Sernau, Scott. *Economies of Exclusion: Underclass Poverty and Labor Market Change in Mexico.* New York: Praeger, 1994.

Staudt, Kathleen A. *Free Trade? Informal Economies at the U.S.-Mexican Border.* Philadelphia, PA: Temple University Press, 1998.

Thomas, Hugh. *Conquest: Montezuma, Cortes, and the Fall of Old Mexico.* New York: Simon & Schuster, 1994.

Wise, Carol. *The Post-NAFTA Political Economy: Mexico and the Western Hemisphere.* University Park, PA: Pennsylvania State University Press, 1998.

Womack, John Jr. *Rebellion in Chiapas: an Historical Reader.* New York: New Press, 1999.

Netherlands Antilles

Brown, Enid. *Suriname and the Netherlands Antilles: an Annotated English-Language Bibliography.* Lanham, MD: Scarecrow Press, 1992.

Sedoc-Dahlberg, Betty, ed. *The Dutch Caribbean: Prospects for Democracy.* New York: Gordon and Breach, 1990.

Nicaragua

Biondi-Morra, Brizio N. *Hungry Dream: the Failure of Food Policy in Revolutionary Nicaragua, 1979-1990.* Ithaca, NY: Cornell University Press, 1993.

Gambone, Michael D. *Eisenhower, Somoza and the Cold War in Nicaragua, 1953-1961.* Westport, CT: Greenwood Publishing Group, 1997.

Hale, Charles R. *Resistance and Contradiction: Miskitu Indians and the Nicaraguan State, 1894-1987.* Stanford, CA: Stanford University Press, 1994.

Kagan, Robert. *A Twilight Struggle: American Power and Nicaragua, 1977-1990.* New York: Free Press, 1996.

Luciak, Ilja A. *The Sandinista Legacy: Lessons from a Political Economy in Transition.* Gainesville, FL: University Press of Florida, 1995.

Merrill, Tim L., ed. *Nicaragua: a Country Study.* Washington, DC: U.S. GPO, 3rd ed. 1994.

Miranda, Roger and William Ratliff. *The Civil War in Nicaragua: Inside the Sandinistas.* New Brunswick, NJ: Transaction, 1993.

Prevost, Gary. *The Undermining of the Sandinista Revolution.* New York: Saint Martin's Press, 1997.

Randall, Margaret. *Sandino's Daughters: Feminism in Nicaragua*. New Brunswick, NJ: Rutgers University Press, 1994.

Ryan, David. *US-Sandinista Diplomatic Relations: Voice of Intolerance*. New York: Saint Martin's Press, 1995.

Sabia, Debra. *Contradiction and Conflict: the Popular Church in Nicaragua*. Tuscaloosa, AL: University of Alabama Press, 1997.

Spalding, Rose J. *Capitalists and Revolution in Nicaragua: Opposition and Accommodation, 1979-1993*. Chapel Hill, NC: University of North Carolina Press, 1994.

Vanden, Harry E. and Garry Prevost. *Democracy and Socialism in Sandinista Nicaragua*. Boulder, CO: Lynne Rienner Publishers, 1993.

Walker, Thomas W., ed. *Nicaragua without Illusions: Regime Transition and Structural Adjustment in the 1990s*. Wilmington, DE: Scholarly Resources, 1997.

Walter, Knut. *The Regime of Anastasio Somoza, 1936-1956*. Chapel Hill, NC: University of North Carolina Press, 1993.

Whisnant, David E. *Rascally Signs in Sacred Places: the Politics of Culture in Nicaragua*. Chapel Hill, NC: University of North Carolina Press, 1995.

Panama

Conniff, Michael L. *Panama and the United States: the Forced Alliance*. Athens, GA: University of Georgia Press, 1992.

Donnelly, Thomas, et al. *Operation Just Cause: the Storming of Panama*. New York: Lexington Books, 1991.

Guevara Mann, Carlos. *Panamanian Militarism: a Historical Perspective*. Athens, OH: Ohio University Press, 1996.

Johns, Christina Jacqueline and P. Ward Johnson. *State Crime, the Media, and the Invasion of Panama*. New York: Praeger, 1994.

Leonard, Thomas M. *Panama, the Canal and the United States: a Guide to Issues and References*. Claremont, CA: Regina Books, 1993.

Major, John. *Prize Possession: the United Stated and the Panama Canal, 1903-1979*. New York: Cambridge University Press, 1993.

Meditz, Sandra W. and Dennis M. Hanratty, eds. *Panama: a Country Study*. Washington, DC: U.S. GPO, 4th ed. 1989.

Noriega, Manuel and Peter Eisner. *America's Prisoner: the Memoirs of Manuel Noriega*. New York: Random House, 1997.

Pearcy, Thomas L. *We Answer Only to God: Politics and the Military in Panama, 1903-1947*. Albuquerque, NM: University of New Mexico Press, 1998.

Perez, Orlando J., ed. *Post-Invasion Panama: the Challenges of Democratization in the New World Order*. Lanham, MD: Lexington Books, 2000.

Ward, Christopher. *Imperial Panama: Commerce and Conflict in Isthmian America, 1550-1800*. Albuquerque, NM: University of New Mexico, 1993.

Paraguay

Hanratty, Dennis and Sandra W. Meditz, eds. *Paraguay: a Country Study*. Washington, DC: U.S. GPO, 2nd ed. 1990.

Lambert, Peter and Andrew Nickson, eds. *Transition to Democracy in Paraguay*. New York: Saint Martin's Press, 1997.

Leis, Paul H. *Political Parties and Generations in Paraguay's Liberal Era, 1869-1940*. Chapel Hill, NC: University of North Carolina Press, 1993.

Miranda, Carlos R. *The Stroessner Era: Authoritarian Rule in Paraguay*. Boulder, CO: Westview Press, 1990.

Nickson, R. Andrew. *Historical Dictionary of Paraguay*. Lanham, MD: Scarecrow Press, 2nd ed. 1993.

Peru

Cameron, Maxwell, A. *Democracy and Authoritarianism in Peru: Political Coalitions and Social Change*. New York: Saint Martin's Press, 1994.

Clayton, Lawrence A. *Peru and the United States: the Condor and the Eagle*. Athens, GA: University of Georgia Press, 1999.

Gootenberg, Paul. *Imagining Development: Economic Ideas in Peru's "Fictitious Prosperity" of Guano, 1840-1880*. Berkeley, CA: University of California Press, 1993.

Gorriti, Gustavo. *The Shining Path: a History of the Millenarian War in Peru*. Chapel Hill, NC: University of North Carolina Press, 1999.

Hudson, Rex A., ed. *Peru: a Country Study*. Washington, DC: U.S. GPO, 1993.

Jacobsen, Nils. *Mirages of Transition: the Peruvian Altiplano, 1780-1930*. Berkeley, CA: University of California Press, 1993.

Lockhart, James. *Spanish Peru, 1532-1560: a Social History*. Madison, WI: University of Wisconsin Press, 1994.

Masterson, Daniel M. *Militarism and Politics in Latin America: Peru from Sanchez Cerro to Sendero Luminoso*. Westport, CT: Greenwood Publishing Publishing, 1991.

Palmer, David Scott, ed. *The Shining Path of Peru*. New York: Saint Martin's Press, 1992.

Peña, Milagros. *Theologies and Liberation in Peru: the Role of Ideas in Social Movement*. Philadelphia, PA: Temple University Press, 1995.

Quiroz, Alfonso W. *Domestic and Foreign Finance in Modern Peru, 1850-1950: Financing Visions of Development*. Pittsburgh, PA: University of Pittsburgh Press, 1993.

Roberts, Kenneth M. *Deepening Democracy? The Modern Left and Social Movements in Chile and Peru*. Stanford, CA: Stanford University Press, 1999.

Seligmann, Linda J. *Between Reform and Revolution: Political Struggles in the Peruvian Andes, 1969-1991*. Stanford, CA: Stanford University Press, 1995.

Sheahan, John. *Searching for a Better Society: the Peruvian Economy from 1950*. University Park, PA: Pennsylvania State University Press, 1999.

Stern, Steve J. *Peru's Indian Peoples and the Challenge of Spanish Conquest: Huamanga to 1640*. Madison, WI: University of Wisconsin Press, 2nd ed. 1993.

Tulchin, Joseph S. and Gary Bland, eds. *Peru in Crisis: Dictatorship or Democracy?* Boulder, CO: Lynne Rienner Publishers, 1994.

Watters, R.F. *Poverty and Peasantry in Peru's Southern Andes, 1963-90*. Pittsburgh, PA: University of Pittsburgh Press, 1994.

Suriname

Brown, Enid. *Suriname and the Netherlands Antilles: an Annotated English-Language Bibliography*. Lanham, MD: Scarecrow Press, 1992.

Dew, Edward M. *The Trouble in Suriname, 1975-1993*. New York: Praeger, 1994.

Hoefte, Rosemarijn. *In Place of Slavery: a Social History of British Indian and Javanese Laborers in Suriname*. Gainesville, FL: University Press of Florida, 1998.

Hoefte, Rosemarijn. *Suriname*. Santa Barbara, CA: ABC-CLIO, 1991.

Trinidad and Tobago

Anthony, Michael. *Historical Dictionary of Trinidad and Tobago*. Lanham, MD: Scarecrow Press, 1997.

Regis, Louis. *The Political Calypso: True Opposition in Trinidad and Tobago, 1962-1987*. Gainesville, FL: University Press of Florida, 1998.

Yelvington, Kelvin A. *Trinidad Ethnicity*. Knoxville, TN: University of Tennessee Press, 1993.

Uruguay

Gillespie, Charles Guy. *Negotiating Democracy: Politicians and Generals in Uruguay*. New York: Cambridge University Press, 1991.

Gonzalez, Luis E. *Political Structures and Democracy in Uruguay*. Notre Dame, IN: University of Notre Dame Press, 1991.

Hudson, Rex A. and Sandra W. Meditz, eds. *Uruguay: a Country Study*. Washington, DC: U.S. GPO, 2nd ed. 1992.

Preeg, Ernest H. *From Here to Free Trade: Essays in Post-Uruguay Round Trade Strategy*. Chicago: University of Chicago Press, 1998.

Rottenberg, Simon, ed. *Costa Rica and Uruguay*. New York: Oxford University Press, 1993.

Sosnowski, Saul. *Repression, Exile, and Democracy: Uruguayan Culture*. Durham, NC: Duke University Press, 1992.

Venezuela

Canache, Damarys J. and Michael R. Kulisheck, eds. *Reinventing Legitimacy: Democracy and Political Change in Venezuela*. Westport, CT: Greenwood Publishing Group, 1998.

Coppedge, Michael. *Strong Parties and Lame Ducks: Presidential Partyarchy and Factionalism in Venezuela.* Stanford, CA: Stanford University Press, 1994.

Coronil, Fernando. *Magical State: Nature, Money and Modernity in Venezuela.* Chicago: University of Chicago Press, 1997.

Enright, Michael J., et al. *Venezuela: the Challenge of Competitiveness.* New York: Saint Martin's Press, 1996.

Goodman, Louis W., et al., eds. *Lessons of the Venezuelan Experience.* Baltimore, MD: Johns Hopkins University Press, 1995.

Haggerty, Richard A. *Venezuela: a Country Study.* Washington, DC: U.S. GPO, 4th ed. 1993.

Hillman, Richard S. *Democracy for the Privileged: Crisis and Transition in Venezuela.* Boulder, CO: Lynne Rienner, 1994.

Rudolph, Donna K. and G.A. Rudolph. *Historical Dictionary of Venezuela.* Lanham, MD: Scarecrow Press, 1996.

A Peruvian Indian and his llama keep a lonely vigil in some of the highest country in the western Andes